ISBN 978-1-330-28806-1
PIBN 10014509

SOCIETY
IN
ACTION

A STUDY OF BASIC SOCIAL PROCESSES

JOYCE O. HERTZLER
UNIVERSITY OF NEBRASKA

THE DRYDEN PRESS · NEW YORK

31 West 54th Street, New York
Manufactured in the United States of America

First Printing, April 1954

PREFACE

THIS BOOK is intended to serve as a foundation text for courses in General Sociology, Principles of Sociology, Modern Human Society, and the like. It may be used in classes where the students have already had a social-science survey course or an introductory one-semester course in sociology, or it may be used as a basic text in departments that introduce their students to sociology after the freshman year.

This is not a simple, "pat" book of cut-and-dried principles. One reason is that human society is immensely complex, and to offer a simple presentation is to underestimate or overlook or understate a multiplicity of intricate problems. Another reason is that sociology as a science is still young and is feeling its way as it proceeds with the study of one of the most complicated and confusing of all areas of knowledge.

Society in Action is intended to provide an overall analysis of human society as a dynamic entity, not only in terms of its structures, but, especially, in terms of its operational aspects—that is, its functions, processes, and relations—and the factors involved in typical and recurrent social situations. Mere descriptions of the more obvious or the more conventionally treated parts or aspects of human society do not provide the thorough understanding of its nature and operation that is theoretically possible or practically desirable today. Nor can this understanding be obtained from an examination of society as a static thing. A treatment which restricts itself to social change, social institutions, the community, or the ecological, cultural, or social-psychological approaches and overemphasizes certain features at the expense of others is also unlikely to provide such understanding. These approaches have their merits, but they are partial—and in some measure deceptive.

This analysis is concerned mainly with modern Western society, although there are some references to other societies for purposes of comparison. The social sciences have, of course, a considerable body of postulates of universal application, but no single study can competently review them or make all the special and scientifically essential qualifications. We do, however, need to know as best we can what our present, fluid, dynamic Western society is like and how it "works."

When the student is led to view human society as a vast "going concern," he has, as it were, a blueprint on which he can perceive and relate the substance of his courses in psychology, social psychology, economics, political science, human geography, and history. And, more important, he is able to bring the more specialized courses in sociology—the community, urban and rural sociology, population, human ecology, poverty and dependency, industrial sociology, social disorganization, marriage and the family, primary and secondary groups, social institutions, and social control—into perspective with the whole of societal operation.

In this book, attention is focused upon social processes. The dynamic conception of society—scientifically essential—has developed in sociologists a pronounced tendency to formulate social theory within the *action* frame of reference. It is here contended that such formulation involves an analysis of processes in relation to structures, functions, and factors. This text attempts to study all the common processes in operation in the societal context. It is not confined to the very general processes and does not overemphasize some simply because of the greater availability of descriptive material or because of great current interest. The treatments found here are based in part on accepted facts and principles and in part upon the most promising current hypotheses. Because there is not full theoretical substantiation for much that is presented, the book offers many hypotheses regarding social functions, processes, and factors which need additional investigation and substantiation. For this reason, the book may be viewed by some as an audacious enterprise. But if progress is to be made, some of the more audacious persons must venture new hypotheses and deductive interpretations. Various important social processes and factors are examined in their *different* functional contexts, for many of these processes and factors have more than one kind of effect. The reader is aided in correlating these different but related aspects of specific processes by means of occasional cross references.

Extensive illustrative material has largely been omitted, but the alert student, possessed of some knowledge of history and living, as he does, in the sociological laboratory, can provide many examples.

This study seeks to uncover core facts and principles. Clues that have proved fruitful in a variety of sociological investigative efforts for more than a generation have been followed, and the accumulated materials have been woven into a more or less coherent scheme of organization. The treatment is devoted primarily to analysis and synthesis.

In the classified bibliography, arranged by chapters at the end of the book, the reader will find frequent reference not only to books but also to articles in the social-science journals, to monographs, and to publications of research symposia, which are evidence of a living, growing, investigative science. These references are not intended to be exhaustive, nor are they "shotgun blasts" at the general theses of the respective chapters. Although there are some references to sociological classics among them, the references consist mainly of recent and readily accessible materials selected for their relevance either as further theoretical elaborations or as specific social-science investigations. In order to enhance their pertinence, they have been classified according to the subject matter of the major sections of each chapter. The references are offered not only as citations for sources consulted but as useful and incitive materials for further study and independent exploration by the students.

Sincere thanks are hereby expressed to the administrative officers, the Board of Regents, the Research Council, and the Department of Sociology of the University of Nebraska for a leave of absence which made possible a semester of uninterrupted application to this study. My colleague Dr. Paul Meadows has been unstinting in his proffer of seminal ideas, highly constructive criticism, and innumerable references and materials. He may, in fact, be regarded as a contributing author. He is in no wise responsible, however, for any of my uses or abuses of his contributions. The members of my seminar in Sociological Theory for the last quarter of a century have also been potent participants, and to them my thanks are extended. My indebtedness to my wife for encouragement and criticism and for assistance in the preparation of the manuscript can never be adequately expressed or repaid.

University of Nebraska
January 1954

J. O. Hertzler

CONTENTS

PART TWO

Culturization

PART THREE

The Social Processes Affecting Natural, Demographic, and Spatial Adjustment

PART ONE

UNDERSTANDING HUMAN SOCIETY

CHAPTER I

HUMAN SOCIETY AS A GOING CONCERN

THE ANALYSIS OF human society is one of the most essential, fascinating, and rewarding activities in which contemporary men engage. The social world, of which we all are unavoidable participants, is a vast sociological laboratory. When we acquire the essential insights and skills of observation, we see our social life as a magnificent experiment in continuous process. Our every personal experience among our fellows and every observation revealed in a newspaper, periodical, book, motion picture, and television, as well as the results of scientific investigations, provide us with valid source materials. Inherent in these are the social facts, governed by determinable principles, which explain *what is* and *why it is.* Without some knowledge of these facts we are social illiterates.

Our Social World

The fact that our society is exceedingly complex in its composition and that its operation is difficult to understand challenges us as citizens and as scientists. In a general way we know that society is not a mere mass but is made up of a great number of *parts* composed of groups and subgroups of human beings—families, neighborhoods, cliques, and other small groups, social classes, sex and age groups, trade unions, corporations and other purposive, institutionalized organizations, communities, and so on. These persons and groups have a relatively stable, unifying arrangement.

All these parts of society *do certain things* for their members and for the society as a whole. They satisfy basic material needs through the production and distribution of goods and services and thus contribute to physical survival and prosperity; they provide personality-gratifying recreational and spiritual satisfactions for their members; they make possible the reproduction, protection, and socialization of the new members of the society. As communities and as a society the different parts counter confusion and conflict and maintain internal peace and order; they perpetuate the culture and develop and acquire new cultural features to meet new conditions, to mention only some of the more obvious and essential things which they *must do* if they are to survive and prosper. In brief, they produce certain kinds of expected and necessary actions which have affects and effects, and which are the reason for existence of the various parts.

Patterned Ways of Action

These actions are continually or recurrently carried on in certain innumerable *patterned ways.* There is a continuous tendency toward equilibrium, consisting of ways (processes and procedures) of organization, disorganization, and reorganization. The persons, in varying combinations, communicate and associate with each other; they cooperate in carrying on numerous tasks, and they form all manner of organizations; they conduct and modify their social institutions; they separate themselves from each other in all kinds of opposed groups and social levels; they move about in physical space and also go up and down the social ladder; they vie with and motivate each other; they fight with each other, commit crimes and nuisances, discriminate against and exploit and persecute each other, and otherwise bring about disorganization; they form agencies of conformity, regulation and maintenance; as unequally endowed and trained persons they are continually adjusting themselves to each other in various ways; to correct inadequacies and inefficiencies in their social life, they establish and participate in all sorts of presumably reconstructive social movements. All individual and social life consists of acting in various ways to accomplish various ends.

Interdependent Relationships of Parts

The parts, as they act in these various ways, are all in interdependent *relationships* with each other. None of them is entirely alone, and each is affected by the others and has some effect upon the others. All operate, interact, and intermesh, more or less dependably, as parts of the whole in standard ways in accordance with certain values and rules; all have their specific social positions with respect to each other.

As the human components, formed into groups of various kinds, interact at any given time, each is *conditioned or influenced*—even determined—*by various elements of the total situation,* such as the physical location and conditions, the unique composition of the population, the arrangement in space of the components, the psychological and social psychological conditions prevailing, the infinite array of culture elements and influences, past and present, of a material, social, and intellectual nature, and so on. The society acts as it does for good and comprehensible reasons. Nothing about it is haphazard; everything has meaning in understanding the whole, great, dramatic performance.

Science of Sociology

The ultimate objective of all scientific endeavor is *engineering.* By this we mean that man is continually attempting to gain such an accurate understanding of experienced things and of the energies that lie behind them and operate in and through them that he can utilize them and possibly even manipulate them for valued human ends. For example, men, through their knowledge of the regular movements of the stars, have been able to utilize them as means of telling time; through their knowledge of the force of falling water they have been able to produce electrical energy that lights our homes and runs our gadgets and machines; through their knowledge of the principles of breeding (genetics) they have, by manipulative procedures, been able to produce horses than can trot a mile in two minutes or corn that ripens in ninety days in northern climates; through the acquired understanding of some aspects of mankind's psychological nature, men, by careful treatment, have been able to restore mentally sick people to a measure of health. In other words, the primary function of science is to give us such a comprehensive understanding of all kinds of phenomena that, by means of appropriate arts, they can be skillfully made serviceable for mankind.

The fundamental objective of the science of sociology is to give us such an adequate understanding of the nature and operation of human society that we are enabled to carry out engineering objectives in growing measure in the field of social phenomena. To do this, we need a consistent, unifying, clearly meaningful, overlying conception of society that relates what we know about it in such proportion and manner that we see it as the complex, durable, fairly efficient operating entity that it is. The older sciences give us some indication of what that knowledge must consist of.

Analysis of Human Society as a Going Concern

The history of the sciences that have made abundant engineering contributions, such as physics, chemistry, biology, and geology, demonstrates that the most comprehensible and useful analysis of a given field of phenomena is the one that examines it as a great dynamic mechanism. In this sense a mechanism is a sum of parts in which energy flows through space-time. The arrangement and operative relations of these parts produce effects. It is a combination of elements or parts and a variety of interrelated activities or processes that enables the system to carry on as a whole and to be preserved. Thus, mechanism may be thought of as a means of achieving ends. Such an examination makes possible the development of a sizable and systematic body of facts and principles that provide a penetrating insight into the nature and operation of the order of phenomena. Such facts and principles can be used to predict the form and action of the phenomena, to establish some degree of mastery over them, and to utilize them for achieving human ends.

A growing number of sociologists believe that an analysis* of human society as a dynamic mechanism, or going concern, leads to the most meaningful and fruitful interpretation. By means of such analysis they are able to get all that is known about society into a kind of moving picture which provides close-ups of the constituent parts at any given moment. It also shows the purpose and use of the parts, the action and flow of occurrences among them, and the combinations of influential or causal factors that in each type of instance determine the actions of the parts. In brief, with such an analysis, human society ceases in great measure to be what William James referred to as "a big and blooming and buzzing confusion." Instead, the mysteries as to *what* the various essential and pertinent elements are that tick, *why* they tick, *how* they tick, and the *circumstances* of their ticking are made clear.

*"Analysis" is the seeking of the nature and the relationships of the aspects (parts) of a phenomenon (whole).

As scientists we cannot get along with anything less than a knowledge of *society in action*. Society is nonexistent as a static thing, and to treat it as such is contrary to the most superficial observation of the ever-changing social scene and taxes our credulity. Nor is society something to be described in a sporadic or partial manner, from this special angle or that. Human society is more than its culture; more than random or organized population groupings; more than spatially arranged and related individuals and groups; more than institutions; more than social control of its various elements. It is all these and much more; it is greater than the sum of its numerous parts and performances. Human society is a vast, many-faceted, complexly structured, multiply impelled and propelled, multiply functioning, dynamic, living entity. Viewing it as a going concern gives us a realistic, comprehensive, balanced, and penetrating interpretation of its nature and operation.

Elements of Going-Concern Analysis

Analysis of a mechanism as a going concern resolves itself into an examination of the structures, functions, processes, relationships, and factors or variables in each common situation. This conclusion has been demonstrated wherever a degree of scientific hegemony has been achieved in a field of phenomena. The general meanings of the terms involved in the analysis can be briefly set forth before we examine them as features of human society.

The structures are the typical and recurrent

identifiable forms of the units, or parts, which, *in toto,* constitute the body and framework of the entity. Depending upon the phenomenal field under observations, they include atoms and elements, cells, tissues, organs, geologic strata, and human groupings and the arrangements and combinations of them. A structure, as Giddings indicated, is a form pattern of space positions of the parts of an entity *as it is* at any given time. (2, p. 4)* In the biological sciences the special study of the form and arrangement of the parts, or structures, is known as "morphology" or "anatomy."

Function is what a structure *does,* that is, what its activity accomplishes in the operation of the whole mechanism of which it is a unit or combination of units. As long as there are energies of any kind, there will be some kind of action and some result. Thus, function is an essential characteristic of any living or otherwise energized going thing. "What ceases to function ceases to be." (3) According to a widely prevalent view, function implies use or utility of the thing or combination of things —the accomplishment of purpose. In general, when we have discovered the function of things, we know their reason for existence.

Process is the sequence of occurrences when a structure functions. It is the *way* or *ways* in which phenomena regularly or recurrently manifest themselves in *time.* A process is an action pattern, or a pattern of change, the operative aspect of a series of changes which is orderly, related, and sequential *in time,* such as chemical reactions and metabolism. As process goes on there is invariably and everlastingly the modification and recombination of structures and often the production of new ones. By means of processes a transition is made from one state to another, involving greater or lesser efficiency as to functioning. In biology, when the functions and processes are paired together, we have the "physiology" of the entity.

Structure defines an organ or mechanism in relation to the three dimensions of space—length, breadth, and height. *Function* applies to that same organ or mechanism as it contributes results or consequences, positive or negative, as it operates. *Process* is the action, the going-on of the structure in time. It involves a four-dimensional set of considerations, *the three spatial coordinates plus the time coordinate. Relationships* are the interplay and interdependence of the structures or parts as they function together unavoidably by means of processes.

Factors

The *factors* consist of all the energies, agents, and circumstances that in combination produce a result. In most sciences they are referred to as the "variables." They include such items as the previous conditioners or influencers of the elements, the particular conditions (place, temperature, light, time, and the like) surrounding the elements at the moment, and the energies or forces operating through or bearing upon the elements. These factors combine in the given situation and affect the elements, causing them to operate as they do at the time.

Societal† Structures, Functions, Processes, Relationships

As *social* scientists we are especially concerned with the conceptualization of structures, functions, processes, and factors as features of a system of sociological theory and with the significance of these features in understanding human society as a going concern.

*Numbers in parentheses refer to the references at the end of the text.

†A prevailing distinction between *social* and *societal* will be used throughout the present work. *Social* relates to whatever transcends the mere biological individual in human behavior; it is the "more than organic." It is a comprehensive term involving, especially as used in sociology and social psychology, any reciprocal interaction of two or more human beings, either as individuals or as groups. *Societal* includes "social" but is more specific. It implies the social action of individuals and groups as they are involved in the structural-functional, the organizational-operational aspects of a human community or society. Societal action is more definitive than social interaction; it means "to function as part of the social mechanism or going concern."

Structures

In the field of social phenomena, with which the sociologist is concerned, we have four distinct kinds of *social structures,* or form-configuration patterns, that must be considered: cultural, demographic, ecological, and societal. The *cultural structure* consists of the community's or society's shared body of artifacts and utilitarian modifications of the physical and biological world plus its system of language, ideas, beliefs, institutions, and so on, which are humanly achieved and socially transmitted. The items of the total culture are the *wherewithal, the material and nonmaterial means,* of social action.

The *demographic structure* of a community, area, or society consists of the configuration of the population, that is, the total number of human beings, male and female, in various marital, familial, socioeconomic, and other pertinent categories. The *ecological structure* refers to the pattern of distribution and relationship in space on the earth, for a given area under consideration, of its various individuals, groups, and institutionalized organizations. It is the "territorial organization" of the constituent elements of the community or society.

The *societal structure* consists of all the socially interacting persons, however combined. It has to do with the characteristic forms taken by the interrelated individuals as actors and the various combinations of individuals—the concrete aggregations, collectivities, or complexes of human beings in some given common habitat at a given time. These structures are variously referred to as "plurality patterns," "form aspects" of human interaction, or, most commonly, "groups" and "communities." The innumerable groupings by means of which men live and act together vary greatly. They are the characteristic relationships between human beings—the way in which the mass of people is constituted. The combined groups of all kinds constitute the societal organization of a given human population, that is, an array of all kinds and levels of groups as units. Each individual unit in the array is reciprocally related to, functionally dependent upon, and interdependent with every other unit.

The rather generally accepted types or categories of associated and societally organized human beings (by no means mutually exclusive) are: genetic groups, such as families, clans, and races, bonded by a common inheritance; neighborhoods and communities with a common territorial basis; occupational, religious, nationality, age, sex, and other vertically differentiated groups, each unified by signal common interests or activities; classes, castes, ethnic groups, or other horizontally divided and hierarchically arranged strata; crowds and other chance and transient gatherings; associations (within or including parts of the above groupings) definitely and more or less deliberately organized for the pursuit of common, expressly formulated, and specific objectives; the over-all assembly and interknitting of all these types of groups under a common political jurisdiction, known as state or nation. Dominant in all of these, in greater or less degree, are the institutions, that is, the established forms, rules, and requirements of procedure essential to group activity and administration. The structural make-up of society can be thought of as "social morphology." Every group, or combination of groups, when examined in action, is resolved into an intersecting network of functions, processes, and relationships.

Functions

Social function refers to the action or performance of which a particular type of social structure is distinctly capable in given situations. Interacting people are incessantly bringing things to pass. Social functioning is what individuals and groups *do* in their physical and social environment as interrelated human organisms and as social mechanisms to meet the requirements of the situation. (6) As in the case of function generally, social functional action involves the use of the actions in so far as they tend toward the attainment of some consequence in connection with needs, interests, or desires of individuals or groups. Thus, social function consists of the activities of human agents directed toward definable objectives or ends in contrast to purposeless or random activity (which is merely motion, strictly speaking). It need not be planned by the performing individuals or groups; it may be unconscious or conscious. But it leads to a result toward which it is logically directed.

Functional social action is a system of solutions to problems of interaction. In the instance of particular individuals and groups, it is what they do to meet their needs, to work toward their goals, and to survive. In the case of a human society as a whole, the functioning is what the constituent units do jointly to maintain their structural continuity and to secure a satisfactory level of performance in the social system as a whole. All the functions performed in a society are interconnected, whether positive or negative in effect; they all contribute to the whole operation; together they determine how well it works. The social scientist is not concerned with "good" or "bad" or any other ethical evaluation of a function, but rather with what is and what occurs according to the best evidence; that is, what the functioning agents and entities typically do as part of the over-all operation of the societal mechanism. Conflict and destruction as well as cooperation and construction have functional effects in the whole.

Processes

The sociological counterpart of the general scientific concept of *processes* refers to all the identifiable, typable patterns of social action and interaction which *two or more persons* of the constituent population of the social structures engage in as they function. They consist of social occurrences, nonpurposive and purposive, associative and dissociative, constructive and destructive, stimulating and enervating, which are involved as human individuals and groups make contact, act, and react to each other. They are the being, the dynamic, living, constantly changing aspects of a society, presenting different types of reciprocal and joint social behavior under varying conditions.

Actually social processes and social functions, like processes and functions in any phenomenal field, are integrally related aspects of the operation of a society. Functions take the concrete form of processes, and processes are functional patterns of social action—action with social "ends" significance. Together, the social processes and functions constitute a sort of "social physiology"; they give us the conception of the dynamic aspect of societal life. In contrast with the still picture or snapshot provided by an examination of structure, the analysis of the processes and functions gives us the motion picture of a society—*society in action.*

Relationships

Social relationships refer to the common categories of interaction of human beings as they function within and between their various societal structures. "Whenever a given interaction pattern is repeated often enough to give rise to relatively stable expectancies among the actors we call it *a social relation.*" (11) The social relationships are always reciprocal interactions, with some degree of stimulus and response among both parties, and may take the form of interaction between person and person, between person and group, or between group and group, or in combinations of these.

Over-all social change, or *the social process,* as it has been entitled, can only be perceived and effected in terms of the modification of relationships among individuals and groups. Where there is no interaction there is no process. In fact, relationships are both cause and result of social processes. All formation and re-formation of structures, all activity of persons and groups, is dependent upon, and conditioned by, the antecedent relations of interacting human beings.

Inseparable Aspects

It must be emphatically pointed out that *societal structures and societal functions and processes are fundamentally and inseparably correlated and interknit.* They are not opposing aspects of social phenomena, and neither can be adequately understood without the other. If they are separated in societal analysis, we get an utterly unreal and inaccurate conception of society as the going concern which it is. The societal structures are the concrete entities in which, through which, and between which all processes occur and for which all essential functions are performed. Social function is social activity producing social consequences; social structure is what acts.

The structures themselves result from social processes operating in the physical and sociocultural environments; because of processes, modified and new structures continually emerge. Every structure is in some kind of action. Thus, the processes operate in and through and between structures and are conditioned by, and dependent upon, structures. The processes are *in fact* the interactional patterns of individuals and groups. The functions performed as the processes occur are the *raison d'être* of the structures. Any change in social structures implies alterations in process and function.

As long as a society *is,* it is ever-changing and reciprocally changing structures, functions and processes. The dynamic occurrence flows from, and is reflected in, the structures of given situations and times and in turn correspondingly affects the structures and effects structural changes. Structures are never, in actuality, static ends in themselves, even when their constituents attempt to make them so; and processes do not occur in a vacuum of some sort. If it were not for the ceaseless flow of social processes, the social structures which at any given time seem to be fixed would collapse and cease to be.

Thus, if we examine only structure, we get a deceivingly static point of view regarding the nature of society. If we look only at processes, we get a false impression of dynamic instability and meaningless motion in time. An examination of the structural-functional-processual aspects enables us to posit a consistent, meaningful, realistic interpretation of human society. We can do what is basically essential to the understanding of social and societal phenomena, namely, to register the known and observable facts and arrange them in order of space, time, and causality. This is not merely descriptive or synthetic but analytical social science.

Significance of the Factors in the Social Situation

In the preceding discussion there have been occasional references to "situation," "circumstances," "conditions," "forces," and "causes." These terms point to a final set of fundamental conceptualized elements essential to an understanding of the operation of any going concern. Wherever there is consciousness of existence and occurrence, we search for reasons. As inquiring human beings we are curious as to *why* and *how* the social forms and arrangements of which we are a part came about; we would like to know why the events that catch us up and make us act and so mightily affect our destiny came to pass. For us as social scientists, concerned immediately with the mastery of the facts and principles regarding societal structures, functions, and processes, and ultimately and primarily with their manipulation and utilization for adjustive and constructive purposes, the understanding of the background circumstances and constituent *elements* is imperative.

Cause-and-Effect Relationships

One of the primary tasks of any science is to seek out and establish cause-and-effect relationships, that is, to discover the dynamic energies, the ingredient elements, and the conditions of relationship which are involved in or are essential to the appearance of an event or phenomenon, or which, if absent, prevent its appearance or, if altered in number, sequence, or combination, bring an alteration in the accompanying phenomenon. Whatever occurs is the result of causes, and there can be no effect apart from causes.

The Social Situation. With respect to social phenomena, such an analysis confronts us, first, with what has come to be conceptualized in the social sciences as the *social situation.* Every social structure, function, sequential going-on, and relationship is a special, significant result or effect growing out of its own peculiar *context,* or *togetherness of elements.* A given social situation is the emergent configuration or totality pattern of all the pertinent components in the social field, in both its inner and its outer features: the physical environment; the population involved in both its physiological and psychological aspects; the sociocultural environment with its ideas and values, its groups and interrelationships, its material and technical equipment, its institutions, as these affect the given phenomenon at the particular place and time as they *appear* to an observer on objective scientific analysis.

Such a conjunction of the elements involved, says Carr, "produces a dynamic pattern which *is* the situation." He continues: "Such a pattern has form, dimension, content, phases, processes, conditioning factors, and relationships to other situations, co-existing, pre-existent, and subsequent." (12; 13) Such a combination of components is the source of all actual or potential experience regarding types and instances of social behavior.

In every situation there are always various conditions, influences, and contents in various stages, orders, levels, and combinations of interdependence. Every social form or occurrence is the resultant of a specific and probably a unique clustering of a considerable diversity of these contributory elements, determiners, and propulsions in its given social terrain, climate, and moment. The whole is not merely the sum of its parts; it is, to use Chapin's fine phrase, a "web of circumstance." (15)

The problem of determining causes, although of supreme importance, is an exceedingly complex one and, at the present stage of development in the analysis of social phenomena, gets us into difficulties for several reasons, which we will discuss briefly. The implication, however, is not to abandon the pursuit of causes or pessimistically to assume that confirmed hypotheses of causes will never be developed.

Multiplicity of Coactive Elements. First, invariably there is a multiplicity and complexity of coactive elements contributing to a given contemporary event or phenomenon. No single, isolable element is solely responsible. There are always, at any given time in any given culture, patterns of causes for types of events. Obviously also there are different levels of pertinence among the numerous causal elements effective at any given time in producing a given occurrence. If multiplicity of causes is determined, can the numerous and interdependent causal elements at work at any given time be scaled as to importance? One-sided or unitary theories of cause usually prove fallacious on even superficial investigation. Moreover, among the multiplicity of elements there is the task of determining whether all are reciprocal or interdependent causes or whether some are correlative effects.

Chains of Cause and Effect. Second, causes are inevitably a matter of chains or sequences of cause-and-effect occurrences, in which causes have pro-

fined as "resolving a phenomenon into components or elements of place, time, circumstance, quality, magnitude, activity, behavior or function, coexistence and sequence." (2, pp. 4-8)

The purpose of factor analysis is to identify the set of variables that seem to have maximum relevance in the situation. It does not attempt the impossible task of discovering *all* the components, influences, and conditions. Of necessity, it resorts to what is feasible at the moment, on the basis of scientific analytical experience and data available to date and is influenced by the principle of parsimony or economy of description. (22)

In the present work, as we examine processes and functioning, we shall attempt to present obvious and pertinent *proximate* factors as determined in the present. We shall draw on known scientific studies made in different social scientific fields of inquiry and on the consensus of more general available treatments. There is no thought of presenting *all* the known factors or of presenting a definitive array for each process, since the array is always changing. But we can attempt to provide a working set of factors, that is, something in the way of an enumeration and description of factors which operate in or accompany the phenomenon in the majority of situations. Admittedly this is not enough. The arrays presented will probably not be adequate or satisfactory, but they will be the best we have, and they can be thought of as points of departure for further analysis. In fact, every process mentioned is a problem for future research, and the factors presented in connection with it need to be weighed, checked, and supplemented. This, of course, is a continuous responsibility in every science.

To attempt to depict factors in any given situation is admittedly a scientifically hazardous task. The faintheart would refuse to attempt it. But we get nowhere if we do not make efforts. Even informal common-sense efforts are better than cautious ineptitude. "Frisch gewagt ist halb gewonnen." There can be no understanding or manipulation of processes unless we are increasingly aware of the factors involved in their occurrence.

The Focal Significance of Processes

Processes in Scientific Analysis

When we examine human society as a great, complex, dynamic, *operative* mechanism, its *processes* are the features of focal significance. In fact, the concept of processes is central and strategic in fundamental scientific analysis in every phenomenal field. For the processes tie together the structures, functions, and factors in a comprehensive and comprehensible relationship. When analyzed they provide the body of facts and principles which indicate what is going on in the way of causal and functional sequence. They are a way—the only way—of explaining all observable products in the form of either structures or actions. Furthermore, the immediate goal of every science is the formulation of scientific laws, and these are simply statements of the way in which events regularly occur under given conditions. In brief, a scientific law is a statement of process.

The establishment of scientific laws, however, is not a final objective; such laws are merely contributory formulas for action. As indicated earlier in this chapter, the fundamental objective, the pragmatic aim, and sole social justification of every science is engineering proficiency in its phenomenal field. Such engineering proficiency requires predictive ability and consists basically of the prevention of some processes and the constructive manipulation and utilization of others. The structures and factors are in a sense "givens" that the engineer starts with. Results in the form of modified structures and functions are what he seeks. But between the elements and the consequences are the processes. The processes are also of central importance in the *analysis* of *social* phenomena. *Everything that happens in any social system in space and time involves social processes.*

Human social life shares with all organisms and mechanisms this eternal transformation with its ceaseless conditionings, formations, differentiations, disorganizations, dissolutions, equilibrations, and reconstructions. It is a succession of ever-changing relationships. A society is a complexity of processes rather than a fixed thing. All modifications and the appearance of all new structures and functions are the result of social processes. The forms that the processes take are the expressions in social action of combinations of factors or variables in every typical social situation.

All sociological investigation is an effort to discover the relations of the operative factors as they affect processes and an effort to predict the processes and their effects. All social engineering is an effort to control, manipulate, and affect social processes. The social processes may be said to be the all-inclusive "object matter" of the social sciences.

The Obligation of Sociology

As scientists sociologists are obligated to present a conception of human society as a going concern and to interpret what goes on in such a society as it functions. These obligations require a wide and diversified scope of analysis. They also involve an examination of *all* the determinable major phases of human interaction that affect the formation, existing make-up and characteristics, and more or less satisfactory functioning of a given society. Otherwise, we have merely an identification and description of *some* changes esoterically considered. The known "changings" should be viewed as an interrelated complex of varieties and sequences of processes that give us *in toto* a conception and an interpretation of a society as an organized functioning whole. (27; 35)

Conceptualization of Social Processes

Social processes are actions, ways of doing, or "goings-on" among contacting individuals that are repeated over and over again in a given society. Their detailed features can be systematically presented as follows:

1. *Social processes are fundamental social acts* growing out of social relations. A social act, it should be emphasized, is always a joint or a reciprocal act in which two or more persons participate in some way, directly or indirectly. It is inevitable that they should make some contact.

2. These social acts are *prevalent* and hence observable and typable. They take the form of *action patterns.* For example, the action pattern may be that of fellow adjusters to, or exploiters or victims of, natural occurrences (building a dyke or fleeing from a flood); of sex partners; of parents and offspring; of rivals; of socially motivated fellow constructors.

3. These processes *repeat themselves over and over again.* These social acts are not historically unique or isolated. If something occurs only once, it is not a societally significant process. The processes may be continuously occurring, or they may be recurrent under given conditions, or they may be cyclical in nature.

4. Social processes are social activities that *involve a time span,* that is, they go on in time. They are more than acts in a moment of time. Most of them are observable as a series of occurrences with duration and movement forward in time. In a social process there is step-by-step transition from one social state or condition to the next; the transition is related and sequential. A process can be described in terms of the initial stage, the intermediate stages, and the final stage, which may be the point of departure for a repetition of the whole series of occurrences.

5. *Social processes are regular in nature.* They are not haphazard events. Each process is the expression in action of the factors operative in the situation. They demonstrate causes and their effects.

6. *Social processes are universal* in a given social area or space. The major ones are present in every society, no matter how small or large, simple or complex, young or old. Some are universal only in a given society, owing to its level of development and its degree of complexity. For example, our American society has processes that are not to be found among primitive peoples.

7. *Social processes always constitute some kind of societal becoming.* The participants in them, whether noted as individuals or as groups, are affected in some significant manner, and the whole community or society will be changed in some degree because of them. The life of any society is made up of series of series, of chains of chains, or processes. Because of them a society is a continual becoming, not a being. As soon as the processes cease, the society disappears.

It is desirable at this point to distinguish, according to current sociological thinking, between social processes and other terms related to processes and sometimes confused with them. A *process,* as has been noted, is a "natural" continuous occurrence growing spontaneously out of the elements in the situation. An *event* is an occurrence of some importance or of some special interest to some person or group. It has a beginning and an end for both the participants and the observers of it. A *procedure* is a conscious and usually intentional and organized utilization of a process or processes, or certain phases thereof, by appropriate techniques; a more or less planned series of steps in operation or performance to accomplish a "purpose," such as the organization of a corporation, the operation of an industrial plant. (12, p. 91; 20, p. 129)

Categories of Processes to Be Examined

A society or any lesser social system has a whole battery of social processes. They are exceedingly numerous. A detailed list of them would be as extensive as the known occurrences in social life. Moreover, the processes are not separate and independent; they are a related array of systems of social action, each of which modifies the expression of every other. A. W. Small presented this idea of the multiprocessual nature of a going concern in his classic statement of railroading:

> When a railroad man speaks of "railroading," he has in mind primarily some or all of the technical processes involved in the building and management of railroads. He is thinking of the financing processes, the construction processes, the maintenance processes, the equipping processes, the train-operating processes, the auditing processes, etc. All this is the machinery side of railroading—its technique, the details of its methods. (32)

In order to obtain a comprehensive and scientifically sophisticated perspective regarding the nature of human society as a dynamic going concern, it is necessary to examine the processes (with their attendant structures, functions, and factors) in accordance with some inclusive and revealing classificatory scheme. The present study will be based on the following scheme:

Proto Processes. The proto processes consist of the master or elemental processes that are found wherever two or more persons are in some sort of relationship as they seek to survive. The processes are general and are involved in all societal action.

Culturization Processes. The culturization processes are those involved in the forming, transmission, re-forming, and domestication of the elements that constitute the culture system or structure of the given society. These processes provide the society with its stock in trade. Unless they are understood, the other characteristic operations of a society will be only vaguely comprehended.

Processes That Enable Men to Meet the Subsocial Requirements of Living. These processes include: (a) the social processes of adjustment to, and control of, the physical and biological environments; (b) the social processes affecting the population—those which effect the vital changes in numbers, flow, composition, and blending of the living human creatures of the society; (c) the processes of areal distribution, location, and relocation of individuals, groups, and institutional organizations.

Processes of Societal Organizations. These processes of structuralization and functionalization involve (a) the general processes of societal organization and operation; (b) the processes of formation and integration of various kinds of groups, especially, in our society, the formation and operation of formal, purposive organizations; (c) the processes and functions of community organization and change; (d) the processes of institutionalization and of the operation of institutional systems; (e) the processes of horizontal and vertical differentiation, with the functions of each; and (f) the processes of mobility between the variously spaced elements.

Processes of Disorganization. Processes of disorganization, or of destructuralization and defunctionalization, that continually threaten the organization, stability, continuity, and operational efficiency of a society include (a) the separative and isolative processes; (b) the opposition processes; (c) the processes making for societal decadence; and (d) those making for societal ossification.

Processes of Continuous Societal Normalization and Equilibration. These consist of: (a) the processes relating to general social order and control; (b) the processes of societal regulation; (c) the processes of societal maintenance; and (d) the processes of reorganization and reconstruction.

Important Aspects of the Present Study

Our primary objective will be to do six things: (1) to identify as many as possible of the known universal and recurrent social processes; (2) to provide an adequate conceptualization of each with definition and description; (3) as indicated in the preceding section, to give a sufficiently comprehensive classification by major divisions and combinations of processes to indicate both the specific functional significance of each, and the interrelationship of all in the total societal operation; (4) frequently as a point of departure to analyze the nature of the major essential societal structures in which, and the structural conditions under which, processes operate; (5) to indicate, so far as possible, the known and proximate factors in the social situations out of which the structures and processes develop; (6) to determine the functions performed and the effects produced by the processes.

There is no thought of repudiating the classical treatments of processes or the later uses of them. We too will be dependent upon them, resorting so far as possible to current conceptualizations and classification. But in order to carry out our objective of presenting a more accurate, adequate, and meaningful interpretation of a society in action, it will be necessary to revise, reinterpret, and copiously supplement the existing materials on processes. Some processes as currently conceived will be redefined, and some thus far neglected, or overlooked, or not identified, owing to existing perspectives, will be named, described, and located. Analytical uses will be made of certain processes which bear only faint resemblance to existing practices.

Neither blanket nor unattached descriptions of processes will do, even though such descriptions greatly simplify matters. We need to see *where* the processes operate in the various areas of society, *why* they operate under the given conditions, and *how* they operate. Otherwise, we do not have information suitable for application.

Conditions and Processes. Several general considerations should be kept in mind. Processes invariably produce *conditions.* These conditions are often given the same name. For example, accommodative or integrative processes can produce conditions of accommodation or integration. We must distinguish between the processes that constitute a type of change and the conditions which result.

Certain of the more common processes will be treated several times at different points in the analysis. This does not constitute duplication or inconsistency of treatment. Various processes, under varying circumstances, are related to varying functions and have varying effects. Hence, they must be examined in these different areas of societal operation. This we deem permissible, since the project is an analysis, not a glossary, of processes. Competition, for example, is involved in the assembling, movement, and ecological organization of individuals and groups, in the relationships of persons and groups within and between classes, and as a motivating and a separative factor in economic, political, religious, and almost every other kind of activity. Social mobility is a basic process in the operation of the class system and in certain aspects of societal and individual disorganization and also operates as an equilibrative-maintenance process. Moreover, the processes are in a state of continual interplay and overlapping with each other, and they are all functionally interrelated.

Dual Relationships of Some Processes. Some processes, depending upon the specific situations, will be found to have both a causal and a functional relationship to each other. Some, as, for example, dissociation and association, or domination and equalization, generate each other, and each is in some measure dependent upon the other for its occurrence. Various processes also permanently and ceaselessly interfere with each other. Similarly, dichotomies of various sorts appear in such an analysis: constructive-destructive processes, cooperation-conflict, integration-disintegration, equalization-stratification, association-isolation, organization-disorganization. The effect of a given process is also often a matter of the degree to which it works itself out. Individualization, for example, in a mild degree may be organizationally and functionally contributory to effective social operation, or it may be neutral, or, in extreme form, it may be highly disorganizing. As in this present discussion, occasional mention will have to be made of processes and functions as phases of a given discussion before they have been competently defined and described. They will be analyzed within the frames of reference where they are of major pertinence.

The various processes ***produce chains of effects.*** For example, acculturation processes are continually producing new aspects of both organizing and disorganizing processes, and both of these bring into effect the necessity of reorganization. The processes of control require exercise of authority and the creation of some regimentation, which in turn require equalization, and this in turn almost inevitably leads to new differentiation and specialization.

Finally, it should be pointed out that our theoretical knowledge in the field of social dynamics has not yet reached a high level of scientific exactitude, basically important though this may be. By compiling and synthesizing the information that *is* available, however, we will be able to formulate reasonably sound working generalizations and present a fairly cogent conception of society in action. No one conceives of these generalizations as 100 percent sound and acceptable. They largely take the form of an informal modalizing of the findings in the way of facts and of the conclusions to date. They should be viewed as tentatives, as hypotheses or working hunches, and points of departure for further investigation. This is in large part an exploratory study in which we are all participating.

CHAPTER II

SOCIETAL LIFE AND MODERN HUMAN SOCIETY

ALL LIVING THINGS have some degree of social life. No living things are ever completely and continuously solitary; they always have some interaction and reciprocity. In certain instances this living together, this relationship between separate but dependent parts, has an over-all structuring and a functioning that we speak of as *organization*. This organization is the essential feature of a *society*. What are the advantages of social life as such? What are the salient characteristics and primary functions of societally organized social life? Human beings, individually and collectively, are markedly different from other creatures in certain crucial respects. How do the different kinds of subhuman societies differ from human ones and why? Finally, not all human societies, past and present, are alike. How do the simpler folk societies differ from the complex industrialized-urbanized society in which we live? In finding working answers to such questions we will gain a clearer insight into the nature of the going concern in which social processes operate. We see human society as a thing of many parts that operate together and have definite functions to perform in the operation of the whole—functions which the parts carry on in certain typical ways and under various typical conditions, and with certain typical effects.

Societal Life

It seems to be an irrefutable fact that at whatever level of life societies are found, they are the major instruments of contemporary adjustment and continuous existence of the given species. The parts contribute to the whole, giving it a durability and persistence apart from that of the constituent individuals. Societies everywhere ensure survival by some degree of mutual responsiveness and influence and some joint and reciprocal action of the organic units of the species living in occasional or continuous propinquity.

Societies are never mere aggregations, that is, a mere gathering or collecting together of individuals —possibly highly heterogeneous individual units— because of their passive subjection to the same external conditions, though under certain circumstances aggregations may be converted into societies. As Herbert Spencer said, a society is formed only when, in addition to juxtaposition, the relationships of the united units are of a cooperative nature and redound to the benefit of the whole. Whether this cooperation is automatic and unconscious or is the result of planned organization, it consists of at least a partial or temporary integration of the activities of individuals with the activities of other individuals. Thus, all are part of a mutual aid procedure. Everywhere individuals are functional parts of societies because more can be achieved cooperatively than singly. (46) Many, if not most creatures, do better living that way.

The elemental fact with respect to societal life is that it is a great boon to survival. In general, societal life means increased efficiency in survival at the lower animal levels owing to combined *life* and at the higher levels owing to combined *effort.* The basic, hypothetical, functional *advantages* of societal life are, briefly, the following:

Maintenance of Population

Societal life enhances the maintenance of the population. Nutriment can be more readily obtained and assured, and the territory from which it is obtained can be more readily monopolized and utilized. The members together can protect themselves better against the exigencies of nature and injury by hostile creatures. Reproduction is facilitated, and offspring are more readily protected and nurtured. In general, strength and safety inhere in numbers, although these advantages are greatest with an optimal number, that is, the number which, under given conditions at a given time, provides the greatest welfare returns per unit of population. There can be too few to meet the conditions of life effectively, and there can be overcrowding.

Network of Relationships

Societal life provides a network of relationships. Within these relationships the individuals of various age, sex, and functional potentiality, as well as the various smaller groupings and functional categories, find their appropriate place. It makes possible the best utilization of all of the different members. Thus, the energies resident in all the component units are organized, integrated, and directed to a definite end—survival.

Division of Labor

Societal life makes possible some division of labor and specialization of function, either on an inherited or on an acquired basis. This means that the energy of more individuals is concentrated more efficiently on more specific tasks of benefit to the population as a whole. Hence, a more elaborate system of cooperation along all lines essential to survival can be provided.

Learning

Societal life is conducive to learning, at least at the higher animal levels where there is the possibility of learning. The interstimulation of association invites some degree and kind of communication, makes possible suggestion and imitation, and offers reciprocal incitement to trial and error action.

Motivation and Cooperation

In societal life there can be motivation and cooperation, Competition as a motivating factor comes into play and, if not too severe, increases the effectiveness of individuals as group members. Furthermore, enjoined living improves the efficacy of the group as a cooperating functional unit, either in competition or in cooperation with other social organizations. Also societal life motivates resistance to, and protection against, outsiders.

In general, societal life is *organization* of some degree and type. With the social stability of organization, members are more efficient individually and socially. (1; 19)

Orientation of This Study

It is important at the outset to indicate the special orientation of this study. The central and essential obligation in any science is to present the facts and principles involved in the ideal-typical aspects of its phenomena. The body of available theory covering the processes, functions, and related factors with respect to human society as a going concern will be drawn upon in this analysis. However, we will not attempt continually to refer to human societies of different historical epochs, different areas, and different cultural levels, either as sources of data or as examples of societal features. Definitive sociology must eventually do this, but at present sufficient data are not available to do it properly. To attempt to encompass all societies invites, and inevitably results in, both piecemeal and diffuse treatment.

We will use as our general *frame of reference* a modern complex society, in most instances our own American society, and our *frame of time* will be the recent past, the present, and the immediate future. Any deviations from this principle will be only for the purpose of highlighting peculiar characteristics, processes, and functions of present-day American society. This does not mean, however, that the available materials regarding the structures, functions, and processes of an ideal-typical society, as well as those relating to specific societies, will be ignored. The massive body of sociological and related materials will be the data upon which the present analysis will be based. The treatment will be synthetic rather than comparative.

The processual interpretation and analysis of human society require first of all an overview of its general nature; a brief spotting of its unique features, as compared with the societies of other living things; the presentation of the generally accepted hypotheses as to its typical and essential functions; and finally, some indication of the special characteristics of modern Western complex societies and the major occurrences responsible for these peculiarities.

Salient Characteristics of a Society

An ideal-typical human society is a complex system or web of relationships between human beings whereby they are enabled to survive and, preferably, also to flourish. It has a number of salient ever-existent and related characteristics. These will be briefly presented.

A Demographic Whole

A society is a demographic whole; that is, it consists of a population—males and females of all ages—with a more or less normal distribution among the age and sex categories. This population has persisted for a period of time, and it must be self-perpetuating through the generations if the society is to endure.

A Common Geographic Area

This population occupies a definite common geographic area, which often is also a common national, political jurisdiction. This common territory is itself a symbol of the population's uniqueness and unity. Not only do the members have a common physical domain, but they have spatial contiguity within it and are distributed according to recognizable spatial patterns.

Variety of Interaction

A society possesses a variety of types of interaction among its constituent human beings. As sentient, psychic creatures these human beings constantly act and react upon each other. Because of intercommunication and a multiplicity of common needs and interests they are interdependent and interfunctional. These interactions take the form of a multiplicity of relationships and reciprocities. This fact of interpersonal relations and of functional interdependence of individuals and groups is one of the central features of a society. It is the background fact in what has been referred to as social organization.

A Feeling of Solidarity

The members of a society have more than communicative and interdependent relations among themselves. *A definite pattern of solidarity feeling prevails* among them. They think of themselves as belonging together, and they live together with an essential degree of unity and understanding which rests upon a common historical experience of some length. They have a common mode of life and an *esprit de corps*. However, they are not completely homogeneous. Because of this common history, combined with the common territory and the common belief that they have a continuity in time, they consider themselves as a greater unit, more or less distinct from other similar human societal bodies. They interact understandingly with one another more readily and more frequently than with outsiders. Furthermore, they have a common purpose, a common and unique ethos or spirit, and think of themselves as having a common destiny.

A Total Culture

A given society has its own total culture. While many of the features of this culture may be shared with other societies, its own geographic setting, its physical and biological resources, its ethnic contacts and composition, its historical experiences, its scientific and technological level, give the culture a perceptible uniqueness. These unique features are traditional, habitual, and socially shared; they stand out in all of the society's techniques, relationships, and ideas. Over a period of time the elements of this culture become better adapted to the needs of the people, to the opportunities and limitations of their geographic environment, and to the demands of survival and collective living. The elements also become better adapted to one another by a process known as "integration." (7)

Societal Organization

Members of a society are societally organized. They belong to and participate in numerous, diverse, but coordinated groups and divisions, such as locality groups, kin groups, class groups, occupational groups, highly functional and purposive organizations, within the larger whole. Each group centers around common needs and commonly held interests. Among the groups some are temporary and others persist through generations. They differ in terms of their strategic position in the society, but the society's total collective life is made up to a major extent of the actions of these groups, which constantly adapt and readapt themselves to each other. Hence, the over-all organization of the society is that of a cooperative entity of innumerable groups with varied functions and varied degrees of organization.

An Essential System of Institutions

A society has an essential system of institutions for maintenance and regulative purposes, in the operation of which the members all cooperate in some degree, consciously and unconsciously. By all manner of chartered directives and established usages and procedures the members are able to support and provide for themselves, more or less autonomously, in the satisfaction of their numerous basic needs and the fulfillment of interests. The people have learned to live and work together and have achieved a considerable degree of stability and regularity of operation.

Functional Differentiation

Members of a society are *functionally differentiated* as to unlike and unequally specialized but interdependent activities *and variously stratified* as to position. They understand their differences, which are, in fact, phases of a unity which consists of an integration of numerous varied and hierarchically scaled but complementary functions.

Difference from Other Societies

The members of a society often think of themselves as set off from other societies by perceptible and sometimes cherished differences and even antagonisms which are demonstrated in typical attitudes and actions and which occasionally greatly complicate intersocietal relations.

Over-All Functioning Unity

In general, the actions, relations, and organized procedures of a society fit together into some kind of an over-all, organized, functioning unity or pattern. Hence, the performance of the society, day by day, in reasonable time, can be predicted, and the society itself is self-renewing, continuous, and possessed of indefinite durability.

A society, however, consists of more than organized individuals and groups; it is also a continuous, interfunctional, operative mechanism. It has an on-going processual existence. The *life* or *action* of it is the fact of supreme importance. Without this functioning the structure is a dead thing. Furthermore, while we may know the position, size, shape, and composition of a structure, or of any organism or mechanism, we still have only a vague and partial knowledge of it unless we understand its functions and its operation. Finally, as already noted, the only real justification of a social structure, a whole society, or of anything that *exists*—that is, its reason for existence—is *what it does.*

Primary Functions of a Society

If a society is to endure there are certain basic functions related to an array of fundamental objectives which it must perform. (15) The primary function of man, individually or collectively, like any other form of life, is to survive. Men, eternally and universally, are confronted with the two inescapable alternatives: survive or perish. They have sought to conform to the first of these compulsions and, like many other forms of life, have achieved greater success when they pursued this quest jointly rather than separately. Hence, no society exists without elemental and determinable reasons; it is not an end in itself; it and its people perish when it ceases to perform its basic functions in sufficient degree. Basically, therefore, a society is an organized, collective, functional device to do certain essential things. It is *a field of action, formed in action,* and *exists for action.* This functioning is, in fact, the *raison d'être* of any society.

Certain hypotheses, based on the current knowledge regarding the functioning of a typical society, are presented herewith. Since a society is a functioning whole, these various functions are related and overlap each other.

Adequate Means of Communication

First of all, a society must provide adequate means of communication, for without communication no social activities can be carried on. In human societies, this means a common language, and in some modern societies, literacy and such symholic devices as media of verbalization, conceptualization, and transmission of human experience.

Satisfaction of Physical Needs

A society must provide techniques for at least the minimal satisfaction at any given time of the nutritive, hygienic and other physical needs of its existing members to ensure their survival as biological specimens. The natural environment must be utilized, manipulated, even reconstructed in some measure, so as to provide food, clothing, shelter, and accessibility. These essentials must be adequately produced, distributed, and enjoyed by the population, and appropriate rules governing their ownership, use, and exchange must prevail. There must also be protection, as far as possible, against disease, accident, and injury by the catastrophes resulting from natural physical or biological causes and from those due to societal neglect or mismanagement.

The provision of these elemental (primary) essentials invariably implies some division of labor among individuals and groups and the rendering of a multiplicity of productive, distributive and protective services to each other by the individuals and groups constituting the society. It involves also procedures and techniques for continually adjusting the population to the ever-changing natural environment.

Continuous Replacement of Members

No society can continue without recruitment of numbers of members at least adequate to replace those lost by death and emigration. Hence, it is especially necessary to provide for the biological reproduction of the population by motivating to, safeguarding, and standardizing parenthood and by protecting children against physical and social hazards to their growth and well-being. No society can safely depend for new members on immigration, adoption, or conquest.

Minimal Societal Disorder

Internal societal friction and disorder must be minimized. Hence, it is necessary to provide for adequate collective stability, security, and continuity by establishing techniques that inhibit individual tendencies contrary to cooperation and order, by suppressing or eliminating antisocial individuals and groups, and, positively, by assigning to persons and groups differentiated but complementary statuses and roles that contribute to order and efficiency of operation. Such functions, properly provided, control human behavior and human liberties, both liberate and limit the activities of men, and set up standards and sanctions for them to abide by. Basically essential also is the protection against external aggression and the maintenance of peace with outsiders.

Socialization of New Members

A society must provide for the socialization of new members, whether acquired by birth or by immigration. The function of primary survival importance here is the fullest possible transmission of the entire cultural system to the younger generations so that they can take their places as functioning adults and make their contribution to the society's operation. The socialization function includes, especially, providing the new members with an understanding of the society's symbols, with as much of its extant knowledge as possible, with an appreciation of its values, and with adequate training in its skills and techniques.

Maintenance of Organization

Growing out of the above is the over-all necessity for a society to provide for and maintain its associational and institutional organization, that is, the concrete forms of accepted and standardized relationship and interaction whereby all the essential functions for working and living together adequately, even prosperously, are (unconsciously or purposively) conducted.

Development of Culture

A society must provide for the continuous development of its system of culture; that is, it must provide the mediums, whether acquired from within by discovery and invention or from without by borrowing and adaptation, of adequate adjustment at the human level to all of the recurrent conditions of existence. Part of this is maintenance of the identity and sufficient integration and consistency of the elements of the culture.

Level of Survival

A society must provide for the survival of the higher forms of development in satisfying, protecting, and expanding men's psychic and spiritual needs and expressions, that is, those over and above the elemental material things essential to mere biological maintenance and the bare requirements for societal order and perpetuity. The human problem is not merely one of survival of individuals and organizations, but also one of *level of survival.* This means that a human society should furnish outlets for man's numerous derived or learned needs. Opportunities for companionship, play, and recreation must be provided.

This higher level of survival is concerned especially with the knowledge of men and their interests, ideologies, and values—the things that men believe in, the ways they think, their definitions of life situations in terms of which they act. In most instances they wish to achieve a *standard* of living and to satisfy intellectual, political, ethical, aesthetic, and religious wants. These give meaning, purpose, and a sense of worth-whileness to the human venture. Of special note are the need for intellectual cooperation and exploration, for developing systems for explaining natural phenomena (magic, myth, and science), for art forms to give satisfaction to expressional urges, and for the means of explaining man's place in the universe and of adjusting his relations to the supernatural. Involved also are techniques for escaping from reality and achieving compensations for the discomforts and thwartings which man's submergence in the corporate existence of his society inevitably imposes upon him. (13, p. 412)

Motivation and Renewal

A society must provide adequacy of motivation for a sufficient proportion of its population to assure all forms of essential societal participation, individual and group performance, and conformity to the society's accepted requirements of action. This involves continuous teaching and the manipulation of both informal and institutional penalties and rewards. Without sufficient motivation the socially essential things are not done. A society must also provide for its own renewal and reorganization as dissociation, decadence, or ossification threaten or occur.

Beyond these lie the over-all objectives of providing for material, intellectual and spiritual prosperity, the essential ego satisfactions flowing from the favorable responses of others, and the fullest possible individual fulfillment consistent with general well-being. All this depends upon a durable, smoothly and efficiently functioning, security-guaranteeing, opportunity-producing social system.

Human and Animal Societies

Although all manner of living forms have some kind and degree of societal life, human society, in addition to the common-animal features, has certain strikingly unique characteristics and functions simply because *man is man.* These will be illuminated in contrast by means of a very brief examination of subhuman animal societies. This will be one of our few resorts to comparative sociology.

On the basis of our knowledge of the animal societies that have been analyzed, they may be arranged along a continuum ranging from the groupings of protozoa or unicellular forms at one extreme to the societies of man at the other. This continuum consists not only of increasing diversity and complexity of social life, though such features are clearly involved, but of increasing consciousness of participation, of learning, of purposiveness, planning, and contriving in organization and functioning, and of the existence of symbolic transmission of what has been learned about desirable individual and social living. The bare outlines of the types of societies arrayed along this continuum will be briefly presented, with special emphasis upon the wide interval between human society and that of the other primates. Man's distinctiveness in the animal world also reveals itself in many features of his societal life.

Protozoan Colonies

The social life of protozoa is derived from the fact that they are single-celled organisms. They exist in colonies and in a medium over which they have no control. Their contacts are accidental and they spend their social life in physical cohesion with each other, acting together as a single organism. The common life involves merely discriminatory reactions to different individuals mainly in relation to mating. In most of the species and varieties that have been investigated there are two sex types. Individuals of the same sex type do not react together, and where the individuals are all of the same sex type, they remain scattered and separate.

If there are different sex types among the mingled individuals, those of different sex types adhere together, forming large clots. Presently some of these unite into pairs by contact of their oral surfaces. These pairs continue in congregation until there has been a division and exchange of parts of the nuclei and chromosomes. Eventually new individuals may develop from each such union. Among some species there seems to be a division of labor based on other physical differences among the individuals composing the colony. In all instances the social bonds between the members are purely physical and physiological and mainly for sexual or reproductive purposes. (37)

Insect Societies

The most highly organized populations among metazoan or multicellular and detached animals below the human level are found among certain species of the social insects—ants, termites, bees, and wasps, although these social insects are a very small portion (some 3 per cent) of the 500,000 or more known species of insects. Among these the individuals are not physically attached to each other. They are sentient creatures, and the bonds uniting them are somewhat psychic as well as physical. The reaction to stimuli provided by other members, however, is always in a manner fixed by inheritance.

The rather extensive division of labor in maintenance functions in some species is based upon physiologically specialized differences between castes of individual insects. There may be such specialized forms as queens, which produce the offspring, drones, workers, and fighters. Members of each group play their unvarying roles and perform their tasks repetitively as a matter of special physiological constitution and instinctive response. Their action is "already learned"—a matter of genetic potentialities.

Communication is of a sensory sort and seems to occur by means of smell and touch through the antennas. Among most of the social species the individuals seem to recognize members of their own colony and discriminate, often to the extent of violent exclusion, against outsiders. In general, the young are produced, protected, and nurtured, and the elemental needs of subsistence, shelter, internal order, and protection against aggression for all members are provided for in an efficient joint manner.

The whole community, however, acts like a single organism, and the behavior of all the members in their respective cooperative roles is entirely unvarying and automatic, a matter of innate, unlearned reflexes, built up through long natural selection. Insect societies are governed by sureness of instinct, and the instincts are limited to specific purposes. Hence, their behavior can be predicted with great accuracy. If anything happens to disorganize the inherited organization of life, it must be re-established according to innate tendencies or not at all. Survival is not through length of life or reflection or any ability to profit by experience, but through enormous fertility.

Societies of Birds and Mammals

These creatures function in fairly durable groups, though some of the groupings are of a seasonal nature. Certain birds, such as pelicans, grackels, crows, and barnyard fowl, live in flocks that seem to indicate some degree of internal organization. Flight organizations take distinctive changing forms. Differences in social position based on superordinate-subordinate relations and a superior-inferior scale (pecking order) seem to prevail, including leadership phenomena. Various noises and other signals lead to different kinds of individual and group action, such as flight, retirement to shelter, advance upon food, or attack upon aggressors and foreign intruders.

Colonies of beavers, which are actually family groups consisting of parents and offspring of the current and past year, cooperate in building dams and lodges and in cutting and dragging trees. Wolf packs, consisting of family groups and larger temporary hunting groups, function jointly. The various herd animals, such as reindeer, elk in season, wild horses, and cattle, have guards and watchmen, warning procedures, defense formations, and social dominance and submission patterns.

Among primates, such as monkeys, baboons, orangutans, chimpanzees, and gorillas, we find various degrees of joint activity. They may have monogamous or polygamous family groupings. The polygamous groups consist of a sort of harem organization with the dominant male, several females, the immature young, and a fringe of young, unemancipated males. Some live in well-organized bands which hunt and feed jointly, and fight trespassers upon their territory. When they fight, however, the cooperation does not seem to be a matter of intelligent apprehension of the situation or of altruism toward band members, but an immediate response to the stimulus of fear.

There is some regulation of conduct among members of groups in such activities as feeding, flea-hunting, sex play, and migration. This intragroup control is largely based upon dominance and submission as determined by competitive interaction. The dominant creature is usually a male though in some cases it may be a female. The dominance mainly rests upon physical strength and prowess with cleverness as an occasional element. The degree of dominance determines the extent to which bodily appetites are satisfied, the females a male may possess, the amount of food an individual eats, and the extent of punishment received.

Birds and mammals have various means of communication, such as vocal sounds (cries and calls), bodily gestures and postures, manual exploration, and, among the primates and possibly some others, facial expression. They make and respond to social stimuli. They receive considerable conditioning, largely by hard knocks, within the group, and they show some capacity to learn. In fact, at the higher animal levels, much of the responsive behavior of individuals toward others is learned. However, each individual must do all the learning which he uses himself and cannot pass on to others the result of his experience, save as the other acquires it by imitation. From the organization along dominance-submission lines, it can be inferred that leadership phenomena exist. Finally, at the higher levels, some of the cooperation seems to be of a conscious nature. This seems to be the case especially with respect to guarding territory, wangling food, and protecting against enemies. However, the consciousness rests on hunger and fear and is a response to instinctive and physical stimuli.

In general, in subhuman animal societies interstimulation is on a mechanistic basis, and the main incitements to social participation are reciprocal feeding, sexual behavior, reciprocal care, need of protection, and shelter seeking. The common participation results mainly from sensory stimuli and is expressed according to inherited, unchanging, or very slowly changing patterns. Even such specialization of social function as exists is a matter of physiological characteristics, with sex and physical strength as the most important factors. While there is frequent evidence of social as well as other contrivance among some of the subhuman species, the fruits of this contrivance either of a natural or procedural nature are not passed on to later generations, except as they can be acquired by direct imitation.

Human Societies

Human societies have most of the characteristics of animal societies as essential aspects of their functioning, but there are certain other unique features that stand out in sharp contrast and give human social life its *special* functional distinctiveness. It should be remembered that there is a tremendous gulf between the social organizations of human beings and those of the most highly social and most highly developed subhuman animals. The uniqueness of human society is fundamentally the uniqueness of man as compared with all other animals. The human distinctiveness will be found to be of stellar and strategic importance in the discussion of every process and function treated in this work. (10, pp. 197-203; 30; 34)

Complexity of Human Societies. The individual units, to be sure, are all *Homo sapiens,* with common biological and psychological characteristics and processes, and not physiologically differentiated elements within the species, as among insects, for example. Human societies themselves, however, are not only collectivities of individuals or of a species living together as simple colonies or reproductive and maintenance groups, but collectivities of collectivities that extend over wide and diverse areas, consist of different human varieties, come from different physical environments, and have different histories behind them.

Mental and Spiritual Social Life. The social life of subhuman animals is almost entirely corporeal and psycho-physical. It is largely based on instinct, that is, inborn, inherited, unlearned patterns of behavior adjusted to a specific past stimulus situation. Species living mainly with the aid of instinct respond automatically in a manner best suited for survival during their past career. Hence, their individual and social life is largely unconscious and a matter of ready-made responses.

Man's instincts are few, and although they are powerful propulsions, they are of a more or less undifferentiated nature, ill-suited by themselves to enable him to survive. They are supplemented, even dominated, by his mental and spiritual capacities. Man thinks. He also remembers. Thus, not only do his peculiar mental faculties enable him to know more than any other creatures; they also enable him to learn more and faster. Thinking and knowing enable him to surmount mere *overt* trial and error. He is able to engage in *inner* trial and error; to find meanings in things and occurrences; to imagine, analyze, and anticipate; to experiment, create, and seek and find solutions to problems. He can sublimate his urges and emotions, make and enjoy beauty, and comprehend the abstract and the unseen.

There is a continual interplay of man's mental capacities and his social life. In its characteristic forms his society is largely a product of mentality, for most of his activities are learned, that is, acquired as a result of interpersonal stimuli originating in group life. Similarly, his very association with his fellow humans not only enables him to execute and realize these mental and spiritual traits, but also stimulates, enhances, and directs them.

These factors point to several interrelated propositions based on accepted facts regarding man in his typical society.

Communication by Means of Symbols. Some of the higher animals, such as apes and monkeys, show some ability to learn and remember during their own lifetime. But lacking all except the most rudimentary ability to symbolize (possibly through a few standardized, developed sounds and gestures), the members of one generation are incapable of transmitting acquired knowledge and attitudes to the next generation. Each generation must, through its own actual participation in experience, acquire the same knowledge and attitudes all over again.

Man is the only animal capable of symbol behavior. (45; 108) He lives his life at the symbolic level. By symbolic expression we mean specifically the fact that man, in association with his fellows, arbitrarily makes, establishes, and uses language. He devises conventionalized systems of expressions and signs, especially words, which carry standard meanings. These systems of words and methods of combining words are used and understood by a considerable number of people.

The animal can simulate impulse or desire by physical gesture, but he cannot describe it. Description implies thinking, and thinking or forming ideas can of necessity be done only by means of words. Without words we have only hazy perception, not conception. Thinking is dependent upon and determined by language.

By means of symbols man can not only conceptualize and specifically, accurately, and fully define his experiences, but can also remember and transmit in detail and completeness what he has learned. Furthermore, both oral and written words enable him to "package" and "store" experience for others remote in space and time.

Culture. Since man is the only animal capable of symbol behavior, he is the only creature to possess culture. (29; 44) By means of symbols and the resultant greatly facilitated remembering and learning and storing, plus his ability to contrive and construct, man creates a vastly significant cultural environment over and above the physical and the biological. Hence, he behaves socioculturally. He thus "adds an extra dimension to existence, and makes human what would otherwise be merely animal." (34, pp. 3, 43) From this all other differences flow.

The subhuman animals begin life where their parents began with respect to behavior patterns and reaction to the material objects of the environment. They have societies, but they lack culture. Man, on the other hand, begins with a rich accumulation of acquired patterns of behavior, contrived modifications of the physical and biological environment, tools, skills, techniques, bodies of knowledge, beliefs, ideas, standards and rules, and a long-developed system of societal organization and operation, which the ingenuity of his ancestors has produced, and which he and his contemporaries and descendants will expand, impair, or reconstruct.

This culture is thus the result of accumulation through the ages, and gives man's social life the historical dimension. (10, pp. 39-40) Similarly, his social life is not only a matter of passive, trial-and-error experience, but of everlasting discovery and invention, of selective borrowing from all ages and peoples with whom any symbolic communication has been possible, and of continuous unplanned and planned reconstruction. Man survives and prospers by means of his culture. (104)

Conscious, Purposive, Norm-Directed Social Life. Man is conscious of his relationships with his fellow beings; he conceives of them as creatures of some worth in themselves with whom he must work out his destiny. With these he exists not merely passively—biologically and psychologically—but constructively and spiritually. Man is ever developing batteries of interests and values, of objectives and purposes, to be achieved, if not always for the whole society, at least *among* his fellows. He seeks not only existence and survival, but ascending levels of living. Most members of the society are conscious of, though not always highly articulate about, these ends, which function as motivators and guides to individual and joint behavior.

To achieve these objectives and purposes men jointly set up norms or standards of performance. These norms define action in the multiplicity of social situations and indicate what ought and ought not to be. Finally, men in society establish positive and negative sanctions to enforce performance.

Constructed Mechanism of Social Organization. Human social organization does not consist merely of stimulation and responsiveness or of something learned on the spot. It consists of all manner of associations and organizations of men to effect particular and more or less well-known and accepted objectives; it consists of institutions which chart and regulate the varied behavior of men in the interests of social order and maintenance and quality of living. Division of labor is effected for more efficient operation, and persons are trained more or less formally for their respective roles. Inequalities among men and groups are more or less fairly arranged for by means of positional systems. The social ways of life are deliberately and systematically transmitted to each generation and practiced under some group supervision. In brief, *the total social organization is not given; it is a constructed means of survival and prosperity.* The society with the most efficient organization has the best chance of survival and prosperity.

Dynamic Quality of Human Society. Human social life is dynamic rather than static. The social behavior of animals is largely determined by inheritable and physical-environmental factors. Hence, it lacks in itself the potentiality for continual and basic change. Every aspect of man's social life is continually changing, not only as the result of natural and automatically operating factors which affect all life, but especially, because of his learning and communicative ability, his inventiveness, his restless striving, his development of new interests and goals, the very accumulation of his culture, the multiplicity of culture materials ever inviting recombinations, and the recurrent, if not continuous, contact with the "contagious" culture of other peoples. His social life is never static and never in a state of perfect balance; it is an ever-going concern. To interpret it otherwise is to misconceive it.

Complexity of Human Societies

Human societies are not only significantly distinct from subhuman animal societies but vary greatly among themselves. They show great variation in their extent, in the heterogeneity and multiplicity of their constituent elements, in the complexity and purposiveness of organization, and in the nature of their ethos and relationships. Three classical dichotomies will be briefly mentioned and a fourth treated in some detail in the ensuing section as a means of depicting the important features of a society such as ours. Each presents a contrasting of ideal-typical* forms of societal organization which can be looked upon, not as polar concepts, but as segments at the extremes of a continuum. Most forms of actual social life range somewhere along the line of the continuum. These four di-

*The term *ideal-typical,* or *constructed,* type, will be used repeatedly. It is indispensable both in conceptualization and definition and as a device for establishing criteria of types and subtypes in the classification of phenomena. Every actual example of a phenomenon—whether physical, biological, psychological, or social—has its unique, divergent, and exceptional features. But science, by its very nature, seeks to create order out of chaos and diversity and seeks to establish the significant uniformities and the recurrent and related aspects of phenomena. Hence, the scientist creates a working conception of the ideal-typical regarding kinds of phenomena as a special instrument of analysis. Scientific knowledge is, in one sense, a collection of ideal-typical concepts. The scientist selects

chotomies are by no means mutually exclusive; all have common and overlapping features.

Gemeinschaft and Gesellschaft

In 1887 Ferdinand Toennies distinguished between *Gemeinschaft* (community) and *Gesellschaft* (society). *Gemeinschaften* are small, spontaneous, intimate groupings of homogeneous persons, in which interrelationships are personal and familistic, based on common, localized interests, and in which a high degree of natural solidarity and mutuality obtains. *Gesellschaften* are larger collectivities, diffused in space, more heterogeneous as to personnel, and characterized by impersonal, contractual relationships and great functional specialization. Solidarity is achieved by rational or willed, even compulsory, action and control. (54; 55; 57)

Mechanistic and Organic Solidarity

Emile Durkheim distinguished between societies with *mechanistic* and *organic* types of social solidarity. Societies with *mechanistic* solidarity are in an earlier and simpler stage of social development. They are relatively small, separate, and self-sufficient. Division of labor and specialization of function are very limited. The solidarity depends upon the mental and moral homogeneity of the members; the social unity is secured by the conformity of members to the same customs, traditions, laws, and moral and religious ideas.

Societies with an *organic* solidarity are artificial mechanisms. They emerge with increasing numbers and density of population and increasing morphological complexity of the society itself. There is great division of labor and specialization of function, with a corresponding decline in self-sufficiency and a vast increase in interdependence of persons and groups. The parts cooperate like the unlike, coordinated units of an organism; social solidarity is *organic*. There is heterogeneity of individuals, the disappearance of mental and moral similarity of individuals, the breakdown of like-mindedness, and the increase of individuality and freedom of action. At the same time there is increase in social isolation and in the emotional and mental insecurity of individuals. The economic and political relations especially are largely governed by contract. Social order and social control are the result of constraint of members by the society itself. There is decay of inherited position, individualization of religion, and increase in cosmopolitanism. (52; 56)

Sacred and Secular Societies

Howard Becker has distinguished between sacred and secular societies. Sacred societies are not sacred in the religious sense of being supernatural or holy. They are societies of piety which cherish and observe the customs, proprieties, and pious observances. They are mentally and socially isolated and may be geographically separated from other groupings. Usually the population is nonliterate and relatively immobile. The relationships are intense and are based on kinship, friendship and neighborhood bonds, and locality contacts and interests. The livelihood patterns and forms of property are simple. Their most distinctive feature is that they are conservative and are molded and controlled mainly by tradition. Behavior rests on the long-standing practices of the folkways, the mores, and the proverbs, folk tales, and parables inculcated in childhood. The traditions are further reinforced by elaborate ceremonials. The elders dominate the entire social regimen. There is not much need of coercion, since social control is largely self-maintaining and self-enforcing. In them there is an aversion to the new; hence, resistance to change.

The secular society is the result of the reduction of barriers to communication, trade, and social intercourse. There is both physical and social mobility, with little or no sacred feeling about the

---

the most significant, common, and most frequently recurring characteristics of an object or occurrence and eliminates the unique and the systematically irrelevant features. The constructed type contains all the *essential* properties or elements (for example, the dog show judge's concept of an Airedale; the businessman's concept of a corporation; the sociologist's concept of a community), but not necessarily *all* the variant features of specific examples of the object or occurrence. It is not ideal in the sense of a desirable type; and it is not typical in the sense of average characteristics. Rather, it is the *hypothetical average,* consisting of the most frequently recurring, constant, standard, and essential characteristics, which distinguish the kind of object or occurrence from all others.

family or locality in which one was born. Literacy is at a high level among the members. The population is heterogeneous. Utilitarian differentiation and specialization characterize the economy. Strangeness, anonymity, individuation, and cosmopolitanism prevail. Law and reason, rather than sacred tradition, regulate the predominantly contractual social relations. Social control requires a continuous expenditure of energy and a high degree of purposive, planned organization that involves the threat of force. Enacted rather than primary institutions chart the behavior of individuals and groups.* The fourth dichotomy is that between folk-agrarian and modern industrial-urban societies—perhaps the most fruitful one in interpreting a society such as ours.

Folk-Agrarian and Industrial-Urban Societies Contrasted

Ideal-typical social systems, examined according to their complexity of structure and operation, can be placed along a continuum: isolated social units → folk-agrarian societies → transitional society → industrial-urban-state society. The small, isolated, homogeneous society of nonliterate peoples has been well analyzed by Redfield, Firth, and others. The folk-agrarian society is the one in which most civilized men have lived their lives through the millennia. It was the predominant type in the United States until well into the nineteenth century, and half to two thirds of the world's people still live in such societies. Contemporary folk-agrarian societies are to be found among the primitives and in the so-called "backward" areas of the earth; they are the tribal, communal, and village peoples. Primitive societies have been copiously described by the anthropologists. Backward and backwoods peoples are today to be found in most of Mexico, in parts of Central and South America, in most of Africa, and in many portions of China, India, the South Seas, and central Asia.

The extensive, heterogeneous, industrial-urban society is mainly a development of the nineteenth and twentieth centuries in the Western world, although its features are rapidly spreading to the outermost peoples and areas of the earth. Our own country in the present century is undoubtedly the supremely significant example. For purposes of general orientation, we will confine ourselves to a brief analysis of the folk-agrarian type of society in comparison with the industrial-urban.

To be sure, folk-agrarian, or communal, societies have been developing complexities for many centuries. For at least five thousand years some of them have had cities which were highly influential economically, politically, and culturally. But in the main the cities were isolated and carried the stamp of the rural countryside; they were, in fact, mainly adjuncts of the country. The great bulk of the population lived in the open country or in villages and small towns.

We still have folk-agrarian communities within our larger modern society, but they are losing their "folk" ways and characteristics as their members participate more and more in the activities of the greater society about them. Similarly, modern complex societies still carry some communal characteristics, since they have so recently stemmed from the folk-agrarian way of life.

At intervals during the last four thousand years, there have been societies with complexities of operation and heterogeneity of population and diversity of culture. These were, nevertheless, mainly collections of communal groups. In very recent times, particularly the last two centuries, as science and modern technology have developed, the new means of communication and transportation and modern urban-centered industry, commerce, finance, social services, and culture have given our civilization a set of characteristics that never existed before. Our societal life has come to have a distinctive stamp.

Ideal-Typical Folk-Agrarian Society

A number of features set the folk-agrarian society apart from the industrial-urban society.

Isolated Communities. The separate communities of a folk-agrarian society are relatively isolated

*The earlier treatment of sacred and secular societies goes back to Toennies, Durkheim, Malinowski, and Shotwell. For recent and current interpretations and analyses, see references 49; 50; 51; 53.

—physically, mentally, socially. The majority of the people live in small agricultural communities. The local groups themselves are characterized by physical proximity within fairly restricted neighborhoods, limited by the available food supply and the means of transportation. On the whole the settlement is sparse; the vast hinterland of each is relatively undeveloped. Although the members are not in complete ignorance of the existence of other communities, they have only limited communication with, or interest in, the outside world.

Intimate Communication among Members. In a folk-agrarian society there is intimate communication among the members who are in face-to-face relationship with each other. Most of the relationships occur in the family, the kinship group, and the neighborhood.

Sense of Solidarity. A strong sense of solidarity prevails in folk-agrarian society. The members are closely bound by their local interests, needs, and functions and by their common culture. The warm, personal intimacy, the cohesiveness, and the sentimental ties of the primary group give the members a strong sense of belonging together. They feel an anchorage in the community.

Relative Homogeneity. A folk-agrarian society is relatively homogeneous—ethnically, structurally, functionally, ideologically. The range of reaction of the members is confined mainly to the primary community. In many instances the members through the generations have lived together and apart from others so long that they have developed some characteristic psychological, and occasionally biological, resemblances. They see these resemblances and feel correspondingly united. Outsiders are not always welcomed.

The members know and feel and believe much alike. They have common traditions and customs, like attitudes and habits. They are molded to a great extent by tradition and so are essentially conservative, even reactionary. They seek to pass on their culture unchanged. The moral and religious conceptions are well integrated and relatively unchanging. In these respects they are a "sacred" society. The main functional differentiations are those related to sex and age. The groupings are relatively few and not highly differentiated.

Local Economic Self-sufficiency. Local communities in a folk-agrarian society are largely self-sufficient economically. The economy is mainly agricultural and handicraft, and the exchange and consumption of material products and services are generally, though never completely, local and direct. The handicrafts are practiced on the farms by the members of the family and the "acquired" or "hired" help and in the villages and towns in small shops. Technology is relatively simple.

The Family as the Basic Unit of Social Organization. The family is not only the reproductive and major child-rearing agency but also the main economic unit of folk-agrarian society. Its members carry on all the farm functions cooperatively and do most of the processing of the raw materials produced. The family for the most part is of the patriarchal type. The neighborhood is the organization for shared economic activities. In it and in the village are carried on most of the educational, religious, and recreational activities. In general there are relatively few highly differentiated associations and highly institutionalized groups.

Scant Mobility. Transportation is slow and limited in a folk-agrarian society, and physical movement occurs as an exceptional act, since persons are bound to the immediate locality by kinship ties, relation to the soil, and inherited handicraft. The classes are relatively fixed and "closed," and social position is inherited and retained. Hence, there is little opportunity or occasion for social mobility.

Mainly Informal Social Control. Social control in a folk-agrarian society is largely exercised through the folkways and mores and enforced by the informal pressure of local community opinion. In so far as there is law—and there is for the larger loosely jointed society—it reflects primary group values and is likely to be a direct outgrowth of the mores. A general pattern of law, political action, and social order prevails. The informal sanctions, such as community opinion, gossip, and supernatural taboos, operate with great effectiveness. If the individual violates the sanctions, he feels anxiety and has attacks of "conscience." Deviations from the standards are penalized by the group (and possibly by the supernatural), which turns against the individual, gossiping about him, ridiculing him, or, as a final measure, driving him out of the group.

Ideal-Typical Modern Industrial-Urban Society

In the last two centuries a set of processes has been at work which has brought drastic changes in the interrelationships of human beings and has produced a form of societal organization with new and distinctive features, an organization that is infinitely complex, massive, and fluid.

Development of Technology. Modern society is a product of an array of revolutions. For some of the factors we must go back to the Renaissance, especially to its scientific phase; to the Reformation, particularly to some of its political and economic residues; and to the commercial revolution of the sixteenth and seventeenth centuries.

In the main, however, modern society is the product of the transformations in the way of life induced by a combination of closely related factors of dynamic change: the scientific revolution, the revolution in communication and transportation, the industrial revolution, the urban revolution, the revolution in agriculture occasioned by mechanization and more recently by electrification, and finally the demographic revolution of the last two centuries. These have resulted in a vast modernization process.

The most extensive of these revolutions has been in technology. Man has always had something in the way of technics (tools and implements) and techniques (skills and operational procedures), and these have combined in the form of a technology, that is, a mechanical and organizational system for carrying on the economy of a society.* The unparalleled advance of science in very recent times has vastly increased man's body of systematic knowledge about all aspects of the phenomenal world. The application of this knowledge to human life problems, which is the essence of technology, is the basis of the profound transformations of the total way of life of modern times. Earlier technologies were based largely on rule-of-thumb procedures rather than on systematic scientific knowledge and method. Today, especially in Western society, discoveries and inventions that proceed from the use of scientific methods have given us a host of new technologies—all of them ways of achieving utilitarian ends.

Major Transforming Processes Derived from Recent Technological Advances. Two social processes growing out of scientific and technological development have been of strategic importance in giving modern complex society its distinctive characteristics. They are the reciprocally related processes of industrialization and urbanization.

INDUSTRIALIZATION. Industrialization is the technological process growing out of the utilization of applied science whereby production is accomplished with the use of power machinery. (76) Power machinery is used in manufacturing or processing raw materials, in the extractive industries, and increasingly in agriculture. It involves many features quite distinct from those of a self-sufficient, localized, rural, or homestead, or village shop handicraft economy. For manufacturing it is necessary to have a central supply of mechanical power. The machines, large, numerous, and expensive, must be grouped in factories according to the production lines, thus constituting a mass-production plant.

In mass-production plants there is a large-scale and intricate division of labor and a large labor force carrying on specialized and automatized operations. The specialized activities and jobs are routinized and serialized. All known mechanical means of transportation are used to bring raw materials and half-finished goods to factories and to take consumption goods from the factories, warehouses, and specialized agricultural areas to the final consumers. Both power and machinery are used for communication, as in the telephone, telegraph, radio, and teletype. Production is for an impersonal market, which consists of an unknown mass of scattered clients. Vast amounts of capital must be publicly or privately provided, and monetary arrangements of all kinds are instrumentalized through a complicated credit system.

In view of the magnitude and complexity of the various functions, it is necessary that huge formal organizations, usually taking the corporate form, carry on these operations. This requires in turn

*See Chap. 6 for an elaboration of these terms.

the concentration of many people in densely inhabited urban or metropolitan areas. Increasingly also, for purposes of maximum economy and efficiency, plants engaged in complementary processes are grouped together, thus saving transportation costs.

As a countermeasure to the huge producing and commercial organizations the workers increasingly form themselves into huge labor unions. Not only does industrialization breed mass production and mass exchange; it involves mass bargaining, both between producers and consumers and between workers and employing corporations. Finally, it creates a vast array of standardized products. So far-reaching is industrialization in its social effects that it produces its own dominant way of life.

URBANIZATION. Modern urbanization is a process consisting essentially of the movement of persons to, and their settlement in, urban areas which is due mainly to the concentration there of production, exchange, social-economic services, government, education, the fine arts and the cultural amenities. (95; 96)

There has been some urbanization in all of the great civilizations of the last five thousand years. *Modern* urbanization, however, received its first impetus from the commercial revolution which in a real sense began with the Crusades, but which had its main propulsion in the discovery of new trade routes during the late fifteenth and sixteenth centuries. The vast increase in commerce resulting from the mounting demand for all manner of commodities and the consequent extension of markets created a need for centers of specialized and complementary handicrafts, of transport and transfer, and of exchange. The very increase in commodities available through the widely extended exchange provided the surpluses essential to urban existence. The industrial revolution beginning in the eighteenth century gave the modern urbanization process its distinctive features as it brought about that complex of processes just referred to as "industrialization."

It was not until the host of modern technologies developed that vast concentrations of population could safely exist. These technologies made available cheap and rapid long-distance transportation of persons, raw materials, and finished commodities essential to the employment and maintenance of large, dense populations. As mechanical, chemical, and biological technologies came to be applied to agriculture, they made possible great surpluses of raw materials and food over and above those necessary to sustain the local agrarian communities, and also released many agricultural workers from the rural districts—in fact, forced them to leave.

These technologies improved the means of communication and increased the transmission of ideas and arts, thus enhancing cities as cultural centers. They made possible modern medicine and sanitation, which in turn have permitted masses of people to live safely in close proximity, avoiding serious endemic and epidemic diseases. They also made possible engineering science; it in turn provided water supply, adequate and safe housing and building construction, internal rapid transit, and so on.

Modern urbanization is the indispensable partner of industrialization. (80) The urban system goes with the industrial system. The city is the scene of industrialism's manpower mobilization, its major organizational forms, such as its factories, its finance, credit and commercial operations, its jobbing and retail businesses, and the multiplicity of economic and social services which stem from it.

Urbanization has been referred to above as a centripetal movement to, and a concentration and incorporation of population in, cities. It is more than that, however; it is a process which, with its related industrialization process, also produces a total way of life. (98) It tends, in a surprisingly short period of time, to produce a population the increasing proportion of which lives in cities or metropolitan areas rather than on farms or in small towns.

What is even more important is the fact that the entire society takes on industrial-urban ways, organizational forms, interests, values, and controls. Not only does agriculture become mechanized and more highly specialized, with emphasis on cash crops, as compared with diversified farming, but large-scale, entrepreneurial, even corporate, farming develops. Rural buying and marketing, rural power and protective organizations, and various forms of commercial insurance are introduced. The rural areas lose their isolated, economic, and cultural self-sufficiency as they become dependent upon urban-made machines, agricultural aids, consumption goods, luxuries, and amusements.

Urban ways, interests, values, and ideas are centrifugal as they move out through all the means of communication and transportation. Even rural religion becomes urban-dominated. The rural areas become dependent upon cities for various specialized services. All areal portions of the society become specialized and dependent communities serving the whole national socioeconomic system.

The folk-agrarian society tends to evaporate; the whole society becomes urban-dominated and urban-oriented. (86; 87; 90; 92; 94; 98)

Characteristics of Modern Industrial-Urban Society. The major characteristics of a modern complex society with its industrial-urban way of life will be briefly presented as a setting for the discussion of processes that follows. While the characteristics are interrelated, they must, of necessity, be treated separately for analytical purposes.

HETEROGENEITY OF POPULATION. The population of a society consists of all the people occupying the given area at a given time. Thanks to communication and transportation, a population like our own is recruited not only from the original indigenous population (negligible in our case), but primarily from peoples of various racial, nationality and cultural origins and backgrounds, attracted from the ends of the earth by high industrial and economic opportunities and superior religious, political and social freedoms and opportunities. Within our country these people have lived under a variety of regional, rural-urban, socioeconomic, social psychic, and cultural conditions. They have blended in various ways and produced diverse "biological and cultural hybrids." Any great national society, especially our own, is a vast, complex mozaic of heterogeneous peoples.

MANIFOLD IMPERSONAL RELATIONSHIPS. The heterogeneous population consists of millions of persons massed together in vast aggregations, increasingly taking metropolitan and cosmopolitan form. The contacts that individuals make as they go about their daily affairs are great in number and many are of fleeting though face-to-face nature. People associate constantly with hundreds and thousands of persons, often in close quarters, but mostly with strangers or with persons with whom they have only occasional contact and very limited acquaintance. Less and less are the contacts personal, positive, sympathetic, and friendly as in a folk or folk-agrarian society. They are largely of a secondary-group nature. The individuals are emotionally detached from each other; they know only small parts of other persons, even of acquaintances, not whole persons. They play only segmental roles in their relationships.

Such contacts do not make for solidarity and mutual understanding. Instead they are conducive to individuation, indifference to others, reserve, and a superficial tolerance of anything that does not affect the given individual adversely.

SPATIAL MOBILITY. Owing to abundant transportation facilities the movement in physical space of persons and goods is greater than it has ever been before, both within and between societies. Thanks to communication, people learn readily of alternative and constantly varying economic and social opportunities elsewhere. We are concerned especially with the resultant intrasociety mobility. The movement from locality to locality within either a rural area or a city, from country to city, from county to county, from state to state, or from region to region involves millions of persons annually in the United States.

The place stability of people is less than ever before. However, permanence or stability of residence contributes to group unity and the preservation of institutional organization. It implies participation in a community, established acquaintances, a known reputation, a status, social and moral, which must be maintained, a knowledge of the mores on the part of individuals, and a regularity in community routines.

High mobility hinders all of these. It continually disturbs the existing community equilibrium and requires a new one. The individuals who move must be continually shifting their social gears. When they move into a different region, they must readjust themselves to different local conditions. Victims of mobility themselves tend to be communally untutored, morally isolated, and spiritually nomadic.

DIVISION OF LABOR, SPECIALIZATION OF FUNCTIONS, AND DIVERSIFICATION OF INTERESTS. In a society of extensive area and great numbers, such as our own, there is a great variation in economic functions conducted between and within subareas. Industry is specialized as to location, resources used, and products. A vast specialization of functions exists in commerce and business, government, religion, education, the professions, even crime. There are literally thousands of different occupations.

Persons are further differentiated, not only along the ancient sex- and age-group lines, but as to occupation, class, educational level achieved, income, wealth, and standard of living, types of property held, ethnic grouping, rural and urban locale, ideology, family membership, personal ability and skills, and so on. This makes for an infinite heterogeneity and diversity of interests, a narrowing of the behavior of individuals, and a multiplicity of patterns of behavior.

Multiplicity of Special-Interest Groups. One effect of the diversification of interests is to splinter the population into an infinite number of special-interest groups. These take the place, in large part, of the very much smaller number of groups of the folk-agrarian society based on physical proximity and lack of mobility. The purely local, intimate group, the neighborhood, tends to disappear as such in modern society.

Instead, persons coalesce more or less spontaneously into groups on the basis of choice mutually exercised by the members. These voluntary groups are almost as numerous as the interests current in the society, and they multiply as the interests multiply. Similarly, the particular groups in which a given person participates may be almost as numerous and as varied as his interests and his needs. He belongs to groups that satisfy vocational, class, age, religious, amusement, fraternal, civic, and other interests and needs. As a more or less atomized creature he resorts to participation in some at least of these groups in order to enjoy companionship and to achieve personality identification. However, in the main, these groups get only fractional parts of the activities of people. No single group has the undivided allegiance of the individual. This is due to the fact that because of the different aspects of the individual's life and his different interests he is a member of widely divergent groups.

Some of these voluntary special-interest groups are small and ephemeral, disintegrating as members move elsewhere or develop new interests. Others are of the extended-contact type, function over a wide area, and are more or less formally organized.

Interdependence. With the rapidly increasing division of labor, the specialization of functions, and the complicated interrelations goes a vast interdependence of persons and groups. There is less and less independence and self-sufficiency. All men are cogs in a vast mechanism of many parts; each and all carry on segmental functions and provide mutual services which are essential to the operation of the society as a whole. All of these parts must function together harmoniously and in a state of equilibrium.

Yet this interdependence is of a rational, impersonal, segmental character. The connections of the multitudinous parts rest chiefly on external, more or less mechanical relationship of persons and groups. (118) More and more the interdependent parts must be organized.

Lack of Cultural Unity. Related to the characteristics of vast size and heterogeneity of population, wide geographical extent, and diversification of interests is the existence of a considerable degree of cultural disunity. In a population such as ours, owing to our peculiar immigrant composition, there are various subcultures: English, Germanic, Slavic, Latin, Oriental, American Indian. We have class and regional patterns of culture and rural and urban patterns. There is the conflict of interests between corporations and unions, between sex groups, between age groups, and so on. There are innumerable centers of cultural organization and influence. As a result there is a diversity of standards, values, and modes of acting, a lack of central unifying value and purpose (other than getting on), and a consequent internal disharmony and confusion.

And yet there is a superficial uniformity. The means of mass communication and mass impression, such as newspapers and periodicals, radio broadcasting, television, and high-pressure advertising, with their great volume and continuous repetition, produce a widespread and large-scale, though indirect, flow of interests and attention and a stereotyped mass culture. (109)

There is also the standardization and universalization of ways that comes of machine production and the mass consumption of its products. In general there is a standardization and universalization continually going on as a result of modern communication and exchange of economic, social, and ideological products. But the resultant universals consist of easily comprehended symbols, mainly taking the form of overt patterns. Notable are the success patterns of action, conspicuous consumption, and very generally phrased verbalizations of beliefs and values.

Such a secondary group culture tends to be a horizontal, rather than a depth, culture. The cultural and social solidarity of a mass society depends mainly on the need of jointly achieving mass utilities and mass survival. It is not, however, a rigidly coordinated and integrated cultural system, even though it gives a *sense* of unity and uniformity.

Social Mobility, Social Distance, and Social Ignorance. The social positions are hierarchically arranged. Achievement is emphasized rather than fixed status, and persons are judged by position won in the social scale rather than by inherited family or kinship connections. Positions are acquired by competitive action. Hence, there is great social mobility. Social climbing by exercising talent, utilizing education, and displaying wealth is engaged in. The reverse can also occur.

Related to this is social distance, the social spacing or separation, even segregation, of individuals and groups. The bonds of kinship and the sentiments arising from living together for generations under a common group tradition, such as those in a folk-agrarian society, function less and less in a modern complex mass society. Free rapport and easy and full communication are made difficult by differences in economic and social status, in racial and nationality backgrounds, in educational level, interests, tastes, and preferences.

This distance unavoidably produces vast ignorance of what goes on inside of other persons. We know them mainly as integers, not as living, believing, evaluating, worrying human beings. We find it difficult to feel with them. Hence, the existence of indifferentism, the difficulty of being "my brother's keeper," the presence of "it's none of my business" attitudes toward others.

Secularization and Anomie. In place of a sacred society, such as the folk-agrarian society was in large measure, we have in modern mass societies a tendency toward secularization and the development of a secular society.

In a secular society, owing to physical and social mobility, utilitarian emphases, anonymity and cosmopolitanism, and higher levels of literacy, the traditions and ancient established ways are deemed of little consequence. There is increasing skepticism regarding them. Individuation reaches a high point; self-interest is the dominant appeal; conscience functions less and less. There is a reluctance to accept things on faith or traditional authority. To do so is considered naïve. Rational grounds are insisted upon as a basis for beliefs. The authority for action rests on personal tastes, momentary preferences, sophisticated points of view; persons insist that they have the right to choose.

This secularism carries with it the disintegration of unitary faiths and doctrines. It results in what Durkheim called *anomie.* (52; 56, Bk. III, Chap. 1) *Anomie* consists of normlessness, or a confusion or conflict of norms. There is a lack of clear-cut, generally understood and accepted goals, values, and interests. There is insufficient motivation for many persons and a perplexity regarding both individual roles and group actions. Much activity does not seem to be worth the effort. A disorganization and disintegration of what Linton calls the "designs for group living" occurs. The resulting frustration may lead to personality disorganization and to various types of extremist and emotional movements, such as aberrant religious sects and other escapist phenomena. (55, p. 401; 110; 115, pp. 532-538)

Formal, Deliberately Organized Social Control. In the simpler, more homogeneous, fixed, and intimate folk-agrarian society, the control exercised by the group over the individual in the interest of social order is direct and largely informal. Group opinion and group reaction are the major instrumentalities. The individual adjusts his behavior to conform to group standards, thus avoiding the disfavor and retaliation of the group, and feels obliged to meet their expectations. Moreover, individuals are also more readily indoctrinated under primary-group conditions.

The impersonality, anonymity, and individuation, the physical and social mobility of the population, the social distance and strangeness, and the general complexity and diffuseness of relationships in the mass society, however, do not permit the informal primary-group controls to operate effectively in the interests of general social order. Save in certain exceptional circumstances, the mass society is unconscious of individuals and smaller groups, and strange individuals mean little to each other. Individuals have no reputation to maintain and no expectations of others to fulfill. Furthermore, there is a great variety of standards of behavior, often of a conflicting nature, to choose among. At the same time the social situations acquiring control increase in kind, gravity, and number.

This means that the sanctions of social behavior must be couched in the form of universal, formal, rational laws and regulations. These grow out of the general consensus of the group; that is, they represent the will of the majority or at least that of an effective minority. They must be planned and devised through a governmental process and administered and enforced through the coercive power of political agencies with delegated power, particularly the police force and system of courts. The resultant behavior may be sufficient for purposes of social order, but it takes the form of outer conformity, of abiding to a sufficient degree by the letter of the law.

There is also much control, mainly for purposes of selfish, special-interest group manipulation, exercised through symbols and stereotypes which are managed by people working behind the scenes through their control of the instruments of communication.

Folkways, mores, and customs are not, however, wholly inoperative in a mass society. They function to some extent in the primary-group relationships wherever these survive. But the important points are, first, that the social-control influence of primary groups is waning, and, second, that individuals can easily escape from the control of their primary groups by losing themselves in the sea of strangers. Hence, the utter indispensability of widely influential and impersonally enforced legal and other institutional controls.

Societal Operation through Large-Scale Formal Organizations. In a folk-agrarian society the essential regulatory and maintenance tasks are carried on in small, face-to-face groups. The tasks are relatively simple and understood by all, and the division of labor is determined by sex and age, status, or simple handicraft specialization. The organization is that of customary routines or informal, on-the-spot procedure.

In a mass society, however, such spontaneous or customary organization is utterly insufficient; in fact, it is hazardous. The tasks are elaborate and complicated and indispensable. They involve many persons, each one of which is crucially important, since in the division of labor each small portion contributes an essential part to the larger whole. The nature of the specific relations of the multiple tasks is incomprehensible to the individual participants. Hence, the bulk of the tasks carried on by modern societies must be deliberately and planfully organized with an established pattern or system of organization. In fact, the larger the society and the larger and more complicated the tasks, the more artificed and more highly organized the operation (or cooperation) must be. Such organizations are referred to as large-scale formal organizations.

Suffice it to say, at this point, that such organizations are great hierarchically constructed mechanisms, specifically planned, structured, and administered to carry on specific processes and provide specific services. The individual is born in a large organization—a hospital with a hierarchically arranged staff—educated in a public-school system and a college or university, and employed by a huge corporation. When he marries, he follows the dictates of church and state. He lives his religious life in a vast church organization. His scientific tasks are conducted by great laboratories or research foundations. He is governed by a massive, centralized political organization. If he becomes dependent, he is cared for by a semipublic or governmental agency. His amusement, recreation, even artistic interests are provided for by organizations. Even his antisocial and illegal activities are conducted by organized rackets and syndicates. He is buried by a corporation in a corporation-owned cemetery. From womb to tomb his individual and social needs and activities are dominated by mass organizations and managerial functions and a vast organized complexity. (103)

The State as the Over-All Service Organization. In the modern complex, secular, mass-society, the state has come to be, not merely an agency exercising ordering and regulatory functions, but the final planner, integrator, arbiter, and administrator of societal needs and operations. In its very nature as the over-all institutionalized organization, we have come to call upon it to do for us what we cannot conveniently or efficiently carry on as individuals or through private or semipublic organizations. It is continually invading new social provinces and administering them for the people; there seem to be no limits to its range of activity. There is a most perceptible drift toward statism.

The modern state, notably the American state, in its local, state, and regional, as well as its national, jurisdictions, conducts a multiplicity of unavoidable and essential services. The state is responsible for police and fire protection; provides, supervises, and endows education, which is universal and compulsory; teaches trades and vocations and makes provision for rehabilitation along these lines; and cares for defectives, delinquents, and the underprivileged.

The state takes the initiative in the conservation of resources, carries on or subsidizes projects in irrigation, drainage, land utilization, and the development of water power and electrical power, and owns public lands and provides public pleasure grounds. The state also operates necessary public industries and utilities, provides for the construction, maintenance, and patrol of highways and waterways, conducts postal systems and regulates communications, in some countries actually operating telephone, telegraph, radio and transportation systems. It cares for health and sanitation and protects against communicable diseases, impure food, and drugs.

The state makes itself responsible for the regulation, improvement, financing, and even the actual provision of housing. It provides art, music, libraries, museums, and recreation and safeguards the population against obscenities in amusements and communications. It has developed the whole array of social security and social assistance programs—public employment service and unemployment insurance, old-age and survivors' insurance, old-age assistance, aid to the needy blind and to dependent children, child welfare and maternal services. This by no means exhausts the services rendered by the modern state.

THE FAMILY AS MAINLY A UNIT OF REPRODUCTION AND CONSUMPTION. In the folk-agrarian society, the family, or more particularly the kinship group, is the central maintenance unit of the society. But in the modern complex industrial-urban society the kinship group has largely disappeared as its members become spatially, economically, socially, and culturally separated. The solidarity of the family is lost as its members pursue their divergent economic, vocational, religious, political, and recreational interests.

The modern family is still the unit into which children are born and in which they receive their earliest conditioning. But it has lost much of its child-rearing and indoctrinating significance. Most of its industrial, vocational, educational, religious, health, security, and recreational functions have been assumed by formalized, specialized, large-scale, institutionalized agencies organized on a community-wide and even national basis.

The home has come to be a dwelling unit, a place where people have residence, receive mail, engage in certain physiological functions, eat a diminishing number of meals, and keep their personal effects.

REGIONALIZATION. Because of the vast geographical expanse of modern societies like our own, with the diversities of climate and terrain, of resources and industry, of demographic factors, of history and interests, there is a definite tendency for modern societies to become regionalized, that is, divided into more or less distinctive, self-conscious, less-than-national geographic-economic-cultural areas—and this despite the centralizing, standardizing and uniformity-producing agencies and processes.* These areas, however, are interdependent, interrelated, cooperative parts of the whole.

Unlike the folk-agrarian society, which is relatively static, a modern society like our own is in process of continuous, rapid, and far-reaching change. With its mobile population, its various subcultures, its multiplicity of contacts, its unceasing flow of discoveries and inventions, its competitiveness and emphasis on activity and achievement, new patterns of thought systems, new value systems, and new action systems are continually arising. Consequently, its structure is never fully articulated, and its functions are ever being modified.

With some conception of the general characteristics and processes of the vast societal organization of which we are a part, we now go on to a more comprehensive analysis of the general and special functions, processes, and factors involved in the total functioning of such a modern complex society.

*For the nature of regionalism and the processes involved, see Chap. 9.

CHAPTER III

THE EVER-CHANGING SCENE: FUNDAMENTAL CONSIDERATIONS

IN THE EXAMINATION of any going concern or functioning system the underlying, elemental, observed fact is its changefulness. Change is omnipresent, universal, incessant, and inevitable. Everything—the universe and all that it contains—is in a state of perpetual alteration and becoming. More than two thousand years ago Heraclitus established a significant though disturbing fact when he discovered the eternal flux of things and definitely stated the concept. Instead of saying there is nothing new under the sun, it is correct to say that all things are ever new.

Omnipresent Change in Space and Time

The statement that the only unchangeable law is the law of change is supported by every science and is a problem of every philosophy. In all our experience nothing has fixity of form or position. Such words as "static," "motionless," "quiescent," and "immutable" are deceptive. There is modification of the variables, or factors, in every situation. As a consequence, the various structurings and functionings are changing both within themselves and in all of their interrelationships. In all living things there is change, and life is ever onflowing and transient. Most significant from our point of view is the fact that the world and the life of mankind share with all else this eternal transformation.

Every occurrence is within the three dimensions of space and the fourth dimension of time. For man space is both physical and social. As individuals and as groups, men at any given time have location on the earth; they live within areas that have boundaries and move about in physical space. As they live in human societies, men have also both horizontal and vertical location and movement in the socially differentiated and stratified structures. Change also constantly occurs in time span. Things in the present are compared with things in the past; that is, they have a history, and they will be different in the future. Occurrences have duration and hence can be quantitatively distinguished from each other. They are movements in time sequence at varying rates and velocities of change. They have recurrence or repetition in time, which permits the comparison of different events with respect to rhythm or periodicity, tempo or number of events per unit of time, and timing or synchronizing of interdependent activities to place them in relative time order.

Space and time are inseparable. Every spatial pattern can be thought of only as it is at any given moment in a temporal pattern; every spatial change is at the same time a change in time. Every event, therefore, must be located in both space and time to be understood, and every movement or action is one in space and time. Thus, all functional activity, all process, is a space-time continnum.

Change itself is merely movement; everything becomes everlastingly something different. The student of change must know *why* change occurs. Wherever and whenever it occurs, it is due to

Social

Human society is perpetually becoming something different. One generation's commonplaces are another generation's antiquities. Any society or any part of a society may foster the illusion of changelessness and permanence. Men may think of a society as static, but it is so only in momentary appearance. This appearance is deceptive because of the limited perspective and insight of the contemporary observers. When viewed over a span of time, however brief, any given society shows changes, endless in variety, though differing in quantity, quality, ease, and tempo for its different parts. There is no possibility of continuing the present unchanged or of returning to an earlier way of life, however nostalgically some may yearn for it. The record of history abundantly attests the kaleidoscopic changefulness that characterizes

human beings relate themselves to one another and carry on functions both essential and inimical to their joint societal life.

The ever-changing societal life involves *all* of the processes and procedures of the given social system. These processes both sustain and disturb the functional equilibrium of all the parts. But, in general, any society as a normally functioning organization is ***a continuing and moving equilibrium of all the processes*** operating interdependently in a relatively established and fairly orderly relation to one another, to the basic, underlying physical and biological environment, and to the general cultural configuration of which they are constituent expressions. The stresses and strains are met, the functional needs satisfied, and the society carries on in space and time. But no social equilibrium is ever permanent or perfect; at best, it is only relative and approximate. As has been well said, a society "is like a web that exists only as it is newly spun." (10, p. 512) The spinning, raveling, and respinning go on continually.

Factors in Social Change

The causal and contributing factors involved in social change will be examined from various angles in the course of this study as the categories of processes are treated. Only a general over-all view of them will be given at this point as a preliminary orientation. The factors, like the processes, have a wide range. Some are relatively automatic in operation and occur without conscious human agency because they are largely beyond human control. Certain psychological, social, and cultural situations, not necessarily intended to produce social changes, often have far-reaching social consequences; whereas other highly conscious and purposive individual and collective efforts produce specific or general and more or less clearly conceived changes.

Natural, or Physical, Environment. Man's natural, or physical, environment constitutes an ubiquitous and potent setting, but it is beset with fluctuations, transformations, and convulsions. The great geological and geographic changes in the earth's contours, climatic and seasonal variations, and catastrophes of nature all frustrate social action. They upset established relations and social configurations and require men to readjust themselves to new conditions and devise new structures and functions.

Biological Changes. Changes in the biological world produce vast social changes. They may take the form of plagues that destroy animals or plants that are important sources of food or of human epidemics which decimate populations. The ordinary biological processes among animals and plants also produce vast social changes. Significant also are biological factors in the life of man himself, such as his own almost infinite genetic variation resulting from the rather unpredictable recombination of genes through successive generations and the shortness of human life.

Demographic Changes. Demographic changes cause vast social changes. Populations and their component stocks increase or decrease according to variations in their birth and death rates. The age groups vary in proportion and size from time to time, with corresponding changes in their influence. Extreme unbalancing of the sex ratio produces certain social changes as do population movements and changes in marital, birth, and death differentials.

Changes in Human Cultural Order. The foregoing are subsocial factors. Above these are the ***changes occurring in the distinctly human cultural order,*** changes which usually bulk largest in human societies. They are due to contact, to communication and transportation, to diffusion and borrowing of culture, to discovery and invention, and the attendant cross-fertilization of culture. Technology is ever changing and modifying man's physical and biological environment, his production and consumption, occupations, wealth, industrial organization, and class structure. A notable example of this is the far-reaching effect of the automobile, which has caused changes in transportation, family life, suburbanism, and even politics and law enforcement. (12; 14)

Man's very ignorance or lack of observation of the effects of his sociocultural processes may bring about vast social changes. Exhaustion of nonreplaceable resources and soil impoverishment through misuse and erosion have caused depopulation, and changed modes of culture including the whole system of social institutions.

Man's attitudes, interests, mores, and laws change. His evaluations, which change with human experience, are factors intrinsically operating to direct social change. New ideas in the form of philosophical concepts, political and economic ideologies, and religious creeds are everlastingly producing profound changes. Culture itself is continually accumulating; in fact, the more numerous the culture elements, the greater the likelihood of accelerated cultural development.

Social psychological currents and social catastrophes, such as depressions, rebellions, and wars, have recurrently played their part in social change.

Some social change arises from unexpected conditions. The social and cultural heritage of any society is selectively cumulative, building up along the lines of current "run of attention" and bringing about accelerated change along some lines while neglecting others. Furthermore, change begets change. The mere fact of the succession of the generations of men is an important factor. Each new generation tries to copy the ways of preceding ones but finds itself unable to do so—and often does not wish to.

Finally, a good deal of social change is due to conscious, deliberate, and purposive effort on the part of men, individually and collectively. Men do not always wait for the slow natural or automatic processes and immanent forces to provide them with the world of their desire. They consciously experiment, invent, utilize, construct, and reconstruct. Advertisers and propagandists work their ways, and leaders, misleaders, and special-interest groups originate and organize social movements. Dictators and totalitarian movements rise, and social, political, economic, and religious revolutions are brought about. In some measure, however, there are intelligently planned and soberly and efficiently executed constructive changes along certain lines, and "Nature's Insurgent Son" effects a good deal of the change.

Critical Examination of Social Evolution

Men have long sought a unifying explanation of continuous social change, preferably in the form of some capsule formula or law that would reveal an over-all pattern or process. Many of the nineteenth- and some of the twentieth-century social thinkers, taking their cue from the hypotheses regarding cosmic biological evolution, developed such formulas. In general their conception of social evolution was that society develops automatically and spontaneously in a preordained, gradual manner in time through regular sequences from the earliest to the most recent forms in accordance with inherent forces and selective-adaptive tendencies. (5; 6)

Herbert Spencer and his followers, for example, presented the actual progression of humanity as a natural fact, a sequel to the general cosmic movement and controlled by the same principles. Evolution was a universal, mechanical, irresistible movement toward perfection. The movement was conceived as inevitably unilinear and consistently upward, from the simple to the complex, from the homogeneous to the heterogeneous, with increasing differentiation of parts, greater specialization of function, and increased general operational efficiency. For Auguste Comte every society passed successively through the theological, metaphysical, and positive stages of sociocultural life.

While accepting certain features of such conceptions, most sociologists have departed somewhat from such precise explanations, because of their false simplicity and the implied automatism or passivity. They cannot accept a concept of social change which implies "the irresistible march of some predetermined sequence of developments, through which all human societies everywhere have passed." * They maintain, on the basis of extensive examination of societies of various eras and areas and states of development, that there is no single law of social change. Furthermore, social change is not purely automatic in the older mechanical sense, nor is it always and necessarily gradual. Automatic factors, to be sure, play an important part in social change, but as we have just noted, they are of an external and subsocial nature. We have also noted that in *social* change humanly devised sociocultural factors due to mankind's creativeness, diversity, contact, movement, and exchange are of predominant significance. Furthermore, in the course of social change there are occasional jumps and crises. Crises, in fact, are

*F. N. House, *The Development of Sociology* (New York: McGraw-Hill Book Company, Inc., 1936), p. 508.

of crucial significance both as effects and causes of social changes, as will be noted later. Social evolution, if we care to use the term, is not an automatic process; it is a matter of a multiplicity of highly diverse social and cultural processes, operating in all manner and number of combinations in different times and places in the same society and in other societies. (8) Although inherent factors are operative in all these, human creativeness must also be accepted as a unique "given."

Evolution literally means "unrolling," as MacIver has indicated. Here is the general, acceptable scientific key to the nature and cause of *social* change. "While the uniformity and unilinearity of development is denied, it remains true that certain things come, and must come, before other things." (7) All that occurs and *is* socially—artifacts, groups, institutions, even large social systems—*emerges* from earlier stages by various determinable and expectable orderly sequences. These sequential changes represent an unfolding of potentialities and tendencies in particular types of situations. Or, stated in another way, the existing combination of factors and conditions in the given situation constitutes the causes out of which the perceptible or discoverable effects flow.

These processes may be similar and even recurrent in different times and different societies, as well as in given societies in some time span; hence, working scientific generalizations may be made regarding them. As scientific insight increases and improves, the nature and flow of these processes become more distinct and elaborate. That is not to imply, however, that some inherent law or force is operating through them which causes a given social system or any of its subforms to unfold through successive stages of ever more complex, better integrated and adapted organization. It simply means that there are various kinds of occurrenees involving transitions or modifications of structure and function of a quantitative and qualitative nature in time and space.

In brief, the course of social change is that of regular processes, operating stage by stage, according to the principle of cause and effect. By means of our knowledge regarding these processes, we are enabled to explain the relatively stable tendencies and regularities in history and society. In some measure we can predict the changes that are to come.

Pattern and Course of Social Change

Having critically examined the evolutionary conception, let us posit, very concisely, a working interpretation of the general course and pattern of change in and of a social system. The general hypothesis is that social change is rhythmic, especially of a qualified cyclical nature. The over-all view is one of continuous alteration everywhere. All sociocultural phenomena change from something to something, from one state to another state. No social system and no part of a system can ever return to its original state; that is, it can never reproduce itself in absolutely identical fashion. However, according to our best scientifically determined present knowledge, the moving picture of a particular social system or subsystem is one of sequential and interrelated development, integration, maturity, disintegration, and decline.

Linear Change. In the process of change of a social system we note various kinds of *linear change* which merge into relatively recurrent or cyclical changes. Linear change is change in a given direction. It takes the *forms* of *spatial direction,* as when a social way of action moves steadily from one place to another; of *quantitative direction,* that is, becoming more or less; and of *qualitative direction,* that is, an order of sequence that may be better or worse according to some standard. The common typical *patterns of linear change* are *unilinear,* that is, accumulation along a straight line, like the course of an invention once started; *oscillating,* or up and down, like many economic phenomena with their rise, boom, and slump; *spiral,* or round and round, but in a given general direction; and *branching,* but in a general line, until stopped, like the growth of a corporation. Linear changes are never limitless, however; they are links in a chain of change.

Cyclical Change. Cyclical change refers to a relative repetition or recurrence of a given state or states of being going on again and again. It is some form of circular movement, which may be spatial, that is, from place to place and back again to the point of inception; or it may be quantitative or qualitative, that is, from high efficiency to low efficiency, and so on repeatedly. The constant repetitions may be periodic, that is, recurrent in fixed periods, or they may be nonperiodic or irregular in recurrence.

These repetitions of change in types of social systems recur rhythmically, but also always relatively; there is never—there cannot be—identical return to a previous position or condition. Each cycle presents new variations of the preceding phase. Thus, every social process represents some degree of old themes and rhythms and so offers the possibility of observable regularity; but it unavoidably involves new elements. Says Sorokin, "All in all the variably recurrent pattern seems to be the only adequate master-pattern of the direction of an overwhelming majority of sociocultural processes." *

To make what seems to be the most typical pattern of social change more concrete, we will examine the elements and sequences of a typical cycle of change. The principles discussed apply to a general societal system or to some part, such as an institution or association. First, it must be emphasized that the processes of change in a social system or part of it are contingent upon the conjuncture and interaction of numerous factors and conditions, as discussed above. These interdependent variables constitute the components of the situation, which generate series of consequences affecting and largely determining subsequent action. Each type of process or recurrence, however, playing its part in the total process of change, has its own particular combination of more or less constant specific factors and occurs according to its own unique potentialities.

In each instance the factors, tendencies, and potentialities converge in the gross cycle of structural-functional equilibration and disequilibration of relationships of the component elements. In the typical cycle there are four steps:

1. There are organizational and functional developments which involve increasing division and variation of parts and increasing specialization of function, together with diversity, complexity, and refinement of structure and function as it adapts itself to its environment and to its epoch as these create demands and needs.

2. The multiple dependent variables become integrated with each other. There are equilibration and stability of elements and high functional efficiency of the coordinated whole. This state may last for a long or a short time.

3. But this state always has within it and surrounding it the seeds of its own destruction. Strains, inertia, overorganization, and the like appear and result in disequilibration and disintegration with loss of function.

4. Finally, there are death and disappearance, or, if the sociocultural system (structural-functional mechanism) is desirable or indispensable in the operation of the particular society at the time, there is resurrection or reorganization and a building up toward the re-establishment of equilibrium on a revised basis, and the cycle is repeated.

This general cyclical pattern of change is found in almost every department of societal life. Communities grow, reach a peak of maturity, and decline. An institution or association, for example, a business concern or a political party, has a typical life cycle consisting of incipient organization, the period of efficiency, then the period of formalism, and finally disorganization.

A cycle that is somewhat similar but results in the tentative adjustment of elements involved or in the completion of the process is found in other aspects of societal operation. Thus, a form of conflict begins with contacts and aggravating factors and conditions, rises to active efforts at reciprocal elimination or destruction, and terminates either in defeat and subjection of one opponent or in some sort of accommodation, only often to be revived in some variant form, possibly with a reversal of aggressors. The life cycle of a new political party might follow this pattern—and in a short time span.

The twentieth century, as well as earlier eras, produced theories of large-scale cycles involving whole civilizations and vast expanses of time. Oswald Spengler and A. J. Toynbee have depicted great terminal cycles, and Sorokin has presented social history as a vast continuous cycle. (20; 23; 24) In general, though, social scientists have found the *small*-cycle theory of change more congenial to their subject matter. The examination of small cycles in terms of their process series, sequence patterns, rhythms and periodicities falls within time spans more readily susceptible to present-day scientific analytical procedures.

*This discussion of linear and cultural directions of change is based largely on P. A. Sorokin, *Society, Culture, and Personality* (New York: Harper & Brothers, 1947), pp. 675-680.

Rate, or Tempo, of Social Change

Although social change occurs everywhere all the time, its rate or degree of rapidity varies. Innumerable rates of acceleration and retardation are possible. Within a given society the general tempo will vary greatly at different times. "Changes in pace" occur with differences both in quantity and quality of change effects. Thus, in our Western society, change was relatively slow and relatively small prior to the twelfth century. Since then both tempo and volume have increased with great rapidity as a result of a multiplicity of events and circumstances, including the Crusades, the penetration of the West by Arabic culture, the Renaissance, the Mongol invasions, the introduction of the printing press, paper, gunpowder, and the compass, the Reformation, geographic explorations and discoveries, the commercial revolution and the industrial revolution, and two world wars with all that they imply. These occurrences have probably produced more social change in the last eight centuries than transpired in all of man's previous history.

Changes also occur at different rates in different parts and phases of a given society during a given time span. Thus, in our society economic organization and the parts directly related to technological development have changed at a furious rate in the last two centuries, while change has been comparatively slow in political, religious, and ethical institutions.

Of special significance is the fact that the rate of social change varies among different societies. Some are slow-motion societies; others are fast-motion. We speak of the former as "static," and of the latter as "dynamic," societies. The general concepts require brief analysis.

Static Societies. In a static society a more or less stable equilibrium of parts and functions obtains. Although this static equilibrium does not imply that all change has been eliminated, since every society is in constant flux, the array of ongoing processes function so slowly and so moderately that changes consist of slight or limited and temporary deviations from the established pattern of life. There is no accelerated and cumulative development bringing about far-reaching fundamental modification in the structures and perceptible and marked disturbance of the functional equilibrium of the parts. The individuals, groups, institutions, and all the other interests of the associated people are so well synthesized and so harmoniously coordinated that, in the main, an uninterrupted and undisturbed reciprocal functioning of all the parts takes place. Changes occur, but they are minor and gradual and not disequilibrating.

Dynamic Societies. A dynamic society is one in which change is occurring at a rapid rate, at least in parts of it. There is much accumulation of effects, either of a progressive or retrogressive character, much transformation, displacement, or elimination of fundamental component societal elements. Various factors intervene to throw the integrating process out of harmony; balances between individuals, organizations, institutions, classes, and so on are being disturbed continually. Most structures and functions undergo marked variation. This does not imply a state of disequilibrium; but it does mean that there is no stable, persisting, normal equilibrium. There is a rapid-flowing, ever-changing, dynamic equilibrium.

If the changes taking place can be kept in a fair state of balance and harmony with each other, such a dynamic society with its dynamic equilibrium presents possibilities of a better state of social health than a static society. By its very nature a static society invariably suffers from stasis, or inflexibility, and fixity of structures and processes. What is remains so. Individuals and groups must either live with and suffer their conditions as they are or instigate violent upheaval to crack the cake of custom. In a dynamic society, on the other hand, rapidity and fluidity of adjustment exist in much greater degree. Almost all elements have the possibility and usually the facility of expression and action. Destructive and constructive factors and situations are more likely to cancel each other, permitting an ever-new stability and functional efficacy to reign.

The distinction between static and dynamic societies is still valid for analytical purposes, but there are fewer and fewer typically static societies. The characteristic ones—those of primitives and most of the societies of the Orient—are being sucked into the orbit of change in which the Western world moves. The last residuary static societies are becoming increasingly dynamic and volatile; they are only relatively static as compared with a highly dynamic society like our own. Another century may see their virtual disappearance.

Sociological Significance of Space

No analysis of going concerns, whether biological organisms or physical or social mechanisms, can avoid dealing with the concept of space. All entities exist in space, have a location in space, and occupy a certain portion of space. All change within entities and between entities involves some degree of movement in space and some relative change of the spatial arrangement and relationship of parts. In fact, change without movement in one or more of the three dimensions of space is impossible.

In order that human beings may deal effectively with limitless space, several means of designating it are necessary.

1. There must be *markers* or points of reference fixed in space whereby the location or position of entities can be determined; for example, a point at so many degrees of latitude and longitude, a position at such an altitude above sea level or depth below the surface of the earth.

2. *Boundaries* must be set up to indicate extent or limits of the earth's territory that is occupied by a particular entity or which constitute an area of some special interest, such as, the city limits or the boundaries of the United States. We also establish boundaries by means of artificially and arbitrarily established lines on the face of the earth, namely, parallels of latitude and longitude.

3. *Units of measurement* must be devised to indicate the amount of distance moved and the amount of space occupied by an entity, for example, so many miles from such and such a place, so many square miles of territory, so many cubic yards in a room.

4. *Directions* must be established to distinguish one line of movement from another—movement which is horizontal or vertical; sideways, forward or backward; north, south, east, or west; up or down.

5. *Areas* must be distinguished with respect to each other in some larger segment of space; for example, the North American continent among the earth's land bodies, the Pacific Coast, the North Side. All these devices for designating aspects of space are man-made.

As the social scientist analyzes social phenomena, he is concerned with two different kinds of space: physical space and social space.

Physical Space

Physical space, especially the surface of the earth, is the physical arena in which human life is lived. Individuals, communities, institutionalized organizations, cultures, and the various essential natural and cultural resources are located at points of reference on the face of the earth. Human beings form agglomerations in space; they are members of different kinds of locality groupings, which are tied to given areas of the earth and have more or less determinable geographic boundaries. Within these areas they have settlement patterns, as well as arrangements of groupings for reciprocity in their cooperative activities and for forms of discrimination and systems of physical segregation.

It is also essential to designate the territorial size of societal units as well as their relative location and spatial relationship. In general, without the concept of space expressed in geometric terms, no location, extent, movement, or relationship of human, cultural, or societal entities can be understood or described. The sociological significance of physical space will be examined in greater detail in Chapters 8 and 9, and in the sections on communities and regions that follow here.

Social Space

There is a societal geometry of great pertinence to the social scientist which involves the concept of sociocultural space in the *social* environment. Individuals, groups, and categories of persons are separated from each other horizontally by sheer sociocultural difference. They are also spaced in the vertical or hierarchical dimension; that is, by their relative positions on the social ladder or in the pyramid of social strata or layers. Where there is considerable social distance, there is little intimacy, friendliness, communication, and free, common activity, and there is greater likelihood of opposition than where there is little or no distance. There is also lateral movement in social space, as from one occupation to another with similar qualification requirements or from one religious denomination to another, and there is vertical movement up and down the social ladder.

The concept of social space is essential as a fundamental referential principle. It enables us to locate sociocultural phenomena in their social universe, to determine their position in regard to one another, to analyze their nearness of relationship, their change of position, horizontally and vertically (usually a combination of both), and their various characteristics and functions. The sociological significance of social space will be examined in more detail in the chapters on differentiation, stratification, and social distance and social mobility that follow.

Sociological Significance of Time

As just noted, everything that happens occurs in space with its three dimensions of length, breadth, and thickness, or altitude. What is equally important is that all events and processes also have a fourth dimension—*time*. Time is a basic factor in any and all becoming. Until very recently it has been neglected in sociological analysis. Its significance in the understanding of human society, especially its relation to social processes, will be briefly examined. No concept of motion or process is possible without the factor of time. Reciprocally our very awareness of time, the continuum of experience, rests upon the observation of the various processes which occur in the universe.

Time is also a necessary variable in all social life, for social life, as we have noted, is a matter of movement or process. Man lives in time, and all that he does occurs in time. His collective life is not to be understood as a snapshot of patterns of action, something fixed and at rest, but as a moving picture of complex structural and functional modifications and transformations in time. Nothing is entirely the same in successive instants. Social becoming, like all other becoming, is a matter of stages or of sequences in time. Each activity requires time for its performance, and all forms of social participation are limited by time.

Conversely, the time sequence presents the connecting links of change and unifies the patterns of relationship and the processes of functioning as phases of a total, on-flowing, variable, but continuous, interaction. To understand the changing occurrences in the whole relationship in time, we examine their order of succession, their tempo, their timing in relation to other events, and their rhythms, or oscillations and cycles.

Social Time, Time Systems, and Time Markers

Time is infinite, but the lives of men and their relationships and actions in it are finite. These events are specific performances in time that must be indicated and expressed in terms of location and duration. The social life of all groups, in fact, is reflected in time expression. Therefore, as men carve out their individual and collective careers, they must have both measures of time and points of reference in time. In brief, men have had to construct symbolic systems of time reckoning. In this respect, men have established some degree of adjustment to, and control over, time, for while time is an ultimate, "given" reality, the systems of reckoning spring from collective life and reflect the round of social activities. Furthermore, their observance is imperatively demanded by social necessity.

Time systems vary among peoples, depending upon the importance of time for them in the intensity and complexity of their lives. There has been current the view that primitive or folk peoples have no time sense and no need of one, but this is entirely erroneous. There has been a past—yes, and the old men know about it; and there is always tomorrow. Among primitives, however, time has more the character of a free good, like air, than it has among peoples in advanced stages of civilization. Time reckoning is not very exact, and time indication is fragmentary and discontinuous. Primitives have a few specific or quantitative time units and no very systematic chronology. Time is reckoned mainly in relation to physical or biological phenomena; only rarely with respect to social events. Things happened at sunrise, before harvesting, or in the reign of Chief X. (30)

But for modern dynamic societies time is of the essence. Their members live by the clock. Each day is precious and scheduled in hours and minutes, even in split seconds. Events begin at a given time and must be accurately placed in time relationship to each other, as before and after World War II. Certain types of action extend over specified periods of time (as a semester). Time is also a cost factor in many business procedures, as, for example, in the close of the market day, eighteen months' installment plan, interest on loans and dividends on investments, contractual obligations with time limits and penalties. The humanly devised and imposed intricate temporal pattern acts as a supreme coercive ruler over our mentality and our individual and social action. We may ignore it only at the risk of isolation from a large part of the collective life. "After consulting Gulliver on the function of his watch, the Lilliputians came to the conclusion that it was his God."

There are also various time systems that exist for specific areas of interest and analysis, such as the terrestrial time system of geology, the time system of biological development with its epochs of growth and decline, and psychological time, that is, psychic developmental periods of mental age. But a general, standardized type of time system exists for conceiving, locating, and measuring the change and movement of sociocultural phenomena. This system is a combination of astronomical-mathematical *and* social time. The qualitative periods of time are reckoned in terms of the rotation of the earth and expressed in astronomical time units—years, months, weeks, and days. But mathematical time is empty; it has no marks to serve as points of origin or end. Therefore, within this flow of years, months, weeks, and days, *the social phenomena are always purposively indicated with reference to particular socially significant historical events, known and meaningful to many people in the social system, and conventionally selected to serve as indicators or focal points.*

In the case of time, human beings arbitrarily establish units of extent, measuring time in terms of intervals between events and locating and relating occurrences in time with respect to known or conventionally established events. Time as an experienced reality for man does not exist apart from events. Each time system has its markers by means of which other events are located and extent of time is indicated, as B.C. and A.D. among Christians and the reckoning of time since the traditional date of Creation—3761 B.C.—among Orthodox Jews. Such arbitrary markers are necessary for past, present, and future time reference.

Sociocultural processes and conditions have even modified the astronomical units in some measure for different social purposes. Our year generally starts on New Year's Day, but organizations have fiscal years which may start and end on any one of the 365 days of the astronomical year. Instead of lunar months we have months variously named after gods and emperors with a conventionally designated order of rotation of 30, 31, and 28 (or 29) days. Weeks are differently oriented with respect to the Sabbath for different religious groups and have different beginnings and lengths (for example, the five-day or forty-hour work week) for different purposes. Similarly, the division of the days into hours is artificial and varies with objectives: the eight-hour working day, the day of the produce or stock exchange, the school day.

The modern world is characterized by widespread communication, growing cultural uniformity and interdependence, and farflung administrative and other collective activities. Hence, there is a definite and essential tendency to depart from local and highly special systems of time, or to use them only for special purposes. Today we increasingly abide by a universal, abstract time system, a kind of time esperanto, for time coordination and time spacing, which is intelligible to, and usable by, all peoples and nations. For this the units of the astronomical-mathematical system, based on two natural occurrences, namely, the diurnal cycle of the twenty-four-hour day and the lunar cycles are universally used. For longer location and duration in terms of years of socially significant occurrences the Christian time marker system is being more and more widely used.

Social Functions of a Time System

Time systems grow out of human experience. They are sociocultural constructs to meet definite societal needs and are constructed because the organizations and functions of groups require time and because mankind purposively utilizes time in all its activities. What essential functions does a time system, especially a widespread, standardized cosmopolitan system, perform? The concise ensuing analysis will be both a pointing up and a summarizing of the significance of time reckoning and time designating in relation to social processes.

Location and Orientation of Occurrences. Man has been referred to as the "time-binding" animal, which in one sense means that he has the ability, by means of his time systems, to locate and relate significant events of all kinds in the endless flow of time. We are especially concerned with the location of social and historical events which are instances and parts of sociocultural continuity. To be meaningful and efficient functional occurrences, our acts have to have time position. In brief, we need dates both as indicators of the beginning of social actions and as points of reference before or after which events occurred.

To start an act we must have a point of time. We must also locate past events in time so that they can be temporally related. When events are thus located with respect to points of reference in time, we are able to conceive of their sociocultural relationship. The relationship may, in some degree, be one of cause and effect, as an occurrence at this point in time was a contributory factor in a later one. But always, we must know that one event occurred before or after another.

Synchronization and Coordination. Closely related to the function of location and orientation is that of synchronizing and coordinating in time the actions of all individuals or of all groups involved in concerted, collective activities. Most human activities demand the complex cooperation of many persons. One of the indispensable conditions for any possible collective action is that it occur at a certain fixed or appointed time. There must also be a mutual, coordinated timing of behavior, for without it no normal social life is possible. Joint activity must be synchronized in time as well as related in space and organized as to functioning constituent parts or agents. Unless you and I meet at 7 P.M. (the time factor in the action) at the corner of Sutter and Gough Streets (the space factor) we cannot attend together the movie (the collective action).

In modern heterogeneous, industrial-urban societies, the significance of synchronization of action becomes more and more pointed. For example, six thousand men must come to work from all over metropolitan Detroit for a given shift of a given automobile production line and must work together throughout a given eight-hour period so many days as a work week, else they lose their wages individually and not a single car rolls off the line.

Designation of Duration. Neither men nor their acts are eternal. To conceive the existence of given social events and to carry on effectively certain functional relationships, we need to know their extent or determine their extent or duration in terms of moments or periods of the endless durability of time. A time-reckoning system enables us to indicate the beginning and the end of given events, as the academic year. It enables us also to measure events in terms of time elapsed: World War II lasted so many years, months, and days. It is possible to arrange functional affairs, such as contractual relations, in terms of time duration: interest and profits are reckoned by the year; leases on property extend for given periods of time.

Designation of Sequence. Many social phenomena, as we have noted, are occurrences of a rhythmic, sequential nature; they consist of a temporal distribution of actions. These must be timed (started and ended); executed at a certain tempo or rate (a certain number of acts per time unit); and spaced in related series in time, as flows of action in the flow of time. The daily life of an individual is a matter of successive acts which are timed, rated, and spaced by the clock. Every functional organization has its daily, weekly, and monthly series of variant, rated, and spaced performances—a university, a department store, communities, all have their time sequences, based on a calendar governed by physical and sociocultural factors.

The various cycles of change are a matter of time, as, for example, the typical business cycle or the rainfall cycle as it affects individuals and communities. Each phase of cyclical phenomena is better understood if determined in time. Without the analysis of the time factor men have little anticipatory or predictive ability.

Time Perspectives

Human beings, as individuals, as groups and categories of persons, and as societies, have some degree of time perspective with respect to the past and the future from their position in the present. Young persons, for example, have a limited range and live mainly in and for the moment, but successive age groups have more extensive ranges.

Societies differ in their emphasis on past, present, or future at a given period. Much can be told about the nature of the particular society or part of society being studied, and much about the dircetion of change within it can be predicted when the emphasis on time is known. Men with little comprehension of the future and little confidence in their ability to effect desired changes in it repair to golden ages in the past for intellectual and emotional comfort in a world of change or escape into problematical messianic states or utopias. Men who have learned to control physical and social processes in some measure look more and more to the altered dimensions of the present as a future of their own devising. (32)

The men of the last millennium have developed a more pronounced historical consciousness. (26) From the perspective of the present they engage in both retrospect and prospect. They have a new interpretation of the past in terms of a temporal flow of related successive occurrences, which gives them at the same time a new prospect of the future. As they become historically aware of the reality of time, they realize that the past is not recoverable, though it yields stern lessons, and that they must accept the present and live in it and prepare for the future. This very ability to comprehend an inevitable future in turn becomes an impulse to both intellectual and social life. (29; 34)

As we gain new perspectives regarding the past and prepare for the future, we realize that our history must be reinterpreted and rewritten again and again. We do this rewriting, not because of a nostalgic devotion to the past, but with the intention of creating a new time perspective for the past that makes the present an inevitable step toward a desired future. Each age produces a conception of history most compatible with its necessities, beliefs, perplexities, visions, and objectives. As we function socially, we continuously reinterpret the past and reorganize and reconstitute the living present in order to live effectively in the foreseeable future. With a time perspective we identify ourselves with the on-going stream of life.

Dynamics of Social Action

All change is concerned with the dynamic factors that lie behind the processes that bring it about and operate through them. To understand the changing processual nature of society in space and time means to analyze at the very outset its dynamics, that is, the factors that initiate and direct social behavior. Processes consist of activated individuals and groups acting and interacting for a great variety of reasons. These human actors *act* because of numerous and diverse impellers, propellers, determiners, conditioners, instructors, and wooers. In brief, the social behavior of human beings, whether they are acting individually or collectively, involves propulsive and impulsive activating, influencing, and shaping factors.

Man, like all else in the universe, is an energy system, that is, "an arrangement of work capacities potential or aroused, which forms a united whole." He is an unusual energy system, however, in that he is not only an expender of aroused energy but also "an attacker of new energy potential." (45, p. 34) The human actors possess energy, are subjected to energy, utilize energy, and expend various kinds of energies in various ways under various conditions. The behavior patterns of man, in fact, whether innate or acquired, are caged energy waiting to be released.

Similarly, "human society, from the dynamic point of view, can be regarded as a system of energy, operating within a field of force in time." The social processes, constituting as they do all the interactions of energized human beings, are manifestations of energy, and the structures of a society "represent the channels along which flow the energy . . . which we postulate as behind all activity." (49)

In the mechanics of action, there are two fundamental elements: the *stimulus,* or that which touches off a tendency to act, and the *response,* or the resultant action. The activity itself is release of energy, which is initiated by the various factors operating as stimuli to move individuals and groups into a complex array of socially significant actions. These factors range from compulsions exercised by environment and by innate biogenic and psychogenic needs, through the various social psychic motivators, to an array of sociocultural phenomena which, in addition to other sociological significance, also function as impulsions or propulsions to action. These dynamic factors are the background energizers responsible for most social processes; many of the factors, especially the psychic and sociocultural, are themselves in large part effects of social processes. The more important categories of these factors which energize human beings to act will be briefly examined, so that we shall have some awareness of the general types of dynamic ingredients which combine in infinitely diverse arrays to induce, accelerate, or retard social behavior.

Physical and Extrahuman Biological Energizers

Wherever and whenever physical influences bear upon human beings, they are moved to act in some manner. They must always adjust themselves to these influences. Sometimes the responsive action is compulsive, as when they are confronted by catastrophes. In the daily life of men various factors of the physical environment, such as temperature, humidity, and light, create conditions that facilitate, stimulate, determine, or inhibit human behavior. Various biological catastrophes have mightily influenced men and societies in the form of plagues among animals and plants which are important to men and plagues and epidemics among men themselves. The ordinary biological processes of reproduction, selection, and survival among both fauna and flora upon which men depend and among the human populations are productive of vast and numerous propulsions and retardations.

In general, the various natural physical and biological elements in the area of a given people affect their health and efficiency, their location, the size of their population aggregations, and their ecological organization, their economy, in fact, almost every aspect of their social organization. Even their typical mental patterns and idea systems are affected.

Biogenic and Psychogenic Needs and Drives

Among human beings the basic bodily organic and appetitive needs and the elemental psychological urges produce imperative propulsions to individual action, but action which affects and involves many of the basic structures, functions, and relationships in every society. In order merely to survive, human beings must have food and water; eliminate wastes and glandular secretions; procreate; have shelter from harmful natural forces and from human and animal foes; balance exertion and rest; exercise the muscular and nervous systems; and be free to develop from infancy to old age.

These needs create tensions which are expressed in behavior by such various names as "drives," "instincts," "propensities," or "prepotent reflexes," with "drives" perhaps most widely used. These drives are the genetically inherited and therefore unlearned energized tendencies to act, the vitalistic energies which make the organism *go.* By means of them the organism is powerfully compelled to reduce or remove the painful or unpleasant tension, to release the impounded energy, to experience satisfaction and freedom from restlessness. This is done without foresight of ends and without previous education in performance.

There are also the elemental psychogenic reactions of individuals bound up with survival, such as curiosity, acquisitiveness, struggling, gregariousness, and imitativeness, which function almost with the intensity of the biogenic drives.

Both the biogenic and psychogenic drives involve other drives in the course of their satisfaction and take place in a social and cultural setting. They are transformed into socially directed and self-restraining purposes. They affect many social structures and become effective through many social functions and processes. In both their elemental and their derived forms they provide much of the motive power that keeps societies operating.

Socially Elicited Expression of Drives

The emotions and the feelings are internal states that are associated with the elemental needs and their drives and that have considerable propulsive significance and play an important part in many of the choices which men make. Although emotions and feelings rest upon the innate biogenic and psychogenic drives, they are socially elicited and socially modified, reflecting the experiences and the particular culture of the actors.

Emotions are the fundamental psychic states of relative arousal that individuals are in when they are under the propulsion of the biogenic and psychogenic drives and under certain physical conditions. They cause the individual to want to act, to perform with intense activity, or they make him temporarily unable to act. The emotions involve the whole organism physiologically, neurologically, and mentally. But, unlike the drives, which are aroused from within the organism by its needs, the emotions are elicited primarily by external stimuli or situations. As the result of the emotions and the circumstances of a given situation, we may act positively, that is, be elated, love someone, have satisfying companionship with others, assert ourselves; or we may act negatively, that is, be angry, envious, hateful, and terrified. Thus, emotions are powerful factors in both associative-integrative and disruptive-distintegrative behavior.

Feelings are bound up with the elemental drives and the emotions. By feeling is meant that agreeable or disagreeable tone of consciousness which accompanies an activity or the anticipation of a previously experienced response. It is a quicker-than-thought subjective valuation which the organism gives, a valuation that is the result of group or individual experience in the past. The feelings are usually designated as pleasurable or painful. In general, the feeling tones accompany action rather than instigate it. They do, however, at any given time function for the individual as guides in approaching or withdrawing and in seeking or avoiding.

Experiential Motivators

Although innate biological and psychological propulsions are the *foundation* factors in human individual and social motivation, they are powerfully affected and effected by environmental conditions. The social as well as the physical environment acts as an influencing, determining, and propelling factor external to the individual. Most of the ways in which certain individuals and groups perform in a given society are a matter of sociocultural stimuli, functioning as cues and dominators, that release human energies—energies expended in socially patterned or channeled forms. We have an array of wishes, tastes, aspirations, ambitions, interests, attitudes, and habits which are interpersonally expressed and are shaped in special social environments. We are sucked or pulled into various kinds of mass behavior by powerful, almost irresistible, social psychic currents and pressed to follow broad planes of practices. These various sociocultural patterns and pressures draw out and develop certain modes of thought and action, mobilize individuals and groups to act, consciously or unconsciously, in certain widespread or standard ways, inhibit other action, and induce striving toward socially induced goals.

The following are among the more important conditioned forms of behavior greatly affected by experience, which motivate to various kinds of socially significant action.

Sentiments. Sentiments are an organized, enhancing or detracting system of emotional dispositions which are related to certain social ideas and values. They predispose us to feel and usually to act positively or negatively in a specific way about some object or class of objects external to us. Thus, we have sentiments and we sentimentalize about the flag. Sentiment predisposes the individual or group to react *toward* (with admiration, respect, or pity) or *away* or *against* (with fear or antipathy). All sentiment seeks expression in action.

Interests. Interests are luminous, culturally defined concerns associated with values characteristic of a particular society. They induce activities which individuals carry on for their own sake. Mention need be made only of interests in golfing and reform activity to indicate their dynamic nature.

Attitudes. Attitudes are deep-seated functional tendencies, predispositions, or proclivities to react selectively and immediately to either specific or general stimuli. They are learned in the course of an individual's development. They are the beginnings of acts, and in certain situations action is the result of the play of attitudes. They are always positive or negative, never neutral; they induce reactions *toward* types of persons, groups, compatible proposals or ideas or *against* them.

Wishes. Wishes are varying combinations of organic appetites, physical and psychic activity drives, emotions and attitudes tied together in the pursuit of a goal of value. Each wish is a driving stimulus toward its goal as well as a persistent effort to avoid the reverse of the goal. In its very nature a wish implies the accumulation of energy and the existence of tension or strain until the energy is expended in accomplishment. W. I. Thomas, who gave the classic interpretation of wishes, presented four main types: the wish for (1) new experience, (2) for security, (3) for recognition or status, and (4) for response. (44; 59)

Habits. Habits are forms of behavior or tendencies to act that are acquired by individuals and groups through experience during their lifetime. They grow out of repeated successful adjustments to types of past situations. They begin as conscious acts, but are repeated so often that they become in large measure unconscious, automatic, a kind of second nature. Hence, they are responsible for action toward objects and persons in common and recurrent situations and occasions with a minimum of attention and strain. They function as automatic, economical, and standardized dynamic elements in the action of individuals. A very sizable part of our essential social action is of a habitual nature.

Intellectual, Expressional, and Spiritual Propulsive Factors

All the dynamic factors thus far examined are innately automatic in operation, or they are various combinations of innate and acquired propulsives that operate more or less automatically in a given situation. All of them come out of the past and motivate to action that is adjustive to past conditions. But man must also function dynamically in new situations.

Intellect. Intellect is a kind of compensatory power that man possesses to make up for the deficiencies of the more or less automatically operating responses. It is the discerning, reflective, formulating and reformulating, projective, correlating side of human nature. Intellect enables man not only to acquire great stores of knowledge, but also to utilize this knowledge and experience which he remembers in order to construct new concepts, new methods, new syntheses of elements. By means of intellect man can discriminate, evaluate, predict, invent, indulge in abstraction, and give concrete form to his expressional and spiritual abilities and urges. Most of man's revised and new action is a matter of intellectual propulsion and direction. One need only mention scientific activity as an example and think of all the propulsion which it gives to both individual and collective action in all departments of life.

Ideas. Through the ages ideas have been known to be intimately related to action, actually functioning as powerful propulsive factors. There is an ancient proverb: Ideas rule the world. Alfred Fouillée posed the doctrine of "idea-forces." He pointed out that ideas, once devised, are forces that tend to assert themselves in action. Any examination of history or of the present reveals that ideas in the form of political, economic, and racial ideologies, beliefs of all kinds, religious creeds, ethical credos, or reformist programs have dynamic social effects. Always they have provided auxiliary energy and action patterns through which innovative enthusiasms were reinforced. (39; 56) The whole literature of the sociology of knowledge provides extensive elaborations of the thesis.

Beliefs. Beliefs are durable organizations of attitudes, perceptions, and cognitions about various aspects of the world of human beings. They include knowledge, opinion, and faith and constitute patterns of meanings. Thus, they take the form of standardized interpretations of meaning of all kinds of phenomena (modern man's belief that the earth is spheroid), of social situations (the Nazi belief in Aryan supremacy), and of supernatural beings and the relations to these beings (the whole array of religious beliefs). As individuals and groups holding these beliefs, men make them the basis of their daily conclusions and of their daily behavior in all situations in which the beliefs are involved or applicable. When men believe something, they are compelled to act in conformity with it or in behalf of it. All social procedures, ranging from planting superstitions or worship procedures to the very latest scientific experiments or engineering feats, rest upon fundamental beliefs.

URGES FOR EXPRESSION. The tremendous, poignant urges for expression in men, usually stimulated by association with their fellow men, cannot be ignored. Through the ages people have been seeking to express their inimitable human potentialities and inner upheavings. They have been impelled to give expression to their yearnings for a better world, for communion and peace with supernatural powers, for giving aesthetic form to words and phrases, things, movements, sounds, and colors, and to their yearnings for contriving, discovering, inventing, and otherwise venting their creative urges. Such expression is felt as a necessity. The effects of these energizers are seen in religious expression and religious movements, aesthetic creation, concepts of ideal social states, social reform, and revolutionary movements, most discovery and invention—in fact, in some of the work and some of the recreational activities of most people.

conformity-producing pressure upon the minorities and upon the newly interested and newly involved persons. We all belong to numerous publics —political, religious, occupational, and so on. Each of these are circles of influence that tug people this way and that. When "everybody's thinking it," few can stand apart—or care to.

Psychosocial Planes. The psychosocial planes are the more enduring, though changeable, widely embracing levels of common action that we all acquire from our culture, which center around persisting and widely sanctioned behavior requirements. They *require* us to act and think uniformly in different kinds of social situations. *Custom* consists of the ways of doing certain things that are transmitted from previous generations. It is especially operative in language forms, religious practices, marriage and family performances, and most institutionalized activities. Customs have the rightness of time and the support of the generations behind them. They are difficult to challenge, since we cannot argue with our ancestors. Much of our behavior is forced upon us by the imperious sway of custom. *Traditions* are the ways of thinking or believing and the rationalizations of most required behavior transmitted from previous generations. They operate much as do customs. *Conventions* are the behavioral planes resulting from the deliberate, noncompetitive, nonrational imitation of contemporaries. They, too, in large measure stem from the experience of the past. They especially relate to the more formal phases of social life, such as etiquette and good manners. They define proper and approved usage, and under their sway we are kept from acting like jungle creatures and are required to act like cultivated persons.

Ego Factor in Human Action

In the treatment of social dynamics the ego is frequently and curiously overlooked. The ego in almost all individuals is a propulsive factor of considerable potency in their action among their fellows. Every individual is a sensitive ego in a social world among other sensitive egos. Every ego has a strong, ever-present sense of personal worth and wants to amount to something among other egos. Every ego is seeking a basis for self-respect, self-confidence, and self-security and at the same time is avoiding a sense of submergence, inferiority, or failure. In every relationship between two or more persons, however friendly and sympathetic, there is this effort on the part of each to reinforce his own ego. Even a comfortable group of agreeable friends vie politely as they tell stories, make points, or recount travel experiences.

The action of ego ranges from the mere avoidance of injuries and slights and various face-saving defense reactions, both inner and overt, to highly forceful self-promotional action. Always, however, vast amounts of human energy and ingenuity are consciously and unconsciously expended in the efforts of every person to maintain and enhance his own feeling of self-regard. Some of the most basic and powerful aspects of social dynamics develop out of the eternal and persistent processes of ego-building and ego-vying.

The action of the ego in *seeking recognition* is one of these ego-building processes. It is, in fact, one of the major motivators of human behavior. Almost universally human beings make a play for attention and notice. They want to be looked upon favorably and to be accepted and respected by their fellows, to belong and not be left out. They seek and crave favorable reflections or mirrorings of themselves in the reactions of others toward them and abhor reproof. Hence, individuals, often unconsciously, by their ego performances, try to obtain favoring reactions to themselves by doing approved things and by avoiding doing unfavorable things.

The normal individual also *seeks prestige.* He tries by one means or another to gain some superiority over *some* others in one or more spheres of action. Prestige means the high esteem of others, but the individual seeks more than that. He wants to be lifted above the common herd, to be on the inside of the groups or activities that are in his opinion the best. Very frequently this ego aspiration expresses itself in the form of striving for leadership, authority, and power. Always, though, prestige is sought for its own sake, as a reinforcement of the ego, as security for the integrity of the person. Its quest is a powerful propulsive in the system of incentives, especially in such a society as our own.

Two features of ego-vying are bound up with the search for both recognition and prestige: avoidance of frustration and aggressiveness. *Avoidance of frustration*—a negative aspect of ego-vying —is highly important in a competitive culture. If the opportunities for individuals to achieve ego-recognition and ego-expansion in a satisfying degree are cut off or blocked, the personality suffers some degree of frustration. And frustration dams up energy until it eventually may reach explosive proportions. Frustration produces various veiled or open forms of retaliation and other more forceful action bent on neutralizing or clearing away the individuals and conditions conceived of as obstacles.

Aggressiveness is a significant, positive dynamic aspect of ego-expression. Most individuals, in at least some of their relationships, attempt to assert themselves over others, to obtain possession of things wanted or had by others, to exercise control or dominance over others, or successfully to oppose others. In many instances such aggressive acts give great emotional thrills to the individual; in fact, indulgence in aggressiveness can be compared to a drinking bout or sexual orgy, for it too is a powerful propulsive factor.

A third general aspect of ego performance, which relates to social dynamics, is the stimulus that derives from the coacting of consciously or unconsciously *vying egos*. This coaction occurs as they participate in common undertakings and even in doing similar things within sight and sound of each other. Not only is the stimulus of the desire to excel or to win approval or distinction present, but the coacting of human beings in physical or intellectual tasks often facilitates the performance.

A final aspect of ego-drive is the necessity expressing itself in *satisfying endeavor,* either work or recreation. The ego must convey itself in overt or dynamic action. But it should be in action which is recognized as acceptable, significant, or good by one or more groups in which the individual functions. He cannot be a meaningless and microscopic cog in a huge machine; he is not contented or balanced if he is only part of dozens of impersonal cycles. This action must not be mere task involvement; it must be socially significant action that requires and evidences ego-involvement.

It may be pointed out that ego-vying has strategic significance in almost every phase of societal operation. It underlies many social facilitations and inhibitions and is directly involved in the status system of every society and all of society's processes of competition and conflict. Ego-vying affects all forms of cooperation and plays a continuous part in both personal and social disorganization. It poses some of the basic problems and tasks to be dealt with by the regulative system and, if socially expressed and utilized, is a powerful resource in all societal maintenance.

Eminent Men

In this examination of the factors in social dynamics, we must take note of the part played by individuals. We shall not be concerned with individuals as vyers for ego-security and prestige and, hence, as blind propulsive units in social action, but with *certain* individuals mainly of an exceptional nature who are direct, conscious, competent dynamic creators and directors of social action.

Vast differences in social potential exist among human beings—differences in intellect, emotion, energy, will, knowledge, ingenuity, enthusiasm, charm, imagination, manipulative skill, and creativeness. Most persons just plod along in their social life. Some, however, can be referred to as eminent or exceptional, rather than as ordinary, men. Although these men are part of their society, subject to its elements and influences and responsive to its stimuli, yet they are to an extent outside it, free from its leveling compulsions and standardizing currents. They have certain qualities in more pronounced degree than the general run of men that enable them to perceive the insufficiencies of life, to be challenged by them, to gain new conceptions of things, to chart new courses and devise means of moving men in these courses. They also function as active agents in crystallizing, organizing, and instigating new social tendencies and occurrences. Exceptional men are unproductive without ordinary men, but ordinary men would not get far without exceptional men. These latter can be simply classified as innovators or as leaders.

The *innovators* are the initiators, the formers of new combinations of facts and principles, the coordinators of thought and activity. They function as the intermediaries through whom the signal forces and tendencies of their area and time pass, meet, and fuse. As they assay facts and trends, they provide conceptions of new desirable and exciting ways of functioning; they rouse possibilities into purposes and set free the potentialities of the mass of men. They are the creative thinkers, the idealists, the contrivers of new or greatly modified ideas, beliefs, and things involving the material, social, and spiritual universe, the constructors of values and goals, the devisers of new blueprints, and the originators of revisionary and revolutionary social movements.

All these innovators are inventors in that they sense needs and gaps, menaces, and thwarted purposes in social life, have premonitory visions of solutions, and have the ability to profit by failures, accidents, and exceptions. Above all, they have the essential knowledge, imagination, and ingenuity to utilize the various extant culture materials and combine them in forms that have new significance and applicability. Their products—the inventions—whether new gadgets, new techniques and technologies, new methods in science, new moral or religious ideas, new organizational forms, new maintenance or regulatory procedures—invariably bring about great modifications of many standard structures, functions, and processes and usually institute new ones. Always they animate readjustments and frequently operate as impulses to experiment; often they initiate chains of innovative action.

Leaders are the dynamic directors and often in considerable part effectors of the processes of social action. Most men depend upon exceptional, self-starting individuals to set up models and goals, to provide the impulse to action, to organize the action, and to command them. They also require leaders in certain situations to coerce them or to deflect them from persistent but deleterious lines of action.

In general, leaders, as dynamic factors, originate action. They appeal to and mobilize pertinent drives, emotions, and wishes of their particular group. They clarify, crystallize, and capitalize dominant interests and aspirations, usually symbolizing them in various ways, and stimulate the people. They pose a line of action to be followed; then they give the orders or "directives" which will realize the objectives. Readers are in some measure human dynamos and indispensable utilities. (Leadership will be more fully treated in Chapter 10.)

Historically and logically, innovators and leaders are the focal determinants in most social decisions and the spark plugs in a large part of social action.

Social Values*

No survey of dynamic factors in human social action, however brief, can be considered adequate unless it calls attention to the social values of a society, especially in certain of their ramifications and special forms, as determinative and propulsive factors. They exist in our sociocultural environment outside of us as individuals, but they bear in upon us as members of our society. They operate as highly pertinent, omnipotent, substantial cultural realities.

Values are treated last in this examination of dynamics of social action because they grow out of, and at the same time react upon, the multiplicity of other dynamic factors already considered. Values are directly related to biogenic and psychogenic drives, the interests, attitudes, and habits, the various intellectual reactions, essential beliefs, and expressional forms, the currents and planes, ego reactions of all kinds, and the actions of exceptional individuals. In a very real sense, values summate the whole discussion of dynamics.

Men make choices between alternatives with respect to all manner of actions, situations, persons, groups, and symbols which they are aware of and which seem to have some bearing on human life. They arrive at judgments regarding these realities which we refer to as "values." Suffice it to say at this point that these values, as constructed products of man's experience, *function as expressions of collective preferential force.* They arise out of, and govern every area of, human interest and action. From them there is no escape.

Their significance in social dynamics can be concisely "pointed up" as follows:

1. Values are what people pay attention to as

*We will analyze social values in their sociologically pertinent forms, expressions, and functions in greater detail in connection with their strategic functional significance in societal organization in Chap. 10. Here we are concerned with them briefly and simply as socially created propulsives, lures, and guides to social action.

valuable and essential; they focus attention upon socially desirable things, conditions, and ways and awaken men to them.

2. Values act as ready-made ensembles of socially acceptable, socially good, and socially ideal forms of belief and action. As such they overshadow and override individual desires and preferences, give us established orders of preference, and serve as guides and regulators. They enable people to make wise choices.

3. Existing values function as creators and formulators of desires and interests, of outlooks and aspirations. As such they are incentives or stimulators which move men, magnets or intensities of desiring which draw out their efforts. Malinowski, in his *Freedom and Civilization,* points out that values are the "prime movers of human existence. Men work to obtain the things they value whether these be objects, ways of life, or beliefs." (p. 137)

4. Values establish metes and bounds and act as restraints upon beliefs and actions that are disapproved of, deemed dangerous, and by consensus prohibited.

5. In certain areas and situations of social life values exist as sternly felt pressures, powers, or dominating musts which, if not heeded, present possibilities of costs to the individual or group.

Every possible action involves choice. The values of a society relate to almost every area of action and choice. Under their pressure and surveillance, in nearly every social situation *we must do or not do this or that.*

Several derived forms of social values of special sociological significance require our attention briefly.

Ideals. Ideals are both accumulations of values around certain ends and the projections of values toward those ends. Ideals grow out of the valuing process. When we value anything, we often move forward beyond, or rise above, the *is* and its consequence, and conceive of something *better* or what *ought to be.* We achieve a new way of seeing and appraising persons and conditions, and we acquire a new and richer perspective. In fact, we develop a hierarchy of values, and ideals are at the top of the hierarchy. They are imaginative representations at any given moment of the most desirable, the most hoped-for, the superior. They transcend the existing situation, express aspirations, and forecast eminently desirable possibilities to be achieved sometime.

Ideals are essentially some of the finest products of the intellect, but they are at the same time suffused with emotion and feeling, which powerfully increase their efficacy as propulsive agents of social action. It also seems to be a fact that most men prefer to steer a course rather than drift; for them ideals function as guide posts or beacon lights. Invariably also, being more or less consistent presentations of the organization and operation of a better state of things, they serve as specifications and blueprints of social action. In many persons and groups ideals seem to instill a sense of obligation, an urge not only to support them but to fulfill them. Most great purposeful social actions—the great, dynamic forward movements of men—have been built on ideals and are, in some part, an externalizing and effecting of them in the social order.

Norms. Norms, or standards, are another specific aspect of the value system of a society and have great motivational significance. They reflect the values involved in almost every recurrent social situation. They are statements or *prescriptions of how one should or should not think, feel, or act in these social situations.* Concretely they take the form of sets of rules for almost every kind of common social behavior. Thus, there are political and legal norms, moral and religious, scientific, aesthetic, and many others. They range along a scaled obligatoriness, the rules saying that some behavior is *permitted,* some *recommended,* some imperatively *required,* and some *disapproved of* or positively and insistently *prohibited.*

All behavior is presided over by norms, which function continuously as stimuli and directives of valued action, and restrainers of disvalued behavior. They have this additional distinctive feature: sanctions attach to the norm-governed behavior; that is, nonconformity to the norm is followed by some kind and degree of punishment, and conformity is rewarded. Some sociologists thus call them "sanction patterns." From them there is no escape.

Although norms motivate and govern in some degree in every process, function, and relationship to be treated in this study, they are of fundamental esses of society. Therefore, they will be more importance in the operation of the regulatory proc-

adequately analyzed as to nature, formation, and operation in Chapter 20.

Roles. Roles are a special set of normative prescriptions that have great dynamic significance in the everyday behavior of individuals in every society. Roles are the socioculturally defined and patterned ways of behaving *expected* of actors by virtue of their social positions in all of the typical relationship situations of a given social system. Thus, my society or various organizations of it have a standard set of generally known principles governing what I am required to do, forbidden to do, and permitted to do as a son, a student, a father, a husband, a citizen, a religious communicant, and so on. All *other* actors in each type of relationship have complementary or reciprocal roles to play toward me because of their similar or opposite positions in the specified interactive situations.

What is expected in the way of a combination of acts in each relationship is in the culture and identified and integrated with the particular set of values relating to the particular kind of interaction. These values, like all others, grow out of experience and reflect the nature and societal significance of each typical relationship. On the basis of this experience as evaluated by many people through time, the society sets the expectations, the requirements, and the limits of action. Each role thus presents the individual performer with a catalogue of specific functions to be carried out and with specific duties, rights, and privileges attached to the action.

Although the roles must be interiorized in the individual to be effective, they exist prior to, external to, and independent of the persons who play them. They are ready-made and omnipresent blueprints for action. But what is equally important in our present frame of reference is the fact that *the roles are felt as imperatives.* If the actors do not play their roles adequately, they suffer the loss of esteem, the avoidance, and even the punishment of their fellows. Hence, roles operate both as propulsions and compulsions among coactors in almost every type of concrete interactional situation in a given society. Roles will be more comprehensively examined in Chapter 10, both for their general significance and as motivating factors.

Significance of Social Crises

All things are constantly changing in relation to each other. This change of relationship means that there is perpetually some degree of disorder or disequilibrium. In human societies the effect of the various factors that produce disorder is known as "social crisis." Some degree of social crisis prevails in some part or other of every social system or subsystem at some time. These social crises range from those that are so minor and continuous or regularly recurrent as almost to escape attention to those that are of only occasional but catastrophic significance. These crises always call for some compliant efforts at readjustment. They have profoundly modified social structures, functions, and processes, and invariably they have necessitated the inauguration of new structures, functions, and processes—temporary or enduring—if the society was to carry on. Their brief analysis, especially in terms of their sociological significance follows as an essential part of the background for our study.

Nature of Social Crises

As social change occurs, any social system, in order to maintain its stability and functional efficiency, must continually balance its equilibrating factors and processes with those that make for disequilibrium. The processes of equilibration—those conducive to structuralization, functionalization, regulation, maintenance, and reorganization—should be continually realigning the societal patterns and re-establishing functional processes and procedures to meet the ever-new needs and demands of societal operation. But no society and no part of it ever functions perfectly. Some disintegration, destruction, disruption, dislocation, or suspension of some basic elements of sociocultural life, which alters fundamental structures and functional rhythms and interrelationships, is always going on.

Some of the maladjustive social changes are the result of the most orderly and regular physical, biological, social psychological, and social conditions and processes. But the changes occur at different tempos and have variant cumulative effects. Other social changes are due to more or less powerful irregular and occasional occurrences in these respective phenomenal fields and have an upheaving effect that may reach catastrophic proportions. Change, regardless of the volume or quality of its effects, always builds up pressures against the equilibrium, always has explosive possibilities, and always requires modifications which work toward the re-establishment of equilibrium on a new or different basis.

There is always somewhere, in some one or more groups, organizations, institutions, or communities of the social system, some departure from the ideal-typical normal, some breakdown and inadequacy, some incapacity and inefficiency, some instability and insecurity. Either the capacity of the social machinery has deteriorated, or its potentialities have not been used or have been misused. Such situations perpetually produce some kind and degree of social crisis somewhere in a social system. In major crisis situations there is a considerable amount of breakdown, imbalance, or inadequacy of functioning. But always, whether minor or major, the deteriorative and disbalancing factors and processes have disturbed the normalizing ones. The social situation prevents the satisfaction of many needs and wants of the population affected. There is some serious disturbance of the habits, customs, standards, and working life patterns of the group. The functional efficiency of strategic organizations, institutions, and conventional patterns of control has been impaired or lost entirely. The personnel, deep in the ruts of tradition and established practice, is unable to cope with the situation. The trend has reached a climactic stage.

Factors Contributing to Crises

Most of the *factors* involved in general social change are also causal or contributory precipitants of crises; but they are factors in crises only when they are uncontrollable, neglected, or permitted to get out of hand. The simplest categories are *environmental (or external) factors* and the *sociocultural (or internal) factors.* The environmental factors take the form of natural phenomena, physical and biological, which have destructive or deteriorative effects upon the people affected, such as hurricane, flood, epidemic, and so on. Also included here may be accidents to or within man-made structures, such as shipwreck and aerial bombardment.

The sociocultural (internal) factors are innumerable. They may consist of any unexpected, unprepared for, or unpreventable occurrences of a social nature that disrupt the normal social processes, such as a bank failure, a strike, or a defeat in battle. These usually grow out of functional disorders or inefficiencies of the social system. Much of mankind's behavior is notoriously inert as to form. It crystallizes in habit and a cake of custom develops. Collective life, in short, is inflexible at many points and, therefore, resistant to change. The disproportionate growth, or unequal rates of change, of interdependent parts and functions of a system are also highly important.

Although there is always the tendency toward inertia, there is also always innovation resulting from discoveries and inventions. But inventions, for example, are more likely in fields of societal life that are receiving special attention. As a result there is an absence of that invention in closely related but neglected fields which makes for compliant adjustment. Thus, to resort to the crucial situation in our society, the techniques and instruments of economic production and exchange have changed much more rapidly than the inextricably related ethical standards, personnel relations, social class alignments, property institutions, and other closely related human-social conditions. This lack of synchronization between relatively fast-changing and slow-changing elements brings about a lack of cooperation and balanced interplay. Any such situation sooner or later presents threats and dangers that may induce crisis.

Social Awareness of the Crisis Condition

It is important to note that the state of disorganization and disequilibrium *must be socially defined as crisis if it is to have the social effect of crisis.* (77, p. 438) At this time when the group defines the situation as a crisis, tensions heighten to the breaking point; the people are projected into the world of the unknown, but are temporarily helpless. The ordinary and expected has been replaced by the extraordinary and the unexpected. Everyone is aware of insecurity. Fear becomes widespread; disorder reigns; morale distintegrates. Chaos seems to threaten. The dangers of irrational and precipitate action are greatly increased. The people want escape or release from the crisis situation. There is a demand for solutions, for order, security, and a tangible program of action. *Regimental action* is often necessary to meet the recognized emergency. (77, pp. 105-110).

Significance

Social crises are inseparable from all the aspects of social dynamics. *They have the strategic place in the ideal-typical cycle of equilibrium*. This cycle, in the form of an adaptation of Becker's analysis (69), can be presented as it is here. There is the combination of factors which produce dissatisfaction among the members of the collectivity affected. These blocked or thwarted impulses lead to tension and frustration, which in turn produce individual and social unrest. This unrest crystallizes in the crisis situation.

When the crisis is defined, there are efforts at resolving it by adjustive actions. If the efforts are successful, there is a lessening of tension and unrest, and a new, though more or less temporary and dynamic, equilibrium is established. If the efforts are unsuccessful, there may be further regression, and the group or society may fail to survive or it may start the cycle anew.

Every crisis, whether major or minor, *poses a series of problems*. The existing means and ends are in some measure inadequate, inconsistent, incongruous, or conflicting, and the problems are insoluble by them. The crisis confronts the group or society with what Hart refers to as "the dynamic of menace" or with what Toynbee presents as "adversity." (73; 84, pp. 80-87) Menace and adversity function as powerful motivators. There are motivations produced by physical pain and suffering and by psychological discontent and resentment.

All sorts of cultural and social maladjustments are possible. They may be due to the disturbance of existing equilibriums by inventions, as in the case of the industrial revolution; or to natural catastrophe, rebellions, or wars; or to the fumbling development, disintegration, or ossification of institutions; or to antagonisms between groups; or to any one of hundreds of other threats to social stability and the satisfaction of personality needs and purposes. These crises generate emotional and intellectual energies which operate toward readjustment. Much of man's career is devoted to solving the problems created by crises.

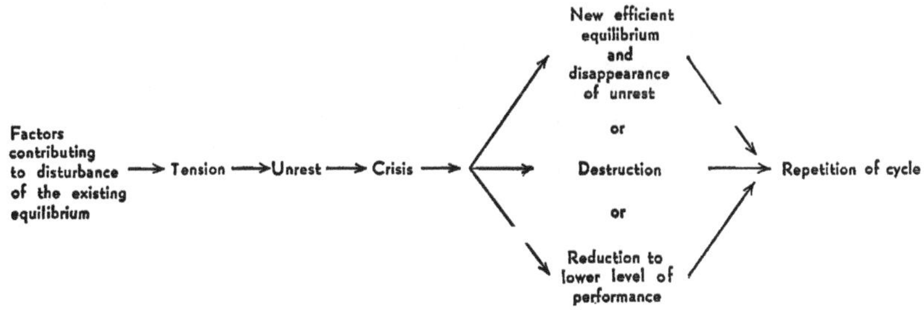

Schematic Presentation of the Equilibrium Cycle

Thus, crises mark a parting of the ways, a point at which transition must be made from an old to a new form of action. Hence, *crisis situations are incentive situations*. Things and events not only present many possibilities for a better or a worse outcome; they focus attention, produce a summons to decision, and demand resolution by social action. Crisis acts as a kind of cultural and social catalyst.

This eternal and universal human situation has been stated by Toynbee as "challenge-and-response." (84) Each problem is a challenge, a stimulus that invites adjustive response. The interplay between challenge and response is what counts above all else in the human career. Ability to meet the challenges means survival, even prosperity; inability means disintegration, reversion to a more primitive form, or, in time, complete disappearance of an organization, a class, a nation, or even a civilization. A stable and enduring society goes from challenge through successful response to further challenge, which meets another successful response, and so on *ad finitum*. Such is the rhythm of societal survival.

Social crises have strategic importance. This is borne out by the fact that in any society *crises have a direct connection with practically every category of social processes.* The processes of destructuralization and defunctionalization, such as isolation, opposition, decadence, and ossification, contribute to situations and conditions that may eventuate in crises. The innovative processes of discovery and invention, the modifications of technics, techniques, and technologies, the demographic processes, the various processes of cultural growth, transmission, and exchange, the processes of physical and social mobility are both cause and effect of crises.

Many processes, if functioning efficiently, tend to produce a social system that forestalls or prevents crises. Pertinent are the various group-forming processes, especially those that produce purposive organizations, the institutionalization processes with their establishment of standardized and codified behavior, the differentiation and stratification processes, the regulative processes, and the maintenance processes, such as ordination, accommodation and assimilation, which normalize and sustain social interaction and assure smooth societal functioning.

Many of the most important social values, such as liberty, equality, and the freedoms, which are themselves the result of typical human processes, exist to avoid crisis situations. The regimenting and the reorganizing processes are explicitly conducted both to prevent and to extricate the given system, if threatened by or actually in a crisis situation, from that deplorable state, and re-establish or construct anew effective agencies of operation. Almost *all* processes, therefore, can be said to be both cause and effect of crises.

Some degree of crisis at some time and at some place is always possible in every social system. If the system is to function smoothly and survive, it must be so constructed that it can deal with any disaffection, impairment, dislocation, or partial breakdown that comes with change, and it must be constantly and constructively poised to re-establish peace and operational efficiency after crises.

CHAPTER IV

THE PROTO PROCESSES

THE PROTO,* or master, or basic, processes are those which are to be found wherever two or more persons are in some sort of relationship and where generation follows generation in maintaining a continuing society. These processes are the over-all elemental occurrences upon which societal existence is contingent.

To date many of the analysts have stopped with association and dissociation and the related processes of cooperation, competition, conflict, accommodation, and assimilation. As a result we have a very general explanation of social occurrence; not a conception of a many-faceted, multi-functioning, continuously operative societal mechanism. These proto processes will here be briefly related to their general place and function in a society; specific forms and instances of them in operation will appear among the several major categories of processes where they play their significant parts in carrying on the numerous functions, essential or unavoidable, in a living, changing society.

Two general processes dominate all human social life—adjustment and interaction. Human beings are in continuous process of adjustment to all their environments and to each other; this is necessary if they are to survive and flourish. As they adjust, they interact, unconsciously and consciously. So fundamental is each of these master processes that they should all be thought of as major aspects of societal operation.

Adjustment

The universe may be looked upon as an equilibrating energy system. The tendency to establish an equilibrium is the basic process among all energy-embodying elements interacting in any en-

*I am indebted to my colleague, Dr. Paul Meadows, for this apt term.

vironment, which may be considered a field of force. The objects or units—mechanisms or organisms—have varying potentials of energy that are exerted at different rates of speed and in different directions. There are attractions, coherencies, and reciprocal dependencies, but at the same time there are resistances, repulsions, and incoherencies to be overcome. The forces constantly tend to get out of balance with each other. Disequilibrium is found in the relationship of everything to everything else.

All natural movement, however, may also be thought of as a tendency to establish an equilibrium within the area of operation. There is a strain toward balance. The forces tend to equalize, though they rarely become equal. The unstable and unbalanced move in the direction of stability and balance. The equilibrium is purely theoretical, however; it is never perfect, never complete, never permanent; it is a "moving balance." (3)

Among purely physical elements this process takes the form of the equilibrium of forces. Water and mountains tend to seek a level; electricity flows from high to low potentials; the hot iron radiates heat to surrounding bodies. Every living thing, in its intake and release of energy, tends toward an equilibrium with its surrounding conditions. Thus, all biological forms are in a continuous process of survival. This process consists essentially of maintaining a balance with all aspects of the encompassing physical environment, and with all other organic forms, including the members of their own species.

Adaptation and Adjustment

According to the best current scientific usage, the processes of equilibration of *biological organisms,* animal or plant, with the conditions of their physical and biological environments are called *adaptation.* The adaptation processes are automatic. They consist of two classes of equilibrative tendencies. (1) There are continuous structural, functional, and biochemical changes within the organism, as it conforms through variation (including mutation), selection, and inheritance to the physical conditions under which it happens to live: altitude, temperature, light or darkness, dryness or moisture, nutrition supply, enemies, symbiotically related other species, and the members of its own species (for example, overcrowding). (2) There is compliant change in physical location, as the result of competition for space and for the physical, chemical, and biological conditions for existence, slow and impeded though the movement may be. The very process of living and surviving among other interacting creatures in the various environments consists of a continuous sequence of modifications in make-up, function, and location.

Human beings as biological specimens undergo some automatic adaptive modification. Social adaptation, however, is an improper term in current sociological usage. The human processes of equilibration are seldom purely automatic. With human beings adaptation passes into adjustment, that is, a more or less conscious, deliberate, and purposeful procedure whereby persons and groups establish systems of action.

Human beings live in a multiplicity of environments. Individually and jointly they must adjust continuously and more or less consciously to the ever-changing physical and biological environments; in addition, there must be the continual fitting of individuals and groups. Man has even conceived of a supernatural environment to which he feels constrained to adjust himself. Without these various adjustments, there can be no survival and no satisfying security.

In the last analysis, all human behavior, individual and social, impulsive or purposive, casual and organized, is of an adjustive nature. No one can live with complete passivity, but must adjust his every activity more or less to the conditions about him. Human life is in some measure an unending effort consciously or unconsciously to work out problems of strain, disequilibrium, or crisis and to find means of enhancing individual and social adjustment. All innovation, exploration, and experimentation have adjustment as an objective. The same can be said for habit forming and learning.

Adjustment is the best single key to the social processes. The formation of culture, the protection against, or the manipulation of, elements in the physical or biological environments, the instruction of the young, cooperation, the devising of all manner of groupings, organizations, and institutions, migration and social mobility, differentiation and stratification, subservience and striving, accommodation of antagonisms, assimilation and conformity, societal regulation and maintenance, amelioration, reformative activity, and reorganization are all adjustive procedures. So too are the forming of values and goals, all planning and engineering, all pursuit of economic, political, moral, aesthetic, religious, and other desires, interests, and goals.

Even when men act destructively, antagonistically, unsocially, or antisocially, they are in their own particular way attempting to overcome some inner or group imbalance, although they are accentuating general maladjustment. For example, in withdrawal and isolation the participants are seeking to adjust themselves by separating themselves from maladjustive factors and conditions; in competition and conflict, the participants are attempting to overcome frustration, tensions, or pressures; the very actions and reactions of disorganized personalities are escapes or other modes of coping with the distracting world about them. Individuals and groups seek to avoid maladjustment by all sorts of negative and positive procedures. Most of man's means or instrumentalities—equipment, techniques, and technologies, all his ideologies, his sciences, his folkways and mores, his complex institutional systems, society itself—are devised for the purpose of adjustment.

Certain Characteristics of Man's Adjustment

1. Adjustment is *partial, never complete.* Man is eternally discontented; he is avoiding pain and seeking pleasure; his goals are ever receding as he approaches them. The very environments themselves are continually changing. Social life is a complex scheme of relationships, and there is constant variation in it due to the geographical, biological, psychological, and cultural forces acting upon it. Hence, equilibrium is never fully attained.

2. Adjustment is *dynamic, and not stable.* Man exercises much control over his environments and is ever doing so; the more he modifies them, the more he must adjust himself to them. This means that his adjustment is a constant shift and flow.

3. Adjustment is *selective and variant.* For man there are myriad environments, and he must make adjustive choices. But he has versatility, mobility, and constructive ability and can cope selectively and by using artifice in some measure with every changed situation.

4. Adjustment is *done jointly* and always involves others. There is joint action in adjusting to the physical and biological environments, as there is interaction in every adjustment of individuals and groups to each other. Most adjustive action is cooperative and conducted in an organized manner with *some* associates, though some forms of action may not conduce to equilibrium in the larger society.

5. Adjustment is *learned and transmitted.* Perhaps the most outstanding feature of man's adjustment is *not* that it is achieved by the biological methods of natural selection, as among other forms of life, but that it is due to vast cultural equipment and conducive behavior patterns which he learns and utilizes in his every action and transmits to his kind.

Social Interaction

Nature and Significance of Social Interaction

It is hardly necessary to state that interaction is the other fundamental prerequisite and condition of all structure and all process wherever these exist, whether in the universe or in any of its parts. Similarly, to posit interaction as the essential requirement for social activity and, hence, the all-important, basic social process is to belabor the obvious. Yet a brief review of its pointed nature and significance and its general constituent elements is essential as part of the general reference.

Interaction in general is "the process in which the action of one entity causes reaction by another. In the course of this action and reaction the course of the original entity is altered as to location, condition, or both." (11) By social interaction we mean "the reciprocal influences that human beings exert on each other through interstimulation and response." (15) It is concerned with the relationship between the activity of one person or group and that of another person or group. The reaction may occur between individuals, between an individual and a group, or between groups.

Interaction is a two-way process, although sometimes it appears to be one-way, as, for example, when a person or group has great power or influence over another person or group and obtains complete submission. Even in such extreme instances, there is actually some two-way action and reaction. Always in the process of interaction each individual or group influences or stimulates the other to some extent, and each brings about some degree of response on the part of each or all. The behavior of all participants is modified. Many different types of reciprocal stimulation and response are going on in every society. In a very real sense they comprise social life.

Human interaction is not only two-way but also circular in nature (20), owing to the fact that any response which one of the parties in the relationship makes to another is at the same time a stimulus to further response from the other. For example, irritation produces irritation; cooperation intensifies in the direction of cooperation.

It may be pointed out that human beings cannot be themselves without interaction. When it ends, individuals are isolated and detached, personality deteriorates, and human action has significance only as biological maintenance in a physical environment.

The causes of particular social interactional acts are biological and psychological in nature and, as such, are problems of these respective fields of study. But when the social acts are repeated, so that they become recognized and established forms or patterns of behavior, the sociologist can study them as forms of *social* interaction *per se,* independent of specific circumstances.

The innumerable special social processes are simply particular forms which interactions take in terms of the functions and persons as various combinations of human beings.

Essentials in Social Interaction

Analytically, social interaction breaks down into two basic subprocesses and conditions, namely, *contact* and *communication.*

Contact is the initiating stage in social interaction. As Eubank stated, it "occurs whenever and wherever two or more persons are simultaneously aware of each other and are conscious of each other's awareness." (12) The question may be raised as to whether contact is not primarily a condition essential to social process rather than a process itself. At any rate, if the contact is not too temporary, or remote, and if there is some degree of sense connection between the persons and groups, the initiation of some sort of interaction, in the sense of some sort of social experience, begins. There is *some* interaction or social action between all sentient creatures if there is any contact at all. The determinable function of contacts is to release interaction.

The contact may be *primary* or *secondary.* In primary contact the persons involved are in spatial proximity and directly and personally influence each other; whereas in secondary contact the units are spatially separated, and the relationships are impersonal; yet, the individuals or groups are aware of each other and influence each other. Contact may be of *short or long duration* with varying attendant effects. *It occurs at different levels,* the most elementary of which is that it is purely automatic and symbiotic—a matter of immediate organic response in the presence of the other organisms. This consists merely of living together on the biological level in the form of either parasitism (one-way advantage) or mutualism (two-way advantage). The relation is largely physical. The more distinctive human contact, however, is at the psychic-cultural level, which will be discussed later.

The contact may be merely a matter of *physical proximity,* with the result that it is limited as to mutuality of responses; or it may be a matter of *social proximity* and, hence, of close social bonds and greater freedom and volume of reciprocal and mutual response. Contact may range from an *involuntary* or purely casual nature to that which is *voluntary* and intentional. Finally, it may be *positive* and lead to relations of approach, or it may be *negative* and lead to relations of avoidance and antagonism and make for isolation. (27, p. 155)

Communication of some kind and on some plane is made possible by contact among individuals and groups and alone makes contact significant with respect to social interaction. Human interaction is communicative interaction. Social life cannot exist in the absence of communication. It is fundamental to all social processes and is involved in every single act of social behavior. *Communication makes community possible.* It can be thought of as a web of signals and expectations and understandings that make living together possible. The members of every group have to be able to communicate with reference to their common tasks, incentives, values, and risks.

The distinctive feature of human communication is that it involves the transmission of meanings through the use of symbols. Human beings have the ability to participate in the symbolic process. *A symbol* is an easily recognizable mark or technique without meaning or importance in its own right, which is used to represent, direct attention to, or recall ideas, actions, emotions, or things that have common social significance. Symbols evoke more or less uniform response in the communicating human beings. They are themselves social products, summaries of human experience, which function as humanly devised agents to bring the world of reality under more effective control. Through mental imagery, by a kind of abbreviated reasoning, symbols monopolize attention, excite reaction, and point easily, quickly, and unerringly to a conclusion. They produce common understandings. With the achievement of symbolism, man's behavior became irretrievably cultural. Whether illiterate or literate, the communication of human beings occurs through one or more levels of symbolism and takes place through various symbolic media and techniques, such as natural actions, signs, language, and mechanical devices.

Natural actions refer to gestures, postures, intonations, movements, grimaces, and spontaneous noises, and communication by these means is necessarily very limited, being confined mostly to the revealing of emotions and simple attitudes. If the contact is continued for any length of time or is repeated, these natural mediums are likely to become conventionalized, as in the sign language of the Indians or the gestural communication which develops between people of widely diverse cultures.

Signs are found in the form of flags, the cross, the crescent, wedding rings, emblems, and so on, all charged with communicable meaning and capable of evoking response.

Especially significant is *language* in its various forms and uses. Common language is the medium of most direct human interaction and the chief instrument of common action. Language consists essentially of a great array of conventionalized, systematized, and standardized sounds in the form of words, each of which has a specific meaning for all who understand the language. With verbalization in the form of vocabulary, concepts of all kinds can be formed and transmitted. Without words there can be no conceptualization; usually without them there is only inarticulate perception and emotional reaction. Language thus makes possible the transmission of thought in all its forms as opposed to mere reactions.

The very extent of social interaction is limited by the development and adequacy of language. In addition, language serves as a cohesive force uniting human groups and setting them apart from other groups. Common speech is an index of the social solidarity of a group. The common language, sometimes even the peculiar dialect, represents one of the differences between the in-group and the out-group.

When the concepts which we express by words or other auditory symbols are translated into the form of physical objects, pictures or pictograms, alphabet or other conventionalized visible figures, we have *writing.* With writing communication can extend far beyond the reaches of the human voice in space and in time far beyond the life span of any individual, group, generation, or culture. By means of it there can be a much more exact and verifiable transmission and a durable recording of experience of all kinds.

Today communication is vastly facilitated by the various *mechanical means of transmitting either language or writing,* such as postal service, printing, telephone and telegraph, radio, photography, motion pictures, and television. These immeasurably increase the speed, range, and volume of communication. In our present-day world of mass organization and secondary contacts, communication by these mechanical means is highly significant.

Certain general features of communication should be noted. Communication may be *direct* or *indirect.* If direct, it is face to face and among persons or groups within earshot or sight of each other. If indirect, it is between persons and groups removed from each other in space and time. Communication, like the contact out of which it grows, may be *one way, two way,* or *many way.* If one way, it is mere communication, and only limited response and exchange are likely. If it is two way or many way, real intercommunication exists.

To be complete and as meaningful as possible, communication should rest upon an *array of common experiences.* Community of experience is a factor which conditions communication. For if communication is to be the conveyance of meaning which has effects on the recipient, then the participants must have a common fund and a common level of sufficiently uniform experience. Thus, a given phenomenon has approximately the same meaning for two or more persons.*

Common Arraying of Interactional Tendencies

The most obvious and general and most widely resorted to portrayal of the various specific forms of social interaction places them on a continuum. At one pole are those processes variously referred to in the recent and contemporary sociological literature as associative, solidary, cooperative, conjunctive, and integrative; at the other pole we find the dissociative, antagonistic, isolative, disjunctive, and disintegrative processes. Most of the social processes of a society can be located somewhere along this continuum.

The major conceptualizations of the two general sets of processes should be known to students, for they provide a general overview. They will be treated here as the associative and the dissociative-isolative processes. Actually, these interactional tendencies complement each other. *The difference between them is not one of kind, but of degree.*

Association

By *association* we mean human beings and groups interacting so reciprocally, so understandingly and sympathetically, so freely on the basis of mutual agreement and common values, objectives and ways, that a strong we-feeling or sense of nearness, partness, and togetherness prevails among them. It is essentially the process of living together compatibly.

Although contact and communication are prerequisites of association, association is not the inevitable result of these preliminary processes. Living together, we-feeling, and cooperative action do not necessarily result. Usually more than one contact, even a repetition and accumulation of contacts, is necessary to produce definite association. Furthermore, although contacts and communication often lead to new significant relationships, they also bring about modification, intensification, diminution, or displacement of relationships already existing. (7, pp. 152-153)

We must distinguish between the process of association and those organizations of human beings, based on common interests and purposes, known as associations, to be analyzed later. However, all *forms* of association (groups of all kinds, informal or formal, spontaneous or durable) rest upon and result from *processes* of association.

The process of association, in some degree or form, is the basis of all effective societal organization. Some of the most important social processes, such as various forms of socialization, participation, integration, organization, cooperation, accommodation, acculturation, assimilation, amalgamation, and circulation, are subprocesses of association; they occur to produce, maintain, or enhance a sufficient degree of unity and positive social action to enable the society, or particular parts of it, to carry on effectively.

The association of individuals may produce groups ranging all the way from the rather simple and small associations such as the family or neighborhood to the large complex associations of communities, states, nations, and various regional and federal combinations of these. Human beings are involved in some degree of association with their fellows from the moment of birth on. The stimuli of association with other persons of varying sex, age, and experience impinging upon the individual from the first moment of social consciousness sound out and help develop the human potentialities of persons into more or less normally behaving personalities. Association in sufficient quantity

*This third aspect of communication is derived from an unpublished paper by Richard Videbeck.

and quality is essential throughout life for the maintenance of individual health of personality.

Dissociation

The *dissociative-isolative processes,* at the opposite end of the continuum, make for a diminution or interruption of general interaction. Some of them produce interaction of an antagonistic and disorganizing form. Owing to this hindrance, or absence of interaction, or to antagonistic, divisive interaction, there is produced for the individuals and groups concerned a detached position with respect to other groups or even to the larger society and culture. The detached elements have a sense of apartness, distance, exclusion, even of antagonism. Isolation thus is a matter of infinitely differentiated association.

Isolation always exists to some degree in every relationship. The very nature of certain types of contacts and the limitations upon the amount and efficiency of communication between individuals, between groups, or between individuals and groups, frequently actually produce a feeling of isolation, especially in its mental and cultural forms. (27, p. 153) The major processes that relate to isolation and dissociation, in most instances taking the form of subprocesses, are individuation in its extreme aspects, the various mobility processes, specialization, competition in some of its aspects, the various contravention and conflict processes, differentiation, stratification, superordination-subordination, discrimination, segregation, ossification, and decadence.

As a result of the various processes of isolation, every considerable population is divided into numerous nonfreely communicating and more or less estranged groups. Also, as will be presently noted, isolation of individuals prevents their proper socialization, and isolation of groups results in their ossification and prevents cross-fertilization of cultures.

As previously noted, both association and dissociation-isolation are matters of degree. There is never absolutely perfect association; some isolation always exists. On the other hand, the only absolute isolation is complete and permanent spatial separation without any means of communication whatsoever. As many and as significant interactional processes grow out of relative or developing isolation as grow out of association.

The associative processes are the essence of societal stability, but the dissociative ones are its great and continuous threat. Although this nearness-farness scale, among other dichotomous ranges, is one on which processes may be fruitfully examined, it does not give us the intrinsic nature of societal process. (28, p. 681) Instead, it presents a conception of a society consisting merely of the combining or separating of its elements, of processes merely as tendencies in themselves.

These tendencies are continually in evidence in a society, but society as a going concern is vastly more than this. The very existence of dissociative processes, for example, requires a concomitant array of equilibrative processes to restore and maintain social balance, unity, order, and efficiency. The key words are not *interaction,* or *association,* or *dissociation,* or *isolation*; but *survival, action, function,* and *operation.* A society as a living ongoing unit is made up of a host of specific and determinable functional occurrences contributing to its operative requirements and its acknowledged purposes. As such, it consists fundamentally of processes of organization, of valuation and norm-forming, of regulation, maintenance, and reorganization.

Socialization

The survival and continuity of a society depend upon another proto process, *socialization,* which in turn consists of numerous subprocesses. Adjustment is the combination of over-all processes that enables man to make himself at home in all his environments. Socialization is the master process whereby the individual comes to be at home in his own society. By it is meant the congeries of processes whereby the inhabitants of a societal area are subjected continuously and persistently to a host of social influences, pressures, and controls, which surround them like an atmosphere and develop them into associates and participants, that is, into members functioning in a tolerable, if not always admirable, manner. Without socialization a society could not perpetuate itself beyond a single generation and culture would be nonexistent.

Aspects of Socialization

Socialization has two important aspects. First, it affects *all* members of a society continuously throughout their lives. Since societal life is an ever-flowing affair, the life of the individual must be an everlasting adjustment. Second, it is the specific process whereby new increments *to* a society—especially each new generation, but also immigrants—acquire the degree of patterned behavior essential to life *in* the society. L. K. Frank refers to the process, although he gives it a different name, as one "educating each generation of children in terms of basic ideas and conceptions, the selective awareness, the sensibilities, the socially sanctioned ways of functioning, thinking, believing, speaking, acting, and feeling." (31) Each society accomplishes some of this socialization more or less informally and unsystematically, but no society can have adequate socialization without resorting to deliberate, systematic, self-conscious, and organized procedures.

Socialized persons and groups have at least the minimal knowledge, attitudes, and habits, including skills and techniques, essential to social action in the society. They feel and think dependably together; they accept the values and conform to the institutions; they perform their various roles. In general, their behavior is sufficiently patterned and established to fall within the limits of tolerance permitted by the society.

Socialization is a molding, inducting, and absorptive social process among interacting individuals and groups, and its over-all function is to achieve unity of purpose and action. By means of it people learn to live with others and become interrelated functional parts of a going concern.

Modification and Interpretation

Socialization is always a relative matter; it never occurs in complete form. Furthermore, its ingredients and criteria are and should be subject to continuous modification and interpretation. But when sufficient socialization has occurred among a large enough proportion of the population, the society's functional structures (groups, associations, institutions, class system) operate adequately and meet the various types of needs of the people, and individuals act, both unconsciously and consciously, in the numerous ways essential to physical existence and to social order and peace.

Socialization thus is involved in a host of societal functions that are of paramount significance. These will be discussed later in a comprehensive manner at the appropriate points.

Among the major specific subprocesses of socialization are the norm-forming (in part), the conditioning and learning, the role-forming, the standardizing, and the motivating processes. Broadly speaking, however, every social process is socializing in some degree and manner.*

Individualization

The proto process of individualization is a concomitant of socialization, for in the processes of interaction, human beings develop not only sociality but also individuality. Because of the complexity of social life and the reactions of persons to it during their lives, no two persons pass through exactly the same socialization experience. Furthermore, while socialization brings about unity of purpose and action, it does not bring about alikeness or uniformity of personality traits or completely similar forms of behavior among individuals within the general minimal patterns. Each individual is unique genetically and reacts uniquely to the multiple conditioners and processes of his total environments.

By individualization we mean that combination

*For the specific part of socialization in societal regulation, see Chap. 20.

of processes whereby the individual, with his particular hereditary constitution (physiological and psychological) and as the result of his personal experiences in growing up and living and responding in a society, is built into a unique, variant, personality *within* and *part of* the society of which he is a member. Individuals do not live in a vacuum; essentially they are products of group living. The very processes of association and dissociation are productive of differences between individuals within groups, and for that matter between different groups.

What we refer to as *personality* is "that organization of individual behavorial characteristics which develop in a social environment and which serve to distinguish one individual from another." (35, p. 287) The individual native potentialities in their infinite variability are encouraged, discouraged, inhibited, or modified by environmental factors. The product is a particular and peculiar person with a special configuration of emotions, a set of characteristic responses to social situations, individual needs for different kinds of dependency upon others, a certain ability to "give" himself to others, special introvertive and extrovertive tendencies, a way of his own of participating in joint and antagonistic activities; in brief, a unique bundle of responses and processes, responding in characteristic ways to other social persons in social life.

There is no implication that the individualizing processes produce an antisocial person, one who is irreverent of values and institutions, refusing to accept cultural patterns or failing to participate in essential social actions, or a person who is oblivious of his associates, although this does also occur in certain instances. Nor are these processes to be identified necessarily with those making for isolation, atomization, or other dissociative or disorganizing processes.

The individualization processes are involved in all other social processes. They are especially significant, however, in group movements like fad, fashion, reform, and other iconoclastic processes and movements, in superordination-subordination processes (including leadership-followership), and in all regulatory processes.

These proto processes do not explain societal operation. They are simply fundamental processes that occur universally and continuously in any society. Primary attention must be paid to categories of specific processes that are generally operative in the major functional areas of a society such as ours.

PART TWO

CULTURIZATION

CHAPTER V

THE ORIGINATION AND ACQUISITION OF CULTURE

ONE OF THE most distinctive features of human life is that it is never merely a passive product of automatic processes but is always dynamic and creative in some measure. Individually or collectively, men do not act merely on the basis of inherited behavior patterns. They are curious and discover things about their total environment. They have intelligence and germinate ideas; that is, they think conceptually and come to conclusions about things and occurrences. They concern themselves with what seems to be essential and desirable and rationally calculate utilities in some degree, however dim and groping. They remember, in part at least, what has succeeded. In a word, men learn by experience.

Even more important than the ability of men to learn by experience is the fact that men have initiative and powers of contrivance and constructiveness; that they intervene in their world and learn in some degree to harness its energies and processes and make them serviceable; that they devise techniques for mitigating the untoward features of their world and expeditiously adjusting to every aspect of it; and that they experiment with ways of modifying and utilizing their world. These utilitarian ways they adopt and develop, although often only partially, belatedly, and haphazardly.

In some measure and in some manner men borrow from their fellows, both near and remote in time and space, ways of living that seem good, modify them, and apply them in their own scheme of living. They profit by the past and build on it, and they usually try and often succeed in some respects in outstripping the achievements of their forebears. These ways they transmit to posterity as they bind human action and human time into a continuous creative and adjustive process.

The Building of Culture

All the foregoing efforts and achievements are summated in what social scientists refer to as *culture*. Unlike other species, man has always been distinguished by the fact that he is the culture-producing, culture-maintaining, culture-transmitting, and culture-perpetuating animal. Culture is his unique and inimitable handiwork. As Kroeber points out, "It is all those things about man that are more than just biological or organic and also more than merely psychological." And, "It is at one and the same time the totality of the products of social men, and a tremendous force affecting all human beings, socially and individually." (14, pp. 8-9) *Culture is both a multiplicity of processes and an array of instrumentalities.*

Cultural Processes

The cultural processes consist of all those processes whereby man cultivates and disciplines his own nature and develops and exploits selected potentialities of the natural physical and social world in which he finds himself. (3; 9) By means of these processess he creates and maintains his peculiarly human world and human mode of living and achieves his numerous ends by collective and implemented action. These processes are for controlling, planning, artificing, utilizing, and organizing natural, biological, psychological, and social phenomena, and for transmitting, exchanging, improving, increasing, and perpetuating through time the instrumentalities by which man achieves this hegemony over phenomena. They are ways of doing things which carry man far beyond mere adaptation to nature, and by means of which man gives himself a self-made environment; that is, he makes himself more or less at home in the universe by what he has wrought. These processes are continually in operation, producing an ever-changing culture.

Array of Instrumentalities

As an array of instrumentalities, culture consists of a collection of behavioral equipment over and above his biological inheritance that has been in process of accumulation and selection since human interaction began. It reflects the historical experiences of the generations of men and is "the precipitate of history, the accumulated treasury of human creation." (13) In this sense, culture consists of all the constantly appearing man-made features of man's life: all the products of his trial and error, his accidents, his observations, his discoveries, his inventions, his imaginings, and the working conclusions arrived at in his attempts to come to satisfying terms with nature, with his fellow men, and with his supernatural and superhuman world.

Culture constitutes a magnificent inheritance for associative human living. Each generation need not start at the beginning; instead, it is provided with effective, tried, ready-made solutions to most of the problems with which it is likely to be confronted. (15) In fact, in its cumulative phases culture is like a cornucopia, narrow at the bottom but wide at the top, and this store at the top is available to each new generation.

All culture is basically utilitarian from one point of view, and almost all of its essential features are reputed to have survival value. From the point of view of the well-being of the whole society, some of these features may not be good, and many are directly harmful among the interlocking societies of the present world, for they include the stupid and vicious practices and instruments of men—implements of war, crime, vice, superstitions, and the like—as well as the enlightened and beneficent practices. Moreover, although culture is an instrument of human gratification, at the same time, as man's way of social life it places serious restraints on certain forms of gratification in the interests of general well-being. Always it is an ever-developing complex affair, the elements of which, however contrived or acquired, require continual adjustment to each other.

What, then, are the more important processes, functions, and factors involved in the originating, exchanging, revising, integrating, preserving, differentiating, transmitting, and fixing of the culture elements of the culture system of a given area or society?

Social Interaction and Culture

Human society and culture are intertwined aspects of a complex of phenomena that regularly occur only in social interaction. Culture originates in and because of the interaction of two or more individuals. Interaction has created the great bulk of needs and the goals that stimulated and motivated the satisfaction of these needs. (18) Interaction provides the reciprocal relations, that is, the contacts and communication, the association, organization, and cooperation that make possible the formation, manipulation, and utilization, as well as the sharing, selection, modification, substitution, and discarding of usable materials, tools and techniques. Cultural processes are part of social processes.

Interaction in space and through time makes possible *transmission* of culture from individual to individual and group to group and *acquisition* of culture, both conscious and unconscious. It also makes possible the *continuity* of culture through time and the *accumulation* of culture elements in volume and variety. The essential requirements of human interaction everywhere determine the universal patterns and schemes of culture. At the same time the peculiar requirements of interaction of a given combination of people in a given environment and with their peculiar history provide each society, even each portion thereof, with its own peculiar culture traits or simple units, its complexes or interrelated and interdependent traits and its patterns or broader configurations, built upon the universal pattern.

Culture, in turn, provides all the essential facilities of interaction. Even more important, since culture consists of the established ways of believing, thinking, and acting of men, is the fact that it is the *determinant* of the manner in which individuals and groups participate in nearly all the social processes and functions of any society; in brief, it is the major determinant of human social events.

Social Functions of Culture

The fundamental significance of culture can be brought out by concisely depicting its major functions in the operation of a societal going concern. Some overlapping is unavoidable, since these functions are carried on together. In any given social situation, however, some functions will be more significant than others.

Culture provides man with a "stock in trade" and a behavioral "set of tools" in the way of necessary physical and social equipment for living humanly in his various environments. Of elemental importance in this inventory of stock are the *artifacts,* the material things that he has fabricated by transforming components of the physical and biological world. Related to these are all the forms of production, transportation, distribution, and exchange of what man has made. These boons are made possible by means of the tools and machines, the techniques and technologies that he has devised. They assure sustenance, protection, controlled energy to supplement his own limited supply, and various kinds of place utility.

Culture provides man with the ways of safely gratifying his biological needs and also with ways of modifying his own biological drives, such as eating only certain things and at certain times and controlling his reproduction. Culture gives him his socially conditioned attitudes, habits, and interests and his ways of satisfying his sociopsychological needs, such as play and companionship, aesthetic, intellectual, and spiritual expression. Man has also acquired from culture all his symbols, including both unmodified objects (for example, stars or mountains to steer by) and constructs to which he has given special meanings and utilities. Of vast importance are the means of communication (language and writing and their extensions), the knowledge, beliefs, values, works of art, ideas and idea systems, and the theologies and rituals by which man adjusts himself to what he conceives of as his supernatural and superhuman environment.

All the structural-functional patterns of human relationship and societal organization by means of which men succeed in living together continuously and more or less efficiently and attain their common ends are signal features of culture. In brief, culture provides man with the instrumentalities for mastering his various environments and hence enables him in some degree to gratify his needs of physical, biological, psychological, and social existence, and to satisfy his yearnings for cosmic understanding and security. It is cherished and husbanded as a precious means of protection, survival, social fulfillment, and self-fulfillment.

Culture gives man a "design for living," that is, it defines, in terms of what is known and available as socially approved and historically effective, the prerequisites and requirements of social action. Its patterns, by defining liberties and restraints, establish the prohibited, the permissible, and the required forms of social behavior. As such it limits or channels the interaction of all human beings within the particular area, group, or society. As Linton points out, culture provides the members of social groups with "an indispensable guide in all the affairs of life." * (16, p. 20) Each human community lives and moves in the grooves of its culture. Its members are thus relieved of much anxiety and strain. It should be noted, too, that because of this channeling function of culture, the social action of human beings can never begin untrammeled by designs for acting, feeling, and thinking which are already in existence.

Closely related to the foregoing is the fact that culture, which is an accumulation or residue of the long and broad experience of men, especially in the way of solid achievements, has developed conceptions of ends of human living as well as means. In it are embedded most of the goals as well as the propulsives. Hence, *culture functions conspicuously in giving meaning, direction, and purpose to human life.* Human beings will strain to do what is presented in the culture as desirable and good, but will hesitate to do something outside the traditional spheres.

These last two functions together enable culture to serve as a structure of expectancies. Thus, when we know a culture, we know what various categories of individuals within it do and what they expect from each other and from outsiders.

Another aspect of culture is as a combination of tools, guides, and goals that surrounds every individual of a given society with a set of conditioning stimuli and pressures. Hence, *culture is "the dominant factor in establishing the basic personality types."* (16, p. 151) Each culture produces its own peculiar attitudes and habits, as the individual discovers when he moves from one culture area to another.

Culture, as the precious common heritage of a given group or society, *functions as a solidarity-producing factor.* It *is* the common ways of life and enables its adherents together to solve the problems posed by the total environments. Hence, it acts as the binder that unites the individuals and lesser groups into a living, continuous, functioning mechanism with a character of its own.

*This treatment of the social functions of culture is in part dependent upon reference 13, pp. 103-106, and reference 16, pp. 19-22.

Society and Culture

In spite of the close functional interrelationship between any society and its culture, the two concepts must not be thought of as synonymous. A *society* is an organized, interacting aggregate of people who are conscious of their unity, structurally differentiated, occupying a common territory, and together working out their major problems of existence. *Culture* is that people's distinctive, complex man-made pattern of ways and means of doing things. It is compounded of elements, some of which are universal and constant among all mankind, whereas others are peculiarly indigenous. (13, pp. 79-93; 19; 20; 23) We apprehend and understand culture only by observing the ways in which the people of a given society act.

Culture consists of the behavioral instrumentalities for living, which have a reality and continuity apart from the individuals or the society that utilizes them or abides by them. Thus, a given society is the temporary steward and modifier of these ways of living. Societies come and go; culture goes on.

But since the culture elements prevalent in a given society constitute the ingredients and mediums of its dynamic action, and since the continuity of any society is dependent upon an adequate and unbroken culture, any systematic and fundamental understanding of human society in operation must necessarily rest upon an adequate knowledge of the cultural framework within which the multitudinous processes of the society operate. Because of the special orientation of this study, we must begin with the culture processes themselves. Hence, we are concerned with the basic social processes that produce the cultural elements; how they are derived from within and from without the society, developed, and naturalized within the society; fixed in individual and group action; and preserved and transmitted through space and time.

All cultures undergo modification continually and will continue to do so, so long as men are dissatisfied and curious and so long as individuals and societies meet and influence each other. These cultural changes take place in response to definite patterns of factors and take the form of typical, regular processes.

Culture Area

The processes affecting culture occur both within the culture area and between different culture areas. The areas involved may be relatively small and few, as among primitive or isolated and backward societies. In the modern highly mobile and communicative interlocking world the areas are numerous and expansive, tending more and more to include the societies of the world.

A culture area is a portion of the earth's surface, a spatial unit or "patch," small or great, in which certain definite and identifiable elements of culture exist. In a given area certain specific traits, complexes, and patterns of acting and believing are found over and over again. In their particular forms they are characteristic of this area, grow out of its influencing conditions and its history, have certain consistency and compatibility, and give it its peculiar character. The size of the area will vary with different items of culture. Most of the earth has traits and complexes related to the automobile; only limited and scattered areas have various kinds of "cattle complexes." Some, in fact many, of the culture forms of a given area will be found in other areas, but invariably will show special regional peculiarities.

Culture Centers

Most culture areas have spots or places where its specific traits or complexes originated, or where these culture elements show their special determining characteristics and are most orthodox and most faithfully followed, or where they are most dynamic, active, and authoritative, most venturesome and inventive, and from which they radiate in the most influential and determining manner. These nuclei, or points of dispersal or greatest density, are known as culture *centers*. Thus, ranches are the center of American cow-country traits and complexes, and New York City is the theatrical center and the center of banking and commercial forms and practices. Within large areas there may be numerous centers for particular culture elements as well as subcenters for each.

Culture Gradient

The culture elements of a given area are not equally dense at all points in the area. The distribution of a given trait, complex, or pattern usually is found to be densest in one part of the area, becoming sparse as distance from its center of origin or its point of greatest concentration increases. It is thus possible to indicate concentric zones arranged about this point, which describe a range from maximum strength for frequency at the center to a minimum at the margin. This increasing weakening or infrequency of the trait as we move outward from the center through the series of zones is referred to as the culture *gradient.*

Flow of Culture

Culture is contagious, however, and its elements radiate, spreading from centers like ripples when a pebble is tossed into a pond. There is thus a rather regular and well-defined *flow of culture* from zone to zone. At the periphery of the culture areas where they adjoin, there are *penumbral areas* in which the elements take on the characteristics of each other area somewhat in proportion to the distance from the other area. At the penumbra, barring absolute physical barriers (though man seems to have conquered most of them) or sedulously established and maintained social barriers (of which there are many), the intercommunication, exchange, and blending begin. New elements penetrate the adjoining areas if they have recognized utility or prestige or both. (24; 25; 26; 27)

Hence, a culture area is not one of uniform homogeneity or density of its elements. Nor can its limits be arbitrarily drawn on a map. The boundaries themselves are fuzzy zones of transition where the culture elements pass into adjoining areas, and culture areas overlap and shade into each other.

Processes of Culture Innovation

How does a given area, even a given society, achieve and obtain its manifold ways of life? How do the innumerable and diverse elements constituting a culture come to be? It would be most revealing if we could go back to the beginning of human time and then follow through the events and processes that spin the threads and weave them into the complex fabric. But this we cannot do. We have to assume something in the way of culture at a given time as our point of departure and then note how it develops quantitatively, qualitatively, differentially, and temporally.

Obviously, a given culture can develop only as the result of processes of innovation occurring *within* the area or society and by means of acquisition from *without*. We will first apply ourselves to the type of changes and the type of culture elements which are initiated within a given culture area or society.

All culture elements have their origin in innovation processes, whereby new ideas, new culture objects, and new usages are developed independently within the framework of a given culture by manipulating and combining existing and available elements. Although these processes are carried on mainly by individuals or small groups of individuals, they nevertheless originate in group life. The individuals function with materials obtained through contact and communication with their fellows and under the influences and stimuli emanating from their total environment. The actual processes of culture modification resulting from factors operating within the culture area or the society range along a continuum from those that are largely of a passive, casual, even accidental, nature to those that are highly conscious, deliberate and purposive.

Processes of Cultural Change

Culture is never static, even in the most tradition-ridden, backward, and isolated societies. There is what Sorokin has called "immanent change," that is, unavoidable and automatic change which occurs simply by virtue of the fact of operation itself. For example, an automobile, all other things being constant, changes continually as it functions, particularly in the way of wear and tear. As long as a culture exists and functions, it incessantly generates consequences which are themselves the results of the system of its activities. (41, pp. 587, 600-601) Largely uncontrollable nonsocial and external phenomena also function as dynamic factors.

More specifically, involuntary processes at both the subsocial, or biotic, and the social levels are continually bringing about changes in the conditions of life and attendant modifications in the culture—modifications often revealed by a short-time perspective. The following are the more obvious of these processes:

Subsocial Physical and Biological Processes. These processes include changes in climate, cataclysms of nature, and changes in biological resources. These in turn force compliant social adjustment, both involuntary and voluntary.

Static-Dynamic Processes. These processes, called *static-dynamic* by Ross, are regular activities or processes of daily living of mankind which leave behind them unintended by-products. In time these by-products accumulate and bring about notable cultural changes. Historically significant are the effects of hunting in wiping out a valuable source of food and clothing and of overcropping in the consequent decline of soil and agricultural produce.

Changes in Density and Composition of Population. As the density and composition of the population change, they affect the economic and political ways of life, sometimes inducing such processes as migration. In connection with these changes, it is necessary to take account of the relative shortness of human life and the consequent rather rapid sequence of generations, each producing, whether they will or not, their own New Deal.

Transmutations. As named by Ross, transmutations are unintended culture changes due to the inability of any generation or society to copy or reproduce exactly the ways and ideas of their forebears, even if they wish to. Such changes are evident in the modifications of a language through the centuries and of religious interpretations.

The Innovating Processes

The actual processes of innovating culture elements that expedite adjustment to ever-changing conditions are discovery and invention, both closely related.

Discovery. Discovery is ordinarily thought of as a rather passive perception of the utility of existing relations among various elements. We stumble upon or "find" some ready-made phenomenon —a useful object, an idea, or a combination of human relationships—already existing in unrecognized form. The result is usually more or less accidental or unanticipated, and the methods used in the apprehension are somewhat haphazard, though discovery may also be a matter of deliberate search. Thus, we discover a useful plant (we do not produce it through genetic manipulation), or we discover an idea or principle that can be applied in a given situation. On the other hand, somewhat deliberately we discover a hypothetical vitamin heretofore missing in a particular series. Perhaps the main feature of discovery is that the phenomenon that has become known and utilized is apprehended as already in existence and represents an addition to knowledge, not a newly constructed element.

The obvious factors involved in discovery are *curiosity* with respect to possible new things, ideas, or ways; *opportunity* to explore, whether physical areas, various fields of phenomena, heretofore unrecognized bodies of ideas, and the like; *observation* of occurrences, things, and ideas; and *appreciation plus imagination* in determining the possible utilization of the newly apprehended phenomenon. (32)

Invention. Invention is the process of actively and experimentally combining or synthesizing and applying in a new, unusual, and meaningful form familiar or known culture elements—objects, ideas, or ways—previously discovered or devised by others. The *specific function of invention* is to recombine, reorganize, and redirect known and accepted elements of culture into new patterns in order to solve the problems of human living, whether these are physical, social, philosophical, or spiritual.

Discovery and invention are closely related, as noted above. The further discovery of new facts or relations depends upon invention of new methods of thinking and acting, whereas invention uses newly discovered elements, facts, and principles. The central innovative process is invention, however, since it is the basis both of discovery and of all subsequent invention. Practically all discoveries have to be followed by or accompanied by inventions if they are to be culturally significant. (34, p. 533) The major portion of our analysis, therefore, will be devoted to the inventive process and the factors involved in it.

The Process of Invention

The process of invention is one of human interaction extending through human time. A given invention is merely a present, temporary, or momentary combination of culture elements. No invention is produced out of whole cloth or is final. Every invention is the result of long processes of contact of thinkers and their ideas, of the transmission, adaptation, selection, combination, and recombination of component elements. Behind each invention lies at least two previous discoveries or inventions; behind each of these are at least two more; and so on back into human inventive time and experience *ad infinitum*. Even the inventions that appear to be most revolutionary are usually the results of slow accretions of many earlier inventions.

Thus, the modern automobile is the product of a series of inventions in connection with internal-combustion engines, gasoline and oil, electricity, gears and drives, circulation systems, rubber, and many other components. The modern American, so-called Christian, Christmas developed through a long, complex, interrelated series of Jewish, Mithraic, Greek, Roman, Teutonic, and early and later Christian and Church seasonal beliefs, practices, and festivals, which were combined and recombined, and finally molded by vast commercial accretions in recent times. The modern plow began as a digging stick, progressed through the forked stick, the crude stone hoe, the forked-stick plow drawn by man or domestic animal, the animal-drawn metal-share plow, to the modern multiple, or gang, plow powered by a diesel tractor.

What then are the interdependent and interrelated dynamics, conditions, and cultural prerequisites essential for the appearance of an invention? Such an analysis of factors puts detail into the understanding of the invention process.

Demand or Need in the Specific Culture Area at the Specific Time. Each region at a given time creates a need or demand for certain types of invention. This does not mean that "necessity is the mother of invention," for history records many inventions which died aborning, so to speak, or were passed over for generations, even centuries, because the general condition and needs of their times did not offer demand or opportunity for utilization. But the given time and place are determining factors in the development of inventions that are encouraged and used. The following subfactors are important in the acceptance of an invention:

NATURAL SETTING AND RESOURCES OF AREA. The invention of physical objects, of ideas about them, and of forms of social organization related to them are of necessity related to the physical and biological aspects and resources of the region. Thus, inventions in the breeding of beef cattle, in forms of local government suitable to widely dispersed ranches and sparse population, and of special springs for automobiles operating on the open range were developed in the open-range cow country of the Great Plains.

LEVEL OF KNOWLEDGE, TECHNIQUES, EDUCATION, AND SUGGESTIVE MATERIALS. What the people of an area know and have been educated up to, what they can appreciate in the way of innovations on the basis of existing culture, including all their previous inventions, opens up possibilities for and suggests innovations. People who do not have mile-long furrows and gang plows do not need tractors. Laws governing social order in complex, crowded urban centers are not needed or understood in villages of "Population 319." The conception of a single Father-God of heterogeneous peoples with sublime spiritual qualities is not devised in a tiny primitive tribe.

THE "RUN OF ATTENTION." The *run of attention* (a term first used by W. I. Thomas) is related, possibly as a refinement, to both of the above subfactors and further emphasizes the social nature of invention. The bulk of the particular inventions appearing at any given time reflect the major trends, interests, and preferences of that time in that area or society. In the United States at the present time, for example, inventions of a technological nature are favored and are occurring in an unprecedented manner. Inventions in social and political organization, such as the formal pyramidal operative organization (bureaucracy) or new aspects of labor organization or social security related to technological development get secondary consideration, and religious inventions are even discouraged in some circles. During a war the "run of attention" is along the antithetical lines of more efficient military machines and of peace-making and peace-maintaining devices.

FAVORING ATTITUDE TOWARD INNOVATION. The appearance and acceptance of an invention in a given area and time depend also on existing attitudes toward change. Attitudes in turn depend upon the prevailing conditions. If the time is relatively quiet, without notable crises, if life is flowing along smoothly and a state of equilibrium seems to exist, the general psyche of the population will oppose upsetting the equilibrium with new things, new ideas, or new ways. On the other hand, when changes are occurring and maladjustments exist, inefficiencies become apparent, needs along many lines are recognized, and the society is willing to try the new—even to search for, demand, and welcome it.

ACTUAL OR IMPLIED REWARD. The keener the need for given types of inventions, the larger the possible rewards for those who make them. The very existence of bonuses of one kind or another invites attention and application to certain kinds of inventive problems. Conversely, the kind of inventions that do come about are in considerable measure conditioned by what the given society does reward at the moment.

The Culture Base. For the occurrence of any given inventions more than a demand is required. All the essential ingredients must exist. A fundamental factor in the amount and variety of invention at any given time in a given society and in the possible appearance of a given invention is the culture base. By culture base we mean the total accumulated culture heritage, framework, or matrix of a specific society, the sum total of its existing and available culture elements and facilities of all kinds.

Invention, as we have noted, is a process of combining and recombining, accumulated culture materials, for improving old utilities or for providing new ones. If the culture base is broad, that is, if it consists of a great store of culture materials of all sorts, including a host of completed inventions, and if knowledge is extensive and the arts and sciences are highly developed, then there are many varieties and an infinite number of culture materials available for combination by the use of innumerable tried and proved skills and techniques. On the other hand, if the culture base is small or narrow, there are only a few elements available for combination, and inventions will be limited and circumscribed in number and range.

The American Indian had a very limited culture base. For thousands of years his culture remained simple and relatively unchanging, and his inventions were very few. European stocks, on the other hand, have had a culture that for millennia has been growing like a snowball rolling downhill. Their inventions have been increasing in number, era by era, like the successive layers of an inverted pyramid.

As Hornell Hart has pointed out (35, p. 529), the need for an invention may be clearly recognized and the general intellectual conception of the method of solving the problem may be fairly clear. But if materials, tools, and scientific principles have not yet been invented, the particular invention must await its proper order in the parade of invention. Thus, for example, Roger Bacon in the thirteenth century and Francis Bacon in the seventeenth century both saw the need of flying machines and visualized their general nature, but not until the twentieth century were the requisite knowledge and other elements available. Then, in less than half of that century, thanks to a culture base that has expanded more during that short period than in all prior human history, the development of airplanes has been phenomenal.

When the *demand* for an invention *and* the appropriate *culture base* exist, then the "ripeness of time" factor is discernible. That is, the time and the people and the culture are ripe for the fulfillment of the next invention along a given usage line in the long series. The modern airplane came when the times were ripe and not before. It should be noted that when the times are ripe, the same invention is often made almost simultaneously by two or more individuals or groups of inventors in the general culture area. (35, pp. 518-524; 38, pp. 90-112) Furthermore, it is generally conceded by students of invention, such as Ogburn, Stern, and Gilfillan, that if a given invention or discovery had not been made by the person or persons who actually did make it, the logic of the demand plus the culture materials available would have caused someone else to create it. Similarly, in culture groups that are isolated from each other, but have had a somewhat similar culture development and have a similar culture base, there is a great likelihood that parallel inventions will appear among them.

Finally, when inventions of a given type exist in the culture base, they stimulate new needs and often produce inventions in the same field or in different but causally related fields. Thus, when a superior invention has been made in government, the people find that they need still better governmental agencies; when the automobile was developed, a host of related inventions, such as traffic laws, drive-ins, automatic garage doors, motels, and so on, made their appearance. In general, invention leads to invention as we have indicated in the cumulative frequency curve.

The Inventor. The apparent demand and the adequate culture base do not automatically produce inventions. There is still the need for the special services of the human devising and combining instrumentality, the inventor. Inventions actually and finally come into being only through the channel of the conscious thought and specialized action of inventors. Although the inventor is a product of his time, he is also the strategic intermediary through which the influences of the time and place pass, meet, and fuse.

Inventive ability is a highly precious capacity possessed by relatively few individuals. Certain persons are inventors for very good reasons. They feel the pressure of desires and needs more poignantly than most people, and perceive the problem situation with its malfunctionings which needs solution. Through their imagination inventors have the premonitory pictures or symbolical reconstructions of known elements of the situation, or they meditate and plan and get the creative idea. They have or acquire the essential knowledge, the theoretical principles, the skills and inventive techniques. They make the struggling experimental searches, discover the defects in the instruments and procedures, and iron out the difficulties, and they are the ones who assay and utilize the past failures, accidents, exceptions, opposition, and criticism of themselves and others. In addition they have the enthusiasm and courage, the infinite patience and good sense to proceed one step at a time, and they have the drive and tenacity to carry on tasks that are often arduous, tedious, discouraging, even heartbreaking. They are the ones who finally succeed or are forced to admit failure.

Not all inventors can make the same kinds of inventions; each works along the lines of his own innate genius and his special aptitude and training. The inventive demands and available culture materials at any given time select some inventive persons and reject others. Moreover, some inventors are able to apply a discovery or invention and yet are not able to make one, for the initiation of a great idea and the consummation of an invention require a vastly different set of capacities from those required to use it, derive benefits from it, or even make minor repairs on it.

In the last analysis the direction and consummation of a given invention depend upon the relative number of special superior individuals we call inventors, though *what* they will invent depends upon the stimulus, the times, and the culture materials of the given society.

Cooperation and Organization of Inventors. Invention in modern, complex civilized societies is less and less an activity of lone, isolated individuals following their own separate gleam. In rapidly changing times with needs multiplying in geometric ratio, it is seen that solo invention is often too slow and inefficient. Isolation prevents contact with its interstimulation and sharing and, in effect, retards invention. On the other hand, anything which enlarges the number of innovators who freely exchange results increases the probability of more rapidly and more effectively combining elements. Hence, more and more invention depends upon cooperation of investigators and inventors at meetings, through publications, and especially in deliberately organized and fostered research organizations.

Today, by means of our scientific societies, research committees, medical centers, research foundations, university laboratories and other combined research facilities, and research laboratories maintained by the large corporations, invention is facilitated. By these means communication between inventors is promoted, mutual stimulation occurs, knowledge and talent are pooled, a division of specialized labor takes place informally or formally, wider-scaled and superior techniques and all manner of facilities can be shared, and economic resources can be used more effectively.

In modern societies the factor of cooperation in invention is indispensable if the internal needs along all lines within a society are to be met, or if the societies are to survive intersociety competition effectively.

Scientific Systematization of Inventive Processes. In the modern world invention cannot be left to chance or individual fumbling. If inventions are to occur in sufficient variety, volume, and quality to meet the multiple and diverse needs of the time, they must be part of a telic or planned process. This process contains the following steps: (1) the determination, as accurately and as fully as possible, of the needs to be met; (2) the accumulation by active and systematic search and adequate definition, measurement, and classification of all the available culture materials that seem pertinent in meeting the need; (3) the marshaling of the known scientific facts, principles, and methods; and then (4) the experimentation, that is, systematic manipulation of the variables, the methodical exploration of the possibility of producing useful combinations of the culture elements, followed by the repeated testing and revising of the results.

The Acculturation Processes

Although all new culture elements anywhere are derived from invention and discovery sometime and somewhere, the great bulk of the culture elements found in any given culture area or society are due to acquisition from elsewhere. The acquisitions of a given area or society are the result of a series of processes of culture exchange usually combined under the general term "acculturation."

The processes of culture exchange take place in some degree and kind whenever and wherever there is some kind of contact between people of differing cultures, whether they reside within a large area or live in different areas. The transportation of elements may be from individual to individual, from group to group, from one society to another, from one international region to another. For if there is some kind of contact, there are reciprocal relationships of a sort; and if there are reciprocal relationships, there is some culture exchange. The processes grow out of the fact that few cultures are completely isolated from others.

These acculturation processes are fundamentally processes of give and take among peoples who interact—processes of mingling, selecting, and partial merging of culture elements, ranging in complexity from traits to whole patterns, and in space from immediately adjacent peoples to all the peoples in the world available by any means of communication. These processes rest upon the fact that culture itself is highly mobile and highly contagious and that all peoples exercise some catholicity of response to the culture of other peoples, regardless of the particular situation of contact. Moreover, mere contact of culturally different groups is always a challenge to each of them.

Consciously or unconsciously, lending and borrowing are sure to occur, regardless of whether the contacts are friendly or unfriendly, and regardless of the similarity or dissimilarity in numbers or in the cultural level of those contacting, or the forcefulness or dominance of the respective peoples or cultures. Purposive isolation may be attempted in defense against foreign ways, but it is impossible to prevent at least some small degree of exchange of elements. And culture contact always produces some, often greatly varying, modification of ways of acting, thinking, and feeling among peoples involved, though the changes induced are not necessarily radical or voluminous.

These social processes, like many others, have been greatly extended in scope and accelerated in time by recent and modern agents of communication and transportation. They are of signal importance in a time when there is world-wide communication and trade, a developing world division and specialization of labor, a world of global wars and global confederations.

The acculturation processes are means whereby different societies or societal elements, consciously or unconsciously, pool their cultural resources, and thus often achieve a greater range of satisfactions and a more efficient and durable society than would be possible by their own unaided efforts.

Diffusion Processes

The diffusion processes are those phases of acculturation that involve the spread, circulation, or dissemination of culture elements *from* a culture center *to* other culture groups. Such diffusion processes are usually gradual but are becoming increasingly dynamic today because of improved and widespread facilities for communication and transportation. Culture elements, even whole systems of culture, are spread and transferred through contacting individuals or groups from one group or culture to another.

In general, the migration of culture elements follows routes of communication and movement established by trade, military conquest, and missionization. The contacts may be *brief*, as when some elements are transported by explorers or migrants passing through an area or by military contingents; or they may be *sustained*, as under the influence of modern ubiquitous means of communication and exchange. Furthermore, the contact may be *direct*, that is, between persons or groups, or *indirect* by means of various communicative devices, such as printed materials and radio broadcasts.

From the point of view of the number of groups, cultures, or societies involved, the different means of exchanging culture elements may be defined as *intracultural* or *intercultural*. The *intracultural, or intrasociety*, exchange of culture operates among different persons or groups *within* the framework of a single culture or larger society. It spreads geographically from one community, section, or region of a given culture area or society to another; horizontally from one group or population segment to another on the same general economic or social level; or vertically from one social class or stratum to another up or down the social scale. The *intercultural, or intersociety*, exchange of culture takes place between one culture or society and another, often without direct or long-continued primary contact between the cultures involved.

The process of diffusion involves a *donor*, or disseminator, usually a center of dominance. From the point of view of the absence or presence of design on the part of the disseminator, the process may be one of two kinds: (1) *natural, unconscious, spontaneous, or incidental*, that is, a matter of gradual and undirected infiltration of culture elements as facilitated by geographical proximity, random migration, trading and commerce, travel, press, or radio; or (2) *purposeful*, that is, a matter of deliberate and often aggressively pursued efforts by such processes as missionization, certain forms of education, or other organized procedures of indoctrination and proselyting, colonization, or conquest.

When diffusion is too rapid or too voluminous, or both, as it makes its impact on members and groups of the receiving culture, thus preventing adequate adjustment to the new elements and resulting in some personal and group disorganization, there may be both a process and a condition sometimes referred to as a *culture shock*.

Borrowing, or Receiving, Processes

The Nature of the Processes. The borrowing, or receiving, processes are those which involve the action of the *recipients* of new and foreign culture elements. They are the counterpart of the diffusion processes. Since in this study we are interested in the development of the culture of a given society, we are more concerned with this receiving and accepting phase of acculturation than with diffusion.

By means of the borrowing processes one segment of a society takes over from other segments certain fructifying culture elements, or one culture or society takes over certain elements from other cultures or societies as the result of interaction. The processes imply some degree of adoption and incorporation into the culture system of the borrowing group or society. During the course of adoption, the elements are usually somewhat modified, and invariably their acceptance and incorporation bring about some modification of related indigenous culture elements.

Most observers agree that any given society acquires the great majority of culture elements existing in and utilized by it by borrowing rather than by invention, chiefly because borrowing is easier than inventing, especially when communication and transportation provide easy access to ready-made ways of dealing with human situations. Invention is arduous, and most human beings suffer from lack of originality and the inertia of habit and routine. Even in times of need, most men will accept what is at hand rather than attempt invention.

Borrowing, of course, has vastly accelerated the rate at which the volume of elements and the enrichment of given cultures have increased. By contrast, primitive cultures of past ages developed slowly because of very limited contacts. They had to depend on invention for much of their culture; consequently, there were few culture changes over thousands of years. Modern cultures, however, borrow far more than they produce internally, and culture change is tremendous both in scope and in amount.

The borrowing or acceptance of culture elements

from without may range from spontaneous, even unconscious, imitation to high-pressure adoption by organized instruction or even the threat or use of force. Under most modern conditions borrowing is a more or less free-will, take-it-or-leave-it process, involving the taking over of elements because of their attractiveness or utility or mere presence. But, in the past and occasionally in the present, culture elements are taken over as the result of careful instruction or even arbitrary pressure. A notable example of the latter is the Americanization movement whereby a deliberate effort was made to obtain acceptance of American ways by immigrants in the United States.

The diffused culture elements, whether single traits, complexes, or patterns, are seldom taken over by the receiving or borrowing people automatically, with complete passivity, by pure addition, or *in toto*. Even when the element is taken over with eagerness, there is some modification. Usually some originality, even of an inventive nature, is exercised unconsciously or consciously in incorporating the borrowed element into the general culture of the recipient people. Invariably the adoption is of a *selective nature* with respect to amount and kind and occurs at varying rates. Usually there is some reinterpretation of meaning. The items adopted are always made consistent with the general system or configuration of culture. Furthermore, many diffused elements are actually *rejected* in whole or in part for reasons that will be discussed below. Thus, the adoption may take the form of (1) *adoption with slight modification,* as when the European stocks in America took over the maize culture of the Indian; (2) *substitution in part of the new for the old,* as in the case of primitives displacing some of their tools and arms with those of Europeans; (3) *fitting the new into the old,* as in the case of Americans fitting all kinds of foreign foods into their diet.

Important Factors in Borrowing. Borrowing is rarely entirely free or without obstructions and deflections. Furthermore, it is not wholesale, but, as just noted, relative and graded. A variety of factors are involved in these peculiarities of the process, which are not mutually exclusive.

Spatial Location and Distance. Cultures or societies contiguous to the point of origin or dominance of given culture elements are likely to borrow them first. Physiographic barriers, however, may isolate given peoples and prevent them from making contact with the borrowable elements. In the modern world both contiguity and physical barriers may be overcome by ease of transportation and communication. Physical space and contiguity of the transmitting and receiving culture are still factors in the borrowing of culture, but they are rapidly losing their determinative significance. Furthermore, the cultural complexion of contiguous or contacting peoples is also an important factor affecting the possible exchange of elements, as will be noted below.

Culture Differences and Antagonisms. Both within a people and between cultures and societies, the presence of sharp culture differences, especially if they involve avoidances or antagonisms, will create barriers and prevent or limit borrowing. Significant are linguistic differences, diverse religious beliefs and practices, ethnic differences and distances, diverse social-political-economic ideologies, and many others. These various culture differences may operate singly or in combination. Mennonite religious sectarians in the United States have for two centuries kept themselves from borrowing many elements of the surrounding culture. In Canada the population segments of French and British origin have had linguistic, religious, and nationality factors as barriers. At present differences in social-political-economic ideology and practice are erecting an "iron curtain" between the democratic and the communistic totalitarian nations.

Similarity of Diffusing and Receiving Cultures. When the cultures are very similar and on nearly the same level, there is likely to be a mutual ability to comprehend and utilize each other's culture elements; there is considerable certainty that there will be mutual stimulation; very often there will be a two-way exchange and a harmonious and fairly complete fusion of many culture elements.

Variation of Culture Elements between Peoples. Where there is a great difference in culture levels, as between the simpler or preliterate peoples and highly civilized peoples, the preliterate peoples as possible borrowers have only a limited comprehension of elements of the higher culture and limited ability to appropriate them. There is, as Thurnwald puts it, a marked difference in "civilizatory equipment" of the two people and a "state of culture tension" exists. (70) In fact, because of these limitations the backward people may lose interest and self-confidence and become deadened rather than stimulated by the contact. At any rate, until the contacts have been long and intimate and sympathetic, the preliterates will be borrowing only the somewhat superficial aspects of the higher culture.

The order of adoption of types of culture materials by the lower culture, from the point of view of their relative concreteness or abstractness, is usually as follows:

First, the more superficial, more comprehensible, more readily applicable material utilitarian elements, such as hand tools and weapons, some items of food and clothing, utensils, ornaments, narcotics, and alcoholic beverages are adopted. These elements from the higher culture are obviously superior to their own. Thus, two generations ago, the typical African tribesman was able to take over gold teeth, but the principles and techniques of operative dentistry were beyond him; he could take over and use the rifle, but not rifle-making by machine processes.

Second, enough of the language of the higher culture to communicate in an everyday manner and the superficial aspects of social intercourse and technology are taken over. The primitive worker can converse with his boss in a version of the boss's language and function as a modern farmer or proficient machinist. On the other hand, while he talks about freedom and equality, the subtleties of philosophical and political democracy are beyond him; and while he can prate the word "Jesus," he comprehends little of Christianity as a complex body of abstract beliefs and dogmas.

Third, and still later, after long contact, the members of the lower culture are able to borrow with fair comprehension and even ability of utilization the forms of social organization, such as the standardized sex habits, the family organization, or the forms of administration of law and order.

Fourth and last to be borrowed and incorporated are the inner culture elements, because of the difficulty of understanding them and appraising their superiority. Notably difficult to take over are attitudes, beliefs, values, philosophical ideas, and ideologies along economic political, ethical, aesthetic, and religious lines. Adoption of these elements requires long experience. Often they are not borrowed at all.

VARIATIONS BETWEEN CLASSES. If class differences and spacing are sharp *within* a given society, a strong class or even caste consciousness is provoked which makes full and free interaction difficult. The flow of elements either upward or downward will be slow and piecemeal, often actually resisted.

More important in this connection, however, is the great variation in culture catholicity between the upper and lower classes both within a society and between societies. The upper strata usually have more diversified and widespread culture interests. They have almost universally a readier and more frequent mobility, contact, and exchange of culture elements than the lower strata, more education and leisure to acquire a greater degree of universality and catholicity in their class as well as in their general cultural attitudes, values, interests, manners, traditions, and customs. The lower strata, on the other hand, are more provincial or parochial, that is, they are dialect bound and habitation bound and have narrow physical and cultural horizons. Hence, they are culturally limited and retarded.

It has been repeatedly observed that people at the higher culture levels throughout history have shown a greater interchangeability between regions, nations, and even to some extent races without experiencing great maladjustments. Notable are the nobility, the learned and professional groups, and the upper levels of the population of Europe during many centuries. The European lower classes, however, especially the rural peasantry, have had less mobility and more limited communication; they have usually been isolated both physically and culturally; they have been bound to racial, local, provincial, class, and primary-group attitudes and usages and have had a narrower set of culture elements that they have rigidly adhered to. Hence, their borrowing has been most limited, and their cultures have been highly variant.

In general, as Sorokin points out, the class levels and persons exposed to culture elements earliest and most frequently are more likely to be the first importers and recipients of these elements. Thus, besides the upper classes, such groups as merchants and traveling salesmen, missionaries, scholars, scientists, intelligentsia, teachers, adventurers, journalists, and government officials are more likely to take over new items, provided that the items are not too inimical to their basic culture. (41, pp. 227-228) Rural groups and classes are slower than urbanites.

The principles governing the borrowing by different strata *within* a culture or society are very similar to those operating between societies of different culture levels. There is likely to be considerable borrowing between adjoining strata, but less between remote strata in the social pyramid. In a steeply and rigidly stratified society there is much that does not, perhaps cannot, pass either up or down. Lower classes, even in the absence of sumptuary restrictions, cannot understand or utilize the abstract beliefs and values of the higher levels, nor can they afford certain forms of consumption, though they will take these over (for example, styles of dress) to the extent that they are able. The upper classes refuse to take over elements that reflect low status, though they will take over novelty items, such as smocks, jazz tunes, certain dances, and so on. In the case of both the upper and the lower cultures and upper and lower classes the principle of "ripeness for acceptance" is involved. (59)

Attitude toward Foreign Culture Elements. For a variety of reasons, peoples vary greatly in their hospitality to, and liberal point of view toward the possible acceptance of, foreign ways, ideas, and objects. Long-standing isolation, a sense of superiority or exclusiveness, an attitude of defensiveness (for example, in maintaining the purity of religion or of domestic relations), general inertia, however induced, inability to comprehend meanings and utilities, and so on, may create great obstacles in borrowing.

Crisis conditions, on the other hand, often point to the inadequacy of existing instrumentalities and procedures and create recognized needs. As a result, people readily try what promises to be a way out. The needs of an ambitious and rapidly expanding society may also create a market for all kinds of new things and ways. Education and sophistication are usually factors. A generalization of the attitude of hospitality to borrowed culture can be cryptically put thus: The Romans had it and built a great empire; the Chinese did not have it and built a great wall.

The Utility and Compatibility of Foreign Culture Elements. The possible borrowers of culture elements must usually grasp the significance and usefulness of the available element. If the new element promises distinct utility under given conditions, it will be taken over. Thus, Europeans and Americans in the Arctic borrowed extensively from the Eskimo, adopting his clothing, housing, hunting methods, and food items and food habits; the Congo Negro took over the white man's rifle and cooking pot. If the element has no utility, it will ordinarily not be adopted. Thus, Eskimos have little use for office desks or electric refrigerators or federated systems of government. To be accepted, an item must have some demonstrable utility alongside of existing items or some demonstrable superiority over items of familiar usage.

Closely related to utility is the factor of compatibility. While there is usually a broad zone of uncertainty, the traits to be borrowed must be in line with the major interests of the receiving group. The principle of run of attention as it applies in invention applies here. Conversely, if much conflict or disorganization is likely, or if radical reorganization of the larger culture complex is threatened upon acceptance of the culture element, and if choice is possible, the acceptance of incompatible elements is likely to be checked and blocked or rejected altogether and their use even forbidden under penalty. Thus, Seventh-Day Adventists will refuse the latest thing in packaged pork. Many features of democratic-capitalist freely competitive American society have no place whatsoever in the communistic Soviet Union or in any dictatorship. In general, other things being equal, the greater the culture differences, the less likely is borrowing to occur. In the phrase of Webster, the cartoonist, "They don't speak our language!"

Relative Prestige and Dominance. The relative prestige of the donor and receiving groups is a factor of significance. Under most conditions, as Linton points out, a group which recognizes its social inferiority will be more likely to borrow from its superiors than will the superiors be likely to borrow from it. (56, p. 491)

Occasionally there is transfer upward from lower to higher classes, although this is seldom a large-scale acceptance. Usually elements that have novelty or piquancy, such as certain foods or decorations, move upward.

Generally the submissive group is eager to be socially and culturally identified with the dominant group. If the dominance is largely a matter of social and psychological lures and pressures, it is not resented, and borrowing takes place freely and spontaneously. But if the dominance is physical or political, or crude and harsh, it may produce negative responses. If force is used by the dominant disseminators, there will be a surface show of conformity, but there will be inner opposition and resistance and often actual retardation of acceptance. Thus, when the use of a language is forced upon a people by a conqueror, the people practice the language in public to the minimal extent, while using their own language surreptitiously on every possible occasion.

The use of force often produces an added consciousness of culture differences; the elements prescribed and required by the dominator become symbols of revolt. Persecuted groups resist borrowing of such elements for centuries. Where a group must accept the elements of the culture forced upon it, the group modifies and reinterprets them for itself in such a manner that these elements will not do violence to their basic beliefs and values.

In general, other things being equal, models of high prestige tend to be copied because their ways of social life carry various recognized social rewards. The copiers anticipate the enjoyment of these rewards.

The last two factors to be discussed relate to the matter of *incentive* in borrowing culture elements. If there are great or perceptible incentives, such as attractiveness or novelty, utility, prestige, and rewards, borrowing is likely to occur. On the other hand, if incentives are limited or lacking, owing, for example, to great diversity of the respective cultures, apparent lack of utility on the part of the available culture materials, reigning antagonisms between the contracting groups, or the existence of active prejudices, inhibitions, and taboos, there will be very little borrowing, and it will be very selective.

THE TIME FACTOR. Although under modern conditions of transportation and communication the time factor has been reduced in significance, it still affects borrowing. Furthermore, sheer inability to learn the complex ways of a strange culture in a short time is involved. Adoption increases with subsequent generations of a people exposed to available elements. The first generation takes over superficial forms; by the third or fourth generation, the more intangible and abstract aspects have been fully incorporated into their ways of thinking and acting.

The Cross-fertilization Process

Cross-fertilization is the over-all process of which the respective processes of diffusion and borrowing are coordinate parts. This simply means that in the course of reciprocal diffusion and borrowing, which go on in some degree wherever there is or has been any interaction whatsoever, there is not only mutual giving and taking, but also—and unavoidably—more or less stimulation of development of each culture. It might be thought of as a kind of bridge building between people of diverse culture.

This cross-fertilization provides the materials and stimuli for innovation in any society or portion thereof. What is more important, however, in terms of total content of the culture of a given society, is the fact that the bulk of its elements is acquired by diffusion-borrowing, and not through innovation, although every culture element is a product of innovation processes, somewhere, sometime, by someone, as noted above. Gillin states, in this connection, "It is probably not an exaggeration to estimate that perhaps ninety percent of the elements of present-day North American culture were originated in societies other than our own, either in modern times or earlier." (48, p. 555; for classic statement, see 57, pp. 326-327)

CHAPTER VI

THE ORGANIZATION AND TRANSMISSION OF CULTURE

ALTHOUGH THE CULTURE of a given society is an ever-changing affair, it is and must be also continuously undergoing organization if it is to perform its essential functions. It cannot be unstable, chaotic, piecemeal, and unbalanced. It must have internal consistency of its elements, a gearing together of its parts, and efficacious adjustment to the environments within which it functions. The time factor is important; different aspects of culture change in various ways in time. Finally, culture is "precious"; each culture group has its processes for transmitting it to, and fixing it in, its new members.

The more important and apparent of the processes involved in this organization will be first discussed.

Organizational Processes of a Culture

The basic process in culture organization, as distinct from the processes of culture origination, is accumulation. Through this process the main body of culture grows both among all the contacting cultures through the ages and within a given area or society. It is a process that has been going on since the predecessors of mankind first began being manlike, that is, culture-constructing. Culture has historical continuity; it deepens and expands; its elements are obtained from the various peoples, periods, and areas.

Jastrow, starting with our American civilization, leads us back into the cultures that have "passed the baton" on to us. He states:

> The history of mankind is a continuous series of links, forming, as Herder phrased it, the "golden chain of culture." Each civilization as it

arises is the heir of the ages that have gone before; every phase of human culture stands in some connection with the preceding phase. Our American civilization is an offshoot of European culture to which we have made some contributions. The culture of Western and Northern Europe represents the extension of Roman civilization. Rome owes its intellectual stimulus to Greece, whose heir she became, and Greek culture, as we know it, rests on a substratum of Asiatic influence and embodies elements derived from Egypt and Babylonia as well as from Asia Minor; and even when we pass to the distant East, the chain is not broken. Persia looks back to India, as Japan to China. Through Buddhism the connection is established between Chinese and Hindu civilizations, and there are good reasons for believing that a direct cultural influence came to China from India at a period even earlier than the introduction of Buddhism. There is also evidence, not yet complete but increasing, which indicates that both Chinese and Hindu civilizations lie within the sphere of influence emanating from such far older cultural centers as the Valley of the Euphrates and the Valley of the Nile. (4)

Accumulation

Within a given society the body of culture grows continually in variety, complexity, and volume as the result of innovations from within and all manner of elements added from other past and present cultures. In a sense, elements ranging from single traits to large portions of whole culture systems are piled up in longer, wider, and higher piles of varied shape, content, and congruity. Nearly everything that is added to a culture tends to stay there because human culture does not keep on automatically eliminating its own waste or outmoded portions. Nevertheless, culture accumulation is not a simple process of stacking or indiscriminately depositing layer upon layer.

During the ages a good deal of culture has been lost as a result of accidents, physical and social catastrophes, foolishness, and bad guessing; other elements have been more or less consciously abandoned or eliminated because of apparent inapplicability or uncongeniality at some time and under certain existing conditions; still other elements as they appeared have been adopted, but restricted in function or located in some different pattern from that which they had been a part of. In general, while there is some loss, some weeding out, and some recombining, these processes within the general process of accumulation do not occur so fast or so consistently as the adding process. Finally, it may be pointed out that, from the qualitative point of view, the cumulative changes that may be taking place in different parts of the culture may be of either a progressive or a retrogressive character.

The process of accumulation may be graphically illustrated as occurring either horizontally or vertically. In the horizontal figure the accumulation is both a matter of a broadening base and linear movement with upward inclination, both quantitative and qualitative, of the elements added.

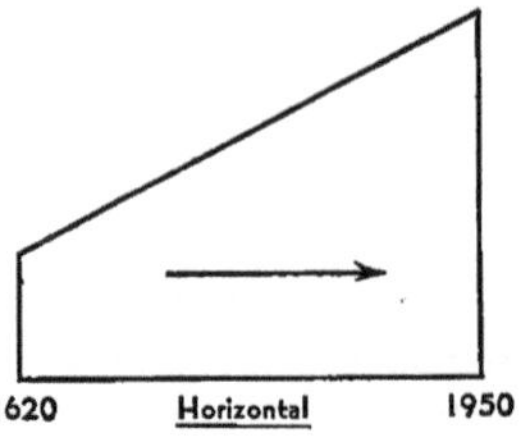

Vertically considered, the process of accumulation may be likened to an inverted pyramid with ever-broader layers successively placed on top of earlier layers:

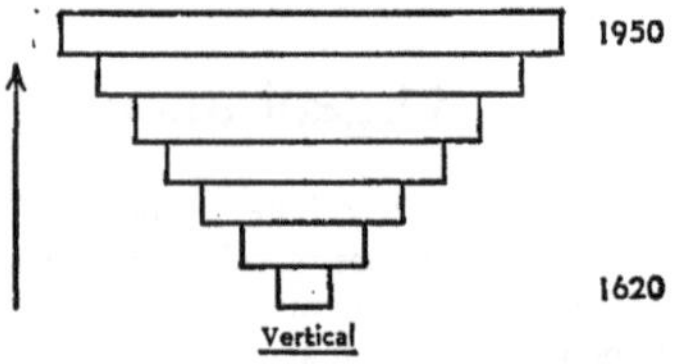

Processes of Resistance and Preservation

A set of processes occurring alongside those of accumulation—in fact, processes which may be looked upon as a special phase of accumulation, though they appear to be the reverse of it—are those that tend to resist modifications and additions and those that tend to preserve culture elements intact.

Processes of Resistance. Processes of resistance both to new culture elements originating within the culture and to the elements diffused from without are continually operating within a given society. Societies differ greatly in their readiness and willingness to adopt the new. Isolated peoples invariably are loathe to accept the new and raise and maintain all manner of obstacles to acceptance. Self-segregated groups within a society, whether segregated by special religious beliefs, adherence to nationality values and practices, or other precious and insistently maintained differentiating culture characteristics, resist modification.

Culture changes in certain departments of a given society will be resisted at the same time that change is eagerly sought in other departments. In our American society new or substitute governmental beliefs and practices come slowly. In the United States we persistently adhere to a two-party system, and although third-party movements are frequent, third parties have been short-lived without exception. Amendments to our federal and state constitutions come slowly and arduously. On the other hand, new technological developments and new forms of recreation tend to be widely welcomed.

In general our ways of life are channeled, and we resist departures from them. The old or the existent is familiar and safe, and a host of symbolic values are attached to it. We crave fixation and security and interpret the maintenance of the *status quo* as a prime essential. The new is usually suspect; it threatens the utility of old charts and charters, causes dislocations, and requires learning and reorganization of thinking and acting. Hence, it usually takes powerful and cleverly used dynamic factors to get our behavior out of the rut. It is often necessary to unseat ancient beliefs, private prejudices, deeply grooved attitudes, established habits, and rigidly adhered-to traditions, mores, and customs, which have a sanctity of their own.

Our own culture, for example, has shown resistance to all manner of inventions, although they were later accepted and highly improved—anesthetics, the germ theory of disease, and vaccination in the field of medicine, coal, laborsaving machinery, new foods, the telephone, and so on. (3) Along social and ideological lines some groups have resisted at one time or another the abolition of slavery and child labor, workmen's compensation, simplified spelling, changes in our conceptions of marriage and the family, geologic time, man's place in nature, and many other changes.

Processes of Preservation. Closely related to processes of resistance are *processes of culture preservation,* by means of which the culture of a people is preserved and protected against loss, disintegration, marked modification, or inundation by foreign ideas and ways. A host of conservative and conserving influences and agencies are working to maintain the prevalent, deep-seated attitudes of people toward their life and culture, their mores and institutions, their elders, patriots, and priests. In quiet and peaceful times these processes are rather obscure. But in periods of crisis they are noticeable, often conspicuous.

Cultural Integration and Assimilation

In spite of the resistance processes tending to retain the old, some culture elements in any given society are always becoming outmoded and ready to be discarded for a variety of reasons. As noted above, passive changes with dynamic effects are continually occurring. These unavoidable changes disturb the relationship and adjustment of the parts of the culture to some degree, thus threatening to impair in some measure the functional efficacy of the culture.

Furthermore, the culture of a given area or society is not a mere aggregate of elements, not a mere sum of parts, not a congeries of scattered, meaningless particles of ways of living. The component traits and complexes existing at any given time are in process of being interrelated and functionally organized into a distinctive, efficient, consistent, meaningful whole.

Cultural Integration. Cultural integration is the process of developing at least a working adjustment, and preferably a more and more nearly perfect relationship, among the various elements that compose the total culture. (5, p. 348) It is a continuous process whereby the diverse and changing indigenous or pre-existing elements and the incoming and borrowed elements are smoothly geared into each other, so that the culture system functions without serious friction or maladjustment. All the elements undergo a main orientation and organization within the particular society's general frame of reference.

This process is in part automatic and in part conscious and deliberate. Glaringly and increasingly incompatible and ineffective aspects of indigenous patterns of behavior, attitudes, ideas, values, techniques, and artifacts are discarded or modified. Diffused elements are examined for comprehensibility and applicability and discarded or accepted. If accepted, they are pared or enlarged, changed qualitatively and often as to meaning. Reinterpretation and refitting of *all* elements are continuous as gaps are filled, slack taken up, and clashes resolved. As Sumner put it, there is a "strain toward consistency" and a general tendency, in the long run, toward some kind of equilibration of all elements.

In the integration process culture elements coming from higher rather than lower cultures and from numerically, politically, economically, ethnically, or otherwise superior groups may be—usually are—dominant and enter predominantly and preponderantly into the integrated product. Furthermore, the resulting equilibrium of elements may be arbitrarily established by virtue of the social power of the dominant group, but the stability of any such equilibrium is usually delicate and precarious.

The time factor is always involved, since integration takes time. In some departments and under certain conditions, it will be precipitate; in others—possibly the majority—the integration will be slow. The process is of course always relative and never perfect or complete in any complex or pattern or in the system as a whole. There is continual movement *toward* an equilibrium. It may even be that complete cultural integration would be undesirable, since it would be evidence of stagnation or rigidity.

Cultural Assimilation. One aspect of the integration of a culture is what is referred to as *cultural assimilation,* the process whereby diverse culture elements that exist at a given time in a given area, regardless of their time or place of origin, are merged and equilibrated with the common way of life. It consists of a common sharing and use of elements with a resultant fusion of basic ways, ideas, beliefs, and values and a unity of feeling and thought about them. It is a continuous process, a "moving," or "flowing," synthesis. Culture assimilation must be distinguished from *societal* assimilation, which is the functional incorporation of diverse groups of human beings into a society. The latter will be analyzed in Chapter 21. These two types of assimilation are related and under some conditions go on concomitantly and simultaneously.

Out of this fusion process a new culture emerges, which is more or less homogeneous and composed of elements of the diverse contributory cultures. The fusion can occur under conditions of relative equality among the contributory cultures or, what is more likely, under conditions of some degree of dominance and submission. The parts contributed by the respective cultures to the new culture are rarely equal, and the majority or indigenous culture usually make the largest contribution. The new culture is not entirely representative of any of the contributory cultures; rather, it is a synthesis of these. Usually all of the contributory parts have been modified in some degree and have lost some of their previous identity as they were fused into the new whole.

We must distinguish between acculturation and culture integration and assimilation. Acculturation occurs among all the cultures or peoples in any kind of interaction; after the diffusion and borrowing, all the parties are still in their own separate territories, and each and all have their own modified, but still distinctive and more or less integrated, culture. Integration and assimilation, on the other hand, take place *within* a given culture area and produce an ever-new, more or less balanced, consistent synthesis of elements.

Intercultural Differentiation and Intra-Areal Regionalization

At the same time that a given culture is undergoing integration within, it is usually also differentiating itself significantly from other cultures. This differentiation occurs in spite of the leveling or unifying efforts of diffusion. Although the fundamental needs, motives, and satisfactions of men are pretty much the same everywhere, the particular attendant circumstances and manner in which they fulfill them differ.

Cultural Differentiation. A number of important general factors are involved in the cultural differentiation, such as the following:

1. Some degree of physical and social isolation, sometimes self-imposed.
2. The peculiar topography, climate, and natural resources, and the resultant economic and other practices.
3. The peculiar composition of the society's population resulting from various demographic, ethnic, and selective biological processes.
4. The cultural and national history of the society, including the accidents of history—changes in climate and resources, cataclysms of nature, military campaigns, internal disturbances, and so on.
5. The predominantly urban-commercial-industrial or rural-agricultural make-up of the society.
6. The special combination of minority and majority groups in the society.
7. The international and intersociety situation and relationships.
8. The special political, religious, and other run of attention in the society.

In many cases there are other peculiar, indigenous, and local social and cultural conditions and combinations of conditions. Cultural differentiation is a process continually going on in every culture and giving each society, each culture area, its special stamp of uniqueness and distinction, for each society has its own aims and values or "ethos" and its own differential cultural landscape.

Regionalization. Within large nation-wide, even continent-wide, culture areas like our own, there is a process going on which further differentiates the given culture along certain distinctive lines and in certain ways. This process may be called *regionalization*. By means of it the culture of the subareas known as regions tends to develop along distinctive lines and adjust itself uniquely and appropriately to the major physical, economic, political, and historical determiners of the area.

Natural factors, such as topography, climate, soil, mineral and biological resources, first shape a region. But as men work and live in such a distinctive geographic-economic area, they unconsciously and consciously invent, discover, select, and shape culture traits and complexes that are well adjusted to the geographic-economic arena and enable them to survive and even to flourish. In brief, they unavoidably *build* a distinctive culture system—one that is in more or less stable equilibrium with the physical features of the area—*upon* a distinctive physical environment. Thus, every region has typical activities, peculiar types of industry, special political attitudes and activities, typical folkways, and other expressional products.

These combined natural factors and the adjustive cultural processes produce variations, concentrations, and coherences of culture materials and give us a distinctive and identifying combination of traits, complexes, and patterns—a cultural *Gestalt*—for each region, as, for example, in the South, New England, the Middle West, the Great Plains, or the Far West of the United States. Because of these competitive and adjustive processes, there are a number of perceptible cultural similarities *within* each region and certain differences *between* regions.

Processes Involving Culture Changes in Time

To understand fully a given culture, it is necessary not only to be conscious of the processes that bring about internal modification and those that make for culture organization, but also to have some idea of what is known about the types of change that occur *in time*. Some or many parts of a culture may show inertia and persist beyond their time; some parts may lapse and later be revived; other parts change in a circular manner, coming back to earlier forms; and still other parts change at differential rates of speed and in varying volume.

What are the more important tendencies that a culture and its parts present in relation to the *time factor*? It should be pointed out at the outset that within a culture all types of change may be occurring simultaneously among different parts. Furthermore, we still know very little about these temporal changes in culture; at best we can only attempt some brief effort at identification and systematization. (8; 12; 16; 17)

Inertia, Survivalism, and Culture Lag

Accumulation is continually occurring, giving us a linear movement, that is, a growth of culture in volume in time, as a result of increasing knowledge, inventions, and borrowings.

Inertia. Within the general process of accumulation, however, there are also retarding factors and processes that cause inertia in few or many parts of a culture. By inertia we mean the tendency of culture elements, ranging from traits to whole patterns, to persist in relatively unchanged form when they have outgrown their usefulness in the total culture. The circumstances which called the culture elements into existence have largely disappeared, and the elements no longer serve their pristine functions or even any other. Inertia, therefore, is a process whereby past and passé culture forms are carried over into the present.

Inertia is the result of a variety of factors, among which attitudes of insecurity held by members of certain groups and special attachments to certain ways are important. There is a tendency to avoid change if a culture element seems to work and is deemed tried and true among many people; they fear change along certain lines which seem to be bound up with their precious and distinguishing interests, seek to avoid the necessity of making new adjustments, hold sentimental attachments and emotional preferences for certain beliefs, ways, and things, and venerate age and give long-term forms and actions an air of sacredness.

Physical and cultural factors also contribute to inertia. The culture of societies or segments of society that are physically or socially isolated and hence remote from the stream of change will show inertia. Lack of communication, for whatever reason, retards change. Until recently the culture of the Appalachian and the Ozark highlanders and of the Acadians of the Louisiana bayous showed vast inertia. The lack of contact or communication on the part of a population segment may be deliberate in order to maintain isolation, as, for example, among Mormons, Mennonites, Seventh-Day Adventists, or foreign nationality groups within a larger society. Many of the culture elements among such self-segregated groups will show inertia.

In a cosmopolitan, complex, fragmental culture like ours, the inertia-producing processes are largely confined to the culture of certain physical areas and certain undercommunicative segments of the population and stem, as noted, from attitudes held by individuals and subcultural groups. And yet, every culture group has some residual culture elements which intrude into the present, prevent the acceptance of more timely culture elements, and hence act as obstructions to efficiency and as complications to integration. Culture elements have a tendency to persist as they are and have been; culture elements and culture systems tend to continue through time in their planes of motion until some set of new forces gives them a new trend.

Survivalism. The outmoded and archaic culture elements that carry over into the present are called "survivals." They are found in every institutional field, notably in language, superstitions, ritual and ceremony, holidays, aesthetics, conventions, and religion. The main justification of survivals is the fact of their existence, although most are rationalized as meeting a real or supposed need, but not necessarily the one for which they were designed. When the survival does pertain to some deep-lying purpose, for example, a practice or belief in connection with religious need, it has great persistence and remains little altered, though it may at times be clothed in new garb. (18)

Culture Lag. In a culture like ours there is no general inertia; the inertia is largely confined to certain segments of complexes and patterns, as compared with relative dynamism in others. This unequal and differential rate of change, lacking synchronization between the fast and relatively slow variables in culture, we call "culture lag." * Inventions and culture contacts, as noted above, are continually producing new runs of attention, new hard-worked emphases in a culture. On the

*The naming and basic analysis of "culture lag" are the work of W. F. Ogburn in his *Social Change* (New York: Heubsch, 1922).

other hand, in the backwaters of culture the tendeney toward inertia prevails. Thus, there is a difference in the rate of development *in time* of different parts of the whole culture. If all traits within a given culture moved or changed at the same rate and at the same time, lags would be impossible. But, of course, they do not. (9)

The classic example of culture lag in our society, as first set forth by Ogburn and subsequently by almost everyone else, is the lag between the present rapid technological development, which has affected the material and economic ways of life, and the relatively slow development of the social values, attitudes, ideas, codes, and other institutional factors unavoidably related to material ways. Inventions affecting the material aspects of life have been occurring at an astonishing rate, but the essential parallel *social* inventions, especially institutional adjustments, have been relatively retarded. During the last half century in China, the lag has been reversed. Many intellectual, ideological, and social changes occurred there much more rapidly than did material changes. (13)

Such time differentials in the development of the various interrelated portions of a culture have significant effects upon that culture. For a culture is and must be, at any given time, a unified, integrated, balanced, synchronized, functioning entity. When one or more highly emphasized parts are developing at a very rapid rate while others, unavoidably closely related, develop at a very slow rate, the time disparity in development may produce a long-run, over-all functional inefficiency.

Revivals and Reversions

Another significant form of culture rhythm appears in revivals and reversions. Often, after a considerable lapse of time and use, culture elements from the past are resurrected or revived and put into some kind of use. Old values are redefined and given appropriate contemporary meanings; traditional beliefs and customary behavior come again to be highly esteemed and cherished; and satisfaction is found in ancient ways.

Cultural revivals are not to be confused with survivals or lags, although revivalism, of course, involves some degree of survivalism. (10) The difference is that a survival has been in active use all along, whereas the revival has been quiescent, lingering or surviving in memory only until reemphasized and reactivated in use.

The revived culture items may be of a retrogressive, neutral, or progressive character in the present. Among retrogressive or malignant items may be ancient superstitions and beliefs, forms of dictatorship, or revivals of dueling embraced as escapes. The present writer some years ago analyzed a set of neutral revivals by modern Americans in the form of renewed interest in ancestors, genealogy, and antiques. (11) Other common neutral revivals are types of clothing, ballads, rituals, and some aspects of architecture. The significant fact is that the past, in some form, again and again, intrudes into—in fact, is deliberately invited or inserted into—various departments of present culture.

Processes of Culture Transmission and Culture Fixing

We have examined briefly the processes whereby culture is originated, transported in space and exchanged between cultures, accumulated and integrated within a given culture area and differentiated from that of other areas, as well as the variations in time. One more major set of processes must be examined, namely, those whereby the life-ways are projected into the future and fixed in each new generation and among incoming individuals of the culture area.

As we have noted, culture is the tested "precious way of life" of any given people; it consists of their basic beliefs and values, their concepts and interpretations, their techniques, their uses of paraphernalia and material possessions, the summation of their experience, and the whole battery of their instrumentalities for living. Therefore it must be passed on without fail and without loss to the next generation. It must also be imparted to all immigrant members of the society. Every new-born member must become a competent participant in the life of the society; the thought-ways and action-ways must become *fixed* in him, and their perpetuation and potency in the future must be guaranteed. Neither individuals nor groups can be permitted to be without the culture or to deviate too widely from it.

As indicated above, culture is not innate, and its transmission is not instinctive; it is acquired by each individual during his lifetime. But man has the *capacity* to acquire culture, and the motivations and conditions under which he acquires it are essentially social. The basic process is *learning,* the elemental psychological features of which will first be presented briefly.

The Learning Process

The four fundamental factors in the learning process are drive, cue, response, and reward.* *Drive* is the strong stimulus which impels persons, individually and collectively, consciously or unconsciously, to act or respond, that is, to want to do certain things in certain ways in order to acquire certain satisfactions. The individual has innate drives such as fear, avoidance of pain, hunger, thirst, cold, or lonesomeness; he has socially acquired drives which motivate him positively, such as desire for conformity and social approval, prestige seeking, desire to match associates along certain lines, and drives of a negative or inhibitive nature such as avoidance of social approbrium.

The *cue* is the characteristic of objects or situations which functions as stimulus and which sets off the drive. The cues are signals to respond, such as the new feat of three-year-old Johnny's playmate which invites emulation, the noon whistle, or the neighbor's new car. Cues determine when and where the individual will respond and which responses he will make. These trigger stimuli vary in strength, kind or distinctiveness, and quantity and quality.

The *response* is the resultant action determined by the cue; it is what occurs after the individual receives the cue if he has the essential drive. When the cue and the response are bound together in such a manner that the cue evokes the response and a new pattern of thought or action is formed, we have a new habit; something has been learned. The strengthening of cue response is the essence of learning.

Any event known to strengthen the cue-response connection is a *reward.* The degree and quality of repetition of the response depend on whether or not it is rewarded. If the response is not rewarded, the tendency to repeat it with the same cues is weakened, and the inclination to respond may be abandoned and become extinct; or if rewards produce reductions in drive or satiation, the rewarding value disappears or is weakened. On the other hand, if the individual or social utility or desirability of what is learned is underscored by rewards of various kinds, such as successes and approvals, the connection between the cue and the rewarded response is so strengthened that the next time the same drive and cues are present, the response is more likely to occur. Without reward of some kind and degree people fail to learn. Hence, if culture is to be acquired, either in the form of specific habits or as a whole (in the case of immigrants), or if phases of it are to be relearned (as in the case of adults), and if it is to be adequately maintained, the rewards for so doing must be apparent and reasonably certain.

For human beings several preliminary advantages exist as far as the learning process is concerned. First, human beings are highly suggestible and susceptible to stimuli cues; and, second, they want to be like other people of their culture, to be well regarded and well received. Hence, they can and do learn what the group has to offer.

Processes of Transmission

The transmission processes, involving the general processes of learning, are those by means of which the internal structuring of the individual under the influence of culture stimuli is going on continually. The culture is being interiorized, or built into each individual, so that every response and attitude and act is in conformity with the society's attitudes and action patterns relating to every typical social situation. Then the culture patterns of the society operate with certainty and smoothness.

As Cantril points out (20), the process of interiorization varies greatly as between individuals

*In general this brief discussion is dependent upon the excellent analysis of N. E. Miller and J. Dollard, *Social Learning and Imitation* (New Haven: Yale University Press, 1941), pp. 1-32. See also G. L. Freeman, *The Energetics of Human Behavior* (Ithaca: Cornell University Press, 1948), pp. 174-192.

of different capacities and temperaments, as between different culture groups, and with respect to different types of culture elements. Says Cantril:

> It would be foolish to expect that an individual living in a backward, underprivileged, bigoted rural community would acquire his ideas in the same manner as an individual in a progressive, middle-class urban environment. . . . Nor would we expect a highly intelligent, introverted boy to acquire his ideas in the same way as a stupid, extroverted boy brought up in the same environment.

The general features of the transmission processes, however, can be presented. They involve all the processes and means of communication and range in deliberateness, intensity, and organization from very informal and casual to highly formalized and purposive processes.

Informal Processes of Transmission. These processes include relatively simple and casual suggestion-imitation and conditioning. At this simplest level the culture is transmitted almost automatically. Cultural elements, especially usages and standards, impinge upon the individual from birth on. He more or less unconsciously and automatically is trained in many of the cultural ways that confront him at each stage of his development or, in other words, at each stage of his expanding social and cultural awareness. Every contact with family, with other associates, unorganized and organized, every occupational, class, recreational, or other institutional contact presents him with cultural ways and standards, often under some pressure to accept and conform.

The techniques of imitation are important in achieving desirable conformity to culture patterns. They take the form either of response to an active signal by a leader or authority or of slow copying in response to repeated cues emanating from models. (24, pp. 11, 183)

Aspects of informal transmission processes range from simple word-of-mouth advice passed on by older to younger members of the society to the transmissive influence exercised by newspapers, periodicals, motion pictures, radio, and so on.

Formal Processes of Transmission. To overcome the deficiencies of the spontaneous processes of transmission, all known historical peoples have resorted to formal, direct, purposive transmission through specialized, organized inculcation and systematized educational procedures. The mediums have taken the form of special ceremonies, schools of all kinds and levels, other organized services and programs for informing people, such as forums, extension services, lecture courses, museums, galleries, libraries, and pamphleteering. These formal transmission procedures are conducted by specially prepared administrators, instructors, and trainers, who use specially devised instructional techniques and materials. (For elaboration, see reference 230)

Adoption of Foreign Culture

This aspect of culture transmission, together with the transmission of prevailing culture to immigrants, will be briefly examined. The learning of culture elements diffused to a given society from without is basically a process of copying and acquiring habits and values. The diffused traits find a place in the actions of the members of the recipient society. The general principles of the learning process apply here also. A degree of drive is needed. If the introduced items are comprehensible and compatible, existent responses can be utilized; the received item can be more readily and quickly learned. The new item may actually reinforce existing responses; for example, it is easier to introduce a new card game among a card-playing people.

On the other hand, the absence of subresponses lengthens the time of learning a new trait or prevents its intrusion. It means that the new trait is incompatible. The reward factor also is important; if a new trait or complex is likely to offer increased facility in drive satisfaction, it is likely to be widely learned and practiced.

Transmission of Prevailing Culture

If the prevailing culture is to be adequately transmitted to the immigrants in the culture area, the essential conditions for learning must exist. The immigrants must have drives which can be satisfied in the new culture. It is essential that they also have something in the way of pre-existing understanding of, and familiarity with, the types of culture items and culture actions in order to be susceptible to the cues and pressures of the host culture. To be able to respond they should have some degree of appropriate and particular response patterns—something in the way of a pre-existing habit outfit. For example, an immigrant who has already learned a language other than his own finds it easier to learn still another. With practice, he develops increasing fluency and greater exactness in the reproduction of the new culture ways. But he must feel rewarded, both in the way of individual satisfactions and utilities and in the way of social acceptances, approvals, and opportunities. In fact, the whole learning process of the immigrant rests on rewards; he copies in order to obtain rewards, not to achieve perfection of response.

If one or more of these four basic learning principles are not sufficiently operative in the case of given immigrant individuals or groups or in the case of certain types of culture elements, the immigrants do not learn the culture in sufficient degree or with sufficient facility to become accepted members.

The Fixing Factors

Beyond these informal and formal transmission procedures are the pressures which seek to fix or reinforce in individuals and in constituent groups of the society the cultural ways and ideas and *make* them conform consciously and unconsciously. These pressures are the propulsive norms that dominate roles and all other required acts and beliefs and the prohibitions and taboos whereby foreign and other antigroup ways are indicated. The society's rituals groove and routinize essential action, and its ceremonials attach a sanctifying sentiment to such acts and beliefs. They woo the individuals to accept the cultural ways and solidify them as attitudes and habits. The myths, legends, traditions, customs, and conventions require conformity, and violation or nonacceptance isolates the individual from the large group and makes him appear uncouth. Above all is the vast system of institutions with their codes, organizations, functionaries, and supporting public opinion which govern almost every aspect of culture and from which there is no escape. Involved in all of these is the system of rewards and punishments. Cultural conformity brings approval, contentment, acceptance, even social prosperity; nonconformity brings disapproval, exclusion, reduction of status, pain, a sense of shame and guilt, and the gnawing conscience.

In most instances these learning and fixing processes are so thorough, so pervasive, that the members of the given society seem to be reacting automatically to their culture rather than reflecting upon it. When these processes have effectively occurred, with respect to the new generation or to immigrants, *enculturation* can be said to have taken place, to use Herskovits's apt term; that is, the individuals have achieved competence in the culture of the area. (22)

PART THREE

THE SOCIAL PROCESSES AFFECTING NATURAL, DEMOGRAPHIC, AND SPATIAL ADJUSTMENT

CHAPTER VII

SOCIAL ADJUSTMENT TO THE NATURAL ENVIRONMENT

ALL SOCIETIES, however simple or complex, must work out their destiny within the elemental arena of the natural physical and natural biological environments. Men are inhabitants of the earth and dependent upon it. All that they are and do, wherever they are, is influenced by the natural environment. These influences are never stilled. Men live and survive and their societies function only when they adequately meet the exigencies of this physical situation. Here is the base upon which all individual and collective human life rests.

The major elements in this natural environment may be classified as follows from the point of view of their influence on man: *Cosmic factors* are those inherent in the universe—beyond the earth—that affect the earth and all on it. Significant are the influences of the sun and the moon and of other planetary systems that affect diurnal, seasonal, and climatic cycles and other great time rhythms, and as they produce various physical and biological benefits and catastrophes on the earth. *Physical factors* consist of space itself and of gravity, altitude, oxygen supply, and barometric pressure.

Geographic factors may be subdivided into *physiographic factors,* consisting of topographic or relief or land-form features, such as plains, deserts, and oceans, and gravity and altitude; *climatic features,* consisting of weather and seasons, with such major factors as wind, moisture and aridity, heat and cold; *inorganic natural resources,* including the minerals and metals and the sources of mechanical power, such as minerals, fuels, wind, sunlight, falling water; *organic natural resources,* consisting of all forms of life.

All these factors affect the sustenance and shelter of people and their general physical and racial characteristics, their energies and health, location, social and cultural homogeneities and heterogeneities, activities, movement in physical space, forms of social organization, special interests and objectives, general survival and prosperity, and historical destiny.

Mankind in the Natural Environment

Below the human level the various forms of life are adapted to the natural environment. As noted previously, adaptation is a process whereby plant and animal species and varieties passively and automatically fit themselves to natural forces, materials, and conditions. Through tremendously costly selectivity, those individuals with the quantitative and qualitative characteristics essential to functioning under the changing conditions survive and pass on these potentialities to descendants; the others perish. While there may be a certain amount of *social* action, especially among certain widely advertised species of insects and mammals, this action itself is the result of selective survival and largely takes the form of reflex or instinctive activity.

Dependence on Natural Environment

Mankind has never been wholly free from natural selective processes and is not now—anywhere. They must always be reckoned with. But from earliest times mankind has never lived in a mere passive, unconscious, submissive manner in the face of nature. Hence, the widely used term *adaptation* in referring to mankind's relation to the natural environment, though a superficially obvious conclusion, is, strictly speaking, a misnomer. To admit some dependence upon natural environment is not identical with an admission of *closest* dependence. While the natural environment is man's "home," he has always tended to make himself "at home" in it. As Febvre points out, man is the only living creature that lives anywhere and everywhere on the face of the earth where life is possible. Yet man is more subjected to nature than any other form of life by the very reason of his ubiquity. (7, p. 8) Every physical environment occupied by mankind shows multiple effects of human and social action in actively affecting and effecting physical conditions and facilitating human life. The natural determiners are always relative.

Man has always been in some measure a dynamic agent in his environments, actively and aggressively meeting their challenges. He has never been purely and simply acted upon by them. He has taken advantage of many of the opportunities for living provided by nature and circumvented or controlled the limitations imposed by it. Nature never surrenders, but neither does man. As he has experimented and succeeded, he has acquired more assurance and facility. Of course, he has also frequently been an active and often aggressive destroyer. But whether his action on the environment has been constructive or destructive he has always "humanized" it. (7, pp. v-xix)

Man the Architect and Engineer

Man has by no means succeeded in emancipating himself from the natural environment. Some courses of action are impossible, and others are permissible. It does not mean that man *must* do this or that; but simply that if he does *this,* he survives and possibly prospers; if he does *that,* he runs into difficulty or danger. Man must make the choices. But with his growing ability to cope with nature, man's action in relation to it has become more and more permissive. To use Lowie's famous terms, the natural environment still furnishes the "brick and mortar," but man increasingly has become the architect and engineer. (13)

So effective has man been as a modifying agent that often what was an obstacle has become a stepping stone, and what had been something to fight against has been converted into an ally against new obstacles. Seas, for example, ceased to be barriers when men learned to navigate and became mediums of communication and transportation. Furthermore, the very changing and controlling activities have led to further action; the more men have changed primary nature the more they are impelled to modify it. To stand still or to retreat is to surrender and suffer loss.

Place of Social Processes in Adjustment

Such human mastery of nature as has been achieved has been due to social action, to functional *social processes.* Men have not acted alone or naturally. By some degree of organized cooperation they have fitted themselves to and modified the physical and nonhuman biological environments in ways essential and conducive to individual and societal existence and, preferably, prosperity. Although the social processes have had to recognize the natural processes and conform to them, they have always also appropriated and utilized them. In fact, as social advance has taken place, the social processes of environmental control have increased in volume and improved in efficacy. A very large number of the elemental processes have been articulated and integrated by social processes. Soil processes, for example, have been accelerated by agricultural practices; climate has been specially utilized by industry, as in the use of areas with a humid atmosphere for textile manufacturing. By means of social processes, the effect of many natural processes has actually been reversed.

It is quite safe to maintain that in ninety-nine cases out of every hundred modern man's relations to the geographical environments involve social interactions that are based on historical and contemporary ingenuity and cooperation of human beings. By means of these social processes man long since has in large part elevated the struggle for existence to the social level and in considerable degree has made it a campaign for physical enhancement. As a result of these *social* processes, natural phenomena become, in an increasing number of instances, merely a precondition for social phenomena rather than specific causes or determiners.

In this analysis we are not concerned with the influences of the natural environment on man, which have been treated in a very sizable body of analytical literature. Rather, our interest is in the social processes by means of which man has adjusted himself to this environment, utilized it, and often wasted it.

Motivations and Culture Media

The social processes enabling adjustment to, and control of, the natural processes have their dynamic in social motivations and operate by means of various instrumentalities of human culture. In their attack upon nature, men are influenced by their drives, their wishes, and their interests in survival, well-being, and prosperity. Their values set the goals of achievement. Creative intelligence, will, memory of past experiences, and logic point them toward the goals. The culture that men have created in its various forms provides the tools, the "ways and means" for the remodeling and controlling processes. The elements of culture that are of special importance in this present analysis are the following:

Man's Scientific Knowledge

Science has been developing through the ages as a method or an art of finding facts. Phenomena are investigated, new facts discovered, new syntheses of facts made. Observations under various degrees of control and experiments in the form of procedures known as the "scientific method" are increasing this body of facts regarding all types of phenomena in an almost geometric ratio. These facts are being classified, generalized, and verified and constitute an ever-growing store of facts and principles governing the relations of facts.

Cooperative Efforts among Men

Cooperative efforts of men range from the very simple ones that involve little organization to the great institutionalized associations purposefully and planfully organized for investigation and for the execution of programs of attack upon nature. All these are pertinent and essential configurations of culture.

The Technical System

The technical system is that phase of man's cultural equipment whereby he adjusts himself to, and partly controls, the natural environment. It consists of ***technics, techniques,*** and ***technologies,*** all means of utilizing artifacts, general knowledge, and scientific facts and laws. The processes are usually known as "applied science" or "engineering."

Technics refers to tools, implements, instruments, and machines, whereas *techniques* are the actual operational actions, with their patterned, sequential mechanical procedures carried on by means of skills. The manipulation and modification of physical materials and living things occurs by means of techniques. Both technics and techniques are mechanical or operational; symbolic, that is, involving ideas, traditions, philosophies, and sciences; and organizational, that is, used and applied by groups in institutionalized ways. *Technologies* are the total organization of techniques as they combine the multiplicity of technics and apply human energy and ingenuity by means of science in carrying on the typical engineering tasks of a society. Every economy is an array of interdependent technologies. Our culture includes a variety of them—biological, physical, psychological, and sociological—which function interdependently and in combination. (6, pp. 223-249; 9; 16)

By means of these three related sets of cultural agencies men are able to comprehend the nature of the universe, work in conformity with it, predict some of its occurrences, invent and otherwise deliberately and consciously innovate upon it, and increasingly manipulate some of its features in a planned and organized manner in the pursuit of human ends. Thus, men override many of the handicaps of the natural landscape by superimposing the cultural landscape upon it. What is more, with each degree of technical, economic, or organizational development, the very nature of the natural environment is changed, and psychic and sociocultural factors become more and more important as compared with geographic and biologic factors.

In general, men with different cultural inheritances, with different degrees of ability and initiative, with different values and purposes, and in different times and circumstances may develop one or another of many different ways of living in a given physical setting and create very different cultural landscapes.

Main Social Processes Involved in Adjustment

The social processes relating to man's successful career in the natural environment are largely a matter of the relative degree of mastery or control of effects of the different types of natural elements. They range along a scale from mere circumvention of the untoward effects to actual transformation of elements and efforts at repair of man's mistakes. All are adjustive processes, as distinct from adaptive processes, in that they involve ingenuity, choice, purpose, and the use of techniques. These processes operate singly or in various combinations, depending upon the category of natural elements existing in the given man-nature relationship.

Circumvention and Protection

The processes of circumvention and protection are involved especially in the case of the cosmic and many of the geographic and climatic features of the natural environment. In some instances man cannot change these because he can exercise no controls over them. But he can *make the untoward or destructive effects recede into the background by some form of escape from, or compliant adjustment to, or protection against, these phenomena,* except only in times of great catastrophe. He cannot influence the movement of astronomical bodies or escape from rain or storm; nor can he prevent earthquakes or other disturbances or the vast weather cycles, such as the rhythms of desiccation and rainfall. But man can protect himself by building his habitations on stilts or high places and constructing dikes and dams and by building quake-proof structures; he can protect himself against climatic conditions; and he can overcome mountain barriers, circumvent space on land and sea, and decrease the expanse of time by various forms of transportation and communication. He can store food against drought and famine, and he has devised various ways of coping with disease carriers, epidemics, harmful bacteria, destructive creatures, and other menaces in the biological world.

When all circumventive means fail, man can escape by *migrating* to a more favorable environment, as he has done through the ages. Nomadism and the unorganized or organized movement of peoples as small groups or as masses are the historically significant forms of this adjustive procedure.

Even these more elemental adjustive processes involve interacting men as active selectors, planners, and manipulators of some aspects of the external environments in order to contend with their menacing phases. It is noteworthy that with experience, men exercise foresight, anticipate some of these effectors of harm, and prepare escape or protection in advance of the uncertain but predictable event.

Utilization

The utilization processes fall short of actual modification of form and substance of environmental elements themselves. By using knowledge and discovered and invented manipulative procedures, mechanisms, and organizations, man has sorted out, controlled, and even appropriated for his well-being certain of the physical and biological elements—both forces and materials. Thus, Nature is made a helpful friend instead of a subtle enemy. In this way man has utilized rain by storing it and diverting it where most needed for irrigation; harnessed the wind with windmills and used the fall of streams for power purposes; converted the indentations of coast lines into harbors and natural barriers into frontiers and boundaries; used the air for transportation. The very rhythms of nature are predicted and utilized for all manner of commercial, recreational, and ceremonial purposes. The processes of utilization are in perpetual flux as man fails, learns, tries, and works.

Transformation*

Associated men have achieved their most notable hegemony over nature in the processes of transformation. By means of these they do vastly more than merely circumvent the hazards and limitations imposed by nature. They do more than appropriate and utilize what nature provides. They modify natural forces and materials and creatures in structure, or function, or both, and thus vastly increase, both in quantity and quality, the energies, materials, utilities, and services for human satisfactions and purposes. Here the technologies, with their unique and highly developed engineering processes, come into full play as men remake nature in all its phases and subject it to their use and desires. By these processes the surface of the earth is modified and manipulated and the physical energies are put to work. Physical materials, such as minerals, metals, and wood are converted into buildings and homes and machines and clothing, and vegetable and animal fibers become textiles. Chemical constituents of matter are transformed from their natural forms and combinations into all manner of substances for innumerable specific uses. Not only are plants cultivated and animals domesticated, thus making them continually available as sources of food, manufacturing materials, and power, but by the manipulation of known genetic principles, types of animals are created for various purposes. Men develop crops suitable to particular soil and seasonal and moisture conditions. Noxious or pernicious bacteria, insects, animals and plants are destroyed or put to work for man in various ways. Space and physical barriers can be converted into aids by mechanical means of communication and transportation, and he can transport himself and all his usable materials on land and sea and in the air.

Destruction and Waste

While man has been uniquely adept as a sidestepper, utilizer, and transformer, he has also been the greatest destroyer and waster of energies and substances among all of the species of the earth. By "destruction" in relation to natural resources, we mean those antisocial processes, unconscious or conscious, due to ignorance, neglect, carelessness, and greed which cause individuals and groups to destroy and spend natural resources and to be wasteful in production and distribution and destructive and extravagant in consumption.

Men have destroyed and wasted valuable bio-

* This peculiarly appropriate term is from L. L. Bernard, *Introduction to Sociology* (New York: Thomas Y. Crowell Co., 1942), pp. 288-330.

logical and physical resources. Forests have been denuded and burned. Grasslands and pastures have been plowed up when they should have been left as they were. Valuable animal and vegetable species have been extinguished and pernicious ones permitted to flourish. Soil has been robbed and allowed to deteriorate or erode and wash away, and the water-retaining capacity of watersheds has been destroyed and water supplies polluted and streams and reservoirs permitted to silt up. Industrial firms have often discarded and wasted more of the raw materials than they utilized, and occasionally, to maintain price levels or monopoly, quantities of finally processed consumption goods have been permitted to deteriorate or have even been destroyed. Finally, use of finished products by the consumer has been and is wasteful. But the crowning process of waste and destruction has been war as it scarred landscapes, destroyed soils, battered bridges, harbor installations, and industrial plants, converted to destructive ends every form of natural energy and useful substance and all of man's innovative ability and machinery.

If we do not cooperatively use our technologies for the conservation and restoration of resources, we become technological vandals instead of beneficent collaborators with, or inspired innovators of, nature.

Conservation, Restoration, Replacement

These processes especially involve the time perspective in man's relationship to his material world. Men must consider what they have done to natural resources in the past and are now doing and what they desire for the future. Conservation applies particularly to what Mukerjee has called "fund" resources as contrasted to "flow" resources. (31) The flow resources are those continuously produced by nature, such as water power and potential water power, air, sunshine, and much animal and vegetable life. Fund resources are those which are nonreproducible or are very slowly renewable, such as mineral and metal deposits. Having characteristics of both, but apparently inclining more toward the form of fund resources at any given time unless wisely utilized, are forests, soils, grasslands, and arable lands. The flow resources represent man's annual *income* from nature; while fund resources constitute the *capital* which nature has stored for men. The conservation processes are essentially those of administering or exercising stewardship in the use of this capital fund.

By *conservation,* then, is meant the processes whereby valuable nonreplaceable or only slowly replaceable resources are preserved from deterioration, extermination, loss, or injury or are restored, or satisfactory substitutes are found for them. Conservation processes have significance for several reasons. Men have discovered that certain resources upon which the whole economy depends are irreplaceable and yet have been used with abandon and no thought of the future, notably coal and petroleum. Others, such as forests and good grasslands, which are only slowly replaceable, have been recklessly used. Still others, like the soil, must be continually restored with respect to physical, chemical and micro-organic qualities and protected against erosion.

In applying the conservation concept through private, semipublic, and public conservation procedures, more and more dependence should be placed on flow resources. For example, water power should be more fully developed and used where possible in place of or to supplement coal and petroleum, and the possibilities of sun power should be more fully explored. The in-between resources should be wisely used and developed as precious and depletable elements. Forests should not be "mined," as they have been quite generally, but "cropped" and continuously replanted, as is coming to be the practice in the United States. The soil of arable land should be protected from loss of essential chemical elements by crop rotation, the use of fertilizers, control of water, and protection from harmful organisms. Soil erosion should be checked by appropriate plantings, the building of dams and embankments, and the employment of contour plowing and other modern farming practices, and grasslands should be protected against overgrazing and plowing-up during the wet phase of the rainfall cycle.

The fund resources should be used with the greatest discretion. Such fund resources as coal, petroleum, iron ore and most of the other metals are exhaustible and are being very rapidly consumed. They should be carefully husbanded by economical mining and used only for essentials, and efforts should be made to utilize inferior grades and to find substitutes before the supplies are exhausted.

The conservation processes are concerned with repairing the damage and replacing the losses arising from man's careless and unwise utilization of natural resources. They are also concerned with the present generation's use of existing supplies of durable and vitally essential material goods. But the most important function of conservation is the creation of a kind of insurance fund and annuity, or a reserve against depreciation, for the benefit of the future. In addition, a considerable part of the conservation process is devoted to training people to maintain a harmonious and fruitful relationship with their natural environments. Nature is usually responsive to these efforts.

CHAPTER VIII

SOCIAL PROCESSES AFFECTING POPULATION

A HUMAN SOCIETY is composed elementally of the total number of human beings occupying its determined territory at any given time. Every population is territorially localized, that is, it has a spatially bounded locale, which is often an area of political jurisdiction—a district, village, ward, city, county, state, nation. All these people are the raw material from which the society's social relations—its social system—is shaped. In brief, *demography,* or the science of population, is *the keystone of societal analysis.*

A census, or comprehensive counting, is the basic procedure for acquiring population facts, and census data are the primary source of population information and the basis for population principles. These data are expressed in statistical form and at first seem to be a vast, complicated mass of dry-as-dust figures. But the slightest insight reveals the fact that these statistics have societal significance and meaning and that they indicate the fundamental bases upon which a society is built and by means of which it operates. From these statistics the organizational characteristics and the social trends of a society—even of a civilization—can be seen emerging.

Behind the statistics and the numerical indicators of various sorts are *contributory* factors, in the form of physical, biological, psychological, and sociocultural occurrences, that affect the *primary demographic facts,* such as changes in marriage, birth and death rates, the size of age, sex, ethnic, and class groups, in internal and international movements of persons, and so on. From the statistical indicators all manner of *conclusions,* implications, and interpretations of an economic, familial, political, military, educational, sociobiological, and sociopsychological nature are possible.

Nature and Sociological Significance of Population

This book is not concerned with the presentation of statistical data or of the generally accepted demographic principles. A sizable body of such literature is available to social scientists. Rather, our purpose is to examine the available facts and reliable hypotheses regarding the significance and action of sociocultural factors and processes in affecting the ever-changing demographic behavior of a society like our own.

Size, Density, and Composition

The general sociological significance of population needs to be pointed out, however, before the examination of the pertinent factors and processes is undertaken. The population of a specific society differs from that of other societies in size, distribution and density, composition, and internal tendencies. Size, or the total number of the population, determines many features of the collective life, and as the size of the social aggregate increases, the behavior of the members changes. Size, for example, affects the extent of specialization in that it determines the number of human beings to be functionally divided, the number of different activities to be carried on simultaneously, and the number of uses of given specialized products and services. Every increase in size indicates the extent to which specialization may be developed. Larger populations are also usually more heterogeneous, thus containing a greater assortment of potential specialists and offering greater opportunity for intensive specialization and more diverse demands.

The members of a given society are unequally distributed within the area. There is greater density, or a larger number of persons per square mile, for example, in very fertile areas and in cities. This distribution roughly affects the frequency and variety of social contacts and the kinds of collective activities that are possible in various localities and involves the potential complexity of group organization. Societies differ with respect to the urban-rural nature and the size of both local and regional component communities within the larger society.

A given society is composed of persons of both sexes of various ages, ranging from the newly born to the very aged, arbitrarily designated as children and adults. Most people, though not all, are members of a type of population unit known as "families," and all fall within one of four marital categories, namely, the single, the married, the widowed, or the divorced. In our country people are divided into various racial and nationality classifications. Their composition is further differentiated in groupings according to socially significant and socially derived characteristics, such as occupational skills, educational level, religious affiliation, and socioeconomic status. Occasionally, also, an effort is made to array them on the basis of their biological quality, intelligence, and social proficiency. Because of its peculiar composition, every population has a distinctive character that sets it apart from other aggregates. These demographic peculiarities are reflected in many aspects of its social organization.

Population Change

Even more important than the size, distribution, and composition of the population at any given time is the fact that every aspect of it is changing in time; that is, it is in continual process. As Vance points out, population is a matter of dynamic conditions, not static conditions. It should be regarded as a "flow," not a store; trends rather than a given state should be considered. (36, p. 7) This flow takes various forms. People are being born and others are dying, and the ratio of these two processes and, hence, the rate of natural increase and replacement, or of growth and decline, are ever-fluctuating.

The vital processes of reproduction and mortality are always governed by selective factors and occur at different rates among the different segments of the population. Marriage varies as to rate among the different levels of the population. The proportion of the population in the different age groups, sex groups, ethnic groups, and all other population categories changes continually. Some groups may be disappearing. Within the society, there is physical movement of people, and there is migration into and out of the society, which augments or diminishes the number of persons in any given segment and area. These processes also occur selectively. These changes continually modify the general and specific numbers, the distribution, composition, and quality of the population.

Effects of Population Change

Population change is a dynamic affair. Needless to say, it has dynamic effects. Increase or decrease of numbers, for example, means a changing adjustment to environment. It also implies altered potentialities of social organization, in that it opens up new possibilities or imposes new limitations. A change in composition of the population, such as a marked increase in the proportion of the aged, requires or brings with it wide changes. In this particular instance it has produced notable changes in the economy (more products for the aged), housing (fewer detached family residences and more apartments), personal services (for example, medical) and recreational services (less participating recreation), the labor force, and education. It has also increased demands for special social services, such as pensions, and possibly a trend toward conservatism in all kinds of organizations and institutions.

In brief, the size, composition, and distribution of the persons of a society are of fundamental importance in its cultural and societal structure and organization, and the demographic processes going on within and about it have both direct and indirect effects among almost all social processes, functions, and relationships. Changes in size and composition *pari passu* bring changes in the relationships and hence in social structure, create demands for new functions to meet the changing needs and desires of the people, and set in motion new and revised processes. Population may be conceived of both as a principal permissive and as a principal limiting factor of social phenomena. Learning how to control demographic processes enables man to determine in some measure not only the size but also the organization and functioning of a nation.

It should be noted too that population bears a close and sharply delineated relationship to such vital aspects of a society as its science and technology, economy, government, nutrition and health, literacy and education, utilization of topographical, physical, and biological resources, ecology, positional arrangements and class structure, family organization, qualitative composition, international position, and even religious make-up. A knowledge of demography is essential in all theoretical understanding of human society, in all determination of policy—private, special-interest group, and public—and for all efforts at practical reconstruction. Social phenomena always involve aggregates of human beings.

Human Demographic Behavior

In general, wherever there is energy, there is a tendency toward equilibrium between the carriers of the energy and the forces of the medium within which they act (Chapter 4). Among living things this means that the organisms are ever seeking a state of equilibrium with all the factors of their environment that affect their life. In brief, there is a continuous and persistent tendency to effect what might be called an "organism-environment equation." Man is no exception to this elemental and essential tendency to achieve an equilibrium. The human species, like every other, is constantly in process of adjustment to its total environment.

Of crucial significance in this adjustment process is the ability to achieve adequate survivorship, so that an unbroken line of succession can be maintained generation after generation. This survivorship, fundamentally, is a matter of preponderance of births over deaths as these processes are affected by the physiological performance of the particular organisms in both fertility and viability. These performances, in turn, are determined in considerable measure by an array of factors in the total environments that augment and diminish both births and deaths. Among human beings, for example, the birth rate is below the fecundity, or potential physiological ability to reproduce, and the death rate is always above that which would exist if all were able to achieve the maximum possible life span of our species.

Any analysis of the organism-environment equation must start with an elementary analysis of the basic biological factors in the organism that are involved in fertility and mortality and those in the natural environment that affect births and deaths. This analysis will be made with special reference to man.

Basic Biological Characteristics of Man

There are three basic biological characteristics of man.

Sex Urge. The sex urge is powerful in man, as in all other species. But in man, a distinctive feature is that this urge is continuous throughout life for both males and females; it is not a matter of oestrus or seasonal periodicity. It is naturally affected in intensity by physiological vitality, which is affected by disease, nutrition, and organic and nervous conditions.

Reproductive Capacity, or Fecundity. The human male is able to inseminate females from adolescence to death, although this capacity tends to taper off in intensity and potency in senescence. Females are normally capable of conception and childbearing from between eleven and fifteen years of age to between forty-five and fifty years, although there are occasional exceptions at the extremes of the conception span. All other conditions being favorable, man has the capacity to double his numbers every seventeen years. Natural factors which reduce this capacity are physiological sterility, malnutrition, diseases of the organism, and injuries.

Life Span and Time of Death. The maximum life span of man is approximately one hundred years. In the vast majority of instances death falls far short of this biological maximum. Even the Biblical "three score and ten" is still beyond usual attainment, though Western peoples are approaching it.

Death is certain and is caused by malnutrition and starvation, disease and organic failure, and natural lethal conditions, including the catastrophes of nature. (25) Science, however, is ceaselessly trying to control these factors.

Basic Factors of Geographic Environment

The elemental factor in geographic environment is living space, that is, land or standing room. Land is never unlimited in amount or quality. Thus, it always sets definite limits to increase in numbers; for numbers can never increase beyond the supporting power of the habitat. There is always a maximum man-land ratio. The land area of the globe amounts to only about 57,000,000 square miles out of a total of 197,000,000 square miles, or roughly 30 percent of its total area, and most of this is not readily habitable and usable. It is estimated that at the present time 5 percent of the entire land area of the earth contains over one half the world population. (26, p. 268)

Three geographic factors limit human life and habitation and contribute to births and deaths. These are:

Terrain and Soil. The land surface of the earth is made up of mountainous areas, tundras, deserts, and swamps which preclude habitation and hinder movement and of great plains and river valleys which are conducive to both habitation and movement. In the main, torrid or arctic latitudes are difficult to live in, whereas temperate latitudes make habitation easy. Human beings normally thrive in the lower altitudes. Good natural soil, ultimately essential to sustain all forms of life, is relatively scarce, and the minerals, metals, and other important chemicals are not evenly distributed.

Climate and Weather. Extremes of rainfall or aridity, sunshine and cloudiness, heat and cold in particular areas discourage human habitation, as do very great seasonal variations. Human beings and societal life flourish during the favorable stages of the great climatic cycles and deteriorate in the unfavorable periods, such as the drought or ice age epochs.

Catastrophic Physical Forces. Catastrophic physical forces include volcanic disturbances and earthquakes, floods and tidal waves, cyclones, tornadoes and hurricanes, lightning, and natural fires which destroy human beings. Men gamble on escaping the devastation of these forces, however, in all parts of the world—our Middle West, Japan, Mexico, West Indies, to name a few.

Basic Biological Factors of Environment

In man's environment other forms of life fall into innumerable categories. But, in general, some of them are useful and beneficial to man, contributing food and a host of other materials essential to his life, and others are harmful, contributing poisons and causing injury, diseases, epidemics, and plagues.

These are the elemental factors in survival. The *actual reproductive performance* is dependent partly on the physiological health of both females and males and partly on the manner in which the instinctive sex urge is influenced and manipulated in bringing about actual conception. Every *actual death performance* results from some combination of insufficient standing room, malnutrition, disease and organic impairment, accident, and catastrophe, and, in the case of human beings, sometimes suicide. Thus, both births and deaths, *as they actually occur,* are due to innate genetic physiological capacity and influential environmental factors affecting the organism physically, psychically, and socially.

Below the human level this balance with nature is largely an automatic adjustment implemented by a process known as "natural selection." At the lowest life levels survival is a matter of enormous *fertility,* usually the maximum that the reproductive power of the various species and the environment permit, countered by an extremely high *mortality,* which is due to a combination of such natural conditions as overcrowding, starvation, fighting, destruction by other species and by conditions and changes within the physical environment. Natural selection acts ultimately through the death rate, for the survival process always involves an enormous expenditure of vital energy.

Higher on the life scale, forms of cooperation and other adjustment procedures which tend to preserve life and postpone death for greater numbers of the species are noted. These procedures, however, are largely reflexive or instinctive and are a matter of *natural selection.* Even at the monkey and ape level learned and creative manipulation is a limited aspect of adjustive behavior.

Another aspect of survival and balance in the organism-environment equation is the tendency of organisms that have any mobility whatsoever to "flow" or migrate. They seek to avoid harm or extinction in an environment by moving to a less hostile or more compatible one. This is also a phase of the process of natural selection. Men, too, individually and in varying numbers, have sought to improve their lot through migration. The movement of men has usually been conscious and has involved an array of socially motivating and socially selective factors, which will be discussed later. The distribution of men is always a temporary affair; there is never any final locational adjustment.

Manipulation of the Elemental Factors

In the preceding chapter we noted that man's adjustment to his physical and biological environment has never been purely passive, never a completely automatic submission or adaptation to physical and biological propulsive and selective forces and conditions. In the present chapter we shall see that his *demographic performance* has at no time been entirely automatic or simply natural, even among the most primitive peoples of whom we have any knowledge. There has always been a considerable measure of social selection by means of sociocultural processes. Wittingly and unwittingly man has intervened and mitigated the factors that affected his survival equilibrium through interactional processes. As he has become more adept culturally he has developed bodies of knowledge, sets of technics and techniques, and a social order that have enabled him to manipulate himself, his land, and a variety of other resources and, hence, in varying measure have enabled him to control his fertility, morbidity, mortality, location, and migration.

Human societies thus have been hostile to mere natural selection and have set limits to the struggle for mere existence. They have developed and utilized values and arts and higher levels of living which freed them from many of the life and death rigidities imposed by nature. Men have exercised preferences with respect to mating, birth, death, place of abode, and movements. These activities have sometimes been preventive, but frequently they have been highly creative and constructive.

Men have not been satisfied merely to subsist and survive. They have eternally sought a comfortable margin of safety and a quality of life. Even primitives have tried to limit conceptions and births and have engaged in euthanasia so that the survivors could weather the seasonal and climatic cycles. (19) Thus, men have persistently attempted to develop and maintain a favorable balance in their behalf. Moreover, in recent times in the Western world, men have been concerned with what the economists call "opportunity cost," that is, weighing the time, energy, discomfort, and inconvenience of child rearing against a host of social and cultural opportunities.

Some of the social action that has affected population performance has, of course, been shortsighted, and some has been highly detrimental to man's survival and has effected unbalance, as will be noted later. But distinctive and characteristic human demographic behavior is the result of sociocultural factors and processes, whether advantageous or detrimental. These sociocultural processes and factors in societies like our own not only influence but even determine the nature of the population and its changes.

Concretely, these processes and factors determine in considerable measure who shall marry whom and at what age; how many shall be born and to whom; who is more likely to die and how death may be persistently postponed; how many can live in an area and where, and what they do; who shall move and when and where. To understand the distinctive population conditions of a given society, it is far more important to understand the social processes, which affect the society, than the biological processes, which are shared with all organisms; for the social processes are ever modifying the biological. Men do not perform merely as biological specimens but as social beings.

Processes and Factors Affecting Population Numbers

The total number of human beings in a society affects the operation of that society in a multitude of ways. In a modern society these are important because they determine:

1. The size of the labor force and hence the human essentials for physical maintenance and for success in economic competition.
2. The man power for military action.
3. A population large enough to provide rich cultural interstimulation.
4. A basis for all the different kinds of division of labor and specialization of functions essential to a high level of group existence.
5. The amount and kind of political administration and other social processes and functions.

The major sets of processes affecting the numbers of a given popoulation occupying a given, usually politically determined, area are (1) those relating to *natural* increase, including the processes and social procedures, such as social movements, affecting marriages, births, and deaths; (2) incorporation procedures, whereby adjoining areas with their population are added to a given political jurisdiction through political or military action; and (3) migration, that is, the voluntary or involuntary movement of individuals and groups into and out of a defined area. The last is so important that it will be treated in a separate section.

Natural Increase and Decrease

The primary determinant of numbers of persons in different areas of the world is natural increase, or the preponderance of births over deaths. But it must be emphasized that natural increase among human beings is not entirely based on *natural factors,* that is, mere biological struggle for existence. Many formal and informal social-control processes, which encourage or retard marriages and births in different manner and degree for different segments of the population, and conditions and movements, which protect or conserve life and hence postpone death, are in effect in modern societies.

Marriage Selection and Marriage Differentials. Mating among human beings is not merely a matter of sex attraction and cohabitation. All known societies prefer that human beings be born of persons married in some combination, such as the almost universal combination of monogamy; hence, nearly all reproduction takes place within some form of marriage institution. The factors affecting marriage—those who do marry differentially within those conditions and the proportion of the total population that is married—are therefore important considerations in reproduction.

The elemental factor in marriage is meeting and the possibility of acquaintanceship. But a host of discriminatory factors determine who may or is likely to marry whom, when, and at what age. Following are some of the more important of these in our society:

INSTITUTIONAL CONTROLS OF MARRIAGE. Widespread political regulation of marriage involves a definite marriage contract, the establishment of a minimum age for both sexes, the proscription of bigamy or polygamy, and, varying among the states, waiting periods and health certificates, specific grounds for divorce, and the prohibition of intermarriage between members of certain ethnic groups. Celibacy is generally one of the conditions for males and females in certain religious orders, and among many religious groups great pressure is exerted upon lay members to "marry within the faith."

MORES AND CUSTOMS. The mores set up the standards on which acceptable or likely marriage depends among different segments of the population. In general the lower classes tend to marry at an earlier age and in greater volume than the upper classes. At higher educational levels people tend to marry later, and the greater the amount of education the less likely are women to marry. People are most likely to marry "within their class" and within their own or with closely related race or nationality groups. Similarly, native-born are more likely to marry native-born. The mores of different segments of the population also vary in the degree to which they permit the remarriage of divorced and widowed persons.

DEMOGRAPHIC CONDITIONS. An important factor in marriage is the *balance of the sexes* in any defined area. If the numbers of each sex of marriageable age are unequal, obviously some of the numerically preponderant sex cannot marry. Thus, for example, if there is an excess of males, there will be many bachelors and few spinsters, and vice versa. The *proportion of the age groups* also affects marriage. If the population is normal or consists principally of persons in early maturity, the marriage rates will be normal or above normal, other things being equal.

SOCIAL CONDITIONS. Marriage is closely related to economic conditions. Thus, in time of business depression with its attendant unemployment, the marriage rate tends to fall off, but the difference is usually made up as economic conditions improve. The birth rate will show corresponding fluctuations. Opportunities for the employment of women tend to reduce their likelihood of marriage or delay marriage, and certain occupations, such as school teaching, tend to isolate women from marriageable men and reduce the possibility of acquaintance. The length of training and the expense of preparation for the professions also tend to postpone the time of marriage and in marriages to reduce the number of offspring.

Urban-rural conditions are also important in marriage. Urban life, with its comfortable celibacy, based on bachelor apartments for both sexes, commercial eating facilities, and so on, and high cost of establishing a home, tends to reduce marriage. However, because of the preponderance of females in most cities, males have a higher marriage incidence in cities than females, and among all age groups, cities have more spinsters and widows and a lower proportion of married women. Urban conditions make both the divorced status and widowhood easier. Agricultural life, on the other hand, practically requires a "home plant," and females have a higher marriage incidence in rural areas than males. Migration directly affects the marriage situation at both the sending and the receiving points. These effects will be discussed later in connection with migration.

Birth Selection. Procreation is a highly private matter between one male and one female and always involves someone else who is going to be procreated in the future. It is not a matter of direct, immediate, individual survival or well-being. In fact, as most view procreation, it involves inconvenience, pain, strain, and expense. Hence, birth rates are subject to intentional personal control.

As is well known, for over a century, the general tendency of the birth rate among Western peoples has been persistently downward, although there have been fluctuations. The factors responsible for this will be discussed below. To get at the significant aspects of this flow, however, it is essential to examine the fertility variations among the different segments of the population.

The potential or actual reproducers are susceptible in different manner and degree to a great variety of social and cultural situations, pressures, and processes. These conditions provide them with diverse social standards and life achievement goals, which in turn affect their respective patterns of reproductive behavior. Hence, the birth rates are never the same for all segments and levels of the population, whether the tendency of the over-all rates is generally downward or upward. Therefore, it is of primary importance, first, to be conscious of the general birth differentials operative in a going society and then to have some comprehension of the sociocultural processes and factors that contribute to them.

The more obvious birth differentials, expressed quite generally and without detailed features or occasional essential qualifications, are noted here. Needless to say, they are interrelated and overlapping.

Regional Differences. The least progressive regions, or those most depressed and retarded, especially along economic and educational lines, have higher birth rates than the more advanced regions. For example, in the United States birth rates are highest in the Southeast and lowest on the Pacific Coast, although they are rising in the latter region as a result of recent changes in the age-group composition.

Rural-Urban Differences. Fertility is generally higher in rural areas than in urban areas. The largest cities have the lowest birth rates, but the birth rates become higher as the cities become smaller. Rural areas usually have the highest birth rates, and the rates among farm populations are higher than those for the rural nonfarm groups. Rural fertility is less near cities and increases as the rural residents are farther removed from cities. However, fertility has been decreasing more rapidly in rural areas than in urban, and also more rapidly among farmers than among nonfarm rural residents. In 1952, in some parts of the country, the rural birth rate was actually lower than the urban birth rate, and the urban birth rate was increasing.

Occupational Differences. In general, the fertility of urban occupational groups increases as we move down the list of occupational categories from professional, to business (these two constituting the white-collar workers), to skilled workers, to unskilled laborers. The birth rates for farm groups are not so divergent, but a differentiation is apparent, with owners lowest, renters next, and farm laborers the highest. Of all the urban categories only unskilled laborers approach the fertility of farm groups.

Differences among Educational Levels. Illitcrates have higher birth rates than literates. Married couples with only an elementary education have more children, on the average, than those with a high-school or college education. The differences between the latter two categories, however, are not great. Higher education, in addition to extra cost and time that are required, has the effect of causing later marriages and higher goals and, especially among women, of producing celibacy. In general, the higher the education of individuals the lower their fertility.

Differences in Socioeconomic Status. The socioeconomic status rests upon a combination of income, occupation, education, nativity, residence, and prestige on a scale of social rating and approval. In general, fertility tends to be highest among the groups with least favorable economic and social status, or those with the lowest plane of living. According to any index of economic status, the fertility rates of the underprivileged groups are generally higher than those of higher-income and propertied segments of the population. There is evidence, however, of a gradual upward trend in fertility among some of the upper classes.

Differences in Dependency. Recipients of relief are more fertile than the general population, but this must not be taken to mean that birth rates increase after families go on relief. The situation of reliefers is due partly to their relative social incompetence and partly to the difficulty of maintaining large families in difficult economic times and the financial inability to obtain contraceptive materials. The situation accentuates the general relation between poverty and high fertility.

Differences in Age at Marriage, Especially of the Wife. It has been consistently demonstrated that the earlier the age at marriage the greater the number of births.

DIFFERENCES IN RELIGIOUS AFFILIATION. In the United States, Catholics, Mormons, and members of fundamentalist sects have the highest fertility among religious groupings. The Mormons have the highest birth rates in the nation, although this is in part due to the fact that they are also predominantly rural.

DIFFERENCES IN I.Q. Families with the lowest I.Q. ratings (short of being feeble-minded) have the largest number of children, and those with the highest I.Q. ratings have the smallest number. In schools children making high scores in intelligence tests come on the average from smaller families than do children with low ratings. Such tested intelligence, however, bears a close relationship to family cultural conditions. Thus, children with inferior cultural-intellectual development tend to come from larger families than do those with superior development as measured by tests. (21, pp. 146-147)

DIFFERENCES IN RACIAL GROUPINGS. Minority racial groups, with a marginal status, usually have higher birth rates.

THE EXTENT OF ABORTION. The practice of abortion is largely in inverse ratio to the degree in which birth control is successfully practiced. The latter is primarily a matter of intelligence, educational level, economic status, and religious affiliation of the respective families.

In addition to these group differentials in fertility, mention should be made of two significant temporal differentials that apply to a society as a whole. The first is *prosperity and depression*. For most sections of the population, births are more numerous when the varied, combined economic processes are operating so as to produce prosperity. The other differential is *war and peace*. When males in early maturity are withdrawn from marriage and family life in wartime, births diminish. Usually there is a compensatory upsurge of births when the males return and normal family life is resumed.

In general, birth differentials rest largely upon *variations* in the diffusion, acceptance, and successful accomplishment of family-limitation practices (birth control) among different localities, different social-economic-cultural levels, and special (for example, religious) groups of the population, and upon *differences* in the socioeconomic ways and places of living of the different elements of the population. All of these are outgrowths of social conditions and situations, which in turn are all induced by social processes—but it is impossible to inventory every one of them.

Major Processes Affecting Fertility. The fertility differentials are due in large part to the varying degrees to which different segments of the population have been affected by, and become sensitive to, several intimately related social processes.

TECHNOLOGICAL ADVANCE, INDUSTRIAL REVOLUTION, AND INCREASE OF WEALTH. These related processes involve the industrialization-urbanization processes, the general significance of which has been discussed in Chapter 2. Here the specific demographic effects will be briefly discussed.

As industrial revolution develops in a society, it quite generally effects a revolution in reproduction. Owing to both urban and rural mechanization of industry, the general utilization of mechanical power, and the advances in transportation, resources can be much more proficiently and economically developed and utilized, and vastly more of them can be made accessible to more people. A great increase in the amount and range of wealth results.

As long as the increase of wealth means merely a movement upward from a bare minimum of subsistence to no more than sufficiency for elemental physiological needs of a population or portion thereof, it results in an increase of births. But when wealth increases beyond this sufficiency level and takes the added form of available decencies, comforts, and luxuries, it begins to have a restrictive effect among all sections of the population which desire these higher forms of wealth surplus. In brief, the standard-of-living factor begins to operate.

COMPETITION FOR A HIGHER STANDARD OF LIVING. Competition for a higher standard of living is essentially a psychoeconomic process. Wealth is a primary factor in the standard of living. But wealth is not equally divided, and there is therefore competition for its acquisition. Individuals desire more and more of the wealth, competitively acquired, for themselves, because wealth, or the more conspicuous and desired evidences thereof in the form of luxuries and conveniences, gives social standing.

Related to wealth are various highly valued social and cultural opportunities. In most instances, among the persons and segments of the population influenced by the standard-of-living factor, the economic and social wants increase in range and volume more rapidly than the means of satisfying them. But always there is the feeling of urgency to achieve an ever-higher standard of living and social position or at least to retain the one achieved. The humiliation of low status must be avoided.

SOCIAL DEMOCRATIZATION. In the case of our society at least, the opportunities for achieving higher standards of living have been accompanied by great gains along democratic lines. Caste barriers have weakened and classes are relatively open. Education is not merely a privilege, but to some extent is required of all classes and levels. The ballot is practically universal, and all can participate in political activity. Both physical and social mobility are possible. Legal sumptuary restrictions have disappeared, and all can buy and enjoy anything for which they can pay. These multiple freedoms and opportunities have given us, and have continually accentuated, what has been called "social capillarity," that is, the straining to reach the higher rungs of the social ladder. Among certain segments of the population a quasi-moral stigma comes to be attached to those persons who do not strive to raise their standard of living.

URBANIZATION. Urban life makes children a luxury, an inconvenience, and sometimes a liability for a variety of reasons. Here the social competition is intensified; the search for pleasure and culture is greater than in the country; the emancipation of women, including their growing economic independence and enlarged and diversified opportunities for employment, is more advanced; the cost of living is higher; housing is more expensive, living quarters more confined, play facilities and self-care of children are more limited, thus requiring more parental or institutional attention; and so on. In the rural areas, children are still an economic asset, in diminishing measure, to be sure. But the city family, as noted on page 36, has almost no productive functions as such. Furthermore, in the rural areas familistic religion and mores and the greater fixity and security of the family still militate less against offspring.

SOCIAL MOVEMENTS. Three types of social movements have contributed to birth-rate changes. *Humanitarian movements,* which inspired different kinds of social legislation, are one type. Child-labor legislation, invariably and of necessity accompanied by compulsory school-attendance laws, has added to the cost of child production. Although every socially minded person approves of these laws, it must be recognized that when children cannot engage in employment (save along certain restricted lines) and must attend school up to a certain age (for example, sixteen to eighteen years), they are an increased and prolonged financial burden that did not exist in a folk-agrarian society. The eugenic movement has also produced social legislation affecting fertility selectively. As a result many classifications of the unfit are legally segregated and confined in institutions to prevent them from reproducing, and sterilization of the unfit has been legalized in certain states and in some made compulsory.

The social movement of most far-reaching importance, however, has been the *birth-control movement,* for this provided the knowledge and the specific technics and techniques which made family-limitation desires effective. With contraception couples have a hygienic and fairly effective method of determining the number of their offspring and of spacing them. In recent decades these techniques have improved, spread to new areas, and percolated to lower levels in the class structure.

A third type of movement that affects fertility—one that is both ancient and modern—involves *birth recruitment* agencies and procedures. Governments have sought by indirect and direct means to stimulate births within the society in general and particularly among the upper class levels. Recruitment is not so widely resorted to in the United States as in Western European countries, but it will be noted that some of the forms indicated are in effect.

The principal positive forms of recruitment include loans on easy terms to couples contemplating marriage, often with the provision that the principal will be reduced with the birth of each successive child; family allowances to fathers in the form of cash grants or additional wages; measures to reduce family expenses connected with child birth; income tax exemptions and reductions for the wife and a certain number of children; special educational assistance for children of large families; maternal and infant clinics; taxes on bachelors; appeals to patriotism; marriage and birth premiums, and prizes for large families; and reduction of railway fares for expectant mothers. The most common negative forms are making abortion illegal and punishing attempts at abortion save under certain circumstances and making the giving of contraceptive information illegal or discouraging the diffusion of such information where it is not outlawed.

The downward trend of the birth rate begins as soon as the various interrelated subprocesses of an industrial revolution become effective in a society. The small-family system, with its more or less conscious limitation of the number of offspring, is one of the most important features of the demographic revolution accompanying industrial revolution. It is *not* due to any decline in marriage; in fact, there is more marriage in the United States. It is *not* due to later marriage; for marriage is occurring at earlier ages, especially for the American middle and upper classes. It is *not* due to incapacity to have children, since among most segments of the population there is probably greater vitality and physiological proficiency and better nutrition and fewer debilitating diseases. It is due to the fact that people *want fewer children,* and they can control the number they have. People attempt to control the size of their families to the extent that they have been affected by these modern processes and conditions.

Death Selection; Mortality Differentials. Life is precious to most people, and there is an almost universal desire to preserve it and to postpone death as long as possible. Hence, most people will gladly do everything they can to delay death. They will also wholeheartedly promote life-preserving social activities to the degree that they believe their own welfare is involved. Direct public action therefore has a much more important and direct effect in the reduction of death rates than is the case with birth rates.

Nevertheless, marked differentials in death rates exist. Deaths are not distributed proportionately according to the different social categories into which individuals may be classified, such as age, sex, race, economic condition, locality of residence, and marital condition. These variations are due in part to demographic and physiological factors, and also in part—and most significant here—to great variations in the degree to which different segments of the population are influenced and controlled by social situations and by *societal action* making for health and longevity.

The more pertinent death differentials follow. Like the birth differentials, they are interrelated and overlapping.

DIFFERENCES IN ECONOMIC STATUS. The economically advantaged in general have lower death rates and live longer. One can almost rank wealth levels inversely with death rates. The differential death rates in this connection are mainly due to differentials in quantity, variety, and quality of food and in housing, recreation, medical attention, and educational opportunity. They imply, in part at least, that adequate income and wealth surpluses are put into nutrition, sanitation, and health.

OCCUPATIONAL DIFFERENCES. Agricultural workers have the lowest mortality rates in the United States. Next above them are professional men and clerical and kindred workers. Then follow in order, with increasing death rates, proprietors, managers and officials, skilled workers and foremen, semiskilled workers, and unskilled workers who have the highest rates of all. (21, p. 188) Unskilled workers have a standardized mortality 2.3 times as great as that of agricultural workers. In general, those in the highest occupations have the lowest death rates and the longest expectation of life, and vice versa. This situation is due to a variety of factors. Unskilled workers are in part the misselected, the incompetent, and the physically unfit and are marginal as to vitality, intelligence, and personality. Occupations generally are somewhat selective as to vigor and capacity. There is also the interaction of the low wages of the unskilled, poor food, bad living conditions, inadequate health and recreational facilities, and the exposure to various types of illnesses and accidents.

RACE. Where there are ethnically heterogeneous groups, as in the United States, the colored, indigenous, and backward minorities have higher death rates than the dominant-majority people. Economic and cultural factors almost identical with those operative in the case of wealth and occupational groups are involved here. Presumed special racial factors can be eliminated.

RURAL-URBAN DIFFERENCES. It is much healthier and less hazardous to live in the country. For almost every cause of death and for both sexes and all ages, the death rate is, on the whole, higher in the cities than in rural areas, although there are occasional local variations. Some of the factors favoring the relatively lower rural mortality rate seem to be the lower density of population in the country, the greater integrity of the family, the outdoor character of agricultural work, the greater peace of mind, and a generally better adaptation of human beings to the rural environment. However, within recent years mortality conditions in cities have improved as a result of the greater provision of medical, hospital, and nursing facilities and services, improved housing, safeguarding of food and water supplies, improved protection against communicable diseases, and extensive health education. These gains have been more rapid in the city than in the country and in part offset the more healthful conditions of the country.

PLACE (INCLUDING REGIONAL) DIFFERENCES. Death rates vary from place to place and from region to region, not necessarily because of differences in natural conditions conducive to health, but because of economic and social conditions. The presence of considerable numbers of underprivileged racial minorities, of mining or other dangerous occupations, or of poverty and backwardness in education and in the development of sanitary facilities may be offsetting factors. The naturally healthy American Southwest has an abnormally high death rate as compared with those of other regions, owing in part to the fact that, as a health resort area, it attracts many persons ill of certain diseases and large numbers of elderly retired persons.

SEX-GROUP DIFFERENCES. Both prenatal losses and losses during the first year of life are much greater for males than for females, and at every age thereafter females generally have lower death rates and hence a higher number of survivors than males. Women seem to have a greater resistance than men to almost all of the more important diseases. Males are especially more susceptible to circulatory and blood disorders (about 50 percent more deaths than females), nervous disorders (about one third more), and diseases of the respiratory and digestive systems (about one quarter more). (50; 52) The life roles of males require a daily wider activity and greater competitive strain and usually entail greater exposure to disease, occupational and traffic hazards, and military risks. The greater life worries and frustrations are reflected in higher suicide rates for males. There seem to be good reasons for believing that males generally have less physiological vitality than females.

DIFFERENCES IN MARITAL STATUS. In general, married persons have the lowest death rates and the widowed and divorced the highest, with the single adults somewhere between. Marriage itself is rather highly selective with respect to both physical vigor and the social adaptability of those who marry. This is especially true of men, for those with ill-health and hence only limited ability to provide for a family are less likely to marry, and others who are neurotic, homosexual, or otherwise lacking in normal adaptability are likely to avoid family ties. Normal married life provides greater regularity of living and a better adaptation to life, physically and mentally.

AGE-GROUP DIFFERENCES. The death rate of children under one year of age is high. But it is somewhat lower for children one to five years of age. In the United States the period when death is least likely to come is between ten and fourteen years of age. The period between fifteen and forty-five is one of relatively low death rates, since the individuals have emerged from susceptibility to the diseases of childhood and have not yet succumbed to the degenerative diseases and organic impairments of senescence. Men between forty-five and sixty-five have higher death rates than women between these ages, and after sixty-five the death rates of men and women are more nearly the same. Males who survive age sixty-five are a pretty vigorous lot.

Infant and child deaths due to acute childhood diseases have been greatly reduced through better community sanitation, wider knowledge of infant feeding and hygiene, better maternal care and education, and improved levels of living. Modern science and the technologies have not been nearly so successful in conquering the chronic and other diseases of the upper age levels, such as cancer, diabetes, cerebral hemorrhage, heart disorders, nephritis, and pneumonia. (46)

Reduction of Death Rates. Certain processes and their attendant agencies are directly involved in the reduction of death rates to the lowest points known to man. These processes are *socially originated* and *specifically designed* to improve health, promote physical well-being, and enhance longevity. Most societies have institutionalized them. Unlike birth-recruitment activities, which have been sporadically and only partly effective, these mortality-reducing efforts have been generally and gladly accepted, supported, and conformed to. The major interrelated over-all processes follow.

TECHNOLOGICAL AND INDUSTRIAL REVOLUTIONS. These processes with their attendant physical and economic advances are among the most important factors in reducing death rates. They have made possible a greater quantity, superior quality, and greater accessibility of food and vastly improved nutrition as new lands were opened and other lands drained or irrigated; as agriculture was improved mechanically and chemically; as food processing in general was improved; and as transportation, distribution, and marketing facilities were developed. Housing and city planning were improved. Increased wealth meant higher real wages, higher levels of living, improved private sanitary and hygienic facilities, and surpluses that could be taxed to provide public health facilities and services. Engineering advance has favorably affected food production, flood control, sanitation, housing, and the development of all manner of protective devices.

MODERN MEDICAL, BIOLOGICAL, AND CHEMICAL ADVANCES. Modern medical, biological, and chemical sciences have made notable progress in the control of contagious and infectious diseases, both epidemic and endemic. The ravages of such epidemic diseases as yellow fever, bubonic plague, typhus, typhoid, measles, and smallpox have been greatly mitigated. Endemic diseases like hookworm and tuberculosis have been almost wiped out, and malaria and venereal diseases are in process of control. The development of serums, toxins, antitoxins, hormones, and vaccines (biologicals and pharmaceuticals) has resulted in a marked decrease in deaths from many other diseases. Contagion and infection have been greatly reduced through special hospital sanitary measures, isolation, quarantine, improved antiseptics, and scrupulous sterilization, and sepsis and gangrene have almost disappeared. Signal advances have been made in prenatal and postnatal care of mothers, in the care of infants, and in controlling the diseases of infancy and childhood. Modern surgery, through improved techniques and instruments, have saved untold numbers of lives.

Any considerable lowering of the death rate and increase in the expectation of life in the future depend upon mitigating the ravages of the degenerative diseases of late middle and old age, such as cancer and diseases of the circulatory and respiratory system, and of the internal organs. In view of the large amount of wealth and energy being devoted to these diseases, one can predict some measure of success. (43; 48)

HEALTH ACTIVITIES OF THE SERVICE STATE. The health activities of the service state have taken and are taking numerous forms, such as the regulation of working hours and working conditions, safety measures for machinery and dangerous materials, dusts, and vapors, and health and accident safeguards in mining. Provisions have also been made for proper care of the working-class ill and injured, better housing, street cleaning and sewage disposal, safe and adequate water supply, regulation of milk and other food supplies, the control of disease by means of quarantine and the provision of clinics and nursing services. Important also are governmental efforts in the prevention, control, and treatment of victims of catastrophes, the reduction of traffic hazards and internal disturbances, mitigation of the effects of warfare, and the provision of public recreation facilities and areas.

SPECIAL SOCIAL MOVEMENTS. Social movements that originate in and are promoted by semipublic organizations have done much to promote health and reduce accidents. Most notable are those that provide hospitals and nursing services for the less populous areas and group hospitalization, combat venereal diseases, and promote "Safety First," education in nutrition, recreation, better housing, city and rural planning, and detection and treatment of cancer, diabetes, and heart diseases.

Process of Incorporation or Annexation

Thus far in our examination of the increase or decrease of population we have been concerned with natural increase, that is, the preponderance of births over deaths and vice versa. There is a second general process that increases the *population of a given area* of interest or jurisdiction, namely, *in-*

corporation. This process does *not* involve the increase of numbers by excess of births over deaths. It is essentially a military or political process whereby an adjoining area with its population is added to the area of a given political jurisdiction. Population (by definition) is increased by extending the political boundaries of the area of count. It may occur through the military conquest of an adjoining weaker people and territory and their incorporation into the national territory, or by a formal procedure combining adjoining areas with the major body corporate, as when two counties are combined into a single one, or a city admits a suburb as part of its incorporated structure.

Migration and Its Effects upon a Population

Migration is the third general process whereby the population of a specific area may be increased or decreased. It also affects the distribution and readjustment of persons and institutions, but these aspects will be treated in later chapters.

The Effect of Migration upon Numbers

The numbers of the *world* population are not affected by migration, but only by an excess or decrease of births in relation to deaths. For any given area or society, however, the inflow or outflow of living human beings will add to, or subtract from, the total number in proportion to the movement. In a society like our own, with highly developed and far-reaching communications and ready private and public transportation facilities and with few political hindrances to movement, migration is a process of great significance.

In any specific area or society, the two major migratory processes are *immigration,* or the coming into an area or society of persons or groups from abroad, and *emigration,* or the departure from an area of persons or groups for another area. Both processes simultaneously affect an area, although at any given time there is usually a preponderance of one over the other. In the United States the criterion of movement is usually interpreted as change of residence, even though it be only to another apartment in the same building. The more significant interpretation from the point of view of numbers in an area is crossing a political boundary, which may be movement into or out of a precinct or ward, a town or city, a county, a state, a designated region, or a nation.

In the United States the numbers of persons added by international movement has been incredibly large—the largest movement into any country known to history. Between 1820, when the United States first began to keep accurate records of immigrants, and 1930, about 38,000,000 immigrants entered the country. Prior to that time an undetermined number of Europeans entered voluntarily as colonists and settlers, and an unknown but considerable number of African slaves were forcibly transported here. Throughout our history, within the national domain, there has been movement to the successive frontiers from abroad and from the older settled portions.

In recent decades there has been a large volume of migration from the Southeast region to Texas, the Great Lakes region, and the Pacific Coast area. The population of the Pacific Coast area has been phenomenally recruited by movement from all the rest of the country. In the United States in 1930 there were more than 25,000,000 persons living outside the state in which they were born and uncounted millions more living in the state, but not in the rural neighborhood, the town, or the city, in which they were born.*

Very great demographic significance attaches to the movement of population from the rural areas to the cities. Cities, especially the large cities, have never been able to sustain their population by means of their own reproduction. The rural areas have been the population reservoir which has supplied much of their replacement. In fact, the more urbanized an area the greater its dependence upon persons moving to it from the rural areas to make up its birth deficit.

Both immigration and emigration have profound effects upon the society concerned. *Immigration* introduces new and often conflicting ethnic and

*For a discussion of internal migration in the United States, see Chap. 9.

cultural elements into the place of settlement, with all the attendant tasks of adjustment. Often the labor supply, especially at the lower levels, is thrown out of balance; other difficult economic situations are produced; and congestion in certain urban areas is brought about. Processes of competition, conflict, ecological distribution, accommodation, and assimilation are involved. *Emigration* disrupts many of the established social structures of the home society, for example, families, neighborhoods, and industries, and distorts many of the essential maintenance and control processes.

Just as recruitment processes may be resorted to in an effort to increase birth, so they are often used to entice migrants into an area. Advertising of all manner of opportunities and benefits has been used to attract people to particular areas of the United States. In the past there were both informal and organized efforts to attract Europeans to American shores. Needless to say, there have been and are discriminations and exclusions.

Selective Aspects of Migration

Certain *selective* aspects of the migration process must be mentioned at this point because of their significance in connection with the composition of the population of given areas to be discussed in the next section. Notable selective aspects of migration are the following:

Age Selection. Except for back-to-the-land movements (in time of business depression), mass movements of refugee populations, and the movement of the elderly and retired to areas of salubrious climate, such as Florida or the Southwest, migration from an area carries away primarily older adolescents and young adults. The sending area, therefore, is likely to have an excess of children and the aged, while the receiving area has an excess of those in early and middle maturity. This condition is most apparent in migration from older areas to newer sections and pioneer or frontier areas of various kinds and in the country-to-city movement of people.

Sex Selection. Long-distance migration and newly settled areas or those undergoing new population-attracting developments are likely to attract an excess of males, while short-distance migration, especially rural to urban, and the areas of older settlement and in more or less static state are likely to have an excess of females. However, cities, with the exception of those of certain industrial types—so-called "heavy industries"—tend to attract more females than males. Hawley, however, points out that, especially with respect to migration from rural areas, females concentrate much of their movement at ages between eighteen and thirty. After age thirty and until age fifty-five males move in larger proportion than females from country to city. (61)

Fitness Selection. There is some evidence, although it is not too reliable, that those more physically fit, those more competent and alert and with energy, imagination, and other dynamic qualities, are more likely to move in free migration, especially for longer distances. The contention of Ross, first propounded in 1920, that migration specifically from the country to the cities attracts from the country those who are better physically, vitally, mentally, morally, or socially, and hence leaves in the country those who are poorer in these respects has not been supported by later evidence. If there is any noted selectivity, it is that the cities attract the extremes from the farms. (82, p. 528; 87)

Education. With respect to education the evidence of migration is more conclusive than in the case of general fitness. Migration seems to be selective of those with superior intelligence, superior scholastic performance, and high educational attainment. There is also some evidence that those with higher intelligence ratings and higher education migrate to larger cities and metropolitan areas and move longer distances.

In general, owing to the selective nature of migration, the fertility and mortality differentials of both the receiving and sending areas are modified, with the likelihood of marked future changes in the population, both quantitative and qualitative, and with respect to its age, sex, marital, occupational, ethnic, and class compositions.

As Hawley points out, migration is the means of effecting various kinds of demographic and societal changes and, at the same time, the most accessible evidence of such changes. (61, p. 346)

Factors and Processes in Composition of Population

The population of a modern industrial-urban society is infinitely complex in composition. It is composed of a vast number of demographic groupings and categories each with societally determinative characteristics. These diversities in make-up vary widely with the size and type of community and with areas and regions of the society. They are the result at any given time of a combination of historical and contemporary factors and processes. The nature and operation of these factors and processes are just beginning to be examined. What is known will be only briefly alluded to. The comprehensive analysis is the province and responsibility of demographers.

Each group, community, and region has a unique combination of these compositional characteristics. Hence, their reactions to stimuli and situations vary; all of their present and future relations and processes are affected thereby. To have some elementary understanding of them is essential to the comprehension of the functioning of a society as a "going concern."

Sex Composition

Sex composition is one of the elemental distinctions rooted in the biological nature of human beings. As noted, although males are in preponderance at birth, they have a greater mortality incidence at all ages throughout life, possibly because of inferior vitality. However, the major discrepancies in sex ratios in any given place at any given time are due mainly to social factors: primarily the selective effects of economic conditions, international and internal migration, and, in the past, war. The nature of agricultural economy and that of the other extractive industries is correlated with a preponderance of males. Heavy-industry cities also have an excess of males. Females are in excess in cities where there are light industries (for example, textile manufacturing), commercial activities, and corporate and governmental administrative activities and where there is much demand for personal and domestic service.

Migration, as noted above, invariably produces distortion—sometimes extreme—of the sex ratio, with males in excess among immigrants from foreign countries, in newly settled and frontier areas, and in areas where the population has been developed mainly by long-distance migration, and females in excess among migrants from rural to urban areas and in older, long-settled regions. In general, also, a young population has more males, an aging population, more females. The American population is tending toward femininity, owing in part to the curtailment of immigration and in part to the rapid aging of the population. An excess of females in a region usually indicates the extent of emigration or the effect of war. The excess of one sex or the other affects marriage, birth, and mortality rates, the status of women, the number and size of families, the type of available labor supply, and social-ethical attitudes.

Age Composition

Populations consist of age groups, designated either by arbitrarily selected years of life, such as birth to five, fifteen to twenty, sixty-five to seventy, or by the more general categories of infancy, childhood, adolescence or the teens, early, middle, and late maturity, and old age. Distortions of the normal age-group pyramid of an area or society are due to many factors. A falling birth rate in general means an aging population, whereas a rising birth rate indicates a younger population. The combined processes that increase life expectancy enlarge the proportion of the aged, but warfare, as formerly conducted only among military combatants with age-selected males, reduced the proportion of males in early maturity. Modern warfare, however, with its mass destruction of populations, is less discriminatory among age groups. Migration brings about distortions of age groups in both sending and receiving areas.

The general population group of greatest importance in the effective operation of a society consists of females roughly between fifteen and fifty and males between twenty and sixty-five. This is the reproductive period of females and the period when males are at their peak as social producers. Both sexes usually make their major cultural contributions during these years and constitute the productive labor force. The very young (under fifteen to twenty, depending upon the level of the society) and the very old (over sixty-five) compose a society's natural dependents. A disproportion of the young implies high and presently higher birth rates, lower death rates, and more child problems, and a disproportion of the aged points to procedures essential to old age security, care, and maintenance.

Age distribution and composition profoundly affect the attitudes and values of a people and determine not only the general run of attention but also whether they are or will be dynamic or conservative in outlook. All manner of future societal conditions and processes grow out of the present age composition. Because of the relative newness of the nation, the high birth rates in the past, and immigration, the United States has had a population preponderantly in the period of maturity; but there is now a definite tendency toward progressive aging. This situation is bringing about profound processual effects.

Racial and Nativity Composition

The presence in a population like our own of people of various races and nativities is mainly the result of slavery and immigration. The continued presence of these people as diverse and more or less separate ethnic types is partly a matter of cultural and marital discrimination and exclusion by the majority, partly, especially among the foreign nativity minorities, a matter of more or less voluntary social segregation and cultural in-turning as these groups maintain their language and culture, especially their customs, traditions, and their folk and institutional ways of life.

The presence of such minorities affects death rates. For example, Negroes, Mexicans, and Indians, who are invariably underprivileged and relatively impoverished, have higher death rates and so affect the society's death rate. The presence of most minorities disturbs sex ratios in a variety of ways, complicates processes of political and economic cooperation, education, and health, hinders religious unity, and develops processes of ethnic conflict, assimilation, and, eventually, amalgamation.

Marital Composition

In our society the general categories of marital status are the single, the married, the widowed, and the divorced. Each category is affected by social, economic, and cultural conditions and changes in the ratios of each category to the others are due to demographic and social processes. Eligibility for marriage is determined by customs and legislation which set a minimum age for marriage; economic and social conditions necessary for self-support and the establishment of a separate family unit; contact opportunities and cultural and class acceptances and discriminations determining who may marry whom; the sex ratios in the age and eligibility group; living conditions and values which make comfortable celibacy attractive; the prohibition of marriage for members of religious orders; and so on. Widowhood is directly related to the innumerable processes affecting health, freedom from accident, and survival. Divorced status depends upon the nature of permissive legislation, a host of conditions—economic, social, cultural—making marriage precarious, and the prevailing attitudes toward divorce, especially among religious groups.

Segments of the population, communities, and regions vary greatly in their marital composition. Foreign-born women are married above the average and Negro women below the average, as a result in each case of the ratio of females to males. In newly settled areas a large proportion of the marriageable women and a smaller proportion of the marriageable men are married. On the basis of rural-urban residence, the percentage of married men is highest in villages and lowest in the rural-farm population; the percentage of married women is highest in the rural-farm population and lowest in the urban population. Widows greatly outnumber widowers, mainly because most men marry women younger than themselves and the life expectancy of females is greater than that of males. Moreover, the tendency to remarry is greater among widowers than among widows. The widowed are more likely to live in towns and cities and in retirement regions.

A much larger proportion of the urban population is divorced, but states and regions differ greatly in the proportion of divorced persons. Each category has its own social psychic characteristics, modes of life, and problems of adjustment, and affects the "psyche" of the community in different ways.

Rural-Urban Composition

The technological and industrialization-urbanization processes of recent times are mainly responsible for the present diversities in a rural-urban composition. Agricultural mechanization and rural electrification are continually reducing the need of man power in rural areas and forcing young males and females to leave the farm. There is, of course, great variation in rural-urban ratios within states and regions. Thus, the state of New York has a great concentration of urban population in the south and is sparsely rural in the north. The northeastern United States and the Great Lakes region are preponderantly urban, whereas the plains regions are predominantly rural.

The fact that a given population is mainly urban or rural constitutes an important factor in its marriage, birth, morbidity, and death rates. Each type of population has its special values and peculiar outlooks on all manner of social issues. The diversity of outlook and way of life and the sharp cleavage of economic interest, despite the interdependence of country and city, create a continual conflict situation that expresses itself in numerous ways to be discussed in a later chapter.

Occupational Composition

The diversity of occupations in a society is both the index of its complex economic organization and the result of that organization. Technological development, the division of labor, and the specialization of functions are the main diversifying factors. The variety of occupations for males is infinitely great and is increasing for females as more married women engage in extra-home employments. In time the occupational categories change with respect to kind and number as industry and levels of living change. During the past twenty-five years, for example, there has been a vast increase in auxiliary occupations relating to transportation and distribution of products and persons, and to rendering various services.

The proportion of workers in different occupations varies from one district to another because of climate, location, resources, and other conditions, and the proportion of male and female workers also varies among occupations and districts. The occupational distribution directly and indirectly influences marriage, birth, and death rates, class differences, income levels, ethnic composition, and migration, to mention only the more obvious situations and processes, and thus affects the character of the social life of the community.

Socioeconomic Composition

The socioeconomic class composition is related to the immediately preceding compositional situation. There are great variations in income and distribution of wealth and hence in social prestige and position among individuals and families. The population tends to array itself in layers, with the broadest at the bottom and the narrowest at the top. A great range of economic, educational, ethnic and distributive processes are involved.

Because people vary in their ability to grasp economic and social opportunities and because there is continuous social mobility up and down the social scale, the personnel in each class category is continually changing. The kind, variety, and number of temporary members of different classes also vary among communities and regions. These differences in economic status help to make intelligible the differences in birth and death rates, cultural standards, and rates of advancement among population groups and areas.

Educational Composition

Since definitions of literacy vary, "schooling" is a more precise concept; nevertheless, the schooling that our population receives shows great variation in kind and amount. There are large numbers of persons who received all or nearly all their schooling in foreign countries. Some of these were just able to meet the reading test required of immigrants.

Among the native-born population a small portion is still unable to read or write, and among the so-called "literate" the schooling ranges from the barest elementary sort to the highest levels of graduate study. The amount and kind of education vary with the economic level of the individuals and groups, race and nativity, sex, and community, state, and regional educational facilities. Thus, we find that Negroes and Mexican-Americans receive far less education than whites; that educational facilities are usually far from adequate in rural areas; that the North and West have the highest general level of education; and that females are slightly better educated than males. Educational levels affect fertility and mortality and the health conditions of communities and regions. They also set the tone of communities and are correlated with almost every type of activity of a society.

Religious Composition

In a heterogeneous, secularized society like our own, there are great differences in religious interest and affiliation. There is, of course, the major cleavage between Catholics and Protestants, and the Protestants in turn are divided into more than 250 denominations, each supposedly having some distinguishing principle of faith. Some of this religious diversity is associated with nationality and the European area of origin of immigrant stocks, but the tendency toward infinite splintering in large measure results from the absence of a state church and our constitutional commitment to the principle of freedom of thought and belief. Various Protestant denominations and sects can be roughly correlated with socioeconomic classes, educational level, urban or rural residence, and section of the country, as well as with race and nationality origin.

As noted earlier, religious affiliation has a direct relationship to fertility. It also affects the conservative or liberal attitudes of people on a variety of social issues. Freedom to proselyte as well as to believe fosters competition and leads to recurrent bickering and conflict among and within religious groups.

The Population-Blending Processes

Amalgamation is the universal population-blending process. It consists of the cross-breeding or intermating and biological blending or mixing of divergent groups, usually racial or nationality groups. Most of the blending of diverse nationality elements in our society has come about through the marriage relationship, but some interracial mixing has been without benefit of matrimony. Amalgamation takes place in some degree wherever and whenever the interactional processes produce physical contact, and it occurs despite antagonistic social attitudes, prohibitory mores, and legislation. The greater the length of time that the diverse elements are in contact, the greater is the tendency to amalgamate.

Although amalgamation is a biosocial process, it is closely related to assimilation, or the cultural and social blending and unification of peoples. There may be much, often unconscious, reciprocal borrowing of culture elements between racial groups in contact with each other. However, if some of these racial stocks have obvious physical characteristics which set them apart, cultural discrimination and exclusion, efforts at physical segregation, and much formal objection to both assimilation and amalgamation, especially on the part of the self-styled "superior" racial stocks, are likely to develop. "Miscegenation" is the term applied to the amalgamation of social stocks deemed contrary to the mores and the laws.

Nationality groups, if not highly diverse racially, assimilate rather readily. When the descendants of nationality groups have achieved a considerable degree of cultural similarity, they are likely to amalgamate freely and without objection. Both assimilation and amalgamation are likely to be accepted not only in the folkways, but in the mores, and both are facilitated by the institutional mechanisms. In the United States amalgamation has proceeded apace among all of the older foreign elements and between them and the native stocks. Assimilation and amalgamation each usually, though not necessarily, lead to and hasten the other.

Amalgamation may be *coercive,* usually taking the form of sex relations between the males of the dominant and the females of conquered or enslaved population elements. Such amalgamation may in time aid assimilation if the ethnic and cultural gaps are not too great; it often tends, however, to accentuate existing antagonisms and prevent or retard assimilation. Amalgamation may be *voluntary or free,* occurring usually after generations of communication and among different nationality groups, rather than among markedly different ethnic stocks. Voluntary amalgamation implies that a high degree of cultural similarity has been achieved, and that no strong feelings of difference, estrangement, or superiority-inferiority exist. Thus, intermarriage is not only permissible, it is in the mores. Voluntary amalgamation usually flows from effective assimilation.

Eugenic and Euthenic Processes

Both eugenic and euthenic processes are consciously inaugurated and largely take the form of social movements, although some aspects of both types have reached the point of implementation through legislation and public administration. The central function of the processes, as developed by their proponents, is to improve the quality of individuals in terms of mental capacity, physical vitality, and energy and the social adequacy of the population generally.

Eugenic Processes. By means of the eugenic processes, people seek to avoid biological drift and improve the hereditary quality of the population by methods of directed selective breeding, the underlying postulate being that vitality and adequacy are first of all matters of inherent capacity. Eugenic processes rest upon cold genetic calculation. Their effectiveness depends upon knowledge of human genetics, which is admittedly inadequate though in process of development, and institutions in so far as these permit the manipulation and influencing of human beings in the highly private matter of procreation. The justification of the efforts rests upon the facts that all procreation is directly related to the efficiency and survival of a society. The processes fall into two major categories, negative and positive, both of which relate to the fertility differentials discussed above.

Negative procedures seek to reduce and prevent the degeneracy of the population by retarding the birth rate among the inferior individuals and segments of the population. They rest on the contention that a variety of social processes affecting the population produce misselection. This misselection results in the societally deleterious procreation of defectives, weaklings, and those liable to congenital mental and physical disease. The misselection of war tends to remove the physiologically and mentally adequate males in early maturity and leave at home for uninterrupted procreation those who do not meet the requirements for military service.

Thus far the implementation of negative eugenic objectives has taken the following forms:

Marriage laws have been enacted in most states to prohibit the marriage of persons with hereditary neuropathic and mental taints, innate physical stigmata of degeneracy, and vicious transmissible diseases, and require medical certification of freedom from these defects.

Information on contraceptives has been made available to, and effective among, the less competent of the population elements. In this country these efforts have included the sporadic provision of semipublic "maternal health clinics," by private organizations, but in some countries, notably the Netherlands, such clinics are established and supervised by the state.

Sterilization of defectives is provided for by the laws of certain states. Upon the recommendation of special boards of examiners and with the consent of relatives, defective persons in specific categories can be subjected to surgical operations which make them physiologically incapable of procreation.

Segregation of defectives and degenerates under supervision in properly equipped institutions or colonies is carried on in many states. The sexes are separated and thus prevented from reproducing.

Positive procedures consist of influencing the physiologically, neurologically, and mentally sound individuals and segments of the population to procreate in greater measure than they do under the small-family system and the fostering of such procreation by various measures. These implementive procedures take various forms, such as the following:

Family allowances and other economic and educational aids are provided for families of "quality."

Class sentiments regarding the desirability of the small family are being subjected to new propaganda. This includes toning down the ideology of sacrificing offspring beyond a certain minimal number to ascent of the "social ladder," moral persuasion, and patriotic pressures.

Eugenic education is provided. This consists of playing up the idea of genetic stewardship and developing a eugenic conscience on the part of the fit and capable.

Certain forms of temporary or permanent celibacy are being alleviated or abolished. Occasional present-day rules in school systems that prohibit the marriage of female school teachers are being modified, and the conditions which practically require postponement of marriage or at any rate progeny among persons working for high professional proficiency are being changed. There is also the suggestion that celibacy requirements in religious orders, whose members are invariably carefully selected persons, be abandoned.

The difficulty with both negative and positive eugenics is that we are not too certain about the distinction of inferior and superior people. We need better biological, psychological, and social definitions and better tests for determining and measuring capacity than we now have. Only about 1 percent of the population consists of idiots, imbeciles, and congenitally malformed persons, and only 1 to 3 percent are morons and borderline feeble-minded persons. (104) On the other hand, superiority is not necessarily a matter of location in upper-income or upper-occupational classes, higher educational levels, or any other opportunity or prestige classification. In our society these segments of the population have been continually produced from, and replenished by, the lower classes. Furthermore, it is well-known that people of all classes resist supervision and preaching in connection with their procreative activities.

Euthenic Processes. The euthenic processes are concerned with the necessity of providing good environment. They are based on the principle that all the invironments of man directly or indirectly affect the quality of a population. If contemporary environments were more adequate, there would be fewer physical, emotional, and mental misfits and a larger number of healthy and adequate individuals. Hence, euthenic procedures consist of efforts at planning and manipulating the physical, biological, and social environments in order to make them more conducive to human well-being. They take the form of both informal and organized activities which are presumed:

To produce good health and vigor or, conversely, to reduce sickness and accident, implying a whole array of physical, biological, chemical, and social controls.

To produce hygienic living through better nutrition, adequate rest and sleep, wholesome and adequate recreation, better conditions of labor, safe and sanitary housing.

To bring about a reduction of poverty, a better distribution of wealth, and the reduction of socioeconomic and regional differentials in well-being.

CHAPTER IX

PROCESSES OF ECOLOGICAL ORGANIZATION

WE HAVE NOTED that every society has a cultural structure and a demographic structure, both of which are the result of various processes and are in process of continual modification. In a later chapter we shall examine the complex group structure of a society. Here we are concerned with the fact that every society has locality. Therefore, it also has a territorial or ecological organization. A society consists of human communities, each located in a more or less determinable area, that are the result of the movement and concentration of people and their essential utilities. At any given time these communities have characteristic areal or spatial patterns of individuals, groups, and institutions, and the different elements of the community are in a state of mutually dependent, symbiotic relationship within the community area.

The different types of communities are scattered about the entire area of the society, but they also are related to each other by various linkages of dependency. The spatial relationships and distributional patterns of human beings, groupings, and institutions both within communities and among the constellations of communities that constitute a society are in continual process of modification in time. In fact, in modern societies with their vast areal extent and all their technologies and accessibilities the movement and redistribution of elements is rapid and great in volume and effects.

The elemental fact is that the areally distributed and separated organic segments are not isolated and self-sufficient units, but are related and interdependent units in a complex organization. Thus, in a city the manufacturing, jobbing, retailing, recreational, and residential sections are functionally related to each other. The city and its hinterland are meaningless and functionless without each other, and the different sections of a country with their varying major functions and cultural specialties are dependent upon each other. Regions too are interdependent, and even nations and larger world areas are to an extent functionally related. At the other extreme, however, every local community exhibits a more or less definite constellation of the individual units that compose it, and all the elements are continually in process of changing location and relationship in the area.

Obviously, the social analyst should have some knowledge of the repetitive regularities in the spatial movement, distribution, and locations of individuals, groups, and institutions as well as of the processes producing their characteristic arrangement and changes in their relationships and positions. Ecological position has a direct bearing on social contacts in determining their direction. Ecological processes mark the boundaries of local communities within societies and set the patterns and sequences of change of arrangement of population and institutions. Ecological organization furnishes the framework of society.

Fundamental Ecological Processes

Competition

Ecological organization and all the processes incidental to the movement, location, and relationship of individuals, groups, and institutions rest fundamentally upon *competition* among these elements within an area and among accessible areas for a place where they can not only survive but exist most advantageously. The struggle for existence within the competitive network produces the division of labor and specialization of function among the population elements and service organizations, and within and among the different areas.

Competition functions selectively in bringing together in particular places or spaces, according to their function and institutional strength, the various types of activities, and the persons and groups that conduct them. It is the propulsive factor responsible for the movement or dispersal in space of individuals, groups, services, and institutions from places of lesser advantage to places of greater advantage. This advantage is more than economic; it includes advantage of status, power, and prestige as well.

Equilibrium

The characteristic distributional pattern of the various functional units of the area or of related areas is based on the tendency of the units to find an equilibrium or balance, although this balance is never completely stable. The continuous nature of competition produces imbalance and disequilibrium, which are countered by continuous readjustment in place and function. Hence, there tends to be a moving equilibrium. The very effectiveness of the differentiation and specialization of function of the interdependent but competitive elements and areas indicates, however, that the relationship is one of reciprocal and complementary advantage and, hence, of cooperation on a large scale. Perhaps Hiller's happy term, "competitive cooperation," describes the general nature of this fundamental process (10)

Sociocultural Human Ecological Processes

The Biosphere

The competitive struggle for existence in plant and animal societies is automatic and entirely a matter of natural selection among the organisms and species within a given physical environment. This struggle brings about a distribution of individuals and species that enables each to live in the place where it can thrive best; that is, to live where it encounters the least stifling competition with other organisms and species and where it can live symbiotically.

This automatic competitive-equilibrative-cooperative struggle for existence and living space and for a place for plants and animals occurs in the ***biosphere,*** as J. Arthur Thompson called it (28, p. 354) and produces a biotic community. Here the interaction is purely that of biological creatures; the activity is at the subsocial and subthought level, and is noncultural in nature. The biotic community is determined entirely by natural phenomena operating in the physical and biological environments.

There is still a tendency among ecologists to

think of human ecological organization and interaction as being primarily at this level. According to this so-called "orthodox" view, the ecological processes operate with a high degree of predetermined and natural inevitability, and the human and social elements follow the line of least resistance. Some ecologists who maintain this point of view may admit, however, that human ecological interaction is always complicated by the presence of social interaction. More and more, one must conclude that human ecological processes are as different from plant and animal ecological processes as human societies generally are different from plant and animal societies, and mainly for the same reasons.

The Sociosphere

Human ecological interaction takes place in what may be called the "sociosphere," or the "biocultural sphere." * The sociosphere is the sum total of environments as modified and created by man. It is the result of human thought, volition, plan, and contrivance. Man's territorial interactions, like all others, are organized and regulated by means of his sociocultural system. Hence, men, through social forces and processes, become in considerable measure the determiners of their physical, biological, and social environments. In human ecological organization and action, the factors of the biosphere *are* unavoidably involved; but the sociosphere has been superimposed upon the biosphere, giving human ecological occurrences their distinctive features.

The significance of social situations and culture becomes clear when we note some of the factors in ecological organization and processes. Geography, in terms of terrain, climate, and resources, is, of course, the fundamental factor. Individuals and groups must have location on the terrain, and the sites and areas occupied must be such that men can live and prosper. They must have natural resources as a basis for sustenance, productive work, and exchange, and they must have routes of accessibility to each other. But an infinite array of cultural and societal factors affect every one of these conditions. For example, sites are often chosen for reasons other than natural suitability. By means of planning and engineering hills may be leveled, swamps drained or filled, arid areas watered, and shore lines extended, if social necessity or desire so indicates. Resources may be modified and barriers to accessibility removed or surmounted so that physical distance is diminished in effect and communication and transportation improved in means and speed.

Thus, man-made changes in agriculture and other extractive industries, manufacturing, communication and transportation, markets, ethnic relations, and other activities become primary determinants in the movement of peoples. Tariffs, transportation rates, and restrictive covenants become primary determinants in the movement of things which people process or consume at different places. Educational, recreational, religious, or political considerations may override biological and economic factors in both location and movement.

All human competition is a *social* process. It is regulated by the folkways, mores, beliefs, values, and institutions of the society. Changes in culture generate changes in the forms and effects of competition among men and hence produce modifications in the spatial relationships. Nowhere are men completely dominated by natural law. Ecological processes cannot be understood solely in terms of "biotic," "subsocial," "natural," "impersonal," or even "strictly economic" factors. Increasingly, the pertinent, even determining, factors are interests, sentiments, traditions and customs, motives, values, plans and policies, sciences and technologies, and institutions with their charters and controls.

Initial Process of Settlement and Typical Configuration

The competing-cooperating people of a society are assembled in different parts of its territory in the form of aggregations or clusterings. We speak of these separate functionally organized clusterings, each occupying a particular amount of the total area, as *communities.* They too are a matter of process.

*Unpublished paper of George I. J. Dixon.

The Initial Process of Settlement

Settlement is the initiating interactional process of collecting or assembling human beings and their utilities as a community in an area or location. The aggregates are formed at places where nature and man have made conditions favorable for the satisfaction of individual and social needs. Individuals and groups take possession of an area and live in it. This is not to imply that the community as settled is one of fixed position or permanent form; it will likely undergo sequences of rearrangement in form as time goes on.*

These communities vary in size and density and in combination of purposes involved in their formation. But each is a more or less separate, self-conscious areal unit, one of a constellation of interdependent and cooperating aggregations constituting the society as a whole. The inhabitants of the community have a demographic structure. They form a characteristic population pyramid with respect to age groups, sex ratio, nativity, and occupational composition. Each community has a pattern or configuration of spatial distribution of its different population elements and its institutions, and each has both a general and a special functional organization, depending upon its part in the general division of labor.

Typical Ecological Aggregations. The typical ecological aggregations of varying size and organization in our society are neighborhoods, rural communities, hamlets, villages, towns, cities, metropolitan areas, and regions. In these, each element and each subarea plays a pertinent part in the total competitive areal organization, which is contingent upon the conditions and the range of functions of the particular elements involved. At the same time a given area may be part of several or many ecological systems, depending upon the particular larger competitive-cooperative situation. For example, the manufacturing section of a city may at the same time have great functional significance (1) alongside the retailing, jobbing, residential, and other sections of the city; (2) as a part of the metropolitan area; (3) in the region; (4) in the nation; and (5) in world organization, especially from the point of view of economic production.

While the whole array of sustenance and maintenance functions must be performed in each community if its population is to endure, the communities may differ considerably in their special functions. They may function mainly as dwelling and service centers for the extractive industries in the area; as primarily resort or recreational towns or cities; as centers for educational, religious, or cultural activities; heavy industry, textile, or residential towns or cities; or they may be so strategically located that they carry on a complex multiplicity of industrial, commercial, communicative, transport, professional, personal, and cultural services for a vast surrounding metropolitan area and, in some instances, for remote areas of the earth.

Factors in Settlement of a Community. The closely related factors involved in the formation and location of communities are: (1) the "natural layout" in the way of topography or terrain, favorable climate, and various natural resources, which may be occupied or utilized; (2) the residential and business buildings, the constructed means of communication and transportation, and the other products of technologies; (3) population, that is, the types of population to be served, the essential labor supply, and so on; (4) facilities for the production of commodities, the transportation of things and persons, and the exchange of commodities and services; and (5) specific cultural elements, such as traditional requirements, educational, recreational and religious facilities, governmental facilities and hindrances, and other interests and purposes. These function as the collective base upon which areal aggregates form and re-form, each factor being interdependent with the others.†

In the process of settlement or concentration, an ecological organization or system is formed that is based upon the dominance of some population groupings, institutional utilities, and subareas and the subordination of others. In the course of the same process there is an integration of the diverse elements into a cooperative whole. Each subarea, for example, becomes specialized with reference to population, institutions, and functions, and each

*The term "concentration" is also used by some sociologists in connection with this initial assembling process, and some human geographers use "occupance" to describe essentially the same process.

†On the distribution of people among cities and the location of cities, see references 49; 50.

area becomes mutually interdependent with others. Only thus can the stability of the territorial organization and the operation of the societal superstructure which functions in it be assured.

The Typical Configuration

Cities and their organizations and institutions dominate the sociocultural life of an industrial-urban society like our own. They function especially as the focal points in the occupation and utilization of the land area. As of April 1, 1950, the urban population was 95,892,000, or 64.0 percent of the people of the United States. Of these, 68,788,000, or 71.7 percent of the total urban population, lived in 157 so-called "urbanized" or "metropolitan" areas. An urbanized area consists of at least one city of 50,000 or more and its urban fringe. Included in these 68,788,000 metropolitan dwellers were 47,988,000 inhabitants of the central cities and 20,800,000 inhabitants of the urban-fringe areas. One quarter of the population of the United States resided in twelve urbanized areas of 1,000,000 inhabitants or more, with a combined population of 37,595,000.

The remainder of the total population of the United States, 53,964,000 persons, constituted the rural population. Of these, 29,629,000, or 19.8 percent of the total population, were the rural nonfarm population, living in unincorporated villages and towns of less than 2,500 population and not contiguous to cities, or living in the open country but not on farms. The number of persons living on farms amounted to 24,335,000, or 16.2 percent of the total population. (51)

The population of a region and its sociocultural instrumentalities thus is a configuration of residents of variously spaced and scattered (on the basis of terrain, resources, and functions) metropolitan areas and cities, each with its hinterland; of small towns and villages; and of open country. All the parts are connected by a communication and transportation network.

The bulk of the population is concentrated in the urbanized areas, and the cities themselves are the centers for the entire society. The cities serve as trade, industrial, political, social, and religious centers and as foci of transportation and break-of-transportation points. They are also concentration points for all manner of specialized services—recreational, professional, cultural, and so on.

The typical and by all odds the most important component of the ecological configuration of the region is the city, involving as it does the largest proportion of the population and its institutionalized agencies. The modern city is not a formless and meaningless agglomeration of people and services, but has an ordered pattern of distribution and organization. Definite areas are allocated to certain kinds of land uses, and certain tendencies of ecological structure are always clearly evident, as in an aerial photograph or land use map.

No two cities show the same configuration. In the first place, each city has its peculiar terrain, and its configuration will be affected by rivers, lakes, elevations, swamps, and other conformations, which greatly influence the location of persons and buildings, the lands reserved for specific uses, and the transportation arteries. Second, cities differ in their combinations of institutions and in the services they render the surrounding area; that is, they may be mainly commercial, industrial, residential, political, religious, recreational, or educational centers.

In general, however, cities are irregularly star-shaped and multicentered. The spine of each point of the star is a transportation artery radiating from the center. The subcenters are at and around the main intersections along these arteries. Usually there is a decline in the percentage of land covered by buildings, a decline in land values, and a marked change in the type of land use as one goes from the center to the periphery and also as one moves back from the main transportation arteries. The general pattern of ecological units is as follows:

The "Downtown" Business District. The "downtown" business district is the center of the community. Here the major transportation lines converge and the density of pedestrian traffic is greatest. Practically all the land is covered by buildings and streets. In the smaller city the retail shopping, financial, and office buildings will all be within a few blocks of each other along a main street or at or near the intersection of several main streets. In the big city the department stores will be at or near the points of greatest pedestrian concentration, with near-by special sectors given over to specialty shops, theaters, financial district, corporation and professional office buildings, hotels, and so on. At the fringes of the central business district there will be smaller and cheaper shops, restaurants, hotels, and theaters, as well as parking areas, garages, and railway and bus depots.

In the larger city there will be bands of commercial growth or string-like development of stores, banks, and office buildings extending along one or more of the main thoroughfares radiating from the main business district.

The Wholesale, Jobbing, and Light Manufacturing District or Districts. These districts are on essential transport lines (streets, railways, harbor, river front, and so on) but readily accessible to the main business district and to the radial arteries of transportation.

The Heavy Industry Districts. Heavy industry is usually on cheaper land where the plants have rail, water, or highway transportation facilities, such as in river valleys, along canals, on the river or lake fronts, or along the outer truck and railway belt lines. Heavy industry increasingly requires much land for one-story production-line layout, storage, and parking space for employees. Hence, there is a tendency for it to move toward the outskirts.

Residential Areas. In American cities residential areas utilize the largest proportion of all privately developed land. Bartholomew, in his study of sixteen cities with populations between 5,000 and 300,000, found such land to be about 80 percent of the total. (31, pp. 25; 36; 46) Residential areas vary widely in type, size, shape, and location and in the preponderance of single-family, two-family, or multifamily structures and the yard space related to each structure. They vary also as to income, ethnicity, occupational level, and socioeconomic class of occupants and include segregated race and nationality districts, slums, rooming-house, workingmen's, and middle-class districts, Gold Coasts, and areas of large, single-family holdings. The various types may take the rough form of curved bands between concentric circles radiating out from the center, of rectangular or circular areas of several or many blocks and parts of blocks, of wedges extending along radial lines from the center toward the periphery, with lower-rent wedges in between.

Usually, as one goes from the center of the city to the periphery, residential use of land tends to become less intensive as multiple-family units are succeeded by two-family structures, and these in turn by single-family dwellings. The amount of yard space also increases. There may, however, be an intensive residential use of land on heights or lake or ocean fronts, near parks, and along fast transportation lines. There are usually transition zones between different adjoining types of residential areas, and high-rent areas shade into intermediate-rent zones and these into low-rent zones. Every city differs in the pattern of its residential areas, depending upon its topography, its industries, its special institutional services (for example, a university or state capitol), the location of its transportation arteries, and its subcenters, prestige areas, and so on. (42, pp. 23-80)

Subcenters. Throughout the city there are *subcenters, or lesser business districts,* on the main arteries at their intersection with crosstown transportation lines. Here more general, continuously needed, and less specialized (neighborhood) services are rendered than at the main center. Land uses and values grade down from the center to the periphery of these subareas. Other significant subcenters may be around an art museum, a college, or a university.

Parks and Other Public Recreational Areas. Parks and other public recreational areas are increasingly found in most cities. The smaller ones are likely to be contiguous to business and intensively used residential districts, and the larger ones utilize accessible river valleys, lake or ocean fronts, or land with special topographical and historical characteristics.

Estates and Suburban Areas. At the outer reaches of the city and just beyond will be the large-estate and country-club areas, the suburbs, the holdings of the rural-dwelling but urban-employed families. Farther out will be the market-gardening, greenhouse, and poultry-raising sections interspersed along the trunk highways with roadhouses, taverns, out-door theaters, motels, fruit and vegetable markets, and so on.

Agricultural Areas. Beyond the city's fringe is the great agricultural area of the city's hinterland, which shades into the hinterland of the next adjoining cities.

Hinterland. In the hinterland are also the more distant commuter areas, the city's separated satellite "dormitory" or residential towns and cities, and its satellite industrial towns and cities. These are usually situated on the rail and highway transportation axes running out from the central city. There is likely to be open country around these towns and between them and the central area.

Primary Determinants in Configuration

The primary determinants in a fairly orderly arrangement of populations and their facilities in community space can be only briefly considered. The following are the most obvious:

The Interdependence of Men and the Land. The interdependence of men and the land requires that the people must have access to each other and be in relatively close proximity to each other to produce and exchange things and services. At the same time, since land space essential to each activity is always limited, men and their works must be somewhat dispersed and distributed.

Land Use and Land Values. Patterns of nucleation and dispersion are the principal results of land use and land values. The most intensive, expensive, and strategic activities (for example, retailing, and major financial operations) must be carried on at the focal center. Here the land is intensively used, and land values are high. Other activities, such as manufacturing and wholesaling, are less intensive and require more land; hence, these can be somewhat removed from the center. Still other activities, such as residence, can be further dispersed and take place where land values are lower or where they are compatible with specific types of residential needs. These limitations of land use and land value thus influence the pattern of activities.

Function of Space and Time-Energy Cost. Space and time-energy cost are dependent upon what Hawley has called "the friction of space." Space presents obstacles and resistances; it is a matter of distance. It is something to be passed over and so calls for an expenditure of time and energy. Transportation and communication to produce the contact essential to activity always encounter this friction, however efficient they may be, and it cannot be overcome. Thus, the territorial pattern of collective activity is largely the product of the friction of space as manifested in time-energy cost, in moving from place to place, in order to conduct essential activities of varying degree of social pertinence. (30; 41)

Primary Dispersal–Migration

In the preceding chapter migration was briefly discussed as a process of demographic significance, especially as it augments or diminishes the numbers of a particular population by immigration or emigration, and one which also exercises various selective effects upon the composition of a given population. Here we are concerned with it as a process of great ecological importance, namely, as the process of distribution and redistribution in space of persons and groups and, unavoidably, of the culture they take with them.

The Nature of Migration

By migration as an ecologically significant process *we mean the physical, horizontal, and linear movement of persons or groups from one locality or community to another, usually in order to establish a more or less permanent new residence.* As such it is the essential enabling process in the change of spatial location of individuals and groups. It may be considered in either its spatial or temporal aspects, the former indicating the direction and place of movement, and the latter the frequency or time of movement. Our interest here is in the spatial aspect.*

Migration bears a direct relation to the two other major processes of ecological importance just discussed. Fundamentally, it grows out of the competition among the residents of an area or society. Because of known or presumed variations in the physical, socioeconomic, and cultural conditions in different areas and under the sway of universal competition, human beings tend under this pressure to move about or are moved about by others so that some individuals and groups can live with greater security and satisfaction.

Migration is also dynamically related to the process of concentration of individuals and groups. Some communities at a given time are mainly "losing" communities, while others are "gaining." Thus concentration in one area usually implies some loss in and movement from another area. Migration is constantly breaking up existing unities and causing the formation of new groupings. Furthermore, there can be no groupings or concentrations if the potential numbers do not take the initial step of moving together. In general, some knowledge of the physical movement of men is essential to an understanding of their spatial configurations. Physical movement has functioned to form and regroup collectivities of people and their culture, and is itself a measure of change of ecological position.

Migration as an ecological process must be distinguished from mobility or locomotion of persons. There may be physical mobility or fluidity of persons and groups without any intention of change of residence. In our own country we find, for example, the daily *movement* of thousands and millions of persons between place of residence and place of work, in the search for recreation and entertainment, among prospectors and migratory workers.

Frequently, of course, when persons *migrate,* that is, make a more or less permanent shift to *another* locality, they also achieve or receive a different status position in the social system of the place of settlement. For example, the farm hand when he moves to the city may become a semiskilled or skilled worker. Invariably migration tends to be accompanied by a break in group relations and in position and role. Social mobility often involves and rests upon horizontal or spatial mobility. (See references 18; 59; 70; 75, pp. 520-534.)

*The classic examination of human migration is in reference 73. See also reference 78.

Why Men Move

Man has always been a restless, roving creature, with a curiosity about other regions and an urge for adventure and new experience. But the main urge in the movement of people, whether forced or free, has been the search for, and the achievement of, more advantageous conditions of living. He must avoid the effects of overpopulation under the existing condition of his technology, that is, escape from an adverse and hazardous man-land ratio. Historic invasions have been movements of people from areas of declining subsistence and threatened well-being to areas where they hoped to find superior land and superior existence. When people form colonies elsewhere for some of their population, or move subjugated peoples in to supply labor, or drive out people as refugees, they are attempting to improve their condition of living. In other words, they move *others* to improve an undesirable condition at home, and they move *themselves* voluntarily to find a place of superior man-resources conditions.

Invariably, however, a host of cultural conditions also enter into the movement. Not only do men seek to escape from want and privation and to gain higher real income; they also seek higher cultural values. By moving they seek to avoid oppression, persecution and exploitation, and seek to enjoy greater self-respect and superior status, comforts and conveniences, religious and educational freedom and opportunity, health and recreation, and so on. In brief, they move to avoid the reduction of their standard and plane of living or to achieve a superior standard and plane of living elsewhere. The new residence is more or less rationally selected in the light of its economic opportunities and its cultural advantages. The anticipation or the hope of more favorable satisfaction of needs and wants in other areas operates to foster a continual and renewed movement to concentration somewhere else. In other words migration is usually from lesser life-opportunity areas to greater life-opportunity areas.

Factors in Migration

Although modern migration is mainly voluntary, it is surrounded by a host of factors which affect its freedom, volume, and direction. These factors may be set forth as follows:

General Factors. The general factors affecting migration may be grouped as follows:

1. Communication with and information about places of greater advantage are necessary. In our day, communication has been greatly facilitated by telephone, telegraph, radio, and press. Information is also circulated among different persons and through all manner of educational opportunities. Unless people know about alternative opportunities, they cannot go to them.

2. Transportation facilities must be available at reasonable cost, since they are the means and procedures of actual movement. Airplanes, railways, free transcontinental highways, and especially the ubiquitous "family auto" are therefore important.

3. Political and social conditions must permit free movement. These conditions include the emergence of huge political units, free choice of residence, political order and peace, and the absence of restrictions on crossing boundaries. Within the United States, for example, political conditions favorable to free movement exist almost everywhere.

4. Loss of ties to place of origin and decline of the closely knit family are also factors. A mobile and migratory people are willing to cut loose from a given place of birth or of present residence. Greater opportunities elsewhere outweigh customs, traditions, sentiments, mores, and loyalties which often have tied persons to location or family.

Push-and-Pull Factors. This has come to be a very common and highly revealing categorizing of factors in migration. (65, pp. 23-40) The impulse toward migration is the result of the flow of people along a gradient. This flow derives its strength partly from the conditions at home and partly from the conditions in the place toward which migration is directed. These factors will be described briefly.

The push, or expulsive, factors are those operating in the area of origin or residence that serve to incite and propel people to move out of it. They may be adverse physical and biological conditions; inadequate development, exhaustion, depletion, or overworking of natural resources; unfavorable political conditions; religious disturbance, intolerance, and persecution; ethnic discrimination; sex- or age-group imbalance; technological developments of a laborsaving type which create an oversupply of manpower.

The pull or the attractive factors in an area are those which draw persons to the area. They include discovery and development of heretofore unworked natural resources; technological advances due to scientific discoveries and inventions which make new industries possible in given areas; industrial advance in an area, creating a demand for many other kinds of manpower; favorable political conditions; cultural opportunities; ethnic equality, or at least tolerance; religious freedom; advertising and propaganda, emphasizing various advantages. The first two pull factors tend to shift the centers of industrial, extractive, and agricultural activity, thus causing drastic shifts in the need for manpower. The other factors are usually less forceful and less extensive in effect.

It must be emphasized that usually both the push and the pull factors mentioned operate in combination.

Hindering and Limiting Factors. The general or the push-and-pull factors never produce a full or instantaneous response in those affected by migration stimuli, because there are always hindering and limiting factors. The more important of these limitations include the following: inertia and lethargy; ignorance of opportunities elsewhere; fear of uncertainty and risk; economic cost; cultural links to the old environment; political barriers to migration; hostile ethnic attitudes; climatic conditions.

In general, the decision to migrate is based upon a rough calculation in which the relative advantages are balanced against all the different costs and disadvantages.

Migration in Our American Society

At the present time the ecologically important migration is that which takes place freely and voluntarily within countries. The United States contains more of this than any other politically stable country in the world. In April, 1947, approximately 70,000,000 persons were *not* living in the same house in which they had lived on April 1, 1940. Some 44,000,000 of these had changed houses within the same county; 13,000,000 had changed counties within the same state; and 12,000,000 had changed their state of residence between 1940 and 1947. During this period the farm areas lost 3,200,000 persons, or one in every eight who had lived on a farm in 1940. The West drew a net gain of about 2,000,000 persons from other regions, while the South lost about 1,500,000 persons to other regions. (82) This period, of course, included the war years. During the single peacetime year of April, 1947, to April, 1948, however, 29,000,000 persons, or approximately one fifth of the population, had moved to a different house, and of these 19,000,000 had moved within a county and 9,000,000 had changed their county of residence. (83)

In our dynamic economy, internal migration is increasing at a faster rate than the growth of population. Let us, therefore, briefly discuss the major types of internal migration in the United States.

Historically the most important movement, and the one which gave the country its original ecological formation, was the migration from the settled centers of the East to the successive western frontiers with their unexploited land and other resources. This was movement to the periphery of settlement and of economic activity. People moved to the frontier to avoid the more crowded urban and industrial areas and enjoy freedom and a higher plane of living. Our economy was mainly organized around the exploitation of natural resources, that is, expansion of the extractive industries. As a result the population was scattered over wide spaces in areas of low-density concentration. But the great natural frontiers were all settled by the last decade of the nineteenth century.

Our economy now is predominantly industrial and commercial. The frontiers to which men migrate are the products of modern technology. Mechanical industry and trade and commercial operations have vastly increased in importance as the extractive industries have relatively contracted. The superior employment and social opportunities for an ever greater number of people now are in the industrialized-urbanized centers of concentration of high density where the people are engaged in manufacturing, commercial, clerical, cultural, governmental, professional, repair, personal, and community service activities and occupations. Consequently, mechanical industry and commerce have come to be the principal controllers of population distribution and concentration.

To revert for a moment to the census data on internal migration in the decade of the 1940's, it should be pointed out that the movements of people from street address to street address within a town or city or from farm to farm within a rural community or county are involved in the discussion in the next section on the processes of movement and transition that occur within a given community. Here we are concerned especially with the distributive movements that involve both greater distance and the crossing of major internal political boundaries, such as the crossing of county lines and state lines, to adjoining or near-by states and the movement across states essential to interregional migration. These movements affect profoundly the ecological organization of a society and are highly effective in the maintenance of its equilibrium.

The primary movement of population in the United States today *to* industrial and commercial centers takes two main, though overlapping, forms. In either case the movement is from older centers of dominance to newer and more active centers. The main determinants of movement to another area in either case are the degree of employment available, the level of income anticipated, and the general level of living attainable.

Farm-to-City Migration. Farm-to-city migration involves the greatest movement of people in our day. According to the Federal census, in 1920, when the national population amounted to 105,710,620, the people living on farms totaled 31,614,000, or approximately 30 percent; as of April, 1951, with a national population of around 152,700,000, only 23,276,000 were on farms, or approximately 15.2 percent. This is due partly to the pull of the opportunities of all kinds in the cities and their increasing demand for labor and partly to the push of the mechanization of agriculture and the electrification of farm life.

Agricultural areas have always produced a surplus of population; now this overproduction is greater than ever. At the same time, many of the agricultural establishment's traditional tasks have been taken over by urban industry; notably, slaughtering of livestock, preparation of hides, the canning of produce, processing of milk, preparation of grains, sirup, and fruit juices. The very mechanization of agriculture, with its demand for all manner of machines and the need for parts, repairs, and services, has increased the demand for urban-industrial labor.

The migrants to the city from the farms are mostly young adults, with a greater proportion of females than males, and the families migrating are mostly those with young children. Farm-city migration is usually *one way,* for people seldom return to the farms from the city, except during times of depression. The movement is reversed when economic recovery begins.

Migration from Declining Areas to New Developments. There is never a general dispersion of changes in either the technological development of extractive industry or the emergence of new manufacturing and market areas. In a technological culture like our own, great variations in this respect are continually developing within and between states as well as within and between regions. Developments in oil and gas production, in irrigation, and the rise of new manufacturing areas are continually providing relatively superior opportunities for immigrants.

The decline of agriculture in the South in the 1920's pushed many people to its newly developing industrial centers, to newly efficient agriculture sections of the West and Northwest, and to the industrial areas of the Great Lakes region and the Far West. The development of intensive agriculture, lumbering, and a host of new industries and markets on the Pacific Coast in recent decades attracted millions from all parts of our country. During the decade 1940-1950 the population of the Pacific states increased by approximately 4,753,000, or 48 percent, and a major portion of this gain was due to in-migration.

While this type of migration is centrifugal to areas of new resources, it is also centripetal to the technologically developed portions of these areas. Thus, the metropolitan areas and their satellite cities are the chief gainers in population. In fact, today, most internal migration is finally absorbed in the cities or the metropolitan areas.

In all internal migration movement is usually to the nearest adjoining counties, states, or regions that have reputed opportunities. In general, as we move from the center of origin, the number of moves stand in inverse ratio to the distance moved. A principle of economy of movement seems to be involved, but this general tendency is distorted if distant points have notably greater compensatory advantages than nearer points have.

Secondary Dispersal – Distribution within a Community

We have examined the general process whereby people and institutions come together or coneentrate into communities, the rather typical configuration which communities take on, and the processes whereby people move to and from communities. Here we are concerned with the processes involved in the continuous locational and functional arrangement and rearrangement of persons, groups, and institutions *within* a community or within a region in which spatial and functional division of labor and interdependence exist. The processes are specialized aspects of growth competition, specialization, mobility, and equilibration; they shape the various functional areas and are details of the general process of community formation.

Expansion

The over-all internal community process following the initiating one of settlement or aggregation is expansion. Contraction is also a possibility, usually implying some decline. In a healthy community, however, there is this centrifugal movement accompanied by certain centripetal tendencies which are often induced by it. The expansion is in terms of physical growth and always involves a redistribution and reorganization of persons, land uses, activities, and institutions.

Centralization or Nucleation

Centralization is the tendency of activity or population to integrate around some center of interest or functional relationship. Different types of centers are produced. There is, as we have noted, the tendency for functions to increase at the center of dominance of a community. This produces the main nucleus of the community or the area, the focal or pivotal point where the greatest and *most basic* economic, social, and cultural activity occurs. This type of center is usually located at the point of greatest movement and highest land values in the area, where the highways and other forms of transportation and communication converge, and is the point of most intense interest and highest functional tension and activity of the given area.

In the rural area the centralization takes place at the crossroads or in the village, possibly the county seat. In the metropolitan area, the focus of activity and services is found in the metropolis, and for the metropolis itself, in the downtown business district.

The second type of nucleation consists of the formation of clusters of human beings and certain institutional activities for the definite purpose of *satisfying specific interests* and *carrying on specific functions,* such as work, play, a specific type of business, worship, education, and so on, such as Wall Street, La Salle Street, Times Square. A community will contain many such centers of different size and degree of specialization, each one constituting a sort of magnet and drawing to itself the appropriate economic and other cultural groups of persons and activities. (88)

Decentralization and Subcentralization

The two closely related processes of decentralization and subcentralization (91, p. 216) are in turn directly related to the preceding process of centralization. They are due to the increase in size of a community, the development of convenient and rapid means of transportation, and the need of establishing local, more accessible centers for conducting services essential to the surrounding population. By means of them human beings and institutional agencies move away from the central nucleus of growth to other points or centers toward the periphery of the community, and create functional subcenters. Thus, in cities at intersections of main arterials at some distance from the main center, subcenters develop with branch banks, retail stores, movie theaters, and all manner of repair and specialty shops. Such centers for special purposes may even locate on the outskirts where land values are low and spaces for parking are available, as in the case of great chain grocery and chain department stores or the newly developing all-purpose shopping centers. (99)

Segregation

This is a special kind of centralization. It is the competitive and selective process, due to the operation of community influences, by which like population types, physical structures, or services and utilities tend to cluster together in special and separate areas, apart from other types. As Hawley points out, these are essentially "corporate and categoric units" and not territorial units; nevertheless, they constitute territorial units and have a special position and significance in the community. (95, p. 276) As a result of this geographic and often societal preparation, competitive maneuvering for position, security, clientele, or other satisfaction or need becomes unnecessary or is greatly reduced. Often economy of time and other conveniences are occasioned by the mutual accessibility and cooperation within the segregated area. Economic function, occupation, economic status, race, and nationality, age, sex, and other cultural traits are *attractive forces of selection* which operate to differentiate one such specialized area from another. Usually several of these selective criteria act in combination.

Several different types of segregated areas may be distinguished, each the result of special selective factors and processes. (1) In many cities, certain functions are included and others excluded in specified areas by zoning ordinances. (2) There are the areas, more or less voluntarily segregated, to carry on similar or identical economic services and utilities. These are similar in economic strength and make a similar use of land. Their mutual accessibility makes for convenience both of the producers and the clients. Notable are the segregation of manufacturing plants in separate factory districts, sometimes even taking the form of intense clustering of particular types of manufacturing, as in the case of ladies' fur and garment factories in New York City. There are also the wholesale and jobbing districts, areas given to eating places offering "foreign" cuisines, sections devoted to pawnshops and second-hand stores, automobile row, newspaper row, and the bank and brokerage district. (3) Certain areas are devoted to special interests, cultural and otherwise, such as Greenwich Village or Hobohemia. (4) Areas of special residential selection are determined by income and social status, such as slums, areas of independent dwelling units, the Gold Coast, the outer areas of commuters' homes. (5) Ethnic and nationality minority-group areas are formed, such as ghettos, Little Italy, and so on. There may also be rural enclaves of these.

Each of these segregated areas within the larger community serves as a selective and magnetic force. It draws into it and segregates, into a separate "niche," homogeneous units of population and appropriate institutions and repels incongruous ones. Each area has its characteristic complex of institutions, customs, beliefs, and other interests.

Such a given functional division of areas is not maintained permanently by given defined areas, however; there is constant transition and overlapping. Several of the ecological processes result in temporal sequences in the larger areas, as well as changes in spatial relationships.

Invasion-Evacuation

By the process of invasion-evacuation new or different population elements and institutions gradually penetrate an area already occupied and drive out and displace the erstwhile population, groups, and institutions. Usually, it is one area of segregation encroaching on another, more often an adjoining one. It implies group displacement and replacement and comes with community growth. Land use and type of occupant both change. Industry invades the business area of the city, and business invades a residential area. Areas adjacent to cities may first be rural farming areas; then they are invaded by suburban population and institutional forms, and then, if the metropolitan center continues to grow, by more urbanized forms, including, possibly, satellite towns and cities.

The correlative process of this is recession or evacuation, that is, the retreat or departure of the elements forced out, implying in turn *their* encroachment upon adjacent groups. An area in process of invasion and evacuation is sometimes referred to as an "area of transition."

Succession

Succession is the orderly and irreversible series of stages in which an area changes *in time*. There is a complete change in type and composition of population, dominant institutions, characteristic social functions performed, and land utilization from the first stage in the process to the last. The changes occur successively from the center outward. Each stage in the series makes the next inevitable. The stages of change are usually sequential, although they may be cyclical.

Succession results from the processes involved in the invasion-recession cycle. When invasion-displacement-replacement in a given area is successful and temporarily complete, then succession has taken place. Where you had a slum you now have a skyscraper apartment area; where you had farms you now have suburbia, and so on. A new social set-up has been produced in a given period of time. Succession leads to either the development or the disintegration of the particular area.

Regionalization as a Complex of Ecological Processes

Within any larger area of interrelationship, whether societal, national, continental, oceanic (134), or global, there are increasingly important and fundamental units known as *regions,* and their study is known as *regionalism*. Regionalism has been referred to as a form of higher ecology. (116)

Regionalism involves certain aspects of the wider spatial or geographic structure of a society. The region itself is a space grouping of human beings and their institutions. It has an over-all homogeneity with respect to associated conditions of land, people, services, culture, and organization. (106, pp. xiii-xiv, 1-11) Both its components and its indices "require a group of people with certain homogeneous attitudes, desires and wants; a contiguous area with certain geographic unities; a certain base in natural and man-made resources, in technology, and economic institutions; . . . and appropriate . . . organization." (117, pp. 25-26) It is "something inherent in the structure of society," (106, p. 7) and "cannot be established solely by edict or enactment." (123, p. 155)

Any given region with its spatially circumscribed combination of characteristics and activities is demarcated from other and different regions. It is more or less spatially inclusive. A given region has more uniformities and homogeneities along given lines than another. It is an area of common living within a larger whole, and the people living in it feel themselves to be part of it and apart from other regions.

By *regionalization* is meant the process whereby a sociocultural structure is developed in a particular geographic area, the structure being adjusted to and reflective of the area. Its significance in forming the unique culture of a region was examined above in connection with the organization of culture. Here we are concerned with it as a process that produces separate but interdependent regions. The process itself is a function of modern communication and transportation and of the consequent mobility of ideas, persons, and products, of competition over wide areas, of an enforced division of labor and specialization and particularization based on space, human and physical resources and various types of technological development, and of the coalescence of interests and activities developed and maintained within given subdivisions of large but interrelated areas. The process produces a certain adjustment or equilibrium among the various forces and the functionally or influentially related elements in the region.

There are different kinds of regions. Recently considerable attention has been paid to international and world regions. We are concerned with intranational regions, particularly those of the United States. Three types of major ecological significance will be briefly discussed.

Geographic-Economic-Cultural, or Geocultural, Region*

The United States, like other large and diversified countries, shows sizable areas, within each of which there is a certain distinguishing homogeneity of physiographic, economic, demographic, and cultural features. These are great natural areas. The various demographic and cultural components of these areas are in considerable part selected, conditioned, and determined by the physical environment. All of the regional areas, however, are coordinate, interdependent, and equilibrated parts of the whole.

Historically, prior to 1860 the United States had, as marks of broad regional variation, the industry-dominated East, the agrarian West, and the plantation South. At the present time, the far-flung domain, extending from the Atlantic to the Pacific, consists of a large number of rather distinct natural regions. Odum and associates, who for more than a quarter of a century have been devoting themselves to the analysis of this type of region, have divided the country into six major geocultural regions: the Northwest, the Far West, the Southwest, the Middle States, the Southeast, and the Northeast. (128; 129) Odum divides the country into the indicated regions on the basis of some 685 indices of dissimilarity and similarity, ranging through land types and land use, natural resources and their use, agriculture and manufacturing, public and private wealth, income and expenditure, demographic characteristics, public services, government, education, religion, and political characteristics.

Factors of Geocultural Configuration. This sort of geocultural configuration of American life is based on five sets of factors. The elemental factor in the development of a given region, among other regions, is its peculiar physical environment (for

*J. M. Gillette has used the term "geocultural" for this type of region. (109)

example, the Great Plains). Next is the factor of economic structure determined by the natural milieu and based upon the natural resources as they determine agriculture, industry and business, occupations, technology, and the unique forms of income, wealth, and expenditure. These point to economic similarities.

The third important factor is the make-up and character of the population of the region—the folk. This involves special ethnic character and the differentiation into specific class arrangements of the region. Important also are sex and age distribution, educational and literary level, the predominant character—urban or agrarian—and so on, of the region. The fourth factor consists of the historical processes of a political, economic, and social nature, beyond the strictly ecological processes, that have affected it, such as frontier experiences, sacred memories, participation in wars, political tensions, and the like.

The fifth significant factor is the unique culture of the area, the product of all the cultural features that flow directly from the regional determiners and inducements and all that have come into the area with successive population increments and all of the other diffusional processes. These cultural elements are adjusted to the natural and economic setting. The cultural features of special significance are the characteristic attitudes and habits, the folklore, the folkways, technicways and stateways, the traditions and customs, the economic and political philosophy, and religious and artistic phases. From all these come the distinctive structural and functional features of institutions as they develop in each region. In addition to the elements that all institutions have in common with those of their field and type, they have special features that give them the greatest functional proficiency in the immediate natural area.

In the wider areas of regions, the nation, and even the continent a variety of selective, distributive, and accommodative forces have been and are in operation, affecting regional economic division of labor and specialization based on the competitive utilization of natural resources and population proficiencies. Processes of settlement, population movements in and out of regions, class and race relations within a region, political philosophy and practices, recreational and expressional activities—in fact, most aspects of life—are affected by competition. The combined factors result, roughly, in integration *within* the region and flow and tendency toward equilibrium *between* regions.

These conditions and processes impose a unique compatible cultural landscape upon the natural landscape of each major area. One need only think of the distinctive social patterns of the South, New England, the Middle West, and other regions to be aware of the nature of each region. There are a certain number of perceptible and accepted cultural similarities *in* each area and certain notable cultural differences *between* areas. There is much point to the concept of the region as an over-all, unique configuration.

Factors Tending to Uniformity. It is significant to note that in the United States the great array of uniformity-producing and massing factors—the means of communication and transportation, the standardizing influences, such as advertising, motion pictures, newspapers, and periodicals, and the vast number of new nation-wide Federal administrative organizations—have accentuated the regional developmental process. The regions have become more important in an economic, demographic, psychological, ideological, recreational, expressional, and especially a political sense. The very ease and frequency of communication, movement, and contact accentuates for the individual the uniformities of his region and develop in him a stronger regional consciousness. As a result literary and artistic expressions show more marked regional emphasis, historical regional traditions and customs are cherished with a new fervor, and deep-seated loyalties, even in the more recently settled regions, flourish. The tendency of government in recent decades to produce centralization has awakened a militant regional consciousness. This increased regionalization shows that we are overcoming the handicap of great size and are maturing as a nation of interdependent, interrelated, and cooperative areas.

The boundaries of these regions cannot be precisely and permanently marked, even though, for purposes of study, they are usually arbitrarily drawn. Where the regions conjoin, we have intermediate zones where the features of each intermingle so bewilderingly that the physical and cultural boundaries are uncertain. Furthermore, the extent of the region depends upon a host of variables that are constantly changing, thus causing a shifting of approximate boundaries. Regionalization, however, can be said to produce a rather substantial and identifiable core area, the characteristics of which are less distinct in contiguous areas.

The Metropolitan Region

The metropolitan region is a roughly bounded special area, usually within a single geocultural region, although it may extend into an adjoining one and also cut across state lines. Thus, the Minneapolis–St. Paul metropolitan area has its central city (or cities) in the state of Minnesota, but its influence extends into the adjoining states. The metropolitan region is an area with a dominant city at its center as a focus of organization, activity, and interest, but extending into the accessible hinterland of agricultural land and lesser towns and cities by series of zones and gradients as well as along communication and transportation lines or axes.

The metropolitan region is due in part to the general process of regionalization as discussed above, but also to "rurbanization" (116, p. 341), that is, the processes that tend to make a society more urbanized and at the same time accentuate the relationship and interdependence of the city and its surrounding area.

The city is more and more the service center of the surrounding area, providing all manner of processed material things and services. At the same time, it is more and more dependent upon the hinterland for its raw materials, its food and water supply, its recreation, its daily working personnel (by commuting), and its population replacements. In any metropolitan region of this type, there is a rough balance and integration between agrarian land and agricultural activities *and* the urban centers with their industrial, commercial, service, and cultural activities. Both city and surrounding country are tending to become the common possession of all who inhabit the metropolitan area. The existence of a metropolitan region implies first-class communication and accessibility to the central city; a homogeneity of areal consciousness and interdependence of its people, that is, a sense of relationship between city and hinterland; and a sense of being distinct from other metropolitan areas.

The processes of general mobility and distribution that are operative in a community are also operative in both the geocultural and metropolitan regions. Especially significant in the larger metropolitan communities in the United States at the present time is the process of decentralization. Because of transportation difficulties and the vast extent of many industrial plants, there is a tendency for both the population and the industries directly related to the city to disperse over near-by areas into smaller and more scattered units in the form of "commuter cities" and satellite industrial towns and cities. Thus, the population in our largest cities is tending to become stationary, while the surrounding towns and cities are increasing in population and in many industrial activities.

The Administrative Region

Administrative regions are specific artificial subareas of convenience and necessity of the national whole that have been arbitrarily established to facilitate the management and operation of predetermined organizational activities. The characteristics that distinguish them from geocultural and metropolitan regions are their arbitrary determination, their limited-purpose use, and the inflexibility of their boundaries. The objective is to avoid the difficulties of overcentralization which are involved in remote, autocratic, and indiscriminate administration from a distant, central headquarters; in brief, to avoid the evils of organizational giantism. Thus, the Federal government has established over a hundred different regional administrative schemes, each with a different number of regions and with different boundaries of the regions in order more effectively to administer its various functions.

Similarly, large business corporations and other nation-wide organizations have operated on the idea that the nation is too large and too complex to permit effective administration through a single central station and for purposes of economy, efficiency, and local good will have established service regions. (129, pp. 213-236) These include such organizations as chain-store systems, mail-order houses, utilities, hierarchically organized religious bodies, the United States Chamber of Commerce, the National Collegiate Athletic Association, the YMCA and YWCA, the Boy Scouts, and many learned and scientific organizations.

The processes involved in administrative regions are those necessary to the development and operation of large-scale formal organizations, which will be discussed later. These administrative regions represent specific functional, rather than ecological, subdivisions of the whole nation and are mentioned merely to distinguish them from the two other types which have distinct ecological significance.

PART FOUR

SOCIETAL STRUCTURALIZATION AND FUNCTIONALIZATION

CHAPTER X

SOCIETAL ORGANIZATION: PROCESSES, FACTORS, AND COMPONENTS

THE KEY CONCEPT in the analysis of society as a going concern is *organization*. Thus far we have examined several different kinds of organization with special emphasis upon the processes involved in their formation and operation, namely, *cultural organization, demographic organization,* and *ecological organization*. The present division of this analysis will be devoted to a fourth highly important type of structural-functional organization—*societal organization*.

Before taking up the concept of societal organization and its specific subdivisions, it is essential to examine briefly the place and content of this concept in sociological theory. Such an examination is one of sociology's primary scientific obligations. Societal organization is as old as mankind. No human assemblage living a life in common has ever been discovered that did not possess some form of societal organization. Nowhere do we find a horde in which the relations between its individuals is completely anarchic. There is always more than a chance ordering of parts, for societal persistence depends upon organization. "The very universality of organization, considered simply as a phenomenon, furnishes sufficient evidence of its necessity in the general scheme of life." (13, p. ix) A society cannot be a haphazard aggregation of disparate individuals and groups; it is *an organized whole*. What are its component elements and how do they jointly operate?

The Nature of Societal Organization

Human society is a network of collectivities of human beings that have varying degrees of systematized unity among them. They exercise different modes and degrees of influence. The different parts function within themselves and are dovetailed with each other in action. It is well to note, however, that no aggregation of human beings remains merely an aggregation if the individuals composing it have any contact in time. Even before it has developed anything in the way of common culture, it will tend to sort itself into various groups with different interests, purposes, tasks, and statuses, but all functionally arranged, related, and systematized. In fact, as soon as an aggregation *does* something, or even attempts to do something, it undergoes some degree of organization, spontaneous or deliberate, informal or formal.

Organization means systematic functional connection and coordination of differentiated but interdependent parts or entities according to certain principles, rules, and limits in order to accomplish some end. All human experience has demonstrated the practical necessity of such organization for the attainment of any of the purposes requiring the joint action of two or more persons.

By societal organization we mean the coordinated system of interdependent social units of a more inclusive social whole as they function interrelatedly with each other and as parts of the more inclusive whole in the pursuit of their values. The units of society are individuals and groups. There is a system of more or less enduring relationships among persons, among groups, and between persons and groups that produces unity, solidarity, division of labor, and functional efficacy for the society as a meaningful, operating whole. At any given time these units are, more or less, in a state of articulation, integration, stabilization, harmony, and equilibrium.*

As indicated above, societal organization consists of both structuralization and functionalization. Each will be briefly examined.

Structuralization of Society

Societal organization as *a structuralization of society* conceives of society as a comprehensive, intricate mechanism, composed of the innumerable ideal-typical and more or less stable, universal or recurrent combinations or configurations of interrelated, interdependent, and reciprocally responding human beings. Concisely, these configurations take the form of many varieties of groups, categories, organizations, vertical subdivisions, and strata. These groups and orders of people are the ways in which associating human beings are combined and arranged and their relationships coordinated and systematized. They constitute the visible framework, the organizational patterns of social life with all its compounded and enmeshed substructures. Without structure, society would not be organization at all; in fact, it would not even exist.

*Closely related to societal organization as a substitute, as a basis for revealing distinction, or (according to Loomis) as a superior analytical tool, is the concept of "social system." (8; 9; 10; 17)

Functionalization of Society

Societal organization is also *process and operation—a system of coordinated functional activities,* continuously developing and going on in time, making for the successful existence of associated human beings. *Structuralization always implies functionalization.* The various configurations and agencies are not ends in themselves, although members sometimes act as if they were. The reason for the existence of the agencies is their functioning—the innumerable service activities carried on by them. Every society and every part of it must become an administrative mechanism, consisting not merely of processes of association but especially of the processes of paramount importance from the point of view of adjustment and survival, namely, those whereby individual and social needs and wants are satisfied.

The functioning is determined by the common value system. The value-orientation furnishes the purposes and objectives which the members of the social system expect to accomplish in their individual and joint functioning. It provides the basis for establishing what is worth while and what is worthless. It includes the norms or standards by which the quantity and the quality (the goodness or badness) of the functional activity are judged. Different subcollectivities may be working for purposes of their own, but at the same time all of them must be so coordinated as to constitute an over-all functional system—a "going concern."

To put it in a slightly different manner, *societal organization is both a societal condition and a combination of social processes.* As a *condition* it is the systematized configuration of interrelated functional groupings or structurings (or, as the term "organization" implies etymologically, an arrangement of the "organs") that constitute the framework of a society as viewed in a relatively short-time or cross-sectional frame of reference. At the same time it is a *complex of processes* continually forming and re-forming the relationships, purposes, and activities of associated human beings as essential functions are performed. This is the action of the combinations in space and *over a time span.* In actuality, structures are combinations of human beings in action.

At the same time that the organizational processes of structuralization and functionalization are occurring in a society or in its parts, the disorganizational or destructuralizing and defunctionalizing processes are also in operation. (See Part Five below.) The *ultimate* condition, therefore, seems to be a moving balance or equilibrium between all of the associative-cooperative-coordinative processes on the one hand and the disintegrative-defunctionalizing processes on the other.

In the main, societal organization is not a static affair, but a living, changing structuralization and functionalization of human beings and their actions—"an extensive, instrumental system of organized activities," according to Malinowski (12) —extending through time. ***Individuals come and go, they fail or flourish, but the social system, the total, complex functioning mechanism, goes on.*** It may be summarized as consisting of many diverse collectivities and categories of persons, variously organized, and vastly differentiated and stratified, mutually and reciprocally serving and supporting each other; a system of coordinated activities on the one hand and a distribution of essential functions on the other, both the activities and the functions being motivated and regulated by general and special values, goals, and norms in the form of a patterned system of "obligation-relations"; and, finally, a large variety of processes which produce a sufficient degree of arrangement, coordination, order, maintenance, and consistency to assure human existence. By means of organization the parts of society are fused into a more or less integrated and consistent, dynamic, functioning whole.

The Reason for Societal Organization

The necessity for organization in a society that is a going concern rests upon both individual and collective considerations. For more than two thousand years wise men have been aware that the individual is *not* self-sufficient biologically or in any other way. Without a supporting social organization, he could not reproduce or satisfy his primary needs; he would have no social and cultural needs; he would not learn very much and would not acquire his habits of response or develop his creative potentialities. In brief, he would not behave like a human being.

Development of Societal Organization

As a collective affair, societal organization has most likely developed elementally from symbiotic conditions, especially those related to biological perpetuation and physical maintenance. As such, it is "natural" in the sense of being largely spontaneous, unconscious, and automatic, produced by processes of trial and failure or success. The forms of action that endured were those that gave the most satisfaction with the least pain. They constituted a form of economy, utilizing and manipulating material, psychological, and social resources in the interests of functional efficiency.

But this organization has advanced beyond the symbiotic and automatic because of the special nature of *human* life. More and more it has come to be a matter of purposeful development, even of conscious planning and intentional, experimental construction. A society in the end is only significant in terms of the societal functions it performs. The important thing is not the aggregations of human beings, the pluralities or collectivities—all more or less gregarious species have this—but the teamwork, the achieved order and pattern of living and working together. The continuous daily life of associated human beings must have purpose and meaning and not be haphazard or chaotic. Living must be harmonized, systematized, instrumentalized, and society must function as a vast, complicated, reciprocally related array of mechanisms and operations. Through these various mechanisms and operations society has to provide for biological existence and perpetuation, physical sustenance, and economic maintenance. (16, pp. 21-22)

Social Needs

The social needs go even further and provide for social adjustment and the prevention of disruptive activities, internal and external peace, and the satisfaction of the sociational, recreational, and expressional urges of men. They also provide for joint supernatural adjustment, the stimulating, ordering, disciplining, and restraining of individuals, and the preservation, expansion, and transmission of the cultural heritage. In general, facilities must exist for societal durability, efficacy, and, preferably if possible, societal prosperity. (See also pages 20 to 22.) It has always been necessary to coordinate actions in the interest of goals and purposes which could not be achieved by individuals acting independently or even by groups. Certain conditions of organization and function *must* exist.

Basic Processes of Societal Organization

The remaining chapters of this analysis of human society will be concerned with a detailed examination of the forms and processes of societal organization. Attention has been called to the major categories of special processes that give us a detailed insight into the organization, disorganization, and reorganization of society. (See pages 13 and 14.) At this point we are concerned with basic, elemental foundation processes that are always in effect wherever and whenever any degree of societal organization exists. All of the various categories of special processes to be analyzed in the ensuing chapters rest upon and utilize these foundation processes or are specialized forms of them.

The over-all process of *social interaction,* the most elemental of social processes is always involved. All other processes are merely different aspects of it. Fundamentally, societal organization is a complicated network of social interaction. Always there is contact, communication, association, and exchange wherever there is a social framework and social action. The elemental processes especially pertinent in societal organization will be discussed in the following sections.

Cooperation

A basic feature of human interaction and societal organization is cooperation. Fundamentally, a human society is a system of cooperation, wide in extent, involving in some measure all individuals and groups, infinitely intricate in its details, and including many forms. *Cooperation is the process by which individuals or groups act jointly, work together, in the pursuit of common interests, purposes, and objectives.* It is a reciprocal relation in which the success of one party in the interaction produces some degree of success for the other party or parties. It enables combinations of human beings to produce together and share what are deemed to be "good things." All the major functions of mankind—the provision of food, trade, government, education, and so on—are fundamentally cooperative. For a society as a whole cooperation consists of combining the activities of the different individuals and groups in order to perform more efficiently the functions essential to the common welfare.

Some activities that are carried on cooperatively could be done by individuals, but at a loss of time, energy, and quality of performance. Long ago men discovered that they could accomplish much more working together than they could proceeding alone. As members of a society, however, they *must* cooperate and perform essential *social* tasks jointly. Failure to cooperate is disastrous to the welfare of the individuals and to the efficacy of the social system. Those who do not cooperate exclude themselves from the objectives, benefits, and responsibilities of the going concern and often become obstacles or hazards to its over-all efficacy. Certainly without cooperation no group, organization, or society can be held together; without it there can be no social survival and no societal functioning.

It may be pointed out parenthetically that cooperation does not imply any kind of concomitant we-feeling. Such a feeling may, however, come about as a by-product both among a small number of face-to-face coactors and in a large impersonal body, as among the members of the United Nations forces in Korea. It should also be noted that cooperation does not require face-to-face contact, but is possible among the members of large groups where there is a common end toward which they are striving.

The processes of cooperation have been analyzed from many different angles involving various dichotomies. Cooperative activities actually range from rather unconscious and spontaneous reactions to calculated, organized, and contractual forms of united effort. For purposes of clarity and simplicity of analysis, these forms may be treated as spontaneous and as organized cooperation, although all concrete instances will represent some blending of both in varying degrees. This dichotomy, in turn, involves the distinction between kinds of groups in which the characteristic types of cooperation occur. The widely prevalent and highly revealing dichotomy of primary and secondary groups will be used.

Spontaneous Cooperation. Spontaneous cooperation is often referred to as "mutual aid" and consists of the spontaneous combining of the efforts of primary groups or even of two or more persons related momentarily and often by chance. Primary groups, as will be noted in the next chapter, are the small, intimate groups in which the contact and communication is direct and face to face and the members are all personally known to each other and are usually sympathetic and friendly. Cooperation in such groups has certain distinctive characteristics. The tasks are usually rather simple in nature, understood by all, and conducted on the spot without premeditation. The participants perform in each other's presence, and their participation is usually conscious and voluntary. While there is some division of labor, it is not elaborate or intricate and is often spontaneously developed on the spot. The cooperation, therefore, is largely unorganized or is not organized or patterned in advance. The entire procedure is informal as in sharing family chores. American pioneers engaged in much mutual aid in house-raisings and husking bees partly from necessity and partly for the sake of social mingling.

Organized Cooperation. Organized cooperation constitutes the bulk of all societally pertinent cooperation today. Modern industrialized-urbanized societies like our own are predominantly secondary-group societies. The population elements are heterogeneous and usually widely dispersed territorially. While there is an abundance of interaction, the relationships are largely anonymous and impersonal, and the communication indirect. A host of tasks, in most instances large-scale and complicated and involving many persons, must be carried on cooperatively by and for the members of such groups. Because of their complex nature, these tasks are incomprehensible to, or uncomprehended by, the great bulk of the involuntary participants. And yet, some degree of participation in these tasks is absolutely necessary.

Spontaneous cooperation or even simply organized, small-group cooperation is increasingly ineffective and so must be replaced by previously planned and precisely patterned schemes of joint action in which relations are contractual and some degree of participation is compulsory. The undertakings involve division of labor, specialization of function, minute coordination, and, hence, usually bureaucratic organization. Each individual and each subgroup contributes a small portion to a larger whole; yet, each person and each group is crucially important and indispensable and must play its part in a definitely prescribed and standardized manner. In fact, as the group becomes larger and the relations more anonymous and impersonal, and as the task becomes larger and more complicated and the total operation more essential and unavoidable, the cooperation must be more artificed and organized.*

Every important field of social life requires organized cooperation, but with varying degree of preciseness and compulsiveness. More and more, the tasks that must be carried on with minimal essential efficiency by the many for the benefit of

*See the discussion by E. A. Ross of the main factors responsible for abandoning voluntary cooperation as a way of carrying on large-scale tasks in reference 28.

the many, require the formal organization of cooperative activity (to be examined in the next chapter).

Social Participation

Closely related to cooperation as a basic process in societal organization is social participation. By this term the social scientist means *the action of individuals and groups in entering into, identifying themselves with, and sharing with others the activities of a group or a community which are directed to some social end.* Individuals and groups take part in cooperative action. Persons *participate* as members, as employees, as officials, as committeemen, as guests, as players, as spectators, as citizens. This taking part varies in intensity, range, and the nature of the contacts and the functions performed by the different individuals and groups of a society, but all *do* participate.

Individuals participate as members of sympathetic or affectional groups, such as families, cliques, and recreational groups, where they share with their associates feelings of affection and loyalty, joint responsibility, sentiment, tradition, and personal friendship. They participate in utilitarian groups and organizations, such as civic, industrial, and political groups, where they share in socially essential joint activities. A small number of individuals participate extensively in groups that are definitely disruptive both to the society as a whole and to the participating individuals, for example, gangs, corrupt political machines, and vice and gambling syndicates.

The interaction ranges from that which is direct and absorbs much attention to that in large associations which touches individuals only slightly and in which activity is distinctly segmental. Some participation is friendly and sympathetic, but there is also aggressive and selfish participation, as in economic affairs. Participation in some activities is free and complete and in others partial and reluctant. In some other activities, such as those of citizens in political affairs, all need to participate.

All sociological research indicates that active participation is essential to the achievement of group ends, if not to group survival itself. Without the contributions of the individual constituents to their churches, civic, occupational, patriotic, fraternal, and recreational organizations and informal and territorial groups, the needs and wants for which these various cooperative systems exist are not met. Unless the individuals participate in sufficient degree, the various groups are not preserved, and unless all individuals and groups participate positively and in sufficient amount in the essential activities of the large society, well-being is impaired.

S. A. Queen points out (34; 35) that there is considerable evidence that social situations in which social participation languishes are those in which indices of social disorganization are high, for example, poverty, broken homes, delinquency and crime, vice, disease, mental disorder, and suicide. All these are evidence of inadequate participation, for whatever reason, or of unsocial or antisocial participation on the part of individuals or of organizations. In general, a high degree of participation indicates *esprit de corps* and functional efficiency of the groups concerned; low participation is related to social pathology and social disorganization.

There are conditions and situations which function as blocks to the social participation of individuals and groups, notably physical and mental handicaps, illiteracy and little schooling of individuals, economic underprivilege (or overprivilege), old age, great ethnic differences, prejudices, physical isolation, high physical mobility, and so on. Similarly, serious crises of all sorts, such as those which affect particular individuals or small groups (mortgage foreclosure, accident or illness or death) and those which may affect an entire community (physical holocaust, economic depression, or war) impair participation. Where these blocks or crises exist, the community suffers a deficit of contributions.

It has sometimes been assumed that the greater the number of social activities an individual participates in the greater his social usefulness. There is increasing evidence, however, that the social contribution is not necessarily proportional to the *quantity* of involvements in social activities. (32) "Joiners" and extreme extroverts do not often make the most or the best contributions with their scattered investment of abilities and skills—assuming that they have abilities and skills.

Furthermore, the drive for ego-enhancement of some persons leads to participation in many showy, notice-producing activity instead of to substantial contributions to much more important but less spectacular or less newsworthy activities of which they are capable. Also, excessive participation often implies a lack of devotion to socially more important functions, as when housewives neglect their homes and families for clubs and committees. An individual may contribute much more to society if he participates with high social effect in a few activities in which he makes his best investment of himself than if he extrovertively or egotistically dabbles in many.

To conclude the broader aspects of social participation, it should be pointed out that much of it may continue to be quite informal. All those forms that are essential to the survival and success of a given group or of the society as a whole, however, must be formalized and made compulsive, and usually the individuals must be trained in some measure for such action. It is also necessary that individuals and groups participate with a sense of mutual responsibility for each other and for the society as a whole. In fact, the degree of free, full, and intelligent participation of individuals and groups in essential societal functions is an index of the effectiveness of societal organization.*

Division of Labor; Specialization of Function

Both division of labor and specialization of function are aspects of cooperation. Cooperation is *working together,* but *at different tasks.* Division of labor is a vast and complicated process of *functional cooperation.* None of the cooperating individuals and groups constituting a society can carry on the *whole* of any particular social task or *all* of the functions necessary in a society; for ***there are many different things to be done, and individuals and groups and categories of persons are variously equipped to do them.*** Everywhere among associating creatures, even among animal groups, there is some division of labor, that is, the tasks necessary to the survival of the society or even the successful functioning of particular groups are apportioned among the members according to ability and are performed by them. The very durability of a society rests in considerable part upon such a cooperative, though unequal, distribution of functions.

*On the nature of indexes of and measurement of social participation, in addition to the references cited, see references 30; 31; 33; 36).

The division of labor takes many forms. Some are based upon natural factors, such as sex and age groups and individual physical and mental ability. Mainly, however, the forms rest upon sociocultural factors. There is the division of labor based on skills and techniques as represented by different occupations and professions, to some extent the result of technological development, and on the major blocks of institutions and their implementing associations: economic, political, educational, religious, scientific, and aesthetic, with innumerable subdivisions.

The different horizontal levels of the population of a society constitute a form of division of labor, and within any given functional organization there is also a horizontal division of labor, as in a corporation, for example, where there are the entrepreneurial level, the executives and administrative level, the skilled-task level, and the unskilled-task level. Within any society of any areal extent whatsoever, there is a territorial division of labor resting upon variations in terrain, climate, natural resources, and regional demographic and cultural factors. In general, the division of labor is both vertical and horizontal.

From the point of view of the society division of labor is a division of functions; whereas from the point of view of the individuals, it is a *specialization of functions.* Thus, an individual has a specialized role or performs a specialized function, depending upon his age, sex, native ability, skill, education, social status, organizational position, or whatever other criterion is involved in the particular situation, in every cooperative undertaking in which he is a participant. This means that each individual plays innumerable specialized and more or less socially standardized roles daily and throughout his life, and that all contribute to the total cooperative division of labor.

The division of labor and specialization of function are integral parts of societal organization because they offer signal advantages in meeting basic needs and goals and are always prompted by the prospect of greater societal efficiency and social convenience and order. The following are among the noteworthy advantages of division of labor and specialization of function:

1. They make possible the maximum social utilization of all degrees of individual capacity and all kinds of acquired skills and proficiencies.

2. The individuals themselves and particular categories of persons *can* engage in tasks for which they have special capacity, thus avoiding frustration and indolence, since the great range of tasks provides an occupational or expressional outlet for almost every type and degree of ability and enables each individual to show his "superior" side.

3. There is usually an economy of time and energy or a more efficient use of energy and proficiency and a consequent reduction of social cost.

4. Many diverse efforts can be fitted into a single, comprehensive, intelligent scheme.

5. The division of labor permits—in fact, requires—a concentration upon, and a development of, special proficiency in the performance of each specific subfunction of the task, obviating the shifting of individuals and groups from one to another with the loss of time, attention, and energy in the "carry-over."

6. Furthermore, this focusing of attention is often conducive to creativity.

7. Various social and material techniques and instruments essential to the tasks can be specialized and standardized.

8. Among the unequal members of a society, the division of labor makes possible a hierarchical arrangement of persons and categories of persons with a sustaining superordinate-subordinate relationship among them and an equitable distribution of rights and duties.

9. With efficient selection and placement of unequals among the diversified opportunities for activity, resentments and oppositions are likely to be lessened and cooperation and social unity likely to be strengthened.*

Finally, it should be pointed out that the division of labor is a vast system of functional interdependence. The various segments of the society become progressively less self-sufficient and find it increasingly necessary to establish working relationships with other segments. Young states: "The most outstanding feature of the division of labor is not the separation of functions but the fact that it renders these functions interdependent in a society." (44, p. 496)

*Most of these advantages of division of labor will be elaborated in Chap. 13.

Specialization binds men and groups to each other and makes every division of function dependent upon other divisions for its efficacy and every specialist dependent upon all others. The degree of division of labor and specialization of functions has come to be an important measure of the intricacy of the social system.

The Opposition Processes

Opposition processes range from the friendliest competition to the deadliest forms of conflict. The most widely known and the most preponderant social effects of the opposition processes are those of destructuralization and defunctionalization, which will be examined more extensively in Chapter 17 below. However, as universal and ineradicable aspects of all social life, they also serve certain strategic functions in societal organization. Individually and collectively men struggle against the threat of adverse natural circumstances and compete with and struggle against each other within groups and between groups. The opposition processes affect every phase of organization and all organizational processes. The outstanding organizational features of these processes will be examined here.

Competition. All forms of opposition, from competition to conflict, grow out of the fact that the things that men value and need and want are scarce and cannot be acquired in equal amounts and that men's abilities to achieve these desired or essential goals are unequal. *Competition* is that continuous and ubiquitous process of interaction whereby all living things, but, especially from our point of view, individuals and groups, try to outdo each other in a peaceful manner and according to social rules in achieving mutually desired goals.

Individuals compete for recognition, response, privilege, power over others, material goods, mates, customers, opportunities, and rights, and groups and organizations compete for such things as members, clients, sales, resources, and public attention. The action is often indirect, impersonal, or even unconscious, and if the competitors do meet, they do not necessarily identify each other as such. Thus, a Nebraska wheat farmer competes with all the wheat farmers of the world, and persons compete for superior social position with all the people in a given class system.

Competition is a notably dynamic factor in social action, for it focuses attention on the ends of aspiration and stimulates achievement by threatening failure as well as promising success. It appears in every social relationship. Every social system, even a communistic regime, allows or deliberately institutes a system of competition, but every system varies as to scope, intensity, and type.

Conflict. When competition becomes a consciously antagonistic process, we call it *conflict.* Now the parties become adversaries or combatants who expend their energies not only in seeking a common goal but in trying by violence or the threat of violence to weaken, injure, dominate, remove from the scene of action, or even destroy the other contenders. The opponent is not a vague rival somewhere; but a personalized enemy that is hated and feared. It may be necessary to marshal all forces and resources and organize for the encounter against the obstructer of the individual's or the group's ends. Families, gangs, sectarian groups, economic groups, classes, nationalities, races, nations engage in conflict as part of the *struggle for power*—power to survive when existence and well-being are threatened.

There are elements of both competition and conflict in all forms of cooperation. As a people becomes more heterogeneous and its interests, objectives, and contentions become more diverse, the groupings become more numerous and diverse. These groups in turn constitute separate cooperative wholes of various sorts within themselves. The efforts of these cooperators are always directed against rivals or adversaries in the form of natural forces, other human groups, or organizations. The very intensity and effective degrees of organization are determined by the intensity of the competition or the degree of menace.

This kind of cooperation, consisting of the combining of efforts of individuals and groups effectively to oppose other individuals or groups that have different and possibly incompatible or hostile objectives is sometimes called "antagonistic cooperation." (46, pp. 35-42) Opposition is thus a great annealing force *within* contending groups; it promotes participation and in-group solidarity at the same time that it produces social distance between groups.

Both competition and conflict play distinctive parts in the division of labor—territorial, occupational, and by classes—and in bringing about the segregations and separations of persons and groups. As individuals and their organizations, especially their economic organizations, compete or struggle for livelihood, place, and opportunity, they are *physically distributed within a society* and over the earth according to a variety of determining criteria, such as the kinds of population elements, the objectives of the functional organizations, and the features of the physical terrain.

Both competition and conflict prompt specialization among individuals and groups. Competition especially serves as a *selective factor in distributing people vocationally.* The rapidly increasing and ever more intricate division of labor in all organized activities gives scope to ever-wider ranges of capabilities. Competition provides a rough, trial-and-error basis for selection and assignment of persons and categories of persons to roles and tasks.

Unequals. Every society is made up of unequals. As these individuals unequally endowed by birth and differently circumstanced by opportunity struggle for livelihood and vie for status, they *achieve position in the class system.* Societal situations, such as degree of personal liberty, the rate of social change, the availability of opportunity, and the fairness and effectiveness of the selective processes, are factors which aid this general process. But if competition is fairly effective, it tends to *assign each individual, each organization, each institution to its appropriate functional niche* in the social system as a whole, thus furnishing one of the indispensable bases of peace and efficiency in sound community life.

The *separation and segregation* of individuals, categories of individuals, and groups on the basis of personality types, ecological (residential) position, culture, wealth, income, or any other social characteristics or factors or of physical or social isolation are due in large part to the opposition processes. This clustering of the like units and their withdrawal into specific areas is another selective effect of these processes. At the same time the units cluster thus to avoid the further costs of competition and conflict, especially the discrimination, antipathy, and domination by rivals and opponents. Within the segregated area the units cooperate and achieve a degree of freedom of action and also competitive strength.

In general, segregation offers the group and the individuals who compose it a place and a role in the total societal organization. It may also be pointed out that competition, though not conflict, is a *motivating factor* in the activity of individuals and groups, stimulating and inciting them to energy and initiative.*

A special and easily overlooked functional feature of conflict, which has great significance in societal organization as well as disruptive effects, is the way in which conflict grows out of situations involving unequals. When an individual or group feels superior or acts superior, or an individual or group holds more power than the other and seeks to dominate the other, there is a lack of communication and of accommodating action and a complete lack of identity and joint action. An intense feeling of tension and hostility exists, and there is an urge to threaten or inflict violence upon the other individual or group in order to remove the cause of frustration and obstruction.

Such a situation always implies extreme lack of adjustment. A crisis situation exists because the limits of tolerance have been exceeded. *The conflict that ensues is an adjustive process*; for the time being, it resolves the confusion, contradiction, and cross-purpose in the crisis or frictional-tensional situation and brings about an equilibrium or routine of relationship between the parties.

As the old saying goes, "A good fight clears the atmosphere"—but only for a time. In this way, conflict reorganizes the factors of a given situation to produce new levels of cooperation, though not necessarily upon an equitable or durable basis, and contributes to the continuity of function in the society. In this connection the statement by Cooley is significant: "The function of struggle is to work out new forms of cooperation, and if it does not achieve this but goes on in a blind and aimless way after the time for readjustment has arrived, it becomes mere waste." (46, p. 41)

*This aspect will be discussed more extensively in Chap. 21.

Social Integration

The final basic process in societal organization, which must of necessity bring together the processes just discussed, is social integration. A human society is made up of numerous heterogeneous individuals, each unique in ability and temperament, displaying various attitudes, holding to various values, and pursuing peculiar private objectives, and of a multiplicity of dissimilar groups and organizations, organized on the basis of common social likenesses, interests, and social purposes, whose members or participants cooperate among themselves, but who are often oblivious of, or unconcerned about, their relationships and interdependence with other groups and organizations.

Within and between groups and organizations there is division of labor and specialization of function, and, although these structural and functional subdivisions are complementary, they also create distance and lack of understanding and often are more or less uncoordinated. The population elements are also stratified in social layers and hierarchies, with gradients of dominance and subordination. Individuals, categories of individuals, and groups and organizations are frequently recalcitrant and are continually opposing each other, operating at cross-purposes, and attempting to outdo, harm, or eliminate each other.

Coordination of Parts. If a society is to carry on the functions essential to survival and prosperity, however, its innumerable diverse and opposed, but interdependent, parts must be coordinated and made to function effectively together as parts of a fairly efficient, smoothly operating mechanism. Furthermore, there must be *more* than aggregation, more than communication, cooperation, and participation in an area. Producing the "more" in societal organization and operation is the function of the various processes of integration. These processes are constantly in effect; in fact, it may be said that there is always a strain toward structural and functional integration.

By integration we mean the processes by which the various segments of a society are brought into harmony with each other, consolidated, and organized as effective and positive participant elements into a complex functional pattern which is fairly consistent within itself. To the degree that integration is effective, the parts of the social system are molded and welded together operationally and function as a total common societal enterprise—as a going concern.

Unity with Diversity. Integration does not mean making the parts more like each other, for that would nullify all the social advantages of diversification and specialization. It is *unity with diversity.* Integration is a constructive process of strengthening, stabilizing, consolidating, harmonizing, and unifying the various elements by the development of common interests and common purposes and aspirations, which are contributory to the common well-being.

It implies (1) the development of the capacity to work together devotedly at diversified tasks; (2) interdependence and over-all cooperation; (3) discipline and willingness to abide by leadership and followership; (4) division of labor and differentiation; (5) an exchange of reciprocities; (6) standardized modes of response in the interests of order; and (7) the absorption of members into the group's activities. Above all, (8) it means a bonding together, through the recognition of its necessity for common well-being, and not through force (though on occasion force must be used). All the diverse and specialized activities are fitted into a larger whole and produce a steady and efficient flow of total activity. As Loomis puts it, in an integrated system there is "community of fate"; all are for one and one for all in true teamwork. (60). Thus, integration is the antithesis of the processes that resolve society into fragments.

Social Disintegration. Social disintegration is the opposite process to social integration. This comes as a final stage of social disorganization in which there is a breakdown of the societally organizing and reorganizing processes. There is a complete collapse of unity of purpose and teamwork in activity, and, if it continues, the disappearance of the group or society.

The integrative tendency occurs at various social levels and in every area of societal functioning. It must occur *within* groups, *among* the members of all essential groups, *between* groups and between all the differentiated and stratified categories of the population, and among all elements and segments of any territorial portion of a society. There must be the over-all integration of all of these for the entire society. Some integration occurs informally, spontaneously, even unconsciously, as the result of all sorts of adjustive and equilibrative processes, but most of it is the product of definite, formal, established, purposive organizational procedures.

Most of the processes thus far examined in this analysis have some bearing on integration, and most of those to be discussed below in some detail and at appropriate points are subprocesses of integration. Notable as integrative processes in some degree and manner are communication, association, learning, socialization, imitation, cooperation, standardization and routinization, uniformation, institutionalization, hierarchization, stabilization, regulation, federation, accommodation, assimilation, amalgamation, and reorganization.

Essential Factors and Components in Societal Organization

If the basic processes just discussed and all their subprocesses to be examined in succeeding chapters are to produce an efficient societal organization, certain sociocultural factors and components must exist, notably social values, social norms, standardized roles and statuses, and leadership. These have been treated (Chapter 3) briefly as dynamic agents in social action, but to complete our general understanding of societal organization, it is essential that reference be made to the *organizational* significance of these factors.

Social Values

The nature, place, and function of social values are being rapidly revealed through social scientific analysis. Certain general features of values and value formation as gleaned from such analyses need to be presented as a basis for our examination of their societal significance.

The Place and Nature of Values. Values exist because men are human. Men are never merely passive and aimless in their world, but are always examining it, checking upon it, thinking about it, and evaluating or judging it with respect to its actual and potential efficacies and inadequacies in producing satisfactions. They are concerned with survival, security, prosperity, satisfying expression, personal fulfillment, social well-being. They are always, in some measure, judges, evaluators, deciders, as to uses, means, and ends. These judgments always rest on choices between alternatives of good and bad, right and wrong, efficient and inefficient, adequate or inadequate, promising or nonpromising. Every object in the universe—every thing, condition, thought, expression, occurrence, situation, symbol, and even the symbols of nonexistent things that man is aware of—is placed on some scale of approval-disapproval.

Every department of life is governed by social values. They operate as determinants of goods and services, family activities, political values, virtues, health and recreation, education, social position, occupation, aesthetic expressions, friendships, religion, and scientific and technological endeavor. As Americans we value highly matrimony and the family, the democratic way of life, loyalty and patriotism, equality of opportunity, community service, the seeking of prosperity, working and achieving as individuals, and so on.*

Values are constructs emerging from experience. Some of the shared values in any given society at any given time are common to all societies; some are unique in it; and some apply only in certain relationships or groupings. But, whether universal or particular, borrowed or indigenously developed, values are created; they are human discoveries and constructs. They are not the vague abstractions of cloistered thinkers or retreats from hard realities; nor are they fiats of autonomous reason or superhuman revelations. They emerge in different physical and social environmental contexts as *products of the collective experience* of many people.

*For an excellent treatment of major value orientations in America with numerous illustrations, see reference 89.

Values grow out of problem situations, out of crises of all degrees of gravity. In these situations, men observe and make inquiry regarding causes and effects, antecedents and consequences. In their long experience on earth men have found, and continue to find, that certain things, conditions, occurrences, actions, expressions, beliefs are in the long run to their advantage, and that others are disadvantageous in one way or another. They arrive at judgments as between right or wrong, good or bad, better or worse, pleasant or unpleasant, beautiful or nonbeautiful, allowable or nonallowable, efficacious or nonefficacious. In some cases these judgments or evaluations may be based on whims, but usually they have grown out of observed and realized facts and involve a certain degree of logical reasoning and conceptualization.

Value judgments demonstrate themselves as preferences in every situation where individuals or groups make a choice and select. Hence, as Kluckhohn points out, a value is always a more or less standardized conception, explicit or implicit, on the part of an individual or a group, of that which is approved or disapproved in the way of things, ways of behaving, ways of believing, means of acting and ends of acting. But it is not just a preference; it is *a preference which is felt or considered to be justified* morally, logically, hedonically, aesthetically, religiously or on utilitarian or other grounds. (80)

Once formed, these value judgments become an integral and dominating part of the culture. They surround everyone like an all-pervading atmosphere, since everything is valuable in some degree, but for this reason many of us are hardly aware of their existence and are not particularly articulate about them. Nevertheless, the objective evidence of the reality of values, as social facts or data, is found in the daily, even momentary, operations or actions of people; in their spontaneous behavior in situations, such as selecting foods, enjoying paintings; in the testimony of witnesses and in self-reporting in typical situations; in demonstrated interests and aversions; in what they exert themselves for, sacrifice for, spend money for; and in what they protect and promote in their efforts. Similarly, we are made aware of these value judgments when we note the dismay or protest that arises when they are violated or neglected. Such negative conduct not only embarrasses us among our fellow group members and makes us liable to censure or punishment, but causes inner disturbance and even conflict. (73; 89, pp. 377-382)

Given values are purely a matter of temporary belief and conviction. They are also no more than assertions whose validity is probable in greater or less degree. Furthermore, like other human creations, they are relative and tentative as to time; they are not finalities. The creative process goes on continually: the truth of one generation is the error of another; the certainty of one, the probability of another; the belief of one, the superstition of another; and so on. Human life is a perpetual and new experience—and a process of developing the experiential and referential principles we call values. (70; 71; 72; 78) Nevertheless, it is only through values that man's actions have meaning and purpose, for values provide the criteria and guides for men's actions and provide men with their living convictions, their patterns of preference, their objectives in living.

The values of a people take different forms and can be variously classified. They may be *positive,* posing what is considered essential or desirable, or *negative,* indicating what is harmful or reprehensible to us as individuals or groups or generally conceived of as antisocial. Values may be further classified as follows: *Instrumental values* are those which have to do with adequate means of achieving things or conditions needed or wanted and include technical standards of utility and efficacy, cognitive standards of truthfulness, regulatory standards of rightness. *Expressive values* relate to the effective aspects of life, how we are to express ourselves appropriately along aesthetic, religious, and recreational lines. *Goal values* govern the purposes, objectives, and ideals of individuals and of a social system, the valid ends that they strive for, and comprise a frame of aspirational reference and determine the potential action of the future.

The social values and the basic attitudes of the persons of a society are inseparable.* The values, as just indicated, are the reigning, empirical cultural entities of groups with an objective reference. The attitudes are the interiorized individual or subjective affective counterpart of the social values and are acquired by the individual and become fixed because he lives in a value-charged milieu. Single social values and individually held attitudes may be paired in individuals. These social attitudes, once fixed in the individual, serve as frames of reference in the situations to which they relate, determining to an important degree the preferences or the likes and dislikes of the individual. Overtly the value attitudes take the form of conscious or unconscious action.

The social values are as numerous and variable as the choices that men and groups must make every moment of their lives. They exist at every level of life and are involved in all fields and departments of human experience and interest. Different persons and groups have variant values regarding things, relationships, or preoccupations and variant interests in given values. Thus, many values are confined to a certain class, a so-called "race," a sex, an occupational or professional group, a region, an organization. Most values are not single or simple. Most religious values, for example, constitute a complex system involving persons, ideas, ideals, and ritualistic actions.

Values may be arranged according to a scale from least important to most important, from the more or less indifferent to the unquestioned and imperative, from immediate or momentary importance to future significance, from the highly individualized to the almost exclusively social. Values are also related to location in space and always vitally related to the given society and culture in which they are functioning. For this reason values are not so easily communicated to another society as are, for example, material techniques and products. The current efforts to impose American democratic values upon the Japanese is a case in point. Finally, the values regarding social purpose may be deceptive, even erroneous, rationalizations or wishful justifications.

Nevertheless, any given society, as distinct from its subgroups, does have a body of social values that are of a relatively generalized, formalized, and integrated character. These are coextensive with the society, quite generally accepted and approved by its members, and operationally potent among them.

The Functions of Social Values. Both the special and the general social *values have central and crucial significance in societal organization.* Their

*For the classic statement see W. I. Thomas and F. Znaniecki, *The Polish Peasant in Europe and America* (New York: Alfred A. Knopf, Inc., 1927), pp. 21-23.

important functions in that organization can be concisely presented as follows:

MOTIVATION. The motivation of men in society is greatly influenced by the social values of that society. They determine the good things, material and nonmaterial, for which men want to expend their energy and time. Members of social systems organize their lives individually and collectively around their values.

PURPOSES AND GOALS. Values state the essentials and qualities of social life that all or most men respect and wish to have established and perpetuated. Thus, values—the estimates of worth—are the matrix from which emerge the purposes and goals of any social system. Without these accepted, luminous purposes and goals, there can be no clarity or consistency of function and no rallying of essential social and societal action in their economic or political life, their education, art, religion, recreation, or any other essential, need-fulfilling aspect of their life. All action must be goal-directed; when it is not, action is haphazard and chaotic (as it is occasionally). In general, the effectiveness, the very existence, of a societal organization depends upon the degree to which the associated human beings constituting it proceed in terms of shared and interdependent values, purposes, and goals.

Most of the processes that are found in a social system are the concrete operational means of accomplishing social purposes. This fact is reflected in all the processes of cooperation, in manipulation of physical environment, in formation of groups, in division of labor and specialization of function, in formation of a stratification system, in the processes of both physical and social mobility, in opposition processes, and in the processes of societal regulation and maintenance and societal reorganization. Even the processes of social decadence and ossification reflect the deterioration, the oversight, or the lack of revitalization of purposes.

CRITERIA OF PERFORMANCE. The social values provide the criteria for testing, sorting, and selecting the individual and social actions, or performances, with respect to their pertinence and appropriateness, their quantity and quality, in pursuing the purposes. These selected requirements are expressed in *norms,* or standards, or bodies of rules, that *prescribe* the imperative, the permitted, and the prohibited action, and in the *roles* that catalogue what different categories of persons are *expected to do* in the way of functions, because of their social position, in the different common social situations.

BASIS OF SANCTION SYSTEM. The values are the basis for the sanction system, that is, the reward-punishment system of a group, community, or society. They determine what is praised, desired, required, and hence rewarded, and what is censured, disapproved, proscribed, and hence punished.

BASIS OF GROUPS. Values *define* groups on the basis of the values held by the members; they *make* groups as people assemble around common values which they jointly cherish; and they *sustain* groups through the cohesion and stability which they provide for the members. Without common, shared values there can be no solidarity, no frame of unity or action, no uniformity or continuity of groups. The same may be said for an entire society. In a very real sense, the critical differences between societies are the differences in their values, since their structures, functions, and processes are expressions of their value-system.

Social Norms

Every social system and every society has a body of norms or standards, rules or codes, and conceptions of acceptable usages which are the basis of all organized life. They define more or less explicitly the behavior essential to support and effect in action the particular values involved in almost every recurrent social situation. They demarcate the zones of tolerance outside which individuals and groups venture at their peril and establish the expectations, the directives and grooves, and the obvious controls essential to order, unity, and all forms of maintenance.

Some norms are expressed in the form of insistent requirements or prescriptions of action (for example, paying taxes, caring for immature offspring); some in prohibition or proscription of certain kinds of behavior (for example, rape, murder, treason); and others in permissive or optional action (for example, marrying, following a particular occupation, joining a particular religious denomination). The sociocultural vehicles or carriers of the norms range in explicitness and imperativeness from the optional folkways, through the customs, traditions, conventions, and mores, to the highly formalized and collectively enforced laws and constitutions of the great organized, regulatory, institutional associations. The norms make social life orderly and systematic; they are the basis of all organized, integrated action.

As in the case of values, upon which the norms are based, some norms are universal among all societies, and some grow out of the peculiar organizational conditions of the society and its parts. In every society there are also the special norms of all manner of special-interest groups, some of which are incompatible with those of other interest groups and also with those of the larger community or society.

In every group and society the norms must be sufficiently numerous and diverse to govern every recurrent relationship and operation. Every social act is presided over by patterned, socially accepted, and more or less enforced rules. Every social act is, in fact, in some degree an approximation of or a deviation from a social norm.

Norms become more and more pertinent in a large complex society like our own. The more complex a society becomes, *the greater the number and the more clear-cut, consistent, and formal the norms of the society must be* and *the more effective and certain the sanctions* (rewards and punishments) *that enforce them.* A more elaborate treatment of norms in connection with their major regulatory significance will be presented on pages 319 to 323.

Statuses and Roles

The functioning of a society depends upon the existence of structured relationships among individuals and groups and of established patterns for reciprocal behavior between individuals or groups of individuals. Therefore, the varying positions, or *statuses,* which the myriad actors in a society hold in relationship to each other and the parts, or *roles,* that they play—that is, what they typically do in these respective positions—are of elemental significance in societal organization; for the statuses and roles are derived from the total structural-functional pattern of a society. At the same time they are the constituent elements in all the standard patterns of relationship and reciprocity (the structures) among the human beings in the society and in all the functions of these individuals in their numerous relationships with each other. In effect, all the statuses and roles make up the total societal organization. All the other structural and functional analyses (which will be discussed in later chapters) are simply more detailed classifications and more specific combinations of statuses and roles.

Every status and every role is always relative to and reciprocal with the statuses and roles of other actors. Furthermore, status and role are inseparable. The individual performs no roles except in one of his various social positions, and his statuses are of no consequence apart from the accompanying functional performance. The individual actor thus is a "composite bundle of statuses and roles." (112, p. 26) The society, or any of its social systems, is an array of status structures with their related role functions. As Linton points out, the more perfectly the members of any society are adjusted to their statuses and the more efficiently they perform their roles, the more smoothly the society will function. (107, p. 115) Statuses and roles will be briefly analyzed.

Status. Status is of basic significance in the structure of a social system, since every individual, every category of individuals, and every group has a social position or identifiable point of location in the organizational pattern of the particular system. This place or position in the scheme of social relations is known as a "status." Every typical social relationship involving two or more persons consists of their status arrangement or positional patterning. Even the newborn baby has a status and as he grows older acquires many more statuses. There are, of course, an infinite number of possible patterns of relationship and hence of possible statuses, but as social scientists, we must confine ourselves to the standard ones. There are such very obvious standard statuses as carpenter, employer, mother, attorney, and so on.

The status, or position of given individuals and categories of individuals in the *societal* organization, must be distinguished from the *ecological,* or *spatial,* location of individuals and groups on the earth. Status has a distinct psychological, as well as societal, signification. The standard statuses of a society exist subjectively, that is, in the minds of the people, in the form of attitudes, beliefs, norms, and ideas bound up with each one. These psychic elements are exemplified in the concrete, overt, patterned performance of each actor in each of his various statuses.

FUNDAMENTAL FUNCTIONAL AND SCALAR ASPECTS. The objective existence of statuses in a social system is revealed in the different functions of the system as carried on by the types of members and in the relative esteem or disesteem accorded the holders of the different statuses on the basis of the graded evaluations placed on the different statuses and evidenced in the prevailing system of social ranks. These different but related aspects of status will be briefly examined.

Statuses are related to societal functions; in fact, most statuses grow out of the great variety of standard functions that must be carried on by the members of a society if its various needs are to be met. These functions are mainly in the economic, familial, political, religious, military, and educational departments of life, although every function as performed has its related status. At the same time, there are some who are primarily only beneficiaries of functions (for example, babies and small children, the congenitally incompetent); others who are not in a condition to engage in many or important functions (for example, the aged, ill, handicapped, isolated); and some who are actually carrying on disfunctions (for example, criminals). These functions and disfunctions are performed by standard categories of persons whom we know by such general designations as father, wife, infant, president, employer, grocer, priest, gambler, and so on. Each category has a status. Functionally, each status has a relationship to the total operation of the society and some degree of significance in it.

Each status is relative to, and usually interdependent with, the statuses of all other individual and group units. The functions or disfunctions must always and unavoidably be conducted in a reciprocal or complementary relationship with other persons; that is, two or more status holders are always involved in a two-way or multiway exchange of activities and effects. Each status implies and requires another status. It is always vis-à-vis others; otherwise it would have no significance. Each performer in a standard social situation has certain characteristic duties and responsibilities, but he also has certain rights and privileges or other gains. Thus, we have such paired reciprocities among status holders as husband and wife, parent and child, official and rank and file, employee and employer, minister and parishioner, doctor and client, criminal and victim.

The rights and benefits of one party imply corresponding duties and expenditures of the other and vice versa. In connection with the societally essential functions, each actor renders benefits and utilities to the other; if this were not so, the societal system would not operate. If it were not for the disutilities performed by the holders of certain statuses, there would be much less societal malfunctioning. But every individual in a society has some kind and degree of function which he performs for others, and some degree of positive or negative demand is made upon him. Thus, function gives him *status*, or position in the system of relationships, and his peculiar significance in the operation of the social system. Each status is part of the functional system. All of them are expressions of the interdependent structuring of a society at a given time and stage of development.

Statuses also involve and reflect the system of scaled values of the society. The social contributions of the various standard functional categories of persons are subject to evaluation according to the values and standards that are accepted and applied by the group or society. The positions are not appraised equally but are ranked on a scale of esteem-disesteem. The value placed upon the different positions seems to depend upon the group's or society's estimation or interpretation of the needs responsible for the functions and of the weight of the social demands made upon the holders. Behind them also are interests, mores, and especially the institutionalized values and practices of the society, and a whole array of historical social and cultural processes. But on the basis of the scale of values as applied to the different types of functionaries, a father usually has high status in his family as breadwinner and protector; the common laborer has lower status than the skilled laborer or the executive; and so on. This is simply additional proof that status is always *social* status. There is no such thing as solitary status. When there are two or more individuals or groups to be compared, they are always subjected to evaluation, and evaluation means ranking according to position on a scale.

Thus, a status system is not merely a means of allocation of social function; it also invokes a set of value judgments according to which individuals, categories of individuals, and groups are ranked along continua, such as superior or inferior, high or low, social or antisocial, and so on, in relation to one another. Since the status system includes every member of a group or society, every individual has some social rank. Each rank, in turn, carries with it some degree of esteem, privilege, deference, or ascendance, as compared with those of different rank. Status is thus both *functional* and *scalar* in a social system.*

Newcomb has referred to the social statuses as the "construction blocks" of societies and organized groups. (111, p. 277) In the same spirit we can say that groups or societies, as functional entities with arranged interrelated and reciprocal elements, are structures composed of statuses. The various classes of statuses are assessed with various degrees of pertinence in the total structure and their holders are evaluated accordingly. All the statuses in the group or society are more or less integrated into a total system of division of function, interlocking rights and obligations, and a value-scaled hierarchy of ranks. In a very real sense the various status interrelations are a kind of cement that binds a social system together.

Ways of Acquiring Status. There are different ways of acquiring status, but most students are agreed that there are two main ways, ascription and achievement, originally proposed by Linton. Hiller has added a third, assumption, that seems to be borne out by observation. (98; 99; 102, pp. 335-337; 107, pp. 115-117)

Ascribed status (*ascription*) is mandatory and unavoidable, since it is due to assignment of functional and value position without reference to the abilities, the desires, or the choices of persons. The occupance of the particular status is the result of certain unchosen and uncontrollable characteristics, such as sex, age, family relationship, order of birth in family, race, nativity, class or caste at birth, locality, and, in some instances, what amounts to inherited occupation. By virtue of such uncontrollable biological social circumstances and such accidents at birth, persons have at least certain aspects of their status, especially the reciprocities involved, predetermined for them and thrust upon them. These differences are made the subjects of special valuations, norms of conduct, and rights and duties.

Although ready-made, assumed status (*assumption*) is optional; that is, the individual chooses it instead of having it ascribed to him or imposed upon him. For example, it is to some extent optional whether a man marries and becomes a father, with consequent special status requirements and prerequisites, whether he joins one vocation or another, whether he joins one religious denomination or another, and so on. But each such position, if he assumes it, imposes requirements in the way of abiding by rules of competence and norms of expectation and obligation.

Achieved status (*achievement*) is acquired by virtue of the individual's accomplishments. It usually requires special abilities and some striving and is due to individual effort exerted under interpersonal competitive or even antagonistic conditions. As Linton implies, achieved status often seems to be designed to serve as a bait to obtain certain kinds of not too abundant but essential behavior from persons of different degrees of competence. Both quantitative and qualitative considerations enter into the values and norms attaching to such status. High achieved status usually involves more social obligation as well as rights and requires high quality of ability and performance.

Key, or Distinctive, Status. Any given individual at any given time usually has several—even many—statuses acquired in the above ways. His statuses are as numerous as his various participations in types of social relationships. Each of these statuses defines his position with reference to a limited sector of social interaction. He has, however, at any given time, a general or over-all status in the community or society. This is his "key status," to use Hiller's apt term. All his statuses enter into it, and to some extent it is a configuration of his behavior patterns and his evaluated social characteristics. His many statuses blend together or cluster or are totalized. But his most *distinctive* status at the moment, in terms of social function and esteem, has major determinative influence. His key status is *weighted* according to his most crucial societal function or disfunction, esteem or disesteem. This weighting involves a quasi-statistical procedure, producing a sort of weighted average of his various statuses. Thus, a particular man is a so-so husband and father, a third-rate

*The *scalar* aspect of status will be emphasized in connection with stratification in Chap. 14.

businessman, and so on, but he has been elected mayor of the city and during his term of office will have that rather high key status. Another man is a devoted husband, a fond father, a generous friend, and devout church member, but his strategic status is that of professional racketeer or gambler.

This key status gives the individual relative rank in the operational and inferiority-superiority order of the total community. On the basis of this status he is classified and his conduct judged. It also determines his social prospects, or life chances, and provides him with most of his rights, advantages, and privileges and his corresponding duties, disadvantages, and liabilities. Finally, it is mainly by means of this key status that the individual obtains his main reflection of himself in terms of how he appears to others. (99, pp. 91-93; 102, pp. 339-343; 107, p. 113)

Relativity of Status. Status functions and values are in force as they exist at any given time. Some of them, however, are ever-changing. Thus, at any given time the evaluation of the statuses depends upon the major trends and contingencies *of the time.* A religious genius may have high status at one time in a society; a political leader or a captain of industry at another time.

Given individuals also have changes of status in the course of their lives, as when they pass from one age group to another (for example, from adolescence to adulthood) or from a lower to a higher occupation or professional standing, get married, and so on.

Societies differ in the types of statuses that constitute their status structure, in the ways in which individuals get into a given status, in the behavior requirements of a given status, in the prestige or rank an individual acquires because of his status, and in the way occupation of a given status affects the life chances of the individual in the general social organization. All societies also have a more or less complex status system, the essence of which is the functional relation and rank location of all its constituent actors.

Roles. Each of the numerous positions or statuses of a social system carries with it a set of socioculturally patterned and established acts which the incumbents are expected, even required, to perform if they are to function appropriately and effectively according to their status in the relational situation. This pattern of expected behavior connected with a particular position is known as a "role." Each role is thus the dynamic, processual aspect of a status. When the actor acts in any status, he is acting out a role, an organized complex of particular acts. Roles thus represent ways of carrying out the functions for which positions exist.

Societal Pertinence of Roles. It is apparent that *roles are of key significance in societal organization in its operational aspects.* In fact, a group or society as a functional system consists elementally of its constituent individuals performing roles. The roles are the means whereby the various essential functions are allocated among the members of that system. The persistence and well-being of the system requires that all the members also adequately perform the whole complement of roles essential to meet its functional requirements. Newcomb puts it well when he points out that the network of prescribed roles is much like a language. Just as a common language is essential to communication in the society, so the role system is necessary if each individual is to be functional and if the society is to operate as a whole.

When persons participate as friends, parents, followers of vocations, stockholders, farmers, members of clubs, lodges, social groups, and social classes, or in any other activity characteristic of or essential to a social system, the action in the particular status is never entirely free. Most of it is specialized and stylized in form according to ready-made, specified role patterns. As the number of positions, types of relationships, and division of labor increase and the allowed or required activities of a society become more diverse, a greater number of voluntary or involuntary parts is assigned to individuals and the necessity of performing them in a standardized manner becomes more imperative. If individuals are to function at all in the recurrent situations and relationships of social life, they must behave in specified, expected, required, or permitted ways to avoid chaos. In brief, all individuals must perform numerous roles; they must have patterns of behavior which are considered by the group to be appropriate to the function to be performed. If, for one reason or another, the individuals do not have the facility to do so, they are incompetents or mavericks, and the society is defunctionalized to that extent.

Finally, the successful operation of a social system requires that the different classes of roles be sufficiently specific to be understood, that they be standardized, realistically appropriate to the functions, in conformity with the common value system, and consistently and coherently integrated with each other.

Relation of Roles to Value System. The prescriptive content of the roles grows out of and is directly related to the value system of the group or society. Needs are recognized and evaluated. Norms develop which specify the correct actions necessary to fulfill the needs values. These norms take the form of rules, of both an informal nature in the folkways, customs and mores, and a formal nature, in the laws and other more or less specifically articulated rules of the social institutions. However, not all of the content of most roles is equally essential in carrying out the basic societal functions. As noted previously some acts are *required* and some are *prohibited*, and in between there is a considerable range of *permitted* behavior. From the operational point of view, however, the necessary part of any role is the expected, prescribed, and required behavior. It is this which enables the social system to operate.

Functional Aspects of Roles. The functional aspects of roles require special mention because of their significance in societal organization. First, at any given time, the roles of the role system are definitely formulated and accepted, and the individuals of the social system do not have to devise their essential social actions for themselves. To use Linton's figure, each role is very much like a ready-made suit of clothes, with considerable latitude in such minor aspects as color, fabric, price, and so on, but with a very similar general pattern and the requirement that *all* men must wear suits, and not togas or coats of paint.

Second, most of the members of a society quite readily perform the great bulk of their roles with at least minimally essential effectiveness. This is due to the fact that the roles have developed through social experience and are based on the limits of proficiency of the vast majority of the population affected and effected by them, and that they are learned successfully. Actually the elements and requirements of the roles for the more universal interactional situations are so much a part of the pervasive role atmosphere that surrounds the on-coming generation (and also the immigrants) that much of their content is acquired by almost automatic conditioning processes.

Many of the roles are learned in advance, and the actors can step into them and perform them without much rehearsal. Thus, familial and civic roles are standing patterns of essential functioning that most individuals perform quite successfully when they achieve the related positions, whereas professional, technical, and official roles are more specialized and require special and systematic preparation. In general, however, most of the standard roles are so important in societal organization that their sufficient acquisition cannot be left to chance. They are the subject of informal and formal and more or less continuous education.

Third, once roles have been acquired and practiced, they function as tendencies to respond that are set off by the occasion or relationship like the pulling of a trigger or the lighting of a fuse. They represent stimulus patterns that impel us to act in modal ways in typical social relationships and positions. Society *gets* its necessary action at the right time in the right way in the particular situation.

Fourth, roles are persuasive and compulsive. Individuals come to know that if they do not play their different roles adequately according to the pattern of expectations, they will be criticized and disciplined. The discipline will range from avoidance, through ridicule, moral persuasion, firing, and ostracism, to legal compulsion and penal action, depending upon the social gravity of the role and the social effects of its violation. The individual discovers also that in order to achieve his own private or selfish objectives in the group, he must meet certain standardized behavior requirements.

Finally, there are emoluments and the positive sanctions attaching to roles. As already stated, roles carry not only obligations and duties but also rights and privileges that the group or society sets great store by and which individuals are anxious to enjoy. Furthermore, when the individual plays his roles with efficiency and completeness, he has the peace of mind which comes from knowing that he is doing his job. What is even sweeter for many is the much desired approval of the group or society and possibility of achieving prestige and higher station. Many of the most precious rewards—praise, success, social recognition—are acquired through role proficiency.

Thus, statuses and roles are the basis of both the structural adjustment and functional coordination of the individuals and groups of a society to each other, by means of which they know where they stand and how they are related in the structural whole, and what is required, permitted, and forbidden in the functional whole.

Leadership

The leadership role is of focal importance in societal operation. Any social system requires more than values and norms, more than statuses and roles. The values need to be clarified and emphasized, the norms exemplified and applied, the statuses and roles functionally coordinated and utilized in the pursuit of societal needs and objectives. Pressures, needs, and potentialities for social action exist in the mass, but masses are not self-starting, self-organizing, or self-directing. No group or combination of groups can exist without originators, organizers, and directors of its processes. It is necessary for leaders, those who possess certain personality characteristics or have been delegated or elected officers of the groups of various degrees of organization, to serve as dynamic and catalytic agents. Before taking up these two major functional aspects of leadership, certain general features need to be examined.

Leadership and the Social Situation. Leadership is both an individual phenomenon and a social phenomenon of a highly functional nature—an integral phase of most group processes. Leaders appear and are necessary in all manner of social conditions and in every department of social life. But always leadership activities are resultants of the interplay of a combination of factors which emerge from any given social situation. The situation invites, secures, and makes the leader. The particular group needs of the moment dictate the choice and type of leader, no matter what the action is to be: a mountain rescue party, a recreational gathering, a religious ceremony, industrial planning, military campaign. The leader, in turn, is the factor that releases, channelizes, and integrates the energies and abilities of the members or participants involved in all societal action.

Leadership and followership cannot be separated. Neither exists save in terms of the other. The functional character of the leader implies a complex give-and-take between the leader and the membership of the group that he is leading. The leader becomes leader through making a contribution to the membership; they follow him because they deem it to be to their advantage, except in situations where they are coerced and must submit. The members are wooed and led, not driven. They "feel the pulse" of the leader and wish to identify themselves with him and his cause. But he remains the leader, or rather the leader-servant, only so long as he satisfies his followers.

Another important aspect of leadership is that many a *potential* leader never becomes an actual leader, because the social situations do not invite and cannot utilize his particular qualities and abilities. Moreover, the good leader in one field of action is not necessarily a leader in others. He may be a follower in all other departments of life. Furthermore, a leader today is not necessarily a leader tomorrow, unless he is flexible enough to change with the exigencies of the situation. The varying social situations in culture, place, and time tend to—in fact, *must*—produce their own "best leaders."

Characteristics of Leaders. Leaders have varying combinations of traits. Each situation requires a unique blend of characteristics and sets up its own demand for particular qualities and skills, as for example, in an army leader, a social reform leader, a labor leader, a political leader, or a dictator. In spite of these diversities of required characteristics, leaders have some traits in common, as recent studies attest. Invariably they have insistent needs for ego-expansion, self-assertion, and some degree and kind of dominance.

In comparison with nonleaders, leaders usually have superior intellectual abilities, a more extensive fund of knowledge and certain essential technical proficiencies for the situation, often good or striking appearance, usually more than average vitality, a persuasive voice and manner, good humor, an air of self-confidence, and demonstrated competence. Other traits commonly found in leaders include keen insight, speed of decision, finality of judgment, dependability, initiative, persistence, adventurousness, self-control, social adaptability, and the capacity to manage men (their emotions, ideas, actions), to meet opponents, and take advantage of opportunities. If successful, leaders call out feelings of liking, respect, admiration, submission, and sometimes even fear on the part of their followers.

Types of Leaders. Various classifications of leaders exist, depending upon the requirements of the varying social situations and the analytical purposes of the analysts. From the point of view of the *organization and purposiveness of the situation,* there are the *informal-group* leaders, such as those at a dinner party or picnic, who are sensitive to the requirements of the particular situation and the feelings of the others and initiate exchanges of services and direct temporary tasks; and the *instrumental leaders of organized groups,* such as administrative and technical directors—all officials —who are specially selected and formally responsible for initiating and directing activities of the organization, according to established rules and routines, in order to achieve specific instrumental objectives.

From the point of view of the *affective or intellectual nature of the leadership services to be performed,* there are the *charismatic leaders,* who provide special and powerful inspiration in emotion-charged situations; the *intellectual leaders,* who provide ideational perspectives and goals; and the *expressive leaders,* who lead symbolic performances, such as at celebrations, exhibitions, rituals, and ceremonials.

From the point of view of *the way power is wielded,* there are *authoritarian or dictatorial leaders,* who in absolutistic fashion determine the objectives, policies, and plans, dictate the activities and relationships of members, function as judges and agents in administering rewards and punishments, and so on; and the *democratic leaders,* who act as the agents or servants of the group in sensing objectives, establishing ways and means, obtaining the participation of the members, spreading responsibility among them, and, in general, carrying out the intentions of the group.

Functions of Leaders. In every social situation leaders perform both dynamic and integrative functions. As *dynamic agents,* the leaders are persons who start action going in their groups. They appeal to and mobilize various pertinent drives, emotions, and wishes; clarify, crystallize, and capitalize the dominant interests and aspirations, which they also usually symbolize; and marshal and guide the energies and latent abilities of the people. Then they pose a line of action, make decisions, or function as dynamic agents in obtaining decisions from the group. They persuade, give authoritative orders, and spur the people on.

Leaders are also the *integrative, organizational,* and *nuclear agents.* They are the key or star persons to whom the group members are attracted and the pivotal persons around whom action revolves. All joint action requires a localizing or centering of attention upon ends and purposes, ways and means. The leaders do this as they function as formulators, bearers, and illuminators of social values and objectives. The leaders embody and symbolize the norms of their group, live up to them, and in general set an example. The mass wants to be *used* in the interest of its ends, to be purposefully organized and directed; it wants essential action. If this is to be, then there must be recognized authority, however it may be established (that is, whether assumed or granted); the execution of decision, however arrived at; the allocation of duties and responsibilities; the direction and supervision of tasks; the administration of rules and regulations; the exercise of discipline and eliciting of obedience; and the purveying of rewards and punishments.

Leaders are the dynamic and integrating factors at all levels of societal organization and in all functional activity. They make all the other factors "work." Every society must have a system of leadership, although the different specific patterns of the system will vary widely for different societal structures and functions of a given society, and the over-all systems will vary according to the major governing—democratic or totalitarian—ideology of different societies. But in all modern societies with their amorphous masses of population, their complex functioning entailed by division of labor and the multiplication of highly organized ways of doing almost all societally essential things, *persons* as special kinds of stimulators, guiders, deciders, representatives, arbitrators, integrators, and commanders become more and more necessary.

CHAPTER XI

GROUPS: NATURE, FORMATION, FUNCTIONS, AND FORMS

THE GROUP is the most general designation of interacting human beings and the most elementary societal unit of observation for sociology. It refers to all unified functional collectivities within the larger societal organization. Not individuals but groups are the basic units into which a society may be reduced, for individuals are without significance save as members of groups. Every phase of the individual's existence involves participation in groups and as a group member with and against other groups. Conversely, every society consists of a combination of social groups. The numerous, varied, ever-changing groups are the interrelated and interacting subdivisions and constitute the more stable *framework* or structure of social life—the main concrete associational forms in which human beings are combined. At the same time, they constitute the *operative* units—connected, interdependent, reciprocal—through which men conduct their activities and enterprises, and achieve their ends and purposes. Members of society cohere and survive in groups.

Wherever men are found, they are conducting their more or less ordered and essential interactions and relationships in groups varying in kind, size, duration of existence, complexity of structure, degree of purposiveness, amount of organization, and specific function. Man lives in groups. What he does is group-determined and -influenced, and with his fellow men he continually creates new groups. The degree of complexity of societal organization is a matter of the number and variety of interdependent groups of which it is composed, and its functional efficacy rests upon their reciprocal and joint efficacy. The facts of social life are basically group facts. The study of groups—their development, structurings, and functions—is a subject of crucial and pivotal sociological concern.

The Nature of Groups

A group is any collection of two or more human beings psychically interacting with each other in some patterned manner, for some period of time, bound by some common interest, who recognize themselves as a distinct social entity and are usually so recognized by others because of their special meaningful reciprocal behavior. Concretely, two or more of us are a group when we function together as a family, when we attempt by our combined efforts to get a car out of a drift, when we belong to a union or a church, or serve as stockholders, executives, or workers of a corporation or as inhabitants of the United States.

To have a group, it is minimally essential that there be some direct or indirect communication between the members, some one or more common interests or objectives, some common participation, and that the collective members possess some unity and compose some recognizable structure. It is *not* necessary that there be compactness or face-to-face relationship or that the members hold all their individual values in common, or understand each other, or agree with each other in all or even many respects, or carry on all of their life tasks together.

When psychic contact, reciprocal influence, common interest, and joint participation cease, persons once united by these no longer constitute a group. This is true, for example, of kinsmen who have moved to unknown destinations and have lost contact with each other, and, hence, no longer have common ties, interests, or participation, and of persons in a club who no longer attend meetings or associate with other members and who do not subscribe to its doctrines or beliefs (1; 11, pp. 117-118; 34)

The concrete groups in a given society are exceedingly numerous and diverse in size, type, and variety of members, in degree of contact, in form of relationship involved, in degree of organization and integration, in specific functions or combinations of functions performed, in spatial scope, and in temporality and durability. Memberships overlap, and persons comprising any one group may be members of many others, depending upon the accident of their different physical locations, the range of their needs and interests, and their urge or their capacity to participate.

Groups vs. Categories and Aggregations

Social groups must be distinguished from *categories* and mere *aggregations* of human beings. A *category of individuals* exists only in thought. It is an invention in the form of a classification of types or kinds of persons based on likeness or difference or some other distinguishing characteristic held in common by the individuals in question which causes them to be considered together for certain purposes in the mind and the investigation of the classifier. The individuals are seen not as persons, but as stereotypes.

The individuals in a given category have certain similar biological, psychological, or sociocultural characteristics or certain similar functional roles and positions in the social system. But they do not have any persisting interaction and interdependence, and as a category, they are not an entity functioning as a dynamic whole. Representative categories are males, females, teen-agers, the aged, single, married, widowed or divorced persons, farmers, the unskilled or skilled workers, Jews, Negroes, janitors, executives, entrepreneurs, the middle class, the wealthy.

If two or more individuals of any category should develop interaction, a common consciousness, and common objectives, they would become a social group, as, for example, when some of those classified occupationally organize as a labor union or a body of strikers; or when the $1,200-per-year persons become an agitating lobbying group; or when some women (a sex category) become a suffrage association or a "public," working for women's rights, recognition, and legislation.

Aggregations consist of collections or assemblages of human beings who are physically contiguous, that is, have relative propinquity to each other in a given territory or space. Their contact is very limited and involves only the slightest interaction or modification of behavior. There is no significantly binding consensus or homogeneity of action. Aggregations are casual assemblages, usually temporary, in which the units are independent of each other and may be pursuing their own ends, unrelated to others. Thus, several dozen people on a street corner or the total population of a county are aggregations.

When an aggregation of human beings begins to interact through the development of some common interest or objective—and it often does this—it takes on the characteristics of a group. Notable forms of this are crowds, congregations, audiences, mass meetings.

Formation and Operation of Groups

Groups, like all other features of human society, come into existence as a result of more or less determinable *factors* and *processes.* Furthermore, their reason for being is the *functions* they perform for their members; they arise and persist because they satisfy the individual and social needs of their members. The needs are those which are culturally defined as such by the members and may or may not be directly related to biological and psychological mechanisms. These needs produce one or more common or complementary interests, usually crystallizing into purposes or goals among two or more interacting persons, the goals being sufficiently impressive to demand joint attention and joint action.

Attraction-Repulsion. The operation of attraction-repulsion among interacting human beings is the basic dynamic factor in the grouping process. Certain individuals and subgroups are attracted to others and attracted by them. Some persons and some groups are repelled by others. Similarities or the complementary nature of characteristics, needs, interests, functions, and physical and social positions, operating with many varieties and degrees of subtlety, draw some persons together in groups. Differences (those of sex excluded) push people apart and cause them to exclude others. The selective responses of different individuals to each other will range by degrees from great mutual attraction, through indifference, to complete repulsion. Usually, persons are also attracted to individuals who can be regarded as nuclei of particular groupings, and who often serve as the "superior" in socially recurrent and essential superior-subordinate relationships. Invariably, the group-forming process is in some degree a choice and rejection process, although such features are of limited significance in territorial groupings. (20; 22; 23; 24)*

What are some of the cohesive factors in group formation? Sex attraction and sheer gregariousness, as Aristotle pointed out, are probably the most elemental ones. Related to these are the parent-child relationship situation and the interest in descent, as exemplified in the family and the kinship group. Unavoidable homogeneous constitution, particularly a pertinent age range, common sex, and race, is a contributory factor that explains in part membership and participation in certain types of groups. Subjective influences involving sentiment relations as persons seek acquaintances, sympathy, love, and mutual attachment and admiration are important centripetal factors. Related to these is the sharing of painful or pleasurable experiences. Common socioeconomic status and interests, educational and cultural homogeneity, and common beliefs are cohesive factors.

The cohesion may grow out of propinquity, or common location or confinement, as, for example, three retired gentlemen sitting on a park bench discussing the passers-by, sponge fishing, or the weather or passengers on a transcontinental bus viewing and discussing the scenery. The common territory occupied by an array of persons with its requirements of accommodation and cooperation, if the people are to live and work together, produces one of the major categories of groups, namely, communities. Physical and social menaces may force individuals or smaller groups to unite for the sake of protection against impending or existing natural catastrophe or hostile groups of men. The possession of a common language or common religion, especially under competitive conditions, will function as a bonding factor.

Much more important, however, from the point

*J. L. Moreno (29), by a system of sociometric tests which allowed each member of an institutional community to designate degrees of attraction to other members, was able to indicate various degrees of intensity of grouping ranging from maximum attraction to maximum repulsion. The intragroup relationships he depicted graphically in the form of a sociogram. By counting interactions the sociometrists have been able to map out "small groups" which are quantitatively distinct from the rest of the population in the "field."

of view of the groups fulfilling pivotal functions in modern societal organization, are the continuous or recurrent needs and interests of a sociocultural nature which unite functionally persons who are relatively heterogeneous. These are of vital concern to individuals in their strategically essential societal actions if they are to survive and live satisfying *human* lives and to the community or society as a going concern. They include economic maintenance, political maintenance, and the satisfaction of intellectual, educational, recreational, aesthetic, scientific, religious, or ethnic interests and ends. (35; 36)

Complex social situations produce and require extensive collective action. As population has increased and the means of communication have improved, men have formed larger and larger societies made up of more and more groups. And as the interests have multiplied and expanded in scope, their satisfaction has required ever more complex functional interrelationships between greater numbers of individuals. Hence, the groups themselves have become larger and more complex. In such modern groups indirect (mechanical) means of communication and interdependence of needs involving organized division of labor are infinitely more important than contiguity, or constitutional homogeneity, or personal sentiment.

Interest Goals in Group Formation. The most important feature of the process of group formation is the fact that there comes a "moment when there is precipitated in the minds of a number of persons the recognition of the mutual value of collective action for the fulfillment of individual interests." (7, p. 28) A number of people in a similar situation and not too divergent in cultural background see the possibilities of joint action. In some cases thwarting or destructive tendencies can be corrected or prevented; in others, opportunities for new satisfactions are evident. The action of leaders and promoters or other controlling personalities within the collection of persons in crystallizing interests and aims and bringing about some degree of actual organization is important, as well as the stimulation of leaders from outside or of conflicting groups whose behavior serves as a counterprecipitant.

The interests are both individual and social. Some are like, and some are unlike, but complementary in character. All are constitutive in nature and draw together large numbers of individuals, most of whom are unknown to each other. Thus, a given society appears as a kaleidoscopic pattern of individuals drawn together into groups for the promotion of their interests.

"Consciousness of kind" as a primary factor has receded into the background as far as the formation of the great bulk of modern groups is concerned.* This is not to imply that there are no groups based on such similarities as sex or race, or common economic position and attitudes, or other precious common interests. But the members of the most significant modern groups are very frequently different as to kind and frequently antagonistic along many lines. In fact, the effective functioning of a modern group (for example, a corporation) often *requires* a variety of members who are widely different and have different functions within the whole. The interest-goal situation is thus the main orienting and bonding factor, and determines in large part the functions in which the particular group engages. The interest goals and the functions are the elements which mutually determine each other, and their interrelation constitutes the group patterns.

Groups may be united into larger groups. Each subgroup is a differentiation of the larger groups and has its own interests, goals, and functions which are often inconsistent with, antagonistic to, or of no material significance to those of the other groups. Although there is diversity in large groups, there is always solidarity growing out of the mutual interdependence of the parts, each of which by itself lacks self-sufficiency in certain major respects.

Summary of Functions. The functions of groups can be summarized as individual and societal. In functioning for individuals, groups provide most of their essential needs and satisfactions. They exist for the individuals that compose them and in the main for all other groups. Through the medium of groups individuals have their social contacts, receive their social stimulation, integrate their personalities, develop their creative potentialities, and conduct their distinctive life functions. Groups

*For a somewhat divergent point of view see T. Abel, "The Significance of the Concept of Consciousness of Kind," *Soc. Forces,* 9 (Oct., 1930): 1-10.

are thus the primary humanizing agencies. They make man fit to live within his kind of society and improve his life chances. (2, pp. 157-161)

Societally, groups are the different constituent social units, or cells, and in all their different forms constitute the operating mechanism and provide it with its functional efficiency as well with its internal frictions and antagonisms. Groups are the main associated cooperating entities carrying on all sorts of activities and enterprises essential to the harmony and survival of the societal organization. The separate groupings make up the indispensable division of labor, and each performs functions as part of the whole. The groups preserve and modify the precious institutions as they ensure social order and maintenance. Society implies interdependent and interfunctioning groups.

Essential Characteristics of Groups

This general analysis of groups as fundamental societal agencies may now be epitomized and systematically summarized in terms of their several universal structural-functional characteristics.

Consciousness of Unity among Members. The members of a group may be of different sex, age, and race, may have heterogeneous cultural backgrounds and many differing, even antagonistic, interests, and may be widely separated in space; but, as a particular group, they are conscious of each other and unified with each other by virtue of an identifiable common interest or compatible interests which they are jointly seeking to realize.

There is a consciousness of membership, a loyalty, a sense of belonging, an intermindedness, and we-feeling or togetherness, although there may be many degrees of this togetherness. The ties or bonds which unite the members into a social group may be either of an elective or of a compulsory nature, but they make the behavior of members closely interdependent and infuse them in some form and degree with feelings of oneness and solidarity. The members are valuable to each other. Furthermore, the group itself becomes a symbol or object value for the members and in many instances seems to take on an existence of its own.

Conversely, others whom the members are aware of as having *different* interests are identified as *not* belonging to the given group. This situation is reflected in the dichotomy of we-groups and out-groups, or others-groups, occasionally found in group analysis. The we-group consists of those sympathetically or cooperatively drawn together by common interests and expressional desires; the out-group is composed of those who are disliked, hated, or at least not understood, and against whom the members have antagonistic reactions. In wartime our nation is the we-group and the enemy the out-group; in labor-employer disputes each is the we-group for its own members and out-group for the members of the other faction.

Interactivity among the Members. Members of a group are co-workers or co-participants and function together in the activities specified as those which develop and satisfy their identifying interests. This common participation and reciprocal functioning may range from mere conversation to highly organized collective action involving heterogeneous population elements. The sociometric studies of groups show that the integration of a group can be measured on the basis both of the intensity of the feeling of unity and belongingness as indicated by its morale and of the degree of reciprocation existing among its members.

A Common Psyche. By virtue of the common interests, goals, and joint activity *the group develops a psyche*; that is, a common, though usually limited, psychological typing appears among the members. Especially is this true among the more durable groups, although it is by no means confined to them. The members show certain typical attitudes, habits, ideologies, and other symbolic features. All are exemplified in *some* of their individual behavior and in *most* of their group performance. (39)

A Separate Entity. The persons in a given group are usually recognized as a separate and more or less stable entity by the larger community for the duration of the active or suspended common interest or common pursuit of some objective. The specific group comes to be represented to all outsiders as a synthesis of its members.

A Common Interest Goal. The interest-goal situation and the corresponding functions operate as selective factors in determining membership. They connect the members and separate them from the nonmembers. As Znaniecki so well points out, the prospective members have already some system of values which nonmembers are not supposed to have. Some or all of the members assume that because of this common interest, they ought to associate together to the exclusion of all those who do not share it. Thus, to some extent groups have a closed membership. (39) Affiliation is based on the inclusion of some and the exclusion of others.

The acceptance and the likelihood of maintenance of a given set of interest objectives function as the basis of admission of new members to the particular group. In the criteria of selection for membership the group shows additional awareness of its identity. The very processes of influencing and conditioning to which the novice is subjected after he has been admitted to the more durable groups (for example, a labor union, a college faculty, a fraternal order) consist of accentuating the interests and values of the group or his subdivision of the group, and of acquiring proficiency in its functions. This also highlights the related consideration that most groups *do* have means of introducing new members into the group and transmitting to them its traditions, ways, and ideals.

Determination of Group Duration. The interest-goal situation is the primary determinant in the duration of the group formed about it, or, to put it a little differently, the persistence of the interest pattern is a cardinal condition for the preservation of the integrity and identity of the group. When the common interest deteriorates or ceases to function as the group dynamic, the persons once united by the interests and goals no longer constitute a group. Furthermore, support of the group's interest goal is essential to continued membership, and the traitor, the apostate, the transgressor against the principles of the group are summarily separated from the group.

Norms of Personal Behavior. Each group has implicit or explicit norms of personal relations and of functional group behavior. If the group is fairly durable, these norms are standardized and systematized until they come to be regarded as group institutions. (39) To these norms, with their minimal rights and duties, the members must conform.

Individual Role of Each Member. A more detailed aspect of the norms just mentioned is that, while acting as a member of any group, *each individual has a role*—some degree of specialization in the way of observable participation or social action—*which is related to and formed by the group function and norms.* This role prescribes his specific behavior and gives him status or honorific position in the specific group. Usually, he has a different role and occupies a different social position in each group to which he belongs.

As far as a particular group is concerned the individual member's status consists of the total "rights" which the group and the individual himself recognize as due him in his role, and his functions are the total "duties" he is required to fulfill. (39, pp. 806, 809) Both the statuses and the functions vary with different categories of members.

Range and Classification of Groups

Every societal system includes different types of social groups. Sociologists have compiled extensive classifications. (4; 6; 8, pp. 289-309; 9; 11, pp. 138-140; 14; 26; 33) Partly as a concise summary of classifications, but mainly to indicate the structural-functional variation, we will confine ourselves here to a presentation of the *range* of groups. Each range represents a continuum, but a given group will qualify under many or all of the characteristics of these ranges. Groups may range as follows:

1. *In extent of membership,* from those with many members (a huge corporation, a political party, even a nation) to those with only a few (a husband and wife, two people conversing, a modern family, a clique, or a dinner club);
2. *In purposiveness,* from those with strategic and fundamental objectives (a health department, an army, a scientific organization) to those with quite trivial purposes (a "wind-jamming" group);
3. *In inclusiveness,* from wide-open ones with a general heterogeneous membership, unified alone by a single social or territorial interest (American League baseball enthusiasts, a political party, the residents of a region) to closed groups with a specific, highly selective, homogeneous, closely in-

tegrated, and exclusive membership (a new labor local, a new religious sect, a Four Hundred);

4. *In temporality and stability,* from those with a high degree of permanence and durability, capable of enduring for centuries, or even seeming to have a sort of immortality (a corporation, a state, a universal church), to those which are ephemeral and flimsy, based on some fleeting interest or psychic current and passing out of existence in a matter of hours or minutes (a "bull session," a street-corner crowd, a mass meeting);

5. *In degree of organization,* from those which are formally organized with contractual relations and an institutionalized body of rules and established administrative procedures and personnel (any of the great political, economical, educational, religious associations or organizations) to those which are quite casual and informal (a clique, a friendship circle);

6. *In spatial scope,* from those which territorially are society-wide, extending over vast culture area, or even almost world-wide (the United Nations) to those which are highly local and restricted (the Tenth Ward Improvement Association, a local boys' club, a street-corner gang);

7. *In voluntariness,* from those in which membership is involuntary or automatic owing to birth (family or nation), location (neighborhood, city, or region), or status or position (class) to those in which it is a matter of individual choice (a dinner-discussion club, a fraternal order), to those in which it is a matter of compulsion because of necessity (a defensive fighting group) or external force (a prison gang);

8. *In type of contact,* from those in which members are in (a) *primary contact,* that is, intimate, personal, face-to-face, shoulder-to-shoulder, and usually friendly and sympathetic relationship, involving individual responsive personalities (small neighborhood, a play group, a family); to those in which members are in (b) *secondary contact,* that is, impersonal, abstract contact through long-range mechanical means of communication without wide acquaintance, involving physical and often social distance, and based on functions rather than on personalities (most modern dispersed groups, including sects, publics, regions, classes, nation-states); to those in which members are in (c) *tertiary contact,* the superficial and ephemeral contact of transients (persons on a street corner, in a bus, or at a ball game), where neither personality nor function is of much pertinence in the relationship;

9. *In equalitarian relationship,* from those in which members are fairly equal (a dancing club, a golf foursome) to those in which they are differentiated and even stratified in hierarchical array, and in which the social distance between the various levels is great, a kind of superior-and-subordinate relationship (any bureaucratic organization);

10. *In functional specialization,* from those groupings where the members have highly specialized functions to perform as part of an essential, complex, interdependent division of labor arrangement, and in which coordination, administration, and line procedures are all important (any large functional organization) to those where specifically designated *societal* function is almost nonexistent and the relationship is largely one of sympathy or gregariousness;

11. *In alignment of members,* from vertical, that is, segments of the population vertically separated from other segments (races, occupations, affiliates of sects), to horizontal alignment or strata or layers of the class system of the society;

12. *In bonding,* from multibonded, with many common interests and ties among the members (a family, a community, the modern state) to unibonded, with a single tie (a skiing club, a public events discussion club, rose-growers association);

13. *In complexity,* from those which are combinations and hierarchies of constituent groups (a corporation, a region, a state) to those which are unitary and all of a piece.

Major Functional Group Structurings

In the structural-functional analysis of a society the kind of organization that prevails among groups is the crucial consideration, since it is the determining factor in their nature and accounts for the special operations which they carry on. Three general types of groups, each with subtypes, are of major importance. They are informal groups; associations or the formally organized purposive groups, including especially the so-called "large-scale" formal organizations; and more widely inclusive, territorially organized or communal structurings. The first two will be examined here and the third in the following section of this chapter.

Informal Groups

Informal groups consist of persons in some kind and degree of communication and interaction with each other. The interest factor, though differing in degree, is always present. They vary in number of constituents from two persons in chance and momentary interaction to culture-wide or world-wide publics. The interaction may be due to gregariousness, sympathy, or kinship; to fear of or antagonism toward identifiable others; to some sudden social psychic current that sucks some people together; to interest in some very local or very widespread issue at the moment; or it may rest upon some ethnic, socioeconomic, or cultural similarity or unity of interest. The interaction may be highly interpersonal and intense, or it may be impersonal and almost unconscious. In many instances, the members act under the sway of all the types of motivation of the society and all the levels of regulatory mechanisms, including the highly institutionalized ones. The groups, as groups, however, *lack a system or organization*; that is, the relations are not governed by prearranged rules and prescribed by methods of procedure. The structure is an unplanned network of interpersonal relations. There are three general subtypes of informal groups:

Primary Groups. Primary groups are the small, intimate, face-to-face, more or less lasting, unorganized forms of association, such as pairs, families, play and congeniality groups, local occupational groups, and so on. The members usually have something in the way of selective common social-cultural backgrounds. The contacts and relationships are direct, personal, sympathetic, intensive, and repetitive. There is deep understanding and considerable fusion of personalities, and the membership has a strong feeling of identification with and belongingness in the group and cooperate freely and abundantly. In general, primary groups are the most cohesive of all groups. They are the chief focus of social satisfactions. They constitute the basic human associational units and are the nucleus of all other organizations—"the unit cell of social structures," to use MacIver's term. (26, p. 236) The groups are the kind of interacting relationship in which we do our first acting and give expression to our first social impulses. They are also the primary personality-forming and socializing agencies, as Cooley pointed out long ago.

The interrelationship of the interacting members (*A, B, C, D, E, F,* and *G*) of a simple primary group can be depicted as follows:

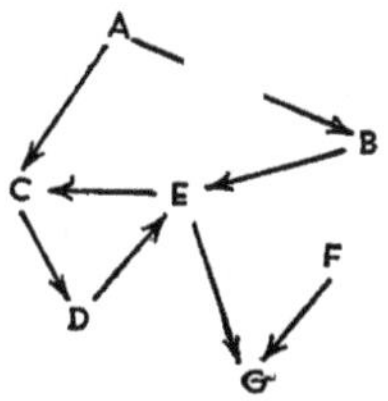

Although the organization is informal, it still may be rather complex. In most of the forms of primary groups indicated, there are codes of conduct for the group members, including customs and norms, regulating both activities within the informal group and the actions toward nongroup members. The members have different rights, obligations, prestige, and influence. There is a scheme of ideas, beliefs, and values, and there are ceremonies and rites related to the activities. The communication system informs the members of the ideas, sentiments, and occurrences vital to group solidarity and action.

Casual Groups. Casual groups are propinquity or in-presence groupings only slightly above the level of aggregations. They do have some *momentary* common interest by virtue of their convergence. In some instances, the momentary interest may be the primary incentive for the convergence (for example, people attracted to a fire). Being in the presence of each other, they are exposed to direct, unselected, often emotion-arousing stimuli. They have a wide range and consist of such chance assemblages as people loitering in a hotel lobby, passengers in a railway station, sidewalk engineers, crowds, and mobs. The contacts are superficial and temporary. Usually there is little likelihood of a common background, common sentiments, attitudes, and habits, or much in the way of congeniality and sympathy among the constituents. The organization is exceedingly sketchy and informal, and there are no conformity producing influences or pressures, save in the crowd, and there only momentarily.

Crowds are highly dynamic casual groupings. The crowd is a highly ephemeral milling herd of human beings. It is not a sustained societal mode of life, but an incident, an eruption. It comes into existence to do something for which no established machinery exists; or if such machinery does exist, its participants are too distraught or too impatient to use it. Crowds appear as the result of tension situations. The occasion may be a crisis or catastrophe (a fire, a labor strike); a spontaneous outburst of group joy or hatred (a victory celebration, a race or religious conflict); or merely an escape from regimentation or discipline (a student "stampede"). The crowd action dispels or releases this tension.

The participants in most instances are sucked in by the emotional tension and high-pressure suggestion. They are randomly contiguous, anonymous, uninhibited, fanatical, and unorganized in relation to one another, but while they are under the crowd sway, they are highly susceptible to generalized mass emotion and sentiment and the physical crowd squeeze. They pursue the objective until it is realized or the tension is broken by summary action of some outside agency or some other distracting event. The crowd's action is irrational, and order and system are in abeyance.

Participation in a crowd has some deteriorative effect upon personality, and crowd action usually creates disorder and menaces social well-being. Nevertheless, the crowd situation and crowd reaction tendency are often utilized by special-interest groups, as in revival meetings and political rallies.

Impersonal Diffused-Interest Groups. The diffused-interest groups are unorganized secondary groups of loose configuration. They consist of identifiable "sets" of people having one or more common and often absorbing interests. But the individuals are spatially scattered (not territorially limited), the contacts mostly impersonal, and communication mainly long-range and carried on by such media as publications and letters. The relations are limited by the subjects of interest, but are relatively enduring. The activities are similarly limited, the members acting mainly as individuals or small subgroups. There are no membership rules or membership lists, and the roles, rights, and duties of the participants are undefined. Some examples are ethnic groups (nationality, race, and other "minority" groups), occupational groups (carpenters, radio technicians, professors), status groups (classes, estates, castes), cultural interest groups (linguistic, religious, scientific, artistic, philosophic, and the like), hobby groups (builders and operators of "ham" radio transmitters, stamp collectors, and many others). If it were not for the common interest, the limited communication and activity, and the feeling of identity among the members, these sets of people would be mere categories. However, local members may exchange views regarding their interest as they meet casually or in specially arranged get-togethers. Certain combinations of the members of such groupings may organize and form purposive associations for the active promotion of their common or joint interests, such as the American Association for the Advancement of Colored People, a labor union of carpenters, a scientific organization.

Publics have some of the characteristics of such groupings. But, except in small isolated communities, publics are loose and widely dispersed groups. As such, they never meet together. Their interaction is not a matter of physical contact, but is through the indirect media of communication, such as long chains of conversation and writing, the press, radio, motion pictures, and television. Incidentally, because of the great recent advances of these media, publics today have attained their highest development in history. *They form around common interests,* which usually center around issues—moral, economic, political, artistic, religious, recreational. Their unity is symbolic rather than physical. Given publics are as extensive as the territorial range of the pertinent interest or interests, which may be local, coterminous with an entire society, or, on some issues, even world-wide. This common interest is the basis of the selection and the unity of the participants. A given public lasts as long as the uniting and attention-producing issue.

Although ready-made sentiments, traditions, and attitudes are used, *information,* false or true, is the primary basis of the end-product of publics, namely, "opinion." This opinion may be a matter of chance formulation through the general availability of information; increasingly, however, it is fostered by all manner of agencies—in the form of propaganda, publicity, releases, instructional material, editorials, pamphlets, sermons, addresses, white papers—or any other color—emanating from special-interest groups and organizations, such as religious bodies, corporations, governments, dictators, chambers of commerce, development associations, and so on. The opinion is registered by means of vocal and written expressions of the members of the public concerned, through influence, representation, polls, and various forms of balloting.

Although publics are not formally organized, they may and increasingly do come about as the result of the manipulative efforts of formally organized groups (for example, the prohibition public, due to the efforts of such organizations as the Anti-Saloon League). Furthermore, some of the members of a public may crystallize in an organization to give effect to the interests and vague objectives. In a sense, many of the religious and political groups are widespread, self-conscious publics.

Associations

Over against the various types of informal or even chance groups, we note *associations* as strategic elements in the structuralization of a society. An association may be defined as *a varying number of persons who are acting collectively and more or less permanently in a formally and systematically organized manner in accordance with deliberately established principles of operation and with an executive personnel to achieve certain more or less specifically formulated common or complementary interests and purposes.* Associations are organized systems deliberately created to carry on effectively in a coordinated manner the more permanent and essential specific types of social activity. All public and private social agencies conducting programs of action are thus manufactured, notably business firms, banks, farm organizations, churches, labor organizations, scientific bodies, art associations, propagandistic organizations, political parties, the state itself.

Associations are not exclusively modern phenomena, but modern society makes them necessary on an increasingly larger scale. Modern industrialized-urbanized societies, as previously noted (pages 32-36), are characteristically complex. The necessity of joint action among heterogeneous and dispersed persons and groups with many special interests in a complex environment has required the formation of associations. The central and signal fact in associations is conscious, purposive, coordinated functioning. This means that process is inherent in their formation and their operation as functional wholes. The features of organization and operation will be briefly set forth.

Organization around Limited Interests and Values. The association is organized around a set of limited and specialized interests and values which its members believe they can realize more effectively through organized concerted action. These interests may be *like,* as in the case of an economic organization where the members act for like ends, namely, economic reward in the form of profits, interests and wages; *common,* as in an organized recreational or artistic group where the interest is one and indivisible for all; or *complementary* in the form of constellations or hierarchies of interests, as in the case of an elaborately departmentalized city women's club or of a labor union, where the economic interests are primary or dominant but accompanied by some secondary interests such as education, recreation, and old-age security. (7, pp. 36-46; 26, p. 440)

It is evident that these interests vary widely from association to association. In a complex society, associations tend to be specialized so that each stands for a particular type of interest or interest complex.* These interests point to definite and specific purposes and objectives and provide the focus in which the activity of the association takes determinate form.

Formation through Covenanting. *The actual formation* of an association is a *process of covenanting or contracting* among the persons and constituent lesser groups devoted to the interest or combination of congenial interests. The interacting individuals with a set of common values and interests combine purposively and create an organized group for the realization of these interests, and the membership of necessity must be confined only to such devoted persons if the association is to

*For a classification of associations according to interests with a chart, see reference 26, pp. 443-449.

meet its objectives. When members become malingerers or recalcitrants, they undermine the organization. Says MacIver, "Every association, every organization of men, came into being through a covenant of men to establish it, and exists in a covenant of men to maintain it." (25, p. 131)

Purpose and Charter. The definite purposes and expectations may be implicit, but usually are explicitly stated in a constitution or a charter, and the modes of procedure for their realization are presented in a body of by-laws, rules, regulations, and resolutions. The charter or constitution usually states the conditions for admission to membership and provides for the administrative instrumentalities—offices, departments, committees, and so on. The rules and precedents present the principles of administration, the rights and duties of members of all categories, and so on. Every association also soon develops an ideology, that is, an official representation of its history, philosophy, and purposes and the justification for and rationalization of its existence. This ideology is generally accepted and advocated by its members.

Determination and Acquisition of Membership. Membership (the people who belong) in an association is variously determined and acquired, depending upon its nature and purpose. The very nature of the stellar needs and interests behind the activity of the association are the major factors in the make-up of its personnel. Associations vary widely both in voluntariness or involuntariness, and in inclusiveness of membership. *Voluntary associations* are those that people want to get into, or enter willingly, because of the advantages and privileges entailed. The great bulk of associations are of this nature. *Involuntary associations* are those that one cannot avoid participating in (the state, for example, into which one is born), or those into which one is forced (an army in wartime, in many instances, a forced labor gang, or a penal institution).

In most instances certain limits and certain requirements of membership exist or are formulated. Thus, one must have not only residence but also citizenship to be an active political participant in the municipality or state; certain skills or employment potentialities to join a union; certain education, experience, and moral qualities for a professional body.

Recruitment of members comes about in various ways. It may be natural or automatic, as in the case of birth or social inheritance, through appointment, as in the case of college faculties, through election as to clubs and lodges, through hiring, as in the case of corporations (really a form of election or appointment), and through purchase in some instances (by purchasing stock to become shareholders of a corporation, or to become members of certain clubs).

Associations vary greatly in inclusiveness of membership from wide-open associations, which admit almost everyone who is willing to join (for example, a political party), to the closely limited groups with carefully restricted entrance requirements (for example, American College of Surgeons, Knights of Columbus). Where the entrance requirements are strict, they are generally based on their relevance to the specific avowed purpose of the organization, although sometimes the purposes are concealed, as in the Ku Klux Klan.

In the larger associations there will be different categories of membership with different requirements for each. Thus, in a college or university there are rather specific requirements for students and a quite different set of determinants for faculty personnel. In a large manufacturing establishment literally dozens of criteria of admission to the different functional levels and groupings exist. In the case of some associations, certain portions of the membership whose functions entail burdens and sacrifices, become involuntary, even compulsory, members. Here the recruitment procedure consists of drafting or conscription or of legitimate or illegitimate (shanghaiing of sailors) coercion.

Similarly, retirement from membership may be automatic or nonautomatic, and voluntary or involuntary. Membership may cease through death, expiration of term or service, nonpayment of dues, nonfulfillment of duties, automatic retirement because of age, voluntary resignation, discharge, expulsion, ostracism, excommunication, banishment, imprisonment, or conquest.

Organization on Horizontal Levels. Most associations conform to a general pattern of internal organization consisting of horizontal levels or layers, on the basis of division of labor and specialization of function. This organization is essential to authoritative relationship between administrators and other personnel and to the location at the most effective points in the total organization of the different essential specialized executive and technical skills and abilities. All personnel from top to bottom, and at every functional level, must be coordinated if the purposes of the organization are to be adequately met. Smaller organizations may consist simply of the minimal number of officers and the rank-and-file membership. A small sect, for example, will consist simply of clergy and laity, or, among the laity, of the minimal lay officers and members. Larger associations may have various levels of executive and supervisory officers and various horizontally and also vertically differentiated categories of workers.

But always there must be functionaries—officers and managers and directors—who are vested with authority and who are required to supervise, direct, and administer the activities and hence to control all levels of personnel below them, in order to carry out the policies, decisions, and programs of the association. In voluntary organizations the authority over members is derived ultimately from the members and delegated by them to the administrative personnel. In coercively organized groups the organization is forced upon the submerged and manipulated strata. The larger the organization, the greater the number of functionaries necessary to integrate and direct the efforts of the entire personnel.

Assignments of Positions, Tasks, Rights. The members of an association have an established assignment of positions, tasks, rights, privileges, and responsibilities. These are based on level of membership and involve skills and personality characteristics, but especially contributive and derivative functions. Often selection, training, indoctrination, and other preparation are necessary.

Leaders as Focal Elements. Various types of leaders are indispensable focal elements in the operation of all associations. Historically and logically they precede all systems of purposive action. In associations the great majority of the members know little about the operations of the mechanism. They play their respective roles. But no collection of individuals can act together without active centers of communication and of concentrated authority and responsibility. Leaders exercise the essential functions of integrating the complex process of organized action. They change potentiality into effective coordinated action and carry the purposive group from one operational state to another. (17, pp. 188, 415-440; 27)

Large Organizations. Large organizations are not separate associations. Rather, each is a system of interrelated associations. A large corporation consists of numerous businesses and industries, each with their separate organization. A university, for example, is made up of colleges, and the colleges of departments. Furthermore, associations are not necessarily or usually self-sufficing, but dependent upon other associations for the continuity of their existence.

In general, the activities of the members of purposive organizations are not those of a random herd, but are specifically functional; they are intentionally and rationally stabilized, combined, and synchronized and are made complementary to each other; for they are part of a plan and an instrumented system for united action.*

Large-Scale Formal Organizations

Large-scale formal organizations are a special, highly developed form of association that has come to be characteristic of huge, complex societies, like the United States. They are not an invention of the last century or two. They were used in ancient and medieval times to organize armies, great construction projects, religious orders, nations and empires, and in early modern and fairly recent times they were the form in which the trading and colonizing corporations were organized.

Today, the novel feature of these organizations is the general application of their principles of formation and operation to almost all of the major functional tasks of society. In their present form they are the particular type of imperative organizational instrumentality occasioned by the revolution by mass production of things and services. (45) Widespread and large societies are impossible

*On an attempt to draw up laws of development of an association, see reference 13.

without them. (17, pp. 466-467; 41, p. 148) In fact, they crystallize and focus the stellar and central structural and functional features of modern societies in operation. They are probably the most distinguishing feature of this age. No analysis of human society is complete without an examination of the sociology of large-scale formal organizations, as they have come to be distinctively named.

Most people do not seem to be aware of either their nature, importance, or universality, and some sociologists have overlooked them. At the same time sociology has much to offer in understanding them as strategic associational forms.

Place of Large-Scale Formal Organizations

There are thousands upon thousands of formal organizations in the United States. All persons are participants in many of them; their daily life is directly dominated, qualified, or conditioned by their activities in them. Human beings live in a new kind of world—one in which highly organized action is the typical channel and area of personal effort. Most people are employed by them, obtain their material necessities by means of them, are regulated and ordered by them, enjoy most of their recreational, intellectual, and religious satisfactions because of them.

This form of organization governs almost all important enterprises, whether governmental, semiprivate, or private. All governments, and governmental agencies, business and industrial organizations, especially in the form of corporations, educational institutions and systems, religious organizations, fraternal orders, service clubs, health and welfare organizations, military and police organizations, professional and occupational associations, larger recreational and athletic organizations, and even criminal enterprises are organized on formal principles. These joint activities could not perform the functions for which they were created if they were not so organized. Most of what we regard as reliable, foreseeable, and stable is a result of formally organized decision and effort.

There is a notable movement toward both the intensification and extension of organization. This has been due to a variety of factors, such as the vast number of heterogeneous persons involved in essential joint tasks, the great differentiation of interests, the completely interdependent relationships among the persons, the high degree of division of labor and specialization, the strategic importance of the decisions to be arrived at and the tasks to be performed, the increasing pertinence of administration, the inescapable necessity of a flow of authority from the top down, and the necessity of over-all functional unity. Large-scale formal organizations are gaining in cohesion, definition, number, and efficacy as the conditions of society grow more complex.

Much analysis, thought, planning, and experimenting, both by the official personnel of large organizations and by social scientists, have been and are being devoted to the nature and operation of these all-important, formal operational mechanisms. Without some knowledge of them the student of society is grossly illiterate.

Bureaucracy

The ideal-typical form of large-scale formal organization is bureaucracy. The word, as used by social scientists and societal managers, is a scientific term, not an epithet or a term of derogation. It involves the very essence of large-scale formal organization. Bureaucracy is the almost universal system of conducting large-scale divided tasks which involve numerous and highly differentiated personnel that simply cannot be satisfactorily performed on the basis of the criteria of and the facilities provided by primary groups or even small-scale associations. It finds its justification in the facts of universal experience.

Bureaucracy is a system of operation—apparently the only one under prevailing conditions—that works. In a bureaucracy we find a functional system that closely approximates the nature, certainly the technical efficiency, of a large modern machine. All is mechanically related and regulated, giving at least a near approach to automatic operation and control.* There is precision, expert control, reliability, continuity, and optimal returns on input.

The large-scale formal-organizations vary in size and in degree and complexity of organization. In order to high-light their special structural and functional features as distinguished from those of smaller and simpler associations, we will be think-

*This has both merits and demerits. The demerits will be discussed in Chap. 18.

ing mainly of such large and complicated formal organizations as an industrial corporation, a state, or a large university.

Major Structural-Functional Features

Organizations of this type have certain characteristic and essential structural and operational features.

The Pyramidal Structure with Departmentalized Layers. Structurally the bureaucracy takes the *form of a pyramid,* consisting of horizontal layers of administrative and technical personnel. *Each successive layer* below the top one is likely to consist of more and more *departments,* representing forms of specialization by areas or related segments of the total function. Each department or area of supervision is presided over by an administrator and includes various categories of technicians. As we move vertically from the top to the bottom of the pyramid, we usually find, not only an increasing number of lesser administrative officers and of departments, but also a larger and larger number of personnel.

Thus, General Motors Corporation as an organization consists of a president at the top and several dozen vice-presidents, each presiding over special divisions of the complex operations of the corporation. Below each of these are superintendents, each with subdepartments or divisions, and below these are supervisors, foremen, and subforemen, all with their areas of operations, arranging the activities of hundreds of thousands of workers differentiated according to clerical, technical, manual and other tasks and skills. Many other organizations, such as universities and churches, have similar pyramidal structures. At each level the personnel is vertically divided into different but related tasks and specialties. Thus, each vice-president, each superintendent, each foreman has a special but parallel task; in a university, each dean and department head and professor has his special area of operation; in a church organization each member of each rank has his area of operation.

The Hierarchy of Authority. These pyramided ranks are the bases for authority relations. There must be authority in large-scale organizations, that is, assigned power and vested responsibility to determine principles of procedure, to make decisions, to give and enforce commands and instructions, to specify and assign tasks, to supervise and guide the entire personnel so as to maintain the organization as an efficient instrumentality of action. *The most familiar form of system is the hierarchy, gradation, or scalar organization of formal authority. Authority is specialized for each rank and is relayed downward from each rank or level to one next below it through the successive layers of the administrative pyramid.* The authoritative unit at the top may be a single individual, several individuals, or a small oligarchic council. The larger units at the bottom of the hierarchy are practically without power.

Through such specification and delegation of spheres of authority and responsibility, and through the establishment of channels for the flow of authority, confusion and conflict are prevented. By means of it, all participants are fitted into the over-all pattern of operation, implying relationship between superior and subordinate, between official and member, between executive and operator. The superior frames, or at any rate transmits, orders and instructions and principles regarding necessary action with the expectation that they will be accepted and executed by the subordinate. In turn the subordinate, in order to carry on his tasks in conjunction with others, expects such commands and instructions; his conduct in the organization is guided and determined by them. He knows to whom he is responsible and for what. If, however, he is remiss in the performance of his tasks as authorized, he is often subjected to social constraint or even coercion.

The control and supervision from above include not only directives to subordinates relating to the operation of the organization, but also often involve power of appointment, promotion, demotion, and dismissal over incumbents of lower offices. Thus, every level and every person in each level in the scalar organization is related to, and dependent upon, every other by a definite pattern of interactions. Each person at any point intermediate between the top and the bottom stands in a position of authority of those below him, but in a position of responsibility and accountability to those above him. This linkage is variously referred to as "line of authority," "chain of command," or "line-and-staff organization."

A pertinent aspect of this scalar system, which

should be emphasized, is that it provides *channels of communication* whereby principles, decisions, orders, instructions, and suggestions can be transmitted to all elements of the organization. Without communication there can be no organization; it is one of the crucial features of management. Although there is much informal communication, from the point of view of operation, formal communication, utilizing the established lines of authority, is more important. Such communication flows in various directions; much of it *downward,* from upper to lower levels, in the form of transmitted decisions and orders, and some *upward* in the form of general decisions of the rank-and-file membership or suggestions, sometimes solicited, from the lower ranks of operating personnel. This upward and downward channeling of information can be likened to flow from the respective ends of a funnel. Some of it also occurs *laterally* from person to person and from department to department within each scalar level in order to facilitate cooperation at that level.

Offices and Officials. In a bureaucracy authority and responsibility for efficacious operation are distributed among, delegated to, and fixed in offices. The incumbents of these offices are officials or officers. They are distinct from, and have a relatively high though varying rank as compared with, the rank and file of participants. Their duties, responsibilities, rights, and grants of power comprised in the special office are defined in the objectives and structure of the organization. However, the formal authority inheres in the office of the hierarchical organization and *not* in the person occupying it. The officer may or may not be esteemed as a person; it is not necessary that he be so esteemed. His is a functional and not a personal authority. The office gives him a specific sphere of authority, but also specific limitation of powers. Within the area of his office he acts as a representative of the power and prestige of the entire organization.

The holders of offices have certain appropriate administrative or managerial abilities, certain qualities of leadership, initiative, and devotion to the aims of the organization, though these characteristics will vary in importance in different types of organizations. Where, for example, technical knowledge or managerial abilities are of great importance, leadership qualities, especially those of an inspirational nature, may have secondary significance.

There are usually two levels of officials, each level selected in a different manner: Those at the top of the pyramid who are generally elected and the purely bureaucratic personnel below the top level who carry on the various supervisory and technical procedures and are appointed, either by the top supervisor or through the exercise of impersonal competition.

The activities of officials of organizations are not always or necessarily confined to executive functions. They may at times and under certain circumstances also be integrators of diverse interests, values, and personnel elements of the organization, stimulators to devotion and action in behalf of the organization, conductors of special rituals and ceremonies, and, on occasion, mainly symbols of the group's interests and activities. (7, pp. 108-113; 51) In the main it may be said that in a large-scale organization a relatively few leaders, natural but mainly official, operate the system in behalf of its numbers and constituency.

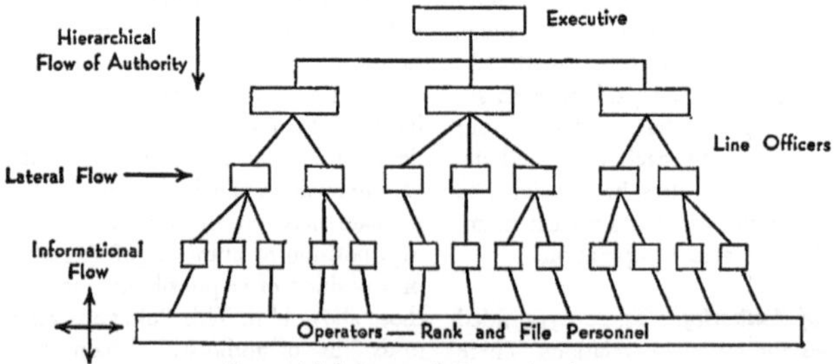

Pyramidal Form of Organization

The "Reign of Rules." Every large-scale organization must have an adequate body of prescribed, pre-existing, and standardized procedural rules and regulations for each operation and each class of personnel. These consist of manuals of procedures, operating codes, standards and specifications of all kinds. They define the obligations, duties, and responsibilities of the various positions of both officeholders and nonofficeholders, and state the sanctions governing the performance of standard activities. There must be a high degree of conformity to these prescribed patterns of action; without them there would be no calculability or reliability of behavior.

Various advantages accrue from these rules. They eliminate friction and unnecessary time- and energy-consuming bickering about procedures. They fix duties, and hence it is unnecessary continually to issue instructions for each specific case. They make it possible for even potential enemies and especially those who would under informal conditions remain indifferent toward one another to maintain cooperative relations. In fact, an important function of discipline, rules, and regulations and of the officialdom that wields the rules is to effect *depersonalization of relationships.* They eliminate from organized operation, in considerable part, the play of private attitudes, emotional elements, such as love and hatred, and all purely personal and irrational elements such as anxiety (about tenure, for example). By no means least is the fact that the subordinate is protected from arbitrary action of the superior, since the actions of both are governed by the mutually recognized set of rules.

In general, a large-scale organization is not concerned with the congeniality of members. It is *an agency to do certain things.* If the members do their jobs, carry out their orders, pay their dues, vote the ticket, and so on, that is sufficient. The organization must be indifferent to personal qualities, except in so far as they are involved in and contribute to function.

Division of Labor and Specialization. In the general analysis of associations above, it was pointed out that they have division of labor and specialization of functions; this is one of their primary reasons for existence. As has already been implied in the present analysis, large-scale formal organizations have these in special and accentuated forms. In general, the different functions instrumental to the main purpose are determined and assigned to subdivisions, subgroups, and other delegated bodies, and within these to individuals, or categories of individuals. The whole arrangement is governed by the principle of competence, which requires that responsibilities and duties be assigned where they can be discharged most effectively.

The division of labor is usually both vertical and horizontal. The *vertical division* ranges from the most complex administrative or technical tasks at the top through the various levels of skill and power to the rank-and-file workers or members who engage in relatively simple or general tasks. Here the distribution is on the basis of levels of function and scalar array of authority. The *horizontal division,* among departments within a given horizontal layer, provides for the selection and distribution of personnel according to particular functions and according to diverse specialized abilities and skills and permits a more effective assignment and coordination of activities at each given level.

Specialization of function may be on the basis of personal qualities and skills, geographical area, departments, types of material or persons worked on, or subdivisions of method and process. However, each unit organization within the whole has a specific objective, specific locational characteristics, specific time schedule, and involves a specific associational structure which determines the selection of the individual contributors to the whole. In most organizations the ends cannot be accomplished without specialization, for it is the way of achieving economy and proficiency of action in the correlation of the efforts of many individuals and groups.

The main objective in specialization of function is to achieve and utilize *expertness of performance,* or *expertese,* as it has been called, and this *requires specialists.* Large-scale organizations depend upon three different kinds of expertness: *experts at administration,* the "management men," who make decisions and issue orders; *experts in technical processes,* the research men, engineers, efficiency men who originate better methods of procedure; and *experts at mechanical, clerical and other occupational tasks*—machine operators of all kinds, stenographers, clerks, draftsmen, salesmen, and so on.

Decision Making and Planning. Governing all action, at every level and in every department and relationship of a large-scale formal organization are policies regarding ends and means, rules and regulations governing all personnel in all procedure, and programs for effecting ends. These are invariably the outgrowth of investigation, conference, and planning, and involve various kinds, levels, complexities, and specialties of decision. Consequently, decision making is another key set of processes in the operation of any large-scale formal organization. It is necessary to get the right things done at the right time and to prevent erroneous action; without it, there is confusion. However, no decision is the sole and uninfluenced task of a single individual, even in a totalitarian regime, and every such organization requires a multiplicity of decisions.

While many varieties of policies must be continually in process if an organization is to carry on, in this more elementary analysis, two very general categories need to be distinguished: general and specific. These two depend upon two correlated types of decision making—again, general and specific.

General Decisions. General decisions involve the processes by which the group will is arrived at; that is, they are made by the entire interested membership or constituency of the organization. In fact, such a wide participation in general policy formation and the making of decisions is essential to the satisfactions of the whole constituency or staff. Here the flow is from the sovereign many to the executive or otherwise specialized few.

In a vast, more or less heterogeneous group, there will be innumerable and complicated interests and values. If the group is to carry on as an organization, some agreement among the divergent interests must emerge which will provide sufficient basis for general action. This is a process of wide discussion in which various agencies of communication and persuasion are employed. Alternatives in issues appear more and more clearly in the process. Unanimity cannot be expected. Eventually, by informal consensus, but usually by some sort of formal balloting procedure, a majority or effective-minority decision is arrived at.

Specialized Decisions. Many decisions, however, are too complicated or involve matters too technical for adequate handling by the entire membership. *A vast number of specific and highly specialized decisions, therefore, must be made* by specifically assigned persons on the basis of the more general policies and practices. Two special principles involving a more special and expert focusing of decision are resorted to, namely, *the principle of representation,* whereby the problem of vast numbers is managed through the selection of representatives who are supposed to have or acquire the special information and make the special decisions for the group as a whole; and *the principle of delegation of power* to experts or specialists with the technical knowledge and training and fixed sphere of authority, or to committees, commissions, and boards which by special study acquire "expertese" to make the erudite decisions. This means competent know-how. The larger and more complicated the organization, the greater the dependence on expertness, as was pointed out above in connection with administrative necessities.

Most organizations (states, corporations, universities) depend upon such experts to make decisions regarding specific aims, which are part of the general aim; technical matters (engineering decisions, legal decisions and interpretations, financing, utilization of different kinds of resources); means and procedures (establishment of standards and specifications, rules, letting contracts); external affairs (advertising, public relations, foreign relations, propaganda); long-time matters (organizational or social planning).

The success in making these more complicated decisions for the whole depends in part upon the efficacy of the processes used to select the decision-making representatives or experts. These are mainly three, as indicated for authorities above: election by the constituency; appointment by administrative officials; or special testing as conducted by personnel management departments and by civil service or merit system boards and other forms of examinations. Each procedure has its merits and demerits with respect to the selection of any given type of expert.

Scientific Research. Three other processes relate vitally to decision and policy making. All large-scale organizations must resort to scientific research in some degree for sufficient and competent facts and principles essential to sound decisions. The days when organizations could depend upon slow and spontaneous emergence of rule-of-thumb generalizations are past. Research itself is a highly organized process. States and municipalities have their legislative reference bureaus and research staffs (for example, for testing highway materials, for collecting health data, and so on); corporations (General Motors, Bell Telephone, and others) have their research and experimental laboratories and staffs to determine physical, chemical, economic, demographic, and other facts; even church bodies have investigating agencies. Specialists and other professionals have been relied upon more and more for the determination of working truth. Here again the flow is from the few to the many. The findings in the way of facts and principles of such specialized groups and agencies are increasingly the basis of organizational operation. (5; 64)

PLANNING. Planning is the deliberate process of drawing up principles and procedures for the present and the future. It is the basis for all decisions, policies, and instructions. In fact, it is essentially a technique whereby the skills of a variety of specialists are brought to bear on the various problems of the organization before the formal stage of decision making is reached. Modern large-scale organization requires planning more precise and far-sighted than anything we have ever witnessed, since action cannot be haphazard and piecemeal. By planning procedure expertness of every kind can be drawn into the decisions. Its conclusions grow out of research in the way of surveys and experimentation, in conjunction with appropriate discussion and conference. (75)

PROGRAM BUILDING. There must also be continuous program building, which is based on planning. Programming is the process of organizing all procedures and policies and personnel elements and plant instrumentalities in such a manner that the planned objectives can be most effectively realized. It is concerned with specific structures and devices and sets forth detailed specifications for action based upon the blueprints.

If these three processes are not continually occurring in an organization, it is dying slowly or rapidly.

Coordination. The final and over-all process in the operation of large-scale formal organization is coordination. By this we simply mean that *the capacities and activities of all the scalarly and laterally divided and specialized personnel must be planfully integrated and motivated in conformity with the ultimate purposes,* taking concretely the form of the plans and programs *of the organization.* All tasks at all levels in all areas are meshed together into a systematic operational pattern. If the organization is to operate effectively, it must have essential unity, coherence, and integrity and must function with the economy and smoothness of a well-designed, relatively frictionless, and adequately powered mechanism. When this coordination exists in a fair degree, one can expect and predict the actions of all participants. This points to certain essentials.

There should be *centralization of authority and command, but also the proper decentralization,* as noted above, with an equilibrium between the two. The organization cannot be top-heavy with authority or bottom-heavy without it.

There should be morale or *esprit de corps,* that is, *the participants need to be infused and buttressed with appropriate cooperative attitudes and sentiments of loyalty,* so that they function willingly and efficiently and to the best of their abilities. They should have a common sense of purpose and destiny, even though so many of the relationships are impersonal and indirect. These are matters of inspiriting and confidence-producing leadership; organizational rules and regulations administered with fairness and certainty; incentives to service and conformity, such as adequate wages, salaries, and increases, promotion devices, security of tenure, seniority, pensions, and so on.

Standardization and routinization of particular operations are also organizational imperatives. The essential details in the performance of specific tasks are uniformly prescribed and the activity of the individual or category of individuals occurs in definite functional and time sequences. The individual does not have to determine how his job is to be performed; he comes to act habitually according to a mechanical formula. Such standardized and routinized actions reduce or eliminate friction, prevent overlapping of action, and aberrant or eccentric action, and obviate gaps in the necessary sequence of action. If properly routinized, all the different but interdependently related standardized performances are followed in their proper order.

Finally, among large organizations that have units which are dispersed geographically, there should be *federation.* Corporations, religious bodies, and other large organizations, have similar units or specialized productive units in various localities and regions of the United States, and even abroad. Each unit possesses sufficient autonomy to function adequately in its particular area. But if they are all to function together as parts of the great whole, their respective particular operations must be compatible with the objectives of the over-all organization. This is accomplished according to the "federative principle," that is, the separate, semi-independent parts are consolidated, by agreement, into the larger whole, as in the federation of the forty-eight states.

Communities

Thus far we have analyzed groups in general and associations in particular as structural-functional entities in themselves. Always, however, individuals and all kinds of groups *exist together in localities. These combinations of interrelated individuals and groups of all kinds functioning together within a given territory, we refer to as communities.* A community is always a collectivity of people occupying and sharing a more or less definitely determined territorial living area in which they carry on a large number of essential activities. It is an organization of interpersonal—but, especially in its modern forms, intergroup—life within a locality. It is a functionally inclusive area. Consequently, each community presents a certain set of common behavior patterns, usually related in certain ways to the nature and scope of the geographic area. Territoriality is its distinguishing feature and one of its chief values.

In Chapter 9 on ecology, communities were examined as *areal* configurations. Here we are viewing them in their other aspect, namely, as bounded, land-based *societal* (interactional structural-functional) entities.

The Territorial Factor in Human Life

One of the elemental features of human life is that it is *land based.* All associated life is conducted in some degree of continuity and cooperation within some physical area of habitation, in a locality. Unavoidably the particular portion of the earth's surface which a given combination of persons and groups inhabit has a great molding influence on their way of life. It is the determinant of many of their most important interests and activities.

It is obvious that in a vast intercommunicative and functionally interlocking society like our own, all local and lesser communities will have in common a vast array of nation-wide and even world-wide values, interests, objectives, and activities *which prevail without reference to particular locality.* But always, at the same time, the particular limited area, because of its peculiarities, *does* produce a somewhat unique common mode of life among its contiguous and interacting people and groups. It induces and focuses common cultural features as represented in certain values, interests, sentiments, vocations, recreations, attitudes, habits of thought and action, traditions, folkways, technicways, customs, mores, and institutions. In the locality the people have their economic and technological reasons for being. Many of its purposive organizations are determined in their objectives and functions by the habitat's peculiar and unique location and demands, as these in turn have affected its composition. The people have been conditioned by and appreciate the historical experiences peculiar to the area.

In general, in the community people build up common interests and activities and function together in the chief concerns of life. All the inescapable physical menaces and compulsives and physical and economic opportunities, the common area-induced interests and values, the localized participations, and the areally interdependent organizations and institutions provide the constituent individuals and groups with a special basis of coherence. These factors weld them together into a territorially unique unity, separate them from, and identify them in distinction to, *other* communities. Furthermore, as long as people live in a community, they cannot completely escape from its influences, activities, and requirements.

Range and Structure of Communities

Communities vary in size and in number and complexity of combined constituent elements. They range along a continuum from small, highly local face-to-face groups, such as neighborhoods, through villages, towns, cities with their immediate hinterland, and geocultural regions, to nations, societies, and in some instances, a world-wide community.

The smallest and simplest locality groups, just beyond the family, are neighborhoods, such as are found in the open country and small villages. In these, persons of all ages live as primary-group members in intimate, personal, frequent, and face-to-face relationships within the restricted area in which they have direct communication with, and ready access to, each other. Some neighborhoods are practically closed. The best examples of these are small numbers of face-to-face associates restricted to limited territorial limits as they are segregated by geographical barriers, such as small isolated mountain valleys, coves, and tiny islands. In most instances, though, the members of neighborhoods belong to other larger communities; they live most of their life activities as participants in nonneighborhood groups and associations.

Somewhat more complex than neighborhoods, although still limited in area, are the "nighdwellers" in modern residential areas. While living in close spatial proximity, such groupings (strictly speaking they may be only aggregations) consist mainly of persons characterized by impersonal relations, considerable mobility, variant culture patterns, and with much social distance between them; they are bonded by very few areal interests. (86, pp. 7-9; 92, pp. 331-336)

Because of the size of typical modern communities as contact and communicating areas, the scope, complexity, and subdivision of their activities, the fact that individuals and subgroups function mainly as parts of many large-scale formal organizations or obtain their goods and services by means of them, the face-to-face factor is limited to relatively private relationships and is practically nonexistent as far as the bulk of the community activities are concerned. The presence in or the interests growing out of or related to the common locality and the need or desirability of certain self-sufficiencies within the boundaries are the binding factors. The communities of major concern are made up of many interdependent and overlapping groups of all kinds, that is, total aggregate groups or networks of groups. These contain all families, sexes, age categories, casual groupings, industrial and commercial organizations, clubs, cliques, ethnic groups, religious bodies—in fact, all manner of temporary and more durable, informally and formally organized groups. They function within the larger pre-existing community and constitute its organs as a self-contained unit. They are manifestations of the common will. (89, p. 130)

The community interests and participations of individuals and lesser groups radiate outward by gradients, in the manner of concentric circles, though often with diminishing intensity, to ever-wider communities. All smaller communities on the basis of certain situational interests are also parts of larger communities. Thus, an open-country neighborhood is usually related to a village- or a town-centered metropolitan community. All these may be part of a broader geocultural regional community, and in turn part of a national community, and, on some issues, part of the world as a community.

Center, Hinterland, and Boundaries

Every typical community has a settlement pattern (see pages 132-135), consisting of a center and an outlying area or hinterland, and rough boundaries. The *center* is accessible to members of all parts of the community; it is a place where their interests, objectives, and activities converge. The *hinterland,* or outlying area, lies between the center and the boundaries and is dependent upon the center for finished products and for services of many kinds. By virtue of the needs and activities of the center, people find it profitable to settle and carry on activities near by. At the same time, the center would have no reason for existence without the hinterland.

The *boundaries,* and hence the extent, of any given community regardless of its size are always determined and dependent upon the particular pertinence, kind, and range of territory-centered interests, purposes, and functions. These, in turn, grow out of areal adjustive problems and interactions requiring different kinds of cooperation.

The boundaries, save where established by physical barriers, are seldom clear-cut and are difficult to establish correctly. They nearly always shade off toward the periphery into a penumbral or interstitial area between adjoining communities, that is, at the edges communities blend and overlap. But the boundaries are spatial and also set by limits of social interaction. Within the general boundaries each community is a sort of "natural" social interactional unit to accomplish certain common purposes.

Some Typical Functions of Communities

By way of summary and conclusion, communities serve certain characteristic functions for their constituent individuals and groups. *First, the community operates as an over-all maintenance organization.* Carr speaks of it as a "residence-subsistence grouping." (79) Bogue discusses it as a sustenance-production locality unit. (78, pp. 12, 146) In the community individuals obtain their physical sustenance. Here they get their living by working; here they consume the material and nonmaterial products, without which they would perish. This does not mean that communities are self-sufficient or wholly self-maintaining. No modern community is. The goods and services that cannot be provided locally are brought into it from other communities by a process of exchange. In the community the population's health is protected; here it obtains its education, recreation, social security, and spiritual satisfactions. Regardless of where the resources of human living come from, they are used to sustain life in the community. It is the survival area.

Second, communities function for their individual and group constituents as media of expression. The community is the arena in which the individual lives his *whole life.* He achieves here his exchange of psychic satisfactions and reciprocities that come from social intercourse. He receives here his values and rules, his obligations and responsibilities, his status and roles, the precious cultural possessions that make life purposive and orderly and worth while for him. It not only sustains his spirit, but gives him outlet for it. He has here his *sense of being.*

Third, the community renders the individual an identifying function. The community is the permanent background of everyone's life. The individual has a *sense of being part of the community,* part of it as a locality, a spot on the earth; part of its history and destiny, its groups, associations, and general societal structure and function, its general and, especially, its unique cultural features. It is his "greater home"; it is what he belongs to, and it embodies all that is familiar and precious to him. Proudly he says "I'm a Nebraska man," or "I'm a New Englander," or "I'm an American." His pride, in fact, may be tinged with ethnocentrism, as his own community functions as an in-group, and he exalts it and depreciates other communities.

Fourth, the community serves as an integrative factor. In consequence of the common consciousness of their common territory, of their common participation in it, of their consciousness of social and cultural resemblance, the community becomes the principal focus of the associated life of the people in it. It integrates diverse people and groups into a living unity of characteristic structure and function. They possess it as a collective symbol; as such, the individual and group attachments gather about it and are reinforced by it. Furthermore, its prevailing norms and its public opinion effectively operate to make it an area of order and cooperation.

CHAPTER XII

SOCIAL INSTITUTIONS AND INSTITUTIONALIZATION

THUS FAR we have examined the group structurings of the *members* of a society. Every societal system, in order to carry on, must also have an *institutional* structuring. The fundamental situation is essentially this: As people interact with each other, *it is imperative that their behavior in almost all relationships, whether continuous or recurrent, be in the form of accepted, standardized, expected, predictable, and enforceable patterns,* that is, long-run and durably established blueprints of action. Without conformity to such established, universal, and known patterns of behavior, there can be no harmony, coordination, or cooperation and not even the minimal efficiency of operation that is essential to satisfactory living and working together. The actors must be normatively oriented.

Social Institutions in Societal Organization

Distinction between Groups and Institutions

In every societal system there are many social mechanisms that define, direct, and limit most of the behavior of persons. These insistently maintained reaction patterns *demand and compel* some forms of behavior, *encourage* some, *permit* some, *tolerate* some, and *prohibit* some, depending upon the type of relationship situation and its place in the total functioning of the society. These crucial mechanisms we call "social institutions."

Concretely, the four Joneses are a group, but they operate as a family in American society, which means that they are governed by a set of institutional standards, rules, and procedures universal in American society and binding upon all members of any family. These apply to all typical relationships among husband, wife, parents, children, and siblings. Our city is a community, but every person in his relations with every other person and every group and organization in it is ordered, regulated, and motivated by rules and principles which govern almost every relationship and action, ranging from how we greet each other on the street to the standardized, established, sanctioned ways of earning a living, being educated, playing games, and so on. The Lancaster County Medical Society is an organization of physicians bound together by common interests and purposes, but written rules and unwritten etiquette govern the relations of the physicians with each other and with their patients and provide the rights, prerogatives, and duties involved in these relations.

The Nature of Institutions

Basically, institutions are rather abstract in nature, since they embody and synthesize the essential values, norms, agreements, and preferences regarding social behavior. Their specific form is that *of* structured requirements of conduct couched in terms of codes, rules, charters (15; 16; 17), by-laws, and ideologies, which may be unwritten or written. Hence, institutions are not concrete and tangible in their key aspects as are the relationships, groups, and associations in which and for which they function.

Institutions are *not vague abstractions,* however; they are as real as any material objects and far more powerful. They manifest themselves *socially* in the uniform usages, practices, routines, techniques, observances, ceremonials, and abstentions that prevail among the people of the group or society. *Individually* they are evident in the attitudes and habits of persons.

Institutions are implemented, that is, given operational proficiency, by all manner of visible symbols, such as the cross, wedding rings, and flags; by codal requirements expressed in traditions, laws, and constitutions; by organizations with necessary administrative personnel and machinery, such as school systems; and by material equipment, such as the Court House. Finally, they are sustained and enforced by social tradition, sentiment, and opinion, which act both informally and formally through various kinds of social-psychological pressures and societal organizations as agencies. (9, pp. 3-6)

The readily observable physical equipment and the associations are the aspects that the man in the street is most aware of. He only vaguely comprehends the basic normative and charter features at the core of institutions, which are made effective in application to social life needs by the equipment and social organizations.

Institutionalized Behavior

The central and strategic importance of social institutions in the existence of a society as a going concern must not be minimized. Institutionalized behavior is a substantial part of all societal behavior. Whenever we examine the behavior of individuals and groupings in the light of what they *do or are expected to do* uniformly, continuously, and persistently in the interests of satisfactory living and working together, we get into the field of social institutions. There is much justification for the contention that the various tasks involved in societal organization are summarized, epitomized, and focused in social institutions; that the societal organization of any culture area as an orderly and efficient affair exists in, and is reflected by, its prevailing institutions and can, in fact, be defined by an enumeration of social institutions; and, conversely, that the basic orientation of social institutions is their strategic position and function in societal organization. (9, p. 23)

The study of institutions may be said to focus one of the primary objectives of sociology, namely, learning the *means* of living and working together in groups. Lundberg said that "the study of institutions is one of the most convenient and fruitful approaches to the formulation of laws of social behavior in general." (12, pp. 414-415) To recapitulate, by way of indicating both the relationship and the distinction between groups and institutions, *groups are the collectivities of interacting individuals* centered around interests and goals; in most instances, they are more or less consciously purposive in action, and increasingly the bulk of them are formally organized.

Institutions are the more abstract but nonetheless highly structuralized and functionalized *mecha-*

nisms or means whereby the behavior of the members of groups is coordinated, regularized, and patterned, so that the goals or purposes may be consistently, certainly, and fruitfully realized. Institutions have implicit or explicit formulation in the shape of charters or bodies of accepted and formulated requirements for satisfactory societal performance. Thus, *interacting human beings in a given society are told how to act*—what the proper, legitimate, expected, tolerated, and prohibited modes of action or social relationship are. Institutions, as such, "represent the relatively stable, uniform, and general dynamic aspects of groups" (12, pp. 378, 411) as they behave, and are functional attributes only of human groups.

Any social group that is identified with some relatively permanent scheme of thought and action must be institutionalized. As soon as an aggregation of persons becomes a *system* of relationships and carries on any satisfying social function, however simple, it must take on the machinery of an institution. The only alternative would be to invent *on the spot* rules and procedures for the particular relationship or function, but this cannot be, for experience is essential.

In brief, institutions define the main modes of the legitimately expected behavior of persons in the various strategic situations of social life; they structure the motivations and practices of people and establish the social sanctions. (21) They furnish a charted course for individuals and groups to follow in meeting life situations. Without them there could be no society. In some way all persons participate in all basic institutions and must conform to their requirements. From them there can be no escape.

Functions of Social Institutions

Any examination of the functions of social institutions supplies some answers to the question, Why do human societies have institutions? Some of the reasons for their existence begin to appear when we examine various situations and conditions in which minimal established standards of behavior, which are stated in widely accepted rules and effected by standardized procedures and agencies, prevail.

Individual Functions

The elemental *biological and psychological urges, drives, and needs* of human beings, some of them most imperative in nature and all of them bearing a direct relation to the preservation of individuals in any society, *must be satisfied in a sufficient, guaranteed, and socially acceptable manner.* Significant among the needs are nutrition, bodily comforts, clothing, shelter, gregarious contact, sex gratification, rest and sleep, relaxation and recreation, health, movement, new experience, self-assertion, self-expression, and favorable response from others. These basic needs produce some, though by no means all, derived needs or *interests.* These interests are concerned not only with what the group members absolutely need for survival but also with what a considerable number of them deem desirable. They might be called "cultural needs" and show the influence of moral, aesthetic, utilitarian, and other cultural standards and values.

Satisfaction of needs and achievement of interests involve competition and conflict between individuals and groups. At the same time none of the needs or interests can be met by human beings acting alone; this requires collective and cooperative action. Furthermore, in meeting these individual problems, which have such far-reaching social ramifications, individuals do not—in fact, are not in a position to—make choices and improvise ways of solving the problems on the spot and at the moment. Nor can individuals be permitted to act upon whim or capricious impulse if other individuals are to be protected and general security and satisfactory welfare are to prevail.

The institutional rules and procedures provide ready-made, well-tried solutions to these problems, and by means of them we avoid nonrational forms of behavior which might be sources of friction, dilemma, doubt, chaos, even ruin. They also give us fixed habits, routine requirements of behavior, and long-standing customary and conventional standards and rules and relieve us of the strain of making decisions and formulating procedures. Through the precise definition of necessary action in each situation, rules and procedures reduce deviations arising from personal differences.

Because the institutions have sustained group support, they function as pressures which buck us up when low or too depressed to act in the essential minimal ways and discipline us when we are too exuberant or energetic and in danger of making foolish and exaggerated responses. Moreover, because institutions routinize action, they help economize human energy, especially psychological energy; for routine obviates the need of much daily inventiveness, ingenuity, thought, or imagination. In the main, institutions function so well in meeting daily needs and interests that only the required and established ways of acting seem possible.

Group Functions

Over and above the elemental individual needs for survival and the more derived interests, and often growing out of them, are the stern and *concrete* needs for group and social survival, perpetuation, and prosperity. The society itself must be preserved; recurring, inescapable life situations must be met; fundamental societal functional requirements must be provided for. Hence, much ordering, regulating, standardizing, cooperating, and correlating of the relationships and activities of all individuals and groups are necessary.

To accomplish all these, the behavior must be so patterned that they cannot be avoided without penalty. Certain societal needs are practically permanent and universal and have undoubtedly existed since the first human groupings. These needs have always called into existence appropriate societal means of dealing with them.

A great array of societal needs present themselves and institutions preside over them and provide normalized and standardized concepts, rules, usages, roles, and purposive procedures and adjustment techniques. For example, it has always been necessary to suppress injury or killing of fellow men, except in certain circumstances where the punishment or execution of some was deemed essential to societal well-being; to satisfy wants for food and other basic material and service necessities through production and exchange without quarreling; and, in a group of any size, to satisfy such wants cooperatively by means of some established division of labor. (9, p. 37)

Major institutionalized systems—the communicative, the economic, the matrimonial and familial, and so on—function to meet the operative needs of the total social system. Every department of ordinary human life creates these charters of action and is organized, directed, and controlled by them.*

Processes of Institutionalization

The institutionalizing processes consist essentially of establishing, as stabilized and formalized requirements of individual and joint behavior, ways of life which have proved to be, or which give every indication of being, effective in satisfying individual and social needs, wants, and interests and in maintaining societal order, harmony, and efficiency and certainty of operation. The institutionalizing processes are actions of the common will, as MacIver has pointed out. Their result is institutional mechanisms. (13, p. 155) The essence of the process consists of the development and instituting of rules, laws, and other generally known and sanctioned requirements of social action in the various fields of social relationships.

For purposes of analysis we will examine the processes of institutionalization from two points of view: the conditions and processes whereby *useful ways and usages emerge and develop institutional stature* and the array of processes whereby institutions *formulate their essential and characteristic structural content and means or agencies of functional proficiency and efficiency.* Actually, these are aspects of the same process; they overlap and occur at the same time. But for simplification and clarity of understanding, it seems desirable to examine *development in time and purposiveness*—the process of emergence—and the development

*For a more extended treatment of the functions of institutions as agents of societal regulation, see Chap. 20.

of *indispensable component parts*—the process of structuralization-functionalization.

Processes of Emergence and Development

Every institution that goes deeply into human life has a long and involved career through which it has developed haphazardly, unsystematically, and cumulatively, mainly by trial and error, although creativeness is always part of the process. The process is one of emergence rather than origination. (20, pp. 394-395) Some elements are very ancient, the products of diffusion and discovery; other features have been added in the course of time; and some may be surprisingly modern, having developed out of and in response to recent or contemporary conditions—even crises.

In treating the problem of the development of institutions, William Graham Sumner distinguished between the crescive and the enacted institutions. (23, pp. 2-3, 30, 35, 49, 53-55, 76-77) Although a clear line cannot be drawn between the two, since all institutions have many elements of both in them, the dichotomy deserves brief attention.

Crescive Institutions. The crescive institutions are those which developed automatically and spontaneously, by more or less discernible processes, out of subinstitutional forms. Many institutions—in fact, important phases of all institutions—appear gradually and largely unconsciously and represent the slow crystallization and organization of ideas, values, and ways of order and operation in some specific area of social relations. They are the result of processes of development which involve experience and informal experimentation, the slow selection of valued and more or less efficacious standards of behavior, and the attachment of various types and degrees of compulsions. They grow out of the test of time, gradually taking the form we identify as institutions.

Some examples of crescive institutions are most of the rules and principles regarding sex relations and parental responsibility, the long-standing rules governing cooperation in economic activity, most of the rule-of-thumb procedures in the primary-group education of the young, and many of the rules concerning relations of superiors and inferiors. Doubtless the great body of institutional content governing most behavioral fields is of a crescive nature.

Enacted Institutions. The enacted institutions, in the words of Sumner, are "products of rational invention and intention." (23, p. 54) He adds that they belong to high civilization. They must be attributable to the cool calculation and deliberate construction of one or more thinking functionaries of the group served. They come when men deliberately systematize and formulate the usages which have become current along certain lines or actually, by planning and experiment, so modify or add to the usages as to create positive institutional forms. Thus, much law today is not a matter of slow development but is due to legislative enactment, judicial interpretation, or formulation by administrative bodies. Rules of property are specifically formulated to meet new kinds and conditions of possession and use of things.

However, pure enacted institutions that are strong and prosperous are hard to find. In general, although given institutions may seem to be primarily crescive or enacted, actually they are both in varying degree. Even recent and unique institutions, supposedly established on the spot for highly contemporary purpose, were not created spontaneously; rather, principles of operation and patterns of organization will have been taken over from other times and other institutional fields. Inventions, as we know, are merely new combinations of existing cultural materials.

The highly generalized process of institutional development is a matter of antecedent conditions and stages. The condition of departure in the long and often slow development of an institutional form is *some kind of crisis*—physical, social, or cultural—which causes a measure of disorganization. As a result, problems arise that appear insoluble by old or existing social machinery. A need for some kind of adjustive solution appears. An incipient institution is on the way.

The *needs,* if persistent, recurrent, and permanent in relation to the situation result in ways, sometimes accidentally hit upon by the group, which seem to be efficacious. When frequently repeated, they become habitual *folkways.* If these folkways work more or less well, they are likely to continue generation after generation and become more and more imperative, acquiring a momentum of their own. Then they become *customs* or culturally inherited usages, with the rightness of the time and the weight of the generations behind them.

When these repeated ways begin to be deemed *morally* right and absolutely essential if calamity is to be avoided, they have reached the compulsive level of *mores*. When the mores are "lifted out of the atmosphere of sentiment and faith" into the realm of the conscious and deliberate and made more definite and specific, when they are given a framework and a more rational, practical, utilitarian, and positive character is added, when they are formally sanctioned, legally enforced, systematized, implemented, and "instituted," they become *institutions*. What was once more or less optional has become mandatory.

> The process might be summarized by noting that institutions start with a mass of scrambling and grouping tentatives . . . that bring favorable results. These become sets of regular . . . procedures. . . . These reactions or their products, subjected to the processes of selection and survival, become stabilized and crystallized; they take on social and cultural sanctions, and even compulsions; they come to be systematized and more or less definitely administered; and thus become institutionalized. Thus institutions seem to be the result of more or less automatic development processes. (34, p. 75)

From this point on in the development of a given institution, there is likely to be recurrent, though usually somewhat belated, revision and addition of all manner of deliberately formulated or enacted features to meet the changing needs of the group concerned.

Formation of Structural-Functional Features

The other aspect of institutionalization is the formation of the *type parts* or component elements, abstract and concrete, which give an institution its characteristic structure and make possible its essential functioning. In any institutionalization of functional activity there must be certain tangible and intangible machinery if the basic purposes are to be met. These mechanisms—valuational, ideological, psychological, associational, physical—are the indispensable prerequisites to its operation. The more important constituent elements are as follows:

Formation of Underlying Values. Fundamental in the operation of institutions, as in all more or less consistent and purposeful social action, is *the formation of the underlying values* of the group or society in question. These define in ideal form the luminous objectives or ends and conditions that are sought in the specific social action. These are continually emerging from the past and present experience of the group members and appear as a consensus of what is good and desirable. Thus, there are economic values regarding material adequacy, political values, educational goals, scientific goals, aesthetic goals, religious goals, and so on. The institutions embody the ultimate and core values that the people have in common and are the main agencies for realizing the values. The institutions will tend to be as numerous as the values that the particular society recognizes as basic.

Concepts and Ideas. Related to the values are the underlying more or less articulate *concepts* or *ideas*—the conceptualization of the guiding purpose—which present the rationalization and justification of the institution's being. These concepts formulate the function attributed to the institution by the individuals controlled by it. Thus, at the heart of the family is the concept of ordered relations of the sexes and the generations; in property is a philosophy of order and usage regarding ownership and use of things and creatures; in all educational institutions is the idea that knowledge and experience needs to be systematically imparted. Behind every ancient or contemporary institution there is an implied or expressed idea of social purpose. When the concept is elaborated and glorified and made the official presentation and justification of the institution's history, philosophy, and purposes, we speak of it as its "ideology." (36, pp. 175-186)

Norms. The values and concepts take more concrete form as norms, or standards. These set, state, and preserve the requirements of behavior insisted upon or permitted in the given situation. They are the rules of the institutionalized game, which prescribe the supreme conditions of formal lawfulness and urge compliance and give calculability to institutional behavior. In general, as norms are formed, they set up new expectations of behavior. Society continually anticipates that individuals and groups will *do* certain things and *refrain* from doing other things in given recurrent situations.

These norms are more or less explicitly formulated in the form of *codes, or rules, regulations, and laws,* which often state not only the general principles and requirements, but also the technique whereby the values and ideology are enabled or decreed to exist in concrete behavior. Unlike the laws of the state, the codes of most institutions do not need to be—although they sometimes are—definite and precise. They may be written in part, but many of their elements continue to be deep-seated in the folkways, mores, beliefs, customs, traditions, and conventions that lie behind the institution.

But all institutions have something in the way of codes ranging in formality and fixity, from written, approved, and sanctioned or punishable constitutions, by-laws, rules and regulations, laws and charters to quite informal and even merely implied taboos and more or less tacit usages. Thus, states have their constitutions, the legislative enactments, treaties, court decisions, common law, administrative rules and regulations, as well as a vast array of unwritten rules, principles, practices, and implications governing the informal relationships of the citizenry. Underlying the family relationships are not only the various legal statutes governing its formation, composition, maintenance, and perpetuation, but also a set of unwritten demands governing relations of husband and wife and parents and children.

All scientific, religious, and educational institutions have both their written and implied requirements that are inherently related to the underlying concept of the institutional functions. Aesthetic institutions rest upon basic canons of beauty, art, and technique which are current in the relationships and obvious in the overt expressions of the artist. Cultural life and the etiquette of polite society are also at any given time a matter of rather precise principles and requirements. Of course, the highly functional adjustment agencies, such as the political, economic, domestic, and health institutions, are more likely to develop effective and binding codes than are the less competitive and less vital institutions.

Attitudes, Habits, and Roles. The current values, ideologies, and codes affect every individual involved in some degree in the particular institutional relationships. The individual is in continual process of conditioning by them. As a result, *the institution becomes concrete and overt and functional in the attitudes, the sentiments, the fixed ideas, and especially the more or less conventionalized habits of the individuals.* This, in fact, is a primary objective in institutionalization.

The attitudes are the institutional fixtures in our being and include most of our stereotypes regarding social relations and activities. They affect our judgment and dominate our thinking in all the more fixed or recurring social situations from early years on. Thus, the particular state, or marriage form, or family practice, or economic procedure among a given people is really a set of deep-seated attitudes as far as individuals are concerned. We hardly realize how deeply rooted they are.

Attitudes relating to property, for example, are so much a part of us that most of us never think of stealing. When American young people think of marriage, the likelihood or possibility of marrying more than one mate—at least simultaneously—never occurs to them. Any criticism of our marriage or family forms, of our economic system, or of our political practices, reveals the underlying attitudes. The common moral sentiments affectively support the rules as "moral imperatives."

The institutionalized habits are the overt expressions of the attitudes. The ordered relations that are the essence of any society with adequate institutions take the form of stable, common ways of individual behaving. As institutions express themselves in daily living, they take the form of more or less standardized habits; it is in this regular habitual behavior of individuals that we experience the institution as a functional reality. In brief, the institutions are largely in the individual persons. If the thought and action of individuals do not rest firmly upon these established values and standards and are not explicitly motivated and channeled with attitudes and sentiments, the individuals suffer *anomie*.

The attitudes and habits combine in the *institutional roles* of persons, that is, in the multiple unique patterns of behavior by all levels of persons in connection with different aspects of institutional functioning. At any given moment the requirements of these various roles are formalized and fixed, even stereotyped, but they are continually in process of change. If they are unclear, the particular kind of institutional behavior cannot be confidently expected.

Ritual and Ceremony. To aid in definitely and securely establishing institutionalized ways, *most institutions develop and maintain ritual and ceremony as effective implementary devices and procedures.* These are prescribed methods and orders of performing important and necessary social acts; they reduce the attitudes and action to common, visible form. They make the action habitual; usually they surround it with solemnity and awesomeness and weight it with authority, sentiment, and tradition.

Personnel and Associations of Human Beings. In addition to these more or less abstract elements, the institutionalizing of societal behavior also involves more tangible and concrete features. The first of these has to do with the personnel aspects of institutions. The institution is a functional agency that serves people that are related to each other by needs and interests.

Most institutions operate for and through associations of human beings, that is, purposively organized groupings. In fact, most of the associations of men, if they have any durability whatsoever, are the organized and living societal aspects of institutions, and no institution can exist without some degree of supporting organizational form. These associations are human beings associated by needs and purposes who require the systematization of action provided by the institution—the family group, the citizens of the state, the persons seeking some form of recreation, the followers of a religious belief, the members of a profession. The association is thus the objective and perceptible machine through which the underlying concept is carried into action, "the only incarnate form," according to Hughes, (35, p. 4) through which the institution can function at the moment.

Thus, political parties, bureaus, legislative bodies, and so on are associations through which different phases of government are expressed; the denominations and sects, the organizations of laymen and clergymen, are associations through which religion functions in American life; the teaching staffs, administrative bodies, school boards, and so on, are associations through which educational functions can be carried on; and so on. These associations promote the concept, embellish the ideology, revise and maintain the codes, and are the source of the stimuli that produce most of the conditioning to institutional ways.

The personnel soon falls into two main categories: the *members,* that is, the general body of beneficiaries and performers, and the special individuals and bodies vested with specialized duties of an administrative or technical nature, usually referred to as *functionaries.*

Symbolic and Utilitarian Physical Equipment. Finally, in order to ensure effective functioning, *it is essential that institutions have the necessary symbolic and utilitarian physical equipment.* Most institutions, in the words of Chapin, include "culture objects of symbolic value; that is, objects charged with sentimental meaning to which human behavior has been conditioned." (5) Thus, the cross is the symbol of Christianity and the crescent the symbol of Mohammedanism as an institution; the wedding ring, of marriage; flags, crowns, and scepters, of government. Many other insignia symbolize a variety of institutional activities.

Even more important are the "physical extensions," the "mechanical cultural equipment," or "paraphernalia," as the Bernards have called them. Most institutions must depend heavily upon buildings and other utilitarian material objects commonly called "property" if they are to function effectively. For example, there are the homesteads and private furniture, land and buildings; offices and their equipment, apparatus for communication and transportation; factories and machinery; chattels of all sorts; and many more that might be mentioned. These are the physical and visible body of the institution; they house its activities. The personnel elements and these physical features are what the average person has in mind when he thinks of institutions, and he often mistakes them for the whole institutionalized content.*

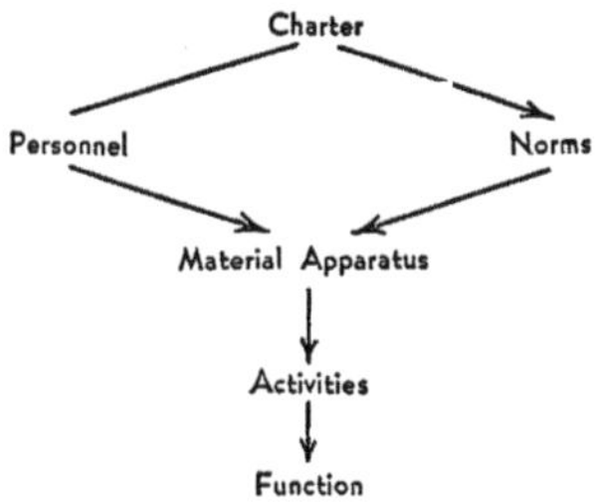

The relationship of these elements in a total institutionalized system is illustrated by Malinowski in the above diagram.

Life Cycle of Institutional Organizations

Although the chartering of societal behavior must be continuous if the society is to endure, the specific associations (formal organizations) that carry on the social functions of institutions are not necessarily so. They have a beginning, undergo modifications of structure and function during their career, and sooner or later have an end. Thus, the total life history of such an organization usually takes the form of a fairly typical cycle. Angell has sketched four successive stages of this typical life cycle. (30) A concise and considerably modified analysis of stages follows:

Period of Incipient Organization. In this initial period, some need as demonstrated in a crisis has become poignant, and tentative efforts are made to meet it. The procedure whereby the particular group extricates itself from the emergency situation sometimes takes the form of social movement. Says Park: ". . . the necessity of carrying on programs initiated in some social emergency has been responsible for many if not most modern and recent institutions." Again: "Every social movement may . . . be described as a potential institution." (39) The institutional organization may begin in an enthusiastic social movement, such as first-century Christianity, eighteenth-century Methodism, or the labor organizations and farmers' organizations in the last decades of the nineteenth century in the United States. Sometimes, of course, the organization may emerge out of the need situation in a more cool and calculated manner as the result of broad consensus; for example, the United Nations or a housing authority.

The significant feature of this stage is that institutionally organized characteristics are developing. The sect, which may have begun as a tangential movement, becomes the organized denomination. Leaders function not only as inciters and crystallizers of sentiments and ideas, but also as formulators of codes, policies, and discipline and as administrative functionaries. The duties of the members and the special functions of the functionaries are established. Constitutions and administrative machinery and ideologies are developed.

Period of Efficiency. The institutional organization is now in its early maturity. The various social needs are met by complementary structures and functions, and the organization is accepted, although not always approved. The functionaries are performing with enthusiasm and efficiency; the potential values and objectives are being realized in considerable part; the codes are accepted and enforced; and the rituals and procedures are still means rather than ends. The need-fulfilling agency is an efficient going concern enjoying its maximum vitality.

Period of Formalism. This is the period when the human purposes implicit in the organization have begun to be obscured, and the mechanisms have become ends in themselves. The positions of the functionaries have become sinecures, and the functionaries themselves function by rote; the codes and ideologies have developed sanctities of their own; the rituals and procedures have degenerated into often well-embroidered but empty formalities. There is much evidence of organization, but less and less vitality and functioning. The whole is a ponderous and pompous machine. It stultifies, misdirects, or fails to utilize the energies of its members in fulfillment of the standing need.

*Institutionalism and the processes that make for institutional rigidity and deterioration will be examined in Chap. 18.

Period of Disorganization. Now the organization is going to pieces. It has lost its effectiveness as an instrumentality, and the members no longer have confidence in it. Those who still embrace it nominally ignore it in practice or conform only half-heartedly. Many have withdrawn entirely and are seeking their need satisfaction elsewhere or are going unserved. Those who are professionally or emotionally attached to it will make efforts to preserve it. But few people can be loyal to a lifeless and futile form after its major utility has been lost.

Death or Reorganization. When an organization is in this final state, one of two things can happen. It may die and disappear, and its need-fulfilling functions will be assumed by some other organization. Or a critical and revolting portion of its membership may put it, in all its significant elements, through a transforming reorganization, after which, in its new form or forms, it may appear as a new institutional organization in the incipient stage. (34, pp. 79-82) Then, again, each stage gives way to the next.

Implementation of Institutions

Questions of major importance are: How are people inducted into institutional ways? Why do people conform to institutional charters? These questions are concerned with implementation, that is, *making institutions work*.

Passive Implementation

All ordinary means of communication and cultural transmission and general exposure to the culture of a society, of course, conspire to breed familiarity with institutions and practice in their ways. By means of these factors, institutional ways are transmitted from person to person, from generation to generation, and from group members to newly arrived outsiders.

Institutional standards and routines impinge upon the individual from birth on in the family, the play group, the neighborhood, the school group, and through all the activities of the larger and more diverse community. From them he cannot escape. He is more or less unconsciously and automatically trained in many of the ways of the institutions that confront him as he rapidly expands into new departments of societal life from age period to age period.

Probably more training in the standardized ways of interacting that constitute institutionalized life is obtained in the informal daily contacts with our fellows and our culture through actual exposure and participation than is obtained through any formal pedagogical or control procedures.

And yet, because the institutional norms and practices so received are unconsciously propagated, are heterogeneous, and are presented in chance and unsystematic fashion, there are obvious gaps and distortions. There is no assurance regarding the necessary quantity, quality, or variety of materials imparted.

Active Implementation

To overcome the deficiencies of the spontaneous and informal processes of transmission and implementation, active and organized efforts are made. *Schools* of various levels and certain other organizations, such as churches, welfare associations, and the press in some of its phases, specifically and consciously act with educative purpose. The more or less formalized aspects of taboos, established concepts of roles, symbols, and ritual and ceremony function as guides and imperatives.

Functionaries as integral parts of institutions are chiefly responsible for making the institutions work. They are the chief dynamic factors in the implementation processes, for they are the administrators of institutional organizations, the disseminators of the specific values, ideas, and mores of the institutions, the preservers and protectors of the roles, symbols, and rituals. To maintain and advance the institution is part of their job or their office. They win or lose in accordance with the manner in which they carry out the policy and program of the institution. The policeman has to police, the mother has to mother, the educator has to educate, the minister has to minister, the governor has to govern.

Public Opinion. Public opinion functions as the chief pressure in achieving conformity, although it is of a somewhat intangible nature. In any institutional field it supports the roles, symbols, and rituals; it motivates and in the long run authorizes and sanctions the activities in behalf of institutional ends for both the general participants and the functionaries; it exerts additional pressures of its own; it often initiates, authorizes, and supports the coercive measures (for example, those of the agencies of the state) that are used as a last resort in forcing conformity to institutional requirements. Human behavior has always been an object of group scrutiny, and when a violation or infraction is discovered, the group rushes into action. Sooner or later every individual and every group realize this fact.

The State. In modern societies, constituted as they are, the state operates as the ultimate and final compulsive agent. There has never been a peaceable and efficiently functioning society which did not rest on a cornerstone of force. No society can permit confusion and anarchy to reign; hence, it cannot allow its institutions to fall below a certain degree of effectiveness in operation. The state is the over-all institution of us, by us, and for us, that *does* for us what we cannot conveniently and satisfactorily do as individuals or as lesser groups.

The state carries our supreme authority, establishes and maintains all indispensable order and function, is our final ordering, regulatory, and constructive agency. It enforces the regulatory measures of many other institutions, such as marriage, divorce, the public health agencies, and is a court of last resort for all moral safeguarding of publicational, recreational, and aesthetic activities. So important are the many enforcing functions of the state that people everywhere permit it to use force in carrying out these functions.

In every institutional field the rights and duties that have been well established and widely accepted as such by the great majority, the compulsions and prohibitions that are deemed so important that neither avoidance nor alternatives of performance nor substandard performance can be accepted, are embodied as the *will* of the group into the specific statements of *law*. These laws are enforced by the police and the courts as agents of the organized people, and infringement and violation are punished.

The essential and fundamental minima in the way of behavior requirements or prohibitions of all institutions must be observed. The modern state designates these in its legal commands and uses coercive force to ensure their observance. The institutions *must* function effectively. (34, pp. 156-177)

Institutionalized Associational Systems of Human Society

The social organization of every society, as historians, anthropologists, and sociologists attest, resolves itself into certain universal and basic divisions or systems of institutionalized activity. These are the pivotal operational entities of societal life. In each historical or contemporary society, of course, they vary considerably in specific content.*

*These systems of institutionalized organizations are the *major agencies* of societal maintenance and their treatment should be thought of in this connection as part of Chap. 21. Because of the abundance of readily available literature on these organizations, their features and functions will be very concisely set forth. The student can easily carry on from here.

What are they and what are their major functions?

The Economic System

Economic institutions in some form are basic for the satisfaction of all other needs, for men must possess the means of physical maintenance in order to exist and perform the functions of life. Food and protection against the elements in the form of shelter, clothing, and tools are necessities without which life is impossible. As civilization advances, the physical minima increase in number and kind and become the bases of many other indispensable satisfactions. The economic system demands the more active participation of a larger proportion of the population, interpenetrates with more aspects of group life, presents more occasions for disturbance, conflict, and maladjustment than any other system.

The processes of physical maintenance are complicated by the fact that they consist of satisfying unlimited wants in a world of limited extent and out of a stock of goods which is limited at any given time. Each individual and group also seeks not only to obtain, but also to conserve and increase, its store of goods. The main economic processes follow.

Production. The various systematic processes and activities whereby the materials of value are put in forms suitable for human use and made available in sufficient quantity (agriculture, mining, lumbering, manufacturing) comprise production. In modern society production is expedited by a vast division and specialization of tasks and conducted by a great variety of organizations. Essential to it is the establishment of *property,* that is, standardized, group-enforced rules determining specific possession, use, and disposal rights over all sorts of corporeal and incorporeal things. *Contract* is the fixed pattern which sanctions, standardizes, and enforces agreements regarding the disposition of property in all its forms and of services of all kinds.

Distribution. The process of dividing the proceeds of production among those directly participating in and contributing to the process is called *distribution.* The participants and contributors include the owner of the land and the capital, the risk takers, and the providers of managerial services, skills, and labor generally.

Exchange. Exchange involves the processes and instrumentalities of commerce by means of which things in various stages of production are made available to those who add usefulness to them and get the final products to the ultimate consumer (jobbing, wholesaling, retailing). Related to exchange are *markets,* established trading places with their special procedures; *money,* the medium of exchange and standard of value of things and services; *banking,* the agency of deposit and process of providing and exchanging credit; and *transportation systems,* the means of moving things and men.

Consumption. The standardized ways of using finished and exchanged products in the final satisfaction of individual and group wants and interests comprise consumption.

The Marriage and Family System

The system of marriage and the family grows out of the fact that the human race consists of two sexes, who are drawn together by sex passion and who mate. Offspring may issue long after the passion has passed. Furthermore, the sexes are complementary to each other in various extrasexual ways and are forced to cooperate. Out of these situations grow two sets of institutions.

Marriage. The basic social functions of marriage are to regulate, stabilize, and standardize sexual intercourse, that is, make it legitimate under appropriate conditions, and to establish in a socially approved way the family as a procreative unit and usually also as a maintenance unit. *Divorce* is the standardized, safeguarded and more or less socially acceptable procedure for the dissolution of unsuccessful marriages.

The Family (a Consequence of Marriage). The primary function of the family is to serve as society's basic institution for its own biological self-perpetuation. It is the group's basic agency by means of which necessary future generations are produced, protected, and reared. A related function is that of major maintenance unit in most societies. It also functions as the chief agency in the socialization of the child.

Political, Legal, and Military Systems

The function of the political, legal, and military systems as they affect us today is to ensure ordered relationships of all kinds between individuals and groups; to establish rules of group living and tranquility as well as to enforce them; to ensure life, liberty, rights, peace, justice, and the pursuit of all socially acceptable individual and minor-group interests and ends; to provide for internal security of person and property; and to set up protection against external aggression.

The State. The state is that system of institutions which unites the inhabitants of a given territory under a single scheme of political administration and control. Its prime function is to enable the constituent beings of areal secondary groups to get along with each other, to secure peace and order among the individuals and classes within the society, and to conduct intergroup relations; in brief, to establish peace and security and maintain justice. In addition to these fundamental functions the modern state of highly civilized societies has assumed a host of service functions.* Today it is the over-all agency that does for us what we cannot conveniently or profitably carry on as individuals or as private groups or what we do not care to turn over to private or semiprivate organizations.

Law. The law consists of the rules of organized social life, summarizing the general principles of social conduct as found in the moral codes of the group, and making them definite, standard, and punishable.

Military Institutions. Military institutions comprise the organized procedures whereby combined force is used for preservation of the group against external aggression and whereby external aggression is conducted.

The Religious and Ethical Systems

The function of religious institutions is to satisfy man's basic religious needs and to canalize the emotions, beliefs, and practices related to these needs. Among all groups, religious activity is a deliberate attempt to get into helpful relationship with powers, personalized or impersonal, that are believed to control the unknowns of human life. People conduct most of these activities jointly.

The ethical institutions consist of the standardized, or systematized, and more or less permanent ideas of right and wrong or good and bad in conduct among a people, along with the accompanying principles, customs, and codes. Their function is to set up ways of acting that are approved and required and designate others that are definitely forbidden and punished in one way or another by the given group or society. Their special significance lies in that men *must act* in certain ways among their fellows. Frequently, for purposes of emphasis and effective enforcement, efforts have been made to place ethical codes under the power of supermundane beings and utilize a posed scheme of supernatural rewards and punishments.

Educational and Scientific Systems

Education is the organized and standardized process in every group to pass on more or less systematically to the next generation the accumulated knowledge, experience, lore, institutions—in brief, the culture—of the group, if the group is to be perpetuated in time, and to prepare the children and youth to assume full responsibility as adults in the society when they reach that biological and social estate.

Scientific institutions have as their function the deliberate and conscious discovery of new knowledge, and the invention of new processes and new methods of producing continually better adjustments of man to his physical and social universe.

Expressional and Aesthetic Systems

The expressional and aesthetic systems are concerned with the expressional urges, such as spiritual fervor, serious thought, the charm of sound, line, form, color, physical rhythm and grace, creative tendencies of various kinds, and any desire to express beauty in its various forms. The expressional system establishes and maintains more or less stable and standardized ways whereby these urges and tendencies can be socially safeguarded, socially understood, transmitted and conserved for future enjoyment by noncreators.

*See Chap. 2, pp. 35-36.

Professionalization—an Aspect of Institutionalization

Professionalization is a special example of institutionalization and as such has very great significance in a modern, complex society like our own. It has, of course, occurred and been necessary in some degree in earlier societies with respect to certain categories of specialized institutional functionaries, especially in religion, law, teaching, and medicine. It is concerned with the *institutional structuring and functioning,* as analyzed above, *of strategic functional personnel in certain occupational areas of social life.*

Professionalization in modern life relates directly to the increase and specialization of knowledge and its use in societal functioning and to chartering of some of the most vital roles—technical, spiritual, instructional, and administrative—that members of certain specialized occupations play. It also involves some large-scale formal organizations, both as combinations of men of given professions organized for various purposes and as operative agencies to perform investigative, technical, and administrative tasks. Conversely, large-scale organizations favor specialization of various functions, which in turn encourages, even requires, new professions. In fact, "Many of the most important features of our society are to a considerable extent dependent on the smooth functioning of the professions." (67, p. 457)

The Nature of the Professions

What is a profession? Occupations range from crafts and trades to the learned professions. The professions are occupations involving specialized knowledge and skill, usually of a highly esoteric or scientific nature, which are acquired by special advanced training. The skilled services are affected with great public interest and are so specialized that the benefiting public cannot acquire the same knowledge and proficiency. In American society there is some degree of professionalization among lawyers, doctors, clergy, teachers, scientists, accountants, actuaries, journalists, engineers, nurses, credit men, insurance consultants, social workers, and many brackets of public servants, and increasingly among businessmen.

Concisely put, the essential attributes of a profession may be analyzed as follows:

1. A profession involves skilled and specialized, expert service (including advice) which is transmitted to others.
2. The service is of an intellectual character and requires persons of considerable intellectual stature.
3. Learning and science are the bases for rendering the service, the actual performance of which involves special training and techniques.
4. The knowledge and training for a profession are acquired through an orderly, highly specialized, usually prolonged educational discipline and often apprenticeship and are tested by rigorous examinations, which in most cases lead to licensing by local or state governments.
5. The members of a profession with minimal acceptable competence hold a monopoly upon the services they render and are in a sense a closed group.
6. A member of a profession is obligated to render the highest quality of painstaking service at all times, with an altruistic motivation, devotion to the well-being of those served, and a strict sense of social responsibility.
7. In the performance of his functions, a member of a profession acts in a professional, and not a private, capacity, and his service is characterized by specificity of function and limited to his particular field of knowledge and skill.
8. In his relationships with his clients or patients, a member of a profession maintains professional secrecy; that is, he does not divulge the personal and private information which he receives.
9. Personality differences, personal prejudices, and whims must not enter into the relationships with clients, nor should discrimination be practiced.
10. The fees or salaries for the skilled services should be adequate to sustain the practitioners, but within the reach of all needing the service.

In general, where the learning and training are complicated and extensive, the services socially strategic and necessary, and the responsibility for a high quality, certainty, and equality of service great, then the necessity of professionalizing the technique and practice becomes more insistent.

Competence and Codes

The actual process of professionalization involves, among several key features, notably *the establishment and maintenance of high minimum qualifications and requirements in the way of special knowledge and practical and technical proficiency* and *the establishment and maintenance of high ethical standards* insisted upon in the relations of the members among themselves and in the performance of services to the recipient members of the community.

Those who have the qualifications and meet the requirements for admission are entitled to use a specially designated title, such as doctor of medicine, counselor at law, professor of sociology, and so on. The establishment and maintenance of adequate qualifications makes it possible for the public to be assured that it is receiving the services of a real professional rather than of a quack or shyster. The standards of professions are usually formally stated in the codes or canons of ethics of the respective professions. These codes emphasize the obligation of the professions to the public as a whole and especially to their clients, patients, or employees; the kind and quality of work or service expected of members; permissible forms of compensation; types of acceptable promotional activity, competition, and obligations to fellow practitioners; forbidden acts; and general educational duties in their specialties.

In order to effect these two major principles of institutionalization, a variety of special organizations exist. The members of the different professions are usually organized into associations of their own, not only to maintain the institutional requirements, but also to preserve and even enhance their activities in society. These include ministerial associations, bar and medical associations, associations of teachers and college professors, engineering societies, associations of certified accountants, actuaries, credit men, real estate agents, and so on.

These associations usually participate in setting and accrediting curricula and training requirement of schools for professional training, defining requirements for admission to practice the profession, administering examinations, determining and developing the ethical codes, and dismissing the incompetents from the professions. Usually, though, the state has general and final regulatory responsibility and authority in most of these matters, since the services of the professions are indispensable to the general well-being and a satisfactory level of quality must be assured.

In general the professional associations work with the state and often act as its deputies. They function in setting standards of admission and acting as examining boards selected by some governmental body under the auspices of the state. These state boards register and certify successful applicants. The professional organizations exercise disciplinary powers over competence and conformity to the ethical code. In the case of breaches of either of these, the association may disqualify and exclude the recalcitrants, but more important, in some professions a state or joint authority takes away the license to practice.

CHAPTER XIII

DIFFERENTIATION: NATURE, FACTORS, PROCESSES, AND FORMS

IN CHAPTERS 11 AND 12 two important related aspects of the structuralization and functionalization of a society were presented, namely, the organization of society into informal and formal groups and the institutionalization of all common or recurrent interactional behavior. Here, societal differentiation as another related major and universal aspect of societies will be presented.

It has been pointed out that differentiation can be profitably studied in two ways: as a static phenomenon and as a developmental occurrence. (7, p. 390)

The essence of differentiation as a *static,* or *cross-sectional, phenomenon* is the fact that every society at any given time is a complex mosaic of innumerable different groups—and especially of different categories of persons*—and that these groupings and categories have distinctive characteristics and carry on dissimilar, though related and interdependent, functions in society. The relations between the members of a society are organized or patterned on the basis of their different socially significant characteristics and around the different functions or roles which they perform. The members have various ranks, statuses, or positions in the social system, with the implication that these are more or less appropriate to the functions or roles. This differentiated arrangement is the basis for all cooperative relations among the persons, groups, and categories of a society and for all exchange relations involving action, remuneration, and the use of the facilities for action.

As a *developmental occurrence* societal differentiation consists of the emergence of new forms due to the addition of new groups, new categories, and new needs and functions and invariably also of the sloughing off of old forms as adjustment is made to new circumstances. As a society grows in numbers and expands, it unavoidably becomes more complex in structure and more diversified in

*By categories we mean in this connection classified types of persons, such as males, the aged, carpenters, Methodists, and so on, rather than true groups as generally defined.

interests and in essential functions. There are always dividing, separating, and specialization of function. Hence, there is a resultant tendency for the differentiated elements to become more numerous and more finely divided, for new functions and roles to be acquired or assigned. However, as some elements are merged with others or as they disappear with the disappearance of the conditions that brought them into being, certain functions also cease to be carried on. The interplay of these two ways of viewing differentiation will be noticeable throughout this examination.

In the simpler societies, differentiation is not so elaborate. Nevertheless, there are age groups, sex division, something in the way of occupational differences, privileged individuals, categories, and classes and other accepted differences due to variations in wealth, sanctity, intelligence, physical strength, social power, and so on. In modern complex societies the differentiation of the population is increasing and is almost limitless. This differentiation is due to the necessity of specialization, ever-increasing division of labor and consequent multiplication of occupations and professions, vast diversification of interests, ethnic and cultural diversities, variations in wealth and income, unavoidable development of an array of offices and administrative and functional categories, variations in individual intelligence, ability, drive, opportunity and achievement, and the desire to profit by opportunity, and numerous other factors.

Differentiation comes with the development of pluralistic relationships. The very increase in size implies increasing differentiation, and there is continual interplay between differentiation and social organization. The organization of society depends upon the articulation of the divergent though complementary units into some sort of working relationship. At the same time, the more complex the organization, the more extensive and minute must be the differentiation among the parts involved if the societal functions are to be carried on.

Elementary Factors in Societal Differentiation

Several sets of elementary factors create the conditions out of which societal differentiation inevitably and inescapably grows.

Extensive Variability of Human Beings

Members of a society are alike only in that they belong to the human race and have a more or less common cultural heritage. Beyond this, and even within some of these general types, great, almost unlimited, diversity exists as to both individual qualities and sociocultural conditions. Great biological heterogeneity occurs. There are differences in inherited natural gifts. Persons vary in physical constitution, vigor, and health, in intellectual capacity, temperament, and spiritual characteristics. The weak cannot do things requiring physical strength; the stupid cannot do things requiring mental ability; the bovine cannot have the insights or ability to do things that those with spiritual capacities have. These unlike types do not comfortably associate with each other.

Human beings consist of two sexes, which differ biologically, and the twain shall never completely meet. There is always some division of the reproductive and child-bearing functions of each sex on the basis of sex; additional acquired differences come about, and every society sets or standardizes the expected behavior and the sex-related functions. A man or woman cannot discharge certain functions of the opposite sex. Human beings fall into different age categories. A child cannot perform various physical and mental functions easily performed by and required of a grown-up person; the old cannot do things that persons in vigorous early maturity can do. Persons differ in visible race features which differentiate them as to cultural environment, position, and often function.

The members of a complex society like our own differ also as to ethnic backgrounds and the acceptance or tolerance of their characteristics on the part of the majority members of the society; their place in urban, rural and regional life; ethical, aesthetic, and religious interests and ways of life; and wealth, occupation, and other economic backgrounds, interests, and opportunities. Other differences are apparent in the prestige of parents or family, social class, and reputation; in educational and other cultural backgrounds and opportunities; individual susceptibility to learning and training processes and ability to utilize life experience; social life objectives; and authority and subservience.

In general, a society would be *undifferentiated* if its members were all alike in native endowment and cultural backgrounds, if they believed the same things, shared identical interests, and followed pretty much the same way of life. Actually, though, they are *infinitely differentiated* as to native resources and equipment, background, training, opportunities, and life situations.

Variability of Complementary Functions

As a society operates, it must perform a multiplicity of diverse and more or less distinctive functions—economic, communicative, familial, technological, ameliorative, and so on. Different individual and social needs require different ways of performing related societal functions, which differ greatly in difficulty and importance and require different types and combinations of characteristics, different degrees and levels of ability, skill, will, and achievement on the part of the performers.

Usually the functionally most important jobs or the socially most strategic require abilities, training, and other qualities that are fairly limited in the population. But all of society's jobs are ranged along a continuum from the easy (for which there are many doers) to the very difficult (for which there are relatively few possible performers). Thus, every society is confronted with the task of providing adequate incentives and appropriate rewards for those relatively scarce population elements that do its hard but important work with a proper degree of efficiency and responsibility. Society solves this problem by giving high position to difficult and important functions and attaching to or building into the position higher honor, prestige, and privilege; in brief, by making rights and privileges conform to duties and responsibilities.

Davis and Moore state:

> Social inequality is thus an unconsciously evolved device by which societies insure that the most important positions are conscientiously filled by the most qualified persons. Hence every society, no matter how simple or complex, must differentiate persons in terms of both prestige and esteem, and must therefore possess a certain amount of institutionalized inequality. (2)

The authors point out, however, that actually a society does not need to reward positions in proportion to their functional importance, but only to give sufficient reward to them to ensure that they will be filled competently or simply that less essential positions do not compete successfully with more essential ones.

Different kinds of social agencies therefore are required, especially associations of human beings with different degrees of organization and institutionalization, different roles, different ranking and degrees of authority, and different superordinate-subordinate relationships within the organizations and the larger society. The society must be divided and diversified into various contributory subgroups, each with distinct capacities and resources, physical and social location, social function, and social rank, responsibility, and authority.

Of course, not all existing differentiations contribute to the efficacy of societal operation. Some grow out of conflict or exploitive processes and reflect past conqueror-conquered or master-slave conditions, and some are formalized injustices based merely on power or force and the ability of certain elements of a population—a majority, a social class, a dominant sex or age group, a powerful ethnic group—to maintain its controlling position. Often, arbitrary legal barriers separate the different elements.

Some differentiation is not complementary diversity, but conflict-inviting and conflict-producing diversity. This latter aspect will be examined in a later chapter. Obviously, a society's interests are best served when the differentiations rest as far as possible on intrinsic differences and as little as possible on special privilege or power.

The Elemental Necessity of Differentiation

Differentiation is an inevitable concomitant and an imperative necessity of any human living together, a universal phase of structuralization, and an elemental functional requirement. One need not wish to abolish social dissimilarities, in spite of the injustices that accompany them, because it cannot conceivably be done. The social objective is to make fair and humane the conditions and circumstances under which diverse individuals and groups function together.

If a society is to survive, many varieties of functions must be conducted, and the several varieties of parts must function together with some coherence. If the activities of the different individuals, groups, and aggregates are haphazard and unrelated, no organized social life is possible.

Without differentiation an organized society would be factually impossible; and even if it were possible, it would be deprived of enormous advantages enjoyed by differentiated society. (8) Each differentiated element has some special characteristic and certain norm- and usage-prescribed obligations, functions, and privileges. All are complementary elements of a system of interdependency. Each must render prescribed or tolerated benefits; otherwise, the operation of the social system as a functional sharing of reciprocities is interrupted or impaired. The various differentiated but interdependent elements constitute a type of equilibrium.

In brief, no society has existed, can exist, or will exist in which social standing and influence of individuals and groups does not differ, and, quite obviously, the differential organization of a society is a procedure for making the multiplicity of heterogeneities socially profitable, of converting unavoidable diversity into cooperation and order.

Processes of Differentiation

As a process differentiation is a normal and continuous aspect of interaction, an essential part of human dynamics. Interaction always differentiates people from each other at the same time that it tends to integrate them. Nor is it always merely a matter of casual occurrence. As greatly variant individuals live in association with each other, they show their differences and tend to develop further differences and to become individualized. The very process of differentiation tends to accentuate and multiply divergences.

Competition and Opposition

Competition and opposition are special processes contributing to and initiating differentiation. As individuals and groups vie with each other in all manner of ways—for standing room, jobs, honors, mates, clients, status, as they seek survival, opportunity, and recognition, they are stimulated to use and develop their special characteristics and abilities as effective mediums of action. As they oppose each other, as they clash with respect to wishes, interests, and objectives, they acquire enhanced self-consciousness, develop aversions, achieve separate unities, and engage in special forms of antagonistic and innovative action.

Individuals become separated into sex groups, age groups, parties, sects, ethnic groups, purposive, defensive, and offensive organizations of many kinds. These processes are forms of safeguarding individuals and groups, and by means of them people make special social niches for themselves. The parts are continually being separated from the whole and are more or less appropriately located in the societal structure.

On the other hand, as indicated above, the very essentials of *functional cooperation,* that is, specialization of parts to carry on a complex division of the whole process of operation of any subsystem or of a society as a whole, demand different persons and different groups and categories of persons doing different things for the sake of the whole.

Continual Selection of Individuals and Groups

In general, differentiation is a process of continually *selecting or sorting out of individuals, groups, and categories of persons* on the basis of a complex array of existing and new criteria, involving individual characteristics and interests, prevailing and changing folkways, traditions, and institutional values and requirements. Because of these diversities, individuals and groups participate in various more or less distinct functions and roles. In the process of participation they are divided, distributed, and located as to functions and roles. Thus, the processes of differentiation assign individuals to certain functions, give individuals somewhat special ways of life and portend what they will get out of life, and break up the members of a whole society into a considerable number of groups, each functioning with something of its own way of life within and as part of the whole.

Social Advantages of Differentiation

Differentiation is of vital significance in the operation of a society, as is apparent when we note some of the advantageous functions it performs.

Functional Advantages of Division of Labor and Specialization of Function

Division of labor and its related specialization of functions are essential features of societal organization.* Both are kinds of differentiation. Many special contributions are needed in a society. The various essential social tasks or activities are divided and subdivided among the various interdependent population elements constituting the entire societal mechanism. Thus, as noted, there is a division of labor between the sexes, the generations, the physically and intellectually diverse, occupational groups, associations and institutions, urban and rural areas and peoples, and so on.

The processes in the division of labor usually operate to produce increased proficiency and efficiency among the various elements through the specialization in the performance of the segments of tasks and usually in terms also of greater volume and greater speed and often of higher quality of output.

Thus, differentiation in terms of division of labor and specialization of functions gives scope to a wide range of capabilities and characteristics on the part of persons and groups. In a rough way it makes possible the location of individuals within the range of their abilities, interests, cultural backgrounds, and opportunities. As far as society as a whole is concerned, it is a form of teamwork in which there is complementary diversity. If the total differentiated-cooperative mechanism is functioning well, the individuals and groups may experience a sense of satisfaction in doing things well. They may feel themselves to be part of an effective mechanism, and the society as a whole may be getting its complicated job done.

*See Chap. 10.

Placement in the Social System

The more or less fair and just placement of individuals, categories, and groups in the social system is a social function that grows out of the great variability and irregularity of mankind.* Men differ vastly as to natural or constitutional endowment, as to physical, intellectual, aesthetic, moral, spiritual, and volitional capacities, and as to needs and interests. Situational factors enhance or diminish the hereditary make-up and the early conditioning of persons. Changing circumstances of life perpetually bring new differences. Persons do not become alike by the availability or use of privileges and opportunities. The very division of labor makes men unlike. The contributions to societal functioning are never alike, and the results are never shared alike by all individuals and groups.

Differentiation makes it possible for unlike persons and categories to function in life somewhat in ratio to their capacities and opportunities, provided, of course, that the selective and placement processes are operating fairly effectively. In this respect differentiation is a condition and a procedure for the protection, integrity, and security of each person in his social environment. What he can give and what is socially required of him are in some degree in balance. Thus, persons of superior ability and those of inferior ability can comfortably live and work together because of such socialized differentiation.

*The aspects of inequality and their functional significance will be treated in Chap. 14.

Provision of Social Integration and Solidarity

The differentiation process results in two apparently contradictory conditions. It often creates potential and actual hostility and divisiveness, since it separates people and usually ranks them hierarchically, and there is usually an implication of socially qualitative differences.* Differentiation and integration, however, go together and are coexistent as processes. Differentiation is a factor in the integrating of activities of many people by forestalling and preventing disruptive activities and coordinating the actions of many persons in the interests of objectives that could not be achieved by these individuals if they were acting independently. (6)

This is simply another way of stating that within a relatively stable social system, differentiation makes possible a functional articulation of the various intrasocial groupings; an equilibrium of sorts exists between them. It acts thus as a mechanism creating social solidarity. A community at any given moment may be viewed as a completed jigsaw puzzle, all of the variously shaped pieces of which are interlocked parts of a whole.

Horizontal and Vertical Differentiation

As has undoubtedly been surmised from the preceding discussion, differentiation takes both horizontal and vertical forms. Individuals and groups are *hierarchically typed, ranked, and socially spaced as horizontal layers or strata or classes* in society conceived of as a pyramid or layer cake. While these strata are complementary, they are *unequal from one angle or another* according to the current yardstick of evaluation of the given society. Prestige, esteem, honor, privileges and rights, responsibilities, and authority are unequally assigned and exist in ascending degrees among the successively higher layers. While there is relative equality *within* them, there is difference of rank and status; there are distinctions of higher and lower, superior and inferior. Usually the situational relationships involve differential treatment and some degree of accepted superordination and subordination. It is somewhat facetious but nevertheless quite accurate to state that these essential and inherent precedences and degrees of subordination among individuals and groups constitute a sort of "pecking order." This ranking is even true in societies that normally subscribe to ideals of equality and fraternity.*

At the same time there is *vertical differentiation.* Groups within the same general physiographic territory are spatially divided from each other, and communities are divided from each other. Within each stratum or layer of the society there are vertically divided groups, equal as to rank and prestige, but different as to functional activity or special interests. Thus, within the rank of skilled workers, there are carpenters, plumbers, plasterers, and so on.

No absolute distinction between horizontal and vertical differentiation, however, can be made in any single case. Always there is some element of each. Any vertical differentiation within a given societal plane invariably involves *some* variation in horizontal space scaling. Thus, the sexes are separated vertically, but usually there is some social superiority (elevation) of males over females; different occupations, although they require similar levels of skill, may carry different social prestige; and so on.

Some Major Forms of Societal Differentiation

Although there is infinite diversification and social separation of individuals and groups, there are certain readily discernible and common forms. Some of these will be briefly examined by way of

*These disintegrative aspects and processes will be examined in Chaps. 16 and 17.

*Stratification, which is horizontal differentiation, will be comprehensively analyzed in Chap. 14.

summary and orientation. These can be roughly classified as biosocial and sociocultural types of differentiation.

Biosocial Forms

The biosocial forms of differentiation are based on sex, age-group, and racial differences.

Sex Differentiation. Perhaps the most ancient recognized differences were those between the sexes, a dichotomy dependent partly on biological differences, partly on social division of labor, and partly on institutionalized roles. Everywhere the sexes have been and are separate societal categories. Sex has been called "the most fundamental cleavage in society." (11)

The naturalistic reason for the differences between the sexes is the respective part played by each in the biological process of reproduction. Each is endowed with the requisite physiological and psychological mechanisms for such functioning, and this is especially significant with respect to anatomical and metabolic characteristics. Males, for example, apparently have better motor ability, greater muscular strength, greater rapidity of motion, and a lower rate of fatigue.

Men and women have also generally differed in their social traits, roles and functions. Owing to woman's relative social incapacity during pregnancy, childbirth, and care of the helpless young, she has had to be physically protected and economically maintained by the man. Thus, she developed a dependency that usually has resulted in some degree of male dominance. The superior physical strength of the male has also been a factor.

In general, a fairly definite division of labor and assignment of tasks exists. Actually, however, in most societies, the diverse social traits and roles of the sexes are decidedly influenced by the folkways, mores, conventions, and institutions of the society. Male dominance has often supported discriminations between the sexes in education, morals, vocations, and other economic matters, legal and political matters, religious activity, recreation, and even artistic life. These differences have usually been well rationalized and well manipulated, even though some of them have little or no relation to the elemental differences between the sexes or to the vital social functions that each must perform if a society is to carry on. Such sociocultural differences have even been extended to sex-appropriate language, clothes, hairdress, and pitch and intonation of voice. Both sexes have been trained for these roles and ways of life.

Age-Group Differentiation. Age-group classification based on stages in the life cycle is a basic differentiation in all known societies. The criterion of relative age reflects the biological fact that people are not identical in ability or function at different ages. Physiological and psychological factors, as they affect physical vitality and strength and physical dependence, are basic considerations. Thus, most societies resort to a rather simple system of chronological classification: infancy and childhood; youth, or adolescence, the chaotic period between childhood and maturity; maturity, or adulthood, the period of highest physical, mental, and social potency and activity and of major social responsibility; old age, or senescence, the period of physical and mental decline with its new dependency and limitation of range of action.

Cultural factors, however, develop patterns of distinctive roles, functions, responsibilities, prestiges, privileges, and power for each age group. Infants and the young are at the bottom of this scale. The immature are nearly always subordinate in most respects to the older groups, and the mature usually, but not always, to the old. The young are dependent upon the old for learning the social heritage and acquiring social status. The mature carry the greatest functional obligations because of ability and experience. The aged gradually relinquish their full social responsibilities, and do less, but are accorded certain rights, privileges, authorities, and manifestations of deference because of their experience and wisdom.

What the age groups do is nearly always a matter of informal rules prescribing the appropriate behavior for each grade and for the relations between them. The distinctions are, in a sense, manufactured and patterned, and each age group has a rough set of culture patterns of its own, as, for example, adolescents in American society.

Race Differentiation. In so far as races exist, they are based on certain supposedly identifiable physical characteristics produced by physical and physiological selective factors over a long period of time. Significant in our society is the fact that there are separate and separated racial groups, each with a high degree of consciousness of its difference as compared with other groups. The members of the respective groups often vary with respect to physical characteristics and the degree of cultural advancement and type of culture. Usually the groups are arrayed as majorities and minorities with the majority accorded greater esteem, opportunity, rights, and authority.

Certain functional specializations based on race prevail among societies with many races. This is due partly to assumption of these specializations by both the majority and minority groups and partly to the imposition of certain others upon the minority group by the majority. Race membership thus is "a primary causal component in the life chances of the individual." (12)

Racial groups are nonvoluntary, interest-conscious unities, generally without formal organization. Each is usually subject to some differentiation in the way of disapproval, prejudice, or active discrimination by the other groups. They often reveal intense hatreds and repulsions against each other, as well as blinding group egoism. (5, pp. 384-416) In our society, even after residence of more than a century and after four and even five generations under a tremendous cultural and social assimilative pressure, positive forces are still differentiating groups on the basis of racial origin.

Sociocultural Forms

The sociocultural forms include vocational, economic, socioeconomic, religious, and rural-urban differentiation.

Vocational, or Occupational, Differentiation. After sex and age, occupation appears to be the most general basis for differentiation and assignment of functions, rights, and duties. Although no one can escape classification by age and sex, not everyone pursues an occupation, although in a broad sense not many are without some occupatiou.

All persons participating in or contributing to the gaining of a livelihood for an individual or some group are pursuing an occupation. The innumerable activities in a society essential to its physical, political, and cultural maintenance provide the occasion for these occupational performances. The occupations involve a wide range of knowledge, ability, and skills, with widely varying standards and obligations, utilitarian and other advantages, and social esteem, ranking, and power accorded each under the current evaluation of functions.

In our society the over-all categories are professional, skilled, semiskilled, and nonskilled, with each having innumerable subclassifications of specialized performance. The increasing occupational differentiation in our rapidly changing and highly mobile society is indicated in the fact that the *Dictionary of Occupational Titles* of the United States Employment Service defines and codes approximately 29,000 titles. A standard classification for the United States, worked out by the Joint Committee on Occupational Classification of the American Statistical Association and the Central Statistical Board in July, 1938, presents the following:

1. Professional and semiprofessional workers
   a. Professional workers
   b. Semiprofessional workers
2. Proprietors, managers, and officials
   a. Farmers and farm managers
   b. Proprietors, managers, and officials—except farm
3. Clerical, sales, and kindred workers
   a. Clerical and kindred workers
   b. Salesmen and saleswomen
4. Craftsmen, foremen, and kindred workers
5. Operatives and kindred workers
6. Domestic service workers
7. Protective service workers
8. Service workers except domestic and protective
9. Laborers
   a. Farm laborers and foremen
   b. Laborers—except farm and mine (26)

Economic Interest-Group Differentiation. Related to occupational group differentiation in the economic sphere is the division of the population into various economic interest groups, such as rich and poor, gradations of income receivers, employers and employees, producers and consumers, buyers and sellers, owners and nonowners. In most known societies wealth especially has been conducive to social differentiation, for wealth or property gives its holders influence and respect quite apart from their personal qualities. The different degrees of wealth tend to divide the population into the separate orders of rich and poor, and the advantages that property brings may maintain and even increase this division. Thus, the rich become more powerful and privileged, and the poor more destitute and subordinate, possibly forming a menial and dependent segment of the population. Wealth is an important factor in preserving high differential status for the coming generation.

Socioeconomic Class Differentiation. In many societies, including our own, there are formal and informal groups occupying different social positions usually equated as low, middle, and high. These social rankings depend upon a variety of factors and indices, such as property, income, source of wealth and income, plane and standard of living, education, family history, ethnic group membership, social power and influence. Social class differentiation will be examined in a later chapter.

Religious Differentiation. Not only are the world religions highly separative, but within a given nation or society an infinite number of religious groupings may exist. In the United States there is the major cleavage between Protestants, Catholics, Christian Scientists, Jews, Mormons, and smaller groups representing other world religions. The Protestants are greatly divided into denominations and sects, and the Jews fall into at least three different groupings.

According to the U.S. Bureau of the Census, there are around 250 denominations in the United States. Some of these are very small, and some are specialized divisions of larger denominations, but all are distinctive enough to have a separate functioning organization. Each is more or less cohesive, and each has its own set of values, beliefs, and norms. Almost all accentuate their differences by proselyting and propagandist activities. Although the groups are mainly open, provided that one accepts the conditions of membership, they are separative as among themselves.

The different cults, sects, and denominations more or less parallel certain class levels, and many of them are also related to racial, nationality, and language divisions. Given sects and denominations vary regionally for a number of historical reasons. There are also cleavages that cut across denominations based on interpretations of fundamental beliefs and numerous other factors. (13)

Urban-Rural Differentiation. The dwellers in the cities and the rural areas are separated and diversified in various ways which have been discussed in earlier chapters. Basically urban and rural populations have different ways of life and goals of life. They differ in social-psychological characteristics, motivations, values, ideas, beliefs, attitudes, and standards along a variety of lines. Only on the most general social matters do they see eye to eye or think alike.

Other Differentiations. Sociologists sometimes examine as other forms of differentiation divisions and diversities stemming from different families and kinship groups, mental status, language groups, different educational levels, different communities and regions, and different political groups, including parties and states.*

Needless to say, these various categories of differentiations are not mutually exclusive, but cut across each other and overlap. All of us are involved in many differentiated situations at the same time.

*For the demographic significance of many of these differentiations and differentials, see Chap. 8.

CHAPTER XIV

STRATIFICATION: CHARACTERISTICS, PROCESSES, AND KINDS

STRATIFICATION, conceived of both as a structural *condition* of human society and as a set of continuously operating structuralizing and functionalizing *processes,* is receiving wide analytical attention from American sociologists. A large number of concrete studies of stratification in American Society have been made, and a maze of interpretations exist. From these it is possible to derive a set of core concepts and principles.

Stratification is a special type and major phase of differentiation. In analyzing it, however, we must go beyond mere individual and group differences. Human society, as we know, is composed of biologically, functionally, and culturally *different* individuals and groups. ***At the same time it consists also of various socially spaced horizontal layers, at ascending levels or strata.***

Each stratum includes both sexes, all age groups, and persons with varying other physical, psychic, and social characteristics and can be conceived of as being somewhat separated from the others by horizontal lines and somewhat socially and culturally isolated. The distinctions between the levels are based on gradations of social valuation and rest upon varying combinations of criteria and determinants. These graded values present a hierarchy or scale with diminishing degrees of prestige, esteem, and power as we descend from the higher to the lower levels.

Even though all members of a society have many things in common, the fact of stratification points to certain differences. The members of different strata have certain qualities and usually certain distinctive ways of life related to similar or common values, attitudes, and goals. They have certain functionally distinctive goals. Different kinds and degrees of social expectations and responsibilities attach to the different strata, and often there are differing key motivations.

The horizontal structuralization of society must be distinguished from the vertical, which is based on population aggregates, areal groups, informal groupings, purposive associations or organizations and institutions.

Stratification—a Characteristic of All Societies

Stratification of some extent has been and is a permanent and universal characteristic of all known societies. Even the simplest, preliterate tribal societies have incipient stratification in which distinctions are based on individual prowess and clan or family property variations and there are usually at least two groups at different levels of prestige and power—the chiefs, or leaders, and others, and the priests and others. In nonliterate societies, however, the social strata are not rigidly defined and membership in a stratum is not automatic through birth. They are more likely to be based upon personal qualities and achieved functional position.

Stratification also exists in some degree in all unibonded groups—racial, economic, religious, and political—whether parts of preliterate or of highly civilized societies. There are always the leaders, the informal or formal administrators and other influential elements, and the varying levels of rank-and-file members and everywhere there are schisms, social distinctions, and rated functional variations.

Complex Societies

Complex societies have universally a higher degree of stratification, and modern industrial-urban societies have the most elaborate systems of stratification. The latter have large and infinitely heterogeneous populations, and there is going on in them a continual proliferation of groups of various levels of functional significance. They have an ever-expanding division of labor and require a multiplicity of services.

In complex societies there is great inequality of wealth, income, and education and other agencies of opportunity and achievement, and there is great variation in freedom of action. Quite understandably, there are great differences in the way individual, family, and group behaviors and positions are evaluated and ranked. Some are always rated higher and some lower, and graded segments are inevitable. It is apparent that the more complex the society, the more extensive and intricate its stratification.

Effect of Stratification on Behavior

This stratification structure is an omnipresent and ubiquitous factor in the concrete behavior of individuals and groups. All of us, in any community, consciously or unconsciously, are constantly making comparisons between persons and between groups on the basis of their social levels, as can be seen in such everyday phrases as the "Country Club Set," the "bosses," the "middle classes," the "wrong side of the tracks," the "proletariat," the "Tobacco Roaders," and numerous others.

Almost every aspect of our social interaction as individuals is influenced by our social level. It is a prime factor in our attitudes and prejudices, our values and standards, our beliefs and ideologies, and affects our habits and institutional behavior—consumption forms, occupations, religious affiliations, marriage preferences and family performance, manners and etiquette, recreations and leisure-time activities.

Demographically, social level is an extremely important factor in differential marriage, birth, and death rates.* It determines many of our free contacts and participations, that is, our neighborhoods of residence, the people with whom we communicate freely and have comfortable companionship, the cliques and clubs we belong to, in fact, most of what we are connected with. Thus, our positional level in the stratification system of our society constitutes much of our way of life and determines most our life chances, that is, the social, economic, and educational opportunities, jobs and job security, chances of health, housing, and survival generally, and possibilities of success and power.

Stratification is an all-pervasive and integral feature of American society that some—especially the upper levels, which so perfectly demonstrate many of its features and privately cherish and seek to perpetuate their exalted positions—prefer to ignore publicly. American social scientists, however, are extremely conscious of its nature and significance. The scientific literature on social stratification is, at present, more extensive than that on any other subject in sociology.

*See Chap. 8.

Essential Characteristics of the Stratification System

The stratification system consists of a variety of distinguishable and related structures.

A Stratified Demographic and Organizational Structure

First of all, a stratification system consists of large, generalized horizontal divisions of the population of any community or society in the form of layers, or strata. If a social system were only a differentiated structure, it could be viewed as a single plane or as a one-story affair with cubicles and rooms of varying size and utility. Actually, it is a many-storied structure, differing from time to time in a given society and between different places and societies.

The stratified population structure may be viewed as a pyramid or, more typically, as a layer cake, composed of uneven and varying strata. Each layer, as indicated above, includes both sexes and all ages. The top layers are usually thin, with relatively few individuals, since there are *few* positions at the top. The layers become thicker further down. The layers themselves are complex affairs, for position in them involves a variety of biosocial, economic, occupational, and sociopolitical factors, which will be discussed below.

Warner and associates have pointed out that the stratification system presents another sort of ecological organization in addition to the familiar one. This is *an ecology of the vertical location, distribution, and movement of individuals and groups among the stories, or layers or strata, of a society,* which also can be indicated by maps, charts, and diagrams. (114, p. 34) In brief, there is a *pattern of strata.*

A similar stratification exists within and among all groups. Within any group the members are divided into layers or ranks in a fairly definite and clear-cut manner; some are at the top, others at the bottom, many in between. This is observable in a family or clan or in an age, sex, racial, language, political, religious, occupational, economic, or other group. There is also *inter*group stratification; different occupations, economic groups, different states, and religious groups are not situated on the same level but are stratified with respect to one another. (33, p. 278)

A Value Structure

Another universal feature inherent in the stratification system is the structure of social evaluations and cumulated norms as they apply to the respective strata. The persons and groups in the different strata are subject to differential valuations by the total society; they have different standing or position, often quite apart from *personal* qualities. The social value system unequally divides people into higher and lower elements, with those in the upper layers recognized as superior (as if they were more valuable or more important) and those in the lower strata as inferior (as if they were less important or less valuable in certain socially important respects). (26; 27; 35; 81, p. 600; 93) These values exist in the tradition and customs and are often institutionalized.

This relationship among strata is never imposed but is implicit in the very existence of the strata and must be understood in terms of reciprocal evaluation. Position in the stratum system is but the objective manifestation of the prevailing social evaluations. The superiority of one stratum implies recognition of that superiority by the inferior strata, and the inferiority of other strata implies the general acceptance of lower status by their members. (35, p. 194)

Usually there are also attitudes of superiority on the part of the upper strata toward the lower strata and of deference on the part of the lower strata toward the upper. Individual incumbents may be dissatisfied with their rank and give their deference reluctantly and jealously, but the general evaluations of rank tend to be accepted by all ranks. There is inequality *between* strata and relative social equality only *within* a given stratum, although the persons within the stratum may differ in renown and personal attributes. Members of the different strata rate themselves and each other in terms of these values and treat each other accordingly.

In the main, the top strata set the values for the

whole system. The given valuations have deep roots in the past, but they may change, and usually do, although somewhat slowly as compared with changing conditions.

A Prestige, Privilege, and Obligation Structure

The value system just discussed produces a *coordinate prestige system.* The stratification system thus presents also a *social hierarchy* based on the gradations of valuation and *a scale of ratings.* Ratings imply inequality, for they grow out of the fact that inequality is known and recognized, although not necessarily approved. The society or community has a *graded series of prestige, esteem, honor, and privilege that the members of the different strata enjoy.* Some people are more respected and their behavior has more prestige than have the actions of others. (9; 81, pp. 330-335) Prestige and privilege diminish as we descend from the higher to the lower levels.

In brief, there is a scale of prestige, and members of the society are roughly categorized according to their location on the scale. The scale presents a kind of continuum from top to bottom with numerous and somewhat confusing in-between or borderline cases.

Differences in prestige and esteem are usually accompanied by differences in opportunity and rights (that is, norm-supported claims) along almost all socially significant lines, especially economic, educational, recreational, leisure, and cultural. Not everyone has an equal opportunity to succeed, since position and rating determine access to opportunities. At the same time, there is a rough apportioning of social duties and obligations, with more being expected in the way of social participation and contribution of the members of the upper strata and less important duties being assigned to those of lesser privilege.

A Power, Authority, and Control Organization

As noted, the system of stratification includes a normative pattern indicated by the prevailing rating scale which is in the institutional pattern of the societal system. This, in turn, usually means something in the way of a *power system,* that is, a scheme of established and more or less accepted superordination and subordination. There are both a pyramid of authority involving the successive strata and a flow of authority downward through the hierarchy of ranks.

Authority is the established right to set values, determine policies, pronounce judgments, and act as social leaders; power is the more or less formalized or institutionalized right to command the services and the compliance of others and acquire the symbols and means of recognition (27, pp. 848-849) along social, economic, and political lines. Hiller points out that these power relations involve property (land, tools, and facilities), administrative positions and managerial functions, ability to utilize the agencies by which public opinion is formed, such as the press and radio, and the ability both to acquire and to control political offices.

These superordinate-subordinate relations usually affect the social control system of the society; that is, there is a tendency to allocate the major social control positions and functions to persons in the upper strata and to assign the routine, noncontrol positions and functions to people in the lower strata, with minor control positions falling somewhere in between. (8; 13; 24) Thus, a stratification system also presents a control hierarchy or a pattern of command-obedience relationship in the institutionalized activities of the members of the strata.

The members of the upper strata with their prestige and power carry the right of directing the activities of the large numbers of persons lower in the hierarchy. Historically, this has been the right of chieftains, feudal lords, generals, and kings in political and military affairs, of chief priests in religious relations, of masters of all kinds over slaves, serfs, and all manner of common people. In our culture it is especially demonstrated in the control power exercised by captains of industry and finance and other holders of property and of organizational authority and influence.

The characteristics of the stratification system up to this point are graphically presented in the accompanying figure. The pyramid in solid lines represents the strata of the population ranked according to status. It has its broad base of popu-

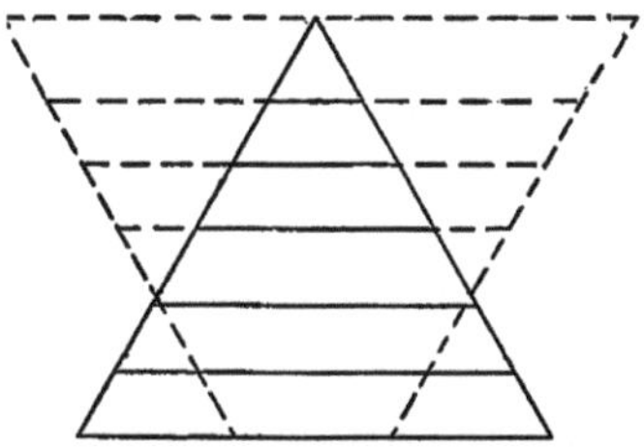

Persons Ranked According to Status

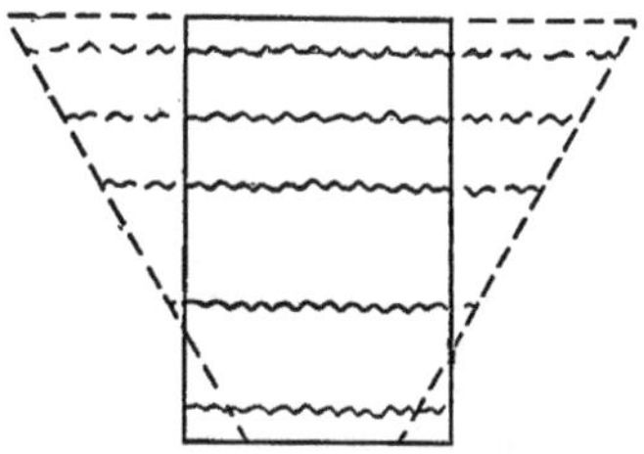

The Layer-Cake Concept

lation in the lower levels and diminishes in size as it rises into the higher levels. The superimposed figure in broken lines indicates roughly the corresponding valuations, prestige, rights, obligations, and social power of the respective strata.

From some points of view the layer-cake concept more accurately portrays the actual situation. A revision of the graphic figure along these lines is shown beside it.

Strata as Subcultures and as Subsocieties

A final signal characteristic of stratification systems must be indicated. While penumbral or transitional areas exist between strata, each stratum in its typical psyche and behavior actually functions as a subcultural group or even a subsociety within the whole. (20; 32; 76) Each stratum constitutes an empirically operative system, however reluctantly and obliquely recognized by its participants or those of other strata, and the members of each stratum are more or less separated from those of other strata in interaction by a variety of situational and cultural factors.

In general the members of each stratum have approximately the same position in the hierarchical structure, consisting of somewhat similar values and attitudes, prestige and esteem, privileges and rights, duties and obligations, power and authority, and societal functions. They think, feel, and act similarly and live and function among other strata as more or less unconscious and unorganized social groups, but nevertheless as real social groups. (33, p. 277)

Human Inequalities—a Basic Factor in Stratification

In the preceding chapter we briefly discussed the significance of division of labor and specialization of function and role in the location of variant individuals, categories, and groups in society as an operative entity. Here we are concerned with the fact that the very variability of these societal elements implies inequality. Thus, any objective approach to human functioning in the societal scheme of things requires the fullest recognition of the inequality of men in physical, intellectual, spiritual, and volitional capacity and of the infinitely wide range of human energy, tastes, qualities, and aptitudes. Men are equal only in their common humanity, although in a democratic society they should be equal in their common opportunities. If all were equal in capacity, receipts, or contributions, however, there would be a dead level of mediocre uniformity in social action.

Attitude of Individuals toward Equality

Parenthetically, we may speculate whether anyone really wants equality. Intellectually or rationally we assent to equality of opportunity, but our personality drives and our inner hopes in many instances seem to be inclined toward the achievement of superiority and domination. As egos we privately resent the implication of equality and find ego-enhancement in superiority. There is in all of us a lurking tendency to believe that everyone is not as good as everyone else. Most persons are trying to differentiate themselves from lower and equal strata and are aspiring to some status carrying higher prestige.

The demand for equality is not a demand for universal common rank, prestige, and privilege, but rather a demand for the right to achieve status equal to some ever-higher rank. The elements most vociferously demanding equality are actively striving for prestige differentiation from their rank and kind.

Effects of Inequality

From the point of view of individual functioning in a societal organization, social inequality is an unconsciously evolved device whereby persons, categories, and groups are assigned, on the basis of reigning criteria, places and functions roughly appropriate and proportional to their essential capacities, qualities, interests, cultural characteristics, and social achievements. That the results are not always morally acceptable and the selective processes—either automatic or socially devised—not always operating fairly and efficiently cannot and need not be admitted. Says Barnard:

> Without differentiation those of inferior ability are constantly in a position of disadvantage, under pressure to exceed their capacities, perpetually losing in a race in which no handicaps are recognized, never able to attain expected goals so long as they are treated as the equals of those who are in fact superior.

And:

> Much experience demonstrates that those who are unequal cannot work well for long as equals. But experience also demonstrates that where differences of status are recognized formally, men of very unequal abilities and importance can and do work together well for long periods. (1)

Ideally the stratification system provides for each individual an approximately appropriate niche in the levels of the social pyramid or layer cake. Certain individuals find in a given stratum an asylum or refuge within which they have a better chance of adjustment than if they attempted to carry on all the activities with all their requirements of the total society. Furthermore, the stratified structure provides a *graded series of asylums* "such that a failure at one level is redeemable by adjustment." (3, pp. 42-43)

One could at this point examine the social functions performed by a stratification system, based as it is upon the unavoidable and eternal inequalities of human beings. These functions will be more appropriately analyzed in connection with the processes of social ordination and accommodation which play a very important part in the *maintenance* of any society.*

*See Chap. 21.

Relation of Statuses to the Stratification System

The array of statuses of a society, which were previously examined as to their general signification in societal organization,* are elemental factors in the stratification system. The statuses, we will recall, are the functional-scalar positions which individuals, categories, and groups occupy in a social system. Not all statuses relate to stratification. There are both nonhierarchical and hierarchical and nonstratified and stratified statuses. The statuses based on sex and age and, in a racially heterogeneous social system, on race, on charm or friendliness, or on other personality characteristics of an individual occur in all strata and exist quite apart from stratum position. But the bulk of the functional-scalar statuses of a society do form the ingredient units of its stratification system.

*See Chap. 10.

Generalized Status

As noted previously, each person has a "generalized" status in which the most socially distinctive and important of his various particular statuses have most weight. In American society the items that carry much weight in the types of generalized statuses are the wealth and income and material equipment of the individual considered with respect to source, kind, and amount, his kind and level of education, the standing of his family, especially his occupation, and usually his affiliation in political, religious, recreational, and ethnic groups.*

This "cluster of statuses" blends or combines into what Davis aptly refers to as a person's "station." (9) Each society has an array of stations, which carry different social valuations. Each station has a locus on a vertical or hierarchical scale of social prestige and power and has attached to it a set of interlocking rights and obligations. Some stations are higher and some lower on this scale.

Members of a Stratum

The fact of significance here is that the mass of persons in a given society who have roughly the same station constitute what is generally called a "stratum." There is vertical social distance* between the incumbents of each social stratum, and those in the same stratum recognize the differences between themselves and the others.

Thus, the generalized, clustered statuses, as broadly conceived and as exercised in usual practice in a society, come to be equated with given strata. Persons, categories of persons, and groups are identified, classified, rated, and marked off from others according to their stratum location. This principle of evaluation and distribution of persons is the essential feature of a stratification system.

Stratification Processes

Undoubtedly the most important consideration in the functional analysis of a stratification system is an understanding of the constituent processes by which such a structural-functional organization is developed and maintained. If we are to have useful engineering possibilities, we must know not only its structural features and forms, but also how it functions and why. This field is one of the most difficult, obscure, and intangible aspects of stratification analysis, since it requires not mere recognition of strata and surface description, which contribute little to any kind of analysis of processes, but penetrating empirical examination.

Unfortunately, such an analysis of the processes of stratification is the least touched upon and least explored aspect of this social phenomenon. At best the data and principles available are most general and are largely incidental to discussions of other more obvious aspects. A vast amount of specific research is needed. Because of this inadequacy our treatment will consist largely of hypotheses regarding stratification processes and the suggesting of types of processes which should be investigated.

*For concrete determinations of objectively established criteria of status, see references 4; 5; 31.

Stratification is a continuous, dynamic aspect of a society. Even the most superficial examination of the known characteristics and functions of a stratification system demonstrates that it is compounded of a large number of complex, subtly operating subprocesses. At this stage of their analysis the following types of processes suggest themselves.

General Processes of Differentiation

The general processes of differentiation were discussed in part in the preceding chapter. They involve the sociobiological processes, the processes producing variant wealth and income categories, ethnic groups, occupational groups, and the religious and political differentiations. They include also all the processes in division of labor and specialization of function as these specialize and separate along functional lines individuals and categories of individuals in all manner of social activities—economic, religious, political, educational, and so on.

*To be treated in Chap. 15.

Processes Creating Social Inequality

These processes involve such varied sociobiological, socioeconomic, and sociocultural processes as those which produce numerous inequalities: in earning power and acquisition of wealth; in getting and holding property; in access to social welfare, occupational selection and advantage, and cultural opportunity; in the transferal to children by their parents of propensities, outlook, objectives, and culture, and the stratum into which individuals are born. (25, p. 488) Persons are not born equal, and many of the situations and occurrences of life preserve these inequalities and create innumerable new ones. The processes that produce these inequalities are the very essence of stratum position.

Processes of Selection and Position Assignment

The processes that determine which people shall perform certain functions and wield certain authority are important to our analysis. The processes of competition and struggle are both involved. By and large, competition tests basic fitness for the various positions. As persons compete with each other, they express preferences, grasp their opportunities, and strive and achieve in proportion to what they have to put into the undertaking. Thus, the achievement of, and assignment to, a more or less appropriate status can be acquired in some measure through competitive accomplishment. (68)

Processes Providing Graded Valuations

We still know relatively little about the psychological and social-psychological processes whereby, through individual and group hedonic and moral experience, values arise and the evaluations of things, situations, persons, and groups are made. Here we are concerned especially with the processes of evaluation through which stratum values are established and accepted, for they are of central importance in the process of scaling. Obviously, there are processes of moral valuation of individuals as units of participation, and these valuations are parts of society's theory of action. (27, pp. 843-844)

Every community and society develops accepted evaluations of rank categories. The position in the social scale of any individual is merely the objective manifestation of social evaluations; this is implied in the way the individual and his qualities are typically treated by those in other strata, and the way others are treated by him. It seems that the value of a stratum is based on what its members contribute in the way of social utility to the society. This is not in terms of usefulness as such, but in terms of the contribution to a scale of values peculiar to the specific society. In the United States, for example, religion is valued less and wealth more.

In general, as we have noted, persons to whom a given set of standardized, even highly institutionalized, values are attached are considered as belonging to a given stratum.

Processes Establishing Norms and Expectations of Behavior

Closely related to the valuation processes are those whereby an integrated set of standards or normative patterns of behavior and functional performance are established and fixed for each category. Every society has processes whereby the effective expectations of behavior in the positions of superior and inferior, of superordinate and subordinate, are developed and maintained. These include processes of informal influence and informal and formal education of all ages and ranks.

Processes of Intrastratum Integration and Distinction

There are operative in every stratification system processes of cooperation and processes whereby common interests, common consciousness of kind and of common objective, and a common ideology are developed and maintained. These give the particular stratum its integrity and persistence.

The standing of individuals within a stratum and the integrity of a stratum are largely determined by the social distance maintained between it and other strata. Strata thus employ various means and develop numerous procedures for creating and fortifying lines of distinction. Among these are the development of domination attitudes and airs of hauteur and snobbishness, interstratum etiquette and ritual, theories of divine right, titles of rank, forms of salutation, speech customs, and many others. The upper strata protect and flatter themselves by organizing exclusive societies, clubs, and religious denominations, maintaining unequal privileges and controls over property, social positions, and life chances generally, practicing philanthropy and charity for the lower strata, inducing the shifting of attention from the bases of tension and antagonism, and very obviously idealizing liberty, equality, and fraternity for all. Various processes are in effect which limit contact and communication and confine these to highly formalized interstratum relations, which are mainly contractual rather than free. (37; 81, pp. 619-622; 101, pp. 152-156; 120)

These imply additional processes of segregation as to place of residence, organization membership, companionship, marriage selection, and so on, and processes of inclusion in and exclusion and rejection from strata, and the bases of such inclusion or exclusion.

Processes of Compliance and Enforcement

A set of processes are in effect which bring about conformity to the status system and the social enforcement of the social privileges and authority. They are the cultural patterning of attitudes and beliefs, the internalizing of values, and the development of emotional reactions against violations of the appropriate patterns. These produce acceptance of, and conformity to, the going system of positions. There are also the system of rewards and punishments and the procedures whereby this system maintains more or less effectively the privileges and power of the ranked groups. Involved also are those processes that establish patterns conducive to the efficient management of the many by the few in society.

Processes of Ego-Enhancement

Our stratification system operates in part as a medium of ego enhancement, a means whereby the potential needs for self-distinction are satisfied. Thus, there are psychological processes that involve the struggle of the *I*'s in association as personality ascendancy, personality protection, and personality recovery are sought. There are also processes relating to the quest for the favorable mirrorings of self in others that are so essential to emotional and mental health. These, in turn, are reflected in *social* processes as persons jointly, and often under great compulsion, seek these essential satisfactions. Any system of graded privileges and esteem and of graded authority carries with it the potential needs of self and group distinction.

Processes of Antagonism and Aggression

The processes that produce antagonism and aggression are both psychological and social processes. In every stratification system individuals and groups have anxieties that come from fear of loss of status and strains that come from unrewarded or punished behavior. There are also the tensions and frustrations involved in striving for appropriate behavior to achieve status and frustrations due to the fact that one group controls the services and rewards of another. These anxieties, tensions, and frustrations produce prejudices, antipathies, antagonistic processes, and efforts at sabotage which are inherent in such a system. (7) They also produce processes of exploitation of one stratum by another as each seeks to preserve its position and use it in its own behalf.

Furthermore, there are invariably processes of aggression, as the upper strata in some measure exploit the lower, and the lower seek to acquire some of the rights and privileges and power of the upper. Aggression is often a consequence of antagonism, and antagonism is a consequence of anxiety and frustration. In brief, aggression is a process of relief from frustration.

Processes of Total Solidarity

Finally, in a society with a stratification system, with its inequalities, strivings, and antagonisms, there must always be processes that are conducive to social solidarity and over-all operation, if the society is to survive. Stratification always involves tendencies toward the equilibrium of the horizontally arranged structure. Thus, there are integrating and coordinating processes whereby cooperation in carrying out the interdependent functions of the specialized strata is assured in large-scale formal enterprises of all kinds.

Other social processes maintain and reorganize working relations among the unequal, separated, superior and inferior, dominant and subordinate, and often discordant elements, and enable these elements to get along with each other. These are equilibrative processes,* and of these accommodation is the most important, for it grows out of the recognition that conflict and inefficiency cannot go on. It consists essentially of various unconscious and conscious formalized procedures by means of which at least temporary adjustment and cooperation are obtained through compromise, toleration, conciliation, mediation, arbitration, coercion, subjugation, and conversion. Assimilation and amalgamation affect adjustment and compromise, but less frequently and less extensively.

Major Kinds of Stratification

There are different kinds of stratification in a society. These different forms are not too distinct. They overlap and run together at certain points, and some elements and characteristics of each occur in the others. For example, closed classes are much like castes; ethnic strata are essentially castes, but tend to have classes within each.

These various forms of social stratification all consist of categories of persons located along a vertical continuum, but each varies in the rigidity of the dividers, or points of transition, along the continuum. In fact, there are various status continua. In some, movement up or down is possible, and is even characteristic of the form of system; in others, rank and status are relatively permanent and fixed. All involve in-group and out-group organization of the society. All the stratification subsystems, however, have common characteristics of a stratification system, serve somewhat similar functions, and develop out of and involve the operation of various combinations of the processes presented.

No all-inclusive inventory and classification of historically known forms of stratification systems is intended here. We are concerned primarily with the more commonly recurring types that characterize the American stratum system. We shall examine the class system, including, for purposes of clarification and contrast, a brief treatment of castes and estates; ethnic stratification; and briefly intragroup and intraorganizational stratification, since this latter is of increasing importance in our structural-functional system.

*To be analyzed in Chap. 21.

The Class System

The class system has certain general characteristics, and it develops under special conditions which distinguish it from other forms of stratification.

Nature and Importance of the American Class System. The American class system epitomizes stratification, for it involves the arraying of the entire population in pyramidal or layer-cake form. Each layer relates to a corresponding level in the social hierarchy, based on gradients of evaluation, and the constituents of each grade have their personalized statuses and also an impersonal hierarchical status determined by their class position. No community is free from class distinctions, and everyone of necessity belongs to some class.

In spite of the universality and inevitability of the class system, the empirical connotation of the word "class" is comparatively loose and is scantily defined. Social classes themselves seem to be somewhat nebulous, and no standard and generally accepted concepts exist. Some usages of the term are substantive in nature; others are classificatory. (60; 76; 77; 88; 93; 103)

There is no general agreement as to the combination of factors or distinguishing characteristics that delineate a social class. The great variety of criteria, or measures, used in different studies to identify class members and of gradations of social appraisal attests the absence of standard identifiable and determinate referents. An almost unlimited number of distinctions is possible. It is equally difficult to specify the number of classes into which a typical community or society is divided. In fact, there are almost as many schemes of class division as there are social scientists who make them.

The traditional American class division is into upper, middle, and lower classes. Warner and associates, in their study of classes, have fixed upon a refinement of this three-part division and use six: upper upper, upper lower, upper middle, lower middle, upper lower, and lower lower. (54; 55; 114; see also 21; 104) Hollingshead found five, which he designates merely by Roman numerals (I, II, III, IV, V). (46) Centers, in his rather comprehensive review, posits four main American classes and the basis of self-identification with a class name: upper (3 percent of the population), middle (43 percent), working (51 percent), and lower (1 percent), with 2 percent of the population saying "Don't know" or "Don't believe in classes." (67)

The number of classes yielded by any method of demarcation will vary, not only with the firmness of the distinctions, but also with the points of comparison. Most differentiations into social classes are more or less arbitrary, and often of the moment.

A further complication is the fact that classes in American society are highly fluid and continually changing and that the class situation in each community is somewhat peculiar and almost unique. The class structure of a community may vary according to age, size, population (especially as affected by ethnic factors), complexity, historical and cultural background, economy, urban or rural nature, and geographic location.

Yet the objectively discernible reality of social classes in American life is unquestioned. All investigations concur that the concept of class deals with a stratification of a population. A class is a horizontal category of persons and families set off from the rest by institutionalized social status. Each class has a place in the rank hierarchy of status groups, and consequently, relations between classes are of a superior-inferior nature. From the standpoint of groups a class is a secondary group with in-group features that fulfills certain functions and, together with the other classes, constitutes a class system that functions as a whole.

In our class system each class has a fairly distinctive pattern of traits, a set of more or less exclusive and restricted participations within the limited group, a stratum solidarity, and more or less formalized out-group relations with all other classes. The individual member is accorded community status based on his class affiliation which is quite independent of his own intrinsic traits or behavior. This gives him at any given time, and depending upon his class, a fairly distinctive set of privileges and disprivileges, esteems and discsteems, freedoms and restrictions, opportunities and limitations. A *working conception* of a class system is a construct, that is, an effort to devise a conception of the structural-functional-valuational stratum situation that corresponds roughly to actuality in a given society. Finally, classes, of necessity, are hierarchically superimposed upon each other, with each class having a hierarchical position.

Classes are a mass phenomenon. This is illuminated by pointing out *what classes are not.* Classes are not natural, organic entities, such as families, or cleavage groupings reflecting biological determinants, such as sex or age groups. They are not mere statistical categories, such as classifications of persons or families based on property owned, income received, or years of formal education. They are not purely occupationally classified entities, such as executives, or professionals, or skilled or laborers. They are not ecological groupings on the basis of residence, however select it may be. They are not communities, that is, fundamental groupings of individuals with homogeneous ends, consciously participating in and sharing a relatively complete way of life. A class does not constitute a homogeneous or completely interdependent system.

Finally—and this is important—classes are not associations, that is, purposive organizations or instrumentalities for the furtherance of particular group interests or ends, for they have no defined ends or purposes. Some of the constituent members, however, may become purposive when they combine and organize to pursue definite economic or political objectives, as, for example, when they become the basic element of political parties or social movements.

Salient Characteristics of a Class System. But what are the essential characteristics of social classes? The extant knowledge regarding social classes enables us to draw at least a tentative list of typical characteristics, most cogently presented in the form of criteria, which distinguish social classes in general from other forms of stratification.

PERMISSIVE SOCIAL MOBILITY. The original position in a class stratum, as in all other forms of strata, is acquired at birth by succession from the parents. Thus, the original class of every person is the class of his family at his birth. However, in a *class* system as distinct from a caste system, an estate system, and a racial-group stratification system, there is no permanent or formal fixity. In a social-class system there is "a constant milling of social-status atoms." (69, p. 149) Theoretically, there is a legal openness, that is, any position in the hierarchy of ranks is open to any individual or family by virtue of achievement. All *symbols* of class (wealth, neighborhood, culture, level of living, affiliations, associations) and all *perquisites* (prestige, rights, power) theoretically are accessible to everyone, provided that he has the necessary requirements in the way of family, earning capacity, and motivation.*

Actually, there is considerable shifting to higher and lower classes. The movement that is aspired to is upward, but it is directed "against a powerful 'social gravity' that brings down the less efficient competitors relentlessly." (69, p. 149)

Nevertheless, as Goldschmidt points out (75), although our class system permits and even encourages social mobility, most community studies indicate that most persons remain in the economic and social status to which they were born, moving neither significantly upward nor downward.

Related to permissive social mobility as a characteristic of a class system is the fact that although most marriage is endogamous, that is, it occurs between persons of approximately the same social class, exogamous marriage is allowed. In fact, marriage with someone of higher class is often sought and approved. Thus, in contrast to a caste system, where marriage is always endogamous, marriage in a class system may be either endogamous or exogamous. (132)

MULTIPLE CRITERIA AND EXPRESSIONS OF RANK AND STATUS. Of primary significance in any understanding of social classes are the bases upon which the rank, status, and roles of any given class of the system rest. Although classes are part of the system of social stratification, they are special types of strata with special implicit principles of evaluation. Sorokin points out that they are multibonded strata. (110, p. 266) Contrary to the views of Marxists and other one-track oversimplifiers of social phenomena, the factors and characteristics that distinguish and tie together the members of a given class are exceedingly numerous and complex. It is not simply a matter, for example, of property holding or lack of property, of high occupation or low occupation, of much education or little education. Obviously, also, the bases of evaluation are not of equal weight. We must distinguish between primary, secondary, and subordinate principles of evaluation, or indicators of quality, and their relative significance in the formation of classes and subclasses.

The criteria and expressions of class are also classified as objective, or directly observable and determinable, characteristics and subjective, or inner and social psychic, characteristics.

Only the more commonly current criteria and characteristics of classes in American society will be examined. Even so, the list is formidable.

The various classes have different *directly observable external, or objective, characteristics,* which take several forms.

1. The *socioeconomic criteria* are primary determinants of classes which differ in economic conditions and activities. There are *variations in wealth or property or property ownership*: the well-to-do, those of moderate means, those of limited means, and the indigent. Long-standing individual or family wealth is usually more honorific than recently acquired wealth (that of the nouveau riche) apparently because in the course of the generations the sweat essential to wealth acquisition has been deodorized, and the quality of activities essential to its acquisition have been ennobled by time and forgetfulness. Finer gradations depend upon income, its amount, nature, and source, that is, whether it comes from interest and profits, rent, salary, or mere wages.

Occupation is an exceedingly important class determinant and closely related to property and income. Innumerable categorizings of occupations exist, but the following list is fairly concise and representative of American society and indicates descending rank and prestige: executives of large businesses, usually corporations, and high government officials; members of the highly qualified professions; operators of medium-sized businesses; semiprofessional and white-collar employees; farm

*This subject will be dealt with in some detail in Chap. 15.

owners and operators; foremen and skilled workers; farm tenants; semiskilled workers; unskilled and farm laborers. Of course, there are always personal and local variations and exceptions. (2a, pp. 305-306)

Important factors in the classification of occupations are the intrinsic characteristics of the occupation, such as its complexity, requisite mental and social qualities, remuneration, prestige, level of skill demanded, attractiveness or freedom from repugnant qualities, routine or manual nature, and degree of domination or subordination which the occupation carries with it.*

The *standard and plane of living and consumption* always constitute an important set of criteria. Wealth, income, and occupation must be translated into appropriate *symbols* of status rank and accompanied by corresponding behavior in the several community contexts. How do the different classes spend their wealth and income and display their social-economic acumen? Notably on the following: the ecological area of residence (neighborhood); cost or rental, physical condition, furnishings, and operation of the home; the car; personal services of others enjoyed and displayed; food and clothing. All these relate to the quantitative and qualitative control and use of economic goods and services and are evidences of social superiority or inferiority.

The upper classes have preferred or more honorific occupations and generally higher economic position, and these socioeconomic factors are of primary importance in determining the class position of any person or family. They reflect the functions that the incumbents perform, determine in considerable part their rank and status, and serve as the bases of their prestige, rights, social power, and authority. In general, the ruling groups in all manner of activities—economic, political, even religious—in a class system are such by virtue of their wealth.

2. Important among criteria of the *cultural and social-political* category are the amount and kind of formal education. Those who have attended or graduated from college rate higher than those who have had only some amount of high school or trade school education, and these, in turn, rate higher than those who have attended only elementary schools. There are also obvious gradations of prestige among the colleges and schools. Skill in the fine arts or at least some patronage of them is important, as is also the devotion of leisure time to intellectual and cultural achievement. The very recreational activities of the individuals or families are determinants of prestige, as are the political and social views that they hold. Additional distinguishing criteria of quality are a cultivated demeanor, polite speech patterns, good manners and conformity to the requirements of etiquette, and participation in certain symbolic social rituals, such as teas, debuts, and the like.

3. *Family, family reputation, and kinship affiliation* are also important determinants of classes. Whether an individual comes of a prominant family or an inconspicuous one, of a good family or a no-account one, is a rating factor that often operates to his advantage quite apart from personal characteristics and economic or other achievement. The length and eminence of recorded lineage is also a factor, for prestige inheres in being the descendant of an old family or a Mayflower descendant, and so on.

4. The *affiliation with, and participation in, different kinds of associations and organizations* comprise another important class-determining factor. Who associates with whom? In the main the members of different classes belong to differently ranked formal and informal organizations. With respect to religious affiliation, there is an important difference between belonging to the Episcopal or Congregational Church and to the Holy Rollers. (91) The upper classes belong to the prestige-carrying leisure-time organizations, such as country clubs, athletic clubs, study and discussion clubs, garden clubs. The lower-middle and lower classes belong to bowling clubs or nationality organizations. Even the fraternal organizations and service clubs have differential ranking and give graded status. Some men belong to the Chamber of Commerce and others to a union.

5. Possibly in recognition of the fact that upper-class position carries with it some element of obligation and the necessity of leadership, many mem-

*Says Sorokin: "The occupations that require a high degree of intelligence, are highly important to the population, and those that consist of intellectual creative work of sociocultural organization and control, have regularly been the superior occupations. The occupations consisting of manual, uncreative work, requiring low intelligence for their performance, have regularly been the most inferior." (33, p. 286; also 14; 15; 81, pp. 479-580)

bers of the upper classes are active in *promoting community interests.* It is desirable to be civic-minded and actively engaged in community service, such as youth activities, community beautification, community philanthropy, and uplift. Such activity is in fact an essential "badge."

6. *Race and nativity* are significant determinants of class standing. Ethnicity is such a weighty divider and ranking factor that it produces its own special kind of stratification, which will be examined below. But it also enters into current American class ranking. Negroes, Indians, Mexicans, and Orientals are practically excluded from white class consideration. European nativity and nationality are important in class determination. In many communities upper-class rating requires Anglo-Saxon or northwestern European origin. To have descended from southern or eastern European nationals places a person in the lower categories. Length of sojourn in the United States is another important factor. Old American stocks are rated higher than the recent arrivals and their descendants.

7. Occasionally, *personality characteristics* enter into class ranking, augmenting or diminishing the prestige and authority of the individual and in part counteracting the significance of other factors. An open-minded, friendly, and helpful person has social lubricants and aids that may help him achieve the higher brackets; the unfriendly and hostile persons, those hard to get along with, the trouble-makers, and those who are just different may find the class avenue closed to them.*

These criteria and factors and some others in special instances all blend together into a configuration for each individual's and each family's class ranking. In locating individuals only certain criteria in special combination will be involved. Economic, cultural, ethnic, and personality factors may override each other, as a given community makes allowances with respect to some criteria and gives more emphasis to others. There are always variations and exceptions.

The respective weighting of criteria and the important combinations of criteria vary also from community to community and in the same community at different times. The ingredients and dimensions of class may and do change. New communities whose growth has been rapid and whose population is heterogeneous and mobile will have rather blurred and fluctuating class criteria; older communities are more likely to have established classes and fixed and readily observable criteria. But always there is an ambivalence, a tendency toward a competitive contrasting and balancing of the socioeconomic, ethnic, cultural, and other factors.

The various classes have, in addition to the objective characteristics, *subjective and social psychic characteristics,* that is, a *class-consciousness.* Class is not only a matter of external aspects, the more or less well-defined and objectively determinable common patterns and types of social action; it is also a "condition within," for both the individual and the family constituents of classes and for a given class as a distinguishable entity. The members of each class as a whole have class-consciousness—a consciousness of membership and similarity—even though they may be differentiated and heterogeneous in many other respects.

This corporate class-consciousness unites and gives cohesion to the whole group sharing similar status. It grows out of the competitive, conflictive, and cooperative relations of the different classes with each other. The more pronounced the competition or conflict, the sharper is this class-consciousness. But it is ever present and is evidenced inwardly if not outwardly in every interclass relationship.

Class-consciousness is compounded of common problems and common interests: common economic, moral, and cultural attitudes, values, aspirations, and objectives; common sentiments and traditions; common convictions on social matters; common patterns of thought; and common code and ideology. It is ingrained through unconscious acquisition and both informal and formal education and indoctrination.

The individual member has a class-dominated state of mind. In his relationship to other members of his class, he is confident that he is in harmony with them and can meet them on equal terms. He has a sense of identification with the given class and a feeling of belonging to it and an accompanying sense of estrangement from other classes. He is more or less antagonistic to all other classes, especially those below him, even though he feels superior to them, and is resentful of his present

*For concrete instances of the appearance of these objective criteria in communities whose class systems have been recently studied, see references 46, pp. 66-120; 57, pp. 38-54.

exclusion from the classes above him, to which he feels inferior. (66; 72; 74; 78; 84; 92)

Unless this class-consciousness is present, no matter what other criteria are used as a means of identification, we do not have that sociological collectivity known as a class, but merely some logical or statistical category or type.

Summarizing the objective and subjective features of social classes, we may say that the members of a class have a fairly uniform set of life conditions and are characterized by similar or common ways of life in the form of common economic production and consumption activities, common organizations, common social participations and informal and formal group affiliations, common cultural level, and similar or related ethnicity. Each class has a certain range and modal average of behavior, and the activities of the members of each class with each other are more numerous and more alike than those with other classes.

Each class is also a psychologically similar entity of persons with common interests, sentiments, and values and common patterns of thought. It is united by a strong in-group consciousness and feels itself to be apart from the other classes and different from them, for they are felt to be out-groups and are always reacted to as such.

A class system, when it occurs, is in a sense a "natural"; that is, in contrast to caste and estate systems, it develops because of certain peculiar and more or less *determinable historical, social, and cultural contributory factors and conditions.* These factors and conditions explain in some degree the rank and status gradations based on differences in wealth, income, occupation, scale of consumption, education, good breeding, ethnicity, and so on; the graded differences in social prestige, privilege, obligation, power, and authority; and especially the key characteristic—permissive mobility up and down the social ladder. Space permits us to allude only to the more important of these contributory factors, but a functional knowledge of the class systems requires an awareness of these special factors contributing to the formation and existence of social classes.

Increase and Differences of Wealth. The increase of wealth arising out of new inventions, discoveries, and technologies always produces modification conditions conducive to modification of class arrangements and the formation of new classes. It relates to a changing, and often an expanding, economy, for class systems seldom exist in stationary economies. Prizes of wealth attract the able and ambitious and also those who are on the spot of economic opportunity and therefore able to exploit new lands, forests, and mineral and other natural resources.

The inequalities of wealth are due to personal dissimilarities, especially in talent and in ability to achieve power. Wealth gives power over others and usually results in actual administration of economic enterprise or the right to delegate that function to others. The absence of wealth means the necessity of working for others and under their direction, for the less wealthy and the poor have subordinate positions. Wealth thus is a badge of achievement, a basis for high esteem and power. It tends to become a more or less permanent element in pre-eminence, since it provides the successive generations with the opportunity for education, political influence, economic security, and so on, thus assuring superior life chances to its hereditary holders.

Social Complexity and Its Related Specialization. There is always a tendency for social ranks to become more numerous and finely divided as the social organization becomes more complex. Significant are the increasing numbers of persons, the growing biological, psychological, and ethnic heterogeneity of population, and the multiplication and specialization of occupations. Many different types of specialization of function appear, each requiring different qualities of personality and life among the members of the society.

The occupations themselves carry different degrees of honor and prestige on the basis of their intellectual and administrative or menial and manual nature. The honored occupations elevate those engaged in them, whereas lower occupations degrade their workers. The various divisions of labor and specializations of function provide infinite shadings of opportunity and achievement. Large numbers of diverse peoples in a society pursuing complex activities and functioning in a multiplicity of ways result in individuals and categories of people being evaluated and ranked. Simple societies have few classes, since the conditions are not conducive to them and do not require them.

Intellectual, Political, and Economic Freedoms. The bases of both physical and social mobility are intellectual, political, and economic freedoms, which are essential features of a class system. Classes can appear only when there is freedom of thought, invention, and research; only when there is religious tolerance and freedom of worship and choice of religious affiliation; only when political conditions permit freedom of physical movement across community borders enabling people to embrace opportunities elsewhere as well as to profit by freedom of political action; only when economic freedom permits utilization of economic opportunities.

These freedoms permit competition to operate with considerable facility, make possible social mobility, and provide the elements of individualism and liberalism by furnishing opportunity for the individual to pull himself out of his class into a higher one. These freedoms make possible flexibility of rank and status and are essential features of a class system.

Movement and Contact of Ethnic Groups. The weakening of political barriers and the availability of efficient, cheap, and accessible transportation facilities have aided the movement and contact of ethnic groups. Frequently, in a given area, a clash of values, beliefs, and ways of life generally of culturally diverse peoples results. The distinction between native stocks and foreigners, or "lower races," appears. The native populations usually have a more homogeneous culture, whereas the other racial or immigrant peoples have no common culture. The native groups concentrate on the managerial, professional, skilled, and other honorific occupations, and the immigrants are forced to take menial jobs. The natives are superior and dominant; the others, inferior and subordinate.

Universal Educational Facilities. In systems of rigid stratification educational opportunities are usually confined to the select few of the higher levels, but with universal or mass education, educational opportunities are at least theoretically available to all. This means that another agency contributing to permissive mobility is available to persons unequal in ability and motivation. The opportunities that the mass educational system provides make possible the climbing of the social ladder. The system also functions as a relatively efficient selective agent in determining abilities and qualities essential to given rank and status.*

*On conditions out of which class systems grow, see 30; 89; 94; 109.

The Social and Individual Effects of a Class System. The class organization of a community has a profound effect upon the organization and functioning of that community as a sociological entity and upon the behavior, psychological reactions, relationships, and destiny of the individuals in the community.

Socially, as can be inferred from the discussion of a stratification system, a class system also gives at least a temporary fixity and a predictability to the behavior of the population which may prove important to the smooth running of the social order. It assigns rank and status, functional obligations and duties, rights and privileges, and power and authority. As such, it has a stabilizing influence, especially in quiet times, but in times of rapid and great change, antagonisms are likely to develop between classes and to have a disorganizing effect.

For the individual his class position constitutes a network of social and psychological influences that affect and effect his personality development and his every act. Especially through the rather definite culture of the class—its ethos, standards, and norms for all sorts of behavior—his class position provides him with many of his social instigations, life goals, and sanctions, and with much of his symbolic world and its evaluations. (7; 79; 114, pp. v-vii, 24-32)

Warner and associates point out that businessmen who make, sell, and advertise all manner of merchandise, including magazines, motion pictures, articles of utility, and wearing apparel, are forever at the mercy of the evaluations of their customers, "for their products are not only items of utility for those who buy but powerful symbols of status and social class." (114, p. vii) Kornhauser, in a recent study of the relations of public opinion and social class, shows that class differences are highly pertinent, especially with respect to the issues that obviously and directly affect the interests of the different class levels differently. He says, for example:

> Rather consistently the lower income groups are more in favor of government control of business and extending government welfare activities, sacrificing certain institutional property rights and unlimited opportunities for individual achievement in the interests of increasing security, overcoming the concentration of influence in

the hands of the wealthy. There is also evidence that the poorer groups have more extreme nationalistic attitudes, greater religious traditionalism, and generally a more restricted outlook on the world associated presumably with limited education. (88)

In general, class offers the individual an almost complete pattern of life and mode of behavior.

Caste and Estate Systems versus Class System. Caste and estate systems occur under different social conditions from those that produce the features of the class system in recent and contemporary American society that we have just discussed.

A Caste System. In a caste system, as in a class system, there is a hierarchy of strata, with attendant social distances and inverse prestige, privilege, and power, and individuals acquire their caste rank and status by birth. The essential difference is that in a pure or ideal caste system the individual's rank and status and that of his descendants are ascribed and mandatory under the customs, mores, and the law and are clearly defined and definitely fixed for all time in most cases on the superiority-inferiority scale. They are not changeable by any option or action of the individual; he cannot rise or fall, irrespective of personal abilities, attributes, desires, or efforts. Permanent stratification is everything.

Often the caste system is originated in, and supported by, religion. The members of the different castes are separated in their living arrangements, recreations, religious observances, and many other institutional activities, and each caste has its peculiar occupations. Marriage is endogamous, that is, it must occur within the given caste. Multitudinous taboos regulate the minutest details of the individual's life and set specific limits in most of his life choices, and a host of physical, social, and psychological rewards and punishments prevail to ensure the purity of each caste.

Purity of caste is maintained at all costs, and often contamination by contact with members of other castes, save those of a highly formalized and unavoidable functional nature, requires institutionalized purification rites. There may actually be repulsion or feeling of antipathy between members of different castes which keeps them separate. Caste systems are closed societies and, in part at least, have grown out of conquest and enslavement. In recent times the classic example of a caste system has been India. (64; 85; 99; see also 69, pp. 1-118; 104a)

By contrast, in a class system individuals are born into a given class, but they do not necessarily have to remain in it for life or presumably for eternity. They may, and often do, move up or down into another class, marry outside their class, and associate with members of other classes. Status and other class emoluments are achieved and maintained competitively and not by hereditary and historical fiat. Thus, a class system is always a fairly fluid affair. In a class system, the classes shade into each other, and interclass dividers may be likened to screens through which individuals and families can move; but in a caste system, the castes are horizontally separated by steel plates.

An Estate System. The estate-system type of stratification existed historically in ancient and medieval times—the feudal system was a notable instance—and forms of it still exist in Latin America and in the Eastern world. Positions are not so precisely defined as in a caste system, but are more rigid than in class system. An estate is a social-status stratum more or less clearly delimited from other strata in customary or statutory law or both. The status is acquired by descent and tends to remain fixed, yet is susceptible to change under certain conditions. In later feudal times a more or less typical hierarchy of estates (or *Staende,* as the Germans called them) consisted of the nobility and higher clergy, the lords temporal (barons and knights) and the lords spiritual; the bourgeoisie, or burgesses or town dwellers, the propertied merchants and the officials of the municipalities; the commoners or free common people—artisans and peasants; serfs and other unfree persons. Each man was in his own estate, and each estate was a matter largely of legal designation, differential legal rights and obligations as to property and political and other functions, and social dignities.

However, membership in an estate was not so rigidly hereditary and permanent as in a caste. The clergy were recruited from all levels, commoners might become nobles, serfs and peons might be emancipated by their masters, and freemen, under certain conditions, might become serfs. A commoner might receive a patent of nobility. Intermarriage between estates, though not invited, was not prohibited and did occur occasionally. In general, there was no mutual repulsion between estates, but cooperation and mutual dependence. (69, pp. 123-126; 101, pp. 149-151)

Ethnic Stratification

Sociologists are quite generally agreed that two major systems of social stratification cut across American society: the class system just examined and the hierarchical arraying of ethnic groups, the latter based on differences of race or nationality background, or both. These ethnic differences are vitally involved in the class system, as we have noted, but they produce such significant cleavages that in practice they operate as separate stratification systems alongside the class system, occasionally overlapping it.

These important forms of stratification grow out of the mingling of racial stocks and nationalities which have different cultures and ways of life. Ethnicity is a complex concept compounded of many variables ranging from highly visible color and other physical differences to differences in language or religion. But invariably, wherever we have ethnic groups in juxtaposition, we have people living in relationships of superiority and inferiority, of superordination and subordination of some people to other people or peoples. These different ethnic groups appear always as competitors and potential antagonists and usually as actual antagonists in some degree.

Ethnic qualities become partial determiners of status according to their definitions in different cultural configurations. Usually a persistent and rigid status hierarchy prevails among the groups. The group that is culturally superior and usually also politically, economically, and socially dominant assumes a higher position in the status scale than that accorded the presumed inferior groups. Out of these contacts between unequals arise involved formalized differences, sometimes taking the form of rigid caste systems.

The so-called inferior ethnic groups are usually numerical minorities as compared with the superior, superordinate, and culturally predominant majority.* The minorities in effect are enclaves, or sociocultural islands or isolated groups within the larger ocean of the majority. The majority is responsible for much of the isolating and practically of all the disadvantaging of these enclaves. Says Lash: ". . . it is the majority which decides the location, the topography, and boundaries of the minority province." (127) Any individuals of the various minorities who escape from their social and cultural isolation must be approved under the rules and standards of the majority.

*In South Africa, however, the superior ethnic elements are very decidedly a numerically smaller portion of the total population.

In this analysis two somewhat distinct ethnic forms of stratification have to be considered: racial ethnics and the corresponding racial stratification and nationality or cultural "ethnics" and nationality group stratification.

Racial Stratification. In the United States racial stratification is constituted of the whites, which make up roughly nine tenths of the population, and the colored stocks, comprising mainly Negroes, but also usually including in this category Mexicans, Indians, and Orientals. In general, the superiority of the whites is formally recognized and exaggerated by the status system and incorporated in it.

Racial inequalities are evidenced in the survivals of legal ranking of the different races into several strata from the highest to the lowest, with decreasing political privileges and increasing disfranchisement of all kinds as we move from the superior to the inferior race groups. There are also the economic inequalities, the variable occupational opportunities, at least by region, in some instances amounting to typical inferior-race jobs, differences in educational and recreational opportunities, and various other discriminations, segregations, and disfranchisements.

In the United States and South Africa this color stratification system takes on many of the characteristics of a caste system. It has developed largely out of conquest and enslavement, with the whites the conquerors and autocratic masters and the colored the slaves and serfs of the whites, and is based on ancient exploitative arrangements, facilitated by corresponding attitudes and habits on both sides. There is little interchange of membership between one caste and the other. Marriage is endogamous, that is, confined to members of a given caste by customs, mores, and in many states by law. Although there are evidences of caste lines in all parts of the country, they are most rigid in the deep South. Says Allison Davis:

> Caste in the Deep South integrates into one system all aspects of white-Negro behavior: social, sexual, economic, political, educational, religious, legal, associational, recreational. The basic subsystem—caste—is a rigid stratification, maintained by physical, social, and psychological punishments and rewards. Everywhere in the South, caste establishes and maintains an endogamous and socially separate system of white-Negro relationship in which by birth the Negroes are all of lower, and the whites are all of higher, status. This caste system is more rigid than that described in the classic literature on Hindu castes.
>
> All white or colored institutions of the southern community, including the church, the school, and the courts, systematically organize and defend the caste system. (117)

Such a caste system is a clear-cut device for the deliberate subordination of an ethnic grouping.

Moreover, a system of social classes prevails within each caste. The white or colored person is born into a social class just as he is born into a color caste. The Negroes in any American community are hierarchically divided into classes based on factors and conditions very similar to those of the class system in general. Permissive mobility also operates within the caste. (129)

Nationality Stratification. Closely related to racial stratification is nationality stratification, by which we mean that form that exists in societies and communities where there is or has been considerable immigration, and various white but foreign elements are numerous in the population. These foreigners are usually distinguished by language and religious differences; by old-country traditions, customs, and institutional forms; often for a time by old-country ties and loyalties; by separate friendship circles and associations of all kinds; and by other different ways of life. Usually for the first few generations, foreigners have inferior occupations, which are assigned to them by the superior stocks of longer residence. In general, the oldest nationality arrivals are highest in the nationality system.

In most communities of the United States the top level consists of the native-born Yankees; on the next level are those of Dutch, German, Scandinavian, Irish, and French descent; next below are those originally Italian, Jewish, Russian, Polish, Finnish, Czech, and Greek nationality. There are many exceptions and variations, of course, depending upon the original class or cultural level of the ancestral immigrants. Great fluidity of position occurs as the result of assimilation and amalgamation.

At any given time, however, if the number of unassimilated or only partly assimilated out-groupers is large, they will form definite strata but will have inferior social status and will be assigned to functions that members of the majority in-group feel are less desirable. Where no color bar exists, time is a factor in reducing these differences. The newer stocks become accepted older stocks, and there is class mobility in time.

In the case of nationalities or culture groups—Jews, for example, in many communities, and French Canadians in New England—an organized policy of social ostracism, or at least avoidance, may exist, which is not reflected in legal or political forms but assumes covert and subtle guises. Such partly ostracized elements take on some of the characteristics of a caste and may have a class system of their own.

Intragroup and Intraorganization Stratification

Sorokin, (33) among others, has pointed out that definite stratification exists within most groups. There are not only the inequalities and differentiation between male and female groups, with the male usually the superior, more privileged, and dominant group, but also stratum differentiation within each sex group. There are always the rulers and the led, the more privileged and the less privileged, the influential and the less influential.

The age groups have been stratified, informally and legally, with different rights, duties, status, roles, privileges, and degrees of disfranchisement. The younger are usually deprived of some rights and privileges of an economic, occupational, political, and civic nature. Within given age groups there are invariably the leaders, the more influential layers, and the plain members. The larger kinship groups have a series of ranks, consisting of the most influential, honored, and dominating persons, several intermediary ranks, and the least influential, more dominated, and lowest ranks.

The great functional organizations, from one point of examination, are systems of stratification. The state has its monarch, president, or dictator at the top, the cabinet members or secretaries of major departments next, chiefs of divisions, petty officials, and plain citizenry at the broad base. Political parties are made up of bosses and members of the central committee, influential members, precinct leaders, and plain voting members. As soon as a religious group is organized, a system of stratification emerges, with the supreme priests at the top, successive layers of clergy and lay members of varying influence, position, and function, and plain members.

The large-scale formal organizations* are highly organized systems of stratification with formally organized pyramids of authority, levels of status, each with its defined and assigned rights, privileges, immunities, limitations, prohibitions, duties and obligations within the total organization, and official and occupational levels.

*See Chap. 11.

CHAPTER XV

SOCIAL MOBILITY IN THE SOCIETAL STRUCTURE

IN ORDER TO UNDERSTAND the structural organization and the operation of any society, it is necessary to have an adequate knowledge of the mobility, or circulation, of its individuals, families, and larger groups and categories. The movements of persons and groups constitute the metabolism of a society, which is continually modifying the constitution and flow of the stratification system. Movements grow out of all manner of conditions, involve various factors, perform various organizing and disorganizing functions and affect others, and produce continual quantitative and qualitative modification of the demographic, cultural, and societal structuring of groups and communities.

Forms of Social Mobility

Physical and Social Mobility

The most general classification of mobility processes is the division into physical and social mobility. *Physical* mobility is concerned with the movement, or migration, of population elements in physical space, that is, from one place to another on the earth. Migration and its effects have been discussed in Chapters 8 and 9 and the movement of culture products in Chapter 5.

Now we are concerned with *social* mobility, or social circulation. By this we mean the movement of individuals or groups from one social position to another in a constellation of social groups and strata. (12, p. 554; 14, p. 405) Usually it also implies the movement of both material and non-material culture products. For example, golf has moved downward. Occupational skills move laterally. All manner of beliefs, ideas, fads, fashions, and codes move up and down.

Horizontal and Vertical Social Distance

Social mobility involves the concepts of social space and social distance, which refer to the social or social-psychological spacing—or lack of it—felt by individuals and groups within a social structure and between social structures. In every community and society recognized *social* differences create some degree of reserve or constraint in social interaction. These differences separate or "space" persons and groups. In their relationships with each other they feel near to or far from each other, intimate with or remote from each other.

Social distance does not exclude the possibility of social contact; in fact, social distance grows out of it. The different persons may be physically contiguous, within sight and sound of each other, and may be interdependent in their social functions, but they feel friendliness, closeness, intimacy, and similarity with some (their own kind and level of folks) and aversion, separateness, strangeness, difference, and preference to avoid where certain others are concerned.

The space or distance felt is based upon such variable factors, in different combinations, as differences in moral evaluations, and the desirability or undesirability of groups and categories of persons, differences in interests, function, and status and rank especially as they relate to superordination and subordination. The degrees of societal space or distance are indicated by the behavior toward each other of the persons and groups in relationship with each other. In some degree we have in-group attitudes toward, and actions with, some and out-group attitudes and actions with others.

Social space relates directly to, and is of supreme and central significance in connection with, societal differentiation and stratification on various *differentiations*: age, sex, temperament, ethnicity, vocation, religion, and urban-rural distinctions. Many of these differentiation situations produce *horizontal social distance,* or a feeling of distance among persons and groups *on approximately the same social level.* Thus, there is to some degree a feeling of strangeness, unfamiliarity, lack of rapport, and difference among skilled workers of different occupations on a job—carpenters and electricians, for example—members of religious denominations of the same level, rural laborers and city laborers. There may be, and usually is, some horizontal social distance among different segments of the same social class owing to the composite and heterogeneous nature of the membership.

Vertical social distance refers to the social space among individuals and groups arising from their positions in relation to others in the hierarchy of social strata of the community or society. Vertical social distance is an essential feature of stratum distinction. It functions as a bar to free intercourse between individuals of the different strata. It rests upon the recognition of scalar differences in rank, prestige, power, and renown, and implies superordination of some and subordination of others.

There is a tendency to move toward persons of one's own level, or at least to feel more comfortable with them, and to retreat or withdraw from or, under certain conditions, to avoid or be excluded from persons of other levels as superiors or inferiors. In general, the members of a given stratum feel that the standing and integrity of their stratum—the position and rank which it carries—are largely determined by the social distance maintained between it and other strata.

Social distance, as well as social nearness, is an organizational principle in society that is fundamental to the operation of society. The systematic distribution of avoidance is as necessary as the systematic distribution of contacts in certain sectors of relationship. Distance supplies a plan for reciprocities and also for refusing them. Conversely, one of the principal functions of a status system is as a main determinant of social distances. The roles institutionally prescribed for the occupants of many statuses carry the expectation of relationships of mutual identification between persons of the same status; they constitute a group. Those with different statuses constitute other, or out, groups with whom formalized relations essential to mutual well-being are conducted.*

Horizontal and Vertical Social Mobility

Social mobility implies movement in social space, change of *social* position. As such, it has both disintegrative and integrative effects, which will be discussed in succeeding chapters. Here we are concerned with the major categories of social mobility

*Social distance can be measured. For the original and still widely used scale see reference 3.

and the part which the processes play in a stratification system. Social mobility relates to social distance; *social distance is an existent fact,* but it is *also something which is transversed and traveled.*

In *horizontal social mobility* there is very little change as to status or plane and no promotion or demotion in the social scale. It consists of the transition of an individual or family from one social group to another situated on the same level, or stratum. (13, pp. 133-137; 14) It is, so to speak, movement within a given degree of social latitude. The individual or family remains within the same stratum and essentially retains the same traits, although changes in social relationships and group location are involved. Thus, a stenographer may shift from one insurance company to another; an auto worker in the Detroit area from the Ford factory to the General Motors factory; a rural cultivator may change from one farm to another or from one rural aggregate to another.

American industry especially is characterized by horizontal transferability of personnel without change of status or rank. Workers can make considerable shifts in specific occupations in an industrial system characterized by a tremendous division of labor without appreciably altering their general occupational rank. At the managerial, technical, and professional level there is also much transferability from corporation to corporation or from one association to another association.

Vertical social mobility consists in the shifting of an individual, family, or even larger group from one stratum to another in the pyramid of social stratification. It may be upward, usually the result of social straining and climbing and implying social promotion, or it may be downward and consist of social demotion. According to the nature of the stratification, individuals are ascending or descending in a socioeconomic manner, social power, social responsibility, cultural attainment, membership in prestige-carrying associations, and status.

Sorokin distinguishes between normal and spasmodic vertical social mobility. (14, p. 423) Normal mobility usually assumes the form of orderly movement up or down the social ladder as the result of individual or family achievement and motivation or lack of these. Spasmodic mobility occurs in times of serious upheaval, such as economic depression, group or mass migration, war or revolution, when the stratification pattern is violently disrupted, and collectivities or whole strata are replaced by new ones.

Social Mobility in Closed and Open Class Systems

Social mobility is a process which has meaning mainly in stratified contexts. The concept of class, as noted above, indicates the existence of permissive mobility, both horizontal and vertical. Vertical mobility especially characterizes a class system; otherwise, we would be dealing with a caste system. Given class systems vary in their fluid nature, ranging along a continuum from closed class systems to open class systems. Historically, no closed system—even a religion-sanctioned caste system—has been completely devoid of some vertical mobility, and no open system has had or has now absolutely unrestricted opportunity and freedom for all to move up or down the social ladder.

The ideal-typical characteristics of the two class systems follow. It must be remembered that any given system at any given time lies somewhere between the extremes with respect to the degree of social mobility prevalent in it. Furthermore, the degree and rate of vertical mobility fluctuate from period to period in the life history of the same society.

A Closed Class System

In a relatively closed, or castelike, system, the positions acquired by the members of the particular class stratum at birth remain fixed for life. This means that vertical social mobility is practically nonexistent, and even horizontal social mobility is often difficult. Each class is rigid, impenetrable, and immobile. There is no ascending or descending, no social promotion or demotion. Intrinsic merits and capacities are discounted; opportunities for advancement are denied; cultural barriers between classes are almost unsurmountable; and personal achievement is unrewarded. When a class system, for example, bars certain population elements from educational or economic opportunities because of color, creed, nationality, family background or similar considerations, it can be said to be closed to that degree. A caste system is an obvious example of the most complete closed-class system.

An Open Class System

In an open system, the position of the members of a given stratum or class may be moved up or down during their own lifetimes by their achievement of class role essentials or lack of them. Such a system does not place categorical limitations on the person with respect to his class position. Vertical mobility is not merely permissive; it is a right, and may be quite general. The membranes, as Sorokin puts it, between the strata are very thin and have holes in them which give access to the stratum above or below. Such a system may be styled "plastic," "penetrable," "mobile." An open class system is highly elastic and flexible; nothing is fixed, and there is much variation, much person-to-person play, and much interplay for divergent behavior.

Our American class system is usually presented as a relatively open one, with relatively rapid social metabolism. We maintain the thesis of equality of opportunity and freedom of achievement. In fact, we have a "mobility orientation," that is, mobility attitudes, aspirations, and patterns of behavior, operating as a persevering, motivating, guiding aspect of individual personality. (8) From both the social and the psychological point of view, vertical mobility is an integral part of our status system. Our American dream, our characteristic idea-value-attitude system, holds in part that everyone has the right to succeed and should strive to reach the top.

This American dream, however, implies continual awareness of our individual class position and a desire to change it upward and enlarge the area of our life chances; for the higher the class, the greater the security, prestige, and freedom. We try to better our position by the utilization of various opportunities and appropriate activities, such as the acquisition of more specialized knowledge and superior vocational skills and proficiencies, the acquisition of wealth, judicious marriage into a higher stratum, the acquisition of political and other social power, and so on.

In such a system, there is always some struggling for position. Social mobility is ceaselessly distributing persons and groups on the prestige and functional scale where they can best contribute and fit into the societal organization. The more freely competitive and cooperative the processes of interaction are, the better they work.

Social descent also may occur in our class system. In fact, as specialization becomes greater, competition is likely to become more and more intense for the relatively few high positions. Hence, the difficulty of not only rising in the social scale but also of holding one's own becomes greater. "From shirt sleeves to shirt sleeves in three generations" has been proved many times over. Since social descent involves what is considered to be retrogression according to the values of our society, it is not widely advertised and it is gradual even when relatively intense. Only a small and incomplete replacement of members takes place at any given time, and the network of relationships of the social organization is maintained virtually intact in spite of the ever-changing composition of its strata. (6; 19)

Channels of Vertical Social Movement

A functional analysis of an open class system like our own reveals an array of social institutions which enable individuals to move up and down the social ladder. These institutions operate as channels or routes—even as social staircases or elevators—of vertical circulation. But the movement of persons by these means is *not* a matter of chance, as T. Lynn Smith has pointed out. (10, p. 533) These institutions also serve as sifters, testing and selecting, sorting and grading the persons of the population and distributing and locating them in the strata where their functions, obligations, and rights are commensurate with their tested abilities. These selective and placement agencies never operate perfectly, however, and some persons and families are always underplaced or overplaced.

Economic Institutions

In the United States the vast material resources available for exploitation and the infinite division of labor and graded occupational specialization offer almost unbelievable advantages and opportunities for social ascent through the acquisition of wealth. Most of the leaders in American industry, finance, transportation and trade rose from obscurity. The existence of graded occupations, each with specific requirements for satisfactory performance, generally functions as a means of testing, selecting, and distributing individuals along the occupational ladder. (21) The way up is through a hierarchy of increasing skill to management and ownership. Position on this ladder, from common laborer to executive and professional man, is roughly commensurate with class standing.

The Army

In time of war, the army provides opportunity for rapid advancement of the talented strategist, great leader, or specialist, regardless of original social position. In peacetime, promotion is based on seniority, and higher social status may be automatically achieved. Through successive promotion to higher military ranks men mount to high social position.

The Church

When religious organizations are growing in social standing, they serve as both elevators and selectors. Both the Catholic Church and the Protestant denominations in the United States offer innumerable examples among their clergy of men of very humble origin who reached positions of great social prominence through the high positions they achieved in their churches. For the layman, affiliation with churches of high social prestige gives social rating.

Political Institutions

Service of the state has always been a ladder. In a democracy like our own, active membership in political parties and the holding of office, whether local, state, or national, provide ascending opportunity for many. Humble folk and immigrants' sons have become mayors and governors, and a frontiersman, a rail-splitter, an Ohio canal boy, a Vermont farm boy, and one from Iowa, and a boy from a small town in Missouri have all become President.

Marriage

Marriage has often led one of the two parties into either a higher or lower social stratum, although a step up is hoped for. The poor but deserving bridegroom marries the rich heiress and achieves working capital and higher social position. The ambitious mother of the poor, but beautiful, daughter marries her, if possible, to the rich young man.

The Educational System

An educational system such as ours, which provides training and specialized knowledge from the nursery school up to the highest technical and professional levels and is theoretically accessible to all members of the society, is a widely utilized and most effective means for social elevation, equal to, or even more efficient than, our economic system. Probably the bulk of students attending state universities have social elevation in mind as one of their primary objectives. Furthermore, schools are testing, selecting, and distributing agencies par excellence for nearly everyone who comes under their influence. In fact, an efficient and just selection and placing of persons are among the major functions of an educational system in a democracy. (22; 23; 24; 25; 26)

Factors Affecting Selective Processes

In general, vertical mobility in the class system involves a whole array of processes of selection. These processes, consisting mainly of forms of personal competition and, due to various conditions prevailing in a given society at a given time, operate with various degrees of effectiveness. Ross (23, pp. 217-218) has pointed out that the effectiveness of these selective processes will depend upon the following conditions:

Degree and Quality of Liberty, Opportunity, and Choice Available to Individuals. In the utilization of media of achievement these conditions will be favorable to the individual's social advance if there is, on the one hand, an absence of blockings caused by family origin, race, and the like; relative absence of special or invidious preferment based, for example, on religious affiliation, membership in a fraternity or fraternal order; and, on the other hand, ready access to earning, educational, political, and other pertinent opportunities.

The Rate of Social Change. In a static society position and rank are fixed, and a castelike situation prevails; whereas in a changing society all is in a state of flux, and the strata themselves may be changing in characteristics and in relationship to other strata. New avenues for both ascent and descent of the social ladder come into existence. It may be said that the greater the rate of social change, the greater is the opportunity for selective movement.

The Efficiency of the Selective Agencies. These agencies consist first and foremost of the educational system as a general tester and selector of intelligence and ability, but various formalized organizations, such as economic and political bureaucracies, also are selectors. These utilize informal and increasingly formal specially and technically designed testing principles and procedures, both for original placement and for advancement.

Industrial and commercial corporations have personnel departments whose business it is efficiently and objectively to test and place employees and determine fitness for promotion. Educational systems have certification and promotion requirements; religious organizations have systems of examination for clergy and admission requirements for lay members; and governmental agencies have long used civil service and merit systems as agencies for selection and advancement of personnel. The better these selective agencies are, the more quickly, economically, and accurately the competitors are sifted and placed.

Factors of Restraint

In a functional analysis of our class system it is just as important to note the factors that curtail opportunity and produce tendencies toward rigidity as it is to examine the historical channels of vertical mobility. Little attention has been paid to this aspect of our class system, since it seems to indicate an undermining of our American ideology, but it will be given comprehensive treatment here.

The processes of vertical mobility have never operated perfectly without checks or restraints, as we have noted. There have always been barriers to rising and artificial supports that held others up. But today, in spite of the American dream, opportunities are apparently becoming restricted; more and more positions seem to be established and fixed, or at least there is a discernible tendency for them to become so; and the likelihood of advancement is not so great. In terms of class structure there seems to be a trend toward lessened interclass mobility and a consequent increasing fixation of boundaries. Some notable reversals are also in evidence. (see especially 36; 47)

What are some of the factors and situations that are introducing restraint and rigidity into the operation of our social ladder?

Original Position of Family

Individuals are born and raised in families of a given class level. Great inequalities exist among families of different classes with respect to property and its inheritance, access to social welfare, culture, occupations and differences in social outlook. These diverse family conditions give some individuals initial handicaps that are more or less difficult to overcome or advantages that protect them from competition. If the family is of the lower classes, the individual is limited as to economic, educational, cultural, and associational opportunities. If he is born into a higher-class family, even though the individual be stupid, incompetent, gross, or even immoral, by virtue of the family's inherited wealth, prestige, and social power, he has a protected position and may stay at that level during his life time. This may continue for several generations. In brief, the race up the social staircase does not start at the bottom or on the same step for all; many have a family head start which cannot be overtaken. (44)

Ethnic-Group Membership

Ethnic-group membership is both a *criterion* of social class and a previously existing *determinant* of opportunity for ascent. In many localities, and under certain conditions, Negroes, Jews, Mexican-Americans, Orientals, and even first- or second-generation immigrants of foreign nationality are subjected to prejudices, discriminations, avoidances, and exclusions, which prevent them from having a fair chance to demonstrate competitively their capacities for achievement and rising. (31; 42)

Curtailment of Immigration

The rather free and abundant immigration that occurred in our country prior to World War I greatly increased the population at the lower levels of the class pyramid, since the immigrants were poor and largely in the common labor occupational categories. The effect of their constant inflow at the bottom was practically to *force* the older arrivals up the ladder. The somewhat greater American sophistication of the older stocks almost automatically gave them a higher prestige rating, and their larger experience enabled them to qualify for and hold more honorific jobs. Furthermore, in many instances, the older stocks seized the opportunity to employ and even exploit the immigrants, using them as means to economic mobility.

The volume of immigration has been drastically reduced by legal restrictions, and such immigration as we have is now of a highly selective nature, consisting not so much of peasant peoples as of skilled agricultural and industrial workers and educated middle-class persons at the technical and professional level. As a result the upper occupational levels are somewhat crowded, and there is less room at the top for American middle- and lower-class young people.

Changes in the Differential Fertility

During recent centuries there has been a decided tendency for the lower-class families to produce relatively more children than the families of the social classes above (see Chapter 8). The low fertility of the lower middle-class white-collar workers was especially noticeable. This situation tended to create poverty, overcrowding, and general disadvantage among the lower classes and greater difficulty of achieving higher socioeconomic status. But it also produced a pressure that literally forced people in the immediately higher classes upward. At the same time, it created a vacuum in the higher social layers that tended to suck up persons from the lower classes to fill the vacancies created by the failure of the upper classes to reproduce themselves. (10, p. 54; 13, pp. 346-360; 46)

In recent times, and especially during and since World War II, a population revolution has been taking place. Not only are we having more babies per thousand of population, thus reversing a long-time trend, but the more highly educated classes, especially high-school and college graduates, and the suburban and city families are marrying earlier and having increasingly larger numbers of children. Between 1940 and 1947 the reproduction rate of women college graduates increased 81 percent, compared with an increase of only 29 percent for women who had completed only five years of grade school. In general, while the lower-education groups still have the largest families, the higher-education groups have made great gains since 1940. (27; 32; 33) The result is a greater tendency of the middle and higher classes to replace themselves by their own offspring, thus eliminating the former vacuum in some measure and diminishing the opportunity for migration to urban jobs by surplus rural young folk. It may also mean that they are creating a situation which will produce intensive competition in the sixties and very likely push some of their more numerous offspring down the social ladder.

Restraining Factors in the Economic Ladder

Our country was once a land of tremendous economic opportunities for the ordinary man. Free land for settlement, easy exploitation of natural resources, rapidly expanding business, the possibility for successful small-scale business enterprises, an accessible and easily operating occupational ladder, and so on, made ascent of the socioeconomic ladder proverbial. From waterboy to boss, from bank messenger to president, from log cabin to White House, from rags to riches were commonplaces. What we seem to be witnessing, however, is a fundamental alteration in the vaunted American ladder of economic opportunity by which people have been supposed to "go up in the world," that is, to the higher economic brackets.

High Cost of Individual Business. The Lynds pointed out that the sharp increase in size, complexity, and cost of the modernly equipped shop makes the process of launching out as an individual entrepreneur or as a partnership more difficult than it was several generations ago. (37) Most industrial, commercial, and transportation processes are conducted by corporations with huge capital investments, extensive division of labor, highly efficient bureaucratic organization, and all levels of technical and managerial skill. Only corporations can compete with corporations in any sizable market.

Curtailment of Opportunities for Advancement. The occupational ladder, with its chance to work up through various levels of skill to supervisory, managerial, and executive posts, is no longer present to any great extent. The very nature of the industrial process, with its production line of semiskilled human-machine parts, ties the worker to a given craft level. He may move horizontally from plant to plant, but he is not fitted in the process to move through the acquisition of higher skills and management experience to a foremanship and above. Furthermore, the supervisory and technical jobs require formal and expensive training owing to their highly specialized nature and rarely can be filled from working-class personnel. Tending a machine and punching a time clock do not prepare them for such tasks.

Technical Training. Today, fewer and fewer men rise from the bottom to the top places of management and ownership in industry and business. There is a growing body of evidence that American business leaders are being *increasingly* recruited from the upper ranks of society. (37; 52) The specialization of technical functions has tended to move up into the higher altitudes of training, and such men come increasingly from technically trained personnel, prepared and contributed by technical and engineering schools and by universities. Also, more and more fathers at the higher technical and executive levels are educating their sons to take their places or to occupy similar places in other industries or businesses, thus leaving fewer positions into which the sons of those on lower levels can climb.

The same kind of occupational fixity is evident at other levels. Davidson and Anderson found that 60 percent of the professionals went directly into their chosen work from similar parental occupations; among the proprietary group, the majority came from either parental farm ownership or from business proprietors; the clerical workers were the principal climbers; the skilled group was least mobile of all; and two thirds of the unskilled came either from unskilled parents or from farmer fathers. In general, between two thirds and three fourths of the workers of the sample came from the level of the father or from the adjacent category. (5) Sorokin also found that "the wealthy class of the United States is becoming less and less open, more and more closed, and is tending to be transformed into a caste-like group." (48)

Restrictions within Professions. The professions also are more and more closed to lower-class persons. The high cost of education and the prolonged training and apprenticeship necessary to meet the high standards of admission fixed by the professional associations and the state certification bodies reduce the number who can get in.

In brief, there are still relatively few positions open at the top, and these positions tend to be filled by the sons of those at or near the top. Higher ambition is in general confined to conditions of class-limited opportunity.

Effect of Labor Unions. Finally, *the labor unions of the workers themselves are a fixing factor* of growing importance. This situation is examined in a brilliant analysis by Tannenbaum.

(51) The worker finds his economic security in his own union. Under law the union is increasingly the labor-supplying agency, and since the workers are limited to those having membership in the union, the job and the membership are precious. The union disburses and also specifies the place of the worker in his organization and within the factory and industry where he makes his living. Such advancement as he enjoys is a matter of seniority in the union. When the worker is thrown out of the union, he is without a job and a future. To be sure, he can voluntarily resign from the union, but under the conditions where will he go and what will he do when he quits?

Furthermore, most of the worker's social security, as it has developed, is paid for by his industry. If he changes his job, he forfeits his right to medical care, maternity and sickness insurance, retirement pensions, and other related benefits. The combination of compulsory union membership and dependence upon the industry for most of his security all but freezes the worker to his job and makes his mobility all but meaningless. His lifelong welfare is that of the union and the industry.

Tannenbaum rightly points out that, without intent or plan, the unions are integrating the workers into what amounts to a separate social order with the unions' members developing into a new type of estate. The unions are re-creating a society based on something very like medieval status and are destroying the hard-won contractual rights of the workers as individuals. The position of the worker in the union is much as it was in the old-time guilds. The union satisfies social and psychological needs as well as economic needs; but it also fixes the economic condition of the worker, and sets for him a status within a hierarchy. (49)

Changes in the Educational System

Our educational system operates as both an aid and a hindrance to social mobility. As a channel of ascent it makes possible regular movement through the successive educational levels without any breaks whatsoever. In actual practice, however, various blocks and obstacles relating to the social-class position of many of the students tend to prevent it from operating as an open-sesame to high achievement and high status and rank. Practically all children of all walks of life start their educational careers in our public schools, but for various reasons, they do not all stay in school and avail themselves of the educational training essential to ascent in our society. The interworking of the social and educational systems tends to eliminate the majority of them, and only a small proportion get through.

Diversion of Lower-Class Children from School. Havighurst and Taba have estimated that whereas 80 percent of the upper-class and upper-middle-class children go to college, where the basic knowledge, training, and social sophistication essential to upper-class position are achieved, only 20 percent of the lower-middle-class and 5 percent of the lower-class children get there. The lower-class children start dropping out of school in the elementary grades and continue to do so in increasing numbers in high school. Warner, Meeker, and Eells say: "The educational conveyor belt drops lower-class children at the beginning and bottom of the educational route and carries those from the higher classes a longer distance, nearly all the upper-class children going to the end of the line." (52, p. 25)

This diversion from education is due to a variety of factors *other* than the innate ability of lower-class children to profit by instruction and training, for many of these have high I.Q.'s. Economic considerations are important. At the high-school level, for example, the maintenance of the young people costs as much as that of adults, and they are a sheer financial luxury for their parents. There is also the enticement of early earning and independence for lower-class young folks and the likelihood of early marriage. Sibley's study in Pennsylvania indicates that "as a boy passes through the sifting process of the educational system, his parents' status assumes increasing importance, both absolutely and in comparison with his own intelligence, as a factor influencing his chances of continuing his preparation for one of the more advantageous vocations." (46, p. 330)

Factors Favoring Middle- and Upper-Class Children. As noted before, high-school education, college education, and higher vocational education remain to a large extent the special privilege of children of superior social-economic backgrounds.

It is also pointed out that the teachers favor middle-class and upper-class children in various ways, and that lower-class children are less likely to be picked for friendships, leadership, and many other favorable personal traits. Neugarten points out that social-class differences in friendship and reputation are well established as early as the fifth grade, and that the lower-class child is often a behavior problem because of this rejection by his classmates. She states: "This may also be one of the reasons why lower-class children often find school unpleasant and unrewarding and why the child of lower-class so often welcomes the first opportunity to leave school altogether." (43)

In view of this educational blocking of lower-class young persons, and the fact that industry and business are depending upon college-trained persons for even the lower supervisory jobs, not to mention the higher technical and administrative positions, there is a definite ceiling over the aspirations of the lower-class young persons to rise in the ranks. Warner, Meeker, and Eells state: "The blocking of the worker's mobility and the encouragement of college-trained men is the ultimate payoff of what began in the grade schools." (52, p. 29) This situation "stacks the cards" in favor of the maintenance of class location in childhood; instead of the actual mobility for the lower classes, it makes for rigidity of the class system. (44, pp. 260-265)

Reduction of Vertical-Mobility Drive

There are grounds for thinking that the fundamental *psychology* underlying the American dream of climbing to the top is undergoing considerable change. It appears that many people in a fluid, laissez faire, competitive society prefer certainty and fixity in some stratum of a more or less rigidly stratified society to the opportunity for success but including also the possibility of social demotion. More and more people covet the peace of mind which security gives; they want a sense of stability at whatever social level they have been able to obtain.

There are several indicators of this change. One is the popularity of civil service jobs. Although the civil service is roughly selective, the jobs are not highly rewarding in money or prestige, but they do, however, offer security of tenure (barring moral turpitude). They do not require highly aggressive competitive action to hold the job, and in most instances, with fair performance of duties, promotion in a given specialty is more or less automatic and a matter of seniority. The stratum fixity in a labor union, with little opportunity of loss or gain save as suffered or enjoyed by the entire membership, is increasingly being sought after and happily enjoyed as a great boon. Even the professional organizations through their regulations and limitations of action embodied in the ethical codes tend to stifle competition and create more or less uniform conditions of action for their members.

People seem to be increasingly interested in avoiding the strains of competition in our complex mass society; they hesitate to "chance" the climb with the attendant possibility of rebuff or retreat. They seem to be less and less sure of themselves as potentially successful movers upward and are adjusting or accommodating their mental states to the life chances of a given level with its status, if it is not intolerable. Many seem to be interested only in such self-improvement as is necessary to hang on or move within their bracket and are willing to accept the esteem of conformity as a compensation for the lack of greater prestige and other social emoluments.

In general, there is evidence that the American dream is becoming less real for many people, that we seem to be settling. The strata are becoming more rigid, the holes in the sieves, smaller. Status is crystalling. There is both a tendency toward restriction of access to the means of personal and family advancement and an apparent reduction in the vertical mobility drive and psyche. Needless to say, in this rigidifying and closing of our class structure and this reduction of vertical mobility, we may be depriving our society of many potential contributions from the lower ranks. The situation limits the use of intrinsic merit; much merit remains undiscovered.

PART FIVE

DESTRUCTURALIZATION AND DEFUNCTIONALIZATION

CHAPTER XVI

ISOLATIVE AND SEPARATIVE PROCESSES

IN THE SIX preceding chapters we discussed a series of processes, with the related factors, which structuralize and functionalize a society. If these processes are operating with essential efficacy, the general effect is societal organization and equilibrium. The individuals associate rather freely and, because of their more or less well-established patterns of relationship, participate fairly effectively in their various functions. The groups and strata cooperate, and the organizations and institutions operate with relative smoothness and efficiency. The general state of affairs is characterized by harmony of relationships and by teamwork. The community or society is a well-integrated mosaic.

Social Organization and Disorganization

We know that societal organization is never completely stable or secure and its functional mechanisms never perform with perfect efficiency. Every society has inherent and endemic in it factors and processes that produce varying degrees of societal disorganization and misorganization.* This disorganization takes the form of both destructuralization and defunctionalization. The *destructuralization* consists of the demolition, disintegration, distortion, decay, atrophy, or rigidifying of groups, organizations, and institutions and of the impairment or destruction of essential enhancing relationships between individuals, groups, categories, institutions, and strata. These elements are weakened and separated. In some instances the structures continue as gross and expensive incum-

*On the use of the term *misorganization,* that is, the "abuses of social action," the fumbling, bungling conducting of social affairs, "the mal-appropriate ends or functions to which they are put," see reference 16.

brances after their usefulness to society has been ended.

The *defunctionalization* consists of the impairment of operative efficiency—the failure to perform certain functional prerequisites—as purposes, objectives, and ends are confused or obscured. There may also be misfunctioning and disfunctioning that is, a working at cross-purposes and a consequent lack of adjustment of the parts of the social system.

Effects of Disorganization

As a result of the destructuralizing and defunctionalizing factors and processes, there is a weakening or partial destruction of the social structurings, a deterioration of interaction, especially cooperation, and an impairment or disruption of the functional efficiency of the society as a reasonably healthy and competent going concern.

Dissociation, defeat, and demoralization also occur, and lack of understanding of, and devotion to, common aims and purposes become apparent. Old attitudes and habits of either the general personnel or the special functionaries and established rules and forms of societal regulation and maintenance no longer function effectively. Nonconformity may become excessive. Traditional values and ideologies are out of harmony with external conditions. In general, there is "relative decline of order and discipline, of unity and rationality, and of integration that renders the social mechanism inadequate to the effective patterning of collective behavior." (22) The behavior of the groups or of the community becomes in some part inconsistent, unstable, and unpredictable, and many contemporary social wants and needs are poorly satisfied. If the processes continue unabated the end is disintegration of the structural and the regulative and maintenance systems.

Pathological Phenomena of Disorganization

Concretely, we have such pathological phenomena as crime and delinquency; personal disorganization in the form of mental and emotional derangement and breakdown and suicide; physical ill-health, unemployment, poverty, dependency and relief, and too much charity; much physical mobility; and social psychological epidemics. Other symptoms of societal breakdown include family disintegration and sexual looseness; economic depressions with reduced production and underconsumption, and economic "booms and busts"; industrial, ethnic, and class conflict and other social dissensions, cleavages, and antagonisms; religious aberrations and conflicts; political corruption; gambling, racketeering, alcoholism, and drug addiction; violation of civil rights, and so on. (15)

Possibly because they lend themselves to sensationalism, these pathological situations and processes have been given more attention by laymen and, regrettably, often by social scientists than have the vast array of processes which together constitute the normal structuralization and functionalization of society. As a result, the impression has grown that society is not successful and that collapse is impending; whereas, in reality, human society is a fairly efficient hardy perennial.

Our purpose here is neither to underestimate nor to exaggerate the importance of these disorganizing and malfunctioning processes, but to present them objectively as continuous or recurrent threats and occurrences in typical societies.

Normal and Abnormal Destructuralization and Defunctionalization

Normal Deficiency and Inefficiency

Destructuralization and defunctionalization are present everywhere and at all times in some degree. (25) The only perfectly organized societies are utopias. Human societies are dynamic rather than static and are never in a state of perfect balance or complete equilibrium. Their balance and equilibrium are always relative, never absolute. In fact, complete harmony and stability are never achieved anywhere and are sheer impossibilities under conditions of modern life.

A certain amount of disorder, confusion, and inadequate functioning of the social machinery appears to be continuously existent in all social systems, and hence more or less normal or natural. (1, pp. 458-460) This endemic disorder or inadequacy does not mean, however, that a major crisis exists. All societies and most of their institutions and organizations can absorb a considerable amount of failure and defeat; they can continue to operate in the face of internal maladjustments and inconsistencies with a fairly wide margin of safety.

Most of the social processes are carried on with fairly satisfactory results; there is no general feeling of unrest or insecurity or dislocation; there are no demands—probably no need—for radical measures of readjustment and no willingness to support them. Like the human body and the human personality, human societies can and must endure many minor ailments and crises; at best, they function only *relatively* well. Even if a generally acceptable conception of 100 percent efficiency of any social instrumentality could be arrived at, it would be unattainable. *Perfect adjustment is an ideal, not an actuality,* for the seeds of destructuralization and defunctionalization are ever present.

The dynamic nature of social interaction requires a constant rearrangement of the constituent elements of a society. The resultant unavoidable modification brings about a dissolution or a marked revision of certain organizational relationships and behavior patterns which are imbedded in the social structure. Ordinarily, in times of fair social stability, the continuous incipient disorganization is continuously neutralized by the reinforcment of essential principles and rules and by the reorganization of procedures and institutions. We have some continuous social reconstruction, some production and application of new schemes and institutions.*

Moreover, disorganization does not necessarily result from some abandonment of existing norms, habits, roles, mores, or even institutions. All constructive "next steps" are a matter of new or revised norms and of intelligent and courageous nonconformity. Much of the nonconformity is stimulating and constitutes a challenge to outmoded ways. Always we must distinguish between the breakdown of inadequate traditional roles and the appearance of desirable, even imperative, new ones. Metabolism is vitally essential to health and function and is an everlasting process of replacement. It must always be borne in mind that

> Each age is a dream that is dying,
> Or one that is coming to birth

and that processes of wholesome change and essential change should not be halted or interfered with.

Normally the processes of organization and disorganization may be thought of as in reciprocal relationship to each other, as operating together in a moving equilibrium of social order. In a sense they represent reverse aspects of the same functioning whole. In a normal and stable society these major sets of social processes go hand in hand: each generates the other; each is dependent for its very existence upon the other; and ordinarily they tend to neutralize each other. Social health rests upon an equilibrium between these two larger types.

Abnormal Deficiency and Inefficiency

There are, however, continual, persistent, lurking tendencies for the destructive and disorganizing processes to get out of normal control and break the equilibrium and become a serious threat to the health, well-being, and functional efficacy of the society. The degree of disorder and confusion in one or more phases of social life slips across the line of what might be called *normal* disorganization and produces situations in which there is a striking and disturbing amount of incapacity, inefficiency, and insecurity.

Here, too, as in the case of the human body and personality, there is a point beyond which maladjustments have a deteriorative or paralyzing effect and lead to breakdown. At such times concern becomes widespread; chaos threatens, social decadence seems imminent, individual and group dissatisfaction, discontent, and even misery prevail. This degree of destructuralization and defunctionalization is our present problem of analysis.

When, then, can such destructuralization and defunctionalization be said to exist? What is the range of deviation from the normal? How is the relative amount of disorganization, misorganization, and malfunctioning determined? Where is the point of disequilibrium and inefficiency?

Whether applied to a given group, institution,

*To be discussed in Chap. 22.

differentiated or stratified relationship, or society as a whole, *a standard, a value connotation of some sort, is implied.* In social organization, there is involved a hypothesis, an ideal construct, that includes stability and efficiency and a certain amount of unavoidable and continuous instability and inefficiency. Social health is fair to good. *Misorganization and disorganization are departures from some norm of organization and efficiency.* There is individual and group behavior and societal operation, which according to useful, convenient, and fairly widely acceptable norms, arrived at discriminately, is deemed pathological. *This is a matter of value judgments among a considerable number of observing people; it depends upon the consensus regarding an actual or imagined deviation or departure from or infringement of some cherished norm or combination of norms.*

"Abnormal" or "atypical" inefficiency exists. Something has gone wrong in some noticeable degree with some of the instruments of societal functioning. The organization or relationship or community has functioned *more* efficiently at other times.* It is believed by many concerned individuals and groups that the continued existence of the situations impairs social order and is incompatible with survival.

There is a state of affairs in some part or several parts of the social system which has thrown it out of joint; that is, its parts are not adequately geared together so as to permit sufficient functioning of the whole according to the desired ends of operation as conceived by many people. The existing situations are unsatisfactory in terms of the needs of the people as they see them. Just as a person decides that he is too ill to work or play, so a group, a community, or a society decides that it has some ailment that does not permit it to work competently. In brief, "social problems are what people think they are and if conditions are not defined as social problems by the people involved in them, they are not problems to those people." (9)

These "problems" are definitions of threatening conditions which many people deplore, disapprove of, worry about, and find intolerable. People believe these conditions need correction; alternatives are conceived and desired, and it is hoped that they are possible. The definitions of the pathological processes and conditions will always be strictly relative to the individuals or the groups which make the judgments. Social action of a corrective nature, of course, must rest upon a rather wide consensus regarding discrepancy beyond the "normal."

Condition of Destructuralization and Defunctionalization

As noted repeatedly, a distinction must always be made between an existing *condition* and the *processes* which in combination produce that condition. In this section we shall devote ourselves to the general characteristics which identify a society that is subject to some degree of destructuralization and defunctionalization. The condition is revealed in various ways. (4, pp. 19-49)

Confusion of Social Norms and Nonconformity of Action

In an adequately structured and efficiently functioning society the norms or rules of behavior (folkways, beliefs, customs, mores, and laws) and the values, goals, and interests are sufficiently clear and consistent so that the great bulk of the population can act with precision and relate their behavior satisfactorily with that of others in the various common social situations. But in a disorganized and malfunctioning community or society there is "a decrease of the influence of existing social rules of behavior upon the individual members of the group," and the rules, goals, and interests are confused.

A state of what practically amounts to *anomie*—the breakdown of the norms of individual conduct, or a state of "normlessness"—exists. Some of the rules and principles of behavior are archaic and have not been replaced with sufficient rapidity by newer and more appropriate and authoritative ones. Consequently, many people have little respect for them. Among the segmented, special-interest groups—organizations, social classes, occupational

*See Chap. 2 on the essential functions of a society.

groups, sex and age groups—a number of the rules and principles are inconsistent with each other, often diametrically opposed to each other, with resultant culture contradiction, confusion, and conflict. Societal behavior is at cross-purposes. Still others, such as success goals, may be widely respected and widely held, but they are of such a nature that their pursuit produces misunderstanding, cleavage, or even conflict.

Thus, because of this confusion of societal norms, there is a loss of universally accepted definitions of social situations, and *a considerable amount of nonconformity in behavior* prevails; there is *violation of legal and other rules; and a consensus as to ends and purposes is lacking.* Individual styles of behavior prevail. In general, there is consistent disparity between behavior and the values by which it is defined.

Disorganization of Roles

The roles are the patterned forms of action for persons and groups and are largely dependent upon the norms of a society for their definition. Thus, if the norms are confused, people are confused as to their roles. There are conflicting and inconsistent conceptions of roles, and the different roles expected of a given individual are incompatible or are in conflict. Individuals may be compelled to choose between two roles, both of which or neither of which they would like to play. Such a choice places a strain upon individuals as they perform as adolescents, or marital partners, or organizational or public officials.

To have unity, harmony of purposes, and teamwork, there must be a high degree of coordination and integration of all roles of all people, but this is lacking in a disorganized or misorganized and malfunctioning society. The responses of people fail to conform to the expectations laid upon them, and there is considerable disparity between aspiration and achievement. Many individuals are defunctionalized, and to that extent the society is also defunctionalized. (14; 27)

Breakdown and Inflexibility of Institutions

The social institutions are the major instrumentalities of societal order and maintenance. In a sick society some, if not all, of the institutions will fail to carry on their essential functions efficiently. The economic institutions may be functioning poorly, as evidenced by reduction of productive efficiency, unemployment or underemployment, and reduced standards of living; family life may be chaotic; political, religious, educational, ethical, and other institutions may show some weaknesses; and political corruption may spread through police and other public services. The malfunctioning of the educational institutions, if it exists, is likely to leave people "uneducated" as to necessary social facts and the assumption of social responsibilities. All these attest to the tendency to breakdown in institutions.

The institutions may also lack integration with each other, and rather than dovetailing and complementing each other, they may be drifting apart and may be in conflict in their objectives and their functions. Some institutions or parts of institutions may have become inflexible, petrified, and survivalistic, resting on charters and procedures whose origins, if not forgotten, have lost some of their importance for the present generations and yet are observed through persistence of habit, sentiment, and tradition. Such institutions are relatively mechanical and unchangeable in operation and are unable to adjust themselves with sufficient dispatch, or to understand, anticipate, or adjust to recent changes and existent conditions. Collective adjustment is thus blocked, and the institutions no longer control, order, and maintain the societal life. (4, 27-28; 10, 240-241)

Conflict Situations

Invariably in a more or less destructuralized and defunctionalized society, there is a decline of unity and harmony among groups, and conflict develops among those with special interests as they promote their various purposes. The socioeconomic classes of the stratification system are in opposition; racial and nationality groups are in conflict; age and sex groups oppose each other; and there is religious and moral dissension and other forms of culture fragmentation and conflict. Instead of understanding and solidarity and cooperation, there is distance and lack of communication between groups, as they conflict and work at cross-purposes.

Social Unrest and Demoralization

Considerable social unrest is one form of evidence that a society is in some degree of disorganization and malfunctioning. It is a symptom of the unsatisfactory adjustment between the societal organization and the social-psychological make-up of the persons and groups living under its conditions, an expression and focalization of their insecurity, confusion, dissatisfaction, and discontent in the general condition of disequilibrium. Many of the standard needs and wishes of the people are not satisfied, and the very processes that have produced the chaotic state have created new wants that the malfunctioning society cannot satisfy.

The social unrest expresses itself specifically in such phenomena as political unrest in the form of new political parties and subversive proposals and movements; religious unrest giving rise to new extremist sects, cults, and blatant evangelism and revivalism; much random wandering (for example, "Okies," "Arkies," hoboes) and change of employment and residence in the vague pursuit of a more satisfactory life; rumors and contagious mass movements, mass hysteria, and other milling and stampeding phenomena; extremes of radicalism and reactionism and the advocacy and organization of all manner of reforms, many verging on the ridiculous.

In brief, many segments of the population are in a *state of social demoralization*. Morale implies identification with supposedly realizable collective purposes and enterprises. Thus, when a community or society is misorganized and not functioning adequately, many people and groups are unable to maintain steadfastness of purpose, to meet their individual and group crises effectively, and there is a lack of belief in significant social causes and beneficent undertakings with consequent inability to participate effectively in them. The people are pessimistic about conditions and in a state of despair and are convinced that the society does not give them the essential satisfactions and security. Under such conditions, the adjustive reactions of the people may change from mere pessimism and defeatism, through random efforts at "escape," to aggressive terroristic procedures.

Personal and Personality Disorganization

Closely related to social unrest and demoralization is individual disorganization. Because of the malfunctioning of the societal system the norms, roles, interests, goals, and expectations are obscure and often conflicting. Old habits are no longer productive. Individuals find that they cannot satisfy their needs in socially approved channels and that many of their wishes, ambitions, and impulses are thwarted. They are expected to do things that they cannot do. They are often deprived of food, shelter, sexual satisfaction, or freedom of expression generally. The lives of many—possibly millions of persons—are impoverished. They suffer shock.

The personality disorganization is expressed in many ways, depending upon various personal and social factors, such as apathy, indifference or boredom, anxiety, fear, guilt, restlessness, bafflement, frustration, tension, irritability, resentment, and even hostility. Some individuals engage in quiet but effective sabotage and opposition, continually alert to frustrate others, while some, feeling themselves unloved and unwanted, spend their lives in a persistent endeavor to get even, to block, attack, or destroy others in order to release the hate they feel. (6) They are in a state of psychic conflict. Other manifestations are extreme selfishness and individualism, crime, desertion, alcoholism and drug addiction, accidents, suicide, neurotic and psychopathic tendencies, and various other bizarre and eccentric compensatory, escapist, underconforming, overconforming, or otherwise deviant forms of behavior.

Such conditions of destructuralization and defunctionalization are due to a combination of change factors. The continuous changes in nature, both of a physical and biological sort, demographic changes, cultural changes with their accompanying lags, changes in societal organization, both those spontaneously occurring and those deliberately induced, produce continuous disequilibrium in the form of crisis situations.*

*For an analysis of change and discussion of crises as cause and effect of change, see Chap. 3.

Destructuralizing and Defunctionalizing Processes

In a functional analysis of human society, destructuralization and defunctionalization can be most profitably viewed as a combination of processes rather than as a condition, for these pathological conditions, as all others, are the result of processes. An array of processes is continually or recurrently upsetting the equilibrium of the societal organization. The major categories of these disequilibrating processes to be examined are the separative and isolative processes; the opposition processes; the processes of decadence; and the ossification processes.

Attention must be called to two primary considerations at the very outset. *First,* many of the processes have both positive and negative effects; that is, in some of their phases and under certain conditions, they produce structuralization, regulation, maintenance, and even reorganization, whereas at other times they have destructuralizing and defunctionalizing effects. This is true, for example, with reference to competition, physical and social mobility, most forms of differentiation, including especially division of labor, specialization of function, and stratification, and, to some extent, segregation. Such processes have been or will be discussed at the appropriate places in this analysis with respect to these different and contrary functions that they perform.

Second, there is some overlapping in functional effect of the disequilibrating processes included in the four major categories just presented. The separative and isolative processes invite or produce opposition and may lead to decadence. The opposition processes may produce isolation and decadence. The processes of decadence often produce separation. Even some of the ossification processes produce lonely, isolated, functionless groups and institutions. The specific processes will be examined under the category where they have their major manifestation.

The Separative and Isolative Factors and Processes

In the present section our main concern is with those social processes that divide or separate persons or groups in varying degree and tend to produce a hazardous degree of isolation or distance between these societal elements. They bring about what Toynbee has referred to as "social schisms." (56, p. 368) The two facts of fundamental importance in connection with the separative and isolative processes are, first, that ***they impair the essential social participation*** of individuals and groups, and, second, that ***they accentuate social distance.*** Social participation is essential to societal operation* and normal and balanced participation is basic in the mental and emotional health of the individual. By social participation we do not necessarily mean extensive social activities, as in the case of joiners, but contributory membership in social groups, spontaneous, happy, and satisfying cooperation and sharing in the interests and activities of others, and being accepted freely as human creatures—even friends—by others.

*See Chap. 10.

By social distance we mean the psychological and sociological nearness or farness, intimacy or remoteness, of individuals and groups, their convergence or divergence in sympathetic understanding.* There is no distance in a literal spatial sense, but only a recognition and acceptance of gradients of *social difference.* Where there is little sympathetic understanding and acceptance as equals, social farness exists; where there is much, nearness obtains. The differences are highly conducive to social ignorance of the parties regarding each other, and to impairment of essential social participation. The difficulty is not merely and solely the fact of distance and separation, though that is grave enough, but frequently the perverted or exploitive use of distance, the lack of proper regulation of differentiation, individuation, stratification, and so on.

Isolation, or separation, is a relative term, a matter of degree. Social isolation is never complete. Nevertheless, it implies some degree of segregation

*For the general treatment of social distance, see Chap. 15.

and creates a vicious circle of difference, avoidance, exclusion, accentuation of difference, increased avoidance, increased separation, and so on indefinitely. Isolation is in part an effect of competition and conflict among variant individuals and groups.

A concise analysis of the more important separative and isolative factors and processes follows.

The Isolative and Separative Factors

Before examining the isolative processes, it is essential that we become acquainted with some of the common factors that are conducive to the separation of individuals, categories of persons, and groups from each other.

Subsocial Separative Factors. The subsocial separative factors may be generally classified as geographic factors and human biological and psychological factors.

GEOGRAPHIC FACTORS. The physical or spatial separation imposed by geographic barriers and obstacles has had a marked isolative effect. Notable are the oceans and other large bodies of water, mountain ranges, desert regions and semiarid plains, tundras, swamp lands, and the very extent of physical space in general. The isolation of island folk and of such groups as the Cajuns of the Louisiana bayous and the hillbillies of the Appalachian and Arkansas mountains has produced not only physical separation but also cultural dissociation and retardation. Because of their isolation, many of these must, until recently, have been viewed culturally as the "contemporary ancestors" of the great body of those less isolated, to use Ross's trenchant phrase.

HUMAN BIOLOGICAL AND PSYCHOLOGICAL FACTORS. Such biological characteristics as sex, age, and race separate individuals and groups. The sexes are more or less mutually isolated, for differences in metabolic processes, physiological functions, and native interests stand as eternal barriers to full understanding. These constitutional differences are overlaid by conventional and traditional differences and historical definition of roles which in some respect increase the social and cultural isolation of the sexes.

People of different ages, by virtue of their varying physical proficiency, mobility, and psychological characteristics, and quite apart from the conventional roles which attach to different ages, are isolated from each other. Infants, adolescents, mature persons, and the aged in many respects live in worlds of different functions and interests. Similarly, race differences also isolate. The various marks of race, such as skin pigmentation, facial features, hair texture and color, and other physical characteristics, differentiate people and operate as barriers to communication and association. The greater the visible differences, the fewer the friendly contacts.

Individual differences in physical, sensory, mental, or other constitutional characteristics are often highly separative in effect. Sense defects, especially blindness and deafness, and physical defects, such as impairment or loss of limbs or organs and illness, often lead to isolation. The mentally deficient and those decidedly superior or mentally exceptional are separated from the mass of their fellows, as are the mentally ill and deranged. Mystics and creative persons are often isolated, lonely, and misunderstood.

Psychosocial and Cultural Factors. The great bulk of isolative factors, and by all odds the most significant, are of a psychosocial nature. Differenees in cultural traits especially are chasms across which social stimuli leap with difficulty. Groups develop different social heritages and sets of mores which produce different attitudes, different ways of acting, different social standards and outlooks. Every human group with unique cultural traits is in some measure isolated from all other groups; in fact, it fosters a system which promotes isolation. The more important of the cultural factors producing or aggravating social isolation will be briefly examined.

LANGUAGE DIFFERENCES AND SEMANTIC DIFFICULTIES. Language differences and the inability to use each other's writing systems most immediately and obviously act as barriers to interpersonal contact, communication, and cooperation. The existence of hundreds of languages and thousands of dialects in the world separates groups and peoples and makes sympathetic relations among them difficult and in some cases impossible. In the United States regional dialects separate many groups, and the foreign-language groups, as long as they retained their European or Asiatic languages, have been suspect and separated from the great body of those who spoke "United States."

Not only are people isolated by different language systems or subsystems, but because of various cultural differences there are semantic difficulties, that is, differences in meanings and appreciations of terms, different, separate and mutually incomprehensible "universes of discourse." Meaningful social symbols and images are differently interpreted by different groups; for example, adolescents and their elders, employers and workers, persons of different religious persuasions. One of the most tragic modern instances of semantic difficulty is the confusion about the term "democracy" on the part of the United States and the Soviet Union. The phrase of the cartoonist Briggs: "They don't speak our langwidge!" has point in innumerable communicative relationships.

These linguistic and semantic barriers make for misunderstanding, isolating the respective groups and often increasing the hostility between them. They also enter into most of the other isolative factors. (4, 35-36; 12; 47, 209)

THE VARIOUS ISOLATIVE CULTURAL DIVERSITIES OF GROUPS. A host of cultural diversities resting upon differences in educational development, moral practices, social and supernatural beliefs, institutional forms and other ways and peculiarities of groups need only be mentioned. *Educational differences* demonstrated in different levels of achievement or accomplishment, different standards and ideals, and different types of proficiencies acquired separate people. The preliterate, illiterate, and literate in many respects live in wholly different and mutually incomprehensible worlds. To a lesser degree, but still significantly, those who have had only an elementary education are poles apart from college graduates.

Different occupational groups, such as common laborers, merchants, ministers, mechanics, lawyers, farmers, chemists, classicists, fishermen, are isolated from each other. Specialists by the very fact of their specialization move in separate orbits. Differences in sex, marriage and family practices create emotional and actional barriers. Because of the Mormons' acceptance of polygamy, they were anathema to the great body of monogamists, and Catholics and most Protestants are apparently irreconcilably divided on the practice of contraception.

Religious differences divide people. Each sect believes itself possessed of the only "truth." Religious folk generally believe themselves superior to agnostics and atheists, and vice versa. Even within the same body of believers there may be sharp cleavage between fundamentalists and modernists. Congregationalists and Jehovah's Witnesses feel a wide gulf between themselves. The members of some sects, such as Mennonites and Seventh-Day Adventists, deliberately isolate themselves for reasons of preservation.

Economic differences in property and other forms of wealth, income level, standard of consumption and plane of living separate persons, categories, and groups. *Class and caste differences,* as noted repeatedly, are highly separative in nature. *Nationality differences,* resting often upon language and religious differences and differences in customs, mores, and institutional ways and frequently accentuated by discrimination and by voluntary or imposed "pocketing" of the alien or proscribed elements, are barriers to interaction.

Closely related to nationality differences are general *majority-minority group differences.* The minority groups characteristically are held in lower esteem and are debarred from certain opportunities or are otherwise excluded from full participation by the majority. The minorities often acquire a conception of themselves as inferiors, as outsiders, as persecuted groups. They develop protective and compensatory forms of action which isolate them still further. *Political differences* separate in some measure, as political parties try to produce diverse platforms and objectives, and the outs vie with the ins.

Ideological differences, whether of an ethical, religious, economic, or political nature, are separative. Nationalisms build up chauvinistic attitudes and haughty and exclusive behavior which deadens communication and cooperation. The followers of world religions and even their major subdivisions within themselves are monstrously separated. The proponents of democracy on the one hand and of communism, fascism, or other forms of totalitarianism on the other live in different worlds of values and purposes and actions.

SUBTLE INDIVIDUAL AND SOCIAL SITUATIONAL FACTORS. There are certain less obvious but nevertheless potent factors that produce isolation, especially of individuals. The *sentimental and emotional pro-*

tective attitude of one person or group toward another may isolate the object of the attention. Thus, an overanxious mother, in protecting and shielding her child from the cruel world, excludes it from many essential developmental contacts and experiences. The chivalrous attitudes of males toward females also has this effect.

Timidity or *bashfulness* makes it difficult for some persons to converse and associate with others, and to that extent they are isolated from group activity. *Mind set,* due to such situations as being poorly dressed, having some conspicuous physical peculiarity, being a member of some divergent ethnic or religious group, or being sensitive about a given name, frequently causes the individual to withdraw from possible contacts.

Prejudice and mutual distrust also isolate. Prejudice against members of other racial or nationality groups, other sex or age groups, other religions, castes, classes, or occupations operates generally to exclude persons from contact and experience. Closely related to this is the tendency of groups to distrust the members of other groups. These mutual suspicions are found in our society, for example, in the schisms between economic and political groups, especially the conservative-radical cleavage, between industrial, ethnic, and religious groups, especially Catholic-Protestant division.

Personal achievement often is an isolative factor. When a person achieves fame or high office, he is cut off from many of his former associations, or at least his contacts with others involve forms of vertical distance that did not formerly exist, as when a professor becomes a dean or a lawyer becomes a judge. Achievement also requires long and undivided attention to the job and thus isolates many from social diversions. Many successful persons develop a sense of exaltation and a certain aloofness which isolates them from the multitude.

The Isolative and Separative Processes

The more important isolative processes or phases of processes that have separative effects are all interrelated. They are, in fact, phases of an over-all process of segmentation occurring in modern societies. In their manifestations these processes cannot always be regarded solely in one category. Several of them, it will be noted, are also decadence-producing processes, and differentiation, for example, although mainly separative, also often produces some degree of disintegration.

Social Segmentation: The Over-All Separative Process. Social segmentation is the general process which breaks up categories of individuals and groups into separate segments, disrupting communication and free, wholesome, and essential social interaction, even though bringing about other desirable and socially necessary effects. It consists of numerous subprocesses, manifestations of which range from personal and involuntary or voluntary isolation, through the separations imposed by modern social trends and those inherent in a complex structural system like our own, to purposeful forms of discrimination and segregation devised and effected by majorities, governmental agents, or other powerful interest groups. The more important of these segmenting processes will be briefly presented.

Personal Separation. Human beings may be involuntarily or voluntarily separated from other human beings. As instances of *involuntary separation,* there are several fairly well authenticated cases of children who were lost or deserted at an early age and grew up as members of animal groups. Later they were found in a wild, or feral, state and returned to human society. When found, they were somewhat less than human, lacking the distinctly human characteristics. They were without language and unable to acquire much language skill, and their mental ability was arrested at a very low level. They lived a vegetative or animal existence, and their reactions were largely automatic. They were generally unconscious of self, lacked social feeling and social ways, were unresponsive to human stimuli, unsympathetic and humorless, and indifferent to social companionship. Even after their sojourn among human beings, they were unable to participate fully as human beings. (33; 35; 51; 53; 62)

The *voluntary isolation* of hermits, trappers, prospectors, sheepherders, and others often produces various forms of personality disorganization and social ineptness. Anchorites and religious mystics also retire voluntarily, as do some scholars and geniuses who wish to shut out the distractions of everyday living. In the latter case the individuals soon lose touch with the world about them, and they and their fellow men are the worse for it.

Atomization. The process of atomization, which is a phase of secularization to be discussed among the decadence-producing processes, in some of its aspects *converts individuals into social-psychologically and,* in some respects, *socially fragmented or fractionized creatures.* It is especially noticeable in modern complex, industrialized-urbanized, secondary-group societies. In such societies individuals, families, and other smaller groupings are separated in many of their interests and in many of the most humanly and socially meaningful contacts from the larger body of persons and are deprived of many of the most normal interactions.

Paradoxically, the very exercise of our heritage of personal freedom in our situation of intense interdependence and collectivization often pushes us into a state of personal and group isolation. As individuals and as members of many of our primary groups, we come to be more and more detached from others as the result of all of the varieties of mobility, industrialism, differentiation, specialization of interests and roles, bureaucratic organization of activities, and stratification. We participate in a formalized way in vast mass activities, acting for the most part as impersonal and anonymous integers.

Many—possibly the bulk—of our relationships do not rest upon the solid social-psychological base of face-to-face groupings, and consequently the fraternal and reciprocally stimulating and expression-satisfying boons of such relationships are lost. Many of us are lost and lonely in the "mass"—impersonal cogs or wheels in the vast machine.

Reference here is *not* to individualization or to the fine and essential combination of processes whereby the individual is built into a unique, well-developed, conforming, contributing personality *within* and *part of* the society of which he is a member. These processes produce a person who understands and reveres the social values and participates knowingly, responsively, and completely (see Chapter 4). This atomization process may be said to be synonymous with *individuation,* which tends to develop, usually through no fault of the individual himself, highly individualized and eccentric traits. It exalts self-interest, selfishness, and mainly personal utilitarian considerations and actions and tends to create or augment social ignorance, nonconformity, disregard, and irresponsibility.* As a result, the community or society tends to be atomized or splintered into countless more or less unconnected, unbalanced, and unresponsive individual fragments.

In a society suffering from such atomization, participation in community functions is more and more formal and often forced rather than informal and spontaneous; there is a deterioration of unity of interest; and an increasing number of divergent values as well as conflicts continually emerge. In general, the social organization assumes a more and more bewildering intricacy, segmentation, and compartmentalization. Certain other contributory processes accentuate the isolation and fractionizing of the individual and the segmentation of the society.

Differentiation and Specialization. Differentiation and specialization have been examined as structuralizing and functionalizing processes in a modern society. Invariably they go together; differentiation is specialization, and specialization in a society with a complex division of labor is a process of integration. As such, differentiation and specialization are essential and a great gain in societal operation. But the integration that they effect is limited to the conduct of the *specific tasks* which are differentiated and specialized. For the individuals and groups they have distinct separative aspects as processes. They break up the society into individuals and groups of people who are segmentalized by the functions of limited scope which they perform. Diverse interests and values grow out of these functions, however well placed the performers may be on the bases of capacity and training.

While the general undertaking, among many other contemporaneous ones, must be an over-all integration if it is to be efficient and successful, the differentiated and specialized parts are separate. Because of the very magnitude of the whole and

*A sort of continuum does exist, however, ranging from fine individualism at the one pole to isolative, separative, atomizing individuation at the other.

the intricate mechanical and formal nature of the whole, the persons performing the tiny and partial roles are segmented. The individual carries on a smaller and smaller part of a larger and larger operation. Usually he uses only a fragment of his potentialities and skills. The organization of the task is on such a vast scale, so complex and carried on so impersonally and mechanically and by such remote control, that the individual participant is hardly capable of comprehending his part in the whole undertaking.

Even if the individual participates in many different divisions of labor, they are not necessarily coordinated or harmonious with each other. Some of his tasks may require excessive devotion and concentration and produce great strain. The unbalanced and chance array of daily tasks may leave vast, frustrating gaps in his expressional life, and much of his life may lack sense and meaning. There is unavoidably a limiting of interests, a shortened perspective, and a narrowing of behavior. All this is socially and spiritually separative.

While modern technology and industrialism, for example, have standardized the product, they have almost incredibly multiplied the specialization of human functions, the division of labor, the variability of interests, and the extent of differences. This technological differentiation of human interests and functions has pulled us as individuals in many directions.

Physical and Social Mobility.* Both physical and social mobility function to locate individuals more effectively in space, among the differentiated social functions, and in the status hierarchy and as such they contribute to societal organization, order, maintenance and even reorganization. But they also facilitate atomization, segmentation, and antagonisms and contribute to both societal and individual disorganization.

In the stable society of immobile individuals everyone has permanency of both physical location and social position. People know each other intimately and have close and long-standing associates and friends; know, appreciate, and support the local values, customs, mores, and laws; persist in their jobs; have an established social reputation and position to maintain; are affected by and susceptible to public opinion, and in some degree participate in various community activities.

But *mobile* individuals are strangers, or temporary sojourners, wherever they are. They feel no definite attachment to their place of residence and participate in many, mainly heterogeneous, groups, shifting from one group to another. This makes identification with any one group difficult and transforms the individual from the component of a group to an individuated person. The possibility of developing satisfying, durable, personal intimacies and friendships is not great, and much shifting weakens the ties that bind persons to birthplace, kin group, or work comrades.

Mobile persons are not firmly founded in community interests and objectives and are indifferent or immune to the opinions of the members of the community. They do not know or care about the requirements of the customs and are only affected by the formal pressure of the law; Hence, they are often not well controlled. They have little desire for involvement in community affairs, and their presence in considerable numbers impairs community integration. The participants in much mobility are to a considerable extent not only socially, psychologically, and morally isolated, but also spiritually nomadic.

For the community as a whole much mobility contributes to the disintegration of the cultural pattern and leads to cultural incongruity. It makes for complexity in social relationships generally, disrupts the established relationships between the various groups and classes, encourages indifference to community affairs, and leads to the disintegration of conventional morals through the impaired inculcation of fixed habits and moral stability. The society itself tends to become a hodgepodge of superficiality and relativism. There is much social distraction and restlessness and a continuous struggle among individuals, groups, and factions. Authority is less effective. Such centrifugal tendencies do not favor social stability or continuity.

Finally, mobility not only atomizes individuals, it also contributes to personality confusion and disorganization and adds to mental strain. Widely circulating individuals show much skepticism and cynicism; they have fewer enthusiastic faiths, fewer firm convictions, more wavering belief in ideolo-

*Mobility as a structuralizing process was treated in Chap. 15. Its significance in societal maintenance will be examined in Chap. 21. Here we are concerned only with its disorganizing effects.

gies, more atrophy of moral sense. This disorganization among highly mobile persons is evidenced in disintegration of the family group, including increased divorce and desertion, crime and delinquency, "selfishness" as a personality trait, suicide, sexual irregularities, social insensitiveness, and in many other ways. (36; 40; 49, pp. 466-468; 54)

As the result of the processes of differentiation-specialization and of mobility, the relationships of human beings to each other are increasingly casual, superficial, formal, anonymous, routinized, contractual, transitory, impersonal, and the individuals perform as players of highly segmentalized roles. Similarly, modern societies, as Wirth puts it, are "splintered into countless fragments of atomized individuals and groups." (60)

Class and Organizational Stratification. The separation of the various levels of a caste system is obvious, but even an open-class system like our own, which has more or less vertical social mobility, tends to isolate the members of the different strata. They have relatively little free and spontaneous communication and contact with each other, and the interactions that they do have are largely formal and contractual. The members of the different levels live in different worlds of friendly assocation, different economic and cultural worlds, and often different political, moral, and religious worlds. They are, in fact, frequently uncomfortable in each other's presence because the distance is keenly felt. The different levels constitute essentially detached horizontal segments of the population with the differences in the social altitude maintained by well-fostered distinctions.

The very differences are the basis of misunderstanding, suspicion and distrust. The individuals and groups of lesser status resent and envy those on the higher levels. Usually, there is fear or surmise of injustice and exploitation.

If the stratification is excessive, the situation produces tension and frustration and usually leads to antagonism. Furthermore, the very efforts at equalization on the part of the lower strata, the existence of barriers to free mobility (for an open-class system never operates with complete efficiency), and always the possibility of some degree of discrimination and resistance by the superior or dominant arouse opposition. In the United States especially the competitive open-class system promotes ambition, but only a few can reach the high pinnacles. This condition intensifies the discontent of the many who fail. Almost all social situations involving social distance produce processes of both segmentation and opposition.

Previously we examined, as an agency of societal structuralization and functionalization, the hierarchically organized large-scale formal organization, more commonly referred to as a bureaucracy. The bureaucratic organization is a characteristic of our sort of functional society and absolutely essential in carrying on its large-scale tasks. Nevertheless, it has disorganizing features in its make-up and operation which lead to separation, decadence, and ossification. These will be examined briefly under the appropriate categories of processes. Since most of us belong to one or more bureaucracies—as subjects, employees, or members of the modern state, great corporations, large nation-wide or even world-wide universal churches, large labor unions or professional bodies, military bodies, universities or other educational or service agencies of various kinds—some knowledge of the processes of disorganization which are commonplace in them is essential.

Bureaucratic organization tends to produce considerable psychical and social, though not physical or functional, isolation and atomization among its constituent human beings. There is a clear-cut division and meticulous grading of roles, duties, and functions at each level of operation of the pyramidal structure, with standardized administrative procedures and formal rules and routines for each class of personnel.

There must be smooth flow of authority, social space between personnel levels, downward relaying of discipline, and specified and entrenched prerogatives for each level. These aspects are essential to division of labor and efficient operation of a vast mechanism, but they tend to atomize individuals and segmentalize the different levels. The organization makes for a depersonalization of relationships and the lumping of individuals, and the standardized rules and procedures usually offer very limited possibilities of individualized treatment of personnel. The relationships within the organization are mainly contractual and largely mechanical.

Bureaucracy is a vast secondary-group mechanism concerned primarily with its own maintenance and little with the congeniality or personality of members. Because of its fixed and routinized character, it usually frowns upon individual liberty of action, initiative, and innovation; hence, it corrupts character and engenders moral poverty. Because of its stratified nature, it unavoidably involves antipathies, discriminations, and varying emphases between the different levels, fosters caste prerogatives, and creates jealousy among the different levels.

In some bureaucracies transferance of persons to higher levels is blocked by requirements of special training which is acquired at a higher class level, and such blocking creates a feeling of resignation on the part of the individual in his fixed place and narrow function in the whole mechanism. In order to reduce competition, each jobholder tends to make his job as self-contained and independent as possible. In bureaucracies the individual is frequently a mechanical atom or cog, psychically, sociologically, and spiritually "dissociated" from his fellow constituents. Willard Waller aptly referred to bureaucracies, examined from this angle, as organizations "for the care of segregated persons."

Ethnocentrism, Group Discrimination, and Group Segregation. Finally, we are concerned with a basic group reaction and a combination of processes which flow out of, and in certain respects summarize, the previously examined separative factors and processes. Individuals and groups recognize the differences between themselves and other individuals and groups. More and more in a society like our own, there is a tendency for people to think of themselves in terms of the group they belong to, whether by virtue of fate or choice, rather than as individuals. More and more the groups are formed through multiple processes of selective inclusion and exclusion.

There has always been a tendency for each group to consider itself and its different values and ways of life as superior to, and hence distant from, other groups—a distance often studiously maintained. To maintain this superiority and exclusiveness, groups engage in a process directed against other groups known as *discrimination,* which leads to processes of social segregation. These processes come into effect (1) among minority groups or other inferiors or groups discriminated against as an in-group expression of congeniality and recognition of kind, interest, and condition and as a voluntary means of protection; (2) as a way on the part of majorities or superiors of imposing exclusion upon minority-group or inferior competitors; and (3) as a self-imposed way of facilitating the organization of special-interest groups, such as religious, educational, economic, fraternal, and convivial voluntary associations.

ETHNOCENTRISM. The basic factor in discrimination is ethnocentrism, "groupism," or group egotism, a social reaction as old as human groups. The tendency of members of every group to approve of and be loyal to each other, to consider each other good and the group superior, and especially to consider their own ways and values as ideal, right, proper, and sensible, while all others (outsiders) and their ways and values are inferior or wrong and, hence, deserving of fear, suspicion, hostility, and contempt, is elemental. Invariably, groups are culturally self-centered and self-satisfied, have an overweening belief in their own culture, are indifferent, or actively antagonistic to the cultural devices of others, and in some instances, have a powerful desire to force their culture on others. Such ethnocentric views and attitudes are supported by all manner of rationalizations, myths, and legends. Ethnocentrism is closely related to xenophobia, or the fear of the stranger; hence, the readiness to be suspicious of, or to hate, the stranger and, conversely, to feel secure and confident among persons who are known and familiar.

Ethnocentrism manifests itself in social groups of all kinds—families, local communities, occupational groups, races, nationality groups, and so on. It grows out of the competition and struggle for existence among groups in their various natural and especially social environments. They have developed ways and codes of life which experience has demonstrated to be effective in these processes. Their ways seem natural and right, and any deviation from them is regarded as unnatural and wrong.

The function of ethnocentrism, therefore, is to emphasize the aims, purposes, and interests held in common by the group; to maintain morale and discipline; to promote group solidarity and cohesion; and to achieve group security and survival. Every group enjoys (or suffers) a swollen ego, although this varies with the nature and momentary situation of the particular groups. Ethnocentrism flourishes, for example, when groups come into active conflict, as in the case of strikes or war. It is also enhanced when two divergent groups come into contact in large numbers; for example, anti-Semitism is probably keenest in the New York metropolitan area where nearly half of the Jews in the United States are located.

Ethnocentrism and social distance are closely related. As ethnocentric attitudes expand and grow, the distance between the groups involved also grows. Usually under such circumstances, groups are exceedingly concerned with maintaining the existing distances and, if possible, increasing them. Ethnocentrism breeds chauvinism, intolerance, prejudice, fear, efforts at acquisition of group power, discrimination, rejection, and, frequently, imposed segregation. (38; 44; 57)

Group Discrimination. Discrimination is one of the active processual expressions of ethnocentrism. The classic definition is that of Hankins: "the unequal treatment of equals, either by the bestowal of favors or the imposition of burdens." (37; see also 31; 48; 50) Although discrimination rests upon differentiation, its essence is the unequal or differential *treatment* by individuals and groups of other individuals and groups. Inherent in social discrimination are the unfairness, arbitrariness, injustice, disproportionateness, and prejudicial treatment of the members of the excluded dissimilar groups by the inclusive, usually majority, group or groups.

America's minorities—ethnic, linguistic, religious, cultural—are the victims of discriminating practices on the part of the majority. The exclusion may be unorganized, or it may be highly organized, even by law; but it is persistent, purposeful, and forceful and is intended to be hurtful, annoying, and vexatious. (42) It reflects disesteem of those against whom it is directed and prevents them from making their full contribution to the community.

One of the most striking instances of discrimination is the treatment of the Negro in the United States. It takes the form, in varying degree in different communities, of denial of the voting franchise, differential educational opportunities, refusal of necessary devices and services even if they can afford to pay for them, "Jim Crow" provisions in education, transportation, restaurants, theaters and other forms of recreation, denial of the right to affiliate with organizations such as churches, fraternal orders, and labor unions, and the denial of the right to be employed in certain vocations.

Usually, the discriminatory treatment of a group intensifies its sense of solidarity, invites antagonism, and often leads to efforts on the part of the group discriminated against to bring about equalization of treatment. The actual intensity of the discrimination, as practiced, is influenced by the intensity of the will to achieve, the emotions, and the aggressiveness of the actions of the objects of discrimination.

Group Segregation. The other major social process growing out of ethnocentrism is group segregation. Here reference is *not* to the subsocial process of ecological or spatial segregation of people, although ecological segregation is involved in some degree. Rather, we are concerned with the social process by means of which isolation of groups from each other and avoidance of groups by each other are established and maintained. The process grows out of group separation and creates social distance by actual physical separation as well as social, and interruption of communication, thereby preventing interaction. In brief, it is the ethnocentric congregating or grouping of people.

The bases of segregation are many—race, culture, religion, morals, social status, language, caste, class, wealth, physique and mentality, talent, and so on. Thus, in American cities we find many immigrant groups segregated on the bases of language and nationality; some on the basis of race; and others on the basis of wealth, morals, or social values; while criminals, delinquents, and defectives are segregated in institutions as a matter of public protection.

In the open country, there are groups, such as Mennonites, Hutterites, and Mormons, segregated to some extent on the basis of religion, and others, such as Indians, Mexicans, Swedes, Danes, Norwegians, and Dutch, segregated on the basis of race, language, or counry of origin. Always, however, the segregated groups are differently specialized from one point of view or another; they have common and compatible characteristics that differ from those of other segregated groups or the larger majority group.

The forces and factors that operate through the

segregating process may be most appropriately classified as positive and negative. The *positive—and sometimes passive—factors are those that bring members of the segregated group together.* Thus, mutual attractions, common interests, common hopes and fears, or special but similar needs operate positively to draw persons into segregated groups, even though not necessarily discriminated against by other groups. The members of artist colonies, religious colonies, immigrant colonies and ethnic groups often either unwittingly or voluntarily build up segregated communities. Among such withdrawn groups there may be the desire to perpetuate an actual or fancied purity of racial strain or to avoid cultural assimilation or contamination, the wish to maintain an accustomed existence free from the intrusion of strangers, the desire to avoid or limit competition or conflict, or the desire to maintain the group's feeling of exclusiveness and superiority.

The *negative and often most actively operating forces and factors are those which cause groups purposefully to set apart minorities or categories of persons.* These rest upon desired superior position on the part of superior or majority groups, who act because of their aversions, prejudices, hatreds, enmities, and fears of the minority groups, or because of their desire to protect themselves against some category of persons. Purposeful segregation may range from actively exercised discrimination, repression, and exploitation to such socially organized agencies as the law. For example, Jews, Mexicans, Japanese, and Negroes in many parts of the United States live in segregated communities, not so much by choice, but because they are excluded by opinion and custom from other areas. In some parts of the South, the Negro is still segregated by Jim Crow law; convicted criminals and committed defectives are segregated for the good of the general community; and in some cities the so-called "red light" district is still prescribed by ordinance.

Closely related to these forms of purposeful segregation are such procedures as ostracism, excommunication, exile, banishment, "transportation," imprisonment, and capital punishment, which are resorted to in order to exclude from the larger group elements that are thought to be grossly incompatible or dangerous. Like discrimination, however, segregation is more likely to be resorted to if the minority group is large or is an active competitor or antagonist and if it is characterized by readily distinguishable physical or cultural characteristics.

The usual effect of segregation is to widen the gulf between the segregated groups, thus reducing the social contacts, increasing mutual ignorance and suspicion, and decreasing mutual understanding, appreciation, and development of common interests. The result is a narrowing, stunting, in-turning, and separating effect upon all concerned, which invites various forms of opposition. (47, 225-227; 59)

Groups that adhere too closely to their ethnocentrism and practice discrimination and segregation may end up in social bankruptcy; for, although these forms of isolation, as many of the others, are means of avoiding conflict, they also invite it. The general effect is to destroy community.

CHAPTER XVII

OPPOSITION: FACTORS AND PROCESSES

THE OPPOSITION PROCESSES are ever-present, regularly recurring, and universal in the interactions of every society and are as natural as the processes of organization and cooperation. In fact, all human collective behavior may be viewed as set in the pattern either of cooperation or of opposition. Cooperation consists of joint action, often in the form of striving or struggling in company *with* other persons or groups to achieve some good, goal, or value, whereas various opposition processes involve some degree of striving or struggling *against* other individuals or groups for some good, goal, or value.

The opposition processes are related to the separative processes just discussed, both as conducive factors and as effects. In some of their phases and effects they may, in fact, be looked upon as additional special types of separative processes. However, the opposition processes, in addition to being separative, all tend, as part of the action, to obtain first, obtain more, withhold from, or take from some other individual or group some good and sought-after thing. In their more extreme forms they have the characteristic of attempting, usually consciously, deliberately, and aggressively, to hurt, weaken, coerce, dominate, eliminate, or destroy the opposing person or the other social group.

Ingredients of the Opposition Situation

Value Orientation of the Culture Area

Before examining the major categories of opposition processes, it is essential to have some conception of *the ingredients of the general opposition situation*. The various forms of opposition, ranging from mild to radical and violent, rest fundamentally upon the *value orientation of the culture area involved,* whether it be purely local, as in the case of some oppositions, or world-wide, as in others. Certain things or conditions of life and being are more or less specifically defined and are considered by large numbers of people to be valuable, desirable, useful, essential, or otherwise worth having. Basically, of course, all human beings have biogenic and psychogenic needs, with a host of attached social values, that must be met if they are to survive. Individuals and groups do not just turn up their toes and die without a struggle. They insist on food or a job; they must have self-esteem and rights.

Beyond these needs are the culturally determined values which condition needs, wants, and desires of persons and peoples as members of economic, political, religious, ethnic, and many other sorts of categories and groups. These values are the basis of various precious goals and objectives. These goals create "drives for satisfaction"; the "good things" are wished for, sought after, striven for, and, if necessary, fought for. Their achievement requires effort, often extreme and arduous individual and joint effort.

Scarcity of Good Things and Conditions

Good things and conditions are scarce. Whether natural or cultural in form, they do not exist in unlimited quantity or quality. There are always limitations of food and other material resources and of suitable standing room. For individuals there has never been enough of prestige, response, recognition, cultural refinements, opportunities, "rights," freedom, status, "glory," authority, office, political preferment, wealth, income, standard and plane of living, objects and amenities, or other top emoluments. Groups seemingly are always objecting to presumed limitations upon their activities in pursuit of ends and are never satisfied with their degree of security or dominance. Furthermore, as the successful opposing units satisfy their needs or desires, they reduce by that degree at any given time the possibility of other units satisfying similar needs and desires. The social units struggle to get what others want. Thus, few goals can be achieved in sufficient amount, and some individuals and groups cannot achieve some goals at all.

Blocking of Activity

The resultant deprivation or difficulty of attainment and the disruption of expectations lead to blocking of activity in the realization of the objectives. These blocked individuals or groups are energy systems. The inhibition of reaction patterns pressing for release sets up intense emotional feeling states in the form of myriad tensions, frustrations, and insecurities, which, in turn, lead to highly motivated action, often in the form of persistent, impelling, even aggressive effort.

Clash of Interests

These tension-resolving efforts produce *clash and cleavage of interests.* So many of the good things have to be attained, if they are attained, at the expense of others. Individuals and groups try to attain them by gaining more from the opponents or the blockers than they are forced to give. In the case of the milder forms of opposition, the clash is impersonal and is simply felt. In the more extreme forms, the clash is against designated persons or groups or against personalized social targets. Always the clash is intensified by existing prejudices, animosities, ethnocentricisms, discriminations, and segregations. Someone has said, "Long-standing animosities keep swords well sharpened."

Lack of Continuous Effective Equalization and Adjustment

Finally, the clash occurs and continues because *there is a lack of continuously operative and sufficiently effective equalizing and adjustive resources, attitudes, information, and mechanisms to maintain unity and cooperation.* The resources are not adequate to permit achievement of the goals. Obstructions to communication and ignorance of other people's legitimate needs prevent mutual understanding. The means of emphasizing common ends as against particular, concrete individual or group ends is lacking. People do not see that not everyone or anyone can have enough of anything. Socialization is inadequate. There is an absence of adjustive traditions and attitudes, conventions, regulations, and other mechanisms of social control. In brief, the social system does not have the means of forestalling or reducing opposition.

Both Organizing and Disorganizing Effects

At the very outset of the discussion of opposition processes, it should be pointed out that they have both organizing* and disintegrative effects upon a society. *The different forms of opposition in varying degree play a distinctive part in setting up, integrating, and maintaining a group or society.* When a group or society is in opposition to another group or society, it is motivated to action, often most arduous action. Furthermore, opposition tends to pull together the group, at least for the duration of action, and requires it to organize itself and coordinate its resources and elements. But, it must be emphasized that these motivating and integrating effects occur only *within* the various opposing groups when the opposition is directed against other groups.

The separative, disintegrative, disequilibrative, and destructive effects are more obvious and vastly more important from the point of view of societal maintenance. Both intragroup and intergroup opposition within a society threaten the necessary solidarity and continuity of the society by rending it into noncooperative, antagonistic individuals and groups. Opposition between nations and societies brings about in some degree universal destructuralization and defunctionalization and piles up debits and costs that often can never be paid off.

In the analysis of the opposition processes we shall distinguish between the less extreme forms and the more radically separative, disintegrative, and destructive forms. Thus, we shall examine, first, competition as the primary mild form. The more extreme and radical forms examined will be distinguished as contravention and conflict. In these latter, the opposition is conscious and is specifically and often violently directed against other persons or groups. The categories of opposition processes, like so many other functionally related processes, can be thought of as a continuum ranging from the mildest competitive striving at one end to the most vicious, violent, and mutually destructive conflict at the other.

The Competitive Processes

The Nature of Competition

Competition among human beings is that elementary, universal, and continuous process of peaceful contest between individuals and groups as they pursue simultaneously commonly appreciated and commonly sought, but scarce, ends. In its ideal-typical form it is a mild type of opposition. The individual or group simply endeavors to outdo or get ahead of the competitor in achieving some mutually desired goal. In competition the efforts to attain goals usually run along parallel lines; the competitors do the same things, but the successful performer does what is necessary first or better. The efforts are not coercive or antagonistic, as compared with the other major forms of opposition; the objective is not to prevent the use of scarce goods or to put out of the running or to destroy the other person or group, but to obtain possession or use or control of the good thing for self. The direct aim is the success of the actor. Hence, competitive action is a race, not a fight.

Jessie Bernard has pointed out (16, p. 84) that competition is essentially a *form of testing* individuals and groups; that is, testing them as they interact with each other, with their respective unequal abilities and opportunities, to achieve necessary or desired material things, spatial location, mates and posterity, cultural refinements, opportunities and, perhaps most significant of all, to preserve or improve their position in the community or the societal system with all that that implies in the way of status, roles, prestige, esteem, and social power.

In its most far-reaching manifestations, competition is largely an indirect, impersonal, and unemo-

*These have already been examined briefly in Chapter 10.

tional form of interaction. In many of its forms it takes place without social contact. The competitors do not meet and are mostly unconscious of each other as contestants and are unaware that their success limits in any way the opportunities of others. If they do meet, they do not always identify each other as competitors. The relations are external, and the communication, if any, is by remote control. In competitive situations the attention of the active performers is focused on the reward.

The competitors may, in fact, be far removed from each other in space, as for example, graduate students competing for university fellowships, the wheat farmers of the world competing in the world markets, and so on. And yet, in most societies, men are aware that their abilities to survive and flourish are being tested by others, even though they cannot be named or located. At least, competition is always present as the egos vie with each other, for ego-vying is part of the process of personality maintenance.

Although competition is present in relatively static societies, its volume and the multiplicity of its forms are greatest in rapidly changing, mobile, rich, heterogeneous, specialized societies with differential opportunities, advanced technology, and complex societal organization. In our culture it is especially noticed and emphasized in the world of economic affairs as persons and groups compete in occupations and for wealth and standard of living elements and businesses compete for markets.

Competition is in fact present everywhere: in political life; in education as students compete for honors and teachers for salary advances, promotion, and professional standing; in class organization as individuals and families strive for higher status; in religious sects and church congregations, racial and cultural groups, communities, recreation and all expressional activities; and even in the family as children vie for parental recognition or favor. It occurs wherever there is the possibility of differential response, recognition, position, and limited reward. In our culture competition is in the mores.

The Major Categories of Competition

The forms of competition may be classified as personal and organizational-institutional.

Personal Competition. Person-to-person competition is the contention between persons for recognition, response, role preferment, security, and approval of fellows in all of the value-dominated areas of interactional life. Among us it is especially a way of acquiring status when status is a matter of achievement rather than ascription. Much of the economic, political, educational, and even sport activity of individuals is competition for status. This interpersonal competition may be intimate and direct, as when children in a family vie for parental recognition and favor, or it may be highly impersonal and indirect, yet interpersonal, as when the wheat farmers of the world compete, or when individuals compete in the form of generalized rivalry for economic goods, official recognition, or class standing.

Organizational-Institutional Competition. Organizational-institutional competition is the contention of institutionalized organizations of all kinds —economic, political, religious, educational, and so on—for common, established, and generally approved social ends. This competition takes several forms. It may be *intra-institutional,* that is, between institutionalized groups and associations within a given institutional field, such as between families, between corporations, political parties, rival schools of art, and so on, as they compete for various kinds of prizes related to their functional objectives.

Competition may be *"cross-field," or interinstitutional, competition* (as Ross called it), that is, between institutional organizations in different institutional fields, such as that between church and state or between the family and such organizations as the Boy Scouts, the religious denomination, and various recreational agencies as these vie for the free time of the children. It may be intercommunity, such as that between cities, states, regions, and nations as they compete for resources, industries, population, and political preferments.

The Place of the Rules

Within a given society most of the standard competition is subjected to controls or rules, which operate to restrict within certain limits the nature and scope of the competitive activities. These rules are both informal and formal, or institutionalized. They are found in regulations, taboos, laws, ethical codes (written and unwritten), and in agreements for business, games, professions, and social conduct generally. What is deemed proper or improper is usually fairly clear. Always the prime effort is to keep competition fair; for when it ceases to be fair, it ceases to be competition.

The Social Effects of Competition

The social effects of competition may be classified as organizational, separative, and deteriorative. As a process which, in certain of its manifestations, makes for *societal organization,* it motivates persons and groups to useful social action and stimulates the efforts of people. (23, pp. 204-209) Jessie Bernard refers to it as a "tremendous dynamo." (16) When it is fair, it makes for the best and selects the best. It produces physical mobility of persons and groups, distributes and locates them in space, and tends to create an equilibrium between people, resources, and standing room. If it is relatively free, it assigns people fairly accurately to their niche in the social system, including their appropriate location in the hierarchical status system.

In this latter aspect, competition also makes for essential differentiation, division of labor, almost all forms of individual, group, and institutional specialization of function. Within groups competing with other groups it tends to knit the members together and increase solidarity. Under conditions of fairness and adequate regulation, these combined effects tend to produce an automatic societal integration and to enhance societal functioning.

But at the same time, even though competition is fair and controlled, in these same manifestations it is somewhat *separative.* It often interferes with cooperation and may obstruct or destroy it. Fundamentally, in its interpersonal forms, competition is an individuating process, in that it tends to dissolve people into separate, vying and striving elements. In its ecological aspects it scatters individuals, families, and other groups, and breaks down existing community cohesiveness. It produces selective residential and institutional concentration and is an important factor in the territorial segregation of people, with the consequent breakdown of communication and free association. As it conduces to economic specialization, at the same time it separates people into vocations and special-interest groups. As it selects people for a given status position and locates them in the open-class system, it isolates them socially. In general, separation is inherent in competition, since the competitive success of one element always shuts out the others from the same advantage.

Finally, competition has *personally and socially deteriorative effects* because it so readily degenerates into disintegrative processes. While it stimulates and incites ambition, it also overstimulates and leads to restlessness, strain, and exhaustion. When intense, it fosters insecurity, has bad psychological effects (for example, the well-known occupational ailment of American professional men—stomach ulcers), and is a factor in personality disorganization. To avoid the costs of strain and the rigorous expenditure of energy and effort in attempting to achieve security, individuals and groups make efforts to circumvent competition, grab opportunity, and erect barriers to its free operation. Business and industrial concerns seek monopoly, make restricting agreements with each other, maneuver for tariff barriers, seek to buy out or absorb the competitor, and occasionally engage in unfair and even fraudulent practices. Labor organizations frequently limit membership and try to obtain closed-shop agreements; religious sects resort to unethical proselyting procedures; political factions make deals with each other; ethnic and culture groups and social classes practice discrimination, create handicaps, and try to effect segregation of competing groups. Nowhere do we find people submitting themselves to complete competition if they can help it.

When competition becomes personal and highly conscious or when the opponent group is identified, especially in uncontrolled or inadequately safeguarded competition, there is the unavoidable tendency for it to degenerate into a form of conflict. The situation is affected by suspicion, mistrust, disgust, repugnance, and hate, and there is always the possibility of competition deteriorating into some more extreme form of opposition. There is then the effort, not to emulate or excel, but to intimidate, eliminate, or destroy.

Contravention Processes

Nature of Contravention Processes

Accurate and adequate taxonomy requires the introduction of a category of opposition processes intermediate between competition and conflict. These are the *contravention processes.* They are more extreme forms of opposition than competition in its ideal-typical aspects, but less severe and more uncertain as to the mode and extent of the antagonism than the conflict processes.

They are the processes involved when segments of a society that are unavoidably interrelated and utterly indispensable to each other in pursuit of common or joint goals, not only vie with and oppose each other, but also, on occasion at least, mildly intimidate and dominate each other. The parties or segments have interdependent functions and are jointly essential to the fundamental situation. The opposing elements frequently cannot get along *with* each other, and they cannot get along *without* each other. Much of the time they want each other. Each side exercises restraint lest the essential relationship be disrupted.

In contravention there is doubt or mental reserve about the willingness of the other person, category, or group to cooperate freely, even along essential lines. Each side, for various reasons depending upon the diverse life orientations, functions, convictions, interests, temperaments, and objectives may have different and occasionally diametrically opposed conceptions of the essential lines of interdependent or joint action. Hence, the emotions, involved are exasperation, dislike, pique, aversion, resentment. Most of the time, though, there may seem to be rapport or at least rather freely given tolerance, and the enmity and antagonism are wholly or partially latent and usually disguised. For example, the young without the old would no longer be able to perform typically as the young; the male without a wife is no longer a husband; country without city has no markets; workers without employers have no jobs.

In actual practice, contravention, like competition, seldom occurs in clear-cut, ideal-typical form. It easily deteriorates into conflict and frequently involves some degree of violence. In particular oppositional areas, contravention situations will include both competitive and conflict forms of interaction. It is always difficult to place common or recurrent forms of opposition fully and solely in any one of the categories of competition, contravention, or conflict. Hence,. any effort at categorizing is on the basis of the modal characteristics.

Major Forms of Contravention

Contravention processes appear in several well-known and easily recognized forms.

Sex Contravention. The sexes, frequently in their particular personal relations and generally as separate categories of persons, oppose each other. Some of the closest and most abiding relationships occur between individual men and women; yet there is continual group antagonism. The fundamental differentiation of the sexes, anatomically and psychologically, and the notable physiological and temperamental differences are factors which have played a part in the basic social division of labor between the sexes and in the traditional roles of each sex. The female is relatively helpless during her periods of gestation and preoccupation with the care of small children, while at the same time there is the necessity of the physiologically freer adult male to engage in economic, protective, and aggressive activities. This has created the basic division of labor. The elemental biogenic and psychogenic differences and the primary division of labor have been overlaid by all manner of cultural factors which have tended to accentuate these differences. Males have arrogated to themselves various kinds of superiorities, status positions, and privileges.

The contravention takes the form of the vying of the sexes with each other for social participation, especially an effort of each sex to achieve authority over the other. Males have sought to maintain and enhance their prestige, privilege, and authority usually by many subtle and sublimated procedures: house segregation of females by differential social codes, including especially taboos along moral lines (for example, the double standard); illusory chivalry; emphasis on the illusion of inefficiency of females along occupational, political, and military lines; sumptuary (for example, dress) and legal distinctions and discriminations. Because of their higher death rates at all ages in almost all known settled and stabilized societies, men have usually been numerically fewer and thus have a certain scarcity value.

To advance their own well-being, females have successfully used sex wiles, cajolery, flattery, craft, and finesse and in recent times have made direct demands for social, cultural, economic, and political equality. In our society the chief points of contravention between the sexes center around the demands of women for the ballot and full participation in citizenship, equal property and contract rights, equal educational and occupational opportunities, and a single standard of morals.

Sex contravention does not become very intense or engulfing as a form of conflict. The opponents cannot work up such strong antagonistic feelings, for the sexes are always cross-linked by countless personal and family ties. Furthermore, there are always women who uphold male dominance, and men who stand up for women's rights. The sexes have more in common than of a divisive nature. Nevertheless, while the sexes are utterly dependent upon each other physically, psychologically, and socially, they are always in some degree dissociated from each other. They never quite understand each other and never see fully eye to eye. Even well-mated husbands and wives have some dubiousness and uncertainty about each other.

Contravention between the Age Groups. Contravention between the age groups is one of the oldest and most persistent patterns of opposition in the history of human societies. Although it has not always been as overt and obvious as it is in our society, it has always existed. The differentiation of the population by stages of physiological development is involved to some extent. Primarily, however, the opposition is of a psychosocial and cultural nature and develops out of the differential roles, statuses, and privileges which society has set up and which are supposedly appropriate to these age categories. The contravention shows itself at two levels: that between children in a limited way, but especially during adolescence in a dynamic way, versus *all* elders; and the more subtle, but more far-reaching, opposition between younger adults and the older adults for the control of society.

When children become socially awakened, and especially in the chaotic period of physical, mental, temperamental, and social transition from childhood to maturity, they are restive under the guidance, discipline, restraint, and punishment imposed by elders, whether parents, teachers, priests, or public agents. This restraint frequently merges into general opposition to, and revolt against, adults as an impersonal, collective body. The young see the older persons of the group as a body which manipulates a complicated order of objects and rules and repressions which interfere with their spontaneous tendencies and valuations. (32; 33)

This level of contravention is strikingly manifest in the interactions of children and parents within the family. Although the children are utterly dependent upon the parents and there are ties of sympathy and even respect, the children, nevertheless, are restive under parental supervision and even in the presence of parents. At least latent hostility is a continual possibility. Nimkoff points out that the constant contact constitutes a source of irritability and tension. Added to this is the unavoidable superior-inferior relationship, with its inequality of action and status in which the parent exercises dominance as he meets his responsibility in bringing the child's impulses into conformity with the society's culture. The child identifies the parent as the source of social constraint and reacts against him. (26; 27) Adolescents especially show this hostility. The father is constructed as the major symbol of authority and restraint, but both parents are agents which stifle the powers of decision and initiative. The wisdom of the parents is doubted, and they are labeled "old fogies."

The opposition is inevitable, since the categories have different outlooks on life. The youths are not fully participant members of society, for although physically strong, they are mentally immature and lack social experience. Yet, they feel the urge to independent action and decision. Frequently, they rebel against the folkways, mores, and institutional practices of their society. Nevertheless, the older generations need to restrain and control the aims, ambitions, and actions of youth in the interest of maintaining the established order.

The second level of age-group contravention is less dramatic and obvious. Deep below the surface there goes on the incessant struggle between the younger adults and the older adults for dominance and for control of the social machinery. The "young" in this arena of opposition may be viewed in our society, as those between eighteen and forty; the "old" as those over fifty; those in their forties are in an amorphous, transitional state—attitudinally neither young nor old. (29) At this level the opposition is noticeable in the areas of politics, religion, education, and economic activity; in fact, in practically every institutional field. The young and the old differ in aptitudes and in major objectives. The *young seek opportunity*; they are interested in whatever enables them to get on, to achieve, to install themselves socially. They want occupation, wealth, social position, recognition, responsibility, and success, and they clamor for open doors and seek adventure. On the other hand, the *old seek security and establishment*; they fear being brushed aside. They want to hold on to their authority and presumed superiority in policy-making and their power over organizations and institutions, which are for them vested interests usually developed and buttressed by organized society. They want to maintain the status quo. (28)

This struggle between old and young persists in government, political parties, the church, business, commercial, and industrial organizations, the army and navy, universities, and the professions. The young feel unnecessarily dominated and blocked by the old and are irritated by the smugness, realism, conservatism, or reactionism of the old. On the other hand, the old are exasperated and disturbed by the brashness and disrespect, the radicalism, fool-hardiness, and inconsiderateness of the young. Thus, we have the contravention between father and adult son, between the chairman of the board and the junior vice president, between the Senior Chamber of Commerce and the Junior Chamber of Commerce, between members of the senior Republican Party and the Young Republicans. Although the relationships are intimate and the sympathy, agreement upon valued aims, and recognition of identity of basic interests are profound, opposition is inevitable. (29) The opposition is not conflict, but rather a sort of factional opposition. It is seldom intense and usually veiled. Both age and sex opposition are not likely to be vigorous, because the parties represent deep and abiding bases of cooperation; and the opposition is always hedged about by numerous and strong counteractants.

Other Forms of Contravention. Aspects of contravention are found in such oppositions as occur within communities, between country and city, between sections of a country, between buyers and sellers, between consumers and producers, between elements within parliamentary bodies, between labor and management, between educated and less educated, between majorities and minorities. However, sooner or later, these almost always take on the characteristics of conflict and will be examined as such.

Conflict Processes

General Nature of Conflict

The conflict processes mainly derive from the deterioration of competition and contravention as forms of opposition. The appearance of conflict implies, among other conditions, the absence of harmless outlets for oppositional impulses, but especially the breakdown of societal regulation and maintenance as equilibrative factors. When competition becomes a conscious personal or personalized, antagonistic process, it passes over into the area of conflict; when the joint goal is lost sight of and the parties go beyond exasperation to efforts at elimination, contravention becomes conflict. Conflict is always a fight for power, for dominance, for supremacy, for the ability to determine policy, to control, to achieve the universal adoption of ideas, beliefs, ways, and ends. As each contestant attempts to preserve, to save, to gain, even to augment, what he considers most worth while at the time and in the situation, he exercises eliminative action against the other. Conflict focuses attention directly upon the opposition as well as upon the goal.

Conflict is universal and pervasive. A certain amount of it is always present, though its volume and intensity vary from time to time and from situation to situation. It seems to have increased, however, in recent times. The incredible increase in contacts in modern society between heterogeneous cultural elements and interest groups through travel, migration, trade, and war, the multiplication of lines of cleavage involving social differentiation and stratification, and the increasing emphasis upon the distributive rewards of wealth, freedom of thought and action, power, prestige, status, or other scarce values have doubtless been primary factors. Everywhere in the world today, we have an intensification of economic, ethnic, class, cultural, religious, and national conflicts. Everywhere there is impaired participation of subpopulations of various kinds.

Ideal-Typical Characteristics of Conflict

Conflict may be analyzed as having certain inherent elements that distinguish it from other oppositional processes.

Antagonists, Whether Persons or Groups, Specifically Identified. Whereas competition is largely unconscious and impersonal, conflict is highly conscious and personal. The opponent is known, hated and feared. When the opponent is a group, it is frequently personalized by some epithet in order to focus antipathy, since it is difficult to hate an abstract group.

Mutually Exclusive Ends of Each Contesting Element Consciously Maintained and Accentuated. In a conflict situation there is fundamental clash of interests, wishes, wills, values, objectives, and interpretations of security and welfare. These interests and objectives are viewed by the opponents as distinctly and diametrically opposed, incompatible, incongruous, and irreconcilable. Each side views the other's objectives as direct impediments or threats to its own security and well-being; hence, each side seeks to have its interests and values prevail over all others. Conflict is an aggressive effort to fulfill needs and desires and achieve insistently adhered to ends. The aims of one party, seemingly, can only be realized at the expense of the other party.

Attempts of Each Side to Remove the Other from the Social Arena. The clash of interests can be resolved only by neutralizing the opponent. In some instances, this can be carried on by nonviolent means in the form of vituperation, accusation, or threats. Usually, however, it eventually takes the form of force, including violence. The enemy is defeated in every possible way. He is subordinated and subjugated; coerced, for example, by purges and pogroms; removed from the scene by imprisonment, residential segregation, exile, banishment, or excommunication; made powerless by conquest or absorption; injured as much as possible. In extremity, an attempt is made to destroy him utterly. The destruction, of course, is not necessarily physical, but may take the form of attempting to destroy his prestige, social status, reputation, and so on.

Intermittent Character. In contrast to competition, which is continuous, conflict, that is, any particular instance of it, is of necessity temporary or intermittent and recurrent in character. This lack of continuity is due to several factors. First, conflict evokes the deepest emotions and strongest passions and enlists the greatest concentration of attention. Such emotional tension and concentration of attention cannot long be maintained. Second, it involves a great expenditure of physical, temperamental, and mental energies in all its forms and, in addition, in its group forms, a vast utilization of physical, cultural, organizational, and technological resources, none of which exists or can be produced in unlimited amounts. Furthermore, in the very process of conflict, these resources are consumed and destroyed in a tragic manner and at a great rate. Conflict is always an outpouring of vital individual and social energies and materials, which sooner or later leads to exhaustion, and one or both sides have to stop and catch up. Of necessity, it is short-lived.

Ideal-Typical Stages of Conflict Process

Conflict as a process is a matter of stages. (41; 46) *Contact* and *communication* are indispensable initial interactional conditions, and *visibility* is essential to the identification of the potential opponent. In the course of interaction with the contacted persons and groups, *differences* will *emerge*. With *awareness of differences* comes the development of fear, frustration, and attitudes of hostility, as the differences become a threat to security of subsistence or status. The *exclusive and irreconcilable nature* of the differences must be accepted. *Hostility* must be *fixed* upon the specific individuals, categories of persons, or groups who act upon the basis of the irreconcilably different views and values.

Once hostility is fixed, the *decision is made to attempt to eliminate or subjugate the opposition.* Action calculated to realize the eliminative objective must be determined and carried out. Defeat of one and *victory* for the other or a *temporary truce* or stalemate until one side again resumes aggression must be the outcome of the conflict. As a result of the conflict, some *efforts at accommodation* are usually made by the contestants or by a third party.

Variations in the Forms of Conflict

The forms of conflict may be distinguished, in a general way, from the point of view of the persons or collectivities involved, its nonviolent or violent nature, and its covert or overt nature.

Persons and Collectivities Involved in Conflicts. Conflict may take any one of several forms: between individuals, as in an acrimonious argument or a fist fight; between groups and individuals or mere categories of individuals, as in the police offensive against lawbreakers; between individuals or factions of individuals within the same group, institution, or institutionalized organization, as within a family, a religious congregation, or a political party. It may also occur among larger units as between groups within a community or society, such as rival unions, workers and employers, or ethnic groups; between nations and societies, as in the case of international war; or between the individual and group members of societal systems organized around widely held ideologies, as in the struggle between democracy and totalitarianism or free-enterprise capitalism and communism.

Nonviolent and Violent Conflict. Not all confliet is violent. Nonviolent conflict consists in the struggle of differing theories, ideas, beliefs, values, mores, and all manner of culture patterns. It is usually pervasive and unspectacular, though persistent, and out of it, in any given community where it occurs, comes the selection, dominance, or blending of culture elements. Usually, however, it invites some use of force, since the struggle cannot be confined to the opposition between the culture forms or culture objects as such. Usually too it involves the individuals and groups which are the carriers and proponents of the culture forms, even though of an abstract nature. (89)

Violent conflict is what most people have in mind when they conceptualize conflict, and most conflict *is* violent in greater or lesser degree. It involves accusation, argument, pressure, and attack as the effort is made to dominate, exclude, or destroy the opponent.

Covert and Overt Conflict. Conflict is not always face-to-face with other persons or groups or directed openly against them. Some of it is covert, that is, surreptitious and undercover. It seeks to undermine the opponent by remote and roundabout means, such as whispering campaigns or quiet discrimination and ignoring. Overt conflict, of course, is the toe-to-toe slugging match out in the open with its direct action against the opponent through violence or threat of violence.

The Functional Effects of Conflict

The functional effects of conflict may be reduced to three forms.

Relief of the Opposing Situation. The ultimate function of conflict is *to relieve the thwarting situation and resolve the issue at stake* in the confused and antagonistic relationships between individuals, between individuals and groups, and between groups. If it results in victory for one side, it in some degree liquidates the accumulated tensions and reduces the social friction by subjugating the enemy or forcing him to acknowledge defeat or eliminating him altogether.

In a sense, conflict is a readjustive process which establishes a new level of routine. After recovery from the exhaustion, the victors at least are free to devote their energies, capabilities, and resources to other ends. The defeated, of course, may have been incorporated as subject elements or may have disintegrated entirely. If not, they must make strenuous efforts to re-establish themselves if they are to survive.

Whether the conflict will end in adjustment or will continue until one or the other of the combatants is disposed of depends on the nature of the arena, as Ross has pointed out. (43, pp. 195-196) If the struggle takes place, as it were, *in a bowl,* which has a concave form, then the farther the stronger pushes the weaker, the harder it is to make him yield. In the case of a well-matched union and corporation, the harder the union presses the corporation, the greater the number of propositions the corporation must prepare itself to meet. As an invading army penetrates the enemy territory, it has longer lines of communication and supply that must be protected, and the enemy offers greater and more effective resistance.

On the other hand, if the struggle takes place *on an inverted bowl,* the situation, instead of stabilizing itself, makes for the rapid defeat of the weaker. For the farther the stronger pushes, the more rapidly is the weaker forced to yield still more ground. Often, for example, as a corporation becomes larger and stronger, its so-called smaller competitors find it more and more difficult to contend and are forced to submit to absorption or be eliminated.

A fundamental question is whether or not other better disciplined and more effective adjudicating and regulatory process for the resolving of tensions, difficulties, and the thrusting and resisting of wills and philosophies can be devised and utilized to take the place of conflict.

Internal Organizing Effects. Temporarily, at least, as conflict is anticipated and engaged in during its earlier stages, *it has organizing effects within the individuals and groups involved.* Within the individuals involved, it produces enhanced self-consciousness and performs an organizing role in their lives in that they must "pull themselves together" if they are to contend effectively. It also increases the self-consciousness of the groups involved, clarifies motives, facilitates leadership and division of labor, and is highly important in fostering morale both in primary and in secondary groupings. It brings about a greater degree of integration and consolidation within the contending groups and produces we-group unity and in-group solidarity. Such in-group differences and antagonisms as exist are translated into out-group hostility and combative action. The more severe the conflict, the less will groups tolerate difference of interests or attitudes or divergent or nonessential activities among members. But this greater individual and intragroup consciousness and organization merely accentuates the general state of dissociation.

Mutually and Socially Destructive Effects. In the long run, *conflict is mutually and socially destructive.* Fundamentally, it is a process of social breakdown and disorganization in any area of social life in which it occurs. It usually creates myriad new tensions and frictions in place of those that it has temporarily resolved. It engenders hate, discord, and prejudice, engulfs people in new frustration and in defeat, perpetuates and strengthens suspicions and antipathies, and misdirects and wastes human and social energy and resources. It divides the people, prevents or destroys social cohesion and cooperation, and disrupts the current social equilibrium. Rarely is anything permanently settled. The margin of superiority is usually only momentary. The costs are always greater than were expected and may be suffered for a very long time after the active conflict has been resolved. Both the winner and the loser lose in the end. Often conflict inaugurates a whole train of new conflicts.

Important Contemporary Forms of Conflict

Although conflict is omnipresent and universal, at any given time in any given society, it is particularly likely and particularly acute in certain areas of social relationships. The more important current forms in our society will be briefly examined.

Economic Conflict. Because economic interests and services are related to scarcities and to those things which some have and others wish to acquire, they create a fertile field for conflict. As consumers or buying customers, producers or sellers, workers, employers, landlords, tenants, stockholders, and so on, all of us are involved in a bewilderingly complicated criss-cross of contentious economic relationships.

Consumers versus Producers; Buyers versus Sellers. As consumers of commodities, housing, and services and as users of loanable funds, we are arrayed against those of us who produce or make available these essential things. Although this conflict usually is not very dramatic or highly overt in its expression, it exists continually and occasionally flares up and gains widespread attention. The consumer-buyers want cheaper, better, and more abundant commodities and services; and the producers and sellers wish to make a profit—in fact, they must if they are to survive. The consumers are thwarted and irritated by various actions of the producers and wish to prevent reduction of quality, sharp trading practices, restriction of output to create scarcity, monopolistic practices, misleading advertising, and reduction of services.

The producers and sellers seek their own protection and advantage by trying to obtain permissive monopolistic legislation, protective tariff barriers, price supports, special trading facilities, and so on, which redound to their own advantage, but to the disadvantage of the consumers and buyers. The issues are fought out by means of buyers' strikes, publicity, propaganda, occasional social movements, and litigations, but mainly through efforts to control legislation affecting the matters in point. (47)

Workers versus Employers. The conflict between workers and employers has existed ever since some persons have had to work for others. In our society the alignment of contestants takes the form of the great mass of workers, unskilled and skilled, organized and unorganized, on one side and the capitalistic, entrepreneurial, management groups, mostly in the form of corporations, on the other. The workers are concerned with wages, hours, job tenure and security, work-place conditions, bases of promotion, principles and rules of hiring and discharge, discipline, recognition, and so on.

The employers or managers are responsible for production; efficiency and output are their goal. They must make as much profit as possible for the stockholders, and as they fulfill their obligations to customers, they must try to control labor conditions as well as possible. "Management would like to treat its labor force as it treats its physical plant: as a means of production, flexible, pliant, and docile." (47, p. 296) But labor wants to be treated as a human end in itself and increasingly wants, not only its share of the proceeds of industry, but also a part in the formulation of management policy. Basically the struggle is for economic rights in labor-management relations. These are the fundamental general bases for the conflict of interests.

The techniques of conflict are characterized by the usual efforts at injury, elimination, destruction, and in many instances they involve force. The force frequently degenerates into violence, because of the provocative nature of the circumstances. Both sides do whatever they can to embarrass, discredit, weaken, or destroy the opponent. The concrete situation develops in sequence from the mutual sources of irritation, apprehension, tension, and chronic discontent to open conflict, consisting of active combative campaigns against the other side. The conflict inflicts great strain on the social system. It may tear communities wide open, and occasionally it results in paralysis.

The public usually takes sides in the conflict. The business and professional classes and most of the farmers are on the side of management, and the great body of workers on the side of labor.

Class Conflict. Class conflict is one of the destructuralizing and defunctionalizing characteristics and by-products of societal differentiation and stratification. Conflict occurs both between classes and within classes.

Interclass Conflict. The struggle *between* classes has taken various forms historically, depending upon the nature and rigidity of the given class structure. Economic distress of the lower classes has occasionally been proffered as the primary factor; but many other factors have entered in. The crux of the conflict between classes is the fact that one class holds itself superior and tries in its own interest to dominate the lower classes. Usually also, this dominant group tries to maintain and extend its own opportunities by exploiting the lower classes. The dominated and exploited classes, generally more or less underprivileged economically, politically, and culturally, become conscious of this inferior situation and strive to liberate themselves. They do this by attempts to subjugate, destroy, reduce, or replace in power, prestige, opportunity, and position the higher strata; at the same time the upper classes resist this pressure by various means, some of them artfully contrived. The interests *may be* religious, political, cultural, or economic advantage; they *always are* related to the struggle for status: the struggle for the achievement and exercise of the rights, privileges, prestige, and power that inhere in the given class structure.

The very processes that produce classes tend to create the conditions and occasions for conflict between classes. Usually, also, there are inequalities of educational and cultural opportunity and achievement, of working and wealth-acquiring opportunities, of income and standard of living, of political opportunity and power, of leisure time and recreational facilities, of health and legal protection. Often there are differences in language, religion, race, and nationality. *All these conditions conduce to invidious comparisons, create dissatisfaction and tensions on the part of the levels with the going system of positions, and accentuate antagonisms.* Always class struggle is struggle between levels of the social hierarchy.

The struggle is not between the classes as such, for they, after all, are indistinct and amorphous categories. It is carried on by ideological groups in the form of parties, cliques, sects, reformist organizations, labor organizations, and other groups, which are wholly or in part initiated and maintained to carry on the struggle. (59) The actual efforts of these groups to effect a change in the *status quo* may range from minor reforms to revolutionary movements designed to change the entire social structure.

The *intensity* of interclass conflict depends in part upon the range and depth of interests involved and in part upon the nature of the particular social terrain in which it occurs. The interests may be numerous and due not only to economic exploitation, but to discrimination and exclusion along political, religious, racial, and other cultural lines, or they may be relatively few and confined largely to differences in socioeconomic status in a fluid society. In a rigidly stratified society with little or no permissible vertical movement, the struggle is likely to be suppressed until the pent-up antagonisms and pressures reach the explosion point and break forth violently as a revolt, as in the Peasants Revolt in Germany after the Protestant Reformation and the revolt of the Russian peasants against the landlords near the end of World War I.

On the other hand, in a fluid, open-class system like our own, in which movement from a lower class to a higher class can and does occur rather freely and where the lower classes are not politically subordinated, the conflict is not likely to be intense. The ideology of class struggle finds it difficult to gain a foothold. In the United States the class lines are always tentative and shifting, and the conflict is fragmentary and intermittent and concentrated on issues of immediate and perhaps only temporary importance. There is simply the constant consciousness of difference of social position and the persistent, though usually mild, jealousy of and antagonism to the privilege, authority, and power of the upper strata. The lower strata do not wish the class system to be destroyed; rather, they wish to profit by it. They simply want more and better social ladders to the top and want the upper strata to get down or move over. In the United States class conflict takes on some of the characteristics of contravention.

The tactics and means used are on the mild side. The upper classes may exercise patronage and use charity as a means of keeping the lower classes in their place and make a show of protecting them. The opponents calumniate each other, calling each other names, lying about each other, and drumming up high-sounding principles to justify themselves. They form their own exclusive organizations, as when farmers form their own cooperatives, workers engage in strikes and lockouts, and so on. There are attempts to control the effects of technological changes as these tend to affect the lower classes detrimentally. Invariably there are efforts to influence public opinion, and especially to gain privileges and rights through legislation and the courts, such as minimum wages, favorable income taxation, housing assistance, and the like.

INTRACLASS CONFLICT. The fact that there is some conflict *within* those broad groups known as classes is not so widely recognized. The members of a given class have many common values and attitudes and accept some common premises of behavior, but various elements are occasionally arrayed against each other in interactional forms that go beyond competition and take on conflict characteristics. There is always rivalry and conflict for status, jealousy for honors and privileges, and efforts to maintain security of position. Within the American working classes, for example, there is jealousy over jobs in the form of jurisdictional disputes (the conflict between lathers and metal workers as to who is to put on steel lathe).

There is the struggle between native and immigrant workers and efforts to exclude foreign workers. There are also efforts on the part of white workers to exclude Negroes, Filipinos, and Mexicans from jobs or segregate them in certain menial occupations; the town-country split, with its occasional feuding between urban-industrial and agricultural workers; the opposition between the craft-conscious and usually skilled workers and the unskilled common laborers. Occasionally, there is a religious rift, as when Catholics or Jews come to control unions. There is also conflict between the sexes, as, for example, when women make a marked influx into an occupation, and finally, there is struggle between radical and conservative wings of organized labor or between craft unions and the general labor unions.

Within the upper classes there are such divisions involving conflict tactics as that between the "old families" and the *arrivistes,* between the "old rich" and the *nouveau riche,* between members of upper class religious denominations, between the managerial employees of large corporations such as Ford, General Motors, and Chrysler in the Detroit area, between families of the Four Hundred, and so on. Ordinarily, the conflict within a class is seldom as pointed and violent as that between classes, for the bonds that tie the diverse elements together are much stronger than the occasional irritations and antagonisms that pit them against each other.

Community Conflict; Urban-Rural Opposition. All conflict, except international war, is community conflict in the sense that it takes place in communities of various extent as the arena. Here we are concerned with that which rends communities as such, and not communities as the seat of economic groups, social classes, or culture groups, religious organizations or other potentially conflicting groups. There are always opposing interests within and between communities which precipitate antagonism and result in conflict. These divergent and hostility-producing interests vary from time to time and in kind, depending upon the issues momentarily at stake. This opposition may take the form of intracommunity conflict and intercommunity conflict.

INTRACOMMUNITY CONFLICT. Intracommunity conflict is that which takes place between factions, segments, or sections within a community and usually centers around opposing cultural or economic values and objectives. Thus, within a town or city, opposition may grow out of educational issues or economic, religious, ethnic, political, or class disagreements.

INTERCOMMUNITY CONFLICT. Intercommunity conflict is that between two or more separate communities or sections of a larger region. Cities and metropolitan regions are frequently in some degree of conflict with each other as they struggle for industries, population, transportation facilities, location of government agencies, public improvements at state expense, water supplies, markets for their products, and other advantages. Different *sections* of the nation have been and are in conflict with each other over all sorts of issues. Often these have their base in geographic peculiarities as these affect economic activities, demographic constitution, cultural variations, and diverse political objectives. One need only mention the sectional conflict over the slavery issue or the persistent opposition between the industrial East and the agricultural Midwest and West on such issues as the tariff, discriminatory railway rates, and money and banking matters.

URBAN-RURAL OPPOSITION. Urban-rural conflict can be most appropriately categorized as intercommunity conflict. Throughout history the unlikeness of the ways of life and the interests of town-city and rural dwellers has bred misunderstanding and hostility. Until cities became numerous and their populations became a growing proportion of the total population of western peoples, the rural population was dominant economically, politically, and culturally. But with the commercial and industrial revolutions, social dominance passed to the towns and cities. Ever since there have been cities anywhere, however, they have exercised great power over the agricultural areas and over the cultural or national areas as a whole owing to the fact that they were centers of government, defense, religion (the seats of the major temples and cathedrals), manufacturing, markets, banks and other exchange facilities, education (the unversities), and art.

The antagonism is not a matter of any one characteristic, but if there is one factor that predominates, it is the basic difference in the economic functions of country and city. The country is engaged in extractive industry and produces raw materials, whereas the city is the consumer and processor of the bulk of these raw materials. Trading, banking, and other financial and exchange facilities, including transportation, have always been centered in cities and controlled by urban organizations. Although the city and country have been utterly dependent upon each other, this essential division of labor, combined with the historical factors mentioned above, has produced a fundamental clash of interests and persistent conflict. The cities in large part have prescribed the economic, political, social, and other forms of organization and control for the rural communities, and imposed their urban schemes, plans, and regulations, and continue to do so. The rural people object to this and fight against it.

The general ways of life of country and city differ so markedly, however, as to further accentuate these fundamental cleavages.

Rural Community Characteristics. Rural areas have rather typical demographic characteristics and functions. The population is recruited primarily from babies born to its own farm members and consists of a larger than normal proportion of children, adolescents, and aged and a subnormal proportion of those in the middle years. The people tend to be more homogeneous in sociopsychological characteristics and economic life, since they are all engaged in agriculture. The division of labor is not great, and there is only limited specialization of occupations, with very limited occupational mobility, since all one can do is climb the agricultural ladder. The population of rural communities is small and the density low because of the nature of cultivation and the dispersion of the population over the land. Thus, families are semi-isolated, the groups are mainly of a rather simple primary or face-to-face nature, with limited communication.

The rural family exists as a production, rather than a consumption, unit, and all its members are directly involved in attaining economic self-sufficiency. The rural class system is not complex, for the classes are fewer and the social distances from top to bottom smaller. Wealth is not so highly concentrated as in urban areas, and social prestige and recognition rest on production and the appurtenances of production—livestock, machinery, buildings, fields—rather than upon conspicuous consumption. Rural people are likely to be conservative in morals and other values and in their general cultural orientation.

Urban Community Characteristics. Demographically cities do not reproduce themselves; instead, they import population from the rural areas at home and abroad. The population in the middle age brackets is out of proportion to the other age groups. City populations are usually heterogeneous, recruited from widely different areas and consisting of people with a variety of race, nationality, and religious views, and different mores, customs, tastes, and patterns of behavior generally. Excessive deviants of population types are found in the city. The population diversity is great, and the people live in crowded concentration, but at the same time they are composed in the main of a multiplicity of complex and diverse secondary groups. Relationships of the individuals tend to be anonymous and impersonal, but at the same time, there is a much greater volume and variety of contact and communication than in rural areas.

The division of labor in urban centers is much greater than in the country, and the specialization of occupations (all outside the family) is almost infinite for both males and females. The urban population is also less rooted in its occupations. Vertical and horizontal societal differentiation is inherently greater than in the country, and with respect to stratification, cities usually have more numerous classes and subclasses; the social distances are usually greater from top to bottom. There is greater concentration of wealth, but the city has more persons who are excessively rich and excessively poor, more who are markedly famous and markedly infamous, more who are notably ambitious and notably ambitionless.

In cities the family is primarily only a unit for reproduction and the consumption of goods. Social valuation depends on competitive conspicuous display. The face-to-face social controls are practically inoperative. There is much greater freedom of action, but usually also much less intimate group support for the individual personality. The people are cosmopolitan, much given to modernity and radicalism, and pursue a diversity of often conflicting interests. In general, urban communities are a hodgepodge of heterogeneous peoples, infinitely differentiated as to values, pursuits, interests, and statuses.

It is easy to understand, therefore, why urban and rural people do not see eye to eye, since they follow fundamentally different ways of life, both economically and culturally. The city folk look down upon the ruralites as uncouth and unsophisticated and the rural people look upon the city folk as smart-alecks. The farmers suspect exploitive designs on the part of the urban "interests" and resent the high wages paid industrial workers on the grounds that high wages increase the prices of manufactured goods.

The farmers' techniques of conflict include such protective and offensive activities as efforts to influence legislation in their behalf governing the regulation of railway rates on their products, interest rates and loan facilities, improved roads and rural mail delivery, grain and livestock marketing, farm subsidies and price supports, tariff adjustments, and so on. They purchase from mail-order houses. They withhold raw materials and engage in such random activities as crop destruction and milk strikes. They form their own cooperative banks and their own purchasing, supply, and marketing organizations and engage in such embattled, highly organized farmers' movements as the Grange, the Farmers' Alliance (the Populist Revolt), the American Society of Equity, the Farmers' Union, the Farm Holiday Association, the Non-Partisan League, and the American Farm Bureau Federation.

The city usually retaliates, although with less heat and agitation because of the greater economic, political, and cultural power which it wields. A notable present example is the attempt of urban "interests" to weaken and destroy the cooperative movement by both propaganda and crippling legislation.

At present, there is in the main a growing awareness of the complete interdependence and indispensability of these segments of the larger community to each other. The isolation is breaking down. Ruralites are becoming urbanized in many of their activities, ways, and points of view, and urban organizations are making various beneficent overtures. The opposition in many respects is ceasing to be a conflict and is emerging as contravention as defined above.

Majority-Minority Group Conflict. Majority-minority group conflict has significant characteristics, utilizes special techniques, and takes certain notable forms.

General Characteristics. There have been many different types of minorities throughout the long course of history. Not all of them have been disliked, treated with suspicion, or discriminated against under all conditions in a given society. Usually, however, their presence as distinctly different, separate, and sizable groups has produced conflict between them and the majority. Group antagonisms seem to be inevitable when bodies of people come into contact with each other if they can be distinguished and identified by differentiating characteristics, whether these be inborn, cultural, or mainly imagined or fabricated.

A minority group is a collectivity of people who are different from the majority in inborn physical characteristics (race) or in national origin, language, religion, or other distinctive cultural characteristics and who are singled out for differential and unequal treatment. The very existence of a minority implies the presence of a corresponding dominant majority group having higher social status and enjoying and maintaining greater privileges and emoluments. Minorities occupy a disadvantageous position. The members have unequal access to economic, political, educational, occupational, and professional opportunities, which largely circumscribes their freedom of choice and self-development. They are held in low esteem and are objects of contempt, hatred, ridicule, fear, and, sometimes, violence. They are usually socially isolated, excluded from voluntary associations, and frequently spatially segregated. (92) The disadvantage of the minority group member is well put by Jessie Bernard: "He is playing a game in his opponents' field; with equipment furnished by his opponents, according to rules set by his opponents." (74, p. 318)

Minorities are characterized by marked self-consciousness and sensitivity. Usually, they have a perpetual sense of grievance and are constantly looking for insults, evidences of economic discrimination, political favoritism toward the majority, cultural ostracism, and attempts at social segregation. They view their exclusion from unimportant activities of the more powerful, socially determining majority as a humiliation, and they are anxious to convince themselves that mundane failures and tribulations are the product of oppression. Moreover, most minorities, being human and craving survival and recognition, especially those with a long, proud history, cannot accept philosophically the social, political, and cultural limitations consequent upon their minority status. They chafe, more or less impotently, not only at their usual numerical inferiority, but also at the indignities, real or imagined, to which they are subjected. (93, pp. 585-586)

In a sense, a minority is penalized for being a minority. Almost every minority has been the victim of the majority throughout history. Minorities are supposed to be different in one way or another and often are until fully assimilated. For one reason or another, they are nonconformists, and nonconformity, which implies unlikeness of beliefs, values, and behavior, even though innocuous, causes suspicion and dislike. In everyday instances, if people do not play bridge enthusiastically, or if they favor cremation, or refuse to attend football games, their reliability and sanity are suspect.

Invariably, those who are unlike, those with whom one does not have complete mental, emotional, and spiritual kinship, are regarded as inimical to the interests and comfort and security of those to whom they are dissimilar. If these unlike elements are a fairly unified group within the larger whole, they are suspected of being disloyal and creating a subversive influence. All societies seem to feel an imperative need to reduce to congruence, or to dispel, their dissimilar elements and to get into focus unfamiliar cultural and behavior patterns. Hence, there is the majority impulse to crush minorities, whether they be racial, religious, political, social, or nationalistic groups.

Sociological Bases. The *sociological bases* of majority-minority group conflict are found mainly in cultural differences and in the fear and hatred of the economic competitor. At the time of conflict the groups invariably have widely different cultures. In the case of some minority groups the culture may have been brought with them and may be foreign to the majority. In other cases, the minority may have been assigned for a long period to a low caste, suffering long physical, economic, political, and cultural exclusion from the life of the majority, as in the case of the American Negro, and, hence, may be unable to become learners of, and participants in, the majority culture; or there have been deliberate, self-imposed cultural and even physical isolation, as in the case of religious sects, to prevent contamination by the surrounding society.

Invariably, the culture of the minority is different, embodying different ceremonies, customs, beliefs, mores, values, standards, goals, and in some instances, different foods, dress, aesthetics, language, religion. Its institutions are different. Many of the cultural features of the majority and the minority are mutually incompatible; they separate, irritate, and produce clash of interests and hence conflict situations. Thus, majority-minority conflict is in considerable part a culture conflict, that is, a conflict between groups with widely contrasting culture elements or on widely separated cultural levels.

Another significant factor in inducing majority-minority conflict is the appearance of the minority members as economic competitors. When the income, or job, or land, or standard of living or some other aspect of the economic security or socio-economic position of members of the majority is threatened by the minority, antagonism and other aspects of conflict are present, even though some more exalted reason, such as racial purity, preservation of a religion, prevention of cultural degradation, may be offered as a justification for the hostility and efforts at discrimination and exclusion. This has been an important factor in the hostility to every new immigrant group in the United States (for example, Irish, Scandinavians, Italians, Polish, Czechs), to the Chinese and Japanese on the Pacific Coast since the sixties, to the Negroes since they were freed in the South and since World War I in Northern cities, to the Jews quite generally everywhere.

The antagonism to the minorities as economic competitors is greatest among the social classes and occupational levels of the majority most directly affected by a minority. In most instances this has been the lower classes, common laborers, and semi-skilled. In the case of Jews, it has been mainly the middle and upper classes—the professions, banking, and merchandising.

Certain other sociological factors in majority-minority group conflict should be considered. In the first place, ethnocentrism appears in its most accentuated form in majority-minority group relations. Each is an ingroup opposed to an outgroup. Each considers itself superior and the other inferior; each is "the best people," a "chosen people," from its own point of view and hence considers itself entitled to dominance.

Second, the intensity of the conflict depends in considerable part upon the relative numbers and degree of concentration of the minority in relation to the majority. If the minority members are few and hence insignificant as cultural and economic opponents, they may actually arouse curiosity and be considered quaint; but if they are numerous, they exist as a threat to the majority's ways of life and a challenge to their dominance. When Negroes came into northern cities during and after World War I, and when French Canadians settled in New England in considerable numbers and concentration, they became objects of antagonism. Anti-Semitism, as already noted, is strongest in and around New York City where nearly half of the American Jews are located, and the antagonism to the Japanese has been strongest on the Pacific Coast where, until forced dispersion during World War II, their concentration was greatest.

Third, the prejudice against the minority rests upon the construction and acceptance by the majority of generalized notions of the ludicrous and reprehensible characteristics of the members of the minority group. It is a matter of stereotypes, or traditional group-accepted images regarding the outgroup. The individual member of the other group is always conceived of through the veil of the group stereotype. Thus, when the Irish, Swedish, Italian, and Polish peoples first appeared in the United States as cultural and economic competitors, each group was regarded according to certain stereotyped conceptions, such as thick-brogued, fighting Irish, dumb, blond Swedes, and so on. All Japanese are automatically assigned stereotyped characteristics, and so too are Negroes. Minority group members are not viewed as personalities aside from their categories.

A fourth set of factors centers around the consistency of the manner in which the mobility and opportunity values are maintained. If a rigid, institutionalized caste system with its supporting values prevails, every element has its place and station. There is no association of ideas and ideals with any other condition. Although there may be suffering and discontent, there is not so likely to be conflict. But if the society's ideals embrace democratic equalitarianism, free opportunity, and general integration, and if vertical mobility is in the mores, then the subordinations, discriminations, persecutions, and exclusions, as inconsistently practiced against minorities by the majority, invite rebellious attitudes and actions. As soon as they are able, the minorities try to fight back and gain admission to the status and privileges of the majority group.

Techniques and Mechanisms. Some of the techniques of conflict have been alluded to in the foregoing discussion. Nevertheless, a brief systematic presentation here is desirable. The tactics that will be described are, it should be emphasized, pursued mainly by the majority in its efforts to maintain its reputed superiority and its societal supremacy.

Patronage of the minority is a downward gesture. The members of the dominant majority group condescend to gestures of doing something for those whom they consider beneath them, thus, subtly reminding them of their inferior position and at the same time imposing a feeling of indebtedness and of low-status obligations upon them. *Ridicule* is making fun, sometimes in a disguised way, of the minority-group members and thereby indicating that they are held in contempt. Jokes and epithets emphasizing the idiosyncracies and disliked characteristics are common forms, such as the jokes about "Rastus" and the sex mores of Negro females, the "Pat and Mike" type of story, and so on.

Discrimination against the minorities takes various forms. In economic relations it includes paying the minority lower wages or refusing to hire them, refusing them services and necessary education or training for economic activity, and denial of union membership. Political discrimination appears in withholding the voting franchise, exclusion from political office, attempts to prevent access of minority members to law-enforcement agencies, or even special discriminatory treatment of minorities by legal enactments, such as are occasionally directed against religious groups.

There is often *avoidance* of the minority through refusal to sell or rent property to them and to admit them to theaters, churches, playgrounds, and restaurants. *Segregation* may take the form of Jim Crow laws and—the most extreme form—legalized ghettos. *Terrorism* is the most severe form of intimidation and involves open hostility and violence. Its tactics include lynching and mob action, internment, persecutions, inquisitions, pogroms, and in some instances organized liquidation. (78)

Characteristic Forms of Majority-Minority Group Conflict. In the United States the most important kinds of majority-minority group conflict are practically synonymous with ethnic group conflict. Three forms will be examined briefly: so-called "race conflict," the conflict between the majority and unassimilated groups of foreign-nationality origin, and non-Jew versus Jew conflict. A fourth important majority-minority conflict is of a religious nature, but religious conflict, both in its majority-minority forms and in its wider aspects and implications, will be examined in the next section.

Still another form of conflict is that between political majorities and minorities within a country. In many parts of Europe and Asia this takes the form of conflict between majority and minority nationalistic groups, whereas in the United States, it takes the form of opposition between the majority political party or combination of factions and the political minority. Although there is an effort on the part of the majority to maintain dominance and withhold advantage from the other side, it is not majority-minority conflict as defined; the sides are ever-changing, and today's majority—the ins—may be tomorrow's minority—the outs. It is essentially a political process. In true majority-minority conflict, the conflict continues along the characteristic lines until the minority is completely assimilated or completely eliminated.

RACE CONFLICT. The struggle that stems from the clash of two or more so-called "racial" groups in contact, one of which thinks itself superior and acts accordingly, is called *race conflict.* These groups are forced by circumstances to live together, but are separated attitudinally and socially by intense and often well-fostered prejudices and antipathies. The superior race tries to maintain and enhance its economic, political, and cultural supremacy, while the inferior group tries to reduce, push aside, and, if possible, abolish the superior race.

Scientifically speaking, *race* is purely a biological term for classifying various members of the human species according to purely hereditary, mainly physical traits, such as skin, hair, and eye color, hair structure, facial features, stature, cephalic index, and certain other special anatomical characteristics, developed selectively as adaptations to the peculiar determining conditions of various physical environments in the past. The proponents of the idea of hereditarily superior races insist that mental, temperamental, and even moral traits are also a matter of biological inheritance and that the inferior races, therefore, always will be inferior socially and culturally. All scientifically valid evidence points to the fact, however, that the existing races are merely varieties—and impure varieties at that—of the common species *Homo sapiens.*

The fundamental biological tests of common species point to the unity of all so-called human races. Cross-breeds of different *species* are hybrids and are usually sterile, but all human races are mutually fertile, and all human crosses produce fertile offspring. For that matter, the supposed physical revulsion of races for each other is without foundation, since most human beings are racial crossbreeds. It is almost impossible to find good examples of pure racial types. Furthermore all four known hereditary blood types are found among all races and can be indiscriminately transfused, regardless of whether the human carriers are whites, Negroes, Mongols, or mongrels. Psychological tests indicate differences in cultural conditioning and opportunity and in individuals *as individuals,* not *racial* difference. Science supports the Scriptures in holding that "God hath made one blood all nations of men."

Race conflict does not exist *as such*; it is always connected with other factors of societal life. It is fundamentally the conflict between clashing economic and culture groups that are distinguished from each other by certain *visible* characteristics. In any given contact situation these characteristics are made the badge or symbol of superiority or inferiority and, hence, of demarcation and efforts to achieve and maintain power. The race-difference argument to justify prejudice, antagonism, and aggression is primarily a studiously maintained and exaggerated rationalization behind which the economic, social, and cultural factors operate. Visible racial characteristics provide merely convenient, ready-made excuses for superiority and inferiority. People cannot change their grandparents or escape from them.

These excuses, however, tend to be fixed in discriminatory attitudes, values, and habit patterns of the individuals of the contending groups or categories. The various peoples may be much alike in all sorts of behavioral attributes, but they are socially identified by their visible "racial" characteristics. Although fanatical race ideology and race conflict are based merely on a well-rationalized pretext, they are among the most powerful, stubborn, and sinister realities in the United States and in the world today.

Racism, or *racialism,* is the most extreme, disconcerting, and dangerous aberration of race in recent times. As maintained by various peoples at times, but especially by the German Nazis, it is a combination of biological, anthropological, psychological, and sociological misinterpretations and deliberate, distorted fabrications about race raised to the status of a pseudo science and used to pursue totalitarian political, economic, and cultural objectives. As presented, the German *Volk*—a highly mongrelized population, owing to millenniums of biological and cultural cross-fertilization—were presented as the only true human race, physically, mentally, politically, and culturally, and all other peoples and nations were stereotyped as lesser creatures, in fact, as subraces and, hence, legitimate exploitative "fodder" for the *Herrenvolk*.

In the United States the race conflict is mainly between the white majority and the approximately 10 percent of the population labeled Negro. Where Chinese, Japanese, Filipinos, Hindus, Indians, and Mexicans exist in considerable number, they are also subjected to white prejudice and hostility. As is widely known, the conflict takes the standard forms of social, economic, educational, and political discrimination, voluntary, involuntary, and even legal avoidance, exclusion, and residential and organizational segregation, and occasionally violent intimidation and persecution. The retaliatory tactics of the disadvantaged race include such less overt forms as jostling on the streets, simulation of ignorance, and resort to slowness and inefficiency; more aggressive action such as insolence and sabotage, occasional open violence; and more and more creative action in the form of organized efforts to achieve favorable legislation and court action which ensures constitutional rights.

Conflict against Groups of Foreign Nationality. The conflict between the "older" and more uniformly assimilated Americans and the more recently arrived immigrant and foreign groups of people has prevailed in our country through most of its history. Since World War I, however, it has considerably abated largely because immigration has been restricted. Ours is a history of the "older" stocks regarding themselves as superior to arrivals from other lands. During the century preceding World War I, considerable numbers of Irish, Germans, Scandinavians, Italians, Poles, Greeks, Czechs, Russians, and other peoples from the Baltic region and from Central and Southeastern Europe and the Near East entered the United States. Here again, the basic conflict factors were economic and cultural clashes. These peoples were always invaders of occupations, threatening the occupational security of the older stocks, competitors for housing and land.

For several generations these immigrants were culturally distinct groups among the larger majority group. They had their own languages, customs, foods, values, ceremonies, holidays, religions—all distinctive products of development in their particular physical, national, and cultural environments. Often they felt strongly attached to their old-world culture heritage and showed distinct ethnocentric characteristics. In many instances, because of discriminations, avoidances, and segregation here, they showed a peculiar loyalty to their former nation and culture, emphasizing their language and literature and maintaining foreign-language churches and foreign-centered patriotic, cultural, and recreational organizations. They were characterized by an internal cohesiveness, a strong sense of belonging together, a feeling of being sharers in a common way of life, and they sought to keep from being engulfed by the different and hostile world about them.

Much of the urban and rural segregation was imposed upon the immigrants by ecological processes and active discrimination by the majority, but some of it was voluntary as a social and cultural protective procedure. Furthermore, as the larger majority held themselves superior and engaged in their active animosity and exploitation, the newcomers tended to develop an oppressed-nationality psychosis, which produced further emphasis upon their own unique characteristics.

Although there is still some of this conflict in certain communities, most of these stocks are now third- and fourth-generation Americans. They speak the same language, dress like everyone else, belong to the Rotary Club, and intermarry with each other and with the older stocks.

NON-JEWS VERSUS JEWS. Anti-Semitism, which includes dislike or hatred of, discrimination against, and occasionally persecution of Jewish minorities, has been a recurring form of social conflict for more than twenty-five hundred years. It antedates the Christian era and even the time of the Jewish dispersion, for in ancient times it was practiced in turn by the Egyptians, Assyrians, Babylonians, Persians, Syrians, Greeks, Romans, Arabs, and many others. During the Christian era in Europe and especially during the last millennium, they have been subjected again and again not only to antipathy and hatred, but to segregations, banishments, and even wholesale extermination by practically every people and nation. Anti-Semitism also manifests itself in the contemporary United States, though seldom in its more extreme overt forms. Here the Jews, in the main, are subjected to a quiet, urbane, but persistent and unyielding negative attitude, and to exclusion from the closer unities and participations of the gentiles —even among educated and cultured non-Jews.

This discrimination rests upon private and personal prejudice, but it also takes group forms. It is not reflected in law or political proscriptions and is not overtly incorporated in class principles, but takes the form of an informal, covert, subtle, but nevertheless effectively organized policy of social ostracism throughout the whole gamut of social life. Although the Jews comprise less than 4 per cent of the total American population, most of them are conspicuously located in the middle and lower-upper classes, since they have wealth, education, social grace, and culture. Hence, the most pronounced discrimination and exclusiveness occur at these levels where group competition is more decisive; for example, in business and the professions.

What forms does the opposition take? Fraternity and sorority exclusion rests upon the well-rationalized policy of "freedom of association," that is, the expression of the gregarious impulse of individuals of similar tastes, interests, and backgrounds to associate together. Universities have their admission quotas, and frequently Jewish applicants for fellowships and scholarships have to be skipped because the corporations that grant funds and employ the finished products do not want Jews either as administrators or researchers. Efforts are also made to maintain a balance between Jews and non-Jews on faculties. Prestige organizations, such as country clubs, university clubs, and discussion clubs, frequently exclude them, and they are refused as guests at certain hotels and resorts and excluded from select residential areas.

Among economic groups Jews are largely excluded from key businesses and industries, such as banking, insurance, trust-company operations, coal, steel, oil, automobiles, railroading, heavy machinery, and construction. They are largely confined to businesses in which a large risk-factor is involved or to which some stigma is attached: personal loan and financial organizations, second-hand shops and pawnshops, liquor retailing, clothing manufacture, amusement industries, and similar businesses. (86)

What are the factors in this discrimination and hostility? The Jews are not excluded because they are members of an "inferior race," although they are frequently referred to as a race. Racially, in spite of reciprocal efforts to prevent intermarriage, they are a conglomerate of Semitic and all the other stocks with which they have intermingled and amalgamated during the many centuries of their dispersion. Most of such original Semitic characteristics have lost their visibility. They have not been a nationality for twenty-five hundred years in the sense of stemming from a common national place of birth. Although the Jews are long-standing and active participants in many societies, the non-Jews often feel that many a Jew, despite protestations to the contrary, is still a foreigner at heart and still divided in his loyalty and sympathy.

The fundamental factor tending toward discrimination seems to be that the Jews are a self-contained culture group not fully integrated in our social system or in any other. This is true even of those who meet the economic and other canons of social respectability. They are usually a marginal culture group. The conflict is one of customs, mores, values, and other cultural norms. The tough attitudinal and cultural unity must be largely attributed to the peculiar circumstances among which Jews have been forced to live. Bereft at an early date, among every people of their dispersion, of various social, economic and political rights and opportunities, they developed a religious faith which became at once the basis and the antithesis of the religions of the numerous peoples among whom the Jews found themselves as conspicuous minorities, notably of Christianity and Mohammedanism.

Judaism was a faith which united its adherents, becoming the prime necessity of their existence and the principal agency of their survival amid the ceaseless assaults of the ages. Although the schismatic reform movement of the last century has divided them into Orthodox, Conservative, and Reformed (or liberal) segments, and emancipation has produced rationalistic and atheistic elements, the common, unique religious tradition is still a basis of unity. The Jews, even the agnostics and atheists, still preserve a feeling of pride in their religious ancestry and a respect for the tribal spiritual qualities of their people. This tends to exasperate the non-Jews and builds a wall about the Jew.

The isolation, difference, exclusiveness, and rigidity of Jewish culture as a whole, including the "chosen people" irritant, has been another factor in discrimination. Here, again, we have a case of a people being damned and discriminated against for something thrust upon them by bitter circumstance—the ghetto factor. Antipathy led first to the voluntary ghetto, which originated as a Jewish device for the protection of their distinctive and sustaining way of life against the inroads of the surrounding alien cultures and also out of fear of the remainder of the population which induced the Jews to be together for the sake of security.

Later the Jews were forced by law to live in ghettos in many parts of Europe. The ghetto facilitated the development and the conservation of a Jewish mode of life, Jewish intellectual activities, and Jewish loyalties and clannishness, and crystallized an entire social nexus with its own life, interests, and diversions. It tended to enhance the group consciousness. The result is that Jewish culture has developed an almost impregnable technique of self-preservation, rigidity and persistence.

The Jew is, in most cases, loath to lose his distinctive identity. Although this solidarity has been defensive, never offensive, it has developed social distance, and Jewish culture is always a foreign element within a larger areal culture. Moreover, it is in many of its features a more readily interchangeable culture from land to land than that of any other people. It has common, unique features everywhere and is a narrowly international culture juxtaposed to specific national cultures.

The economic factors of anti-Semitism also have their roots in historical circumstances over which the Jew had little or no control. Their functions as money-changers, as moneylenders, as traders and middlemen, and as risk-takers were largely thrust upon them because medieval Christians were forbidden to carry on these activities. Then later, entrance to agriculture, the trades, and industrial occupations were denied the Jews.

Because of these and many other factors the Jews are deemed to be different, somewhat insulated, and alien culture groups wherever they are. They are an out group, suspected and feared by the majority. Because of their difference, they frequently become a symbol upon which to project many of the failings and misfortunes of the dominant group—"symbols of free-floating aggression." They make excellent targets or scapegoats because of their position and their comparative helplessness. (80; 88)

Religious Conflict. Individuals and groups representing different religious points of view always try to absorb each other by proselyting or coercion. Failing these, one group tries to exclude the others in one way or another from the area of contact or, on occasion, to destroy them altogether.

Religious conflict grows out of the fact that religion is fundamentally a matter of beliefs about the extrahuman and the supernatural which have been rationalized and systematized in the form of theologies, creeds, and, usually, mythologies. Each religious group is convinced that it has "the only true faith" and the only assured method of salvation. Since the efficacy of these beliefs, articles of faith, and sanctified practice, because of their very nature, cannot be proved by any mundane means —the only ones available to men—every divergent set of beliefs is a standing criticism, challenge, even a nullification of every other. The followers of any given belief can feel secure in their faith only when all contending or contrary faiths have been eliminated.

Every religious group is always, in its very nature, a highly ethnocentric group. It is not only superior; it is always right. In fact, it cannot continue to exist if there is doubt as to its sole and fundamental rightness and truth. Other religious groups are always benighted "heathen" or nonbelievers. Hence, there is always some degree of at least quiet intolerance, always some latent—and often active—prejudice and antagonism.

In addition to the conflict between groups holding divergent religious beliefs, religious conflict carries with it certain other types of conflict. It takes on the form of intra-institutional conflict. Each religious group from the most recent cult, to the far-flung, massive, centuries-old world religions is institutionalized. Each has its structural "type" parts, its body of ideas, beliefs, doctrines, dogmas, articles of faith, and other ideological elements, standardized and systematized in the form of a theology and creeds. Each has its standardized practices and rituals and other essential forms of communicating with and worshipping the deity. Each consists of rather closely knit organizations of human beings embodying priesthood or clergy and laity and has its emotion-charged and emotion-eliciting symbols consisting of church buildings and sacred images and objects. Each has its unique "right" regulatory functions that must be performed. (96)

While the structural and functional features are common as to type, of necessity they differ greatly in their specific characteristics. Each theology must offer its own distinctive aid to salvation for its particular proponents and adherents. These institutionalized organizations are, therefore, almost unavoidably antagonistic and undertake both defensive and offensive procedures toward each other. The organized nature of religious conflict, as compared with the more blind and haphazard nature of much other social conflict, grows out of this high institutionalization of religious groups.

Religious conflict also partakes of the nature of majority-minority group conflict in areas where the majority is predominantly of one faith and organization but minor heretical or nonconformist sects also exist. Occasionally, it takes the form of ethnic-group conflict, as when a racial or nativity stock in a larger and more uniform ethnic sea has its distinctive religion (for example, the Jews), or the form of intracommunity conflict, as in a community divided on certain issues between Catholics and Protestants or one divided between formal religionists and nonchurch members.

FORMS OF RELIGIOUS CONFLICT. Religious conflict as such may be subdivided into interreligious and intrareligious conflict. *Interreligious conflict* is that which occurs between individual adherents of organized and institutionalized religions and also between representative organizations of world religions. Examples are the age-long antagonism between Christianity and Mohammedanism and, notably in recent times, the actual strife between Hinduism and Mohammedanism in India.

Intrareligious conflict is that which develops between sects and denominations or between more widely divergent groups within a given world religion. In the United States it takes various forms. First of all there is conflict between Catholics and Protestants, which began with the Reformation. This conflict rests upon the uncompromising stand of the Roman Catholic Church that it is the only true Christian Church, a point of view firmly contested by Protestants who insist upon free choice, and upon sharp differences regarding religion-related social and cultural issues, such as attitudes toward marriage and the family, public and parochial schools, contraception, and sex education in the public schools and differences growing out of class or nationality divergencies, moral principles, and other supposedly fundamental cultural values.

There are also conflicts within Catholicism and within Protestantism. Within Catholicism there is occasional conflict, with laity and priests on both sides, over congregational or universal Catholic organizational ownership of church property, attendance at public or parochial and sectarian schools at all levels, the separation of Church and state, and there are also ethnic cleavages between Irish, German, Italian, Polish, and other national Catholics. This is matched in the Eastern Catholic Church of Europe and the Near East by the conflict between the different national divisions of that Church. In addition there is the major historical split between the eastern and western divisions of the Catholic Church, which is very much in evidence wherever there is any contact between adherents.

Within American Protestantism there is the continual contention between the nearly three hundred sects, denominations, and subdenominations. Sects and denominations, in their very origin and nature, are groups that have separated themselves from some main religious body in order to emphasize their peculiar doctrinal principles, specialized worship, and other religion-related practices, such as diet, costume, forms of baptism, and so on. The justification for the continued existence of these groups rests upon studiously maintained contrasts and antagonisms. In general, the denominations "hug their differences."

Within some of the larger denominational bodies there have been ethnic divisions and conflicts as well as various subdoctrinal differences, and some of these still persist. The Lutherans, for example, have their various synods and language-nationality divisions, which the Methodists and other denominations also had until quite recently. Within given denominations there may be conflicts centering around orthodoxy, such as between fundamentalists and modernists, between the orthodox and the liberal factions in theological and ethical interpretation. (94)

Techniques of Religious Conflict. The techniques of religious opposition range from mild forms to extremely violent forms. There is nearly always *active proselyting and missionization,* that is, active efforts to alienate members of one religion from that religion and draw them into the religion of the aggressive group. Teaching and merely peaceful and hortatory means may be used, but, all too often, political and even physical pressures and procedures are resorted to. Proselyting often takes the form of the *competitive use of rewards, promises, cajolery,* and *bribery* and emphasizes superior qualities, the special blessings, the assurances of salvation, and, occasionally, superior social prestige. Other inducements, such as educational and medical services, are used as baits both at home and in mission fields. Nearly always the conflict involves positive and direct antagonistic tactics.

Criticism, polemic, and villification of opponents may be resorted to, and propagandist methods of all kinds are employed in denouncing, misrepresenting, belittling, and discrediting antagonists and even arousing racial, class, or other prejudices. Frequently, there is *avoidance and denial of certain relationships* in the form of discouragement or prohibition of intermarriage among members of at least certain more dissident religious groups, refusal of social integration and economic relations, and noncooperation in community enterprises.

Efforts at *legal prohibition of worship* or of certain proscribed acts or *even efforts to outlaw minority religious points of view altogether are made.* These take the form of laws restricting religious freedom, discrimination in favor of one or more religious faiths, sabbatarian (Blue Law) legislation, and judicial decisions supporting such laws against dissident individuals and groups.

Forceful proselyting and coercive demonstrations have frequently been engaged in. There have been banishment, expulsion, and forced migration (the French Huguenots in the seventeenth century, the Puritans, the Mormons); persecutions and torture (the Inquisition of the fifteenth and sixteenth centuries in Europe and America); massacres and pogroms; and actual warfare between organized political-religious groups (the Crusades, Zionists versus the Arab League, and Mohammedans versus Brahmans in India).

Religious conflict is always separative and disintegrative in its effects. As Ross has pointed out, a society's elite is often eliminated by expulsion or liquidation. France lost many of its best "brains" and "spirits" in the Massacre of St. Bartholomew and expulsion of the Huguenots from France, and Holland, the Rhine Valley, and America gained thereby. The Spanish Inquisition not only destroyed some of Europe's most rare individuals, but deprived certain countries of superior Jews by expelling them. And many other examples could be listed.

Finally, religious conflict, unlike almost all other kinds, does not fade and disappear. It always rests upon faith and belief about the supramundane which is factually unknowable and unprovable. The tenets of faith, in turn, rest upon well-marshaled, but nevertheless mundane, logic and authority. The infinite truth cannot be known by finite creatures, however advantaged by consecration and revelation. No given faith *dare compromise.* Hence, differences cannot be finally settled. Nothing short of one universal faith will resolve religious conflict, and that is inconceivable in the light of the nature and history of religion.

War. The forms of social conflict thus far examined, with the exception of certain phases of religious conflict, have been intracommunity, intrasociety, or intranational conflict. War, save as civil war or internal rebellion, is ***inter***national, ***inter***-society, even world-wide conflict. Hence, it is the most engulfing, most far-reaching, and most destructuralizing and defunctionalizing of all forms of social conflict.

Civil war or rebellion is conflict ***within*** a nation between two or more portions of the nation and is usually due to a sectional, racial, nationality, religious, or socioeconomic class group, or some combination of these, seeking redress of grievances and aspiring to greater political recognition and power. It is directed against the larger body of the nation which considers itself the main guardian of the national sovereignty. On occasion rebellion may be the revolt of a dependency against the controlling power.

Our main concern here is with *inter*national war, that is, war between two or more sovereign nation-states or between two opposed coalitions of such states. Usually, it is an effort to resolve or liquidate a crisis situation, which involves friction, tension, maladjustment, and profound fear and hostility, by attempting to subordinate or destroy the opposing nation or allies or remove it or them from the international scene. (101) Through the centuries war has come to be a highly institutionalized use of force whereby nations, singly or in combination, have sought to preserve or advance themselves in the arena of nations. Wars are conducted by governments and are, in fact, the most highly organized and historically the most consistently glorified function of government. (111)

The analysis of war as an institutionalized form of conflict, especially with reference to its causal and contributory factors, functions, processes, efforts to prevent it, and accommodative procedures at its conclusion, is an infinitely complex and herculean task. Though a most voluminous literature exists at all levels of discussion and analysis, no one is satisfied with the conclusions, social scientific or otherwise, that have been arrived at. Our treatment, of necessity, owing to limitations of space and the confused nature of the working conclusions, will be brief and of a hypothetical nature.

THE NATURE OF MODERN WARFARE. *Modern warfare,* as distinct from primitive, ancient, and medieval warfare, is all encompassing. The radius and depth and degree of involvement have been vastly extended. It is now three-dimensional and three-planed. It is fought on land and sea, below the surface of the water, and in the air with weapons undreamed of half a century ago. Every element of the civilian population, as well as the military, is involved, and the whole population is vulnerable to attack and destruction. Both attack and defense have come to require the marshaling of the ***total*** resources of the nations involved. Never again can military conflict remain a purely political and local matter in which large portions of the population are only remotely and indirectly affected. Now there must be ***total conversion*** of all resources, equipment, and population *to carry on total war.*

Finally, modern war sooner or later becomes world-wide. The world has become a compact communicating area and has shrunk both in facility of transportation and in transportation time. It has come to be a single interlocking area—an area of mutual and reciprocal supply and commerce, of common economy and techniques, an area of interwoven political arrangements, an area of functional interplay and synchronization, and an area of vast cultural and especially ideological unities. As a result, partial crisis becomes general crisis; every local war develops into global war. The situation is like that of a fire breaking out in a huge, drafty, wooden, multiple structure, with many open hallways and shafts and no fire walls. Two world wars in a third of a century and the tragic threat of a third global involvement are concrete evidence.

CAUSAL AND CONTRIBUTORY FACTORS. Recently much space and attention have been devoted to the *causal and contributory factors of war* and many interpretations offered—economic pressure, population pressure, psychological, especially "instinctivist factors," imperialism, militarism, and the plotting of international munitions makers. Actually, war is due to many infinitely complex causes, some of which doubtless have not yet been recognized. Some are incidental and others fundamental, some accidental and others purposive, some unpremeditated and others premeditated, some transitory and others continuous.

Some of the more obvious and recurrent recent and present causal factors follow. Population pressure, that is, the tendency of population in certain areas of the world to outrun the means of maintaining itself, has been a factor. In the modern world demands for *Lebensraum,* however, are not efforts for mere survival, but are usually rationalizations for economic and imperialistic expansion.

Modern peoples cannot sustain their population by agriculture alone. They must turn to manufactures and commerce to get not only food, but great quantities of raw materials and finished goods. They want markets and fields for investment which they can monopolize. Colonies, protectorates, or other forms of subject or dependent peoples and territory provide them. These aspirations combined with nationalism have led to so-called "imperialism" and, in achieving territorial aggrandizement, have created various attempts to remove rivals from the arenas of friction or to halt the extension of other empires. Related to this is the desire to acquire strategic economic and military sites, such as the Dardanelles, the Suez and Panama Canals, the Straits of Singapore, and many others. The clash of economic systems has been an additional factor.

In the past wars have been fought for national honor and revenge, to preserve and perpetuate culture, to achieve freedom and independence, to maintain or advance a religion, to liberate oppressed peoples, to protect small countries against tyranny and aggression. In the modern world, war is conducted mainly to preserve, salvage, or advance the hegemony of a socioeconomic or political ideology, such as democracy, free-enterprise capitalism, communism, or some form of fascist totalitarianism.

The War Process. The waging of modern war is a process that reveals a fairly definite pattern. It is a matter of stages, not necessarily sequential and usually with considerable overlapping, somewhat as follows:

The first stage is the *combination of inciting factors.* Irritating situations and incidents that constitute a threat to the security of a people, nation, or similarly circumstanced combination of nations produce fears, suspicions, frustrations, and tensions. These factors lead to the second stage, the *milling process.* (116, pp. 18-21) The incidents, fears, and tensions are subjected to examination. The agencies of information and propaganda review the incidents. Myths and stereotypes of various kinds are fabricated, and a ground swell of war opinion is formulated. The tensions develop into ethnocentric prejudice and hatred. Patriotism and loyalty are emphasized, chauvinism is resorted to, and sentiments and attitudes are built up to accept war.

The third stage is the *war resolve.* The physical, ecological, economic, cultural, and political factors are now related specifically to "incidents" and to fears, tensions, and hatreds. In brief, they are fitted into the institutionalized war pattern. War is now the only way out, and usually, sooner or later, there is a "declaration" of war.

Mobilization, the fourth stage, sometimes begins prior to a declaration of war. In the present era mobilization consists of the marshaling of all manpower, military and civilian, all material resources, all psychological and political aids, and every form of technology in order to conduct an effective offensive and ensure protection of the nation or nations. It usually involves also a coordination and integration of all resources and agencies—economic, political and military—of the participants on each side.

During the stage of *actual combat* each side tries by means of all the technics and mechanisms of intimidation, confusion, and destruction to reduce and, if possible, to eliminate the other side. The *involvement of neutrals* almost inevitably follows the beginning of combat. Once war has begun between nations or alliances of nations, it tends to spread. Other nations, sooner or later, must take sides. (116, pp. 21-22) Few can stay out. The final stage, *accommodation,* develops as war weariness sets in on both sides and destruction takes its toll. The firing and destruction cease. The diplomats sit down together to work out a peace—for the time being.

The tragic thing about war is that it accomplishes nothing. Everyone is the loser. In its very nature it is separative and incomprehensively destructive in multitudinous ways. It breeds more hate than it exhausts. It is provocative of retaliation and further conflict, often with some recombination of antagonists, as soon as resources and conditions permit. Let us hope that mankind may in the very near future make certain concessions to nationalism and sovereignty and ethnocentrism and effect a world organization that can maintain peace and prosperity. (See especially the comprehensive treatment in 118, Part IV)

CHAPTER XVIII

PROCESSES OF SOCIETAL DECADENCE AND SOCIETAL OSSIFICATION

ALL OF THE PROCESSES that contribute to destructuralization and defunctionalization are related and overlap in action. Some processes—in fact, many of them, as already noted—have several disorganizing effects, some of which are reciprocal. Careful analysis, however, reveals certain general distinctive types based on kinds of destructuralizing and defunctionalizing effects. Thus far, we have examined the separative, isolative, or disintegrative processes and the processes of opposition, especially those of conflict. Two other major categories will now be considered: the processes of societal decadence and those of societal ossification.

Processes and Conditions of Societal Decadence

The processes of societal decadence bring about a crumbling, rotting, undermining or other decaying and disintegration of important parts. They may affect—and occasionally have affected over long periods of time—entire social systems, lowering the functional efficiency of individuals, groups, and institutions to the point where the system disintegrated at the slightest attack from within or without, as Toynbee's studies so brilliantly demonstrate. (8, pp. 244-359) Since function is structure in action, they tend to impair or destroy societal functional efficacy. Where there is decadence, there is a diminution of participation, discipline, control, and societal strength; loyalty and teamwork are on the down grade, and a spirit of each for himself prevails. The web of common or interlocked interests and actions, which must enmesh men in an effective going concern, gives way.

Decadence must not be thought to be universal.

Usually it is more noticeable in certain departments of life than in others, and it may be only temporary. But there is always a tendency to dissolution, and wherever and whenever it occurs, it causes deterioration of structures and reduced functional efficiency.

In general, the processes that make for societal decadence can be divided into four categories: subsocial and extrasocial processes; processes related to the secularization of modern social life; certain general social processes that produce decadence; and those impersonal, inherent, and internal social processes related to the social diseases to which institutionalized organizations fall heir.

Subsocial and Extrasocial Processes of Decadence

Changes in Physical and Biological Environment. Such environmental changes as marked climatic swings, drought, floods, earthquakes, deforestation, erosion, and soil exhaustion, and such biological catastrophes as insect plagues and great plagues and epidemics among human beings—typhus, bubonic plague, Spanish influenza, and so on—may lead to decadence. Any loss of command over the physical and biological environment is likely to be a cause of societal breakdown, though it may also be a consequence. (7, pp. 594-598; 8, pp. 255-272)

Deterioration of Human Biological Elements. A variety of adverse selective processes may bring about deterioration of the human biological elements of a society. They include: cityward flow and eventual dying-out there of dynamic human types; selective emigration, for example, of those approaching maturity and full social participation; extirpation of the superior of one type or other or the disproportionate increase of the inferior as a result of war; the attraction into celibate religious orders of the mentally and spiritually select; unwisely dispensed relief; unfavorable birth differentials and death differentials due to various cultural and social situations. Whatever produces a deterioration of the human elements of a society, especially among its youth, its talented superiors, and key classes, dissipates its original and fundamental capital and makes for decadence with accompanying functional impairment.

Decadence Processes of Secularization

The decadence processes of secularization are actually those which characterize modern so-called "secular" societies, with their high communicative and mobile populations, their breakdown of spatial, social, and mental isolation, and, hence, their vast accessibility along these lines. Secular societies are also characterized by great technological development, complex differentiation, stratification, division of labor and specialization, urbanization, multiplied and varied groupings, complex forms of opposition, cosmopolitanism, and, above all, rapidity of social and cultural change and paucity of fixed patterns of the life organizations of their individual members, with its consequent demoralization.

This situation must be contrasted to that of ideal-typical "sacred" societies where there is considerable physical, mental, and social immobility and vicinal, social, and mental isolation. Notable also are relative stability and common acceptance of values, folkways, and mores, much dependence upon tradition and ceremonial, stability and fixity of institutions, relatively unchanging and ready-made definitions of interactional situations, and rather rigid static life organization and character attitudes of the individual members. The people generally live in terms of the past.*

Secularization as a process consists of what occurs when a society goes through the transition from sacred to secular form. It is an extremely inclusive process. It implies a departure from an impermeable value system, a partial release of men's minds from established systems of belief, and the breaking down of the norms of relationship with consequent *anomie.* There occurs a growing irreverence for the folkways, mores, and institutions, a loosening of the bonds of tradition, and a tendency to view almost everything functionally rather than traditionally. In most kinds of social action, the criterion is utility, and in individual action, the determinant is the hedonistic and egoistic wishes of the individual. People increasingly respond to the new, and the new things, ways, and experiences are prized above the old. Attention is paid to discovery and invention, and innovation accelerates. Change is viewed as normal rather than abnormal.

*Attention was called to the dichotomy of sacred and secular societies in Chap. 2.

Individuals become members of more and more groups, and group membership is rather loosely defined. Social control is not primarily informal, face-to-face, and through the customs and mores, but by means of formal, rational, legal controls and contracts. The specifications for a growing proportion of social relationships, functions, and responsibilities are not exact and specific, but variable and left to be worked out expediently as occasion demands. Principles are flexible. There is more and more milling about and dynamic disequilibrium.

The process, of course, is not sudden. Not all of the elements and features of the sacred society are set aside or lost. Not all of its effects are disequilibrative and decadence-producing; many of them constitute highly essential and suitable new organizational structures and functions. In a changing world secularization makes possible a smoother and more rapid adaptation of new conditions. But there *are* certain decadence-producing subprocesses inherent in it that will be briefly examined.

Individuation, Demoralization, Marginalization. Individuation, or atomization, was discussed in Chapter 16 as an isolative process. It is also one of the inherent subprocesses of secularization that has profound decadence-producing effects. In this respect it may be said to be synonymous with *demoralization*. As secularization proceeds, there are fewer and fewer established and prescribed behavioral patterns and more and more freedoms, but, paradoxically, at the same time, there is a greater and greater volume of often seemingly contradictory controls over persons *en masse*. Furthermore, with the rapidity of change characteristic of secularization, the old rigid and static life organization of the individual must often be consciously set aside, since it no longer functions properly.

Nevertheless, life organization, as Becker points out, is no more than a set of rules or formulas for meeting relatively constant situations in the corporate life of social groups (1, p. 272) Moreover, in a secularized society not only is it permissible and possible for individuals to go their own way, but they are more and more on their own. And yet, many persons cannot seize upon or form an adequate life organization that will enable them to prevent disaster. Thus, the individual personality disintegrates to a point where there emerges "the man without conscience, the woman without shame, individuals cut loose from the laws of common humanity." (1, p. 273) Owing to this condition of demoralization all sorts of irregular, amoral, immoral, and illegal behavior as adjudged both by primary- and secondary-group standards is likely to occur.

Secularization also produces a type of "marginal men," that is, human beings on the margin between sacred and secular ways of life. They are controlled in part by character attitudes derived from the hold-over sacred society and at the same time are liberated and individuated by the influence of the secular society. They are not at home in either, but are in a continual state of inner conflict and social maladjustment. Depending upon their particular temperamental make-up, they may react in the way of abnormally aggressive self-assertion or they may show marked introversion. (1, pp. 279-280)

Both individuated and marginalized behavior are at the same time evidence and cause of social decadence. Both societal structures and functions are impaired by the presence and the socially inadequate behavior of such denormalized persons. Various of the component building blocks are rotten and crumbling; collective, cooperative, and regulatory necessities are not met, and essential individual and social satisfactions are not provided.

Individual and Social Segmentation.* In a secular society there is an infinite differentiation of the population in the form of innumerable groups and a complex specialization of functions. The members are characterized by anonymity and lonesomeness and by extreme diversification of values, interests, and functions. Because of their particularistic nature, few of these groups provide adequate sociability or permit full expression of the individuals. This is true even of the modern family, as well as of recreational, religious, occupational, professional, and other groups. At the same time, individuals and groups are more and more specialized as to economic capacities and activities. In fact, there is a tendency to overspecialization, which causes individuals and groups to develop lack of transferability and lack of ready adjustment to changing conditions. Individuals tend to become

*This term is Becker's. (1, p. 281)

like some of Lord Avebury's ants that starved to death in sight of food because they were not the food-carrying ants.

For the society there is the danger that the multiple differentiations and specializations will not permit adequate integration of parts and functions. The result is a societal machine whose parts are not working together, but are strewn about, so to speak, or are in continual danger of falling apart. Only with difficulty can the various parts be adequately integrated, and there are always likely to be gaps.

Massing. In a secularized society, massing is the other side of the individuation and segmentation shield. Individuals and separate groups are not all of a piece, but modern collectivizing processes treat them as though they were. Modern populations are huge and both densely concentrated and widespread over great communicating areas and are treated as impersonal masses. Thus, we have a mass culture in religion, recreation, language, literature, and humor; mass communication and public opinion; mass government; mass production and consumption; mass fashions; mass patriotism; mass Americanization; mass security and well-being; mass standards and patterns of behavior; and a mass character. (2)

Population is an amorphous mass. All is for the average, or "lumped," man. There is a growing invalidation of the individual as the unique, precious creature he is. He is lost in a person-destroying giantism, and is more and more a passive, complying unit, less and less a personalized responsible agent. The individual as such is the real forgotten man of modern life. These collectivizing and externalizing tendencies of modern society encourage an individualism, *not* based on civilized traits of fine expressionism and socially responsible and cooperative behavior, but on devil-may-care, self-seeking, personally aggressive, dog-eat-dog attitudes, which are more and more untouched by friendly societally centered considerations.

Societally speaking, there is a growing tendency toward mass behavior as the structure of mutual confidence and regard weakens and falls apart. At the same time there may be public frivolity and public apathy toward important matters. Cultural epidemics and phobias are a possibility and occasionally an actuality, as witness Orson Welles's famous radio hoax of the invasion from Mars. Panic is likely to occur and engulf many people. There are crowds and crowding. Rumor and suspicion and misrepresentation spread readily and often lead to mob action and mob violence, as in race riots.

Any kind of irrational excitement spreads more readily and rapidly increases in intensity. Fashions and fads in every department of life are widespread —new religious cults, card games, dress, foods, walkathons and dance marathons. Economic and financial inflationary "booms" and depression "busts" have to be carefully guarded against. The very mass behavior is a collective reaction to a general feeling that the existing order is not functioning in a satisfactory manner. A spirit of unrest and dissatisfaction pervades the population; attention turns to all sorts of escapes. (5, pp. 371-407)

General Social Processes of Decadence

Certain general social processes in a society like our own lead to decadence and therefore should be mentioned here.

Radicalization. The process of radicalization (9, pp. 370, 389-390) is frequently bound up with segmentation. It is the product of excessive orthodoxy in values and beliefs, insufficient satisfaction of social wants and needs, and rigidity of social structures. It is a form of hyperindividuation and consists of a fanatical belief in the need for one-sided change, either in regard to certain aspects of social relations and processes or to the whole social order, and an aggressive activity in furthering the new thing or way. Always the change should be speedy. It may be merely revisionist or reformist, but occasionally the objectives and efforts are revolutionary —deep, thoroughgoing, sweeping, and carrying the threat of violence. The action is usually premature and hence upsetting. Toynbee speaks of this as "futurism," an attempt "to break away from an irksome present by taking a flying leap out of it into another reach of the stream of time without abandoning the plane of mundane life on Earth." (8, p. 515)

Mobility. Mobility has been previously discussed as both an organizational and a separative process.

Whether physical or horizontally or vertically social, mobility has a disorganizing effect on both the individuals and the communities involved and tends to amoralization and demoralization. Individuals are isolated from kinfolk and other familiar persons of the primary groups of which they have been an accepted and supported functional part. In the new environment they may be unknown and anonymous and through ignorance or design free from primary-group controls. The migrants are separated from familiar culture elements, especially norms, customs, mores and some institutional features, which not only leaves them without disciplines and directives, but impairs values and order in the community.

Culture Contact and Culture Shock. Culture contact, invariably related to mobility, brings people of divergent cultural backgrounds into intimate contact with each other. The result is confusion and perplexity as to values, standards, and everyday life procedures, for people have no common definition of the situation, no foundation of mutual understanding or appreciation, no basis for cooperative action. The processes of continuous adjustment are unavoidably complicated. Conflicts, lags, and other inconsistent behavior are certain to be in evidence. The difficulties between white men and Indians, between old city dwellers and new arrivals from the country, between the older or indigenous population and immigrants are cases in point. (6)

An obvious related process is culture shock. In this process an emigrant element, a heretofore relatively isolated minority, or any population element is brought into sudden contact with a more complex, widely dominant culture, many features of which are incomprehensible and overwhelming, and breaks down under the confusing and disorganizing impact. Modern communication and transportation have at times been the means of causing culture shock.

Exploitation. and Parasitism. Exploitation is closely related to various processes of social conflict. Usually it is one of the primary objectives of conflict. It consists of the use of conscious and purposive efforts on the part of both experienced and amateur individual manipulators of groups to obtain control over other individuals and groups in order to use them without adequate compensation, to advance the interests of the special manipulating parties, or to accomplish other objectives incompatible with the general well-being.

The exploitation may be conducted for egotistic, sexual, political, religious, or economic purposes and takes many forms—flattery, gossip, and ridicule; some types of reward; misrepresentation and misdirection; lying, deception, and intrigue; intimidation and terrorization (Ku Klux Klan, Gestapo); racketeering, confiscations, and robbery; supernatural controls; and slavery or selfish and conscienceless utilization of backward people and colonies. Exploitation always tends to produce individual decadence among all concerned and a general state of societal malfunctioning. (3, pp. 16-49, 179-214, 262-302; 7, pp. 172-191; 9, pp. 377-385; 10)

Closely related to exploitation is *parasitism,* a frequently occurring condition and process both in nature and in human society. It is important because of the harm it causes. In human society it connotes the radical exploitation of one individual or group by another individual or group. The parasite is a dead loss to the individuals or groups it lives on, usually receiving a maximum gain from a minimum outlay. But the parasite loses its independence or its power to be self-sufficient and self-supporting and degenerates inherently and socially, becoming a mere appendage to the host. Caste systems, slavery, and dictatorships involve parasitism.

The presence of parisitism in a social relationship means that the parasitic elements are not "pulling their load." In the long run it has an adverse selective effect, destroying or weakening the more fit and useful and preserving the relatively worthless. A society with many parasites is ultimately destroyed. (2, pp. 479-482)

"Diseases" of Institutional Organizations

Institutional organizations are peculiarly susceptible to certain "diseases" which bring about their deterioration and cause them to fall away from the purposes they were devised to serve. Some of these disease are results of ossification or are contributory to it and will be treated in the next section. At this point we shall briefly examine the diseases that produce decay.

Favoritism, Patronage, and Nepotism. Through the related processes of favoritism, patronage, and nepotism administrative boards and officials and others who exercise selective authority in societal organizations, especially in connection with economic, political, religious, charitable, and educational institutions, place friends, relatives, and political or factional affiliates in functional positions without regard to their proficiency, skills, or abilities. The selection and placement are made in order to take care of relatives or to pay some kind of debt.

Perversion. Perversion is the process whereby a college, charity, religious sect, or almost any institutional organization departs from its original objectives and ceases to perform its essential functions. The structure may become infested with self-seekers. It becomes more interested in administrators than in inspiring and dynamic leaders. As a result its members lose their sense of consecration; its jobs become sinecures; its members are held by hand-outs of favor and privilege; and the organization becomes an end in itself, conducted for the sake of its operating personnel. (7, pp. 619-622; 9, pp. 392-394)

Commercialization. Commercialization is the excessive subjection of an occupation, calling, profession, or organization to the profit motive. It is closely related to perversion and is in a sense a form of exploitation. It is a continual threat in all economic organizations and may become dominant in noneconomic institutional activities. People even marry for money. "Commercialization" means a subversion of creative or service activity, of standards of excellence, of solicitude for the welfare of customers, clients, or patrons, and may be found in business, professional, and artistic organizations. (7, pp. 559-569; 9, pp. 391-392)

Corruption. Corruption is the procedure whereby antisocial persons or groups induce or seduce members, constituents, or functionaries of an organization by bribes, graft, or fraud to render them special, usually illegal, services not otherwise obtainable. Governmental departments and agencies on every level are especially susceptible to this disease. It can also occur in other kinds of organization. Corruption undermines decency, confuses people as to objectives and methods, and produces vicious waste and malfunctioning. It is contrary to organizational and general well-being and is distinctly disintegrative in its social effects.

Red Tape. What has come to be called "red tape" is the result of efforts to forestall corruption and dishonesty in the conduct of societal organizations by requiring endless and complicated reporting, auditing, checking and double checking, and detailed supervision of all activities of the operating personnel. Some of this control is vitally necessary, but frequently there is a tendency for it to become excessive. The procedure may grow so cumbersome, so consuming of time, energy, and resources, so obstructive of prompt action and destructive of efficiency that it becomes an organizational disease as serious as the diseased procedures it seeks to prevent.

Processes of Societal Ossification

General Nature and Factors of Ossification

The processes of social ossification are those whereby social structures or important parts of them undergo a petrifying or crystallizing action which tends to retain, even accentuate, the visible organzational form, but results in a loss of flexibility and consequent loss in functional utility.* There is a devitalizing excess of organization. The tendency of the processes is to produce organizational monuments rather than flexible, living, operating social agencies.

*The term "social ossification" was first used by E. A. Ross at the beginning of the present century. Von Wiese and Becker also use it.

The end results of the processes of decadence and of ossification are essentially the same; in both instances there is serious functional impairment of societal structures. But the processes whereby this impairment has come about are different. Some years ago, in the cutover country of northern Minnesota, the writer came upon a curious mound several feet high, three or four feet wide, and about fifty feet long. Digging into it, he found that it was the prostrate, rotting, and crumbling remains of what had once been a magnificent tree. The following summer, in the Petrified Forest of Arizona, the writer saw dozens of great logs, showing evidences of bark and rings that could be counted. But the logs were as hard and impervious as stone. In Minnesota there had been decadence; in Arizona, ossification. In both instances, however, there were only dead remainders of once-flourishing trees.

Not only do the ossification processes produce petrifaction of social structures; they also make for "archaism," as Toynbee calls it, and the "back-look." They cause the departments of social life that are affected by them to get out of step and fall behind the rest of the societal procession.

Ross has presented some of the *factors involved in ossification.* (7, pp. 585-590)

Mental Laziness. Human beings are loath to exert themselves mentally; they shrink from recognizing a changed situation, rethinking the problem, and reorganizing the task and the agencies devised to carry it through. They roll along in the rut of habit and routine.

Control of Social Structures by Older Members. Social structures tend to be controlled by older members of the society. The old are inclined to abide by their earlier values, judgments, and ways. They are concerned with security and wish to preserve the familiar status quo.

Veneration and Sanctification of Precedents and Long-Established Ways. Says Ross: "The long-established becomes an Ark of the Covenant which we fear to lay hands on lest we meet the fate of Uzzah." The things our forefathers fought and bled for and the things we have cherished and lived by so long have become stumbling blocks. The Bible becomes a kind of "scientific manual," and the amendment of the Constitution is hedged about with all sorts of restrictions. There is the sedulous preservation of antiquated rules and ways.

Assumption or Hope That Society Is Static. Change means adjustment, and adjustment requires planning and policy-making and vast expenditures of individual and social energy in putting the plans and policies into effect. Hence, people like to imagine that society keeps to the track, and that it does not take new directions. Most of us view the future with some misgivings and hesitancy.

Vested Interests Resistant to Change. Persons who have come to depend upon an institution resist proposals to abandon or alter it. Many lawyers do not want the statutes or court procedure to change; some professors do not want their subject matter to change; theological seminaries long resisted the incorporation of sociology and economics in their curriculums, and many ministers do not want theology to change.

Dominant Social Class Resistant to Change. Their present position and power rests upon the past and present policies, relations, and institutions. The new thing is "radical" or "socialistic."

The Masses Probably Most Resistant to Change. The masses tend to resist all change save where it is to their advantage. They recall what they have experienced in the past and fear losing what they now have. Innovation presents unknowns that, because of their uncertain and untried nature, are often feared and avoided, with the result that antiquated mechanisms and stupid routines persist.

Formalism or Institutionalism

The most notable effect of the processes of ossification is the organizational and societal condition known as "formalism"* or "institutionalism." We

*The term "formalism" and the classic analysis of it as a social process and condition is that of C. H. Cooley, *Social Organization.* (12, pp. 342-355) For a comprehensive treatment of the factors and processes involved in producing inflexibility of institutions and of the effects, see Hertzler, *Social Institutions.* (6, pp. 237-255)

shall examine briefly its nature, the processes and factors involved in its development, and its effects.

Nature of Formalism. Institutions are the agencies whereby the life of a given society is maintained and perpetuated. No society whose institutions are insubstantial or flabby can prosper or even long endure. If the institutions are too easily modified, they are pernicious and do not serve their strategic functions. They should have a degree of durability and permanence. And yet, social prosperity demands that this fixity and persistence should not be carried too far. Unfortunately, there is a tendency for this to occur.

The relationship of institutionalization to eternal social change is well stated by Toynbee:

> Ideally . . . the introduction of new dynamic forces ought to be accompanied by a reconstruction of the whole existing set of institutions, and in any actually growing society a constant readjustment of the more flagrant anachronisms is continually going on. But *vis inertia* tends at all times to keep most parts of the social structure as they are, in spite of their increasing incongruity with new social forces constantly coming into action. (8, p. 280)

Institutionalism is this tendency of institutional organizations to concentrate on archaic and irrelevant forms of procedure and increasingly to go through the motions of rendering their specific societal services or merely fulfill requirements that may be empty of content. It is "mechanism supreme." The institutions tend to become bearers of social fossils—crystallized depositories of archaic attitudes, beliefs, codes, habits, and social procedures.

Factors of Formalism. Various quite understandable *factors* specifically related to the nature of institutions and the characteristics of their personnel account for institutionalism. Although societally unfortunate, they are quite natural. *Institutions are established structures,* and structures, in order to endure, must become stable and fairly rigid. The first requirement in the processes of institutionalization is to construct and standardize its machinery and activity. *Institutions are products of the past,* the products of experience and contrivance, and *have* functioned as useful instrumentalities. *Institutions are agents of control and conservation,* bulwarks against disorder. They preserve the conserving pattern.

Institutions are in charge of administrators who often become conservative, even reactionary. Leaders and administrators often become comfortable, once their position is secure, and they are flattered by their own pre-eminence. They also tire and try to avoid new and complicating, energy-requiring situations. Hence, they attempt to routinize their duties. Furthermore, old men usually are in charge of institutions; and old men are invariably conservative. They abide by their earlier judgments. The outgrown condition, the effete thing, escapes their notice. New and unfamiliar procedures are anathema. *Some institutions have a protected position.* They safely hide behind some doctrine of expediency, some generally accepted fiction of inspiration, revelation, or unchallengeable wisdom of the Founding Fathers, some time-honored apology, some major social fear, some vested thoughtway, or even some appealing figure of speech. *Institutions engender loyalty, pride, and sentiment which promote their longevity. New institutions must be made out of old materials.*

Varied Societal Effects of Institutionalism. Some of the more important effects of institutionalism follow.

PERSISTENCE OF ANTIQUATED MECHANISMS AND STUPID ROUTINES. Men become slaves of their ancestors' machines. The time and energy of the functionaries, and sometimes of the personnel as a whole, is given to stupid preoccupation with nonessential machinery or superficial details. There is lack of vital thought and energy to keep the social mechanism pliant to its task. The disease is to be found in various forms in the church, in government, education, industry, and the so-called "service" agencies. The personnel drifts into a perfunctory and mechanical way of doing its work; the standardized curriculum of the school or college becomes a convention and then a tradition, and the teachers tend to become routinized and lose their power to inspire; the religious belief is crystallized into a creed and a vast organization, and the clergy becomes more intent on ritual, orthodoxy, and observation of creeds and forms than on kindling religious fervor.

Not only does age ennoble these institutional

ways, but their administration is put into the hands of self-perpetuating boards or other professional functionaries. Thereby an inertia sets in which maintains them far beyond their legitimate time.

RESTRAINT OF INDIVIDUAL AND GROUP ACTIVITY. The set patterns establish limits and tend to discourage or even inhibit further learning and experimentation. Frustrations and repressions galore are developed, individuality is suppressed, and the energies of human beings are repressed or misdirected. The dynamic spirit of the group is also crushed.

INSTITUTIONS AS ENDS IN THEMSELVES. Institutions tend to develop a sanctity and an inherent infallibility which causes them to become ends in themselves and above criticism. The institutional personnel has become a more or less self-sufficient in-group and conducts the institution for its own sake rather than for its social function. What was developed originally as a means is still cherished when the ends have been secured or are antiquated and the means no longer necessary. As Cooley pointed out many years ago, there is an overemphasis on symbols, not as embodiments and vehicles of the underlying idea and purpose of the organization or institution, but as objects of worth in themselves, as substitutes for reality.

DISTORTION OR LOSS OF FUNCTION. The very stability and persistence of an institution may result in its conversion to uses for which it was never intended. Basic aims and principles may in time come to be sacrificed, as when a church founded to promote unity and catholicity becomes extremely sectarian and bigoted, or a political party dedicated to personal freedom and equality becomes the champion of special interests.

VESTIGIAL CHARACTERISTICS OF INSTITUTIONS. Institutions are likely to have forms left over from earlier days. Such institutional forms are often quite ineffective in satisfying existing needs. Their current existence is an anomaly. Vestiges are likely to, and frequently do, become seats of dangerous disease, paralleling in this respect the human vermiform appendix and the tonsils. Often, a dead or nearly dead societal carcass is lying about and an array of essential social functions are being conducted inadequately or not at all.

SPECIAL DANGER OF BUREAUCRACIES.* A bureaucracy sets an exaggerated value on the maintenance of the institutional scheme of which it is the guardian. The individual member of the bureaucracy magnifies his own function and is jealous of any encroachments. There is often an unchallenged insistence upon punctilious adherence to formalized procedures and mechanical regulations, resulting in the subdiseases of ***routinization, ritualism,*** and ***rule by rote.*** Experiment and innovation are complacently rejected. The personnel is often overtrained for minute jobs and incapable of being transferred. Seniority is given priority, and correctness is more esteemed than ability, while responsibility is shunned. The public, for whose benefit the organization exists, is regarded as a nuisance which ought to accommodate itself to the convenience of the personnel. The organization tends to grow stereotyped, inflexible, and mechanical. (17; 18; 20, pp. 362-366; 21; 22; 23)

*For treatment of the nature of bureaucracies, see Chap. 11.

Some Special Diseases of Ossification

Ossified structures, especially institutional organizations, are prone to develop defunctionalizing diseases, such as the following:

Institutional Separatism. An accompaniment of institutionalism, and in some instances a result of it, is what has been termed "institutional separatism." (15, pp. 430-437) This process has separative and decadence-producing, as well as ossifying, effects. There is a disposition of institutions to regard themselves as both independent of the communities for which they exist and as separate and apart from each other. This develops from the tendency of every institution to become an end in itself. Its functionaries act as if this were so.

Only in times of crisis do leaders of business, religion, social work, political bodies, recreation and other institutions come together for the purpose of discussing and shaping community policies. In universities there is the temptation for each department to operate as a separate administrative unit on its own jealously guarded budget, adhering religiously to its own curriculum, and insistently maintaining the reputed distinctiveness, and possibly the superiority and indispensability, of its field and subject matter. The personnel of institutional organizations refuse to face unitedly the fact that they are fantastically interwoven.

Social—Especially Institutional—Lag. Cultural lag as related to cultural processes was discussed in Chapter 6. A phase of this is social organizational lag, which is the relative ossification of some structural part of society as compared with other parts that have been more or less prompt in their structural and functional adjustment to the changing society. Some part has remained more or less static in spite of the dynamic demands upon it. The parts changing slowly lag behind the others. Since all parts of a society are interlaced and functionally interdependent, this lag and relative immobility of some parts produces stresses and strains and overloading in the closely related parts of the web.

This tendency may take several forms. Certain parts of the institution may lag with respect to other parts. Thus, the code may persist, in all its sanctity, but the practice may change. Certain institutions may lag as compared with others that are vitally interdependent. There is a dangerous lag today between ethical, political, and religious institutions as they are related to intellectual, scientific, economic, and technological advances of present-day society. Politicians, for example, are full of inertia and self-interest, and legislatures are slow to provide laws for soil conservation and water control, transportation and traffic control, new corporation practices, new forms or technologies in crime and in anticipating essential public works or services or military situations. Such lags invite "harebrained," rushed, inadequately planned schemes when crisis strikes.

An entire organized group may lag behind the rest of the society because of involuntary or self-imposed isolation. Some sectarian and ethnic groups are in part illustrations. Socially they are only partial participants, not carrying their load; they persist as a sort of vestigial element in the body politic.

Reactionism. Reactionism is the converse of radicalization, which is a premature leap into the future. Reactionism is a nostalgic disposition and effort to leap back into the past. It seeks a reversion to, and a renewing of, some previously current but now abandoned mode of thought and system of organization. The reactionary fears both the future and the present. For him only the past is safe. He yearns for the ways of the good old days in moral conduct, business, government, art, religion! This is definite evidence of ossification. The reactionary is muddled and socially illiterate. The past provides lessons for those who read it aright, but time and change make its continued existence impossible.

Indifferentism. Indifferentism is a senile disease of social structures which develops when the entrenched functionaries of a social agency, neither subject to competition among themselves nor enlivened by the competition of similar agencies, lose their zeal, their competency, and their sense of service and perform merely as "chairwarmers." They become indifferent to their functional obligations to the organization's constituency. It is a disease which attacks military organizations in peacetime. Semipublic and public agencies which serve the ignorant or the lowly are particularly susceptible to it. Effete churches, universities, and religious orders suffer under its torpor. (20, pp. 611-612)

Absolutism. The disease of absolutism is closely related to both indifferentism and obsolescence. It comes when social structures are *absolved* from obedience to the judgment and wishes of their time. There is the imperious sway of archaic needs and principles. Autonomous corporations and self-constituted and self-perpetuating boards of directors or administrators and controlling cliques can easily produce this disease for their organizations. A particular bias becomes a basis of selection of the new personnel, and the bias becomes chronic. There may be occasional new blood but not new ideas and new ways based on study and experiment. An ancient outmoded formula is perpetuated and administered absolutely by people who are "already dead" as far as their ability to make efficacious, present-day, societal structural and functional appraisals and directives is concerned.

Obsolescence. Obsolescence is due to the retention of old and outmoded forms, equipment, and procedures until they become sanctuaries of antiquity rather than contemporary, dynamic, operating entities. These forms constitute "vestigial remains," which time and changing functions have canceled, and which at best are useless or nonusable and at worst may be cancerous growths. Obsolescence is the sway of the dead hand, to use a legal term, trying to operate or regulate the present according to the will and ways of those long since dead. It is often found in wills which set up endowment funds in perpetuity. There are still funds accumulating to carry on services for nonexistent categories of recipients simply because no legal way has been found to break the grip of the dead hand. For example, there are funds to provide for the widows and orphans of American seamen killed fighting the Tripoli pirates, to care for old fire horses and stranded migrants moving westward in prairie schooners, and so on. (20, pp. 614-619)

We have examined a vast array of destructuralizing and defunctionalizing processes, all of which impair the operation of any society as a going concern. No society, if it is to endure, can ignore them or leave them unchecked. To avoid the serious consequences of these processes and to ensure adequate and satisfactory functioning, every society has an equally extensive array of agencies and procedures which make for continuous regulation, normalization, and reorganization. The examination of these procedures follows.

PART SIX

MECHANISMS AND PROCESSES OF NORMALIZATION AND EQUILIBRATION

CHAPTER XIX

SOCIAL ORDER AND SOCIAL CONTROL

IN PART FOUR we learned that a functioning society must have adequate structuralization of its constituent members into groups, associations, formal organizations, communities, institutions, and interdependently differentiated segments and strata. As individuals and as members of groups, human beings must get along with their fellow men, and many actions and relationships must be made to fit into some kind of functioning unity. Associated individuals, however, do not play their social roles with equal degrees of proficiency and responsibility. Shifting of relationship and power among the differentiated and stratified elements is continuous, and cultural processes constantly produce modifications and confusions of values, norms, attitudes, and habits. In Part Five we examined the various separative, oppositional, decadence-causing, and ossifying processes that continually produce or threaten to produce some degree of destructuralization and defunctionalization.

In Part Six we shall examine the mechanisms and processes that determine normalization and equilibrium. Our examination will begin in this chapter with social order and social control.

Normalizing and Equilibrating Mechanisms and Processes

If there is to be not only survival but also individual self-fulfillment, adequate group life, security and certainty, and the possibility of prosperity and progress, these weaknesses of organization and the ever-present tendencies toward disorganization must be continuously and persistently countered. This counteraction is the function of the normalizing and equilibrating mechanisms and processes, for they regulate, maintain, restore, reorganize, and, in certain situations, reconstruct essential social structures and functions. They grow out of the fact that any considerable degree of fluctuation from the normal or the adequate threatens the stability and continuity of the society and the well-being of its members. Giddings's example from physiology is very appropriate. (10, p. 207) The temperature of the healthy human body fluctuates about the normal 98.6° Fahrenheit. When the range of variation is considerably widened either below or above the normal, it means that a serious state of shock or disease exists. Similarly, there is a certain "98.6°" of order, maintenance, restoration, and construction—in brief, of function—from which a community or society cannot widely depart without suffering "ill-health." As Giddings pointed out (10, p. 201), if society is to survive, it cannot withstand very wide variations or deviations of individual or group behavior. It cannot allow individuals or groups to fall too far short of behavior essential to order and operation. Equilibrium must be perpetually restored. Every fairly healthy society, therefore, is a dynamic, moving, flowing equilibrium of processes of organization, disorganization, and reorganization.

The task of maintaining this equilibrium involves two related conceptual fields, namely, *social order* and *social control*. Social order comprises the norms of harmonious relations between the individuals or parts of a community or society, that is, the norms of conformity of behavior and functional adjustment. Social control refers to the congeries of mechanisms and processes whereby society as a living thing resists deflection and *controls* variations from itself. Factors which produce "high social temperature" must be regulated, reduced, corrected, or otherwise adjusted. Where there is "low social temperature," there must be boosting and restoration. Always there must be inculcation and discipline.

In all societies the social control is continuously in operation. By means of the controls the behavior of individuals and groups is regulated and standardized in the interests of social order and efficiency; a sufficient degree of physical, psychological, and social maintenance is provided for; procedures and mediums of accommodation and equalization exist; reformation, reorganization, and construction are being carried on continually in some instances and recurrently at certain times and under certain conditions in other instances. The concepts of social order and social control will be examined in the next two sections.

Social Order

There is no absolute social order. There exists in any society a zone of toleration and permissibility of variation, schism, opposition, individualism, antisociality, lack of participation and responsibility, and relative inefficiency and inadequacy of function. A fairly normal society is a "flexible" society. (1, pp. 497-498) Nevertheless, no society can have its constituent elements working at cross-purposes beyond these limits or have more than a certain amount of inefficiency, waste, friction, or lag in its operation or of stalemate or disorder among its diverse and often antagonistic individuals or groups.

Social order is that indispensable and crucial harmonization, coordination, and correlation of interactions wherever and whenever two or more persons are trying to live together. No combination or plurality of human beings can persist without mutual adjustment, good conduct, social peace and constructive action. Order is the first requirement, the life necessity, of the diverse, specialized, interrelated activities of men. To have this order, there must be an organization of requirements for social living, both within and between the groupings of men. As MacIver puts it, there must be a "firmament of order." (35, p. 75)

Individual Factors Affecting Social Order

We have already noted the fact that variations exist among individuals because of biological and psychological differences. Peculiarities of cultural background and training produce differences and create possibilities for irritation and opposition. Inequalities of wealth, income, education, and other affectors of social position produce jealousy and dissension. It must also be pointed out that individuals differ enormously in their capacities to understand social requirements in social situations of different levels of social and cultural complexity, in their sense of responsibility, and in their willingness and ability to participate in a societally adequate manner.

There are always persons who do not hold up their end of necessary joint undertakings which benefit all. There are the socially ignorant and the socially infantile who are unconscious of, or immune to, any conception of their social obligations and responsibilities and some who are callously indifferent and inconsiderate. Many people are egoistic and selfish, even brutal, as they compete with their associates, and some—moral idiots and lunatics—are downright predatory and criminal in their behavior toward others. There are always persons ready to commit social sabotage. Still others spend much of their time and energy in a persistent endeavor to "get even," to retaliate, to block and destroy others in order to compensate for the jealousy or to release the hate they feel.

Sects, cliques, minorities, and other special-interest groups may pursue their own distinct and often conflicting desires and objectives in buccaneer fashion. Routineers try to prevent necessary social change, and innovators sometimes bring on change prematurely. Because modern societies are vast and complicated, even the best intentioned and most socially minded are sometimes unable to comprehend and perform their parts in an accurate and timely manner.

Social Conditions and Social Changes

Contemporary social conditions and changes make more pointed and more difficult the problem of social order. We have already examined the social complications produced by physical and social mobility, by technological changes in a "mass" society, by the increasing impersonality of relationships, by the division of labor and social stratification. Our society is also characterized by the accelerated appearance of new knowledge. New knowledge tends to make much old knowledge uncouth and useless, and invariably, if it is to be utilized, it requires new ways of life. For example, the germ theory of diseases, the new light on human heredity, the new views regarding the utilization and conservation of natural resources, the knowledge of conditions conducive to mental, and other developments, have thrust a host of imperative individual, informal, and organized group responsibilities and functions upon us. Yet, we lack the imagination, the social intelligence and will, and the cooperative organization to carry them into effect. Where there should be orderly, concerted action, there is disfunction, frustration, and confusion.

These personal and social factors making for social disorder underscore the importance of social order.

Some Implications of Social Order

What specifically do socially informed citizens and social scientists have in mind when they are trying to determine the substance of social order. That is, what does social order actually consist of? Some of the more important implications of social order are the following:

1. *An enforced absence of discord, disorder, conflict, and the maximum possible freedom from exploitive or predatory behavior.* Men must be able to assume that others will commit no intentional aggressions upon them.

2. *The development of, and the conformity to or compliance with, established standards and patterns of cooperative relationships which are accepted by most of the associated human beings.* Mankind needs patterns for joint living, not only in relationships with those who are unlike and who are disliked, but also in order to live with those like them and whom they love.

3. *The organizations, customs, institutions, bodies of ideas and values, and patterns must be comparatively stable and orderly and consistent in relation to each other.*

4. *The individuals,* regardless of personal inclination or social position *are actually and in large measure participating in behavior in all pertinent and continuous or recurrent social situations which produces harmony, coordination, and cooperation essential to satisfactory living together.* This involves both constraint of some behavior and eliciting of other types. There is always some curtailment of liberty, not to mention prohibition of license as well as encouragement of and insistence upon positive action.

5. The careful and effective *observation of unavoidable and essential precedences and degrees of subordination among diverse and discrete individ-*

uals and groups—the "pattern of distinction" and the "social pecking order"—inherent in all successful organization of function.

6. The *necessary enforcing authority prevails,* which is usually a matter of gradations and degrees, differing in source, amount, and kind for the different types of relationships.

7. As significant as any other feature of this ordering is the fact that *the standardized and coordinated conduct,* which is channelized, directed, and enforced by the various established social processes, mechanisms, and pressures, *becomes so regular that it makes possible not only the prescription but also the expectation and prediction of essential, desirable, or satisfactory behavior* of the vast proportion of persons in any given, more or less current social situation. Every relationship must be ordered and standardized so that individual caprice and variation in interpretation and procedure are limited or eliminated to the extent that general uniformity and dependability of behavior can be anticipated and predicted.

There can be no order without a *system of expectations*; without this individual or social life would be impossible. Men must be able to assume that those who are engaged in some course of conduct will act with due care not to cast the risk of injury upon others. This predictability of socially adequate behavior of other persons has the additional advantage that it makes it possible for each person to plan his own conduct in view of the probable reactions of other people under prescribed circumstances, thus producing not only general order, but more secure, more satisfying living for everyone. Such social order comes about by means of social control.

Nature and Significance of Social Control

"Control in its broadest sense may be defined as anything that exercises a modifying influence on anything else." (6, p. 207) In this sense the whole range of the universe constitutes an unbroken series of controls, for everything in it is affected in some manner and degree by every other part. All going concerns, whether physical, biological, or human, are characterized by order. Whenever there is order there is control. The orderliness we find in the physical universe is due to physical forces establishing a continuous equilibrium. Such social order as we find in animal groups below the human level is largely automatic—almost entirely an outcome of the controls exercised by geographical conditions, biological constitution, and the common instincts of the species.

The concept of control is fundamental to an interpretation of the life of every individual as well as the functioning of every society. As individuals we are not as "free" as we think. We are not physically free, since physical forces and processes limit us; we are not psychically free inasmuch as determining factors within and conditioning factors without are continually directing us; we are not culturally free, since from the moment of birth we live in the culture box of our own area and era. We are only *morally* free within the limits of choice established by all of our environments.

Social order is a result of *social control*; conversely, social control is concerned fundamentally with problems of orderliness—problems of the regularity of behavior, of maintenance, of equilibration of societal elements. As such social control in all its multiform aspects is one of the central and strategic features of any meaningful analysis of human society as a "going concern."

Meaning of Social Control

When we think of *social* control we mean the way social power and social influence *function* to regulate, direct, adjust, and organize the social conduct of individuals and groups. It is concerned with the comprehension and analysis of needs of human associative living, with the establishment of appropriate ends and criteria of such living, with the operation of the various essential processes, procedures, techniques and programs, and with the social instrumentalities for bringing about —by suggestion, instruction, persuasion, or compulsion—prescribed and expected actions and operations, or prohibiting, constraining, or preventing unsocial or anti-social or otherwise unwanted behavior. Social control is a matter of both "musts" and "must nots." In social control there is always social interaction, there is always 'causality" and "consequence"; there is always the action of societal units, individual or group, to influence or manipulate. (5).

Social Control—a Human Construct

Social order and social control cannot be taken for granted. They do not come from some mysterious cosmic mechanism; knowledge of, and motivation to, orderly patterned social action are not inherited biologically, nor do the processes of social control operate automatically. Social order must be achieved by man. (8) Control in human societies is a discovery. It is purposive and requires contrivance and effort and to be conducted and continuously maintained. In other words, social order is mainly a man-made condition, and social control is a set of man-made operations and mediums. The mediums take the form of common obligatory norms and usages which define the relations of persons to each other in all manner of social relationships, of persons to important things, such as in the case of property controls, of persons to ideas, beliefs, and ideologies, as in the case of religion. (12)

The established order and the effecting controls may, in some respects, be a result of ages of trial and error, random observation regarding social experience, bungling and hit-or-miss devising; they may occasionally—increasingly today in some departments of life—reflect expeditious, deliberately devised, inaugurated, and administered procedures and instrumentalities. But always social order and social control are *artificed* in large degree; they are a matter of directive and regulative actions, rather than of automatic, nature-given mechanism.

A *Guide to Human Behavior*. Effective social control is a guide to human behavior and gives direction to it. Without it, community living would be impossible, because each person would do what he wanted to do at will, without regard to other people or their desires. People do not respond to stimuli willy-nilly. Their responses are usually channelized and expressed in terms of prevailing standards and according to current processes. Social control tells each person when and how he is expected to act in almost every social situation. Behavior of all members of the entire society must be controlled not only along lines essential to peace and order, but within associations, including the great formal, operative organizations, where behavior of all members must be kept in line with the objectives and operative principles of the particular association if the basic functions are to be performed.

A *System of Conduct*. So complicated and fundamental is the problem of social order that even agreeable, socially well-intentioned persons need a *system* of social control to live by. If every individual loved his neighbor as himself and conscientiously observed the Golden Rule, there would still be necessity for a central controlling system. Two friends cannot go through the same door, cannot share in the same meal, or participate decently in the same conversation (to keep matters on a simple plane) without established and standardized, informal or formal principles of precedence and procedure. An assembly of ministers or a sorority of college girls in chapter meeting must conduct its affairs by means of Robert's "Rules of Order," regardless of the universal, reciprocal love prevailing. Intelligent and understanding people generally need the assistance of regulative agencies. We all have to do or should do a certain amount of thinking in every social situation and relationship, but by ourselves, however well informed, motivated, and self-controlled, we cannot establish a universal *pattern* of action each time; there must be standardized, tested, and widely accepted procedures for action in the various typical social situations.

Thus, organized social control is necessary, not simply as the major set of devices and procedures for order in the society, not simply as an assurance of stability, solidarity, and continuance; but *also as a means of preserving the well-being of every individual constituent of that society.* This point has been well developed by Landis. (14) He indicates that the individual develops a system of patterned behavior and an integrated personality only to the extent that he absorbs the patterns of an orderly, organized social environment. If he does not, he is a misfit in the social whole, a creature of abnormal stresses and strains. The social control system gives him an established frame of living, including socialized and moralized attitudes, consistent habits, and socially cultivated norms for his roles, his status, and other modes of life within his groups.

Social Organization as the Basic Orientation for Order and Control

Thus far the nature, significance, and processes of social organization have been examined in relation to the over-all structuralization of human society.* Now let us consider the relationship of social organization to the actuality of social order. Social organization is of special concern, since it constitutes the more or less established and formalized machinery in which people live their socially ordered and controlled daily lives. In fact, social organization and social order are inextricably related and supplement each other. Each implies the substantial existence of the other. It is impossible to have social order without organization for that purpose. It is equally unthinkable to organize associated human beings, that is, have effective functional structurings, unless these are ordered and controlled within the groupings themselves and among and between them.

For social organization, among other things, means that some sort of continuous and functional ordering arrangement or patterning exists in the world of associated men. The different parts of human society are in a state of articulation, integration, stabilization and equilibrium. In order that this may be possible, behavior is organized and standardized, and the requirements of essential behavior are enforced in all the significant contacts, relationships, and activities of social life. Thus, through the organizational framework unity is achieved among the discrete units within groups and between diverse groups; they behave in a manner expected of them and are enabled to act purposively and concertedly.

Aspects of Social Control

Although a system of social control exists to maintain order, the *conditions* under which it is exercised vary widely, and great variations and ranges exist among the processes and instrumentalities, especially with respect to the consciousness of intent, the play of personal and impersonal elements, the amount of social organization that is involved, the amount of social force used, the positive or negative nature of the controls, and the social objectives of the controllers. If the functioning of the social-control system is to be understood, the processes and instrumentalities must be comprehended at least in their elementary aspects. Unavoidably there will be some overlapping of concepts in such an examination.†

Range of Consciousness of Intention

The great array of social controls may be arranged by general categories and dichotomies from the point of view of the degree of individual and societal consciousness that enters into their operation.

Unconscious Control. Some of the control at the human-social level is a matter of random diffusion of, and spontaneous response to, stimuli emanating from fellow men, individually and collectively, past and present. Much behavior of the random suggestion-imitation variety is of this sort. Perhaps the most elemental control is that exercised by the play of suggestion under the influence of instincts (fear or hunger, for example) and evidenced in such rapport and uniform collective action as the "milling of the herd" in the form of crowd and mob phenomena and much of the behavior due to the submission to, and participation in, crazes and manias.

Many of the instrumentalities of control create a persistent "atmosphere" of control and dominate the controlled in a manner which is largely unconscious because they have been conditioned to them. In large measure this is true of control by folkways, customs, traditions, conventions, revelations, the moral codes, and even much of the control exercised by the long-standing deeply seated institutions. Here the control, though effective, is casual

*See Chap. 10.

†I am obligated for some of the concepts presented below in modified form to an unpublished prospectus on social-control systems by my colleague, Dr. Paul Meadows. He is in no way responsible for the uses made of his materials.

and without the intervention of invention, either on the part of the sources of stimulus or in the compliant behavior of the controllers.

Conscious Control. Other controls are intended as such by the individuals or social groups manipulating them; they have specific conformity-producing objectives. The controllees also are mostly conscious of wanting to conform or of being required to conform to their requirements. Notable examples are conformity to fads (by some—possibly the soft-headed) and to fashions (by most eventually), both of which are largely fostered and manipulated with deliberate intent nowadays, the conformity to the dictates of group or public opinion, to advertising with its conscious omnipresent and insistent pressure, to organized propaganda, to the laws of legislative bodies and the decrees of courts and administrative bodies, to the requirements of the organizations of which we are members, involuntarily and voluntarily, and to many of the chartered and enforced requirements of the institution, especially those that have come into being to meet recent and present needs, wants, and interests of the great majority of the community.

Personal and Impersonal Control

Control ranges from the personal, through the mainly impersonal, to the completely impersonal.

Personal Control. Some control is seated in, and exercised by, persons both living and dead. The obvious dead personal controllers are great rulers, heroes, reformers, idealists, deliverers, and so on—those of whom ideologies, associations, and institutions are sometimes "lengthened shadows"—who have influence on considerable portions of a society. There are also others, such as ancestors, that are of special significance to smaller groups. At any given time there is much control of both large and small groups by living persons—leaders and misleaders, organizational officials, persons of high class status, parents, persons with the prestige of age or learning, and so on. They exercise this control through their immediate or their visualized presence and actions.

Group Control. Both primary and secondary groups as collectivities exercise controls over the individuals composing them. Persons and lesser groups feel the weight of the control exercised by the neighborhood or the larger community through its action, whereas groups which are organizations with specific purposes—recreational, religious, political, military, professional, economic, civic—have more clearly defined control over their constituent elements.

Situational Control. Various social situations require uniformities of behavior because they are recurrent phenomena and have developed patterns of behavior through long historical experience or because they have a peculiarly inherent, possibly momentary, character. The situations presided over by familial, political, or religious institutions are examples of this kind of control, as are those governed by conventional requirements, contractual regulations or class or caste relations, celebrations, socioeconomic activities, and so on.

Formal and Informal Processes and Instruments

When control agencies and the processes related to them are examined as to degree of organization, they are usually placed in one of two major categories, which are distinguished by informal and unorganized controls and by organized and formal controls respectively. It might be more accurate, however, to point out that they range along a continuum of formality and organization with completely informal and noninstitutionalized controls at one extreme and highly formalized, institutionalized controls at the other. It must be kept in mind that every society institutionalizes, or incorporates into its institutions, the procedures and agencies essential to the ordering of the supremely important continuous or recurrent social relationships and situations. This range usually also involves degree of intention as discussed above.

Unorganized and Noninstitutionalized Controls. In themselves, the unorganized and noninstitutionalized controls may range from the utterly informal and implicit to those having an element of consciousness in their formulation and utilization but showing no social organization. These are all rather elementary controls and include, as examples, the imitation of parents and other adults by children as they engage in ordered social behavior and such other spontaneous personal-influencing actions as ridicule, gossip, name-calling, praising and blaming, and so on; illusions and belief in luck, magic, and other supernatural sanctions; and the milling control formed in crowds and mobs.

Unorganized Subinstitutional Sociocultural Controls. These controls are deep-seated cultural structures that have accumulated through time and experience and are perpetuated and emphasized because of their efficacy as control mediums. But they are only incipiently institutional. Many of them are the bases of institutional controls and supplement the institutions, but they are mainly subinstitutional in character. Legends, myths, dogmas, parables, admonitions, aphorisms, and proverbs belong to this group, but the most distinctive examples are the folkways, traditions, customs, conventions, including etiquette, the technicways, the mores, and all other unwritten laws.

Institutional Controls. The great battery of social devices contrived and organized through time to establish and maintain social order and operation in every major department of social life comprise the institutional controls. Their very *raison d'être* is the establishment of standardized, universal charters of action, based on imperative moral and utilitarian considerations and supported by general consensus. The controls have related purposive associations, including special functionaries vested with authoritative power and in many instances administrative officers obligated to carry out the regulative and maintenance objectives.

Institutional controls also have time-tried symbolic elements, including ceremony and ritual, and the physical equipment essential to their functioning. Notable, of course, are the matrimonial and familial institutions, the educational institutions, the economic institutions, the ethical-religious institutions, and especially the political institutions which have their own distinctive domain, but also exercise a final supporting and enforcing influence upon all the others. The state, the supreme institutionalized organization, establishes laws, constitutional, statute, judicial, and administrative, and has organized police power and the essential forms of administrative machinery to enforce them. These have been discussed above as social structures and will be occasionally referred to below with respect to their regulative and maintenance functions.

Range of Force

By force is meant the application of constraint or compulsion, to which it is necessary to yield or comply. Force means the reduction, or limitation, or closure, or even total elimination of alternatives. (27, p. 733) The means of control range from those that function with almost imperceptible force to those where the threat and actuality of overt societal constraint is omnipresent and omnipotent. Only the extremes will be discussed.

Barely Perceptible Force. In some situations no particular force or pressure, either physical or psychical, is left. The control is by suggestion in a given social situation with symbols of an incidental gestural or verbal nature as the cues to compliant behavior. The reactions are largely spontaneous or imitative. A man sees another man's coat collar awry and almost unconsciously makes a move to adjust his own, whether it needs it or not.

Highly Forceful Pressures. At the other extreme we find the deliberate, studied and organized employment of highly forceful physical and psychic pressures, or "musts," including the threat and the imposition of the death penalty at the hands of the state, with concomitant, all-powerful enforcement procedures and agencies. This is the realm of control in which there must be powerful compulsions or powerful prohibitions or constraints if men are to survive and if social order and continuous, effective societal operation are to be assured.

Between the extremes just described we find an ascending range of ever more forceful devices. There is the direct use of suggestion to obtain compliant behavior by such lightweight controls as hints, examples, commands, personal models, announcements, encouragements, slogans, shibboleths, catchwords, advice, promises, and flattery. At about this same relatively low level of forcefulness is the use of symbolic artifacts which elicit emotion, feeling, and sentiment and operate through their suggestive potential. Examples are art forms, such as poetry, paintings, and statuary, music (standing at attention when *The Star-Spangled Banner* is played), the control exercised through flags, religious symbols (the crucifix, the crescent), books (the very presence of a Bible), badges, uniforms, and even sacred or political edifices. At this level there is also suggestion through the symbolized ceremony of particular occasions and events.

At a level above these in forcefulness is the control exercised by abstractions in the form of fairly widely effective social beliefs, convictions, principles, stereotypes, ideals, interests, and the sublimated group expressions of power. Here also must be placed the rational controls involving the use of instruction and enlightenment, as well as false instructions and fostered illusions.

Next most forceful are the intentional, though not necessarily organized, forms of persuasion, inducement, and dissuasion, such as the use of the superiority appeals (praise, flattery, prestige, smiles), blame, insinuation, satire, ridicule, request, pleading and preaching, and the use of annoyances. Most forceful and violent are the threatening or coercive deterrents and prohibitions, with the obvious possibility of harm and punishment, such as intimidation, ordering, forbidding, warning, demotion or withholding of promotion, fines, pain or injury by violence, excommunication, ostracism, compulsory labor, banishment, imprisonment, death, and threat of punishment after death.

The range of force may be graphically presented as follows (24, p. 544):

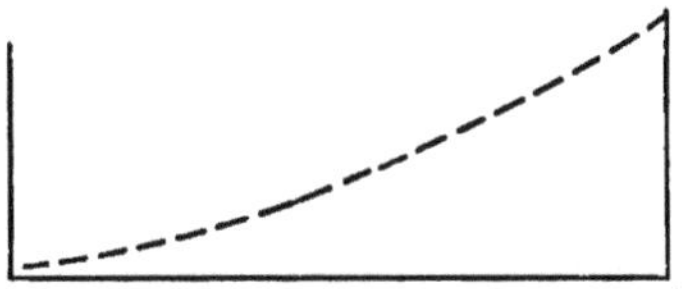

The amount of force used in conscious control is usually that needed to get action in any concrete type of situation. People do not use bulldozers to move a bit of fluff.

Nature of Controls

As has been implied in the immediately preceding discussion, the controls are either negative or positive. Each type has its special place in the manipulation of individuals and groups.

Negative Controls. The negative controls involve processes which deliberately restrain, repress, inhibit, or prohibit antisocial conduct. These are directed mainly against those incompletely socialized and antisocial individuals whose conduct is destructive of the rights and interests of others. By its very nature, all control is in part restraint, and all individuals and groups, however socially intentioned they may be, require some negative control. These constitute the mass of prohibitions.

Positive Controls. The positive controls involve processes which deliberately persuade, induce, stimulate, direct, excite, and motivate to acceptable, desirable, and essential conduct. These give the persons and groups controlled satisfying outlets for their energies, invite positive action and social expression, and lead to the establishment and cultivation of cooperation, self-control, respect for others, and general good will.

Objectives of Conscious Social-Control Action

Social-control techniques and instruments, like all techniques and instruments, are ethically and purposively neutral. They may be used to fulfill various objectives, personal, antisocial, asocial, and social. The ways in which they are used and the ends for which they are used depend entirely upon the individuals and groups appropriating and manipulating them. The objectives may be classified generally as follows.

Exploitative and Predatory Controls. In mass societies like ours, much control is exercised by individuals and organizations for the specific purposes of advancing their own special interests, without regard for the interests of those controlled or the effect of the control upon the well-being of the community or society as a whole. Such control generally runs counter to the morals of the community or society and sometimes constitutes a violation of the legal codes of the political state.

All types of control techniques and instrumentalities can be used for such ends, but special mention should be made of the many practices of competition and conflict; the control exercised in certain instances by various organizations, such as professional associations and unions over members; racketeering; publicity; political-machine activities; monopolistic activity in all its phases; censorship; and propagandizing. In some instances such control involves violence, intimidation and fear, graft, corruption, and fraud, and unscrupulous forms of psychic persuasion. Although examination of the operation of these means of control is not part of this analysis (they are especially involved in a treatment of social disorganization), the student of social operation should be forewarned regarding them and should acquire a good working knowledge of them. (2, pp. 51-335)

Regulatory and Maintenance Controls. The regulatory and maintenance controls involve the use of control techniques and instrumentalities in the interest of society as a whole. (They are the main concern of the next two chapters.) Control is used in order to obtain and maintain orderliness and effective cooperation in the human world. As indicated above, such control resolves itself into the following forms: the restraint of parasites, exploiters, criminals, and all other imperfectly socialized and antisocial persons whose behavior threatens the well-being of society as a whole; the direction of the actions of all the diverse individuals and groups into conformity with the society's *system* of order; the establishment and preservation of that degree of social adjustment, equilibrium, and social solidarity among the various parts that will make possible effective joint action on common needs and objectives and ensure the efficient operation, stability, and continuity of the society.

Reorganizational Controls. Social-control instrumentalities and techniques have been used repeatedly throughout history in conscious, purposeful, and deliberate efforts to remold the human social world. These activities have ranged from trial-and-error corrective efforts to those that were and are intelligently creative and constructive and in some instances based on scientifically determined facts and principles, from those with purely special-interest-group objectives to those concerned with the advancement of community-wide, society-wide, and even universal well-being. Social movements, especially reform movements, dictatorships, and social revolutions, have involved in their preparation and execution the whole gamut of social-control agencies and processes.

Although at times the participants may have been misguided and the movements themselves socially deleterious in both immediate and long-time effects, the objectives in most instances have been a better society in some or many respects from the point of view of the groups promoting the objectives and engaging in the reorganizing efforts. Related to these are all the social policy-making, programming, and engineering activities, regardless of the social scale in view, ranging from those of particular groups (for example, unions or corporations), through community planning, up to the efforts of the United Nations to procure world peace and prosperity.* Dominance, variously expressed, is involved in all these controls.

Dominance-Submission Relationships and Related Factors

We have noted that social order is not automatically achieved through natural forces or inborn patterns of behavior, but is the product of a social control system which is in continual process of construction. To be sure, men learn to live in a more or less orderly way, and much of this satisfactory daily social living comes to be unconscious, so effectively are we molded. This orderly social conduct occurs in omnipresent and unavoidable types of dominance-submission relationships. Moreover, various persistent and interrelated factors contribute to the orderly living in these relationships. In these are the psychological and social "whips" that drive men into socialized conduct or

*This category of controls will be examined in the concluding chapter of the present analysis.

into conformity with advocated or required patterns of ordered living. These answer, in a way, the question: Why do men behave in an orderly and even a socially constructive manner to the degree that they do?

Dominance-Submission Relationships

Although dominance is primarily a social-psychological concept (27), it has profound sociological implications. By its very nature, social control always means that dominance-submission patterns exist, that some societal elements dominate and others are submissive to them. Neither domination nor submission is necessarily conscious or organized, and the dominance of individuals and groups for social-control purposes has a wide range of levels, forms, and sources. By way of introduction to the discussions of social influence, social power, and authority in society, the major categories of dominance will be defined.

Dominance of Larger, Over-All Society or Community over Constituent Groups. This type of dominance is exemplified by the relationship of the national state to the separate states and other political subdivisions and to corporations and other associations and lesser groups within it. This is the most pervasive and powerful form of dominance and is very pertinent in modern mass societies.

Dominance of One Category or Group over Another. The control of old over young, men over women, cities over rural areas are instances of categories of persons or unorganized groups dominating others. The control exercised by a corporation over a union or by a union over a corporation is an example of the dominance-submission relationship between organized groups.

Dominance of Individuals over Other Individuals. Examples of individual dominance are individuals commanding other individuals, laughing at, admonishing, or instructing others, threatening to gossip about others, exercising physical force over them, and so on.

Dominance of Individuals over Groups. Individuals exercising dominance over groups are the exceptional individuals and the officially designated individuals, who affect their society for good or ill. Notable examples are dictators throughout history, various leaders and "misleaders," delegated officials, and the concrete instances of the control exercised by such persons as John L. Lewis, James C. Petrillo, and the Roosevelts, "T. R." and "F. D. R."

Dominance and submission in interpersonal and intergroup relations imply types of factors that are utilized in a society to bring about the submission of the various societal elements. The factors to be briefly examined are the *socially potent influences,* which are of a persuasive nature; *social power,* which is organized compulsion; and *authorities* in whom the right to wield influence and power is vested by some sort of formal or informal grant.

Influences as Factors in Dominance-Submission Relationships (27, p. 731)

Influences attach to acquired knowledge, ideas, doctrines, beliefs, sentiments, creeds, wishes, values, and other social-psychologically and culturally induced dispositions to act on the part of a given people. They are persuasive rather than compulsive, and many people submit to them voluntarily. They are, however, frequently components of power and are manipulated in the wielding of power, but they do not have the distinctive attributes of social power itself. The following are among the more notable forms involved in social control.

The Fear of Social Disapproval. Men are sensitive to the reactions, especially the rejections or acceptances, of their fellow men. All egos wish to be in rapport with others and, if possible, receive from others favorable mirrorings of themselves. Hence, they fear and avoid being the victims of gossip, name-calling, ridicule, or any other form of social disapproval.

Mass Psychical Pressure and Mass Action. This form of influence is met in public opinion, fads, fashions, crazes and social movements, and the pressure to patriotic conformity. "Everybody's doing it!" and "Everybody's thinking it!" are powerful monitors.

Ego-Vying Drives. The ego-vying drives include especially the compulsion to achieve ego status in a competitive society. This is exemplified by the standard-of-living requirements. "Keeping up with the Joneses" amounts to the "Dictatorship of the Joneses." Under the sway of their egos, individuals seek prestige, power, status, rank, wealth and property, and so on.

Persons or Categories of Persons. Many persons as individuals or as groups influence others through their knowledge, skill, competence, ability, charism, social position or social status, or other bases of eminence. These persons or categories have some kind of social prestige and are held in high esteem by greater or lesser portions of the society. Their views and the ways of life that they advocate are frequently prized and followed.

Intelligence and Information. Acquired knowledge, developed reasoning and rationality, appreciation of the relationship between cause and effect, and education by experience and formal instructional procedures have considerable effect on many people.

Ideologies and Social Myths. The well-rationalized and widely accepted patterns of social belief and interpretations of social destiny among a people are often extremely influential.

The Socialized Conscience. A socialized conscience is developed through the growth of ethical-mindedness, altruism, a sense of justice and good social sportsmanship under the dominance of the values and the moral codes of the community or society. It is reflected in the desire to be an acceptable "gentleman," "lady," "good sport," "father," "wife," "mother," citizen."

Belief in the Supernatural. Belief in the supernatural has been widely used throughout history to support ethical and legal codes and class, caste, and political arrangements, as, for example, the divine right of kings. The fear of divine or supernatural disapproval and the use of magic and taboo have combined with belief in future rewards and punishments to produce very potent forces in the regulation of the lives of individuals and groups.

Social Power as a Factor in Dominance-Submission Relationships

The fundamental ordering of a social system requires more than social influences. There must also be social power, that is, the ability to present and employ force in the form of sanctions for nonconformity to the various kinds of behavior requirements of a society or certain of its elements. These requirements are more or less explicit in various rules. The sanctions range from mere threats of personal or property damage, through various legalized prohibitions, to actual imposition of the death penalty. Every society, in fact, has a power structure for the sake of social order.

MacIver has provided the classical treatment of social power, referring to it as "the capacity in any relationship to command the service or the compliance of others" and "the capacity to control the behavior of others either directly by fiat or indirectly by the manipulation of available means. (34; 35, pp. 82, 87)

Bierstedt in turn uses MacIver's analysis as the point of departure in his brilliant treatment. He holds that power is coercive in some degree, not merely persuasive, for all upon whom it is exercised; it requires, even commands, submission. It expresses itself in all social relations and stands behind all social organizations. Especially significant in our present discussion is the fact that it is the omnipotent basis of the social order of a society and the essential support of all social organization. "Without power there is no organization, and without power there is no order." (27, p. 735) In brief, without it the social order would disintegrate.

Locus of Social Power. The locus of social power is in the various groupings of a society, namely, informal groupings, the organized community, and formal organizations. In the informal groupings and the unorganized community the power inheres in the force and the general support of the mores. In the formal organization, it takes the form of a specific grant to various levels of the organization to use different kinds of force to obtain effective action.

Sources of Social Power. As Bierstedt (27, p. 737) points out, the sources of social power are also of three general categories, namely, the number of people, usually taking the form of majorities (28); some form of organization and crystallization of consensus through which the operation of the effective mores and rules is implemented; and, the resources at the disposal of the more or less organized elements in the particular grouping, such as the use of natural resources, money, property, prestige, fraud, secrecy, the application of supernatural sanctions, and many others.

Pyramid of Power. Invariably, also, if the dissolution of the social order is to be avoided, there must be a pyramid of power, to use MacIver's apt term. (35, pp. 98-105) The power exercised appears in a graduated order, flowing from the top to the bottom of every grouping's hierarchical arrangement through the more or less spontaneously developed or the formally organized ranks and stations.* Every rank has power exercised upon it from above and, in turn, wields power over the ranks below it.

The pyramid of power, however, undergoes incessant change, and continual shifts of social power are occurring. Every change in social organization —every technological advance, every economic development, every change in the composition of the population, and every social movement or cultural accumulation—changes the pyramid of power.

Authority as a Factor in Dominance-Submission Relationships

Authority is the group-delegated right to use social power in the ordering of social relationships. It is made effective through "authorities," which, with their variously vested social power, have the form of certain persons, groups, specialized categories of persons, organized groups, or associations, and institutions. These authorities are informally or formally granted the right to wield power. In many instances, because of the specific, strategic functions of the authorities in the social system, they are socially obligated to wield power. Without such authority, no group or social organization of any kind could function; without authority, social power is spasmodic, undirected, futile, even destructive, for authority is a way of channeling and utilizing social power economically for purposes of social order and social well-being and is an elemental and indispensable feature of all social control.

*The sociological principle here involved was discussed in other connections in Chap. 11 and also in Chap. 14.

In the authoritative use of social power, there are always two elements—the agent exercising the power and the persons on whom it is exercised. The agents for exercising authority require certain action and in many control situations are able to enforce the requirement. The subjects of the authority accept the communication as authoritative. They usually have attitudes of responsiveness and deference and admit the necessary degree of subordination involved in the particular functional control relationship. (25; 26; 27, pp. 733-735; 35, pp. 16, 83-86)

Authority in Different Kinds of Grouping. Authority is always in the mores. But it has various degrees of specificity and articulation, depending upon the kind of grouping or the relationship of categories in which it is exercised. Although it is always present and potent in informal groups, it is somewhat vague, since it rests upon the esteem for certain persons who wield it, the roles they play, and the ancient principles of leadership-followership. In the differentiated and stratified positional relationships, it is more definitely specified and articulated through the accepted and more or less explicit norms governing the relationships of the respective elements. In the rigidly organized formal association the social power is formally institutionalized by means of clearly specified and articulated norms in the form of stated rules, statutes, and laws. Here, as Bierstedt states, "power is resolved without residue into authority." (27)

Kinds of Personal Authority. We are especially concerned at this point with the examination of authority to wield social power for control purposes as it is assumed, traditionally granted, or formally delegated to persons or categories of persons, for it must be borne in mind that it is always within the power of the majority to confer actual as well as statutory authority upon persons and to retain the granting of authority residually in any informal or formal organization. These persons or categories act as accepted superiors in influencing and directing the larger bodies of men, or they act as the selected, assigned, and authorized agents of organized, purposive groups. There are three major forms of personal authority.

LEADERSHIP AUTHORITY. This type of authority rests upon the capacity to persuade, direct, or dominate other human beings that comes from personal qualities. (29; 30; 38; 41) Exceptional personalities—great men, heroes, receivers of revelations, innovators, fulminators, indoctrinators, persuaders, men "out in front"—through ascendancy over their fellow men achieve their intentions among them and influence them. Physical qualities have some part, physique, voice, and so on, but mainly psychological characteristics, such as imagination, courage, insight, knowledge, idealism, persistence, and strength of will, are more important factors in their ability to perform as leaders. Oratorical ability, the ability to arouse ecstasy, reputation based on previous exploits, and so on are additional assets.

Leaders may wield their authority on behalf of the established order, or they may be opposed to it and seek to create a new type of authority and order. The informal, spontaneous grant of authority to the natural leader inheres in the very act of followership. It is the right to command—and even to coerce—given by the majority of the particular grouping in which the leader functions.

POSITIONAL AUTHORITY. This type of authority is the traditional and informal one that inheres in persons and categories of persons because of their position, rank, or "sacredly" vested power in the differentiated and stratified structuring of society. The authority here depends, not on personal qualities or achievements, but on the recognition that a person, group, or category receives within the established scheme of social evaluation of a given society. Examples of such exercise of authority are that of the old over the young, males over females (in a male-dominated society), the wealthy over the less wealthy, the upper classes over the lower classes, the "holy," or those with charism, over the less holy, the wise over the ignorant, parents over their children, teachers over pupils, and so on. In these situations authority is conceded in the mores of the community and society.

OFFICIAL AUTHORITY. The planned, assigned, specifically delegated, and institutionalized authority which attaches to the various levels of office in formal social organizations is termed "official authority." It does not inhere in them as persons. The administrative person holding the office or position for executing managerial or other regulatory functions is invested with the right and charged with the obligation to exercise certain kinds of supervisory and directive controls. Obvious instances are the authority which the president of a corporation and all successively lower ranks of officers exercise over subordinates, the offices of president, deans, and departmental chairmen in universities, the delegated authority of lawmakers, judges, law-enforcing officers, clergymen, and priests in their respective formalized social organizations.

Having now examined the A B C's of normalization and equilibration as they relate to the basic concept of social order and to the general nature, principles, functions, and factors of social control as the over-all ordering process, we may now proceed with the examination of the major categories of social processes and societal instrumentalities that function as normalizing and equilibrating media in human society.

CHAPTER XX

PROCESSES AND INSTRUMENTALITIES OF SOCIETAL REGULATION

SOCIAL CONTROL is a concept that includes, in addition to the exploitative ways of producing desired behavior among others, all the processes, techniques, and cultural and societal instrumentalities involved in producing social order. The essence of this order is not found in the widely described agencies or means of social control, since they are merely aiding instrumentalities by which specific behavior is manipulated within some aspect of the organizational complex and with reference to it. In a functional analysis, the crucial revealing aspect of social order inheres in the processes and techniques which produce and continuously assure social order, social solidarity, social security, and social survival and continuity. These are the processes whereby the ends of order are attained, the ways in which the principles and compulsions of order get into the very being of the persons involved, and the ways in which disorder is forestalled or corrected and continuous, unswerving peace and order are assured. These processes resolve themselves into two major, but continuously overlapping, categories—the regulatory and the maintenance processes—which seek to forestall destructuralization, disfunction, and disorder or repair these when they appear and to preserve and safeguard what has been wrought in the way of satisfactory mechanisms and functional efficiency. In brief, the examination of these processes and of the conditions which they produce points up the integral aspects of social order and social control.*

In this chapter and in the following one the reader will find the discussion of certain very important societal processes which have been examined individually by social scientists, sometimes at great length. Here they are treated in their regulative or maintenance context. Through this method of presentation their true functional significance is revealed.

*In the section on social dynamics in Chap. 3, we discussed an array of factors potent in inducing social action in its various phases. Here some of the same ones will be examined, but with respect exclusively to the manner in which they arise and operate as factors in those social actions that make for social order.

Social Order—Regulation and Maintenance

Regulation

Regulation of human society means to bring about regular and recurrent actions or responses on the part of its constituent individuals and groups. Only thus can there be any of that predictability of behavior upon which order and stability depend. The regulatory processes and techniques, as the term implies, have to do specifically with ordering according to rules (the Latin *regula*). Wherever men live together in any sort of permanent association or carry on any common enterprise, they have to develop complexes of rules of social interaction for all the recurrent types of interaction. These rules state the necessary uniformity and conformity of the actions of the variant persons and groups involved in the social situations, and they must function effectively or the enterprise is not accomplished.

These rules establish minimal permissible action. They do not eliminate chance or choice, and they do permit much freedom, but all acceptable behavior must be above this level. The rules also guide and direct and incite to useful and socially positive behavior as well as constrain and prevent ways of acting that, in the light of experience, are potentially productive of disorder. They set standards of behavior and fix limits. Deviation or variation beyond these limits, if permitted, would produce disequilibrium or even disaster.

Such regulation always implies some restriction upon the complete freedom of action of individuals and groups, for it is not possible, in an orderly community or society, for them to do entirely as they please. To abide by standards, regardless of the high ethical nature of one's intentions, is always to be restrained or constrained in some degree. Hence, under this reign of rules, there is always some recommendation, some requirement, some scrutiny and supervision, some imposed discipline, some compulsion, some checking and prohibition, and some enforcement by the society, just to "play safe."

From the functional point of view, however, regulation goes beyond these checks and propulsions. It involves the *organization* of the behavior of individuals and groups under the rules. The social order is what Sorokin calls a "sociolegal order."

How are the rules inculcated and made socially effective? How is the firmament of order assured and continued?

Maintenance Processes

The maintenance processes are as important as the regulative. If a community or society is to be orderly and stable, if its functioning is to be continuously normal, and if an equilibrium of its various elements is to exist and persist, the processes and techniques of social control must go beyond regulation. The members of the community or society must be continually and effectively adjusted to each other in the interests of sustenance, stability, and perpetuation.

Persons must be deliberately arrayed and persuaded to accept a system of satisfactory and harmonious working relations which operate in as economical a manner as possible. This is accomplished through an array of *maintenance processes and techniques,* which perform various essential functions. They motivate people as individuals and as groups to expend energy in a positive way and perform in top form in the essential common organizational and operative undertakings. They also maintain morale; establish and secure rights and freedoms; enable men to acquire, exchange, and consume the means of material sustenance and to render the reciprocal services essential to good living; distribute, align, and locate people more or less efficiently in the system of differentiation and stratification and locate them more advantageously in the areal and ecological organization; repair breaks in, or departures from, cooperative participation due to dissension and strife and seek to forestall and prevent such breaks. They seek to prevent and correct ossifying and decadence-producing tendencies, protect the members against internal disorder and external aggression, and provide safe and satisfying means of venting the various expressional impulses of human beings. In general, they seek to diminish the failures and multiply the successes of associated human beings in the management of the social household, to use Aristotle's phrase, and to maintain and perpetuate the society.

The regulatory processes and instrumentalities will be examined in the present chapter; those contributing to maintenance, in the next.

Regulatory Processes That Establish Order

Establishment of Norms

The processes that *establish* order constitute a sequence. Through some basic ends the requirements of order are set up and continuously developed. Others build these principles of order into the consciousness, attitudes, and daily behavior of the individuals and groups of the society, and still others instrumentalize and enforce the requirements of order.

General Nature and Function of Norms. A regulated society of necessity consists of a vast array of required and permitted usages, which, as indicated, are expressions of rules or norms. The foundations of order, therefore, are to be found in the norms. The norms themselves are a specific, dynamic phase of the *value system* of a society. The nature, formation, place, and function of values in a social system were examined in Chapter 10. Suffice it to say at this point that values are the collective estimates and representations of what a given society considers good, essential, and desirable. They comprise "a frame of aspirational reference" and are a basic, but not exclusive, component of what Linton has called "designs for group living." The positive values express what people wish to retain or to increase their possession of, whereas the negative values express what they wish to decrease, discard, or avoid possessing. By means of its value system a society sets its goals and upon them bases all programs of action. Most of the activities of a society are assessed in terms of the values as are most individual and group choices regarding action.

The norms are embodiments and expressions of the basic values regarding social relations and function as specific implementations of the values. They consist of a complicated set of authoritative rules in the form of postulates and definitions of action and imperatives, permissives, and prohibitions of action. Their purpose is to standardize and channelize behavior in all the frequently recurring interactional situations in the life of a society. They are criteria of conduct, plans and specifications of order, and standardized expectations and requirements of conforming action which give a considerable degree of predictability to human behavior. They point out lines of obligatory action, interpret situations, imply or declare areas of rights, and, as statements of ends as well as means, provide ways of achieving social approval for individuals and groups.

In fact, so far as the individual is concerned, most of his stimuli, other than biogenic and psychogenic, stem from norms, and most of his innate tendencies are modified, controlled, and organized to meet social standards. Every human act is in some degree an approximation of a social norm. The continuous and imperious sway of norms standardizes his attitudes, likes and dislikes, preferences and aversions. Conformity to the codal requirements makes or breaks the person among his associates, for without conformity, he has no friends, no fellowship, no status, and is a nobody. Most action is reacting to the various group norms, and as far as societal functioning is concerned, they are ways of avoiding aimlessness, confusion, and disorder, allaying friction, encouraging good will, and improving cohesion and cooperation generally. They are the essence of regulation, and without them societies could not exist. A society as a functional unit is a unity of individuals and groups resting on systematized relations which are normatively directed. In fact, a functioning society *as regulated* can hardly be understood and defined otherwise than as a system of both implicit and explicit norms actually determining conduct at a given time and place.

Formation of Norms. Norms grow out of the interactional, especially interstimulational, experience of all the peoples who have contributed to the entire body of culture of a given area and epoch, as well as the experience of the particular communities and societies in question. The processes are the results of more or less groping, emergent, trial-and-error formation and of purposive, organized enactment.

In the emergent phases of norm formation, the norms appear as the result of common comprehension and definition of social situations, of coalescence of ideas, and of a consensus of views. They attest to mankind's ability to learn by experience, to profit by and communicate failure and success, and to establish the ways which make for order and, hence, the survival of individuals and groups. (11, pp. 89-112)

In modern, mature societies and their highly purposive organizations many of the norms are more and more deliberately artificed constructs for various specific regulatory and maintenance ends. Committees, boards, commissions, conferences, and formally organized representative or appointive bodies (for example, legislatures and congresses) are charged with the task of evaluating existing standards and setting up new and more appropriate ones. Expert investigation, experimentation, testing, and planning are more and more resorted to.

The formation of norms is a continuous process. As the community or society changes, the social conditions requiring regulation also change. Some norms become outmoded and are devaluated; then group or societal functioning dictates the devising of new ones. Hence, the norms are always in process of re-formation as to kind, content, and compulsiveness.

Carriers, or Vehicles,* of Norms. In what social constructs are the norms more or less specifically defined? By means of what kinds of social carriers or conveyances or vehicles, as they function, are the norms expressed, perpetuated, and brought to bear upon individuals and groups? The range is tremendous.

Norms are found in the *folklore* of most peoples. The aphorisms, admonitions, parables, fables, and proverbs have as one of their primary functions the crystallization and purveying of norms in preliterate, illiterate, or other simple primary groups. Myths, as imaginative and often cunningly constructed embodiments of what is considered good or truth by the dominant element of a people, are more than merely stories. They express, enhance, and codify beliefs and values, validate and justify principles of order through the moral unavoidably attached to them, and contain models and practical rules for guidance. Legends, although based on historical incidents or personages, have their facts distorted, fictionized, or rigged so as to convey and support the prevailing social norms. The superstitions of a people, which have a very slight foundation in fact and are largely well-fostered fictions, also do this.

The *folkways,* the elementary, useful ways of a folk, are socially selected ways of doing things expediently. Although they exist mainly in unwritten form, they carry in themselves the simple codal requirements accepted by a great majority of the people for almost every detail of daily living at any given time and place. The *mores,* or ethically founded and insistently compelled right ways, and the more formally organized moral codes, as couched, for example, in lists of commandments, are in their very nature the obvious vehicles of these requirements.

Customs, traditions, and *conventions* constitute a set of normative patterns. The *customs* are folkways that have become fixed and are passed down through the generations and have the weight of time and practice of many men behind them. The *traditions* consist of the knowledge, beliefs, standards, and values handed down from the past. The *conventions* are the special, noncompetitive, proper ways of acting in prescribed and usually unavoidable situations in order to avoid friction and embarrassment and include rules of etiquette and codes of good manners.

Another notable type of carrier is the *ideologies,* the rationalized and official presentations of beliefs, creeds, purposes, and justifications of organized groups and social movements. To a limited degree *fads and fashions* carry purely contemporary norms in phases of social life that are not necessarily very important from the point of view of social order, stability, and continuity; nevertheless, they produce conforming behavior among many people. Norms governing many special relationships and functions are found in the *codes* of all manner of clubs, of occupational and professional groups, in rules for various sports and forms of

*Sorokin's term. (12, pp. 51-63, 390-399)

recreation, books of discipline of religious bodies, charters of corporations, and generally in the constitutions, by-laws, and administrative rules of all the purposive associations that are found in modern societies.

In modern societies like our own, which are scientifically and technologically advanced, a set of ways that transcend folkways and are called by Odum *technicways* function as special normative vehicles. They carry the norms governing conformity to the new and ever-changing requirements for living with the continuous flow of new physical, industrial, and commercial mechanisms and procedures—in brief, for living with technological forces and products, including mass-production lines, installment buying, automobiles, telephones, radios, and many more. (10)

The most far-reaching, most highly organized, most imperious, most widely supported, and virtually inescapable, carriers are the laws and rules of governmental units, especially those of the nation-states, the *stateways*, as MacIver calls them. These take the form of the constitutions of states, their legislatively enacted laws, the decisions of their courts in interpreting the constitutional and enacted law, and the rules of their various constituent administrative bodies.

Variations in Norms. Norms are exceedingly numerous and varied, since they regulate every area of human life and every type of social action and relationship however obscure or important. Jessie Bernard (1; 2) in her excellent analyses of norms shows that they differ among themselves in three important ways: in the number of persons and situations involved, in the degree of compulsiveness, and in the degree to which they are formulated into either oral or written codes. These three aspects will be briefly examined.

PERSONS AND SITUATIONS INVOLVED. Not all societal norms bind all the members of a community. We are indebted to Linton (8) for the most cogent analysis of norms in terms of the number of persons governed by them. He distinguishes three kinds of regulative patterns which he calls "universals," "specialties," and "alternatives." His basic theory will be applied to our analysis.

The *universals* are binding upon all members of the society. In our society, for example, *everyone* is supposed to abstain from murder, theft, adultery, incest, infanticide, and the creation of public disturbances or nuisances; everyone is supposed to conform to the required minimal standards for marriage, and parents are required to maintain and protect their children and assist them in preparation for adulthood. Members must function with a reasonable degree of competence in the various essential associations, as citizens observe the political ordinances and laws essential to general safety and well-being, and support, morally and financially, their organized state, and so on.

The *specialties* are those regulations which apply only to certain categories of persons or types of groups and relate "to those varied but mutually interdependent activities which have been assigned to the various sections of society in the course of its division of labor." (8, p. 272) In our society, women are sometimes required to observe different behavior patterns from those of men. Occupational and professional groups create standards of observance and performance which apply only to themselves. The different technically specialized groups and levels in the large functional organizations, such as corporations or public administrative bodies, have their special rules and standards. The different social strata or classes or castes have their own characteristic and special behavior norms.

The *alternatives* are those norms "which are shared by certain individuals but which are not common to all the members of the society or even to all the members of any one of the socially recognized categories . . . they represent different reactions to the same situation or different techniques for achieving the same ends." (8, pp. 273-274) For example, in our society, if we marry, we may meet the requirements of *either* a religious or civil procedure; if we wish to select a trade, we may choose among a considerable number of them.

RELATIVE COMPULSIVENESS OF NORMS. We have already referred to controls in general as imperatives and compulsions, permissives and prohibitions. Here we are thinking of the relative compulsiveness of the "carriers" of norms discussed above. The norms range in compulsiveness from the laws of the state and the fundamental moral rules, which are the most insistently and sedulously supported and enforced by the society, to those superficial norms that are practically in the take-it-or-leave-it category. The preceding categories of universals, specialties, and alternatives in part determine the compulsiveness of the norms.

The more generally experienced types of norms may be arranged in the following *descending* degree of compulsiveness:

1. The legalized and moral norms (the mores) are the most compulsive. They incorporate the indispensable minima of social order or of action in the various social organizations of a society. Violations are accompanied by ostracism, social isolation, or more specific forms of punishment, including, if necessary, physical coercion by the constituted authorities of the state or of the special organization in question.

2. Customary, traditional, and conventional norms are less coercive. They have the rightness of time and the support of generations behind them and are difficult to challenge, but they have no formally constituted authorities to declare them, apply them, or to safeguard and enforce them. Custom and traditions die and are replaced by new ones. Violation of the conventions is not immoral or illegal, merely unconventional.

3. There is little coercion behind the folkways, as such, before some of them with utility are transformed into the customs, mores, and laws. Alternatives flourish among them.

4. Creeds and the beliefs of particular groups, while highly essential and strongly enforced, apply only to the special groups which subscribe to them. In most instances, members are free to withdraw from such groups if they wish. The "social myths" and ideologies of particular groups and social movements also have high compulsiveness only among those dominated by them.

5. The norms embedded in the folklore carry relatively little weight in modern secular societies. Many, in fact, are unknown and most can be ignored.

RELATIVE CONCISENESS OF FORMATION OF NORMS. The norms differ in degree and conciseness of their formulation. Norms couched in laws and commandments are objectively and specifically formulated and codified in written form—constitutions, statutes, judicial decisions, decalogues and pentateuchs. Moral norms may or may not be in written codified form. Creeds, beliefs, and ideologies are often specifically expressed for those adhering to them. Customs, traditions, and conventions are usually relatively specific during their reign, and many of them may actually be in written form. The many norms in the folklore and folkways are quite general in nature.

Socialization and Inculcation of Norms

Next to the formation and conveyance of norms the most important and most basic processes in regulation and, for that matter, in maintenance as well are those of norm indoctrination or inculcation. These loom large and important among the processes of socialization, which are the most powerful of all the regulative elements. The significance of socialization as a condition and as a process lies in the fact that effective and orderly social living according to the values and norms of a society inheres quite as much in the attitudes and beliefs and ingrained behavior patterns of individuals and groups as in the over-all formal implementing structures, such as organizations and institutions. The arbitrary application of physical, psychological, and social force is arduous, requires a great expenditure of a society's energy, and means that much attention must be devoted to mere ordering as compared with the satisfaction of an ascending series of wants. Hence, both to ensure good order and to practice economy, societies do all they can to avoid the use of compulsion and coercion through external social agencies.

The most certain, most effective, and most economical regularization is *inner* regulation. Thus, unconsciously and consciously, much of social order and social control is interiorized or built into the character structure of individuals as societally established and socially acceptable self-controls. As far as possible, for every regularized act, communities must rely upon the properly conditioned and adequately socialized person automatically pursuing socially acceptable patterns of behavior.

Socialization "implies a kind of solidarity based on participation in a common enterprise and involving more or less complete subordination of individuals to the intent and purpose of the group as a whole." (30; see also 22) Socialization as a basic process* is one whereby the common stand-

*Briefly examined in Chap. 4.

ards, objectives, definitions, and rationalizations of orderly social living of a given community or society are ingrained in the personality of the individuals to such an extent that their behavior is largely in conformity with these norms and ends. These interiorized social norms and values are the *social* in individuals. The socialized person conforms generally in his likes and dislikes and in his actions to the requirements of his social system. The socialized person has what has been well called "situational learnings" for the essential positive activities of normal social life. (16, p. 260) He has become conditioned to society.

The reverse of socialization is *desocialization,* which is a form of disorganization. In such a situation the individual is a disfunctional actor in the community. Hence, the reverse of the socialized person is one who is amoral, unmoral, or antisocial, with criminality the zero point of socialization. (15; 22)

The process of socialization—essentially a social-psychological one—begins at birth and goes on throughout life. It is one of continuous conditioning, orientation, instruction, and incorporation. It organizes and motivates the related persons of the group to the set of values and goals of the group and leads to the fixing of group-contributing attitudes and habits and the assumption of group-relevant roles. The individual is identified with the group with a reasonable amount of consistency and functions in the social situations he meets sufficiently well to command the tolerance, if not always the admiration, of his fellows.

In general, the individual has not been equalized with others, but he is harmonious with others in thought and sentiment, acts in conformity with general well-being, and feels himself to be part of the whole. He has come to be a more or less responsible, dependable, self-controlled, cooperative, positively functional, and interrelated part of society. He has achieved a feeling of solidarity with, and an attachment to, his particular social order and the codes that regulate it. He has become "community-centric."

Socialization is fundamentally a process of acquisition. It consists of conditioning, impression, inculcation, instruction, training, and discipline and comes about as a concomitant of the individual's lifelong participation in the sociocultural life of his society. The basic subprocesses will be briefly presented.

Attitude Forming and Habituation. As Aristotle noted long ago, behavior, to be secure and dependable, should be in the form of habits. Social control is accomplished mainly through the processes of habit formation, especially through the processes of attitude formation. Basic are the *attitudes,* that is, fixed mental patterns in the form of both affective beliefs and motor sets regarding social conduct and social relations. They are actional fixtures in our heads and include most of our stereotypes regarding social relations and activities. Once formed, they dominate, mostly unconsciously, the thinking and the action of the individual in all the more fixed or recurring social situations from the early years on. They come into action prior to thought and often act selectively in determining what is admitted to consciousness. They affect the judgments and motivate acceptable and required conduct.

Habits are in a large part the overt expressions of attitudes. They are the dispositions and facilities to act in a certain manner, mostly unconsciously acquired step by step and act by act. *Habit formation* itself is an active process of modification and elaboration of the stimulus-response patterns of individuals. By repetition of the act the responses are canalized, routinized, and integrated into specific patterns; the native tendency to respond in a similar way to a similar situation has come to be defined, confirmed, and grooved by organic and psychical modification.

Thus, habits come to be organized responsiveness to social stimuli. When the individual is habituated to act in a certain way, it becomes easier, both mentally and physiologically, so to act and more difficult to act in alternative ways. As such, habit economizes energy, reduces drudgery, saves needless expenditure of thought, and guarantees exactness and dependability of response. Habit is an automatic stabilizer.

Significant also is the fact that there is a strong tendency for persons to build up habits or acquired behavior patterns that are in keeping with what is expected of them. The social values and norms of the various groups in which they participate are the directing stimuli.

The important feature of the process of attitude fixing and habituation in relation to social regulation is that, if habituation has been effective, the individual is unaware of much social direction or constraint and acts spontaneously and automatically in any common social situation in conformity with the social standards or codes prevailing in his conditioning environment. In fact, the normative action has come to be congruous with and serviceable to the individual's own desires.

The Educative Process. Attitude formation and habituation are not sufficient in themselves to develop and insure adequately regularized behavior. They are supplemented, in fact dominated, by the educating process which provides information, training, and discipline. This process in all its ramifications may be looked upon as the universal, master process in socialization. Its purpose is the mental and actional adjustment of individuals to the significant requirements of social life and their effective participation therein. It is the consciously controlled and usually more or less organized process of inculcation of knowledge and social induction. Its mediums range from the family, through other primary groups, through all manner of special-interest organizations, to the highly institutionalized agencies like church and school, whose sole or primary objective is that of education. Some of these, of course, do some miseducating.

As a primary socialization procedure, the educating process has several functional objectives. It seeks to discover and develop the socially pertinent capacities and powers of individuals. It is the main process of inculcating social values, norms, and directives and is an important developer of right attitudes and habits, and furnishing most of the basic patterns of social behavior, including the various categories of social skills. Education provides the facts, principles, insights, and reasons upon which human beings as more or less rational creatures can base their socially acceptable and socially essential and expected behavior. It is a way of cultivating, supervising, and manipulating ways of thinking and acting and provides much practice, training, and discipline in the various appropriate forms of social behavior. All other processes of establishing regularized behavior, regardless of the agencies which employ them or through which the processes operate, are specific forms or utilizations of the educational process.

In a matter of days, months, or years education accomplishes what would take several generations by the processes of slow, spontaneous, fumbling, trial-and-error acquisition and inculcation of social attitudes and ways and would still be inadequate. As a procedure it is also a powerful means which society places in the hands of each of its members for achieving social control through self-control. It enables the individual, in so far as he is capable, to understand his own and his society's adjustment problems and to work intelligently and voluntarily toward effective adjustment without compulsion or autocratic or deceptive manipulation. (21; 31)

Role-Exercising Processes. To ensure orderly and correct behavior, the responses of individuals must also be pointed to the specific recurrent actional situations. This involves the processes of role forming and role exercising. A social role, as has already been noted, is a specific pattern or configuration of attitudes and behavior, consisting of specified functions and duties, which persons assume in a particular type of relationship or situation and perform according to prescribed rules. The acquisition of these role rules is also part of the internalizing and especially of the learning processes. Thus, W. K. Smith, growing up in American society, has learned his various roles, as husband, father, dinner guest, employer, owner of landed property, church member, citizen. By virtue of these roles, his behavior in these various situations is regularized and in considerable part can be predicted.

At any given time and place the requirements of the various roles essential in a given society are formalized and fixed. Although very few members of a society could set forth systematically every specific detail of behavior required in every one of the innumerable roles, even those which they themselves play day in and day out, a fairly clear conception of the requirements of each given role exists as a consensus.

Each role is formed as a product of history, of trial and error, of accretion and selection, and consists partly of folkways, folk values, mores, and even rules and formal codal elements. It may be encrusted with age and tradition and be descriptive of abstract ideals and standards of conduct. Social groups, in the roles set up, establish not only specifications regarding concrete social performance, but also ideals of behavior which they seek to make effective in the lives of persons.

The significant feature of roles and role exercising from the point of view of social regulation is that the group looks upon the roles essential to social order as *imperatives* in social behavior; they are "obligatory norms." They are also made *compulsive forces* by the group and contain values and action elements that *must* be observed in almost every type of recurrent social situation. The society as a whole or the group or organization sees to it that no very wide departures from the patterns of the roles are permitted. Fathers must perform their various functions as fathers; physicians must play their part; and so on. Society is vastly concerned about the business of responsible and orderly everyday living; the roles define especially the duties essential to this living. The role thus is a strict social disciplinarian, a sort of strait jacket in different standard situations of life. (17; 33)

Conscience-Forming Processes. The processes whereby selected social taboos and requirements are rationalized and organized in the consciousness of individuals are conscience-forming processes. The elements of conscience are acquired both by conditioning and by instruction. Conscience regulates solely through the sense of guilt and the likelihood of self-censure when the individual acts contrary to the criteria of social action or through the sense of inner harmony and joy, with the likelihood of self-praise when he acts in conformity with the criteria. These criteria function as the voice of one's group. Or we might say that conscience is the group, with its social-ethical values and insistences inculcated in you, "looking over your shoulder."

Conscience is compulsive. Violation of the taboos, of the role specifications or of the broader social requirements brings to the individual unfavorable mirrorings of himself and develops in him a consciousness of separation from the group. He has let down himself and his group. He desires to reconcile and regularize himself with himself and with his group. Sooner or later, after such experience, he learns to forestall the painful twinges of conscience by refraining from tabooed behavior. The kind of conscience, of course, depends on the kind of group to which the individual belongs. (18, pp. 39-41)

In general, socialization is a matter of learning processes, conducted by informal but ever-active social stimuli and pressures and by the vast array of massive, carefully devised, formal institutional and organizational media. The learning processes reorganize and reinvigorate personality continually and reduce norms, ideas, and actions to standardized expressions which are in conformity with society's need for constructive order and function.

Uniformation Processes

Uniformity is a social product and condition. Uniformation is a set of related processes found everywhere whereby a uniformity and similarity in time and space of practices actually or reputedly essential in the different social relationships are established. They too are necessary in order to overcome or prevent the socially unsafe eccentricity and deviation of performance of social actions. Without such uniformity and regularity of sequence and coordination, societal regulation is not easy or systematic, and the societal operations carry no guarantee of certainty, preciseness, or efficacy. (34) Three significant subprocesses of uniformation will be examined.

Standardization. Standardization occurs under the determining influence of the various norms or standards just discussed, including those involved in roles. It consists of the reduction to uniformity, by authority or by accepted or established custom, organizational decree, or general consent, of the necessary functions of social life and human intercourse or of such functions of special significance to particular societal organizations. Standardization involves the establishment of uniformly ordered procedures, practices, types, and qualities of performance. It is what the norms have men *do* as they are conditioned by them, habituated to them, and instructed in them and as they are affected by all sorts of massing influences (for example, under large-scale advertising). Standardization molds men's attitudes, ideas, tastes, and ways of acting.

It is more than uniformizing of products of commerce and industry, of weights and measures, of mechanical productive processes; it is more than abiding by a given standard of living as this relates to the display and use of articles for consumption. It is a process of typification, or establishment of more or less uniform types of behavior, for almost every typical daily process of living in the common and recurrent social situations. Language, modes of attire, forms of salutation, requirements for almost every job, arm signals for getting through traffic, forms of worship, and most of our social performances are standardized.

Standardization in sufficient degree is essential in both societal regulation and maintenance. Without the externally imposed constancy of action in given situations, there cannot be predictability. Standardization concentrates and conserves attention, removes the necessity of choice, diminishes fatigue, and reduces much essential behavior to habit. Thus, it makes for economy of individual time and capacity. From the over-all societal point of view, it not only gets more necessary work done, "but work is accomplished in shorter time, with greater ease and with greater accuracy, and dependability." (34, p. 439) Standardization in all fields of behavior in modern complex society is becoming more and more important as a process in regulative procedures.

At the same time, in some of its forms and effects, standardization stultifies many a fine, socially desirable and culturally enriching uniqueness and diversity among persons, and tends toward a prosaic "dead-levelism."

Regimentation. Regimentation is actually a subdivision of standardization. It is the process whereby standardized behavior for different functions at different social levels is brought about under the rules by means of an authoritative, planned, highly systematized, and hierarchically arranged organization and direction of social tasks* The interpretation of the rules, the initiative in their transmission, and the procedures for obtaining obedience to them are allocated to and concentrated in certain designated persons or administrative groups. The lines of command, from the apex down, are rigidly defined. (38, pp. 362-363)

Regimental action, to use LaPiere's term (38, pp. 105-110), is necessary to meet both the recurrent and the exceptional emergencies of a social system or subsystem. Many of these are predictable occurrences. Such emergencies should be—and many are—prepared for in advance by appropriate social agencies and procedures. Commonplace examples are fire and police departments, with a skilled and drilled personnel operating under officers and authorized by the community to deal with any situation arising in connection with their responsibility.

Regimentation as a continuing process, however, has a function of some degree of importance in the regulation of all social activities. There cannot always be disputation about tasks to be performed, and there cannot be complete freedom. Not all people recognize their proper functions and perform them conscientiously. Some lack intelligence and insight, some are not trained properly, and some lack good will even though they logically recognize their obligations. All such persons must be directed, even regimented ("pushed into line"), by some one or some group in authority. Things cannot be left to run on in their own way and order themselves in a complex society with a multiplicity of often-conflicting interests. Some regimentation of component elements is especially necessary in large-scale functional organizations, whether they be commercial or industrial corporations or class or caste systems. In general, as Bernard states, "Factories have to be managed, governments must be administered, children and others require advice and direction." (34, p. 447)

Better, more scientific standardization of motivation and conduct may remove the necessity of much regimentation, because it makes possible a wiser and more adequate self-direction, but even self-applied standardization can never wholly dispense with regimentation. (34, pp. 447-448) Furthermore, because of the very absence of socially adequate, appropriate, and carefully devised regimentation procedures and agencies dictators appear. Recurrently, during at least the last twenty-five hundred years, great misleaders have taken advantage of the crisis situations, insinuated themselves into them and forced their own particu-

*The wide use by dictators, totalitarian organizations, centralized hierarchies, and other exploiters and the general "bad" connotations of regimentation should not lead us to ignore its basic regulatory significance.

lar brand of "saving" regimentation upon the distraught societies.* At the same time, history records the names of many great men and great groups that have unselfishly but effectively extricated their people from crises by establishing new systems of regimental behavior.

Symbolization, Ritualization, and Ceremonialization. These closely related procedures are often overlooked or pooh-poohed. They are frequently viewed as of no great consequence in societal regulation or as part of the froth of social life. This opinion is especially prevalent among Americans with their emphasis on supposedly practical and utilitarian procedures and their wide dependence upon all manner of organizations to conduct their activities. And yet, as Herbert Spencer remarked many years ago about ceremony, "The earliest kind of government (that is, regulation), the most general kind of government, and the government which is ever spontaneously recommencing, is the government of ceremonial observance." (40, Vol. II, p. 11) Symbols, ritual, and ceremony are triggers and regularizers of essential social behavior, especially on crucial occasions, and their use goes far to guarantee proper performance.

Symbols, beyond the general ones of language and writing, function actively to induce and maintain conformity. They range from verbal formulas to physical objects. Thus, to ensure and enhance the performance of the proper role as citizen in political life, one notes declarations, documents, songs and literature, flags, insignia, uniforms, medals, pictures and statuary of heroes, watchwords and slogans, thrones and scepters, palaces and capitols, all redolent with sentiment and tradition. The family has its songs and pictures and reunions. Religious institutions have their creeds, prayers, hymns, vestments, crosses, altars, shrines, and so on. Symbols fascinate, appeal to the imagination, allay doubts, titilate long-standing feeling states, emphasize ideals of behavior, glorify practices, define and limit social expression, and stimulate or lure people to conforming response. They are visible or audible "trigger phrases" or "trigger objects" which mobilize and set off preformed patterns of behavior.

*This will be discussed more fully in Chap. 22.

Ritual and ceremony are also highly regulative procedures, closely related to symbols, in that they are in a sense the manipulation of roles and symbols. They are not mere survivals or empty forms. They are prescribed and right forms or methods of performance of some important and necessary social act, highly charged with group values.

To ritualize means to establish "a formal rhythmic procedure controlling a succession of acts directed to the same end and repeated without variation on appropriate occasions." (39, p. 150) Ritualization involves habituation, but a ritualized action includes more than habit or routine. It implies standardization and even regimentation. The performance of the succession of acts is accompanied by a peculiar sense of rightness and inevitability. Departure from it is felt to be undesirable, even outrageous, for it breaks the rhythm and disturbs the emotional response.

Among us, most of our religious observance, both personal and in association, is a matter of ritual. Contract making, property transfer, court procedure, baptism, marriage, and burial, assumption of citizenship, induction into office, voting are all matters of ritual. Observing the requirements of social etiquette, participating in vocational and professional duties, eating and drinking, and personal care have their ritualistic aspects. To do these in the "right" way—the "ritualized" way—gives us as individual members of the society a feeling of satisfaction, a feeling that what we know needs to be done is being done in the correct way. For the society, ritual renders the essential performance automatic and enables it to be carried out with a minimum of responsibility on the part of the performer. This reduces the necessity of using external pressure to maintain conformity to the predetermined, value-charged pattern of situational interaction.

To ceremonialize an action or occasion is to add further features to its ritual which enhance its peculiar significance. To ceremonialize is to add to or invest the rhythmic precision and undeviating repetition of ritual with a mystic element, an awesomeness, a solemnity, a dignity, a gravity, even a sanctity, which charges it with sentiment and emotion. This gives the performance or occasion vastly more than everyday routine significance and even lifts it beyond mere formality. The ceremonial procedure often is long established or has ascribed to it an ancient and sublime lineage and usually has much precious symbolism attached to it. Ceremony always impregnates the occasion with rich meanings and values, evokes reverential attitudes toward the principles embodied in the occasion, and conveys an almost ineluctable impression of the high and enduring worth of the values and occasions which it glorifies.

In most ceremonies the elevation, fixity, and preordained importance of the larger group that is involved is implied or proclaimed, and conversely, the subordination and suppliant nature of the individual in the group is brought out. Thus, respect for the occasion and its social implications is fostered and criticism is lulled. Ritual and ceremony give the occasions—religious events, state events, institutional events generally, public and private celebrations, and so on—importance and solemnity and make them weighty with rightness and social power. Without ritual and ceremony, the maintenance of social order would be greatly jeopardized. Realistically considered, however, both often become rigid and tend to survive their usefulness without undergoing questioning and revision to bring them up to date.

Sanctioning Processes

When a society has formulated its norms or rules, when it has done as much as it can to socialize them, and when it has uniformized the practices by more or less effective procedures growing out of experience, it still has to take precautions, for the conduct of individuals tends to deviate from the requirements defined in the norms. This is due to several factors. Hiller points out that members of the groups make different estimates respecting the validity of the norms, at least as applied to the given situations; are faced with unlike situations involving choice between personal and collective or public interests; and are not uniformly brought into contact with all norms. Hence, there is a lack of unanimity and uniformity of social behavior among the sections of a society. (6, p. 49) Whether these are due to lack of sufficient comprehension of the norms or insufficient acceptance of them because of individual stubbornness, whim, or selfishness, or whether they are due to alternate or competing norms or insufficient habituation to perform according to them adequately and competently *all* the time, the fact stands out that there is a continuous and universal tendency toward some degree of nonconformity at least to some standards. Norms and social behavior never coincide completely, as witness the statistics of crime, moral scandals, and unconventional behavior.

Society and all of its subsystems must enforce the other regulative procedures by establishing a *system of sanctions,* that is, procedures which confront individuals and groups with, and bring to bear upon them, the *social consequences to them* of their conforming or nonconforming behavior. In brief, society sets up and administers sanctions of approval or reward, and sanctions of condemnation or penalty. Sanctions often utilize the different kinds of *social power* mentioned in the previous chapter—the positive powers of promise, satisfactions, and social approvals and the various precious securities, and the negative powers of threat, disapproval, denial, and actual painful punishment. Long social experience shows that no social system which fails to provide adequate rewards and penalties can long exist.

Rewarding. Rewarding utilizes the positive controls to induce, incite, and motivate to desirable and essential social conduct. Individuals and groups are granted various kinds of bonuses or gains for their socialized efforts, which may be in the form of material inducements, such as physical and economic good things and desirable physical conditions that contribute to sustenance and comfort; personal or group signs of approval—special attention, praise, and the like; diversions and pleasures, such as vacations; objects or conditions that contribute to respect and esteem, as, for example, medals, prizes, promotion, high status, fame, authority; admission to higher associational opportunities and participations, such as clubs; or the promise of ideal, even supernatural, benefactions. Individuals and groups do much giving because they want or need to control people, for experience shows that it is an effectual control procedure. (41; 46, pp. 31-55)

Penalizing. Penalizing is the application of negative controls. Penalties are coercive, and their application involves various degrees of restraint, repression, inhibition, oppression, or prohibition, all with the intent of threat and punishment. Thus, through penalizing, social disapproval and concern for breaches of the social code are actively expressed. No rule is secure if it can be transgressed with impunity; therefore, disobedience must be prevented if possible, but if it has occurred, the transgressor must be penalized both as a lesson to him and as an example for others.

The threat and actual use of force in any regulatory system cannot be abolished. There must always be some organized, socialized force to restrain the antisocial manifestations of power itself in the society, whether exerted by individuals or by groups, and to restrain within limits the greedy, the unscrupulous, the socially illiterate, the intolerant, the combative, the lawless. Penalizing is necessary ultimately to prevent disorder, to settle disputes and conflicts, and to curb the encroachments of the strong and unprincipled, whether individuals or organizations. Force alone, to be sure, cannot maintain order and operation, but without it no social order can be secure.

Among the mild, more or less personal and unorganized disapproving procedures are blaming, frowning, ridiculing, criticizing, reprimanding, brusqueness of manner, and so on. At about the same level are forms of economic intimidation, such as withholding trade, cutting or threatening to cut wages, sabotage, impugning of the economic good will, and the like. More extreme penalties are demotion, studied avoidance and discrimination, denial of privileges, ostracism, intimidation, persecution, terrorism, and excommunication, which are carried on both informally and formally. Most extreme and unavoidable forms, usually resorted to only after formal determination of guilt, are punishments inflicted by the authoritative and organized political state, ranging from fines and other temporary or permanent deprivation of property, through cancellation of constitutional rights, to death for what are deemed heinous offences.

Agencies of Regulation in Modern Mass Societies

We have briefly examined the fundamental processes and conditions of societal regulation. We are especially concerned with regulation in a society like our own, that is, one that in considerable part has undergone a transition from sacred, primary-group relations to secular, secondary- or derivative-group relations. Modern societies, as we have noted repeatedly, consist of widely dispersed, mobile, heterogeneous populations which communicate mainly through a multiplicity of indirect, mechanized agencies.

Individuals no longer live wholly or largely in primary groups. The relationships have become varied and extensive and are characterized by many forms of horizontal and vertical social distance. The relationships between individuals are more and more impersonal, anonymous, external, and formal. The norms multiply, becoming specialized for groups and often confused and inconsistent in so far as the over-all problem of societal order is concerned. More and more activities in every department of social life must be regulated, for example, those in connection with marriage and divorce, industry, transportation and traffic, labor and capital, occupations and professions, recreation and welfare. The more complex the relations become, the greater are the possibility and probability of exploitative control. (47; 51, pp. 151-184) The task of maintaining order among the standardless and confused individuals and among the multiplicity of specialized, uncoordinated, heterogeneous, stratified, and often conflicting groups is tremendously complicated.

All the elementary and fundamental processes and instrumentalities *do* operate in such an industrialized-urbanized mass society. Norms are formed and conveyed in space and time. The primary controls, which rest upon the desire to maintain personal reputation, and involve close and mainly informal personal supervision, still operate more or less effectively. They function in primary groups, such as families, true neighborhoods (where they still exist), small groups of close acquaintances, congregations, and so on, where individuals are known or known about by others with whom they live in frequent relationships. Some of these primary-group controls operate in a limited or exceptional way and to some extent in some of the broader social relationships. Folklore elements, such as aphorisms, admonitions, parables, fables, and proverbs, have some effectiveness, especially in the backwater areas of modern life, and legends and myths, especially the social myths, are effective for the groups that believe them.

The time- and experience-rooted controls that have come out of the sociocultural heritage and operate informally or in a semiorganized manner still have influence, though it is somewhat mixed and haphazard. Reference is through control by the mass of folkways, mores and moral codes, customs, traditions, and conventions. Fad and fashion, crazes and movements, propaganda and advertising, and other currents, standardizations, and regimentations may produce vast uniformities.

But all these, in so far as they contribute to societal regulation, must be combined and focused, must be made specific, uniform, and binding upon all peoples and over the wide areas of a society. A society must function in all essential, minimal aspects of order as one people. These controls must also be revised and supplemented to meet modern regulatory needs. Thus, if modern societies are to be orderly, they must be more and more institutionalized and organized.*

Institutions

Social institutions are not only the major general operational agencies in satisfying the great array of wants, needs, and interests of a society; they are also the basic instruments for stabilizing and regularizing the social life of individuals and groups. They embody the ruling ideas and the codes of the society and have incorporated in them most of the motivating pressures and devices. Public opinion and public will function through them. Most of the specific control mediums, including customs, conventions, mores and moral codes, civil and religious law, ritual and ceremonies, the conditioning, educating, and other influencing, indoctrinating, and shaping procedures, personal leadership, operate in and through institutions. Moreover, since every crucial field of social relationship and essential functioning is presided over by institutions, a great number of specific ends in regulation are realized. Without institutions social order could not be maintained.

The reasons for this crucial place of institutions in societal regulation should be clearly understood. (48, pp. 43-46) The institutions have incorporated in them most of the generally accepted norms or charters of social action. They embody the organized force of associations and in most instances that of the community as a whole. With the aid of the group opinion that supports them, they are prepared to compel obedience and punish disobedience. They literally coerce persons into behaving in the expected or required manner; their requirements are imperatives.

If individuals disobey the institutional dictates, they are punished in some manner. Violations of regulations governing sex and marital relations, parental obligations, economic responsibilities, property rights, the sanctity of life, citizenship duties (including the military), religious practices, the moral minima for expressional forms, and innumerable other everyday institutionalized relationships and practices call forth variations and gradations of penalty, including victimization by gossip, deprivation of certain rights and privileges, social ostracism, imprisonment, and in some instances death. Institutions are the most stabilizing, best organized, most far-reaching, and most deeply rooted of all the forms of social control in operation.

All institutions exercise a high degree of effective social control over all of the associative activities of human beings, whether these are of a face-to-face primary nature or of a complex, secondary or derivative nature. Under the influence of each institution, we regulate our activities or actions in relation to others along a given line according to the rules and established practices of that institution.

Certain institutions are, however, more definitely intended and utilized for purposes of social control than others. Some institutions—the communicative, aesthetic, and to some extent religious—regulate only in the sense that they provide a standardized means of expression. Others, such as those inherent in real estate boards, credit men's associations, and professional organizations generally, exercise a very special type of regulation for groups of limited size,

*On the general institutional structuring of a society, see Chap. 12.

interest, and purpose. But the great mass of institutions are definite and purposive means of regularizing and standardizing individual and group conduct and of establishing and compelling certain social habits involved in the various pertinent relationships that are socially necessary or at least acceptable.

Institutions are peculiarly effective as regulative agencies in modern complex, heterogeneous societies in that they more and more substitute an organized external, objective, depersonalized social control of conduct for the impulsive, subjective or individual control or the control of separate, special-interest groups. In modern societies, institutions provide and maintain society-wide regularized patterns of behavior. Katz and Schanck wisely state: "Today we are not a nation of communities but a nation of institutions." (50, p. 23)

An important phase of the social control exercised by social institutions hinted at above is the patterning of the social behavior of individuals. One of the primary functions of any institution is to reproduce, preserve, and transmit to persons the uniform patterns of behavior by which they can meet the recurrent types of situations arising in human society. For the institutions serve not only as compellers, but as conditioners and guides, as cultivators of habits of conformity and of social understanding in individuals. Our institutions *tell us how to act.* Without the institutions, we would be lost. Institutions also mold social groups. Business corporations, families, athletic teams, university faculties, neighborhoods, nations, even many spontaneous but occasionally recurring groupings, like mass meetings, follow institutionalized patterns of activity. They cannot exist and function unless they do.

Finally, a distinct advantage inherent in the controlling and patterning function of institutions should be mentioned. If the control has been successful, both individual and group behavior in most relationships and situations can be predicted in large measure. Behavior will not be a matter of impulse, whim, or caprice; social life will not be chaos or anarchy. Each individual can face each new day with the assurance that he will know how to meet most of the problems that will confront him; that he will know how most of his fellows will act 99 per cent of the time; that he will have high certainty that the life of the society will be orderly. In short, he can count on security.

Associations or Organizations

Institutional, customary, and many other regulatory requirements function mainly through associations and organizations. Especially important among these are the economic, educational, religious, and governmental associations. As noted before, they have definite purposes and objectives set forth in their rules, regulations, and laws, which create a continual, pervasive atmosphere of guidance. Each formal organization has its pyramid of power, its administrative set-up, and its system of discipline and enforcement which leads members to conform to the rules and regulations. Through their direct influence they suggest, ineulcate, persuade, and compel appropriate common action.

Membership in almost all associations short of the state is largely voluntary, although unavoidable, if individuals are to function and survive in modern societies. Hence, the associations have the consent of their members and are able to enforce their rules with disciplinary action with comparative ease. (54, pp. 458-459) Moreover, each association has its appropriate array of officials or functionaries charged with duties of disciplining as well as coordinating the efforts of members in meeting the organization's objectives.

In the field of economics a great array of organizations have come into being for the express purpose of acting collectively in deciding conflicts and maintaining order in meeting the threat of want and scarcity. Notable among these are corporations, trade associations, boards of trade, employers' associations, trade unions, cartels, cooperative associations, and the Federal Reserve System.

In the recreational field all manner of associations formulate rules for conducting sports and games, determine eligibility of contestants, and discipline violations in various ways. In the field of morals and religion various organizations are intermittently or continuously operative. In all societies religious organizations constrain individuals through their manipulation of beliefs and actions relating to the supernatural power or powers. Religion also aids custom and law in maintaining what the society considers to be right and prohibiting what is wrong. A host of other specific organizations operate in American society with obvious regulative functions, such as the Boy Scouts, Girl Scouts, CYO, YMCA, YWCA.

The State

The universally dominant and indispensable institutionalized organizations for the regulation of modern societies are those of a political nature. Their significance and hegemony have been consistently increasing and seem destined to continue to do so. All other organized agencies maintain order in and for limited groups only. The *state* is the over-all regulative, directive, and ultimate compulsive and enforcing agent of the rules of social life. It is omniscient, omnipotent, and ubiquitous.

Through its various legislative and administrative bodies the state makes and remakes the essential laws governing every action construed in the public interest. These laws are the concrete formalized expressions of the community's insistent norms. They supplement and predominate over all the informal controls and the rules of lesser organizations; define certain acts as offenses and state rights, duties, and liberties; specify penalties for disobedience; carry the massed and supposedly impartially applied authority of the community and enforce it in the name of the whole community. Through its courts, the state interprets law and determines guilt or innocence; and through its innumerable departmentalized policing, administrative, and service organizations it assumes the responsibility of providing for, regulating, and directing a host of societal needs.

The state is the final arbitrator, advisor, moderator, and coordinator among societal elements and has the ultimate creative role. Through its power to limit individual and group action and property rights and to force action, it can penalize its constituents and carry out enforcement of its decrees. It has the ultimate authority and the supreme power to exercise the essential and, if necessary, unlimited force, since it is the only social agency having a complete and unquestioned monopoly of force in any society. (53)

If individuals or various groups are ignorant or learn slowly or refuse to be guided by the pressures and controls emanating from roles, symbols, functionaries, and the various social-psychic propulsions of informal public opinion, or if the lesser formal organizations are out of line, they must submit to final regulation by the state—the over-all political community.

In the last analysis all other institutions and organizations depend upon the state to enforce their indispensable and irreducible social-action requirements. The state enforces the regulatory measures, for example, relating to marriage and divorce, parent-and-child relations, the public health institutions, most industrial and commercial institutions, many occupational and professional organizations at least as final arbiter, and is a court of last resort for the final moral safeguarding of recreational and aesthetic institutions. Furthermore, all of the other regulatory agencies are held to exercise disciplinary authority subject to the law of the state and within the bounds fixed by that law. The state represents the common will and is endowed with the united power of the entire society to maintain a common, united, orderly, secure, and reasonable living together.

The state has also assumed and is continually assuming a greater and greater array of general maintenance functions in addition to its more specific regulatory functions. As the institutionalized agency bearing the ultimate responsibility for general well-being, it has had to take on many functions once conducted by other institutionalized organizations but lost by them in the transition from primary- to secondary-group life. It has also had to take supervisory responsibility for many others and actually develop many systematic new functions heretofore carried on sporadically or not at all. For example, the state, through its various departments has had to assume responsibility for the provision of education and the support of much research; for much of the moral and social training and protection of the young; for the care of the aged, the dependent, and the defective; for disease control; for food and drug protection; and for public sanitation and health.

The state guarantees religious rights and most of the other freedoms. It has had to set standards for and regulate building construction and housing, industry, agriculture, finance, business, transportation, communication, and water utilization; to supervise the relations between industrial groups and the standards and practices of certain vocational and professional groups; and recently, to provide public utilities, sanitary facilities, water supply, and even facilities for aesthetic satisfaction and cultural achievement. It is well on the way to becoming an all-encompassing, but nonetheless benevolent, giant.

Public Opinion

In the last analysis the fundamental and supreme implementing agent in societal regulation and operation is public opinion, a force of unfathomable potency in influencing and directing people. None of the regulatory procedures or instrumentalities is effective without its firm support. There must be an underlying community of interest, understanding, agreement, expression, and will to give *force* to all regulatory and maintenance aims and efforts or to any kind of collective organizational action. In a very real sense, the rules and machinery of societal life must first be in the shared ruling ideas, values, objectives, preferences, anticipations, expectations, requirements, permissives, prohibitions, and spirit and will *of the people.*

Public opinion is the support of all norms, codes, and laws. Law, for example, in itself is useless. A law is nonenforceable unless it is actively supported by the beliefs, values, and wills of a majority or an effective minority of the community. As we say, such a law is a "dead letter." Public opinion reflects and supports both the informal and formal controls. The informal elements, such as folkways, mores, beliefs, customs, traditions, and conventions, which grow out of sociocultural experience, rest upon it for compliant performance. Most organizations exist only by virtue of public permission, and the functions they perform must meet with its approval. Public opinion gives approval and power to the social institutions; supports the institutional roles, symbols, and rituals; motivates and in the long run authorizes and sanctions the institutional activities of both the general participants and those of the functionaries. It is the ultimate rewarding factor, and it authorizes and supports the coercive and penalizing efforts and measures of the community, including especially those of the state as the last resort in forcing conformity to all essential regulatory requirements. In the last analysis, it shapes our attitudes, beliefs, desires, and motives and is behind every social movement that has any efficacy.

By public opinion is meant the more or less definite set of ideas, beliefs, and judgments formulated as a sort of decision by a group—it may be three persons, a neighborhood, an association, a community, a nation, even world-wide mankind—in connection with matters of concern to that group. It is the resultant of the attention which the concerned members of the group give to the issue at stake, although the concerned members are seldom all of the members. The decision represents a sort of general conviction or consensus, including all the positions maintained by the attentive members of the group, but it is not a superindividual opinion nor a uniformity of opinion, nor a majority or effective-minority opinion. Rather, it is a certain preponderant trend and direction of the individual opinions and judgments of the members and represents the general level of what men believe and how they feel about a given subject at a given time. It may be only momentary, or it may be persistent on matters of continuous or recurrent concern within a given societal unit.

The Bases of Public Opinion

Public opinion is the result of social interaction, communication, stimulation, and experience. The interstimulation may be spontaneous or designedly created. Public opinion may be disseminated by private conversation between neighbors, friends, and associates or developed by chance talks or by speakers in the lecture rooms, pulpits, or radio. It may be shaped in part in the conference, discussion group, or deliberative body, partially or wholly organized for that purpose, and propagated through drama, motion picture, television, or literature in various forms, especially periodicals and newspapers. Attempts at propaganda, with its combination of truth and lies, and censorship, unofficial and official, usually are involved, especially in the case of far-reaching issues.

In content public opinion is a conglomerate, compounded in some part of facts, principles, and rational considerations. But it also reflects the attitudes, prejudices, stereotypes, sentiments, feelings, and emotions as these are shaped by all of the sociocultural conditioning and inculcating influences of members of the group or public, both as individuals and as interest-group participants.

Group opinion differs from group to group, although in the end the opinion of all the groups is incorporated in the larger opinion of the whole on all issues pertinent to the community or society. In spite of the haphazard manner of its formulation, it is usually sound at the core. Public opinion cannot exist apart from the individual minds that hold it and the various subgroups and associations that contribute to it; yet each individual and each lesser societal element acts toward it as if it were something apart from and above it, an autocrat whose fiat must be obeyed. It is the basis of most public action and the mentor and censor of most individual behavior. Once public opinion is formed on any issue, its weight tends to accumulate, even in sheer numbers of supporters.

How Public Opinion Functions

How and why does public opinion function as a regulative force? It is felt by almost all individuals and lesser groups and organizations as an inescapable pressure. Men, individually and in association, are social creatures. There is among us an insistent and omnipotent concern about what others will *think* about us and what they may *do* to us. No matter how heterogeneous or homogeneous, scattered or local, a public is, it usually acts as a judicial agent, making decisions, rendering judgments, exercising its irresistible power of approval or disapproval, and selecting, checking, and punishing. In considerable measure, it holds the position and well-being of all societal elements in its hands. Even a large, powerful corporation, a region, or a nation cannot stand out against public opinion in its activities for any length of time without loss. When public opinion is ignored or defied, sooner or later it makes itself felt and often does so without bringing to bear upon the dissenter any special means of punishment. Its quiet persistence is sufficient. Submissiveness, fear, and shame bend our waywardness into line, for public disapproval, ridicule, scorn, distrust, rebuke, avoidance, and condemnation are powerful procedures. Every societal element feels the need of being an accepted and approved part of the larger social going concern.

Thus, the power of public opinion as a regulative agent does not necessarily rest upon the peculiar wisdom of its decisions or upon its special enlightenment, but upon the tremendous force of its public approval or, at least, absence of disapproval. It is the major regulatory check upon individuals and groups.

Its difficulties and weaknesses as a regulatory agent derive from several factors. The public is not always sufficiently homogeneous for public opinion to form and operate. Control of public opinion can only occur among "a body of individuals who are held together by the bond of common ideas and sentiments and who have at least a dim desire to maintain and continue their union. . . . In groups in which there is a really deep cleavage there can be no public opinion." (60, p. 140) Public opinion often lacks explicitness and clarity, especially in modern secondary groups with their multiple and divers sets of opinions. Furthermore, owing to much deliberate misleading and much confusion, public opinion is often not sufficiently enlightened or governed by sound and tried facts and principles. It merely reacts. Finally, ". . . the public has a short wrath and a poor memory, and the offender, if he dodges into obscurity and waits until the gust of public indignation is over, often goes unpunished." (68, p. 96)

Nevertheless, it must back the norms if they are to be effective. It must sustain in sufficient degree every association that wishes to continue. All the informal procedures and instrumentalities regulate to the degree that they do because of its support, and all going regulative and maintenance institutions have it behind them. All new functions in the institutions and all new forms of them must be accepted by it; in fact, they are often the result of the pressure of public opinion.

CHAPTER XXI

PROCESSES AND INSTRUMENTALITIES OF SOCIETAL MAINTENANCE

AS INDICATED in the introductory section of the preceding chapter, social order and continuity are matters of *both* regulation and maintenance. The rules must be established and inculcated, social behavior uniformized in essential details as far as possible, rewards, penalties, and effective regulatory instrumentalities supported by public opinion. But the regulatory elements are not sufficient to ensure order and functional efficiency in societies as they are typically constituted. There must also be continuous bolstering of socialized conduct and adjusting of individuals and groups. Both the flesh and the spirit need to be stimulated by more than rewards and penalties. Morale must be maintained and the very standardization and regimentation that are imposed by regulation must be limited by rights and freedoms to the extent that is functionally safe. Where diversities of individuals, categories, and groups are unavoidable and are essential to societal operation, they must be ordered by fair niche-assigning procedures. Separation, dissension, and conflict must be prevented or alleviated, and processes making for automatic uniformation and compatibility of the society's various elements must be permitted, even aided, to operate. (23) These are the *maintenance* processes.

In addition to all the regulatory processes and instrumentalities involved in societal maintenance, there are socially motivating and continuously or recurrently adjusting and restoring processes and procedures that enable the society to carry on.

It should be pointed out that the actual agencies or instrumentalities for societal maintenance are the great purposive institutionalized organizations of society. The major typical organizations are those that constitute the economic system, the marriage and family system, the political, legal, and military systems, the religious and ethical systems, the educational and scientific systems, and the expressional and recreational systems. The nature of these great institutionalized organizations and their maintenance and other functions were examined in Chapter 12. In the present chapter we shall examine the general conditions and the better known basic maintenance processes, not the processes of operation of the great battery of societal organizations.

Two essentials must be present if any society is to be continuously and prosperously maintained. The persons and groups must be motivated to act along all desirable and essential lines, and they must have morale—a tone of cooperative life and societal loyalty. Beyond these essentials are the specific adjustive processes and procedures.

Social Motivation

Nature and Function of Motivation

Motivation in itself is a subjective matter occurring in and through individuals, but *social* motivation is a social-psychological process of profound, *objective,* sociological significance, for the maintenance of any social system requires adequate motivation. (17, pp. 159, 161) The process of social motivation is concerned only incidentally with human energetics as they express themselves in human behavior.* It is concerned primarily with all those energizing factors, processes, and procedures that produce, or can be marshaled to produce, that positive individual and group action which contribute directly to effective societal functioning.

The individual survival of the members of a social system must be ensured, to be sure; but they must also be so impelled from within and without that they adequately perform the minimal activities necessary for meeting the functional needs of the social system. Human beings must *want* to act in the way they *must* act as members of the society or of any of its lesser groups. They have to *desire* what is objectively necessary for them to do. It is best if *outer force* is replaced by *inner compulsion.*

Social motivation has both positive and negative aspects. In its positive form it is the manipulation in individuals and groups of the urge to act in so far as this urge exists. Always, however, it must develop socialized will and purpose, for the production of every good thing and every service essential to societal self-preservation depends on these. In its negative aspects, social motivation seeks to overcome lethargy, diffidence, unsocial deviance, lack of cooperation, and antisocial behavior.

In general, social motivation means to illuminate and aggrandize the established goals and norms of indispensable social participation, cooperation, and social production; to get people to pay attention to these goals; to press them upon individuals and groups continuously and persistently; to get individuals and groups to want what the functional goals include for themselves and all others. But above all, the function of motivation is to stimulate activity. Adequately motivated individuals do their part to the fullest extent of their abilities, facilities, and positions in working for social ends.

Social motivation consists specifically of inciting and inducing individuals to tolerate and to perform effectively their various social roles in the differentiated and hierarchically organized network of roles that constitutes the social system, to strive to achieve a particular position or status, to exercise the various contribution-eliciting prerogatives and rights provided by the social system, and to do these things according to the normatively oriented channels. These various roles must be filled and their functions adequately performed. The roles and the performers must mesh smoothly; otherwise, we do not have societal prosperity or even bare maintenance. We have social deficit.

Concretely, social motivation incites persons to want to live fully and express themselves with all their socially acceptable and socially useful capacities and propensities, to act among their fellows in an orderly manner, to provide population replacements for themselves, to have adequate work habits and work aims, and to produce according to their best abilities their share of essential goods and services. Under its stimulus the members of a society cooperate with others in their respective fairly achieved status positions and seek to play all their various socially relevant roles in a purposive, competent, fair, nonparasitic manner, thus maintaining their society in all its essential familial, economic, political, ethical, religious, educational, scientific, aesthetic, and recreational processes and functions.

An important consideration in social motivation

*For the examination of these, see Chap. 3.

is the stimulation, utilization, and manipulation of all the dynamic factors in individual and group behavior. This includes the incitement and appropriation for regulatory and maintenance objectives of the basic, constant human-nature needs and drives, habits, socially derived wishes, desires, and expressional urges, and propensity to imitate. Another important consideration is the social utilization and manipulation of the push of aspiration and the desire for gain, self-preservation, security, and, paradoxically, the craving for freedom and adventure. A third and even more important consideration is recognition of the fact that human beings are social by reason of their need to interact with others. This means that probably the greatest single force in social motivation is the anticipation of satisfying response from others. Thus, a maintenance system appropriates for social ends the ego-enhancement factors, such as ambition and desire for favorable recognition, social reputation, position, distinction, prestige, and power.

Finally, social motivation involves the purposive performance of all *social agencies* that exercise influence, authority, or propulsion, directly or indirectly, consciously or unconsciously, *persons* in their leadership, positional, or official capacities; *associations and institutions* through their massed, organized power in the employment of instruction, propaganda, power, sanctions, and other incentives and pressures; and *publics* as they decide issues and act impersonally but powerfully as conformity- and action-demanding propellants.

Unless the group or society has this continuous sufficient social reinforcement of the socially motivating factors, it cannot long continue, for it will lose both its cohesiveness and its functional effectiveness. Without this reinforcement there is vast individual and social waste. Newcomb appropriately points out: "It would probably not be an exaggeration to say that the principal source of human waste, in our society at least, lies in our failing to take advantage of group resources for individual motivation." (15, pp. 425-427) He goes on to indicate that such failure is not due to human perverseness, but to the fact that we have not learned to take advantage of the resources. Social motivation is in considerable part an "undiscovered country." We have no adequate statement of the principles involved and we need to devote more attention to the discovery of such principles and their verification and to making them available for social use. Finally, if social motivation is informed and adequate, it removes the necessity of regimentation through organized regulatory agencies because it makes possible a wiser and more ample *self-direction* of social behavior.

Competition as a Motivating Process

Competition as a general motivating process and as an opposition process was examined in Chapters 10 and 17. Like many other social processes, competition in some of its aspects may have societally deleterious effects, and in others societally beneficial effects. Here we are concerned briefly with competition as a universal, inevitable, and largely unintentional and automatically operating process of motivation. It functions as such in some degree in all societies, save absolutely rigid caste systems.

Competition functions best as a motivating process when it is fair and just and governed by good rules well understood and enforced, and when the objectives are socially acceptable or desirable and competitors have opportunities and training to pursue their competitive course according to their respective abilities. (7) But any social system that is alive and moving must be, in some sense, competitive, for by means of competition individuals and groups are motivated to carry on the common enterprises of the society in a cooperative manner.

As previously indicated, competition consists of the largely impersonal process whereby individuals and groups, including organizations, endeavor to gain relatively scarce identical desirable objectives which other individuals and groups are attempting to achieve at the same time. The objectives will vary from society to society and from time to time within a society in nature, quality, and social pertinence. But it is a motivational process which underlies and pervades all aspects of interactional life, and it always has some special significance in the achievement and maintenance of operational ends:

Under competition individuals and groups are impelled to function with intensity. It stimulates, selects, and develops potentialities and abilities, places a premium upon initiative and resourcefulness, and brings about a vast expenditure of energy and a creative utilization of energy in socially useful and essential activities. Success depends upon achievement under its rules and conditions, that is, success in achieving personal popularity, marriage, occupational performance, improvement of social position, acquisition of material goods, and other social emoluments. Competition stimulates the social laggards and illiterates as well as the socially informed and ambitious, for some have not been conditioned adequately to the proper discharge of their duties either to themselves or to society. These persons can be motivated only by such a strong and acid stimulus as competition. As such, competition is often a process of self-discipline as well as of motivation.

Among organizations it fosters a continual effort to keep operations at maximum efficiency by weeding out incompetents and inspiring technological innovations and reorganizational activities to enhance efficiency, thus getting much maintenance work done in a highly energetic and efficient manner. Consequently, in a dynamic, relatively free, and open-end society like our own, many social situations are actually arranged so as to be competitive. In our society, because of the multiplicity of competitive standards, opportunities, and requirements, both individuals and groups have a vast array of possibilities of demonstrating competence and of making contributions which are satisfying and profitable to themselves and redound greatly to societal output and efficiency. Competition as a potent motivational process is involved in various other maintenance process and procedures to be discussed below, especially those relating to ordination and mobility.

Social Morale and Morale Building

Nature of Social Morale

Social morale is closely related to social motivation as an indispensable factor in societal maintenance. Nevertheless, a society needs more than mere motivation, more than the push of competition. It needs also what has come to be called *morale*. Social morale is mainly discussed in connection with major social crises (for example, war and revolution), undoubtedly because at such times it is lacking in sufficient degree and societal maintenance has been impaired. What needs to be appreciated, however, is that *a high degree of morale is a continuous necessity* if unity and the effectiveness of operation are to be maintained.

As has been noted repeatedly, a society like our own is characterized by great diversities, differentiations, and cleavages. Relationships are largely anonymous and formal and almost incomprehensively complex. The population is vast and heterogeneous, and different elements of it are held in different degrees of esteem, have differing degrees of opportunity, and receive different degrees of treatment. There is considerable cultural fragmentation, and no sufficiently consistent general design for living prevails.

All manner of cleavages between groups, especially majority-minority cleavages between nationality and racial groups, religious cleavages, political cleavages, and cleavages between social classes and economic groups are to be found. There are quarrels within organizations, urban-rural and sectional differences, diversities of attitudes and aims, excessive partisan aggressiveness and much lack of allegiance to essential community and societal objectives and functions. In a very real sense a state of crisis exists *all the time,* and a continuous crusade for societal maintenance must be conducted.

Morale is a dynamic unifying factor in human action, which is essential to the identity, stability, and continuity of any group, large or small. It holds groups together, gives them their tone, and determines to a large extent the directions and effectiveness as well as the quality of their activities. *By morale is meant a unified state of attitude, emotion, and thinking among the members which makes for a dominating, over-all loyalty to, and oneness of, that group; and an effective devotion and commitment to its common essential objectives.* As Hocking puts it, "It is a will-to-give to the job in hand." (32)

When there is high morale, there are settled convictions as to the worthiness of group beliefs and ideals, a high level of mutual and reciprocal good will, a unity of resolution and purpose, a freely granted obedience to the directors of the undertakings, a focusing of action in the form of intelligent and organized teamwork, and an abiding belief that the cause can and will be realized. People have a firm faith in the supreme importance of their common undertakings and an impelling sense of obligation in seeing them through. There is a free, even sacrificial, willingness to act and a merging of the many wills into a single will for the performances at hand. When morale is high, the "best" of the individual members is brought out; they conform to the group ideas and ideals with willingness and zeal; they have faith in each other and in their leaders; they respond freely to the group controls and they subordinate deviant tendencies. They have *esprit de corps*. There is a maximum of individual and collective efficiency and output. In brief, the group or society is in a state of individual and organizational fitness to conduct its undertakings.

Morale is poor, that is, *a state of demoralization exists,* when there is much atomization, suspicion of others and discrimination against them, callous indifference, distrust, dissension, studied diversiveness, rank partisanship, apathy and defeatism, skepticism about the rightness of goals, criticism of, and lack of confidence in, group leaders, and much uncertainty regarding the future of the group. Individuals are discouraged, disheartened, frustrated, separated, and as members of groups they have little feeling of identification with, and involvement in, the group. Groups and organizations do not cooperate. The people can find no energy for rebuilding their individual and group lives, and they have no feeling of urgency for attempting any achievement beyond mere survival. They are paralyzed and have ceased to live as a people. (30) A group or society in such a state cannot long maintain itself.

Morale Building

The process of morale building, although it is of continuous, strategic importance, has not been adequately analyzed. We will attempt, however, to draw together some of the scattered points that have been contributed. At the very outset, it must be kept in mind that morale has something to do with the *release* of the springs of socialized action and the *control* of the energies that go into right social action. The functional task is both to *invoke* and to *sustain* morale. As Creel has pointed out, (29) morale cannot exist in a vacuum, but must have specific content and must be continually fed. It must also be remembered that morale is a conditional quality of a people.

The development and sustaining of morale is first of all a leadership phenomenon; it requires leadership which is wise and patient. It depends also upon the fullest utilization of the various mechanisms of communication. The objectives of the group must be presented in a simple and clear-cut manner, and their relationship to individual and over-all needs and aspirations should be emphasized. Cognizance must be given to the fact that the objectives are ways of escape or release from an actually or potentially low-scale order of existence, that they are ways of achieving higher ends in satisfactory living and acting.

A positive goal is a magnetic pole toward which the aspirations of men are drawn. This means that the process of morale building has an intellectual aspect; it is a response to meaning. The essential basic and elucidating ideas should be propagated; the facts of their nature and the requirements for carrying them out should be given; and the reasonableness of the endeavors should be emphasized. These require effective mobilization of the instructional and indoctrinating agencies, including the use of forthright constructive propaganda. At this point it is usually desirable to emphasize the rooted traditions and other precious cultural heritages of the people, those that have a long, noble, and successful past. There should also be emotional preparation, for the emotions, properly elicited, invested, and controlled, are the dynamic factors in human action; through them ideas come to lively, purposive action. People need to be inspired with enthusiasm and confidence in the purposes of the group, though not to the point of energy-allaying overconfidence.

Furthermore, it should be emphasized that the objectives are realizable in reasonable time with the proper assumption of responsibilities in the unified endeavor. A time perspective is important. The relevance of present to successive activities gives a feeling of security regarding the future. By no means of least importance is the eliciting of actual participation in common endeavor itself by presenting opportunities, even requirements, for joint action. There is both unification, or togetherness, and vast expenditure of energy when individuals *give* themselves when others are also doing so, when men *give* with devotion to a common idea and task which is stronger and more luminous than their segmental private ideas and actions. Finally, the successes and the victories resulting from the loyal joint action should be stressed. Men are encouraged by even small successes. "Nothing succeeds like success" and "nothing fails like failure." The victories jointly achieved give all the participants a lift.

Equalization: Granting and Maintaining Freedoms and Rights

The equalization processes are absolutely essential in a society such as ours for several reasons. They are necessary to support, supplement, and further implement motivation and morale, to counterbalance the ever-potential stultifying effects of uniformity, conformity, standardization, and regimentation as these are affected by the regulatory processes and instrumentalities, and to produce some compensatory gains over and above the unavoidable submission to rules and restrictions. (56, p. 38) They are essential in neutralizing some of the effects of differentiation and stratification, especially the effects of such a disfunctioning process as discrimination.

As will be noted below, the equalization processes, along with competition, are indispensable aids in the processes of ordination as these operate in a differentiated and stratified society. Finally, the equalization processes are necessary in the maintenance of any society because of the tremendous positive gains that a society derives through their operation in the form of all permissible variations of individuals and groups, and from well-selected and well-placed abilities and skills. They are boons to the economical utilization of a society's individual and collective energies, as well as indispensable processes for fluid adjustment.

Nature of Equalization

Equalization as a process consists *not* in bringing all to a dead level or even to an average of performance, position, or social reward, *but in equalizing the opportunities for social achievement* —educational, economic, political, cultural, and so on. It gives each individual the chance to ascend or descend the social ladder until he reaches the point where his abilities and skills are matched and *equalized* by the requirements and prerequisites of his attained social position. Concretely, the equalizing processes usually take the form both of reducing the restrictions upon the opportunities of those of lower status and of reducing the special or artificial advantages of those of higher status in a given society.

There always has been and always will be great variation in individual capacities and abilities, and some of these are susceptible of great change in the lifetime and career of individuals. A dead level of equality (absolute equalitarianism has never been possible historically, although it has been experimented with) would be utterly undesirable even if it could be achieved, for it would impose vast strains upon the part of the population below the level and have a stultifying effect upon the abilities and aspirations of those above the level. Equalization thus does not mean producing human equality in the sense of some sort of mathematical or mechanical equilibration of persons, but in having societal provision of *equality of opportunity* in development and self-expression and in having some choice of life goals.

If opportunity is made as equal as possible, the various functions of a society are better performed because there is a wider and more effective selection of persons to perform them. The main need of men is self-expression, but with the vast differences in personal abilities and social requirements, not all can render equal services. If the possibilities for self-expression can be made general, inequalities will excite little resentment, and all can serve with equal eagerness. In brief, equalization consists in providing equal chance or opportunity to develop and express unequal capacities and to produce unequal results. (59)

Essentials of Equalization

Equalization provides equal access to, and the equitable distribution and guarantee of, freedoms and rights. The freedoms imply independence of, and immunity to, restraint and submission to the power or control of others. They are privileges of self-direction in belief, thought, and practice, privileges of knowing, learning, acting, and enjoying results. The rights are the specific freedoms claimed, permitted, guaranteed, and enforced by a society for that society's constituent elements. These social rights define the areas and the boundaries of the various freedoms. They are rooted in the values of a society and are based upon the principles of the morality, custom, tradition, convention, religion, and, especially in secularized civil societies, constitutions and laws of the given society. In brief, rights are the socially granted freedoms.

Essential Social Limitations on Freedom

Rights, as specifically defined, established, and limited freedoms, point to the fact that there cannot be unlimited freedom or, as Malinowski puts it, "free-floating, pervasive, omnipotent" freedom. (56, p. 82) In fact, equality and absolute freedom are incompatible in almost all conceivable social relationships, for absolute and unrestricted freedom means lawlessness, anarchy, and license, and these lead to disruption, subversion, and destruction. Unlimited freedom would result in the impairment, even the abuse, of freedom for most because of the power of the wealthy, of factions, and of those capable of exercising physical violence or exerting mental and spiritual intimidation.

Consequently, every society must reconcile the privileges of freedom or liberty among its variant and often dissident individuals and groups so that all these elements live together in an orderly and prosperous manner. The quantity or range and the quality of freedoms permitted are assets which depend upon how the given society is organized. The freedoms inhere in the values that the society cherishes, its established and accepted norms, the efficacy of its instrumentalities for order, the accessibility of its means of achievement, and the guarantees which ensure the equitable distribution of benefits. Freedom is organized and implemented in the interests of the well-being of the greatest number. Therefore, it always means *some* degree of submission, *some* renunciation, *some* sacrifice on the part of all individuals and lesser groups under socially authoritative discipline. It too is a social construct, a social grant, a by-product of institutionalized life, and a function of community power.

In spite of the limited nature of socially granted rights, the alternative in the form of none at all is unthinkable. It implies the complete use of power by *some* persons or groups and the complete regimentation of all other members of the society.

Standard Rights of Our Society

Our own American society has an unbroken tradition of democratic freedoms and rights that has accumulated through the centuries. Some of these are implicit in our widely accepted moral codes, and many of the most important ones are stated in our constitutions, bills of rights, and other statements of civil rights. The more common rights will be merely mentioned here. Always it must be kept in mind, however, that certain moral and legal conditions as usually determined and interpreted by majorities under the guise of protecting the health, morals, and safety of the community, prevail in the case of every one of them.

Ours is a long list of "rights." We have the right to live in places of our choice and to move about and change our residence; to marry whom and when we choose within certain defined limits or not to marry; to carry on our occupations and exercise choice among a wide range of occupations; to carry on legitimate business; to hold property and administer it within a range of permitted uses and abuses and transmit it; to make contracts; to associate, assemble, and organize for a wide range of purposive activities; to embrace a great variety of economic opportunities; to speak freely and express opinions on many subjects; to hold religious beliefs and worship as we please; to embrace educational, cultural, and expressional opportunities; to experiment and invent; to vote and to be represented in government and to hold office; to receive equality and justice before the law; and, as important as any, to be considered as persons, regardless of age, sex, class, educational level, occupation, race, and other characteristics. This is by no means a complete inventory, but it indicates a proud and noble heritage. It represents the limitation of many historical governmental, ecclesiastical, class, caste, and special individual prerogatives.

Maintenance Gains of a System of Rights

These socially established, limited, controlled, and enforced freedoms are indispensable requisites in a system of social regulation and maintenance. First, where we do not have recognized rights, there is the actuality or the continuous threat of violence, insecurity, suspicion, and disorder; where rights do exist and are fairly equitably enforced, they make for peace, security, and order. Second, rights make possible the release and effective mobilization of human potentialities and abilities and provide opportunity for variation and spontaneity of expression and a high degree of self-realization based upon personal choice, free contract, and individual initiative. Persons are free to be themselves, to achieve a sense of personal value, and to build the best career.

Third, society gets positive contributions from the diversity of abilities and roles. Men are free to explore and experiment, to plan, to find and develop new forms of material wealth and well-being, to form new socially useful instruments and techniques and enhance technological advance. They have scope for developing new social organizations, new enterprises, and new forms of cooperation and the opportunity for religious inspiration, intellectual and artistic expression, and access to the finer gifts of cultural development and enjoyment. They are free to develop new values and achieve new goals. The cultivation of learning, science, wealth, art, recreation, health, and religion all grow out of them. The freedoms do not guarantee any of these contributions, but without the freedoms there would be none of them. Social life to be adequately maintained must expand, it cannot be "frozen." The freedoms are the bases of expansion.

Fourth, the exercise of the freedoms provides a society with safety valves, that is, they make possible the reduction of frustration, tension, and protest. Dissension and resentment can be converted into competitive effort. Decadent and outmoded ways can be corrected by trying out new ways. Through free assembly, discussion, and decision, problems can be worked out, and the social atmosphere cleared.

Finally, such freedoms as we have make possible the most efficacious recruiting of leaders and elites. Careers are open to the talented and able. From the freedom of learning, of searching, of choice, of expression, and of action come the scientific, technological, economic, cultural, religious, and administrative leaders and elites, without which no society can maintain itself.

In actual practice the degree to which the declared rights function as equalizing factors or, in other words, the quality of the guarantee and the actuality of the realization of rights depend upon local interpretation and the impartiality of the administration of justice, which, in turn, is a matter of public opinion.

Efficiency and Economy of Positive Social Controls

The discussions of standardization and of sanctions in the preceding chapter and the examination of the freedoms in the present section point to an important consideration regarding the regulatory and maintenance behavior of human beings. The freedoms are positive, that is, they relate to, and in many instances are embodied in, the positive social controls. By contrast, the negative controls are based on prohibitions and use threats and penalties. Social experience shows that positive controls are conducive to vastly more efficient and economical societal regulation and maintenance than are negative controls, but negative controls are necessary in dealing with certain kinds of antisocial behavior and certain human weaknesses of will and deficiencies in social intelligence and insight.

Nevertheless, the negative controls produce fear, and fear is a poor motivator, for it either suppresses and paralyzes human beings with resultant inertia or leads to frantic and inconsiderate action. Furthermore, since all men are in some measure self-expressive creatures, the prohibitions invite resentment and breed recalcitrance. By the very fact of their forbidding certain acts, the prohibitions arouse curiosity regarding those acts, invite a test violation, and frequently tempt people to try to "beat the rap" and "see what they can get away with." In general, negative controls and regimentations quench enthusiasm, reduce energy, suppress initiative, and discourage or crush imagination. Such effects are bad for the social morale and for social productivity.

Every society desperately needs the positive behavior that comes with the positive rewarding sanctions and with all the permitted and encouraged freedoms. These allow regularized self-expression and self-direction, stimulate and release personal energy in socially wholesome, even ideal, directions, utilize self-esteem and the craving to excel in every sphere of available activity—physical, intellectual, economic, and so on—arouse ambitions and hopes, provide opportunities for creative and constructive activity, and, above all, provide luminous, rewarding goals. Indeed, if energies are put to creative and constructive ends, they are not available for harmful ends.

Positive action and opportunity mean growth and socialized strength and the most efficacious investment of human energy. In our present ever-changing and ever-expanding world with the ever-new and ever-more complicated problems of adjustment, we need versatility, talent, self-starting, construction, and willing emulative service as never before. All these underscore the importance of the wise and circumspect extension of the freedoms and the facilitation of the various processes of equalization.

Adjustment of Unequal Persons and Inequalities of Opportunity

The processes that bring about the universal differentiation and stratification in society were discussed in Chapters 13 and 14. A differentiated and stratified society is one of divided and unequal individuals and groups; hence, one continually in a state of disequalibration. In such a society processes must be continually occurring which structurally and functionally readjust the various differentiated and stratified elements to each other. This adjustment is essential if relative order and efficiency of operation are to be maintained.

Moreover, there are continually accumulating unequal ratios of persons to available spátial and economic opportunities and dissatisfaction with political, educational, social, and other desired opportunities at any given place and at any given time. Because of dislocation in given class or organizational systems, there are thwarted ambition pressures of some persons and frustrations and inferiority feelings of others caused by demands upon abilities in the way of a required level or quality of performance that cannot be met by them. A range of processes permits some adjustment of these recurrent contingencies.

Processes of Ordination

The inequalities inevitably create different levels of social ability; certain social processes, more or less efficiently, assign human beings to their appropriate levels of action.

Societal Situation Requiring Ordination. If a society is to maintain itself, a great number of functions must be conducted. These require various degrees and levels of proficiency and involve human beings as actors with their unequal capacities and preparations for social action, contribution, and responsibility. All these enterprises, if they are to be successful, and all these variant human elements must be coordinated and solidified into a working whole. (70)

The very division of labor in a society is both horizontally differentiated as between more or less similar and equal tasks and functions and vertically differentiated as between tasks and functions involving different levels of proficiency, complexity, and responsibility. Some positions and functions require innate talents of such high degree and involve training processes that are so long, costly, and elaborate that the persons qualified to fill them are rigidly selected and are bound to be rare. Unavoidably, there is grading according to efficiency and achievement.

These *socially* selected and qualified persons are usually in the upper strata. Thus, many of the persons in the upper strata perform predominantly organizational and managerial functions or provide services of a highly professionalized, learned, and skilled nature. Persons in the lower strata carry on manual operations involving routine and more easily performed tasks and roles. But each stratum needs the cooperation of all the others. Hence, as the strata are each performing their respective functions, they are bound together, and the common divided but coordinated enterprise serves as a basis for mutual solidarity. No stratum is self-sufficient or separable from others. The very distributions of functions inherent in stratification are part of the inalienable traits and fundamental necessities of organization and operation of any group or undertaking.

Nature and Function of the Ordination Process.* Ordination in the sociological sense is a special kind of ordering, arranging, or *placing of the variant individuals, categories, and groups in the different functional and prestige levels of the stratification system* in order to secure relatively effective reciprocity and coordination of services and to provide stability in individual and community life. In brief, it is the process of allocating statuses and hierarchical niche assignment and is a phase of the proto process of integration. It must be distinguished from the role-performing processes which consist of the acquisition of patterns of behavior for specific functions and relationship situations.

It may seem almost paradoxical to discuss ordination immediately after equalization. However, they are co-related processes even in a democratic society. After we have the freedoms and opportunities, we still have the inequalities of abilities, performance, and responsibility. The societal task is to get individuals and groups placed most justly and appropriately so that they can render their most effective services to the total organization or society. It should be noted that, strictly speaking, ordination belongs in the general category of accommodative processes (to be discussed below). But since it is a process of major significance in the maintenance of any society, and especially of a democratic class society like our own, it will be discussed separately.

As noted in Chapter 14, a stratification system in its very essence is a status, power, authority, and control organization. This means, in turn, that the process of ordination, which continually maintains the organization, *is essentially one of superordination-subordination*. Each of these is both a condition for some elements of the society and a process. Superordination as a process consists of granting or acquiring high status, prestige, and authority in the various higher categories or ranks of an organization or society. Subordination is the process of acquiring or being forced to accept at least temporary lower status and prestige and also followership on the part of all lower categories or ranks of an organization or society.

The joint action of these two processes in producing the respective conditions is functionally necessary in almost every known social relationship if there is not to be confusion and dysfunction. Some persons must precede and others follow; some must direct and coordinate at least some of the behavior of those below them if there is to be social order and efficiency, and they must have the authority and prestige to make this control effective. Others must look to them for direction in the particular social situation, obey, and be coordinated, whether this be the daily living of a given family, the seating of guests at a dinner party, the operation of a formal organization, or the maintenance of a class system.

Thus, the function of superordination is to hold the various parts and levels of a society together in the acceptable and essential relationships with each other; there must be some fixing and enforcing of the imposed distribution of rights and obligations. Conversely, the function of subordination is to recognize with deference and loyalty and functional response the authority of socially placed superiors and to cooperate with them in the achievement of common purposes. Thus, the father should admonish and the children comply; the foreman supervise and the workers act accordingly; the priest instruct and the laymen follow the instructions.

All cannot have equal authority in any group or society. If such a hierarchy and flow of authority did not exist, the interacting individuals would be in a state of incessant conflict. All voluntary or purposive organizations need to have ordination of the authorities and ranks of the group members. Such relationships quickly assert themselves even in the simplest and most pliant of common human activities. This does not mean that all individuals and groups in all of their relationships are subordinate to, and controlled by, others, for many have reciprocal relationships of mutual equality.

*This necessary name for the process is that of von Wiese and Becker. (71)

Moreover, in the variety and multiplicity of relationships and situations of life, all of us are commanders in some and obeyers in others. But always in any given going concern there must be a hierarchy of authority and control, and the authority and control must move downward through the strata. The decision of each superior authority or stratum is mandatory upon the respective inferior ranks or authorities.

In brief, one of the functions of ordination is to provide social-control hierarchies and mechanisms. These control hierarchies are basically command-obedience relationships. The major control positions of an organization or society are usually at the top, as in the case of a pope, king, general, or corporation president. The minor control positions are distinguished by submission to various levels of superiors and control over a smaller number of persons below, such as is exercised by factory superintendents and foremen, lower church and military officers. Farther below are noncontrol positions characterized by the requirement of purely routine duties and the absence of any directive power over the activities of others—in short, the rank and file.

Although in general the social-control positions may be open to achievement by individuals from any stratum, they are usually limited, at least in their higher reaches, to the upper strata, simply because the selective processes tend to place the best controllers and authorities in the upper levels. The major control positions go to the upper strata and the noncontrol positions to the lower strata. (63, pp. 315-320; 64, pp. 368-369; 68)

The ordered condition that comes about through ordination is usually institutionalized. Under the conditions of mutual interdependence, the privileges and duties of all differentiated elements are standardized sufficiently to permit predictable reciprocities. Individuals and groups may not be satisfied with the statuses, but they know where they stand, what they can do and demand, and what is expected of them. The norms define and the values underscore the arrangements and placements; the sentiments, folkways, customs, traditions, mores, and the institutions are adjusted to them and support them; the arrangements are fixed in the attitudes and habits of all concerned. Nonconformity and objections are constrained, even coerced, by public opinion. Forms of etiquette serve as guards.

Thus, the relative functions and rankings are agreed upon and ordered by standardized arrangements and procedures; incessant confusion and strife are forestalled or prevented; cooperation, reciprocity, peace, and order are facilitated and in large measure ensured. Ordination is absolutely essential to societal maintenance, for by means of it, in some measure, "all the statuses of the society intermesh like a series of interlocking wheels," to use Florence Kluckhohn's phrase. (66)

Principles of Niche Assignment. In all societies to some extent, but especially in a society like our own, two general sets of principles govern the acquisition or assignment of niches or positions in the ordered and generally accepted status-authority-prestige ranks of an organization or society. They are the principles that are predetermined by established rule or procedure and those that operate upon an experimental-competitive basis. (71, p. 257)

The predetermined principles of niche assignment are pre-existent in the cultural values and ways of a differentiated and stratified society and almost automatically place an individual, category, or group. Some of these positions are matters of tradition, inheritance, or family or other group affiliation; some are due to the impersonal embodiment of position, such as old age, superior sex, valued occupation, wealth, office, class, caste position, or the majesty attaching to kings; others are acquired by seniority, standing in line, or some more arbitrary appointment to office or position; and still others rest upon some myth of authority and relate to authority and prestige based upon religious revelation and insight, or some other reputed acquisition of charism or superhuman power and significance (for example, Hitler and Stalin).

Although these predetermined principles are relatively uniform and usually quite effective in assigning niches, they have the marked disadvantage of hampering and lessening energy and initiative, and they frequently impair morale and in some instances do not permit full play of the equalization processes and the expression of freedoms and rights. They are often directly antithetical to the functional selection of competition and are not necessarily based on abilities and achievements.

The experimental-competitive principles of niche assignment operate alongside the predetermined principles in our society. Many positions are achieved by individuals and groups as the result of experimental behavior in active competition with others. The attainments are rated according to the prevailing standards of success, for every group and society has its special scales of values and symbols of achievement for its wide range of activities. The niches thus acquired are the result of capacities and achievements demonstrated in the course of the often vigorous selective, or sorting out, and advancement processes. Individuals strive to secure respect, honor, reputation, power, rights, wealth, and other evidences and emoluments of success.

Ideally, as we have noted, competition assigns individuals to a place in the social system, the quantitative and qualitative requirements and responsibilities of which are appropriate to, and compatible with, their native and acquired capacities and skills. Position thus achieved through competitive processes rests in large part upon the degree of personal liberty, the fairness and justness of the rules of the game, the availability, guarantees, and enforcement of the freedoms and rights, and the rate of social change. Organizations and communities likewise are subjected to the selective effects of the competitive process. It helps to determine which cities, markets, corporations, churches, schools, and so on shall survive or gain ascendancy and the forms they shall assume.

But in all niches assigned under the experimental-competitive principles of action, the individuals and groups are not only permitted, but compelled, to determine their positions thereby. Furthermore, the freer individuals and groups are to choose, and the wider the range of choices, the more active they must be in the processes of acquiring place.

The chief disadvantage of this procedure is that individuals and groups, as they compete, are self-centered as to both means and ends. They do not necessarily seek the welfare of others in their striving. There *may* be vast acceleration, facilitation, and improvement of things and services for others; injuries and illth may also result.

Principles of Motivating and Rewarding. One other main functional necessity explaining the universal presence of ordination processes and a system of ordained ranks is the use of the hierarchical positions of such a system to motivate persons to perform and reward them for performing the more important, upper-echelon societal functions. Because the positions are graded, many persons desire to occupy the higher ones. However, the duties associated with the various positions are not equally easy or agreeable or important. Different positions require different abilities and different degrees of effort and responsibility, and it is highly important to the well-being of a society that the functions of the more strategic positions be performed with conscientiousness, diligence, exactitude, capability, and skill. Invariably, however, the demand for persons to fill the highest positions vastly exceeds the supply of those qualified to assume them.

A society, therefore, has a system of rewards and ways of distributing them in proportion to the significance, difficulty, and quality of the services rendered. The ordination processes attach different incentives and rewards to these different levels of positions and duties that are in some measure proportional to their importance. In brief, it makes the rewards for services high enough to attract capable persons.

These rewards take the form of economic compensation (wealth, income, and standard-of-living satisfactions), cultural advantages and enjoyments, social prerogatives and privileges, social esteem and prestige, and various other contributions to self-respect and ego and family enhancement. These are usually dispensed unequally as between the different levels, but always, as Davis puts it, they are "built into" the different positional levels as accompaniments and perquisites. Thus, an ordained system, with its institutionalized inequalities of position and reward, functions as an unconsciously devised but highly effective means whereby society makes provision for the filling of its most important positions by the most qualified persons, and so on down the strata. (64, pp. 366-371; 65, pp. 242-244; 67)

Mobility Processes and Maintenance

The mobility processes have been previously discussed with respect to their demographic effects, their ecological aspects, and the various general functions that they perform in differentiation and stratification systems and from the point of view of their effects in producing or contributing to different kinds of individual and societal disorganization. Like most other social processes, the mobility processes are involved in a variety of social functions and in their many manifestations have many different effects. Here we wish to examine them briefly with respect to their positive effects in contributing to societal maintenance and enhancing it.

We are concerned with both physical and social mobility, that is, freedom of movement as to spatial location and social position. As such, the mobilities are two-edged social tools, having both negative and positive effects. They make for disorganization, in the way of irresponsibility, root pulling, isolation and anonymity, unconventionality, and normlessness (*anomie*), and also for adjustment, stability, and superior maintenance by providing means for better place location and more appropriate societal niche assignment.

Both physical and social mobility relate to what has already been presented in this chapter. If these processes have wholesome maintenance effects, they must depend upon competition, the freedom of competition, the adequacy of testing methods, the availability of certain social and political rights, and the flexibility of the social structure. When such conditions prevail, for example, a young man with ability and ambition can move from his physical and sociocultural position on "the wrong side of the tracks" to both a locale of greater opportunity and a social level that matches, even challenges, his abilities.

Maintenance Contributions of Physical Mobility. Migration has numerous beneficial and disturbing effects in the areas of both departure and admission. This physical mobility, as we have noted, has greater possibilities than ever before as a result of modern means of communication and transportation and in the larger federated societies like our own the elimination of political obstacles to movement. Dissatisfied and disadvantaged persons have a chance to move from places of lesser opportunity to those of greater opportunity, provided that they have the means. Its outstanding effect is thus that of an equilibrative nature. It adjusts the disharmonious distribution, or the dislocations, of population as environmental, especially economic, changes occur.

Whether peaceful or violent, migratory movements are expressions of a trend toward equalization of economic density, which is the ratio between the number of inhabitants and the resources at their disposal. Industries, trades, and services flow to areas of new resource and market development. Surplus and stranded population elements from relatively disadvantaged areas flow to these places with labor demand and other opportunities and advantages. There is thus a continual tendency to effect a balance between distribution of population and distribution of resources. It makes possible a more advantageous ratio of men and resources, improves and equalizes the standards of living and the standards of satisfaction for many people, makes for the more effective utilization of newly discovered or developed localities and a more adequate selection of population for given tasks.

Physical mobility may also have an integrating rather than a confusing or demoralizing effect upon both individuals and groups under certain conditions. Albig (73) points out, especially with respect to residential mobility:

> The removal, at times, of newlyweds from the geographical vicinity of relatives, of conflict groups or sects from an area where their status is fixed at a low level, of some types of psychological variants from their neighborhoods and groups, is undoubtedly beneficial.

He also quotes C. H. Cooley with respect to the integrating effect of the automobile:

> Automobile travel tends to domesticate the whole country in every man's mind; his patriotism is enlarged without becoming less concrete. I cannot agree that it is making us an unstable, because nomadic people. Is it not rather a flying shuttle that weaves the strands of our life into a broad and flexible fabric? It is not fixity that makes people stable, but possessions, hopes, contentment.

Physical mobility generally also tends to produce among the migrants more plastic and versatile behavior, larger mental vistas, and less narrow-mindedness as compared with less mobile persons, as Sorokin has repeatedly pointed out.

The process of physical mobility is essential to the general welfare. It preserves peace, order, and stability, makes for effective utilization of physical, industrial, and human resources and hence enhances prosperity, and conduces to optimal conditions of life in both the emigrating and immigrating areas. (75; 76; 77; 79) It provides these maintenance benefits in the least expensive and least harmful way. But although migration is salutary, it is not a panacea. The process is rough and incomplete; it never accomplishes a complete equilibrium of population and opportunity. Errors in choosing new locations, physical and cultural isolation, inertia and ignorance, overenticement, lack of private and public planning, all interfere with the full efficacy of the process.

Maintenance Contribution of Social Mobility. The possibilities of *social* mobility of individuals and small groups, usually families, has still greater maintenance significance in that advantageous movement within a stratum as well as between strata is possible, in fact, invited, even required; thus serving as a means of relieving discontent, relative misplacement, and tension. Two major forms will be briefly discussed.

Horizontal Social Mobility. The relatively free movement of individuals and small groups within the same general social stratum makes possible enhanced satisfaction and greater productive contributions. For example, it permits a redistribution of persons among occupations at a given level of skill; a family head can move from an outmoded occupation or vocation to a somewhat similar one brought about by technological changes (from wood lathing to metal lathing, from hot-air furnace tinworking to air-conditioning tinworking, and so on). Similarly, individuals may move from one political party to another, and individuals and families may move from one religious denomination to another.

Vertical Social Mobility. The selective movements of individuals and groups up or down the social ladder that connects the strata of the social pyramid is in some respects the process par excellence for maintaining social equilibrium and inviting and securing the most satisfying, most appropriate, and most socially productive services. Regardless of his status at birth, the individual, with appropriate qualifications and efforts, may move upward from one rank to another, from mediocrity to a high level of expert achievement and a position of prestige, affluence, and influence.

An open-class society with a substantial democratic tradition holds out hope for all who desire to advance themselves by whatever legitimate means—ability, specialization, acquisition of skill, learning, or wealth, the utilization of political opportunities, and so on—so that they may achieve success, social recognition, elevated rank. The very existence of such possibilities makes endurable for many people their present economic insecurity or inadequacy, their political insignificance, their limited culture, and their lowly social position.

Conversely, vertical mobility also permits a downward flow from a level where the requirements of the position are beyond the general abilities of the individual to a lower economic, vocational, or cultural level where his abilities are appropriate to and equilibrated with the lesser requirements of the position.

Some of the more specific maintenance gains derived from vertical social mobility will be briefly presented.

First, like physical mobility, it encourages breadth, versatility, and open-mindedness and reduces provincialism and occupational and other idiosyncracies. As Ross points out, in a frozen society individuals are indelibly stamped at birth with their life roles and many are bound to be dwarfed or warped and have a narrow outlook; but in a mobile society, an individual in his own lifetime "may have been both servant and master, hand-worker and brain-worker, underling and chief."

Furthermore, in a mobile society the individual can go from role to role, from status to status. He is not so likely to build up rigid attitudes and habits, because he has been obliged repeatedly to alter his behavior as every change of status requires a corresponding adjustment of body, mind, and reactions. As Sorokin points out, as a result of such shifting, individuals pass into a different social atmosphere. They breathe different social air, experience different standards, habits, morals, ideas, customs, and beliefs and acquire different mental vistas and points of view that are incentive-laden. In fact, in a mobile society, one who is not versatile and adaptable does not rise far. (85, pp. 466-468; 86, pp. 508-509)

Second, social mobility facilitates intellectual life and is conducive to discoveries and inventions. The multiplied contacts, opportunities, and strivings lead to a cross-fertilization of ideas and an intensive creation of new economic, religious, philosophical, scientific, aesthetic, and moral values and corresponding ways. There is also the likelihood of material and nonmaterial discoveries and of more diversified and more numerous combinations of ideas, values, and things, which is the essence of invention and the indispensable prerequisite for expansion and enrichment of life. (86, pp. 511-515)

Third, social mobility contributes directly to social prosperity and stability in various ways. It facilitates the distribution of individuals among the skill and responsibility levels, permitting selection to work itself out with relative freedom and efficacy, so that the round peg is more likely to get into the round hole, the square peg into the square hole, and so on. When an individual is carrying on a function compatible with his inclinations and abilities, he is satisfied and enjoys his job. Thus, he is not only more peaceful and stable, but also more efficient and likely to be making his maximum contribution. The increase of inventions usually makes for increased productivity, helps raise the standard of living of the whole society, and contributes to more rapid and competent adjustment to social change. Such conditions work for both prosperity and stability. (80)

The most important stabilizing effect of social mobility is doubtless the reduction of radicalism and the maintenance of attitudes of conservatism and social conservation. The fact that the able can rise draws off the high-explosive personalities from the lower classes or lower opportunity levels where they would be restive and puts them to work intensively in the upper strata where they become conservative though aggressive competitors with their own level of talent rather than discontented radical leaders. Thwarted ambitions, blighted hopes, rankling grievances, and unreached goals make for radicalism, but when a man has reached his best competitive level, he is likely to be conservative. Moreover, the gifted and ambitious persons are not likely to assail the social order that gives them a chance to rise; in fact, they are likely to defend it to the last ditch. They are not revolters against it, but protectors and conservators of it. Being in the main well-selected persons who have risen through grit, ability, and experience, they have the know-how for coping with potentially disturbing individuals and movements.

Furthermore, when people have discovered that many doors are "swinging doors," as Ross puts it, class conflict is not likely to be so bitter and intensive. Instead of a disintegrative subservience toward the upper classes on the part of the lower classes, there is a tendency to envy and idealize upper-class positions and privileges, even though existent members of the upper classes may be criticized. The members of the lower strata look upon position in the upper strata as possible and desirable goals for attainment. (85, p. 468; 86, pp. 533-534) The actuality of such mobility also makes the resemblance between the members of the several classes stronger than the differences. Thus, a society with vertical fluidity is not likely to develop a highly class-conscious proletariat, which is always potentially rebellious. This explains why the proletariat in America has been less clear-cut and less organizable than that in many European countries, and why class conflict has played a less conspicuous role in the United States than in Europe.

In conclusion, the mobilities, both physical and social, under certain stated conditions are positive and integrative in effect and hence contribute potently to societal maintenance. They tend to function as safety valves and relieve social pressures. At the same time and as part of the same processes, individuals and groups flow to areas of less social pressure and fill social vacuums. In general, much troublemaking and much individual and social disorganization are avoided, and vast unimpeachable gains in social stability, productivity, and progress accrue.

Processes Adjusting Social Dissension, Conflict, Differences

Opposition is always present in any society, and it is probably impossible to avoid or eradicate it entirely. But given instances of social dissension and conflict cannot continue and intensify if the society is to maintain order and operational efficacy. These opposition processes are too time-consuming and exhausting of essential human and social energies, too wasteful and destructive of limited resources, too disruptive of other social processes, and too separative of unavoidably interdependent elements.

Any state of incessant opposition may lead in the end to impotence or even annihilation of one or all parties to the struggle. In a well-maintained society there must be a safeguarding of general social interests, some possibility of recuperation, and hence, some composition, reconciliation, and harmonization of opposed elements, some demarcation of spheres of interests and rights, and something in the way of adjustive processes and techniques. There are always conscious desires for the amelioration of strife.

In such oppositional situations there are two somewhat related sets of major conditions and two corresponding sets of adjustive outcomes. One set of conditions occurs when one opponent is destroyed or conquered or there is a deadlock. Even the winners get tired and suffer a variety of losses. Hence, most conflicts have an end. Ways and means of reducing or resolving conflict in its particular forms and instances are devised and used. At least the overt expressions disappear through various sorts of adjustive procedures, and the conflicting elements settle down to some state of working arrangement, possibly even to an equilibrium that is usually more or less temporary in nature, but sufficient to enable the society to carry on and to enable the particular segments involved to get along together in some manner, not necessarily satisfactory to either.

The other set of conditions occurs where the two or more opposed or socially separated heterogeneous elements are unavoidably thrown together and *get acquainted,* usually over a period of generations. As the contact and the inescapable living together continue, there is a reciprocal, though not necessarily equal, osmosis of values, ideas, and ways of life. A blending and merging occur, and the bases of irritation and opposition weaken, recede into the background, and may in large measure disappear. The formerly diverse and opposed elements have become one people.

The processes operating in the first instance are those of social *accommodation*; in the second instance those of social (as distinct from, but also including, cultural) *assimilation.* The latter processes usually involve biological amalgamation in some degree, either as a contributory factor or as an effect, or as both. Both sets of processes are central in the establishment and maintenance of social equilibrium.

Accommodation

Accommodation is the major social process adjusting opposed elements to each other. The objectives depend upon the situation. Inequality-equality factors are involved and determine the degree to which the immediate participants and the larger community exercise power in the adjustive process.

Nature of Accommodation. The concept of accommodation, like many others involved in the analysis of human society, implies both a *condition* and a set of *processes.* The *condition* consists of an arrangement or equilibrium of contending elements that is more or less effective for the time being in securing or permitting social functioning. A set of working relations has been established. A condition prevails which assures for all the parties concerned a recognized and temporarily fixed relationship and a degree of security and certainty in the pursuit of their different but usually interrelated interests. The condition of *complete* accommodation exists when external control and enforcement of peace are no longer necessary. This rarely occurs.

The *processes* are the sequences of procedural steps and occurrences whereby competing and conflicting individuals and groups effect "working relations" with each other, permitting the parties to function either separately with a degree of peace or cooperatively—at least in certain immediately essential respects. In the course of the processes attitudes are often rationalized, redefined, or transferred so as to permit adjustment to "peace" conditions and habits and conscious action patterns are modified in some degree. Often new relationships and organizational procedures are effected. But there is no implication that discordance and opposition have been permanently and effectively resolved; there may be much latent hostility. Full reciprocity and free, equalized participation have not been achieved nor differences eliminated or reduced; nor have understanding, harmony, unity, uniformity, affection, or justice necessarily been established.

The many accommodative procedures are acts of expediency or necessity in resolving opposition and setting up ways of getting along together in the prevailing situations. Only occasionally are they long-time stabilizing actions. Nevertheless, since some opposition is always actual or potential, they must be unceasingly conducted, unconsciously and consciously, informally and formally, in the interests of societal maintenance.

As "accommodation" is used, it consists of both the adjustment or equilibration of *individuals* to life situations and the establishment of working arrangements between opposed *groups*. The two are inextricable, but we are more particularly concerned with the accommodation of groups to each other and the adjustment pressures wielded by groups over each other and over individuals. The accommodation of *individuals* refers to the increasing adjustment of individuals as they interact with each other in the ever-changing competitive and conflict relationships. Individuals become fitted to and accept their position in the social order and play their various roles with some sense of satisfaction to themselves and with some contributions to the group as a whole.

For *individuals,* accommodation is essentially a *learning process,* whereby they undergo changes in habits, sentiments and ideas that enable them to get along with others. The accommodation of *groups* also involves learning, but it implies in addition all manner of social-psychological and institutionalized techniques and mechanisms. This accommodation among groups is in some extreme instances a resolving of opposition through the exhaustion or extinction of one adversary. Mainly, however, it is a process of maneuvering or jockeying in which each group tries to achieve the most advantageous position in the effected arrangement.

Objectives of Accommodation. Situations requiring or resulting in accommodation are always situations of opposition for which some sort of adjustment is consciously sought. The objectives in these conscious efforts vary. One objective may be the softening or mitigating of opposition between persons and groups in order to permit healing, or at least adjustive, influences to bring about some sort of identity of interests and joint participation, as in the case of older stocks and immigrant groups. Another objective may be the postponement or prevention of overt conflict for agreed-upon periods of time, as in peace truces and contracts of various kinds.

A third objective may be the provision of means whereby persons or groups who are widely separated by social distance (for example, racial, nationality, religious, and other sharply different cultural elements) are able to carry on, at least temporarily, life activities in the juxtaposition of close spatial relationship, as in the case of some sort of caste system. A fourth objective may be the prevention of what would be, in the opinion of one of the several parties involved, undesirable assimilation, as in the enslavement of one element, the involuntary segregation, voluntary withdrawal, or other exclusion of one or more elements from common participation, or some combination of these. (104, pp. 2-3)

The Inequality-Equality Factor. The particular forms or types of conditions of accommodation and the particular processes and techniques whereby accommodation is effected depend upon the relative oppositional strength and thus upon the respective ability of the parties to maneuver and bargain with each other. With respect to any given situation, there is a wide range from great inequality at the moment of contact or inequality developed during the oppositional processes to approximate equality of adversaries. Hence, the conditions and the processes adjusting the opposition situations will range along a continuum from those involving various degrees and kinds of superordination-subordination to procedures working themselves out on the basis of relative equality of power and conditions consisting of approximately coordinate relationships of adversaries. This inequality-equality situation is one of the key factors in the functional analysis of accommodation, for it determines whether there are to be processes of coercion and a condition of domination or processes of adjudication and conditions of equilibration.

Parties Exercising Adjustive Power and the Types of Involvement. The nature of inequality-equality in the particular opposition situation determines the degree to which the parties directly involved and the larger community exercise power in the adjustive process. There are three categories of possibilities: there is *one-sided accommodation,* in which the patently stronger party forces some state of submissive adjustment upon the weaker party, or the weaker adversary, in order to avoid coercion and conflict, engages in self-motivated forms of escape activity (for example, a 200-pound plug-ugly bullying Caspar Milquetoast). There is *bipartite* or *multipartite reciprocal accommodation,* in which the two or more parties involved either arrive at some condition of deadlock or adventurously or experimentally bargain with each other to remove some barriers, possibly develop some conscious regulation, and produce some kind of more or less permanent, coordinate working arrangements for joint participation (for example, in the case of an interracial congress or an employer-labor controversy).

And finally there are *accommodative procedures, depending upon* the accepted assistance or the authoritative intrusion of *an outside agency,* in which third parties are invited to function or make themselves available for adjustive purposes. Although this last type of procedure is not new, it is being increasingly applied in modern societies where any opposition deleteriously affects the whole community or society and must be resolved if possible. More and more, the state, in one or another of its jurisdictions and through one or another of its agencies, and in the interests of the participants in the opposition as well as the greatly affected nonparticipants, has intruded with some degree of its granted authoritative power to attempt to effect accommodation.

Accommodative Processes

The objectives, the inequality-equality factors, and the respective compliant types of adjustment are demonstrated in the major known types of accommodative processes now to be briefly examined. These are ideal-typical conceptualizations of the processes. It must be kept in mind that every concrete opposition situation is unique. Furthermore, each kind of opposition has its own kind of accommodation, whether it be a form of competition, contravention, or conflict, as in class conflict, the various forms of majority-minority group confliet, economic or religious conflicts, or conflicts between communities or states. The actual procedures depend upon the social terrain, or the nature of the arena, and the importance of the issues involved to the participants and to the larger society. The procedures will be treated under two major categories: those among unequals and those among approximate equals.

Accommodation among Unequals. The situation among unequals always implies the existence of the weak and the strong. The strong exercise some sort of coercion in which actions, states of minds, and social relationships of the weak are constrained or compelled. The coercion may be physical or psychical, and often it is a combination of both. The resultant accommodation consists of some sort of domination and submission, in which there is victory of the strong for the time being and power is exercised by the strong. The weaker party makes most of the adjustive concessions and must accept the arrangements of relationships laid down by the stronger. Various degrees and kinds of adjustment (physical and psychical) on the basis of domination-submission or domination-escape result. The following are the more frequently occurring processes and resultant conditions of adjustment.

DESTRUCTION. In this process the weaker adversaries are exterminated entirely by the stronger element, (as in the wholesale massacre of Indians by the Spaniards in the sixteenth and seventeenth centuries and of the Jews by the Nazis in the 1930's) or because of the might and strategic situation of the strong, the leaders and other key persons of the weaker adversaries are imprisoned, exiled, excommunicated, or liquidated and their organization and equipment destroyed or so weakened that resistance is impossible. Hence, there is no more opposition and the destroyer reigns supreme.

For various reasons most opposition situations fall short of destruction of the weaker part. Notable is the fact that destruction is impossible, or, that if attempted, it would dangerously weaken the stronger. Moreover, it is inexpedient and undesirable from the point of view of the victor to destroy the adversary, since he can be profitably exploited.

VOLUNTARY WITHDRAWAL OF THE WEAKER. Voluntary withdrawal consists of physical or mental retreat or escape of the weaker element or elements. The weaker seek to avoid conflict by avoiding participation in the life that produces it. This withdrawal may take one of several forms. There may be physical withdrawal from the scene of operation and the creation of a space barrier, as in the final flight of the Mormons to the Great Salt Lake valley. Or there may be voluntary segregation in urban and rural ghettos on the part of ethnic minorities or in colonies, such as those of the Shakers, Quakers, Owenites, Mennonites, House of David, and so on. Or minority dissident or heretical elements may split off from the main organization, with which they have come to disagree irreconcilably, and form a special group of their own, as numerous Protestant sectarian elements have done.

In the case of individuals, or even of groups, as opposed to the larger group or consensus, withdrawal may also be accomplished by some sort of psychological escape process. Such individuals or groups may revert to some romantically constructed Golden Age or resort to mysticism or religious experience, or through rationalization and idealization reach a mental state in which they justify their position. By such processes persons and groups create for themselves a "world within" which is also a world apart in which they can dwell in peace. Persons in such mental states are resigned to their overt condition and acquiesce to the actual oppositional situation without loss of self-esteem.*

So long as weaker or minority elements are thus self-withdrawn, either physically or mentally, there is much less overt expression of opposition. The field is deliberately left to the stronger.

Defeat, Conquest, or Imposed Dominance. These processes of accommodation consist of conquest and consequent subjugation or some other imposition of conditions of submission, compliance, and social distance upon the weaker or dependent by the stronger. The resultant relationships are those of superordination-subordination, and the regulations governing the relationships and the respective positions of all involved are largely determined by the stronger.

The imposed and enforced relationships may take any one of various forms. (1) The defeated weaker element may be made innocuous by enslavement and exploited by the stronger. (2) It may take the form of informally or formally organized physical or social segregation, or both, of the weaker elements by the stronger, as in the case of the discrimination against, and the segregation of, racial groups or other cultural elements that are out of step with the majority. (3) It may take the form of effective dominance on the part of the stronger on the very scene of action, as in the case of the imperious control of labor by capital before unionization and governmental action equalized the fighting and bargaining power of labor. (4) It may, as already mentioned in a preceding section, take the form of societally organized ordination of the differentiated population. Caste systems are the most extreme form of such accommodation. Every class system, however, is also an effective, though more flexible, form of accommodation of unequals.

It is obvious that most of the processes of accommodation among unequals are of the one-way variety. The only notable exception is the accommodation of strata in an open-class system.

Accommodation among Approximate Equals. As noted above, most of the accommodation among equals is of the coordinate rather than the superordinate-subordinate variety. None of the combatants can prevail, or the general social situation is such that social well-being does not permit the prolonged dominance of one over the other. The power relationships may reach a state of approximate balance. The interests, wishes, wills, and goals of the contestants are somewhat modified in the direction of compatibility. There may even be some coalescence of interests and objectives and active cooperation which redounds to everyone's advantage. (87, pp. 49-52) In the processes of accommodation there is usually two-way or multiway participation, and outsiders are often brought in to facilitate the processes. The relationships that are established are usually of an implicit or formal contractual nature rather than those of imposition and hierarchical arrangement. These equilibrative processes take various forms.

The Truce. The truce is the process whereby a cessation of opposition is agreed upon for a definite or indefinite period, but with no change of attitudes and none of the issues settled. It may be a period of preparation for further hostility or one of preparation for adjustment of differences.

The Alliance. The alliance is the process whereby heretofore diverse or antagonistic groups join some of their interests and unify some of their efforts, not necessarily on an equal basis, for mu-

*"An individual may achieve accommodation by finding reasons, sound or unsound, that justify his conduct, views, or status, thereby avoiding frustration, mental conflicts, feelings of inferiority, or other unsatisfying psychological states . . . members of exploited groups may endure the unpleasantness of exploitation by rationalizing that it is 'God's will' and therefore right."—N. P. Gist (94, p. 407)

tual functional benefit. The arrangement may be formal or informal and more or less temporary. Historically, it has often been a procedure for protection or for more effective aggression against another combination of actual or potential adversaries. Thus, competing farm organizations may temporarily combine their efforts to fight the big grain-buying corporations, or one array of nation-states may combine to fight another array.

TOLERATION. Toleration is the process whereby each of two or more diverse or contending persons or groups who cannot agree and who believe that they cannot make concessions to each other bear with each other and go their own way for the sake of mutual peace. It is one of the first steps in accommodation among hostile but approximately equal elements and produces a state of suspended animosity. There is recognition that the possible gains from further opposition are more than offset by those of peaceful cooperation. It usually takes place without formal decision, but the parties accept certain principles of behavior that make it possible for them to carry forward their divergent interests. There is no change in the basic policy of either party, and there are no arrangements for settlement.

Toleration does not necessarily produce greater good will, and it may make for studied indifference. However, long contact and better acquaintance or a clearer understanding of the reasons for the opponent's beliefs and ways often makes toleration of them easier. This procedure is frequently found in situations of religious or racial controversy, where any closer form of working relations seems to be impossible, an unthinkable retreat or concession of precious principles.

COMPROMISE. The process of compromise occurs in situations where each party feels that it can give up something for the sake of compensatory or even greater gains and where reciprocal adjustment is possible. It is not a case of all or nothing, but consists of each of the contending elements consciously making some reduction or even surrender of viewpoints and immediate objectives, while retaining the right and power to engage in further contention. Each usually gives up as little as possible but endeavors to obtain as large a concession as possible from the other. It is essentially a nonviolent give-and-take or sparring procedure in straightening out controversial issues. It involves joint discussion, deliberation, and negotiation, and results in some decision as to temporary working relations.

Compromise occurs especially in opposition situations where the participants are unavoidably interdependent and integrally related by ultimate objectives but divided into embattled, self-conscious elements by self-interest. It is an effective procedure in democracies in adjusting the claims and efforts of opposing political parties and factions, in industrial conflict, in controversies among nations, and in fact wherever collective bargaining can bring about a temporary balance and cooperation of opposing elements.

A good deal of compromise is effected entirely among the opposed parties directly concerned and is thus a bipartite or multipartite form of action. In opposition situations where the well-being of the whole is at stake or in situations which do not readily resolve themselves by means of collective action, outside agents are called in to facilitate the process of compromise and adjudication. These forms of compromise are in some measure and degree directed. The main types follow.

Conciliation as a special compromise procedure does not necessarily involve the assistance of a neutral outside agent. It always implies, however, some joint effort or joint-and-assisted effort at reconciliation among the disputants. There must be some effort to bring about a willingness to compromise, to develop friendly attitudes and relationships. It may take such forms as the National Conference of Christians and Jews, where an endeavor is made to build up a spirit of friendliness among people of different religious faiths, or an interracial commission, which seeks to develop better attitudes and relations between whites and Negroes. Conciliation is also employed in industrial disputes to iron out differences before they become acute.

When an outside agent is brought in, usually at the invitation of the disputants, it is his function to offer advice and suggestions, to encourage, and, if possible, to direct frank discussion and effect some sort of agreement. A common example is the action of ministers, social workers, or marriage counselors in attempting to bring about the reconciliation of estranged husbands and wives. The conciliator, however, does not have any grant of power, and his position is usually somewhat anomalous.

Mediation is closely related to conciliation. Here too a disinterested person is introduced whose function it is to bring about a peaceful settlement of the issues, although he has no power to do so. The distinctive feature of mediation is that it is employed when conciliation has failed, when matters have got out of hand and the negotiations have reached an *impasse.* The acceptance of a mediator by the disputants, however, indicates that both parties have a genuine interest in continuing negotiations and avoiding a reversion to conflict. Special procedures are required because of the peculiar nature of the situation.

The mediator must have the confidence of both sides, since his primary function must be to act as a go-between. He confers with each group separately, advising and suggesting, but avoiding any hint of command or coercion. His purpose is mainly to find how far the disputants are willing to go in making concessions and then to whittle down the extreme demands on each side so as to bridge the distance. He does not try to bring the respective parties together until he is fairly certain that he has worked out a set of conditions satisfactory to both sides. If he fails, the situation may revert to open warfare or the parties may agree to arbitration.

In *arbitration* a dispute is brought to an obligatory settlement by the legalistic and judicial action of an arbitrator or an arbitration committee or board. Arbitration may be compulsory under the law of the state where conflicts affect public interest or agreed upon by the deadlocked disputants. At any rate, the arbitrator functions as a judge. He has a grant of authority and arrives at an independent and impartial decision. The decision is assumed to be binding and is sometimes enforceable, if necessary, through sanctions. Arbitration in present-day society is found most frequently in industrial controversy and in international relations.

CONVERSION. Conversion is a process of accommodation that may take place among relative equals or among unequals. Those to be converted may have the choice of avoiding or resisting, but where force can be used, the weaker must submit. Conversion is the process whereby individuals and groups, having been subjected to great emotional, intellectual, and sometimes physical shock and threats, abandon certain former attitudes, beliefs, and practices and embrace those of the pressure-exerting individuals or groups. Conversion is the formal defeat of one set of attitudes, ideas, and ways by another through suppression. All are henceforth on the same side, that of the successful persuader.

Conversion is used in all aspects of life where there are differences and opposition. The older generation invariably tries to convert the oncoming generation, and majorities often try to convert minorities. Conversion is generally associated with religious difference and opposition, but it has been widely demonstrated in the political area, notably by dictatorial regimes which use not only propaganda and other psychical pressures, but also physical violence to accomplish their aims.

Since conversion is essentially an inner process, the new points of view are usually accepted with some discrimination and reservation. The dominator can only insist on outer conformity, and there may be merely transference, not a fusion, of points of view. Hence, it may not be permanent. There is always the possibility of backsliding when the pressure is relieved and the necessity of reconversion.

Social Assimilation and Amalgamation

The two sets of processes involved in social assimilation and amalgamation invariably operate concomitantly and sooner or later are the final and most closely interrelating and integrating processes operating among diverse and hostile population elements in a given area.

Social Assimilation. Social assimilation goes beyond accommodation in producing the integration and cooperation essential to societal maintenance. Accommodation, as we have noted, produces the best kind of working arrangements possible under conditions of diversity, estrangement, and hostility. Among unequals it results in superordination-subordination, and among approximate equals it produces toleration or informal or formal and more or less temporary contractual relations growing out of some sort of collective bargaining and maneuverings. Both types of accommodative conditions are somewhat unstable, and potentially likely to resolve themselves back into hostility.

Social assimilation is a long-time process, continning over generations, and results in more permanent adjustment of the elements through unification of aims and ways. Social assimilation may and often does grow out of accommodation, for in the very tolerating, compromising, and converting the diverse elements may become better acquainted and more closely knit together and learn to be more freely cooperative.

Social assimilation originates in social situations where there are various heterogeneous, alien, and even antagonistic elements in the population occupying a common territory, usually a political state. They are all *physical* parts of the population. In the United States we have had the Indians, the Negroes introduced originally as slaves, and the various voluntary immigrant elements of diverse race and nationality and with widely variant cultural heritages.

These diverse elements have constituted various kinds of minorities in relation to the dominant, earlier assimilated, culturally and politically integrated white majority. The minorities are differentiated both vertically and horizontally from the majority by the discriminatory and segregative action of the majority and often by the minority's own voluntary separative action. The situation is one of physical, social, and cultural isolation and spacing between the majority and the various minority elements. For a time these minorities may be discordant, recalcitrant, nonparticipant population elements, and distinct conflict situations may exist.

THE PROCESS OF SOCIAL ASSIMILATION. The process of social assimilation is one in which the various elements eventually come to be merged, coalesced, absorbed, and incorporated into a relatively solidary and cooperative society that is unified and homogeneous in essential attitudes, ideas, values, objectives, loyalties, and major social activities. There is considerable sloughing off or disappearance of characteristic differences on the part of the minorities, or the differences lose most of their significance. The majority also undergoes some modification, although it is usually slight. Many of the social distances and antagonisms are weakened or evaporate entirely, and there is nondiscriminatory common participation of the formerly diverse elements in the general life of the community or society.

The very unavoidable contact, participation in common activities, and living together in relatively intimate relations, which function as both cause and effect, tend to develop an organic, sympathetic responsiveness to the other's attitudes, views, and claims. (115) The minorities no longer think of themselves as different or act as such and are not viewed as such by the larger body. They have achieved some agreement as to the ways of life, and they join relatively freely and wholeheartedly in the common teamwork and have a shared social life. In the main, the minorities have gradually taken on the ways of the larger society.

The process of social assimilation may be said to consist of two concomitantly operating subprocesses: *denationalization*, or *social divorce*, that is, the abandoning of old-country or other minority group ways, ideals, master loyalties, and allegiances, and (2) *naturalization*, that is, the acquisition of loyalty to, and participation in, the majority group, involving formal political induction procedures in the case of nationals from elsewhere.*

Social assimilation processes also range from spontaneous forms to highly organized procedures. *Spontaneous assimilation* is an automatic, unplanned, and casual merging through interaction in a common area. Some of this always occurs, regardless of the nature of the contact situations. It is aided by favorable attitudes toward innovation on the part of all groups concerned, equal access to the freedoms and rights, a feeling of general security among all groups, and fairly free participation of individuals and groups in general societal activities.

*Social assimilation as a maintenance process must be distinguished from cultural assimilation or acculturation (Chap. 6). While cultural assimilation is definitely involved as part of the total process, social assimilation goes beyond it and has additional connotations. Not only are those who were formerly divergent now culturally alike, but they are also free, common participants in all the major societal operations. For example, American Negroes and American Jews are culturally like the rest of the population in almost all pertinent details, but they are still very obviously excluded from various forms of social participation. In general, total assimilation is a cultural, a psychic, *and* a societal phenomenon: there are transmission, borrowing, and fusion of cultural heritages (acculturation); there is modification of attitudes and sentiments (psychic assimilation); there is a social, functional incorporation of once alien and separated elements into the larger body, which we are concerned with here.

In *organized assimilation,* that is, organized by dominant or majority groups, there is a deliberate and systematic effort to hasten and direct the processes of transformation and merging. Extreme illustrations of this are the efforts of the medieval Catholic Church to assimilate the pagan religions, by the sword if necessary, and the forcible imposition of the German language and German education upon the Poles in East Prussia by the Germans. The patriotism-inspired "Americanization movement" in the United States during and immediately following World War I was a milder instance of organized assimilation.

The difficulty with much organized assimilation, especially if coercion is used, is that it defeats the very end desired. Any arbitrary or long-continued external pressure to bring about acceptance of majority beliefs and ways tends to make the minority self-conscious, to organize it in defense of its special values, to create a militant group spirit, and to enhance rather than allay antagonisms. Such pressure may produce externally submissive accommodation, but it actually produces an accentuated in-turning and inner insulation against the majority and often retards or entirely stops the natural process. (122, p. 370)

Even under ideal conditions, social assimilation is never complete; absolute homogeneity and perfectly equilibrated participation are never achieved. In a mobile, rapidly changing society like our own, not only are there old rigidities to be overcome, but always new differentiations arise that complicate the process. Although it is continuous, it is always approximate—a matter of degree. Some persons are off on the fringe of culture and hence of the social life generally. These persons or groups are referred to as "marginal men." Usually they are somewhat disorganized both as members of groups and as individual personalities, as, for example, the American Indians.

Factors in Social Assimilation. Assimilation does not occur with equal facility, effectiveness, or speed in all the different majority-minority relationships. It depends upon a variety of factors, the more obvious of which will be concisely presented. In general, any factors or conditions that hinder free association and participation will delay or prevent assimilation; conversely, all factors and conditions that favor and facilitate such association and participation promote assimilation.

If the *attitudes of the majority* toward minorities and strangers are hostile or superior, assimilation will be retarded, whereas if they are tolerant and friendly, assimilation will be accelerated. Similarly, actions of discrimination, avoidance (for example, opposition to intermarriage), exploitation, persecution, or enforced segregation constitute serious obstacles, but those of acceptance and invitation to participation are aids. If immigrants or diverse racial stocks are only permitted certain menial jobs and other limited economic opportunities, assimilation will be retarded. Moreover, if barriers and discriminations of a political nature against minority elements exist, such as the denial of various civil rights, the maintenance of definite barriers, as in "grandfather clauses" and the poll tax, or the creation of difficulties in the way of formal or political "naturalization," then assimilation will be retarded.

Ethnocentrism of minority groups is an important factor in assimilation. If the immigrants insistently and persistently adhere to their foreign language, foreign-language press, nationalistic sentiments and phobias, nationalistic societies and foreign recreational and mutual-aid societies, parochial schools and foreign-born religious leaders, and so on, their assimilation will be slow.

The *relative number of the immigrants* affects the speed of assimilation. Other things being equal, when the ratio of newcomers to the existing population is high, the rate of assimilation will be low. Real assimilation at best is a slow process; too many foreigners produce assimilative "indigestion" in the larger population. The slower the rate of entrance, the more likely is absorption.

The *demographic composition of the immigrant groups* is a factor in their assimilation. If the various sex and age groups are normally represented, which means essentially that the immigrants come as families, the assimilation is usually more rapid and complete than if these groups appear in abnormal numbers. If the immigrants are preponderantly male, for example, the absorption will be much slower than it is with family immigration.

The *class composition of the divergent elements* will affect the rate of assimilation. If the recently introduced elements are of the upper classes, they will be more readily assimilated than if they are of the lower classes. Because of the greater opportunities for contact, communication, and higher education and the very fact of participation in common or related economic, recreational, aesthetic, and other cultural interests and enterprises, the upper classes, regardless of nation or nationality, have greater uniformity of experience, and hence, a wider catholicity of spirit. They have much in common to begin with. Among the lower classes the situation is usually the very reverse; hence, their ready changeability is slow.

The *manner of settlement of immigrants or dissident elements,* that is, whether diffused or segregated, regardless of causes for the type of settlement, will influence their assimilation. The more diffused the settlement, the more frequent the contacts and the greater the opportunity for cultural exchange and common social participation, the greater the likelihood of assimilation. On the other hand, segregated settlement by huddling of racial or nationality minorities in city districts or rural pockets, the detached life on an Indian reservation, or the isolated life in colonies of eccentric religious sectarians, such as the Mennonites and Dunkers, produces physical and cultural isolation and enables or even requires the so-called foreign elements to avoid contact and to maintain their exclusive cultural and social organization.

Similarities or differences in general cultural backgrounds of majority and minority elements affect the ease of assimilation. Where the general culture of the minority groups is similar to that of the majority, assimilation is usually speedy and considerable. Where there are great differences, there is limited possibility of common understanding. The majority group, supposedly with a higher culture, finds little to interest it and much to oppose in the culture of the highly diverse minorities. The lower culture minorities, at least in the early stages of interaction, can only understand, appreciate, and absorb the more superficial elements of the majority culture. Thus, immigrants to the United States from Great Britain and the other countries of northwestern Europe (which historically provided the basic American stocks) have been much more readily assimilated than those from southern and eastern European countries and the Orient.

Where marked physical differences exist among the minorities, as, for example, different colored skin, different form and color of hair, peculiarities of facial features, notably different stature, and so on, the social assimilation is usually difficult and retarded. The physical peculiarities of the minorities may be looked upon as badges of inferiority and they may become grounds for discrimination and exploitation by the majority. The relationship of majority and minority under such conditions is often merely symbiotic, as between discrete entities, and not that of free and equal social participants.

Positive assimilative agents in the larger community include, in the United States, for example, a variety of associations, institutions, and social conditions that contribute to the assimilation process. Notable among these are compulsory nation-wide public schools and free access to a higher education on the basis of ability, of a nation-wide language, nation-wide, one-language newspapers, radio, motion pictures, and television, nation-wide law and justice, free, nation-wide physical mobility without political restrictions, ready social mobility in an open-class system, unrestricted opportunity to work together in all economic activities and to aspire to various levels of standard of living, unlimited opportunity for political participation, common nation-wide organizations, such as fraternal orders and labor unions, community centers, common civic activities, and so on.

Amalgamation in Relation to Assimilation. Strictly speaking, amalgamation is a biological process, but it has significant demographic (see Chapter 8) and sociological implications. It consists of the fusion of originally distinct ethnic groups by interbreeding and intermarriage. Wherever and whenever diverse human stocks come into contact with each other, regardless of the conditions under which it occurs, there is some cross-breeding. Under most conditions, it has distinct equilibrative significance and is directly related to social assimilation both as cause and effect. The two processes are favorable to each other. That interbreeding *always* aids assimilation, however, is not implied. When interbreeding is objected to or proscribed, especially by the dominant or majority group, it is called *miscegenation.* Under such circumstances it occurs illicitly between stocks that are racially or culturally highly diverse or both. The offspring are often stranded between both groups, for example, the offspring of French *voyageurs* and Indian squaws and of white males and Negro females in the antebellum South. But under most conditions there is eventually a socially integrating effect.

In the first place, amalgamation promotes assimilation. The offspring of the cross-breeding have physical and psychical characteristics of both stocks and acquire something of the sentiments and loyalties of both. Moreover, the primary contacts and sympathetic association usually produce reciprocal appreciation and understanding in time. It aids cross-fertilization of culture and leads to common ways of life and to much common participation. In the second place, when interbreeding has reached the level of accepted intermarriage, it represents one of the surest indexes of assimilation. When groups have lost their diverse visible characteristics or their social spacings and cultural diversities sufficiently to intermarry freely, they are assimilated, or at any rate, they are on the way of being an ethnically and a socially homogeneous society. Assimilation is not complete until intermarriage is permitted by the mores and the institutions, especially by the legal institutions.

Correction and Prevention of Decadence and Ossification

Decadence and ossification, discussed above (Chapter 18) as destructuralizing and defunctionalizing processes, are characteristic of groups, organizations, and institutions, whether due to physical, biological, psychological, or social factors. Preventing and correcting decadence and ossification are of paramount importance in societal maintenance. The processes involved have adjustive aspects, and some hints have been given as to procedures. (138)

It should be pointed out here that a community or society should be constantly alert to the ominous fact that the processes of decadence and ossification continually threaten all organized phases of a society, and that these phases should be subjected continually to rational examination and constructive control. This means several things. There should be a continual, or at any rate a periodic, audit to determine whether the organizations and institutions are satisfying the needs for which they were designed. An effort should be made to detect the presence of the social diseases and other factors that make for decadence and ossification. The objectives in the particular field of action should be critically reexamined as to their sufficiency in the light of old and new needs. The public should be reliably informed as to the facts and conditions. The programs of action should be revised with the intent of discarding their outgrown, diseased, and useless features and incorporating the fruits of new knowledge and innovation wherever they apply. Finally, there should be careful, timely, and creative modification of the organizations and institutions, utilizing the best available technical and administrative personnel and procedures.

This, of course, is an ideal procedure. History pointedly demonstrates that the countertreatment of decadence and ossification, along with that of many other disorganizing and disintegrating processes, is effected by various kinds of more or less spontaneous and planned, partial and far-reaching, uneconomical and efficient processes of reorganization. These processes will be examined in the next chapter.

CHAPTER XXII

PROCESSES AND INSTRUMENTALITIES OF SOCIETAL REORGANIZATION

THE ANALYSIS of social reorganization heads up the whole of social organization, since social organization is never completely stable, adequate, or permanent. The very processes of regulation and maintenance must be supplemented by additional procedures to assure a normalized, equilibrated *status in quo* and obtain possible advances in well-being. We have to run to keep from going backward. A society's structural instrumentalities tend to become ossified, obsolete, decadent, and distorted, and its operational procedures become overly routinized, perverted, and archaic. Various interrelated structures and procedures get out of gear, and consequently various functional lags and disproportions become accentuated.

The factors in the various social situations change in kind, number, and combination. Old wants and needs are of necessity reconstituted, often embellished, under the changing conditions of the physical and social environments, and new wants and needs arise. The changes attendant upon the growth, decline, or rearrangement of the population, upon the scientific and technological advance, and upon the increasing complexity of the society must be met.

As the culture meetings between the people of different regions and different societies increase in frequency and number, some of the indigenous practices and forms come to be deemed archaic or obstructive. Also, because of these contacts, new wants appear which existing procedures and instruments cannot satisfy. Moreover, there is invariably some incubation—among at least some parts of the population—of new values, such as conceptions of the "good life," which are reflected in new or greatly revised dominating ideas, ideals, and ideologies and are effective in the setting of new goals. People also realize that social action must be cast in new time perspectives. The past and the future must be brought into the manageable present.

Finally, the very boredom of some persons with things as they are, the craving for something "different," and the upsurge of constructive urges are occasionally potent factors in reorganization activities.

Reorganizational Procedures in the Operation of a Society

Avoidance of Crises

In situations like those just described mankind has been continually subjected to minor crises and occasionally to major crisis conditions. (On the general nature and significance of crises see Chapter 3.) Crises imply that from the point of view of either a small or a large segment of the population social action is falling far short of the reigning goals and norms. There is serious impairment of function of persons and groups due to internal and external factors. There is a commotion, a stirring, an unrest among the people, an attempt to escape a tension-producing, frustrating, or otherwise critical situation, and a desire to approach a visualized goal. In general, there is imbalance and the stern necessity of re-establishing balance. Human society in a very real sense appears to be determined by the need for adequacy in the face of crises.

To our best knowledge mankind has always sought to neutralize, counteract, or stop processes of destructionalization and defunctionalization, and hence disequilibration, which make for crisis situations, before they reached the state where they might bring about societal dissolution; conversely, mankind has sought to stabilize society and secure some equilibrium of forces and functions. In brief, there have always been processes and schemes of social reorganization to provide flexibility and efficiency in the operation of any society.

Societal Reorganization Defined

By societal reorganization is meant the more or less conscious devising and utilization of social practices and procedures to *restore and rebuild social organization* whenever and wherever, in the opinion of smaller or larger bodies of members of a society, weakness is revealed or breakdown threatens. It involves, depending upon the particular circumstances, both the modifying or reinforcing of existing instrumentalities and procedures and the borrowing or constructing of new ones. Or, to put it differently, social reorganization consists of those processes whereby human groups, usually belatedly, establish in some degree revised or new systems of values, schemes of behavior, relationships, organizations, institutions, and operations to meet the requirements of continual re-equilibration of the ever-changing social order. Social reorganization is not necessarily social progress or betterment, although these are often stated as the objective among the active participants in reorganizational actions.

In the last analysis, social reorganization is simply a form of the general societal organization processes. Once the condition of organization is established, reorganization keeps the social concern going by reacting against the ever-present effects of societal disorganization.

Modes of Attack in Reorganization

Mankind has had much experience in devising and conducting procedures and projects of reorganization. Some of it has been largely in the nature of ingenious wishful thinking, sometimes accompanied by efforts at realization. Such thinking has taken various historical forms, depending upon the prevalent social, economic, and political conditions, the degree of cultural insight and perspective of the peoples, and especially their intellectual grasp and effective manipulative control of the phenomenal world.

Reiterated failure properly to adjust themselves to a world which seemed to them to be changing continuously for the worse and a feeling of pessimism and impotence in coping with the situation have led men, early and late, to seek in the realm of imagination that satisfying and sustaining social state which was so stubbornly denied them in actuality. These treatments have taken three general forms: a return in spirit to fantasies and myths about an idyllic past, to golden ages and good old times (1; 3; 6); a yearning and hope for the appearance of a more than human religious savior or redeemer who would establish for them a messianic state or a millennial epoch (4; 5; 9); and the design of utopias, those magnificent never-never lands. (2; 7; 8) Although most of these have been largely intellectualistic escapist constructs, many useful principles for reorganizational purposes have come from them, and some of their proposed elements have become effective parts of modern societies. (2, pp. 279-300)

The forms of societal reorganization that we are especially concerned with, however, are the various kinds of social movements that have incidental or purposive reorganizational effects and the special scientific techniques deliberately developed to carry on continuous inventorying and readjusting of conditions. Most of these, it will be noted, are actually effective only in part. Even when they have over-all effects, they have been and are still confined to specific combinations of objectives. They are seldom coordinated and seldom provide a consistent general pattern or procedure for societal reorganization.

Social Movements as Effectors of Societal Reorganization

Throughout human history most actual reorganization has occurred through social movements of one kind or another. The term *social movements* is a general one for collective actions involving smaller or larger numbers of human beings that have dynamic reorganizational effects. As McCormick has pointed out, they appear in those aspects of the social order that are man-made —economic, political, educational, religious, class, or other social and cultural relations—and hence are susceptible to human manipulation, rather than in aspects that are attributable to fate or supernatural agencies. (24, p. 227) In addition, they may also be efforts to modify the natural environment in so far as this can be done by collective action, a notable example of which is the soil and water conservation movement.

In the course of any enduring movement there is some modification of social life and the emergence of new forms of action. Social movements are motivated by unrest arising from social disequilibrium, which has brought tension and frustration or at least dissatisfaction to large numbers of persons, and by hope of the relief and anticipated satisfaction that will result if certain changes can be effected. (26) Often new incitements to change develop from discoveries and inventions along various lines or from diffusion borrowing from other cultures. Social movements usually start with the break-up of one or more phases of the institutional structures of the existing social order and frequently take the form of schismatic groups or groups to inaugurate some new scheme of life.

Social movements may seem at first to be mere collective responses to needs and therefore more or less amorphous, spontaneous, and blind. The unrest may produce mere excitable and ephemeral action and never develop into an observable social movement. Usually, however, if there is substantial incitement, and if the movements are not killed at their inception by dominant opposition forces, the action may assume cumulative aspects. The needs, wishes, and hopes become articulated in the form of more or less specific ideas and values; objectives are clarified, principles and mechanisms vaguely or clearly developed, and the personnel organized through leadership and division of labor. (10, p. 255; 14, pp. 678-679)

A social movement is usually slow to develop, but once it does develop, its participants come to have purpose, means, and concerted action. It may die out after its purpose has been accomplished or if the social situation changes and no longer requires it, as in the case of the women's suffrage movement. Usually, though, whether the movement continues or dies, it brings some change of, or reassertion of some neglected aspects of, the established folkways, mores, and institutions. Some, even many, of its objectives come to be embodied in some or many of the institutions of the society.

Types of Social Movements

Social movements can be variously classified. (10; 14; 15) They may range along a continuum from mass uniformities of behavior that are almost entirely unorganized and have only the most vague social objectives to movements that are societally organized for the pursuit of specifically defined objectives. The relatively unorganized mass actions are fairly large-scale collective-action phenomena based on suggestion-imitation and include fashions, fads, crazes, booms, and rushes, which are largely "pushes" or "drifts" as far as most of the participants are concerned.

Closely related to these forms of mass action are expressive movements, such as dancing manias and ecstatic religious demonstrations, in which the participants have a common incitement, some common sentiments, feelings, emotions, and interest, and some uniformity of practices, and in which the phenomena follow a fairly predictable course. These movements often have both great disorganizational and great reorganizational effects, but they do not necessarily build up into a social organization. The persons and groups involved are merely psychologically propelled participants, usually with no conscious leadership and only informal and implicit control. These phenomena do not seek to alter any part of the existing social order for reorganizational purposes, but function simply as release mechanisms for unrest, tension, and dissatisfaction.

Most sociologists are inclined to think of these, *not* as social or societal reorganization movements, but as more elementary, spontaneous, imitative phenomena of mass action, either with some reorganizational effects or with effects requiring reorganization. Heberle cogently expresses the sociological point of view. He says of a social movement:

> A sense of group identity and solidarity is required: only when the acting individuals have become aware of the fact that they have social sentiments and goals in common, and when they think of themselves as being united with each other in action for a common goal do we acknowledge the existence of a social movement. (18)

A prevalent classification of social movements in the accepted sociological sense divides them into *general* and *specific* movements. (10, pp. 256-272)

General Social Movements. The general social movements are relatively uncoordinated affairs, such as the labor movement, youth movement, women's movement, and world peace movement. These are groping efforts and have only a general direction along which they slowly but persistently move. They are unorganized and have neither established leadership nor recognized membership and little guidance and control. But much discussion is devoted to the general objectives, and many persons participate as evangelists and promoters. Specific social movements are likely to develop from general movements when the aims crystallize, a leadership is developed, and at least some of the participants effect an organization.

Specific Social Movements. In contrast to the general movements there are specific social movements. These are movements with well-defined goals and an ideology, a set of rules, a definite organization, including a conscious and devoted membership, recognized and accepted leaders, a division of labor, established procedures, and also a general body of expectations for society as a whole. All these aspects in concrete instances will vary in degree. Such movements develop stage by stage over a period of time. They run a wide gamut of interests as movements of revival or restoration, or withdrawal, or of direct approaches to modification. (15, pp. 408-426; 27; 28)

REVIVALS. Revivals—although *not* of the religious sort—or what might be more appropriately called "restoration movements" are efforts to return to actual old ways as a means of checking a trend toward what appears to be disorganization. Thus, we have movements to revive old folk arts, the communal square dance, to return to antiques in furniture and glassware, and so on, and even the restoration of former institutional features, including economic, religious, political, and artistic forms. (15, pp. 408-409; 20)

WITHDRAWALS. Movements of withdrawal are in essence attempts at collective escape from the larger social situation.* They are group protests against frustrations and dissatisfactions. The protest is made effective by actively withdrawing from all or most of the vexing greater society. *They seek,* however, *by their example, ultimately to bring about the reconstruction of the entire society* along the lines of their special model forms of life. Meadows distinguishes between two general types of withdrawal movements, the sectarian

*They have been alluded to in their accommodative aspects in the preceding chapter.

and the communitarian, though the differences are mainly in degree. (27)

Sectarian movements consist of the withdrawal of dissident elements from a larger religious body which the withdrawing elements think needs reorganization or of specialized religious groups which are actively discriminated against by the traditional and conventionalized bodies. Some examples are the initial Protestant withdrawal from the Roman Catholic Church and within Protestantism itself such withdrawals as those of the Anabaptists, Mennonites, Levellers, Society of Friends, and Methodists. We have already mentioned the special withdrawal of such religious groups as the Mormons.

Communitarian withdrawal movements are mainly secular movements, consisting of withdrawal from the larger society in the form of insulated communities in which the ideal values and practices are supposed to reign, and the general operation of which is to serve as an object lesson. In the United States we have had Owenite communities, such as New Harmony, Yellow Springs, and Nashoba; Fourierist communities, such as the North American and Brook Farm; and Icarian settlements, such as those at Nauvoo and on the Red River.

MOVEMENTS DIRECTED TOWARD SOCIETY. The movements directed toward the society as it is seek actively and premeditatively *to change* a given social condition of greater or lesser scope and significance or a combination of situations *by direct attack*. They operate within and as a special part of the society. These specific organized social movements usually have both negative and positive objectives, although these vary with each movement. They combat and seek to prohibit or eliminate certain folkways, mores, social differentiations, and institutional values and practices which their adherents believe to be outmoded, decadence-producing, or vicious. Sometimes they seek to reconstruct the entire society and eventually and as soon as possible the whole world. The movements may be prohibitive, preventive, remedial, positively constructive, or any combination of these.

Movements directed toward society range from what have been called "cultural movements" through social-reform movements, with their more fundamental but still partial reorganizations, to social-revolutionary movements, which seek to reconstruct the entire society or even the whole world. Faris has analyzed unconventional, crank, or fanatical, movements, (15, pp. 412-426) and Dawson and Gettys have treated the so-called "cultural movements." (14, pp. 680-688) As typed, the two conceptualizations have much in common. The unconventional crank movements seek some quick, easy, simple solution of the world's problems, often through some single principle or practice, such as vegetarianism, prohibitionism, nudism, new thought, ethical culture, technocracy, or some other cultist ideal.

The cultural movements as analyzed are distinct from movements that have economic and political objectives. Their distinguishing feature is that they seek to effect, through some measure of collective response, a larger satisfaction of the sentiments, emotions, ideals and values, and moral principles of men. The active proponents in such movements are convinced that they have a monopoly on truth and that this truth should be subscribed to and shared by everyone. They function as evangelists, persuaders, pleaders, crusaders for their particular religious, nationalistic, cultural, artistic, literary, linguistic, ethical, or other "perfect" segmental way of belief and action.

From the point of view of the present analysis, the social movements that have had the most fundamental and far-reaching effect in societal reorganization historically and at present are semi-political. These are the social-reform movements and the social revolutions. The social-reform movements in most but not all instances and the social-revolutionary movements invariably try to effect their reforms through control of some part of the political machinery of the society. The reason, of course, is that the state has come to be the primary agent of all significant social occurrences, including those with reorganizing aspects. The state is our major corrective, constructive, service-rendering, administrative agency, and sooner or later anything of social importance that needs doing or redoing must have at least the approval of the state. In the vast majority of cases the state will be expected to support the measure in whole or in part or to assume major or sole responsibility for providing or conducting it.

The characteristics that distinguish social-reform

movements, social revolutions, and dictatorships (in some respects a special type of revolutionary movement) will be examined in separate sections below. All three, however, have certain common features.

Characteristics of Specific Social Movements

This presentation will be both a concise summary of points thus far made and a systematic analysis of essential features. (10, pp. 258-269; 25)

Basis in Untoward Social Conditions of the Time and Place. The objective basis of organized social movements lies in critical situations, as viewed by the proponents and participants, such as economic, political, moral, or religious crises or events of physical or cultural change. The subjective base lies, on the one hand, in the frustrations, tensions, and thwarted dissatisfactions of a considerable number of individuals and, on the other, in the values, hopes, and specific demands of persons.

Conscious and Purposive Action. The nuclear group or groups of participants seek to make societal modifications, to actualize, and to terminate the social movement. The background of both the objective and subjective bases in the particular situation will provide the purposive orientation of the individuals and the group. These elements vary in combination in any given social movement. Men have never depended entirely upon laissez faire, that is, as little interference as possible with what are presumed to be natural processes of adjustment and readjustment, through competition and conflict, selection and survival. In fact, many of the most vociferous proponents of laissez faire during the last two centuries have been the greatest experimenters with, and promoters and conductors of, deliberate reorganizational procedures and movements in their own spheres of special interest.

In modern, and especially in democratic, societies, many members believe that they can do something constructive about their society, approach a realization of their social values, and engage in purposeful collective, manipulative activity. Increasingly, also, there is the conviction that social situations should be continually assayed, and, where necessary, foresighted and constructive processes of readjustment should be initiated *before* there is serious social injury.

Functional Relationships. Social movements directed toward society have causes; that is, they grow out of certain situations involving all sorts of physical, psychological, and societal factors which produce conditions of individual and social crisis. But they also have effects or consequences, both unexpected and expected, for they are specific means to consciously conceived ends.

A Developmental Pattern. These social movements show stages or typical sequences as they become organized, solidified, and persistent and also in many instances as they decline upon accomplishment of their objectives and die of success, or as they are crushed by opposition or ossify or decay from within for various reasons. This typical developmental pattern will be examined in connection with social-reform movements, although it is also found in its general forms in revolutionary movements and dictatorships.

Objective Embodiment of Social Movements in Societal Structures. The movement may be expressed through, and identified by, a single group, or by many groups. Because of its purposive nature, it is likely sooner or later to assume the form of an administrative organization. These groups and special organizations serve as the foci of the movement, the vehicles, the originating and modifying centers, as the major mode of definition and redefinition. (25)

Objective of Obtaining Modified or New Action Patterns in the Institutions of the Society. The institutions are the crucial agencies in societal operation. What is not in them has little enduring importance or effect. If reorganization is effected, there is, in the areas of social life where it has occurred, a modification of the scheme of chartered and organized relationships of collective living together. There may be the formation of *new* institutional techniques and component structural features, but some elements have been discarded and some added to the system of patterned expectations and organized action of the society.

Techniques or Procedures for Realizing the Goals. These social movements engage in agitation to jar people loose from their traditional ways of thinking and believing and to arouse new motives. They also seek to develop *esprit de corps* and morale among the participants. ***An ideology must be developed*** if a movement is to maintain itself against its opponents. This ideology consists specifically, in the excellent analysis of Blumer, in the following:

> . . . first, a statement of the objective, purpose and premises of the movement; second, a body of criticism and condemnation of the existing structure which the movement is attacking and seeking to change; third, a body of defense doctrine which serves as a justification of the movement and its objectives; fourth, a body of belief dealing with policies, tactics, and practical operation of the movement; and fifth, the myths of the movement. (10, pp. 267-268)

A set of procedural tactics for both offense and defense are devised to establish the movement in power. These have a wide range and include: discussion and propaganda to gain adherents; symbols and ritualistic and ceremonial devices and procedures; organizational tactics and strategies, such as mass meetings, petitions, pamphleteering, and so on, to influence publications, and especially to influence legislation along political, economic, religious, or civil rights lines, effect the formulation of constitutional or legal reorganization, and achieve the development of public administrative machinery.

The successive aspects of a social movement as a type of social action may be indicated in the following figure:*

Equilibrium → Social Change → Problem Situation → Crisis Situation → Definition of the Situation → Corrective Action → Resolution of Crisis through the Development of New Institutional Techniques and Controls → New Equilibrium

Social-Reform Movements

From the earliest civilizations on, individuals and groups—usually very small minority groups at first—have sought to correct what they deemed to be bad social situations by specific *reform* procedures. These *specific* and intentional reorganizational social movements range along a continuum from social reform to social revolution. For purposes of clarity of conception, however, each will be separately presented in its ideal-typical characteristics.

Specific changes in the conditions of living are always taking place which upset existing arrangements and actions and attract and focus the attention of certain groups. These changes are due to inventions; economic activity, such as inflation or depression; industrial conditions, such as long hours and bad factory conditions; new conceptions of urban-rural, sex, ethnic, and class group relations; insecurity of certain portions of the population, such as children and aged, and unemployed; corruption or perversion in certain strategic societal organizations, especially those concerned with social control; and so on. Institutions in the different departments of life must be readjusted to protect individuals, groups, and society as a whole. There are always people who conceive of schemes of direct action for relief from the adverse conditions. People organize to effect changes for themselves and others. The resultant adjustment is social reform; the collective efforts to achieve it are social-reform movements. (39, p. 4)

Notable examples of social-reform movements in the United States in the last three quarters of a century have been those in the fields of taxation, labor, and immigration; the farmers' movements; railway regulation; municipal reforms to counter political "machines" and local corruption and bring about slum clearance; public recreation; safety and health regulation; the abolition or sharp regulation of child labor; women's rights; civil service reforms; Progressivism, both the Bull Moose

*Suggested in part by my colleague, Dr. Paul Meadows.

and the La Follette varieties; and the whole array of reforms constituting the New Deal.

Characteristics of Social-Reform Movements

The more pertinent and distinctive characteristics of social-reform movements follow.

Acceptance of Existing Social System. The social-reform movement *accepts the existing social system and desires its full and efficient maintenance.* It approves the underlying values and most features of the mores and institutions of the system. In fact, it reaffirms the basic values and ends, and attempts to utilize and more effectively objectify them by means of its reorganizational actions.

Restoration of Normality and Well-being. Certain features of the mores and some of the institutional performances, however, fall short of the ideal values and ends in the opinion of the proponents of the movements, and eventually, if the movements are to succeed, of at least an effective minority of the general population. *The movement seeks to restore normality and well-being by some modification of one or more related practices in the community or society.*

Spasmodic and Sporadic Appearance of Reforms. The reforms usually come spasmodically and sporadically. Needed adjustments are postponed, and in general people do not exercise great foresight in the different areas of social life. Only when conditions become unbearable are people willing to make the effort required for the overdue modification.

Efforts at Modification. The modifying efforts may take one of several forms: *eliminating some institution or institutional practice,* such as slavery, dueling, and war; *prohibiting certain practices,* such as the consumption of alcoholic beverages or the employment of children; but usually a *remedial or ameliorative* action seeking to remodel or supplement certain existing institutions or practices, such as the reform of justice, penal reforms (for example, expansion of probation and parole), administrative reforms, alphabet, spelling, and calendar reform, the promotion of cooperatives, world federation, racial equality, social security, marriage and family improvements, and so on.

Wide Range of Objectives. The particular objectives range from the fantastic or the perverted to those which are based on intelligently and practically conceived needs and effected through hard-headed, opportunistic, well-planned, well-organized action resulting in concrete social gains.

Agents of Reform Movements. The reform movement may be carried on *by outsiders,* usually middle-class groups, *for the distressed elements, or* they may be initiated and conducted *by the affected groups themselves.* In the first instance the proponents are not themselves the victims of the societal malfunctioning. Because of outrage at the performance of so-called "social sinners" or because of humanitarian feeling and vicarious sympathy for the ignorant, socially illiterate, distressed, exploited, or repressed elements, reformers seek to bring about the change of mores and practices *for* them. Usually the reformers do *not* work *with* these elements. Appeals are generally made to those who are more strategically placed to do something about alleviating the situation. Notable examples are antislavery, the abolition of child labor, and the prohibition movement.

In the second instance the affected elements themselves agitate and conduct the reform *by* themselves, although they try to enlist the aid of various sympathetic elements. Such groups or classes have their own special interests and aims and confine themselves to satisfying them. In the United States the agrarian movements, operating under such leaders as Albert S. Goss, and E. A. O'Neal, and labor movements, such as the American Federation of Labor and the Congress of Industrial Organizations under leaders like Samuel Gompers, John L. Lewis, and Philip Murray, each with their own limited, integrated membership, are examples. They have been admittedly selfish rather than broadly humanitarian, and their cohesive organizations have produced immediate results.

Sometimes, as in the case of the woman-suffrage movement and the movement for improved relations between Negroes and whites, there is a combination of efforts of groups of outsiders and organizations of the distressed elements themselves.

Controversial Nature of Goals. The goals of social movements are usually of a controversial nature, and the process is one of opposition between interest groups. The parties on the one side are the persons and groups with a good deal of moral and social idealism and humanitarianism who see evils and try to correct them, or those who wish to improve their own condition. On the other side are those who profit from the evil or whose position would be disturbed by the reform and usually the great dead weight consisting of those who are too disinterested to do anything about the condition and prefer to let sleeping dogs lie. The contention ranges from mere persuasion through crusading and conciliation to highly militant action accompanied by bitterness which engenders much emotion and heat. Reforms, like most innovations, regardless of whether history labels them as absurd or highly beneficial, have invariably been opposed in their day on various grounds. (51 to 57) Usually, though, social-reform movements are conducted in a relatively peaceful manner.

Use of Existing Institutions and Organizations. The reform movement uses, as far as possible, existing institutions and organizations, such as the church, press, civic organizations, state agencies, and so on. It seeks to arouse public sentiment and opinion in its favor by all manner of publicity, education, and public discussion, for its ultimate objective is to obtain semiformal or formal public action, that is, some change of policy and administration, especially to get its reform into legislation and obtain the support and enforcement of the state. Invariably the movement, if successful, is a procedure of imposition of will upon unwilling opponents and is highly opportunistic in nature.

Limited Scope and Objective. Finally, social reform movements are limited in scope and objective. They aim to prevent further deterioration and, if possible, produce some improvement in the given social framework by a single or a few social measures which, in the opinion of the reformers, are of supreme and all-absorbing importance. Reform seeks not to build adequately, consistently, and relatedly, but to patch the old, to reorganize here and there. Because of this limited and particularistic nature of reforms, they often fail, for all aspects of a society are interrelated, and change anywhere requires reciprocal change elsewhere.*

In general, social-reform movements have usually been prompted by a combination of moral indignation, frustration, and good intentions. Some have been conscience salving, paternalistic enterprises; some have been dominated by sublime idealism, sometimes bordering on utopianism; and some have been little more than selfish rackets, regardless of the pretentions of their proponents.

Many reforms of history have been based upon some real vision of the underlying causes of the difficulty and have demonstrated some grasp of fundamental changes essential to the improvement of the particular situation. But they tend to place sole stress upon, or at least focus their attention upon, a single measure or a few related measures as a corrective for a single problem or a few closely related problems. Reformers seem to be unaware of, or unconcerned about, the relatedness of structures, factors, conditions and processes. Causes of a given situation are always multiple and complex in nature. Conversely, in an interrelated society, the effect of given reformist changes may create, and often have created, much more serious problems than those they aimed to cure. A notable example of this is the prohibition movement. Furthermore, no one reform is able to solve the problem which brought it into being. The reformist movements of a prohibitory character have almost universally stressed eradication without formulating satisfactory substitutes for the habits, customs, or institution under fire.

And yet social reform, though piecemeal and unilinear, has been responsible for much of the positive reconstruction of the past. Reform movements have almost universally called attention to troublesome conditions, even though their advocated procedures were often maladroit and incomplete. At best, some of them have actually remedied conditions which laissez-faire attitudes might have permitted to exist indefinitely or worsen until

*The above discussion of the nature of social reform movements has been suggested in considerable part by Blumer. (10, pp. 269-272)

they led to revolutionary action. Much in the way of reform movements can be expected in the future. In fact, many of the scientific social engineering features have had their motivation and origination in reform movements, and the reform movements have served as highly informative experimental procedures.*

Ideal-Typical Stages of a Social-Reform Movement

One of the most revealing ways of studying reform movements, with respect to both their organization and their operation or actional aspects, is to examine their stages of development. Each such movement is a complex process exhibiting a temporal course of development in which the different phases or stages—emergence, maturation, and often decline—may be distinguished. Each stage, with its fairly distinctive and appropriate mechanisms and procedures, grows out of its predecessor in time and anticipates its successor. Thus, a reform movement is a dynamic thing, ever becoming something different. Both the processes of its operation and the functions that it performs change with successive stages.

The following study is based upon the examination of more or less successful reform movements, which have been mentioned earlier in this chapter. The information, although obtained from specific, piecemeal movements, provides in composite and synthesized form a substantial conception of such movements and some basis for prediction and guidance. (14, pp. 689-709; 31; 36; 37; 38; 44) It must be remembered that these stages are not precisely defined; there is much overlapping and running together, and wide penumbral areas exist where each merges imperceptibly into the next. Many variations will be found as specific movements are examined, and in some instances a stage may be skipped.

Period of Aggravation and Incubation. The period of aggravation and incubation is usually a long one. There is gradual awareness that certain social conditions are threatening certain cherished values and evidence that certain existing social arrangements are being weakened internally and show signs of being overtaxed. At first the concern may be vague and confined to very few persons, since any class arrangement, social practice, or institution, no matter how false, defective, or pernicions, if firmly fixed in the social organization, will be widely accepted. But outmoding forces are at work, sometimes operating for decades or even centuries.

If the situation is strategic in well-being, the unrest and dissatisfaction that were vague and amorphous become strong and noticeable. A perception of new needs develops. The issues begin to be defined, and some individuals and small groups become aware that a situation exists which is undesirable and intolerable and think that "something ought to be done." Others oppose the views. The existing equilibrium of interests is very definitely disturbed. But there is no established leadership; the behavior of the reformist participants is unsynchronized and random; the protest is expressed in general terms. But there has been a focusing of attention.

Period of Initiation and Discussion. The more severe the aggravation, the more general is the recognition of a need for change. Community-wide excitement develops as far as the specific problem is concerned. At this stage the success of the movement is not assured; it may die aborning. The possibility of the initiating stage developing successfully depends upon the quality and ability of the leaders; the procedures that are adopted; the general intelligence of the people; the peculiarities of the situation, such as the political, economic, and moral conditions prevailing at the time; the degree of entrenchment of the challenged practice or institution; the alertness and strength of the opposition; and a host of other factors.

The most important launching factor is the initiating leadership. The leader at this stage is usually of the visionary, fanatical, even charismatic type, and his chief function is to make such an impression on the community that the movement begins to take shape. Consequently, he agitates, preaches, and harangues, pictures an ideal world, and prophesies dire consequences if the criticized condition continues. He arouses small groups to action, and they in turn convey their point of view

*On American reform movements, see references 39, pp. 3-6, 274-287; 42; 45; 46.

to larger numbers of persons. The nascent reformist group develops its literature at this stage, including its own journals and pamphlets. There are public addresses, newspaper and magazine editorials and articles, and semipublic assemblies of interested parties, both pro and con, to debate the issue.

If the process of initiation has been properly carried on, the problem and its alleviation or correction become a matter of widespread public controversy, in the course of which many people make up their minds and take sides, as they did in the case of the slavery and prohibition issues. The vested interests and other parties who approve of, or profit by, the challenged activity become alarmed and active. Seeking to evade the issue or detract attention from it, they try to stop discussion, cut off agitation, and humiliate or calumniate the leaders of the reform.

The intensity of this opposition will be in direct proportion to the degree that the opposed activity or institution is institutionalized, commercialized, and otherwise entrenched. So, all manner of institutions, interests, and social agencies are enlisted, if possible, on both sides of the question, including especially the press (a controversial issue is always news), influential nation-wide organizations, political parties, churches, schools, and colleges.

At this stage there is an integration of unrest. Collective myths and doctrines are appearing which strengthen the reformist group's power and rally others to its support. There is some coordination around an objective and a fairly well defined program is developing. Many people are becoming convinced that what has been proposed *should* be done.

Period of Organization. At this stage the movement develops into an organization to do what has been proposed. The form of organization depends upon various factors, but especially upon the nature of the constituency to be organized and the peculiar nature of the cause being advanced.

The movement is now beyond the stage of sentiment and sensationalism, beyond evangelism. This is the stage of both private and public action. Hence, the movement is converted into an administrative organization with specialized functionaries. The leadership now consists largely of persons of the statesman type, who are aggressive, astute strategists. The emotional and evangelical fringe has been pretty much pushed aside. Several courses of action usually take place at this stage: (1) The *ideology* is clarified and systematized, repeatedly affirmed, and pointedly and effectively directed against the neutrals and the opposition. (2) The motives are now formulated into *concrete policies* and placed before the public by means of systematic educational, publicity, and propagandist procedures. (3) *Informal and formal planning is carried on* by the skilled nuclear body of the movement. (4) A *program of action is devised,* which incorporates both the concrete proposals for effecting the ends sought and the specific methods of action and constitutes the method of attack.

Period of Institutionalization. The period of institutionalization follows the preceding one almost imperceptibly. The organizational process has gained an identifiable body of adherents and moral and financial support for the cause among a majority or an effective minority. The movement takes on the characteristics of an institution. A body of established customs, traditions, rules (in the form of constitution and by-laws), and rituals has developed which disciplines and directs the entire personnel. There is division of labor, effective procedures for action have been developed, and the essential nonmaterial and material equipment is available. The leaders are now official administrators who translate policies and programs into action. The movement has developed into a labor union, a cooperative, a new religious denomination, a new political party, or a state, national, or world organization.

The movement now seeks to effect favorable decisions for semi-public or public action, or both, in behalf of its constituents. The administrative experts try to get action through semipublic organizations, such as clubs, civic organizations, church groups, and so on, especially in exercising pressure upon public bodies. In most instances, though, they also try to obtain favorable legislation, both outlawing the old practices if the movement has been one of substitution or proscription and specifically permitting, or prescribing, new enabling action. This, then, includes the administration of the law by public executive or administrative agencies, and the sustained approval of the judiciary. This stage may be the end of the social reform movement. However, two additional stages are usually found.

Period of Rebuilding and Enforcement. Crystallizing the decision in the form of law, even if properly bolstered by administrative and judicial agencies, does not end the matter, as is commonly believed. Irreconcilable minorities and ignorant individuals and groups must still be dealt with. The law must be applied and enforced before it becomes effective. Also many persons in the general population must be re-educated, and some of the existing social machinery must be revised in function and administration. If this is conscientiously and successfully carried out, a social evil, weakness, or incumbrance has been in large part overcome, and a new plane of social activity in the form of a re-formed or new institution has been achieved and is accepted as a regular aspect of the community's way of life.

Period of Formalism and Decay. This stage must be alertly guarded against. The beliefs and ways of the reform group become stable, and the general public becomes accustomed to them. Or, as often happens, the changes effected may become increasingly tiresome to the public and to the individuals and groups regulated or taxed. When the public loses interest the popular support is stopped. A reaction sets in, and the people return to "normalcy." This is what happened to the Progressive movement and to some extent to the New Deal. But even if the movement still has urgency and some popular support, it may deteriorate or collapse because of internal weaknesses. The zeal of the members themselves cools, and they make accommodative concessions to the world at large. The movement's organization and power may be too greatly centralized to allow enough local autonomy, or there may be too little coordination, control, and cohesion.

At this stage also the diseases of excessive bureaucracy—inflexibility, indifferentism, even reactionism—can set in. The movement may settle into a routine. The leaders often become "swivel-chair warmers" and mere salary receivers going through set motions. The human purposes implicit in the movement have begun to be obscured, the mechanisms have become ends in themselves, and the positions of the functionaries have become sinecures. Many of the procedures have degenerated into pompous formalities. The overstructuralized, ossified reform movement suffers from what has been called, all too truly, "hardening of the categories"; it sits and possesses; mostly it just sits. When this occurs, if the adverse situation which produced it still exists, it may become the subject of a new reform movement.

Revolutions as Processes of Reorganization

Nature of Revolutions

To regard revolutions as pathological or criminal phenomena, as is commonly done by millions of persons who are the beneficiaries of revolutions enthusiastically participated in by their ancestors, is evidence of lack of information or understanding regarding the nature and the significance of revolutions as adjustment procedures in the history of human societies.

Revolutions are usually looked upon as wasteful and expensive disorganizing, even destructive, processes, and they are; but through most of the history of civilized peoples, revolutions have at the same time been the means—often, under the conditions of the time, the only means—of conducting large-scale, long-due equalizing, corrective, and reorganizing activities. Under certain current conditions revolutions are "natural" occurrences, as natural, in fact, as struggle, selection, and survival among and within biological species, or as natural as the readjustive shifting and faulting of the earth's strata which produces an earthquake.*

Revolutions are social phenomena inherent in history, and their effects are in the very fabric of social systems. As Lederer states, "No one can

*"Revolutions are not made: they come. A revolution is as natural a growth as an oak. It comes out of the past. Its foundations are laid far back."—Wendell Phillips, 1852.

know how the world would have developed without revolution." He goes on to point out that no prevailing deep-rooted economic and political system of the past has been rebuilt by evolution alone to a structural and functional form resting upon new principles. For every fundamental social change there has been revolution *somewhere,* either within a given social system or acquired from a revolution elsewhere at some time. (73)

A revolution is a combination of widely influential and deeply penetrating social processes that tends, in a shorter or longer period of time, to bring about a marked and usually a rather general alteration of the entire social system. As the term implies, there is a "revolving," a general turning or shifting of societal structures, and a relocation of functions and responsibilities in different societal elements. Most revolutions originate in one or several related institutionalized segments of the system, but if they are true revolutions their ultimate effect, owing to the interrelatedness of the pivotal institutional system, is to bring about a very considerable remodeling, transformation, or reconstruction of most of the important functional mechanisms and procedures of the society.

A time perspective shows a marked change, a break, in the continuity of development and orientation of the society, a recasting, recombining, and recrystallizing of the given social order on a new and different plane. There has been a considerable overthrow and destruction of the customary and traditional order or of some considerable portion of it and a rebuilding of certain fundamental features. While revolution involves the disintegration of one system of social organization, it at the same time consists of the reintegration of the society along different and it is hoped usually along more efficient and appropriate lines.

Revolutions should be distinguished from social-reform movements, which, as we have noted, are *limited* secular movements that endeavor to patch up one or several of the most objectionable (to the reformist) parts of the existing order. *A revolution,* in so far as it is consciously conducted, *seeks to replace most of the old with something supposedly new and better.* Whether largely unconscious or conscious, it is a society-wide development which involves revamped social goals shared by most of the populace and very considerable change of the existing societal structure, rather than sporadic and partial accommodative or corrective actions within this structure. Nevertheless, a revolution has many of the features of a social-reform movement—factorial, processual, organizational.

Reorganization is a matter of degree both in volume of changes and in ultimate effects. Similarly, it may be pointed out that a revolution is usually a multiple and related combination of reforms occurring contemporaneously. But the primary reason for a revolution is the inadequacy of specific reforms in the society under the conditions of the time, their insufficiency in number and coverage of various social lacks and lags, and their delay in time.

Fundamental Contributory Situations. Fundamentally, revolutions are due to two major sets of related factors. The first set consists of inefficiency in a considerable portion of the strategic institutions of the society or the perpetuation of anachronistic institutions that have become decadent and perverted from their basic purpose. In either case, the institutions have broken down and become parasitic or infectious. There is usually also a disruption in the alignment, a lag, of social or institutional functions. Many of the institutions are out of step.

The second set of factors is based on a marked deterioration of formerly accepted values, norms, and controls and the dawning of new values and goals and new conceptions of more efficient societal mechanisms and functions. The general factors thus are tenacious old institutions and values which have been thwarting and cramping the new expressions of life.

Over-All Characteristics of Revolution. Revolution is a long-time equilibrating process characterized by (1) an accumulation of repression among large segments of the population, which is demonstrated in social tensions and widespread unrest and dissatisfaction; (2) an attack upon many of the basic social values of the society and upon the institutions which embody them, and a considerable modification of strategic values, objectives, and attitudes; (3) diminishing social power of the dominant social classes or other population segments who support the out-moded, inadequate, and repressive values and institutional structures and procedures, often accompanied by showy overcompensations on the part of these social elements on the defensive; (4) a more or less successful shifting of social power to different and newly strong and competent social classes or population elements, accompanied in the final stages of certain kinds of revolution by demonstrations of violence; (5) the rearrangement of the relationships between the opposed social groups; and, consequently, (6) a noticeable transformation of the ideologies and some of the structurings and operations of some of the major social institutions, especially the political and the economic, although all are affected in varying degree according to the nature of the revolution.

Revolution, it should be noted, is an adjustment phenomenon of societies in an advanced stage of development—societies that are populous, established, highly differentiated and stratified, and complex as to culture and that have a multiplicity of highly organized institutions. So far as can be determined most have occurred during the last three millennia. There is little evidence of revolution, as we know it, among tribal peoples. Among them social change has been slow, their social organization relatively simple, social and cultural shocks due to innovation few and moderate, and adjustments have come about gradually.

Kinds of Revolutions

The term *revolution* has been applied to social upheavals of many kinds, which have a wide range of importance and extent. It has been applied to spasmodic and random revolts and factional coups, such as those frequently occurring in Latin-American countries, which are mainly substitutes for national elections or are even forms of election. They produce no fundamental change in the arrangements and functions of the society, but substitute temporarily one faction's names and faces for another's in the barracks and administrative offices. This is an untenable special usage of the term.

Sociologically authentic revolutions are political, economic, commercial, industrial, intellectual, ethical, religious, ecclesiastical, theological, even aesthetic. (59, p. 337) They may be divided into two general categories: those that are more or less unplanned as revolutions and those that are studiously planned and organized in order to bring about a conquest of state power and effect purposively a fundamental reorganization of the social system. They always overlap, however.

Unplanned Revolutions. Relatively unplanned revolutions are more or less spontaneously developmental or evolutionary in nature. They occur slowly and more or less peacefully and often originate in a particular institutional field, but their effects spread to other departments of social life. They go far beyond social reforms in the ultimate changes that are brought about. They are due to the accumulation of a variety of contributory factors. They may be due to new cultural contacts, such as those effected by the Crusades and the new access to the Far East in the fourteenth and fifteenth centuries, resulting in, among other things, the introduction of printing, the compass, and gunpowder. Or they may be due to new discoveries and inventions, such as discoveries of previously unknown and distant territories and discoveries and inventions of an intellectual, ethical, religious, scientific, or technological nature.

Many stupendous events have had the effect of revolution if all their ramifications are examined within a time perspective, even though they were *not* set in motion deliberately to effect the specific kind of reconstituted society that evolved. Notable instances of this general type in our own culture are the intellectual, humanistic, and scientific revolution developing from the Renaissance; the so-called "commercial revolution," which started in the twelfth century with the Crusades and was especially pertinent in the fifteenth and sixteenth centuries owing to the new means of communication and transportation and the discovery of new lands all over the earth; the Reformation with its innovative religious ideas and organizations as introduced by Wycliffe, Zwingli, Luther, Melanchthon, and Calvin; the industrial revolution, with its vast scientific and technological changes, which began in the eighteenth century and is still going on.

Although the changes were at first determined by the institutional field or fields with which these revolutions were most directly and effectively associated, they have had far-reaching effects upon *all* institutions. They have brought about basic relocations, realignments, and reconstructions and many new features in the major emphases, attitudes, interests, values, relations, controls, activities, and structures of our Western system of life.

Purposive Revolutions. Purposive revolutions are the great social movements that come to have a direct, studied, purposive, and organized character. They are consciously and pointedly directed against the entire *status in quo*. Although the general objective is the swift and radical alteration of the entire social system and a complete redirection of its functions, their specific objective is the conquest and transformation of the political and economic institutions. They are mass action by groups and are specifically directed against the government because it is the most conspicuous feature of the social system and supports most of the institutions that are under attack. Thus, there is a basic shift in the locus of political power when the existing government is overthrown. New forms of political organization appear.

Accompanying the political realignment there are often marked modifications of production techniques: new forms and location of ownership of economic goods; modification of the distribution of the proceeds of production among the major factors; revision of the system of exchange; and even different standards and planes of consumption. There is a new alignment and often new differentiation of groups. Different classes gain ascendancy and in some instances new classes appear. Some classes grow numerically, others shrink; some achieve greater power and higher status, others lose. But, invariably, because of the crucial nature of these changes, every other department of life—familial, religious, scientific, aesthetic, recreational—usually undergoes some alteration. Nevertheless, although the new social order is markedly different in its orientation, it arises out of the old regime, never departs completely from it, and often reverts back to many features of it. Notable examples of such revolutions are those in England in the seventeenth century, the French Revolution in the eighteenth century, and the Mexican, Chinese, and Russian Revolutions of the present century. Our main concern is with these social-political-economic revolutions as deliberate, more or less organized reorganizational procedures.

Political-Economic Revolutions

The Time Factor. Revolutions are commonly assumed to be sudden, unpredictable, and exceedingly rapid in their development, and some persons refer to them as catastrophic events. This is largely due to the special attention given to certain spectacular occurrences near the end of a long process, namely, the violence and disorder when the break comes—the period of crowds, mobs, riots, barricades in the street, bloodshed, purges, and forcible taking over of institutional functions and offices.

Actually this is merely the violent culmination of a long preceding development, an incident rather than a process. A revolution is not made in a day; it has a long history behind it. The violent overthrow is preceded by a spiritual process disintegrating the pattern of ideas and a social process disorganizing the institutional arrangements, which reaches through the whole social structure. There is invariably a succession of effects arising from long and silent changes which have been felt but not fully understood, frankly faced, or competently coped with in a timely manner. Revolution is the inevitable product of obstruction to the processes and mechanisms of orderly social adjustment.

Causes. Behind every revolution there have been notable changes in technology, new inventions, discoveries, and improvements, economic progress, new conceptions of the good life for men generally, and expanding knowledge of superior human and social values and of more efficient institutional functioning. It is thus a product of social enlightenment among large elements of the population. Paradoxically, it comes when the conditions of life generally are in a state of improvement—when the abuses of which the revolutionists complain have already been abated in some measure.

The immediate cause of revolution is thwarted self-expression and hampered activity among the masses of people; in brief, the restlessness and pressure that come with the repression of normal human impulses and activities. Beyond this are a host of subsidiary and implementing factors. (62, pp. 1-67; 64; 66; 76; 78; 84, pp. 365-463)

This repression is mainly due to the fact that the ruling classes have selfishly tried to keep the subject masses in ignorance and poverty, weakness, confusion, and disorganization by withholding every right and opportunity possible and have exploited and dominated them. Through their manipulation of the institutions of social regulation and social maintenance and in order to preserve the *status in quo,* the ruling classes, shortsightedly, selfishly, and often desperately, have interfered with all the power at their command in the mechanisms of normal adjustment. Usually certain outmoded economic institutions and arrangements are insistently adhered to and enforced; government is controlled in the interests of the ruling class; a self-perpetuating clique is in power; law is not the joint product of the various segments of the population and is not fairly enforced; the rights of free speech, press, and assemblage are abridged or denied; grievances and needed social adjustments cannot be openly discussed. Religion and the other expressional institutions are forced to conform to the wishes of the reigning theory of class supremacy, and the church is appropriated and manipulated. Education, in so far as it exists, is controlled for ulterior purposes as to diffusion, quantity, and quality, and misinformation and misguidance are deliberately engaged in.

The favored and dominant classes seem insensitive to the well-being of the general body politic. Born and reared under the protection of time-honored rights and arrangements, they are entirely ignorant of the bases and the ephemeral and perverted character of these rights and arrangements. The ruling classes fancy themselves invested with them forever by some sort of divine right. For their own sakes they attempt to maintain a static system and obstinately resist change by every power and usage that they can muster.

Constituent Processes and Sequences. As previously stated, a revolution is a phenomenon of social dynamics. Social life is an incessant and inevitable alteration of social equilibrium, and a silent revolution is always in process. Those who move with it intelligently survive and flourish. A new governing social class, or classes, is always in the making, though their development within the old social framework at first is so slow as to be almost imperceptible.

As the top weakens, strength appears farther down in an ever-greater degree and at accelerated speed. Often the situation is accentuated by a special crisis situation, such as war or economic depression, which reveals the ineptness of the top and provides those below with opportunities both for protest and for appropriation of some power.

The revolutionary personnel does not consist of a single class, but of practically all of the classes below the topmost ones. Furthermore, the strategically important elements are not the lowest, most abject classes, but the middle classes, the skilled workers, the members of the professions (save those who are hangers-on of the aristocracy), the newly important and successful commercial elements, the intellectuals—all population elements with ability, knowledge, insight, resource, energy, and will. The intellectuals voice the accumulated suppressed and heretofore inarticulate discontent and aspiration of the bulk of the population. They undermine the social myth that lent support to the older and would-be-discarded institutions and construct and illuminate the myth of the new order with its promises of well-being. Also, they point the way to the new order and develop plans and programs of procedure. They function as leaders who organize the groups and direct the concerted action.

The other important effective elements in the population are the resentful and excited masses. These are an amorphous potentially dynamic power in secondary-group societies. When they are given concrete goals and are properly motivated, led, and organized, they are molded into a mass movement with momentum and power. They become the battering ram of the revolution.

In general, among those at the top there is growing inability to maintain their status and power and the organizational bulwarks of their system and a growing unwillingness farther down to tolerate the situation. A fundamental change in the attitudes of the general citizenry toward the underlying bases of the institutions has come about. Actively or passively they are already united behind the aspiring regime. The machinery of the state and the economic institutions give way at various points some time before the break. The violence at the break is simply due to the exuberant release of the masses and the desperate death struggle of the die-hards of the old system. The confusion is like that of moving day, as new administrative tenants move in after forcibly ejecting the old or taking over the offices of those who left frantically.

Before the new equilibrium is achieved, there is much shifting in the functioning of institutions, such as new property arrangements, legislative and judicial groping and experimentation, and the practical certainty of some reaction and counterrevolution by the unpurged survivors of the old system or by disaffected elements of the newly ascendant classes. It may be pointed out, however, that the changes brought about by revolution are usually not so marked and divergent from the older order as is often imagined. When the overt activities of revolution are over, we find a great deal of the old merging with the new.

By way of summary, the sequence of stages in the process may be systematically presented as follows:

A Long Period of Gestation. During this period the irritants accumulate; the revolutionary movement is formulated in its ideological and organizational aspects; and there is struggle for power, with the gradual weakening and undercutting of the groups "sitting on the lid" and the development of spiritual, political, and economic strength on the part of most of the other groups.

A Period of Violence. When the break comes, with its mobs, strikes, economic disruption of all kinds, and general disorder, the reactionary and conservative elements that have been in control are removed through flight or liquidation.

A Period of Seizure. In this stage the governmental and legal system, the production and exchange system, the means of communication and transportation, and often the educational, religious, and other strategic organizations are taken over by the revolutionaries.

A Period of Consolidation. The revolution acquires, not a going society, but a disrupted, confused, even collapsed one. Many of the new ideas and schemes do not work. The chaos has to be converted into orderly functioning. The governmental machinery, now in new and often inexperienced hands, has to be made effective. The economic system has to be established along the lines of the new blueprints. There is redistribution of property, power, status, and privilege. Often the attack of aggressive nations, worried about the possible international effects of the new regime, has to be contended with at this stage.

The new and revised institutions generally have to be coordinated and a working regulatory and maintenance system organized. Although there has been a breaking away from the prerevolutionary system, the basic functional features have not been —could not be—entirely destroyed without disaster. Hence, the new and much of the old must be geared together.

A Period of Retreat or of Counterrevolution. Some temporary retreat always occurs, and often there is counterrevolution. The process of establishing a new system proceeds too fast, and the break is often too violent. There is insufficient carry-over; Utopia has not come. There may be some retreat in ideology and invariably a partial return to the older institutional forms and procedures in order that the rebuilding process may go on step by step, as it inevitably must. There may be counterrevolution, that is, some effort to unseat the new occupants and procedures and to restore some of the old. The counterrevolution draws on both the elements of the old regime that have been abroad or underground and the jealous factions and disgusted and disillusioned elements of the revolution itself.

A Period of Re-establishment. If there has been a period of retreat or counterrevolution, it is followed by a blending of elements, objectives, and programs and a settling-down of the society. Always, the new system is a combination or an accommodation of the best and most workable features of the revolution and of the indispensable aspects of the preceding order. (68; 71; 77; 84, pp. 229-359; 88; 89)

Results of Political-Economic Revolution

The results of any political-economic revolution are of two kinds—constructive and destructive.

Constructive Results. It cannot be denied that some satisfactory social reorganization has come through revolutions. Often, in their area and era, revolutions were the only means of accomplishing the desired and necessary adjustments. Most revolutions have ended the worst abuses and inefficiencies of the old economic-political regimes. For a time the political machinery works more smoothly, and there is usually the transfer of property into hands of individuals and groups that use it in such a manner that it contributes to greater well-being. Often superior industrial and commercial processes are affected, and many outmoded features of other institutions are discarded. Frequently, new humane attitudes and ideas, mores, and practices come to prevail. Occasionally new cultural peaks are achieved, new capable personalities appear. An array of new social rights (and responsibilities) for the average man are often produced. And above all, the tradition of successful revolt is established and social energy is purposefully utilized, which is a wholesome experience in any society. (60, pp. 272-285)

Destructive Results. The objectively minded student also notes numerous and widespread costs of revolution. There are psychic costs; the mental stability and sanity of many are often wrecked. Revolution often destroys or weakens realistic thinking, because the excessive danger and the overstimulation of passion unsettle disciplined thought, and breed fanatics.

Periods of chaos come both during and after the revolution and impair the agencies and processes of social control. There is a loss of respect for law and order, and with it countless other evils. It brings also, in many cases, the destruction of the choicest products of culture, expression, and intellectual achievement simply because they have some association with the hated and despised former dominant classes.

Economically, at least for a time, revolution reduces working power, dissipates energies, or directs them into socially useless or even harmful channels, destroys wealth, disintegrates distributive processes, and interrupts or destroys the international as well as the national trade of the nation involved.

For a time also, it produces great moral and spiritual costs. Mutual hate and suspicion are engendered among the citizenry, sentiment and feeling are brutalized, good will subverted, moral restraints relaxed, and a general brutish state produced. The crowd and mob behavior release and induce qualities in human beings that should never be encouraged. The unseating of the disciplines and regularities of conduct that make us socialized human beings leads to violence, and the employment of violence starts a process of rebarbarization that destroys many fine qualities and controls.

The acts of violence, inseparable from revolution, produce with almost mechanical precision an equivalent reaction, which, unless stopped, results, as noted, in counterrevolution. To avoid this reaction, the revolutionary leaders must become dictators and despots; they must rule with a hand of iron, destroy opposition at any cost and by any means, and centralize control. The populace must be cowed into loyalty. This produces a new feeling of oppression and strain, crushes much initiative, maintains fear, arouses new hate, and produces much distortion of self even among the supposedly freed classes.

Finally, there is a tendency to slip back after the revolution until the recuperative forces have been painfully and slowly developed.

Every revolution has presented a bill of stupendous costs. The Russian Bolshevik revolution, which has been running its course during the last three and a half decades, is typical. Both laymen and specialists have described and documented it with a voluminous literature. It presents a record of political upheaval and civil war, economic disorganization, invasion, famine, pestilence, both flight and forced movement of people, wholesale murder, fumbling and bungling reversion and perversion, terror and terrorism, extremism and fanaticism, misselection, deformation, expropriation, and suppression.

Inadequacy of Revolution as Reorganizing Procedure. In spite of its historical significance, today revolution as a reorganizing procedure is incompatible with modern knowledge of possible constructive action. It has become logically unsound, and, what is more, it is becoming increasingly unnecessary, because there are more economical and effective methods and agencies of adjustment available.

Revolution is essentially very expensive. It is mostly negative, seeking the destruction of certain institutions and the elimination, at least from power, of certain classes or population elements. It is a more or less blind, ignorant, and spontaneous, hit-and-miss groping for means of adjustment.

Much energy is wasted, many basic institutions unnecessarily maimed, many fine values distorted, many extremes resorted to from which retreat must later be made, much positive social momentum lost or misdirected, much that is good, transferable, and usable irreclaimably lost, and many essential human beings are killed or lost through flight. It usually waits too long.

Revolution is always a substitute for orderly, systematic development and reorganization. It is a matter of ignorance of or unwillingness, impatience or inability to utilize telic procedures. As a matter of fact, in so far as revolutions have effected permanent advances of almost any kind, they have been both accompanied and followed by telic processes.

Dictatorships

Evidence of dictatorships or totalitarian regimes can be found all through recorded history, for they have recurred in many different eras and in almost every region of the earth. They are not sporadic and abnormal phenomena, but a sinister reorganizational movement and temporary pattern of social life which threaten among peoples from time to time when certain sets of conditions occur. Totalitarianism, whether socialistic, communistic, fascistic, monarchic, or autocratic in form, or any other form of absolutism continues to be a menacing possibility. The following brief analysis is based upon a study of some thirty-five dictatorships of history, including some ancient Greek and Sicilian tyrants of the seventh and sixth centuries B.C., the Roman dictators, the European dictators prior to World War I from Cosimo de Medici to Louis Napoleon, the outstanding Latin-American dictators of the nineteenth and twentieth centuries, and especially the array in Europe and the Near East following World War I.

The conception of dictatorship dominating the present analysis is that of a social, especially a government, system in which "the principle of the separation and mutual control of the different agencies of government is replaced by a concentration of supreme power in the hands of one man or a group of men who are uncontrolled by a free and unrestricted public opinion, and who wield an absolute power over the executive, legislative, and usually also the judicial branches of government." (105) To this must be added the fact that usually the supreme power is held in an unorthodox, irregular, or extralegal manner, although there is invariably the ex post facto invention of some fiction of regularity or some strained or bastard adaptation of constitutional procedures.

Dictatorships have some of the characteristics of social-reform movements, but they are hurried, multiple reforms on a nation-wide scale. They also have some similarity to revolutions in that they produce a vast, although usually temporary reorganization of the social system. But they develop out of highly contemporary conditions, are hurriedly and frantically engineered, and almost without exception, sooner or later, terminate in a completely effective reversal of the forms of organization by counterrevolution.

Causal and Contributory Factors

Dictatorships are a pattern of control which the logic of circumstances tends to thrust upon a people when certain kinds of *crisis conditions* prevail. These situations constitute a collection of red flags that should be heeded by all who cherish stable ways of societal readjustment. The crises develop through various social processes and have as their precipitating factors such occurrences as financial panic and depression, poor harvests, invasion or threat of invasion, war and national humiliation and prostration following military defeat, revolution, civil strife, or threat of violent class cleavages, folk depletion, the multiplication of political factions or parties, the breakdown of strategic institutions, and so on. Physical catastrophes and epidemics and plagues may also be involved.

In the crisis situation tensions heighten to the breaking point, suppressed fears become panic, and everyone is aware of insecurity. The problems presented are seemingly insoluble by the old or existing social machinery, at least in its disorganized state, and the old regulatory and maintenance personnel is unable to cope with the situation. Confusion and disorder reign; morale disintegrates. Many individual crises are induced. Problems of survival and group solidarity become of paramount importance. There is a demand for solutions, for order, fixity, and a tangible, even though temporary, program of action. The great majority are willing to pay a price for these.

The situation creates a demand for immediate regimental behavior. Obviously, however, such unprecedented disorganization cannot be prepared for in the organizational machinery of the society. There is the need of centralized planning and of facilitating orderly and constructive procedures. The entire community must be organized and marshaled for quick and decisive action. Thus a befuddled and fearsome mass in time of great crisis is nearly always ready—nay, anxious—to give over control to anyone who gives evidence of ability to wield it efficiently.

This situation, in turn, both demands a leader and provides the opportunity for a leader or a cohesive minority group which offers a ready-made formula of social procedure and promises a dynamic attack upon the problems. Hence, in time of crisis, an imperious and audacious leader and his aides, either by invitation or by insinuating themselves into the affair, are often gratefully accepted and permitted to arbitrarily re-establish the routines of social life on their own terms. Any kind of societal operation is better than none. The crisis creates the demand for a deliverer; it has been invariably the avenue to dictatorship. The ambitious man, the imperious hero, the savior, sizes up the situation and takes over. Dictatorships are not normal forms of societal operation, and dictators are not the kind of men who would be ruling under normal conditions. (97; 98)

Some Features of the Totalitarian System

The traits presented here do not occur in every dictatorship, but they recur so frequently as to constitute a fair pattern. There is *concentration of control,* almost complete regimentation of all social activities, and sharp opposition to democratic procedure, even though there may be some pretention along such lines. Parliaments must be abolished, hamstrung, or converted into dummies, for no dictatorial regime can withstand the loss of power that would result from being held responsible to a body of legislators. Government must be centralized as to authority, administration, decision, and the making of laws. The citizen disappears, and the individual inhabitant becomes the slave of the state.

There is *emphasis upon leadership and the tendency to symbolize, even deify, the dictator.* The "leadership principle" prevails in extreme form, and the incompetence of the masses is exaggerated. The leader is beyond human fallibility and frequently becomes an almost mystical symbol of authority and group greatness.

Dictatorships have always been characterized by the *use of force,* the inevitable army and semi-private police force, and an espionage system. The dictatorial regime dares not allow opposition to develop. Related to this are the *systematic use of terrorism and ruthlessness* by terroristic bands and in concentration camps and the threat of or actual summary execution of all who do not willingly submit. There has invariably been some variation of *the one-party system and always a manipulated judiciary,* both essential to carrying out without let and hindrance the policies of the regime.

A considerable number of dictators have emphasized *militant, even fanatical, idealistic objectives of a nationalistic or militaristic nature,* and in many cases they succeeded in converting these objectives into a secular religion. They also provide physical construction projects (rebuilding the Forum) that elicit adoration and love. All include in their programs ideals based on sublime and flattering national or racist hopes, and many depend upon real or fabricated rabid historical fervor and past glory. Such tactics drown out fears and sour memories, unify or lull discordant elements, and submerge all under waves of patriotic emotion.

Finally, dictatorial regimes *control public opinion, and all the agencies of education, information, communication, recreation, and, if possible, religion.* While they have always placed primary reliance upon military and police power, they have always also utilized all available agencies for holding the people from within by selecting the thought materials at their disposal, by shaping their convictions, by keeping constant control over their emotions, and filling their spare time with "safe pursuits." (100)

Typical Life Cycle of Dictatorships

Like other reorganizational procedures, a dictatorship is also a series of interlocked processes and sequences of action. The study by the present writer has revealed the following ideal-typical stages:

1. The period of chaos, depression, and governmental breakdown.
2. The preparation for power by the rising dictator or dictatorial party.
3. The thrust at power, the *coup d'état.*
4. The conquest or the revolution.
5. The entrenchment.
6. The decline.
7. The uprising and overthrow.

The whole cycle may occur in a relatively short time—in as brief a period as two or three years, or it may take as much as several centuries and include the rise and fall of a family (the Medici) or a dynasty. The study indicated an average duration of about sixteen years. After the collapse of a dictatorship or the overthrow of a series of dictatorships, there is usually a temporary reversion to the previous type of social-political control—a "restoration." If this does not work—and usually it does not, because the defects of the previous regime were partly responsible for the appearance of the dictatorship itself—there is a period of confusion until a new and more appropriate and adequate form of social organization is developed. (92, pp. 130-148; 96, pp. 8-21; 99; 105, pp. 581-582)

Effects of Dictatorship

An analytical examination reveals unmistakably the effects of this reorganizational phenomenon, good and bad, in terms of the general well-being of the people and the functional stability and health of the nation. On the credit side can be mentioned the fact that dictators do temporarily produce order. The imperious strong man does marshal men and events and social machinery with force and dispatch. There is also a temporary restoration of the morale of the population. Dictatorships occasionally bring about some cultural and material advance, part of which occasionally takes root.

The preponderant number of effects is on the debit side, however. Dictatorships are impermanent, and rarely are successors prepared to take over. The overcentralized regimental machine, under the necessity of quick and imperious action, provides no margin for compromise, no margin for experiment. Furthermore, the dictator cannot turn back, for to do so would be a confession of failure. Consequently, he is frequently run down by the juggernaut car of his own contriving. Dictatorships thus are inherently unstable and do not inspire abiding social health and popular confidence. Since all nonconformity is a crime, and all sources of information are controlled, there is moral and intellectual degradation of the populace. Also, the absolute power in a dictatorship is as corruptive to its holders as it is oppressive to its victims.

Frequently, the dictatorship may involve the nation in war, both as a means of refocusing slipping power and morale and as a defense against surrounding nations. Thus, finally, dictators prepare the way for future confusion and decline. Practically every dictator could say, "*Après moi le déluge*!" Fundamentally, totalitarianism is the most illusory and destructive of all of the specific forms of reorganization that men have resorted to historically. It is not a cure or even a remedy, but a harmful nostrum for the ills of a nation, one that tickles the palate and gives temporary exhilaration, but eventually produces debility and prostration. The price paid for dictatorship is great, and the bill must be paid.

Prospects of Scientific Societal Reorganization

There is good reason to think that we are on the threshold of a considerable degree of scientifically conceived, directed, and achieved societal reorganization. This reorganization would be on a higher level than has been achieved in most efforts to date, a level that will enable man to avoid much of the slow, blind drifting and the human and social expense of the automatic, natural adjustive processes, the partial and episodic palliatives, tricks, and frequent bungling of social-reform movements, the unevenness of laissez-faireism with its aggressive-competitive action of various uncoordinated special-interest groups.

Within the last few centuries men have grasped the idea that there is a possibility of controlling social change and directing it into desirable channels in some degree comparable to that control over physical and biological phenomena which is the glory and wonder of this age. Many have expressed this thought, especially since the middle of the eighteenth century, but it has been focused in the conception of "social telesis" by the American, Lester F. Ward. (163; 164; 165) By this he means the conscious, purposeful manipulation of social forces and processes in conformity with scientifically determined facts and principles and their direction toward equally rational, socially approved, and scientifically possible goals.

Social telesis is an artificial (in the sense of "artificed"), previsional, and calculated process. It consists of the utilization of all man's knowledge and experience regarding the physical universe, man's psychical nature, and social factors, structures, processes, and techniques in the most economical manner in order to produce societal self-direction and improvement. As Ward expressed it, such a procedure can be likened to the calculated course of an ocean liner as compared with the drifting of an iceberg.

Ward's view, which is increasingly that of many of our contemporaries, is opposed to that of fatalism, also still widely prevalent. It rests upon man's ability soberly to conceive possible but luminous goals, to profit by social experience, to engage in scientific research in ever-expanding areas of concern and interest, to amass tested facts and laws, to develop workable techniques, to assay trends and predict possibilities, and creatively and constructively to employ these elements for mastery—step by step, but a persistent step every time—for the sake of ever more effective and prosperous social living.

Social Planning

The contemporary forms of societal self-direction are referred to by the general term *social planning.* It is one of the most controversial and misunderstood of all subjects occupying the attention of both lay and professional students of modern society. Some look upon it as the grand panacea of our age; others think of it as a menace that will thrust upon us complete regimentation and the destruction of many of our most precious liberties. There are all shades of opinion between these extremes and much inconsistency, and frequently, there is more heat than light on all sides. However, since social planning embodies our best possibilities of rational, orderly, and progressive reorganization, it deserves an objective examination, a brief analytical synthesis of the best contemporary thought and practice.

Misuses of Social Planning. At the very outset it must be pointed out that social planning, like all other techniques and instrumentalities, can be used and has been used by all sorts of groups to further all sorts of objectives. Social planning is widely used by dictators and totalitarian regimes. In democracies it is resorted to by selfish but strategically situated groups and organizations, such as political machines, predatory unions or corporations, or vested interests generally. Most of the senseless blueprinting and ill-advised and precipitate action of so-called democratic groups have been planned in a sense, although many of these misadventures have been frantic efforts to "catch up with the procession" rather than considered and well-founded implementations of public needs and public opinion.

Nevertheless, planning is a fundamental characteristic of modern secondary-group societies which has come about as the result of the acceleration of determinable trends and is essential in some degree for the satisfaction of a host of needs. As Merriam put it, it is "doing what otherwise we could not do at all or could not do as well or as efficiently." (149) Throughout his history, man has relied on planning with greater or less success and on an ever-expanding scale. He has always acted with some anticipation of the future. It is an ancient and universal procedure, but also, in its present forms and scope, something very new.

Prevalence of Social Planning. Every successful, consciously pursued, individual, group, or societal occurrence is a matter of planning, whether it be the shaping of the first eolith or the garnering of the first harvest, the quarrying and transportation of materials and the construction of the first Egyptian pyramids, the engineering and military feats of the Roman Empire, or the activities of the great modern industrial and commercial corporations. In our time social planning has come to be one of the major formulas of joint action among primary and neighborhood groups, formal organizations, communities (rural, urban, or metropolitan), and of all manner of regional, national, and international enterprises.

> Planning . . . is not a political philosophy which can be accepted or rejected. It is a mode of exercising foresight in action and is indispensable to effective action in any walk of life. (145, p. 8)

Every business, every public enterprise, every special-interest association whatsoever has become a planning unit, and there is no likelihood of any abatement of social planning in the future. Obviously the question is not whether to plan, but rather the nature, extent, methods of establishing the projects, and procedures to be used in our society under fully democratic auspices.

Group Effort. By social planning is meant the effort of some group—increasingly one with political jurisdiction—to direct consciously and at an accelerated rate its development toward socially approved ends, by means of appropriate and efficient procedures and instruments. Social planning accepts the existing social order as its base and its point of departure. It admits that all is not well, but it insists that correction is a matter of careful diagnosis, timely and expert therapeutics, with occasional skillful surgery, rather than attempts at wholesale purging and amputation or emotion-charged, amateurish first aid. It is action with some anticipation of the future, a preventive and a building process over and above its mere ameliorative and corrective functions. It may take place in any, many, or all related departments of social life.

Planning in Our Society. In our own case we have unbelievable technical and industrial assets, highly developed educational institutions, numerous private, semiprivate and public constructive social activities, and we are the wealthiest nation in the world. Yet there is an increasing lack of equilibrium and balance. In modern industrial-urban secondary-group societies social life has become so complex and interdependent, so fundamentally important in satisfying almost every individual and group need, that it cannot depend on chance or spontaneous forces, and it is too complicated to be self-regulatory. Nor can it be left to anything less than the most efficient consciously devised and organized procedures. Modern man must organize and operate the involved mechanism that he has brought into being. Hence, many have come to realize that they cannot acquiesce in haphazard, partial, and inefficacious methods of doing the necessary things that vitally affect large numbers of us. The more difficult and complex the situation, the greater the need for timely, considered, and systematized action.

Therefore, we seek increasingly to create a more or less comprehensive design for action and attempt to guide and coordinate the forces that play upon us, knowing that we cannot repress or turn back trends that they produce, and knowing that many have vast constructive potentialities that should be utilized. We realize also that such a telic procedure should be continuous, flexible, coherent, and sufficiently comprehensive, for planning is a dynamic phenomenon and is based on the fact that no permanent, final, definitive, blanket solution of social problems can be found. It is always tentative, a flowing, growing procedure in which new experience is constantly enlarging the understanding of those concerned and increasing the adequacy of the means—one of continuous learning, manipulation, and adjustment. Planning is a long-range task. Hence, we cannot conceive of a definitely planned society on the basis of some universal formula or master blueprint that will be good for all time, but only of a continually planning and replanning society. It is an everlasting "organized foresight plus corrective hindsight." (130, p. 5)

The future will be achieved by deliberate, concerted, scientifically founded, guided, and organized human effort. Modern civilization has imposed on man the ordeal of practical planning. The conditions have changed and the time has passed when man can afford to muddle through. (142; 143)

Finally, by way of general orientation, it should be pointed out that social planning of sufficient scope and authority is almost of necessity under the auspices of government or actually conducted by various governmental agencies. Any planning by other agencies suffers the incompleteness and ineptitude, as far as essential well-being and reorganization are concerned, that are characteristic of social-reform movements. Owing to the division of labor and specialization of function, each scientist or scientific organization, each functional organization, each constructive agency works in its own narrow groove, helpless to contemplate the larger whole in its multiple perspectives and relationships. Government, despite its inadequacies, is the only body capable of an overview. Furthermore, as we have repeatedly noted, government is the only general institutional agency of any society that is established and maintained for the purpose of promoting the general values, of integrating all other institutions, and of planning and acting for the satisfaction of communal needs and the achievement of communal ends.

In a sense social planning epitomizes the entire analysis of this book. It involves all the dynamic factors operating in a society, all the existing structures, interdependencies, and relationships, all the essential functions, all the social processes both positive and negative, all the values, norms and goals, and all the techniques and mechanisms used in the manipulation of nature and of men.

Requisites of Social Planning

Limitations of space permit only a skeletal treatment of the widely and voluminously discussed essentials of social planning. The planning situations to which they relate are those widely prevalent in the United States, such as the conservation and utilization of natural resources (water, forests, land use, soil, river basin development, and so on), community planning (traffic and streets, slum clearance, health, housing, recreation, and so on), communication and transport, economic planning for production, distribution, and balance between production and consumption, population policies and procedures, educational planning, social security for various elements of the citizenry, planning relating to ethnic groups, planning of intercultural group cooperation, and so on. Typical planning operations range from those of local semipublic and public activities to those involving regions and the nation as a whole.

Knowledge and Research. Planning must be based upon a substantial body of the best data and principles that can be obtained through analysis and appraisal of conditions. Without this foundation, planning may easily become a matter of emotion, or belief, or surmise, or "loaded" opinion of special-interest or pressure groups. In this connection, adequate planning has been defined as "a process of work, involving fact-finding, fact-organizing, and fact-using for the purpose of formulating policies, designing appropriate methods, and integrating necessary behavior." (122)

The first essential is painstaking investigation and research, utilizing scientific methodology with its careful collecting and recording of the facts by experimentation and controlled observation, classification of facts, sober generalization, cautious interpretation, and continual verification. It is necessary to know what is wrong with the present adjustment and why and to determine and list the critical needs. A knowledge of causal factors—physical, psychological, social-psychological, and sociocultural—involved in every situation is required.

A careful inventory of past successes and failures and the reasons for each, in so far as they can be discovered by penetrating historical analysis of the types of social situations under consideration, should be made and there should also be an examination of both historical and contemporary trends. The nature and potentialities of the materials, energies, activities, and capabilities to be dealt with should be determined, including the numbers and characteristics of the people, the structuring and functioning especially of the political and economic power, the efficiency of the pertinent institutions and of the technology, the resources, natural and man-made, that are available for development and utilization. (132, pp. 165-166; 145, p. 9) Probabilities, feasibilities, costs and liabilities, and alternatives, as well as facilities, should be appraised and calculated as far as possible. All these facts, principles, and conclusions should be brought together in the order of their importance and relationship. They are the foundation for all other requisites.

Defined and Feasible Goals. A second basic essential in planning is the discovery and definition of what we are planning for at the moment. The determination of feasible goals rests upon the previously mentioned factual examination and is an expression of purposes in the optimum use of all resources for the rational functional integration of the group concerned. It is futile to plan without rather clearly defined and widely understood and accepted goals. Much of the failure and misfiring of our planning to date has been due to the lack of perception of the integral place of substantial goals in the process.

Specific Procedures. In planning it is necessary not only to have the facts and some indication of where we want to go, but also to know how to get there. A set of telic procedures, of ways and means of accomplishing the objectives, is essential. These fall into three closely related categories.

DECISIONS ON POLICY. A social policy is a specific formulation or statement of corrective, preventive, or constructive objectives to be pursued in the particular planning operation. It grows out of a comprehension of the needs that should be satisfied and the cause-and-effect facts that must be dealt with. It is founded upon the major social values and goals of the socially conscious group and consists of a specific adaptation of these to the specific social situation. In general, the broad policies governing planned action are best decided by all persons concerned or by their properly chosen representatives.

BUILDING A PROGRAM. A closely related aspect of the planning process is building the program of procedure. This consists of preparing creatively and in line with the policy the blueprint or design for the reorganization that is sought, drawing up the specifications of elements required, and setting the order to be followed. The task of building a program is one of determining *how* the resources and tools for the attainment of the goal can be marshaled, developed, and utilized and of determining *which* techniques are likely to be most appropriate in obtaining the release of the essential human and social energies and of coordinating them in a successful constructive enterprise.

The conflicts that invariably arise must be kept in mind, and modes of adjustment contrived; all the pertinent institutionalized organizations—scientific, governmental, economic, and so on—must be brought into the movement; educational and other informational procedures must be set up; and finally, the program must provide for the coordination of the efforts of these various groups and agencies. The actions recommended must be set in priority schedules of time. Concretely, this is usually done by program-making boards or councils.

SOCIAL ENGINEERING. Strictly speaking, social engineering is the actual execution of the policies and the programs of action. Its basis is social technology or applied social science, that is, the technical know-how and the use of techniques or methods for organized societal manipulation, control, and reconstruction, which in turn is based upon the established facts and principles of the social sciences. Social engineering is the task of technical and administrative experts and authorities who have special competence. It includes, for example, using ways and means of changing attitudes, beliefs, stereotypes, and convictions and thus developing appropriate, supporting public opinion and will; of bringing pressure to bear upon various groups and organizations, especially upon legislators and strategically located administrators in private, semipublic, and public bodies in order to obtain necessary legislation, revised organizational practices, and new procedures; of reorganizing social institutions and other social structures; and, in general, of deliberately manipulating a great variety of social energies, resources, and processes in order to reduce strife, inefficiency, and disequilibrium, and to increase cooperation, efficiency and peace. The tasks of social engineering are far more intricate and delicate, and also more massive, than any that confront civil or mechanical engineers.

Adequate Coordination of Efforts in the Various Social Fields. Incomplete, one-sided, unilateral planning produces lags and often creates less, rather than more, all-round well-being. Planning should be a multilateral, dovetailed procedure. The operations should be related and wide enough in scope to include major interdependent phases of social life. Planning for conservation, production, transportation, consumption, public works, public services, social security, housing, health, community development, recreation, and so on must be coordinated and unified. The planning for and by rural and urban local areas should be integrated with that of the state and the region, and, in turn, with that of the nation. In specific fields, for example, child labor, planning must be accompanied by educational and recreational planning if an increase in juvenile delinquency is to be avoided. Planning always involves extension from the narrower to the broader and the coordination of units. The evolving situation should be dealt with as a whole. This means not only interlocking planning boards and commissions ranging from local to nation wide in scope and authority, but a host of multipartisan interareal and interagency clearing, advisory, and cooperating arrangements.

Democratic Essentials. Social planning in a democratic society is a vastly different matter from that in a totalitarian system. When it is carried out according to democratic principles, it is a movement of, by, and for the people—a joint process of self-education, self-direction, and self-expression, rather than a forcible imposition of a system of control by the dictatorial power. Social planning is not general regimentation, for this is precisely what the democratic society is trying to avoid. Regimentation springs up only when democratic social planning is halted or is inadequate to meet the needs of the society. Social planning affects the people; its objectives must stem from them and be understood by them; its procedures involve them as participants and as beneficiaries; its disciplines are self-imposed. The layman, the technician, and the administrator have distinctive and necessary roles to play in the common reorganizational process.

CRITERION OF SOCIAL PLANNING. The well-being of the greatest number is the criterion of social planning. In a totalitarian set-up all planning and control are for the perpetuation of the party machine and the paranoiac individual at the apex of the hierarchy. The aim of democratic social planning, as of all democratic social action, is to provide the opportunity for the development, at an accelerated rate and on an ascending scale, of the largest number of persons with respect to resources, capacities, security, and the amenities of life. The general objective, of course, must be broken down into specific but compatible subobjectives for the various fields of endeavor. But the attention is focused on people as a whole and on widespread human needs and values; in brief, on a quality of existence for the citizens. There should be no promotion of segmental well-being unless in the long run it is consonant with the well-being of the whole.

CONSENT AND CONSENSUS OF THE MAJORITY. Planning should be based on the consent and consensus of the majority. In a democracy planning is a rational fulfillment of the people's desire. There must first be agreement that a cherished value demands attention and action. This comes about only through the processes of communication and decision, of getting together, talking over, and pooling ideas. The objectives should be worked out in the forum of the public affected. If planning is to be successful, it can go no further along any given line than the public majority decision is willing to allow. Even the police power in a democratic state is merely a grant of power to restrain or impel some in the interests of the majority. The broader the plan, the broader must be the favoring base of consensus and consent.

The willingness to accept planning along a given or a general line is expressed by petition, voting in a referendum, approval of party platforms or party accomplishments, or the granting of power by constitutional procedures. Only in such a manner can a socially satisfactory balance be effected between the essential regulation and coordination in the public interest and the rights of those whose interests and activities are affected. The public always participate in determining what is good, and the executing authority must be responsible and accountable to the bulk of the people. (129) In brief, it must stem from the "grass roots."

PRINCIPLE OF DISSEMINATION OF INFORMATION. Democratic procedures are a matter of direction from within, but this does not preclude informative efforts on the part of informed persons. In fact, the consent and consensus develop from the competition of ideas and the presentation of facts, objectives, and plans in the "market place," as Justice Holmes put it. Educational procedures and peaceful, honest persuasion and argument are fundamental in all democratic action. What occurs comes not by dictation or coercion, but by generally disseminated information.

PRINCIPLES OF REPRESENTATION AND DELEGATION OF AUTHORITY. Obviously, all citizens are not in a position to participate directly in all the processes of planning. Where large numbers of persons are involved, we use the principle of representation and assign to the representatives, who are sensitive to the majority will, the power to make all manner of general decisions. In highly specialized tasks of fact-finding, technical review, and administration, we delegate authority to experts and specialists. There is nothing in the democratic process which denies the right to use special skills at any stage in any field of its program of action. Planning objectives and procedures need not originate on the farm or in the street or with the average citizen, but they do need the approval of the people, and the representatives and technical and administrative specialists act as their servants, not their lords. Thus, democratic planning is a two-way process. One of its fundamental principles is interaction between authorized, experienced, and specialized experts and the sovereign people. (127)

MINIMAL ESSENTIALS. Planning should be confined to minimal essentials. Our society is an extremely complicated one, and planning is a difficult and complex process. Although we need vastly more efficient planning than we have, not everything must or should be planned. If only those aspects of social life most pertinently and drastically in need of foresight and cooperative reorganization are planned, a relatively limited though strategic number of segments of life will be subjected to it.

STEP-BY-STEP PROCESS. Planning should be a step-by-step process. In a democracy it cannot be a process of arbitrarily establishing the visionary, completed, master blueprints of utopians or totalitarians, nor is it brought about by some social magic. It is necessary to start with things as they are and deal first with the most pertinent problems. The plans cannot be projected too far into the future, for, with the rapidity and volume of social change, they will be outmoded at an early date and cause confusion and discouragement. Furthermore, the plans must be confined to possibilities of action; otherwise, the planners lose the people's confidence. Each step of the process in advance should develop out of preceding step, and each step should be a matter of fractional improvements and temporary adjustments as experience increases. Experimentation on a small scale is desirable before there is wide application of principles. It is better to build with tested materials and procedures than to risk endangering the whole social edifice. In addition, we need continually to rebuild and rearrange elements. For all this we need learning, time, techniques, and patience.

The observance of such democratic essentials makes planning slower, more cumbersome, more expensive, and far more complicated than totalitarian planning; but it also makes it far more secure and durable.

Possibilities of Adequate Social Planning

What are the possibilities of social planning on an adequate, scientific basis in the United States? Let us attempt a brief inventory of factors pro and con.

Pro Factors. First, we are in some respects in a better position than any other people to plan on the scale that is essential today. We have great developed wealth and vast potential wealth; we have made stupendous advances in invention and technological development and developed a tremendous productive capacity. (126) This means that the economic and social position of all the population can be improved without lowering that of any segment of it. It means also that hoarding, or a scraping economy (the resort to *ersatz*), is unnecessary. In brief, we have a broad, sound economic base and a wide margin of safety and security on the physical side which permits experimentation and even some temporary mistakes in planning without greatly endangering general well-being.

Second, social planning among us is not a "shot in the dark." We have behind us a great array of examples of private and public planning that were both practical and successful. These have ranged from small-scale tasks to great, multiform operations on a nation-wide scale and have given us much useful experience in the development of social policies, the organization of social programs, and the fulfillment of these through forms of social engineering. Furthermore, we have an enormous amount of planning—economic, social, political, community—on local, regional, and national levels actually in process. Much of this only needs to be brought into equilibrium in more comprehensive design and practice.

Third, we have a considerable body of physical and social scientific knowledge, the literacy, education, and the other cultural institutions necessary to develop the capacity and will, and the technical means for planning on an expanding scale. We have much knowledge of historical processes as completed experiments. The social sciences, with their data regarding factors, processes, and structures have developed to the point where they can be of considerable assistance, and social research is developing ever-better methodologies and thus a growing body of verified social theory. Social inventory is a more accurate and a more persistent process than ever before; knowledge is more widely diffused among all population elements; and there are improved means of bringing social facts and principles before the public. We are also an alert, literate, and educable people, accustomed to change in many spheres of life and having some flexibility in accepting new facts and ideas, especially if they have some relation to the expanded well-being of the populace. Classes are more open and the movement of ideas and persons is relatively free.

Con Factors. There are human, social, and scientific limitations and difficulties in planning. First, many persons are unable to comprehend the necessity for, and the implications of, planning in our age. They fail to grasp the fact that planning is the method or means and not the end, that it is not an esoteric, academic preoccupation or an attempt at domination by experts or politicians, but a sternly necessary procedure in avoiding chaos. Akin to this is the informational lag among many classes, that is, the inability to grasp the full implications of complex, interrelated, artificed modern society. Many persons still regard the world through the narrow windows of primary or special-interest groups and assume that if each one as an individual or as a member of a special group goes his own way and minds his own business all will be well.

Second, there are the limitations of human nature. There is the tendency to act unsocially for individual gain or for our own little in-group, while at the same time admitting rationally the value and necessity of the opposite action. People are likely to be emotional in a social situation and to do the habitual or the customary thing rather than the rational or social-scientific thing. Planning is "an uphill pull," and people tire from the sustained and integrated effort that is necessary. There is much resistance to what are admittedly the incredibly complex processes and requirements of planning.

Third, there are the difficulties imposed by vested interests and pressure groups. Groups with vested interests in the *status in quo* and traditionalism, especially in religion, industry, professions, constitutionalism and State rights, private property, and institutionalism in general, as well as pressure groups of all kinds—business, labor, agriculture, political parties, and so on—resist the larger efforts at well-being at the moment, in spite of the fact that they would all be primary beneficiaries in the long run. In fact, the inability or unwillingness to take the long-run point of view is in itself one of the supreme difficulties.

Fourth, there are the limitations of social and political jurisdiction. Successful planning always implies an equilibrium between private, nonpolitical social forces and agencies and those of a local, state, regional, and national political nature, as well as the development of effective working relationships between the various political jurisdictions themselves. The state is the indispensable final agent in planning. At the same time, the will, the willingness, and much of the effort must stem from the people themselves. There is always the danger of too much state, and when the state takes over, individual and group efforts tend to relax.

There is also the inadequacy of many of our politically constituted agencies to participate in effective planning. Government as now constituted is not an engineering job of getting a clearly conceived task done with the greatest economy of energy and expense, and with the utilization of established scientific principles and procedures. The successful politician satisfies popular, momentary desires. Furthermore, many administrative officers have relatively short terms and there is no carry-over, whereas most planning in its very nature must be continuous and of long duration. At the same time, where there is continuity there is the danger of most of the evils of formalism or institutionalism.

Finally, there are the admitted, though correctible, inadequacies of the social sciences themselves. They are still in a relatively nascent stage. Much more and much better scientific knowledge is needed. Much of the experience and knowledge that we do have has not been systematically inventoried, reviewed, and codified. There are serious deficiencies in contemporary social-science research. New and more adequate techniques need to be developed. Social research needs to be developed in universities, governmental and business units, and specialized research agencies and research liaison between all the investigative agencies should be effected. Social-scientific research needs adequate financial support. The lack of familiarity with established social-scientific knowledge and the misuse of it need to be corrected. Finally, it may be pointed out that the social scientists themselves have been rather ineffective in advertising and pushing their very considerable body of theory and the products of their research.

It cannot be gainsaid, however, that there is in a sense a race between the development, acceptance, and application of social-scientific knowledge and the threat of great social loss, retardation, even catastrophe.*

*For an elaboration of these and many other relevant points in connection with the utilization of social theory and the products of social research, see references 171 to 198.

REFERENCES

Periodical Abbreviations

In order to save space in listing the extensive references, most of the periodicals have been abbreviated. The following list shows both abbreviated and full forms.

Amer. Anthrop.	American Anthropologist
Amer. econ. Rev.	American Economic Review
Amer. J. Econ. Sociol.	American Journal of Economics and Sociology
Amer. J. Sociol.	American Journal of Sociology
Amer. polit. Sci. Rev.	American Political Science Review
Amer. sociol. Rev.	American Sociological Review
Ann. Amer. Acad. polit. soc. Sci.	Annals of the American Academy of Political and Social Science
Ann. Ass. Amer. Geog.	Annals of the Association of American Geographers
Brit. J. Sociol.	British Journal of Sociology
Bull. Amer. Ass. Univ. Prof.	Bulletin of the American Association of University Professors
Canad. J. Econ. polit. Sci.	Canadian Journal of Economics and Political Science
Comp. Psychol. Monog.	Comparative Psychology Monographs
Curr. Hist.	Current History
Elem. Sch. J.	Elementary School Journal
Fortnightly Rev.	Fortnightly Review
Hum. Relat.	Human Relations
Int. J. Ethics	International Journal of Ethics
J. abnorm. soc. Psychol.	Journal of Abnormal and Social Psychology
J. Amer. Folklore	Journal of American Folklore
J. Amer. statist. Ass.	Journal of the American Statistical Association
J. Business Univ. Chicago	Journal of Business of the University of Chicago
J. comp. physiol. Psychol.	Journal of Comparative and Physiological Psychology
J. educ. Sociol.	Journal of Educational Sociology
J. Farm Econ.	Journal of Farm Economics
J. Hered.	Journal of Heredity
J. legal polit. Sociol.	Journal of Legal and Political Sociology
J. Phil.	Journal of Philosophy
J. royal statist. Soc.	Journal of the Royal Statistical Society
J. soc. Issues	Journal of Social Issues
J. soc. Psychol.	Journal of Social Psychology
Milbank mem. Fund Quart.	Milbank Memorial Fund Quarterly
Pedagog. Sem.	Pedagogical Seminar
Phil. Sci.	Philosophy of Science
Plan. Age	Planning Age
Popul. Bull.	Population Bulletin
Proc. Amer. philos. Soc.	Proceedings of the American Philosophical Society
Proc. Pacific sociol. Soc.	Proceedings of the Pacific Sociological Society
Psychol. Bull.	Psychological Bulletin
Psychol. Rev.	Psychological Review
Pubs. Amer. sociol. Soc.	Publications of the American Sociological Society
Quart. J. Econ.	Quarterly Journal of Economics
Rur. Sociol.	Rural Sociology
Sci. Mon., N. Y.	Scientific Monthly
Soc. Forces	Social Forces
Soc. Sci.	Social Science
Sociol. Rev. Brit.	Sociological Review (published in Britain)
Sociol. soc. Res.	Sociological and Social Research
Sth. Atl. Quart.	South Atlantic Quarterly
Sth. Econ. J.	Southern Economics Journal
Sthwest. soc. Sci. Quart.	Southwestern Social Science Quarterly
Technol. Rev.	Technological Review

References

I. Human Society as a Going Concern

Structural-Functional-Processual Analysis

1. Bennett, J. W., and M. M. Tumin, *Social Life: Structure and Function* (New York: Knopf, 1948), pp. 63-85.
2. Giddings, F. H., *The Scientific Study of Human Society* (Chapel Hill: Univ. North Carolina Press, 1924), pp. 1-22.
3. Kallen, H., "Functionalism," *Encyclopedia of the Social Sciences* (New York: Macmillan, 1931), Vol. 6, pp. 523-525.
4. Malinowski, B., *A Scientific Theory of Culture* (Chapel Hill: Univ. North Carolina Press, 1945), pp. 147-176.
5. Merton, R. K., *Social Theory and Social Structure* (Glencoe, Ill.: Free Press, 1949), pp. 21-81.
6. Parsons, T., Introduction, in Max Weber, *The Theory of Social and Economic Organization* (A. M. Henderson and T. Parsons, trans.) (New York: Oxford, 1947), pp. 18-24.
7. ———, "The Position of Sociological Theory," *Amer. sociol. Rev.*, 13 (Apr., 1948), 156-164; or in T. Parsons, *Essays in Sociological Theory* (Glencoe, Ill.: Fress Press, 1949), pp. 4-14.
8. ———, *The Social System* (Glencoe, Ill.: Free Press, 1951), pp. 3-23.
9. Phelps, H. A., *Principles and Laws of Sociology* (New York: Wiley, 1936), pp. 32-56.
10. Radcliffe-Brown, A. R., "On the Concept of Function in Social Science," *Amer. Anthrop*, 37 (July-Sept., 1935), 394-402.
11. Williams, R. M., Jr., *American Society: A Sociological Interpretation* (New York: Knopf, 1951), p. 445.

Factors in the Situation and Factor Analysis

12. Carr, L. J., *Situational Analysis* (New York: Harper, 1948), pp. xi, xiii, 1-7.
13. ———, "Situational Sociology," *Amer. J. Sociol.*, 51 (Sept., 1945), 136-144.
14. Cattell, R. B., *Factor Analysis: An Introduction and Manual for the Psychologist and Social Scientist* (New York: Harper, 1952).
15. Chapin, F. S., *Experimental Designs for Sociological Research* (New York: Harper, 1947), pp. 140-141.
16. Furfey, P. H., and J. F. Daly, "A Criticism of Factor Analysis as a Technique of Social Research," *Amer. sociol. Rev.*, 2 (Apr., 1937), 178-186.
17. Holzinger, H. J., and H. H. Harman, *Factor Analysis* (Chicago: Univ. Chicago Press), 1941.
18. Lewin, K., "Field Theory and Experiment in Social Psychology: Concepts and Methods," *Amer. J. Sociol.*, 44 (May, 1939), 868-896.
19. ———, *Field Theory in Social Science* (D. Cartwright, ed.) (New York: Harper, 1951).
20. MacIver, R. M., *Social Causation* (Boston: Ginn, 1942).
21. ———, and C. H. Page, *Society: An Introductory Analysis* (New York: Rinehart, 1949), pp. 626-630.
22. Price, D. O., "Factor Analysis in the Study of Metropolitan Centers," *Soc. Forces*, 20 (May, 1942), 449-455.
23. Sorokin, P. A., *Sociocultural Causality, Space, Time* (Durham, N.C.: Duke Univ. Press, 1943), pp. 38-96.
24. Thurstone, L. L., *Multiple-Factor Analysis* (Chicago: Univ. Chicago Press, 1947).

Social Processes: Their Importance in Sociological Theory and Analysis; Critical Treatments

25. Bain, R., "The Concept of Social Process," *Pubs. Amer. sociol., Soc.*, 26 (Aug., 1932), 10-18. 10-18.
26. Case, C. M., "Scholarship in Sociology," *Sociol. soc. Res.*, 12 (Mar.-Apr., 1928), 323-340.
27. Eubank, E. E., "Social Processes and Their

Accompanying Relationships," *Pubs. Amer. sociol. Soc.*, 26 (Aug., 1932), 44-54.

28. Hayes, E. C., "Social Process, Social Relation, and Social Structure: A Vital Distinction," *Sociol. soc. Res.*, 12 (May-June, 1928), 403-410.
29. Lundberg, G. A., *Foundations of Sociology*, (New York: Macmillan, 1939), pp. 244-280.
30. Mihanovich, C. S., "Social Processes according to Von Wiese," *Sociol. Rev. Brit.*, 37 (Jan.-Oct., 1945), 1-9.
31. Reuter, E. B., "The Problem of Sociology," *Sociol. soc. Res.*, 13 (Nov.-Dec., 1928), 118-132.
32. Small, A. W., "The Category 'Human Process'—A Methodological Note," *Amer. J. Sociol.*, 28 (Sept., 1922), 205-227.
33. Sorokin, P. A., *Social and Cultural Dynamics* (New York: American Book, 1937), I, 153-191.
34. Sutherland, E. H., "The Biological and Social Processes," *Amer. J. Sociol.*, 32 (July, 1926, pt. 2), 58-65.
35. Thomas, W. I., and Znaniecki, F., *The Polish Peasant in Europe and America* (New York: Knopf, 1927), I, 36-38.
36. Wiese, L. von, "Systematic Sociology as the Science of Interhuman Behavior," *Sociol. soc. Res.*, 15 (Nov.-Dec., 1930), 103-115.
37. Znaniecki, F., "The Analysis of Social Processes," *Pubs. Amer. sociol. Soc.*, 26 (Aug., 1932), 37-43.
38. ———, *The Method of Sociology* (New York: Farrar and Rinehart, 1934), pp. 319-331.

Classic Treatments of Social Processes

39. Cooley, C. H., *Social Process* (New York: Scribner, 1918).
40. Eubank, E. E., *Concepts of Sociology* (Boston: Heath, 1932), pp. 261-330.
41. Park, R. E., and E. W. Burgess, *Introduction to the Science of Sociology* (Chicago: Univ. Chicago Press, 1921), pp. 226-272, 339-434, 505-852.
42. Ross, E. A., *Foundations of Sociology* (New York: Macmillan, 1905), pp. 98, 149-255.
43. ———, *Principles of Sociology* (New York: Appleton-Century-Crofts, 1938).
44. Small, A. W., *General Sociology* (Chicago: Univ. Chicago Press, 1905).
45. Wiese, L. von, and H. Becker, *Systematic Sociology* (New York: Wiley, 1932). A translation with supplement by Becker of L. von Wiese, *System der Algemeine Soziologie* (Leipzig: Duncker and Humblot, I, 1924; II, 1929; 1-vol. ed., 1931).

II. Societal Life and Modern Human Society

Societal Life and Its Salient Characteristics

1. Davis, K., *Human Society* (New York: Macmillan, 1949), pp. 24-31.
2. Giddings, F. H., *Civilization and Society* (New York: Holt, 1932), pp. 31-35, 246-262.
3. Hiller, E. T., *Social Relations and Structures* (New York: Harper, 1947), pp. 650-670.
4. Jennings, H. S., "The Transition from the Individual to the Social Level," *Biological Symposia* (Lancaster, Pa.: Science Press, 1942), Vol. 8, pp. 105-119.
5. Linton, R., *The Cultural Background of Personality* (New York: Appleton-Century, 1945), pp. 5-18, 55-73.
6. Malinowski, B., "The Group and the Individual in Functional Analysis," *Amer. J. Sociol.*, 44 (May, 1939), 938-964.
7. Murdock, G. P., "Anthropology and Human Relations," *Sociometry*, 4 (May, 1941), 140-149.
8. Znaniecki, F., "Social Organization and Institutions," in G. Gurvitch and W. E. Moore (eds.), *Twentieth Century Sociology* (New York: Philosophical Library, 1945), pp. 172-217.

Primary Functions of a Society

9. Aberle, D. F., A. K. Cohen, A. K. Davis, M. J. Levy, Jr., and F. X. Sutton, "The Functional Prerequisites of a Society," *Ethics*, 60 (Jan., 1950), 100-110.
10. Bennett, J. W., and M. M. Tumin, *Social Life: Structure and Function* (New York: Knopf, 1948), pp. 40-57, 197-203.
11. Faris, R. E. L., *Social Disorganization* (New York: Ronald, 1948), pp. 4-7.
12. Linton, R., "Present World Conditions in Cultural Perspective," in R. Linton (ed.), *The Science of Man in the World Crisis* (New York: Columbia Univ. Press, 1945), pp. 203-206.
13. ———, *The Study of Man* (New York: Appleton-Century, 1936), pp. 401-421.
14. Murdock, G. P., "The Common Denominator

of Cultures," in R. Linton (ed.), *The Science of Man in the World Crisis* (New York: Columbia Univ. Press, 1945), pp. 123-142.
15. Parsons, T., *The Social System* (Glencoe, Ill.: Free Press, 1951), pp. 26-36.

Human Societies and Animal Societies

16. Allee, W. C., *Animal Aggregations* (Chicago: Univ. Chicago Press, 1931).
17. ———, *Animal Life and Social Growth* (Baltimore: Williams & Wilkins, 1932).
18. ———, *Cooperation among Animals* (New York: Schuman, 1951).
19. ———, "Social Biology of Subhuman Groups," *Sociometry*, 8 (Feb., 1945), 21-29.
20. ———, *The Social Life of Animals* (New York: Norton, 1938).
21. Allport, F. H., *Social Psychology* (Boston: Houghton Mifflin, 1924), pp. 154-167.
22. Alverdes, F., *Social Life in the Animal World* (New York: Harcourt, Brace, 1927).
23. ———, "The Behavior of Mammalian Herds and Packs," in C. Murchison (ed.), *A Handbook of Social Psychology* (Worcester: Clark Univ. Press, 1935), pp. 185-206.
24. Carpenter, C. R., "A Field Study of the Behavior and Social Relations of Howling Monkeys," *Comp. Psychol. Monog.*, 2 (No. 2, 1934), 1-168.
25. ———, "A Field Study in Siam of the Behavior and Social Relations of the Gibbon," *Comp. Psychol. Monog.*, 16 (Nov., 1940), 1-212.
26. ———, "Concepts and Problems of Primate Sociometry," *Sociometry*, 8 (Feb., 1945), 56-61.
27. ———, "Sexual Behavior of Free Ranging Rhesus Monkeys," *J. comp. physiol. Psychol.*, 33 (No. 1, 1942), 113-162.
28. ———, "Societies of Monkeys and Apes," in *Biological Symposia* (Lancaster, Pa.: Science Press, 1942), Vol. 8, pp. 174-204.
29. Case, C. M., "Culture as a Distinctive Human Trait," *Amer. J. Sociol.*, 32 (May, 1927), 906-920.
30. Davis, K., *Human Society* (New York: Macmillan, 1949), pp. 31-50.
31. Forel, A., *The Social World of Ants* (New York: Putnam, 1928).
32. Freitas Marcondes, J. V., and T. L. Smith, "The Caipira of the Paraitinga Valley, Brazil," *Soc. Forces*, 31 (Oct., 1952), 47-53.
33. Friedman, H., "Bird Societies," in C. Murchison (ed.), *A Handbook of Social Psychology* (Worcester: Clark Univ. Press, 1935), pp. 142-150.
34. Gillin, J. L., and J. P. Gillin, *Cultural Sociology* (New York: Macmillan, 1948), pp. 34-43.
35. Haskins, C. P., *Of Societies and Men* (New York: Norton, 1951).
36. Hooton, E., *Man's Poor Relations* (New York: Doubleday, 1942), pp. 1-412.
37. Jennings, H. S., "Social Life and Interrelationships in Certain Protozoa, *Sociometry*, 8 (Feb., 1945), 9-20.
38. ———, *The Beginnings of Social Behavior in Unicellular Organisms* (Philadelphia: Univ. Pennsylvania Press, 1940).
39. Michener, C., and M. H. Michener, *American Social Insects: A Book about Bees, Ants, Wasps, and Termites* (New York: Van Nostrand, 1952).
40. Plath, A. E., "Insect Societies," in C. Murchison (ed.), *A Handbook of Social Psychology* (Worcester: Clark Univ. Press, 1935), pp. 83-141.
41. Scott, J. P., 'Group Formation Determined by Social Behavior: A Comparative Study of Two Mammalian Societies," *Sociometry*, 8 (Feb., 1945), 42-52.
42. Wheeler, W. M., *Social Life among the Insects* (New York: Harcourt, Brace, 1923).
43. ———, *The Social Insects* (New York: Harcourt, Brace, 1928).
44. White, L. A., "Energy and the Evolution of Culture," *Amer. Anthrop.*, 45 (July-Sept., 1943), 335-356.
45. ———, "The Symbol: The Origin and Basis of Human Behavior," *Phil. Sci.*, 5 (Oct., 1938), 369-389.
46. Yerkes, R. M., *Almost Human* (New York: Century, 1923).
47. ———, and A. W. Yerkes, *The Great Apes* (New Haven: Yale Univ. Press, 1929).
48. Zuckerman, S., *The Social Life of Monkeys and Apes* (London: Kegan Paul, Trench & Trubner, 1932).

Complexity of Human Societies

49. Becker, H., "Sacred and Secular Societies: Considered with Reference to Folk-state and Similar Classifications," *Soc. Forces*, 28 (May, 1950), 361-376.
50. ———, *Through Values to Social Interpretation* (Durham, N.C.: Duke Univ. Press, 1950), pp. 248-280.
51. ———, and R. C. Myers, "Sacred and Secular Aspects of Human Sociation," Parts I, II,

Sociometry, 5 (Aug., 1942), 207-229; Parts III, IV, *Sociometry*, 5 (Nov., 1942), 355-370.
52. Durkheim, E., *Le Suicide* (Paris: Alcan, 1930), Bk. II, Chap. 5, Sec. 1.
53. LaPiere, R. T., *Sociology* (New York: McGraw-Hill, 1947), pp. 176-181.
54. Loomis, C. P., "The Nature of Rural Social Systems—A Typological Analysis," *Rural Sociol.*, 15 (June, 1950), 156-174.
55. ———, and J. A. Beegel, *Rural Social Systems* (New York: Prentice-Hall, 1953), Chap. I.
56. Simpson, G., *Emile Durkheim on the Division of Labor* (New York: Macmillan, 1933).
57. Toennies, F., *Fundamental Concepts of Sociology* (C. P. Loomis, trans.) (New York: American Book, 1940).

The Folk-Agrarian Society: Theoretical Essentials

58. Becker, H., *Through Values to Social Interpretation* (Durham, N.C.: Duke Univ. Press, 1950), pp. 45-57, 66-92.
59. Boskoff, A., "Structure, Function, and Folk Society," *Amer. sociol. Rev.*, 14 (Dec., 1949), 749-758.
60. Davis, A. K., "Conflict between Major Social Systems," *Soc. Forces*, 30 (Oct., 1951), 29-36.
61. Firth, R., *Primitive Polynesian Economy* (London: Routledge & Kegan Paul, 1939).
62. ———, *We, the Tikopia* (London: Allen & Unwin, 1936).
63. Freedman, R., A. H. Hawley, W. Landecker, and H. Miner, *Principles of Sociology* (New York: Holt, 1952), pp. 255, 266-272.
64. Lewis, O., *Life in a Mexican Village: Tepoztlan Restudied* (Urbana: Univ. Illinois Press, 1951).
65. Miner, H., "The Folk-Urban Continuum," *Amer. sociol. Rev.*, 17 (Oct., 1952), 529-537.
66. Redfield, R., *Tepoztlan, A Mexican Village* (Chicago: Univ. Chicago Press, 1930).
67. ———, *A Village That Chose Progress, Chan Kom Revisited* (Chicago: Univ. Chicago Press, 1950).
68. ———, *The Folk Culture of Yucatan* (Chicago: Univ. Chicago Press, 1941), Chap. 1.
69. ———, "The Folk Society and Culture," *Amer. J. Sociol.* 45 (Mar., 1940), 731-742.
70. Tax, Sol, "Culture and Civilization in Guatemalan Societies," *Sci. Mon., N.Y.*, 48 (May, 1939), 467ff.

For specific descriptions of folk-agrarian societies, see the copious literature of anthropology on primitive societies. For example, R. Linton, *The Study of Man* (New York: Appleton-Century, 1936), pp. 491-494, lists some fifty studies of such societies.

Industrialization: Essential Features and Societal Effects

71. Brozen, Yale, *Social Implications of Technological Change* (New York: Social Science Research Council, 1950).
72. Chapple, E. D., and C. S. Coon, *Principles of Anthropology* (New York: Holt, 1942), pp. 138-140, 223-249.
73. Cole, G. D. H., "Industrialism," *Encyclopedia of the Social Sciences* (New York: Macmillan, 1932), Vol. 8, pp. 18-26.
74. Drucker, P., *The Future of Industrial Man* (New York: Day, 1942), pp. 74-112.
75. Gillin, J. P., *The Ways of Men* (New York: Appleton-Century, 1948), pp. 357-368.
76. Heberle, R., "Social Consequences of the Industrialization of Southern Cities," *Soc. Forces*, 27 (Oct., 1948), 29-37.
77. Mayo, E., *Human Problems of an Industrial Civilization* (New York: Macmillan, 1933).
78. Meadows, P., "Culture Theory and Industrial Analysis," (*Ann. Amer. Acad. polit. soc. Sci.*, 274 (Mar., 1951), 9-16.
79. ———, *The Culture of Industrial Man* (Lincoln: Univ. Nebraska Press, 1950).
80. ———, "The Industrial Way of Life," *Technol. Rev.*, 48 (Mar., 1946), 285-288, 312.
81. ———, "The Motivations of Industrial Man," *Amer. J. Econ. Sociol.*, 6 (Apr., 1947), 363-370.
82. Moore, W. E., "Theoretical Aspects of Industrialization," *Sociol. soc. Res.*, 15 (Sept., 1948), 277-302.
83. Ogburn, W. F., "How Technology Changes Society," *Sociol. soc. Res.*, 36 (Nov.-Dec., 1951), 75-83.
84. Phelps, H. A., *Principles and Laws of Sociology* (New York: Wiley, 1936), pp. 283-301.
85. Weber, M., *The Theory of Social and Economic Organization* (T. Parsons, ed.) (New York: Oxford, 1947).

Urbanization: Essential Features and Societal Effects

86. Barnes, H. E., *Society in Transition* (New York: Prentice-Hall, 1939), pp. 485-496.
87. Bennett and Tumin, *op. cit.*, 418-451.
88. Freedman, *et al.*, *op. cit.*, pp. 360-374, 411-424, 489-503.

89. Hatt, P. K., and A. J. Reiss, Jr. (eds.), *Reader in Urban Sociology* (Glencoe, Ill.: Free Press, 1951), pp. 127-219.
90. Hoyt, Homer, "Forces of Urban Centralization and Decentralization," *Amer. J. Sociol.*, 46 (May, 1941), 843-852.
91. Meyer, J., "The Stranger and the City," *Amer. J. Sociol.*, 56 (Mar., 1951), 476-483.
92. Mumford, L., *The Culture of Cities* (New York: Harcourt, Brace, 1938).
93. *Our Cities: Their Role in the National Economy* (Washington: Nat. Resources Commission, 1937), pp. 29-41.
94. Phelps, *op. cit.*, pp. 261-282.
95. Thompson, W. S., "Urbanization," *Encyclopedia of the Social Sciences* (New York: Macmillan, 1931), Vol. 5, pp. 189-192.
96. Tisdale, H., "The Process of Urbanization," *Soc. Forces*, 20 (Mar., 1942), 311-316.
97. Turner, R. E., *The Great Cultural Traditions* (New York: McGraw-Hill, 1941), Vol. 2, pp. 1289-1333.
98. Wirth, L., "Urbanism as a Way of Life," *Am. Jour. Soc.*, 44 (July, 1938), 1-24.

The Characteristics of a Modern Complex Society

99. Becker, *Through Values to Social Interpretation, op. cit.*, pp. 46-57, 66-92.
100. Davis, A. K., *op. cit.*
101. Davis, K., *op. cit.*, pp. 24-51, 329-336.
102. De Gracia, S., *The Political Community: A Study of Anomie* (Chicago: Univ. Chicago Press, 1948).
103. Drucker, P., "The New Society: Revolution by Mass Production," *Harper's*, 199 (Sept., 1949), 21-29.
104. Frank, L. K., "Man's Multidimensional Environment," *Sci. Mon., N.Y.*, 56 (Apr., 1943), 344-357.
105. Hiller, *op. cit.*, pp. 650-672.
106. Landis, P. H., *Social Control: Social Organization and Disorganization in Process* (Philadelphia: Lippincott, 1939), pp. 151-208.
107. Mannheim, K., *Man and Society in an Age of Reconstruction* (New York: Harcourt, Brace, 1940).
108. Markey, J. F., *The Symbolic Process and Its Integration in Children* (New York: Harcourt, Brace, 1928).
109. Meadows, P., "An Age of Mass Communication," *Psychiatry*, 10 (Nov., 1947), 405-411.
110. Merton, R. K., *Social Theory and Social Structure* (Glencoe, Ill.: Free Press, 1949), pp. 125-149.
111. Miller, D. C., and W. H. Form, *Industrial Sociology* (New York: Harper, 1951), pp. 829-858.
112. Park, R. E., "Modern Society," *Biological Symposia* (Lancaster, Pa.: Science Press, 1942), Vol. 8, pp. 217-240.
113. Rogers, M., "The Group Approach to Community Organization," *Sociometry*, 5 (Aug., 1942), 251-257.
114. White, L. A., "The Symbol: The Origin and Bases of Human Behavior," *Phil. Sci.*, 5 (Oct., 1938), 369-389.
115. Williams, R. M., Jr., *American Society: A Sociological Interpretation* (New York: Knopf, 1951), pp. 449-461, 532-538.
116. Wirth, L., "Consensus and Mass Communication," *Amer. sociol. Rev.*, 13 (Feb., 1948), 1-15.
117. Wood, M. M., *The Stranger: A Study of Social Relationships* (New York: Columbia Univ. Press, 1934), pp. 221-242.
118. Young, K., *Sociology: A Study of Society and Culture* (New York: American Book, 1949), pp. 17-28.

III. The Ever-Changing Scene: Fundamental Considerations

Social Change

1. Becker, H., *Through Values to Social Interpretation* (Durham, N.C.: Duke Univ. Press, 1950), pp. 175-178.
2. Chapin, F. S., "A Theory of Synchronous Culture Cycles," *Soc. Forces*, 3 (May, 1925), 596-605.
3. Davis, K., *Human Society* (New York: Macmillan, 1949), pp. 621-636.
4. Freedman, R., A. H. Hawley, W. Landecker, and H. Miner, *Principles of Sociology* (New York: Holt, 1952), pp. 312-315, 323-324, 329-330, 554-560.
5. Ginsberg, M., "The Conception of Stages in Social Evolution," *Man*, 32 (Apr., 1922), 87-91.
6. ———, *Reason and Unreason in Society* (London: Longmans, Green, 1947), pp. 27-34.
7. Goldenweiser, A. A., "Leading Contributions of Anthropology to Social Theory," in H. E. Barnes, H. Becker, and F. B. Becker, *Contemporary Social Theory* (New York: Appleton-Century, 1940), pp. 433-453.
8. ———, "Social Evolution," *Encyclopedia of the*

Social Sciences (New York: Macmillan, 1931), V, 656-662.
9. Hawley, A. H., *Human Ecology* (New York: Ronald, 1950), pp. 319-323.
10. MacIver, R. M., and C. H. Page, *Society: An Introductory Analysis* (New York: Rinehart, 1949), pp. 509-635.
11. Ogburn, W. F., "Change, Social," *Encyclopedia of the Social Sciences* (New York: Macmillan, 1930), Vol. 3, 330-334.
12. ———, "How Technology Changes Society," *Sociol. soc. Res.*, 36 (Nov.-Dec., 1951), 75-83.
13. ———, *Social Change* (New York: Viking, 1950).
14. ———, *The Social Effects of Aviation* (Boston: Houghton Mifflin, 1946).
15. Parsons, T., *The Social System* (Glencoe, Ill.: Free Press, 1951), pp. 487-503.
16. ———, and E. A. Shils, *Toward a General Theory of Action* (Cambridge: Harvard Univ. Press, 1951), pp. 23-233.
17. Phelps, H. A., *Principles and Laws of Sociology* (New York: Wiley, 1936), pp. 386-406.
18. Sims, N. L., *The Problem of Social Change* (New York: Crowell, 1939).
19. Sorokin, P. A., 'A Survey of the Cyclical Conceptions of Social and Historical Process," *Soc. Forces*, 6 (Sept., 1927), 28-40.
20. ———, *Social and Cultural Dynamics* (New York: American Book, 1937-1941), 4 vols.
21. ———, *Social Philosophy in an Age of Crisis* (Boston: Beacon, 1950), pp. 279-292.
22. ———, *Society, Culture and Personality* (New York: Harper, 1947), pp. 635-713.
23. Spengler, O., *Decline of the West* (New York: Knopf, 1926), 2 vols.
24. Toynbee, A. J., *A Study of History* (1-vol. ed. abridged by D. C. Somervell) (New York: Oxford, 1947).
25. Williams, R. M., Jr., *American Society: A Sociological Interpretation* (New York: Knopf, 1951), pp. 538-545.

Sociological Significance of Space

See the references of Chapters 9 and 15.

Sociological Significance of Time

26. Cassirer, E., *An Essay on Man* (New Haven: Yale Univ. Press, 1944), pp. 171-206.
27. Cottrell, W. F., "Of Time and the Railroader," *Amer. Sociol. Rev.*, 3 (Apr., 1939), 190-198.
28. Engel-Frisch, G., "Some Neglected Temporal Aspects of Human Ecology," *Soc. Forces*, 22 (Oct., 1943), 43-47.
29. Frank, L. K., *Society and the Patient* (New Brunswick, N.J.: Rutgers Univ. Press, 1948), pp. 339-358.
30. Hallowell, A. I., "Temporal Orientations in Western Civilization and in a Preliterate Society," *Amer. Anthrop.*, 39 (Oct.-Nov., 1937), 647-670.
31. Hawley, *op. cit.*, pp. 288-316.
32. Hertzler, J. O., " On Golden Ages: Then and Now," *Sth. Atl. Quart.*, 39 (July, 1940), 318-329.
33. ———, "The Sources and Methods of Historical Sociology," in L. L. Bernard (ed.), *Fields and Methods of Sociology* (New York: Long & Smith, 1934), pp. 260-273.
34. Hulett, J. E., Jr., "The Person's Time Perspective and the Social Role," *Soc. Forces*, 23 (Dec., 1944), 155-159.
35. Lundberg, G. A., *Foundations of Sociology* (New York: Macmillan, 1939), pp. 503-534.
36. Sorokin, *Social and Cultural Dynamics, op. cit.*, II, 413-428.
37. ———, *Sociocultural Causality, Space, Time* (Durham, N.C.: Duke Univ. Press, 1943), pp. 158-225.
38. ———, and R. K. Merton, "Social Time: A Methodological and Functional Analysis," 42 (Mar., 1937), 615-629; and rejoinder by G. Devereaux, *Amer. J. Sociol.*, 43 (May, 1938), 967-968.

Dynamics of Social Action:

PHYSICAL, BIOLOGICAL AND PSYCHOLOGICAL ENERGIZERS

39. Andrzejewski, S., "Are Ideas Social Forces? *Amer. sociol. Rev.*, 14 (Dec., 1949), 758-764.
40. Bennett, J. W., and M. M. Tumin, *Social Life: Structure, Function* (New York: Knopf, 1948), pp. 301-312.
41. Dawson, C. A., and W. E. Gettys, *An Introduction to Sociology* (New York: Ronald, 1948), pp. 604-625.
42. Dodd, S. C., "A Tension Theory of Societal Action," *Amer. sociol. Rev.*, 4 (Feb., 1939), 56-77.
43. Eubank, E. E., *The Concepts of Sociology* (Boston: Heath, 1932), pp. 171-205.
44. Folsom, J. K., *Social Psychology* (New York: Harper, 1931), pp. 137-165.
45. Freeman, G. L., *The Energetics of Human Behavior* (Ithaca: Cornell Univ. Press, 1948).

46. Krech, D., and R. C. Crutchfield, *Theory and Problems of Social Psychology* (New York: McGraw-Hill, 1948), pp. 29-75, 150-156, 417-439.
47. Linton, R., *The Study of Man* (New York: Appleton-Century, 1936), pp. 422-442.
48. Lundberg, *op. cit.*, pp. 159-234.
49. ———, and M. Lawsing, "The Sociography of Some Community Relations," *Amer. sociol. Rev.*, 2 (June, 1937), 318-335.
50. MacIver, R. M., *Social Causation* (Boston: Heath, 1942), pp. 123-160.
51. Malinowski, B., *Factors Determining Behavior* (Cambridge: Harvard Univ. Press, 1947).
52. ———, "The Group and the Individual in Functional Analysis," *Amer. J. Sociol.*, 44 (May, 1939), 938-951.
53. Miller, N. E., and J. Dollard, *Social Learning and Imitation* (New Haven: Yale Univ. Press, 1941), pp. 218-234.
54. Murdock, G. P., "The Common Denominator of Cultures," in R. Linton (ed.), *The Science of Man in the World Crisis* (New York: Columbia Univ. Press, 1945), pp. 123-142.
55. Park, R. E., and E. W. Burgess, *Introduction to the Science of Sociology* (Chicago: Univ. Chicago Press, 1921), pp. 435-500.
56. Parsons, T., *Essays in Sociological Theory* (Glencoe, Ill.: Free Press, 1949), pp. 151-161.
57. Sherif, M., *An Outline of Social Psychology* (New York: Harper, 1948).
58. Symonds, P. M., *The Dynamics of Human Adjustment* (New York: Appleton-Century, 1946).
59. Thomas, W. I., and F. Znaniecki, *The Polish Peasant in Europe and America* (New York: Knopf, 1927), Vol. 1, pp. 72-73.
60. Young, P. T., *Motivation of Behavior* (New York: Wiley, 1936).

THE EGO FACTOR IN HUMAN ACTION

61. Allport, G. W., "The Psychology of Participation," *Psychol. Rev.*, 52 (May, 1945), 117-132.
62. Cantril, H., *The Psychology of Social Movements* (New York: Wiley, 1941), pp. 35-46.
63. Newcomb, T. M., *Social Psychology* (New York: Dryden, 1950), pp. 246-254.
64. Sargent, S. S., *Social Psychology: An Integrative Interpretation* (New York: Ronald, 1950), pp. 201-219.
65. Sherif, *op. cit.*, pp. 248-314.
66. ———, *The Psychology of Social Norms* (New York: Harper, 1936), Chap. IX.
67. ———, and H. Cantril, *The Psychology of Ego-Involvements* (New York: Wiley, 1947).
68. Young, *op. cit.*, 388-405.

INNOVATORS AND LEADERS

See the references under Leadership in Chapter 10.

SOCIAL VALUES, NORMS, AND ROLES

For references on these propulsives, namely, social values, norms, and roles, see the references in Chapters 10 and 20.

Significance of Social Crises

69. Becker, H., "Processes of Secularization," *Sociol. Rev. Brit.*, 24 (Oct., 1932), 266-286.
70. Beckerath, H. von, "Crisis and Reform in the Western World," *Soc. Forces*, 14 (Dec., 1935), 167-185.
71. Bidney, D., "Culture Theory and the Problem of Cultural Crises," in L. Bryson *et al.*, *Sixth Symposium Conference on Science, Philosophy and Religion* (New York: Harper, 1947).
72. ———, "The Concept of Cultural Crisis," *Amer. Anthrop.*, 48 (Oct.-Dec., 1948), 534-552.
73. Hart, H., *Technique of Social Progress* (New York: Holt, 1931), pp. 613-619.
74. Hertzler, J. O., "Crises and Dictatorship," *Amer. sociol. Rev.*, 5 (Apr., 1940), 157-169.
75. Jensen, F. B., and L. H. Jensen, "Progress and Disequilibrium," *Sociol. soc. Res.*, 22 (May-June, 1938), 439-445.
76. Kutak, R. I., "The Sociology of Crises: The Louisville Flood of 1937," *Soc. Forces*, 17 (Oct., 1938), 66-72.
77. LaPiere, R. T., *Collective Behavior* (New York: McGraw-Hill, 1938), pp. 105-124, 437-440.
78. Malamud, I., "A Psychological Approach to the Study of Social Crises," *Amer. J. Sociol.*, 43 (Jan., 1938), 578-592.
79. Mannheim, K., "Crises and Culture in the Era of Mass-Democracies and Autarchies," *Sociol. Rev. Brit.*, 26 (Apr., 1934), 105-129.
80. Meerloo, J. A. M., *Patterns of Panic* (New York: International Universities, 1950).
81. Mowrer, E. R., "Social Crises and Social Disorganization," *Amer. Sociol. Rev.*, 15 (Feb., 1950), 60-66.
82. Rader, M., "Toward a Definition of Cultural Crises," *Kenyon Rev.*, Spring, 1947, pp. 262-278.
83. Sorokin, P. A., *S.O.S.: The Meaning of Our Crisis* (Boston: Beacon, 1951), pp. 83-142.
84. Toynbee, *op. cit.*, pp. 60-139.

85. Znaniecki, F., 'Group Crises Produced by Voluntary Undertakings," in K. Young (ed.), *Social Attitudes* (New York: Holt, 1931), Chap. XI.

IV. The Proto Processes

Adjustment

1. Hankins, F. H., *An Introduction to the Study of Society* (New York: Macmillan, 1935), pp. 29-34, 382-384, 397-398.
2. Keller, A. G., *Societal Evolution* (New York: Macmillan, 1931), pp. 1-20.
3. Lundberg, G. A., *Foundations of Sociology* (New York: Macmillan, 1939), pp. 207-211.
4. MacIver, R. M., and C. H. Page, *Society: An Introductory Analysis* (New York: Rinehart, 1949), pp. 73-80, 122-124.
5. Meadows, P., "Balance and Imbalance in Human Social Adjustment," *Soc. Forces*, 22 (May, 1944), 415-419.
6. Smith, T. L., and C. A. McMahan, *The Sociology of Urban Life* (New York: Dryden, 1951), pp. 624-629.
7. Sorokin, P. A., *Social and Cultural Dynamics* (New York: American Book, 1940), Vol. IV, pp. 670-693.

Social Interaction

8. Bales, R. E., *Interaction Process Analysis* (Cambridge: Addison-Wesley, 1950), pp. 30-84.
9. Bennett, J. W., and M. M. Tumin, *Social Life: Structure, Function* (New York: Knopf, 1948), pp. 116-126.
10. Bernard, L. L., *Introduction to Sociology* (New York: Crowell, 1942), pp. 611-630.
11. Dawson, C. A., and W. E. Gettys, *An Introduction to Sociology* (New York: Ronald, 1948), pp. 295-296.
12. Eubank, E. E., *Concepts of Sociology* (Boston: Heath, 1932), pp. 315-317.
13. Freedman, R., A. H. Hawley, W. Landecker, and H. Miner, *Principles of Sociology* (New York: Holt, 1952), pp. 117-120.
14. Gillin, J. L., and J. P. Gillin, *Cultural Sociology* (New York: Macmillan, 1948), pp. 487-504.
15. Gist, N. P., "Communication," in S. Eldredge (ed.), *Fundamentals of Sociology: A Situational Analysis* (New York: Crowell, 1950), pp. 363-381.
16. LaPiere, R. T., *Sociology* (New York: McGraw-Hill, 1946), pp. 212-241.
17. Park, R. E., "Reflections on Communication and Culture," *Amer. J. Sociol.*, 44 (Sept., 1938), 187-205.
18. ———, and E. W. Burgess, *Introduction to the Science of Sociology* (Chicago: Univ. Chicago Press, 1921), pp. 339-346.
19. Pieris, R., "Speech and Society: A Sociological Approach to Language," *Amer. sociol. Rev.*, 16 (Aug., 1951), 499-505.
20. Porterfield, A. L., "Social Interaction and Peace," *Sociol. soc. Res.*, 30 (July-Aug., 1946), 431-438.
21. Reuter, E. B., and C. W. Hart, *Introduction to Sociology* (New York: McGraw-Hill, 1933), pp. 256-272.
22. Sapir, E., *Language: An Introduction to the Study of Speech* (New York: Harcourt, Brace, 1921).
23. White, L. A., "The Symbol: The Origin and Bases of Human Behavior," *Phil. Sci.*, 8 (Oct., 1940), 451-463.
24. Wirth, L., "Social Interaction: The Problem of the Individual and the Group," *Amer. J. Sociol.*, 44 (May, 1939), 965-979.
25. Young, K., *Sociology: A Study of Society and Culture* (New York: American Book, 1949), pp. 59-63.

Association-Dissociation

26. Lundberg, *op. cit.*, pp. 256-268.
27. Wiese, L. von, and H. Becker, *Systematic Sociology* (New York: Wiley, 1932).
28. Wilson, L., and W. L. Kolb, *Sociological Analysis* (New York: Harcourt, Brace, 1949), pp. 681-687, 713-716.

Socialization

29. Bennett, and Tumin, *op. cit.*, 259-270.
30. Davis, K., *Human Society* (New York: Macmillan, 1949), pp. 195-233.
31. Frank, L. K., "Man's Multidimensional Environment," *Sci. Mon., N.Y.*, 56 (Apr., 1943), 344-357.
32. Gillin, and Gillin, *op. cit.*, pp. 643-664.
33. Lundberg, *op. cit.*, pp. 291-299.
34. Parsons, T., *The Social System* (Glencoe, Ill.: Free Press, 1951), pp. 201-248.

Individualization

35. Bennett, and Tumin, *op. cit.*, pp. 271-276.
36. Giddings, F. H., *Civilization and Society* (New York: Holt, 1932), pp. 256-262.

V. The Origination and Acquisition of Culture

General Nature of Culture: Functions, Distinction between Culture and Society, Component Elements of Culture

1. Bennett, J. W., and M. M. Tumin, *Social Life: Structure, Function* (New York: Knopf, 1949), pp. 197-258.
2. Bernard, L. L., *Introduction to Sociology* (New York: Crowell, 1942), pp. 725-808.
3. Bidney, D., "Human Nature and the Cultural Process," *Amer. Anthrop.*, 49 (July-Sept., 1947), 375-399.
4. ———, "On the Concept of Culture and Some Cultural Fallacies," *Amer. Anthrop.*, 46 (Jan.-Mar., 1944), 30-44.
5. ———, "On the Philosophy of Culture in the Social Sciences," *J. Phil.*, 39 (Aug., 1942), 449-557.
6. Blumenthal, A., "A New Definition of Culture," *Amer. Anthrop.*, 42 (Oct.-Dec., 1940), 571-586.
7. ———, *The Place of the Term "Culture" in the Social Sciences* (Hanover, N.H.: Sociological Press, 1935).
8. Ellwood, C. A., "Culture and Human Society," *Soc. Forces*, 23 (Oct., 1944), 6-15.
9. Frank, L. K., *Society as the Patient* (New Brunswick, N.J.: Rutgers Univ. Press, 1948), pp. 375-385.
10. Freedman, R., A. H. Hawley, W. Landecker, and H. Miner, *Principles of Sociology* (New York: Holt, 1952), pp. 55-62.
11. Gillin, J. P., *The Ways of Men* (New York: Appleton-Century, 1948).
12. Herskovits, M. J., *Man and His Works* (New York: Knopf, 1948).
13. Kluckhohn, C., and W. H. Kelley, "The Concept of Culture," in R. Linton (ed.), *The Science of Man in the World Crisis* (New York: Columbia Univ. Press, 1945), pp. 78-106.
14. Kroeber, A. L., *Anthropology* (New York: Harcourt, Brace, 1948), pp. 8-9, 344-444, 538-571.
15. Linton, R., "Present World Conditions in Cultural Perspective," in R. Linton (ed.), *The Science of Man in the World Crisis* (New York: Columbia Univ. Press, 1945), pp. 201-221.
16. ———, *The Cultural Background of Personality* (New York: Appleton-Century, 1945), pp. 5-80.
17. Lowie, R. H., *An Introduction to Cultural Anthropology* (New York: Rinehart, 1940), pp. 78-106.
18. Meadows, P., "The Cultural Organization of Action," *Phil. Science*, 13 (Oct., 1946), 332-338.
19. Parsons, T., and E. A. Shils, *Toward a General Theory of Action* (Cambridge: Harvard Univ. Press, 1951), pp. 6-8, 21-24, 159-162, 237-239.
20. Sorokin, P. A., *Social Philosophies in an Age of Crisis* (Boston: Beacon, 1950), pp. 202-228.
21. Wallis, W. D., *Culture and Progress* (New York: Whittlesey House, 1931), pp. 3-34.
22. Willey, M. M., "Society and Its Cultural Heritage," in S. Eldridge (ed.), *Fundamentals of Sociology* (New York: Crowell, 1951), pp. 65-138.
23. Williams, R. M., Jr., *American Society: A Sociological Interpretation* (New York: Knopf, 1951), pp. 443-448.

Culture Area: Center; Gradient; Flow; Penumbra

24. Hawley, A. H., *Human Ecology* (New York: Ronald, 1950), pp. 81-91.
25. Kroeber, A. L., *Cultural and Natural Areas of Native North America* (Berkeley: Univ. California Press, 1939).
26. Wissler, C., *Man and Culture* (New York: Crowell, 1923), pp. 55-63.
27. ———, "The Culture-Area Concept in Social Anthropology," *Amer. J. Sociol.*, 32 (May, 1927), 881-891.

Innovative Processes

28. Barnett, H. G., *Innovation: The Basis of Cultural Change* (New York: McGraw-Hill, 1952).
29. ———, "Invention and Cultural Change," *Amer. Anthrop.*, 44 (Jan.-Mar., 1942), 14-30.
30. Bernard, *op. cit.*, pp. 674-695.
31. Brozen, Yale, "Invention, Innovation, and Imitation," *Amer. econ. Rev.*, 41 (May, 1951), 239-257.
32. Dixon, R. B., *The Building of Cultures* (New York: Scribner, 1928), pp. 33-58.
33. Gilfillan, S. C., *The Sociology of Invention* (Chicago: Follett, 1935).
34. Gillin, *op. cit.*, pp. 532-552.
35. Hart, H., *The Technique of Social Progress* (New York: Holt, 1931), pp. 511-606.
36. Linton, R., *The Study of Man* (New York: Appleton-Century, 1936), pp. 304-323.

37. Lundberg, G. A., *Foundations of Sociology* (New York: Macmillan, 1939), pp. 504-511.
38. Ogburn, W. F., *Social Change* (New York: Huebsch, 1922), pp. 80-102, 159-280.
39. ———, and M. F. Nimkoff, *Sociology* (Boston: Houghton Mifflin, 1950), pp. 514-520.
40. Ross, E. A., *Principles of Sociology* (New York: Appleton-Century, 1938), pp. 623-641.
41. Sorokin, P. A., *Social and Cultural Dynamics* (New York: American Book, 1941), Vol. IV.
42. Stafford, A. B., "Is the Rate of Invention Declining?" *Amer. J. Sociol.*, 57 (May, 1952), 539-545.

Exchange Processes: *Diffusion-Borrowing*

43. Barnett, H. G., "Culture Processes," *Amer. Anthrop.*, 42 (Jan.-Mar., 1940), 21-48.
44. Benedict, R., "Two Patterns of Indian Acculturation," *Amer. Anthrop.*, 45 (Apr.-June, 1943), 207-212.
45. Bogardus, E. S., "Cultural Pluralism and Acculturation," *Sociol. soc. Res.*, 34 (Nov.-Dec., 1949), 125-129.
46. Bowers, R. V., "Differential Intensity of Intrasocial Diffusion," *Amer. sociol. Rev.*, 3 (Feb., 1938), 21-31.
47. Freedman, *et al.*, *op. cit.*, pp. 312-330.
48. Gillin, *op. cit.*, pp. 553-569.
49. ———, and V. Raimy, "Acculturation and Personality," *Amer. sociol. Rev.*, 5 (June, 1940), 371-380.
50. Hallowell, A. I., "Socio-Psychological Aspects of Acculturation," in R. Linton (ed.), *The Science of Man in the World Crisis* (New York: Columbia Univ. Press, 1945), pp. 171-200.
51. Herskovits, M. J., *Acculturation: A Study of Culture Contact* (New York: Augustine, 1938).
52. ———, "Some Comments on the Study of Culture Contact," *Amer. Anthrop.*, 43 (Jan.-Mar., 1941), 1-10.
53. ———, "The Significance of the Study of Acculturation for Anthropology," *Amer. Anthrop.*, 39 (Apr.-June, 1937), 259-264.
54. Kroeber, A. L., "Diffusionism," *Encyclopedia of the Social Sciences* (New York: Macmillan, 1931), V, 139-142.
55. ———, "Stimulus Diffusion," *Amer. Anthrop.*, 42 (Jan.-Mar., 1940), 1-20.
56. Linton, R., *Acculturation of Seven Indian Tribes* (New York: Appleton-Century, 1940).
57. ———, *The Study of Man, op. cit.*, pp. 324-346.
58. Mead, M., *The Changing Culture of an Indian Tribe* (New York: Columbia Univ. Press, 1932).
59. Miller, N. E., and J. Dollard, *Social Learning and Imitation* (New Haven: Yale Univ. Press, 1941), pp. 253-273.
60. Pedersen, H. A., "The Emerging Culture Concept: An Approach to the Study of Social Change," *Soc. Forces*, 29 (Dec., 1950), 131-135.
61. Pemberton, H. A., "Culture Diffusion Gradients," *Amer. J. Sociol.*, 42 (Sept., 1936), 226-233.
62. ———, "The Curve of Culture Diffusion Rate," *Amer. sociol. Rev.*, 1 (Aug., 1936), 547-556.
63. ———, "The Effect of Social Crisis on the Curve of Diffusion," *Amer. sociol. Rev.*, 2 (Feb., 1937), 55-61.
64. Price, M. T., "Culture Contact in China: Some Natural Trends and Their Conditioning by the Cultural Setting," *Soc. Forces*, 7 (Dec., 1932), 270-278.
65. ———, "The Assumed Isolation of China and Autochthony of Her Culture," *Amer. sociol. Rev.*, 10 (Feb., 1945), 38-44.
66. Redfield, R., "Culture Contact without Conflict," *Amer. Anthrop.*, 41 (July-Sept., 1939), 514-517.
67. ———, R. Linton, and M. J. Herskovits, "A Memorandum for the Study of Acculturation," *Amer. Anthrop.*, 38 (Jan.-Mar., 1936), 149-152.
68. Siegel, M., "Religion in Western Guatemala: A Product of Acculturation," *Amer. Anthrop.*, 43 (Jan.-Mar., 1941), 62-76.
69. Steward, J. H., "Acculturation Studies in Latin America," *Amer. Anthrop.*, 45 (Apr.-June, 1943), 198-204.
70. Thurnwald, R., "The Psychology of Acculturation," *Amer. Anthrop.*, 23 (Oct.-Dec., 1932), 557-569.
71. Wallis, *op. cit.*, pp. 77-106.

VI. The Organization and Transmission of Culture

Organization of Culture

1. Danhof, R. M., "The Accommodation and Integration of Conflicting Cultures in a Newly Established Community," *Amer. J. Sociol.*, 49 (July, 1943), 14-23.
2. Gillin, J. P., *The Ways of Men* (New York: Appleton-Century, 1948), pp. 515-526.

3. Hart, H., *The Technique of Social Progress* (New York: Holt, 1931), pp. 619-632.
4. Jastrow, M., *The Civilization of Babylonia and Assyria* (Philadelphia: Lippincott, 1915), pp. 2-3.
5. Linton, R., *The Study of Man* (New York: Appleton-Century, 1936), pp. 347-366.
6. Stern, B. J., "Resistances to the Adoption of Technological Innovations," in National Resources Committee, *Technological Trends and National Policy* (Washington: U.S. Government Printing Office, 1937), Sec. IV.
7. Wallis, W. D., *Culture and Progress* (New York: Whittlesey House, 1931), pp. 107-122.

Culture Changes in Time

8. Chapin, F. S., *Cultural Change* (New York: Century, 1928), pp. 207-222.
9. Choukas, M., "The Concept of Cultural Lag Re-examined," *Amer. sociol. Rev.*, 1 (Oct., 1936), 752-760.
10. Krout, M. H., *Introduction to Social Psychology* (New York: Harper, 1942), pp. 523-534.
11. Hertzler, J. O., "American Ancestor Worshipers," *Sth. Atl. Quart.*, 36 (Apr., 1937), 189-200.
12. MacIver, R. M., and C. H. Page, *Society: An Introductory Analysis* (New York: Rinehart, 1949), pp. 519-528, 574-580.
13. LaPiere, R. T., and Chen Wang, "The Incidence and Sequence of Social Change," *Amer. J. Sociol.*, 37 (Nov., 1931), 399-409.
14. Mueller, J. H., "Present Status of the Cultural Lag Hypothesis," *Amer. sociol. Rev.*, 3 (June, 1938), 320-327.
15. Ogburn, W. F., *Social Change* (New York: Huebsch, 1922), pp. 146-154.
16. Sorokin, P. A., *Social and Cultural Dynamics* (New York: American Book, 1941), Vol. IV.
17. ———, *Society, Culture and Personality* (New York: Harper, 1947), pp. 675-695.
18. Wallis, *op. cit.*, pp. 125-140.
19. Woodward, J. W., "Critical Notes on the Culture Lag Concept," *Soc. Forces*, 12 (Mar., 1934), 388-398.

Culture Transmission and Fixing

20. Cantril, H., *The Psychology of Social Movements* (New York: Wiley, 1941), pp. 3-5.
21. Freeman, G. L., *The Energetics of Human Behavior* (Ithaca: Cornell Univ. Press, 1948), pp. 174-192.
22. Herskovits, M. J., *Man and His Works* (New York: Knopf, 1948), pp. 39-45.
23. Hertzler, J. O., *Social Institutions* (Lincoln: Univ. Nebraska Press, 1946), pp. 132-140, 156-160, 178-182.
24. Miller, N. E., and J. Dollard, *Social Learning and Imitation* (New Haven: Yale Univ. Press, 1941), pp. 1-32, 253-263.
25. Park, R. E., "Education and the Culture Crisis," *American J. Sociol.*, 48 (May, 1943), 728-736.

VII. Social Adjustment to the Natural Environment

General Treatments

1. Bennett, J. W., and M. M. Tumin, *Social Life: Structure, Function* (New York: Knopf, 1948), pp. 30-34.
2. Bernard, L. L., *Introduction to Sociology* (New York: Crowell, 1942), pp. 209-337.
3. ———, "A Classification of Environments," *Amer. J. Sociol.*, 31 (Nov., 1925), 318-332.
4. ———, "Environment as a Social Factor," *Pubs. Amer. sociol. Soc.*, 16 (1921), 84-112.
5. Brunhes, Jean, *Human Geography* (Chicago: Rand McNally, 1920).
6. Chapple, E. D., and C. S. Coon, *Principles of Anthropology* (New York: Holt, 1942), pp. 96-272.
7. Febvre, Lucien, *A Geographic Introduction to History* (New York: Knopf, 1925).
8. Frank, L. K., "Man's Multidimensional Environment," in L. K. Frank, *Society as the Patient* (New Brunswick, N.J.: Rutgers Univ. Press, 1948), pp. 359-379.
9. Gillin, J. P., *The Ways of Men* (New York: Appleton-Century, 1948), pp. 357-368.
10. Huntington, E., *Mainsprings of Civilization* (New York: Wiley, 1945).
11. Kelsey, C., *The Physical Basis of Society* (New York: Appleton-Century, 1928).
12. LaPiere, R. T., *Sociology* (New York: McGraw-Hill, 1946), pp. 90-135.
13. Lowie, R. H., *Culture and Ethnology* (New York: McMurtie, 1917), pp. 50-53, 62-64.
14. MacIver, R. M., and C. H. Page, *Society: An Introductory Analysis* (New York: Rinehart, 1949), pp. 98-109.
15. Markham, S. F., *Climate and the Energy of Nations* (New York: Oxford, 1944).
16. Meadows, P., *The Culture of Industrial Man*

(Lincoln: Univ. Nebraska Press, 1950), pp. 9-130.

17. Mills, C. A., *Climate Makes the Man* (New York: Harper, 1942).
18. Mukerjee, R., *Man and His Habitation: A Study Social Ecology* (New York: Longmans, Green, 1940).
19. Ogburn, W. F., and M. F. Nimkoff, *Sociology* (Boston: Houghton Mifflin, 1950), pp. 85-100.
20. Peattie, R., *Geography in Human Destiny* (New York: Stewart, 1941).
21. Pomfret, J. E., *The Geographic Pattern of Mankind* (New York: Appleton-Century, 1935).
22. Semple, E., *The Influence of the Geographic Environment* (New York: Holt, 1913).
23. Thomas, F., *The Environmental Basis of Society* New York: Appleton-Century, 1925).
24. Whitbeck, C. L., and O. J. Thomas, *The Geographic Factor* (New York: Appleton-Century, 1932).
25. Young, K., *Sociology: A Study of Society and Culture* (New York: American Book, 1949), pp. 137-158.

Processes of Adjustment

26. Bennett, H. H., *Soil Conservation* (New York: McGraw-Hill, 1939).
27. Chase, S., *Men and Machines* (New York: Macmillan, 1937).
28. ——, *Rich Land, Poor Land: A Study of Waste in the Natural Resources of America* (New York: Whittlesey House, 1936).
29. Forbes, R. J., *Man the Maker: A History of Technology and Invention* (New York: Schuman, 1950).
30. Hart, H., *The Technique of Social Progress* (New York: Holt, 1931), pp. 49-91.
31. Mukerjee, R., *Political Economy of Population* (London: Longmans, Green, 1944), pp. 146-147.
32. Mumford, L., *Technics and Civilization* (New York: Harcourt, Brace, 1934).
33. National Resources Committee, *Our Energy Resources* (Washington: U.S. Government Printing Office, 1939).
34. Randall, R. H., "Conservation of Natural Resources," *Ann. Amer. Acad. polit. soc. Sci.*, 206 (Nov., 1939), 142-146.
35. Renner, G. T., *Conservation of Natural Resources* (New York: Wiley, 1942).
36. Roberts, W. H., *The Problem of Choice* (Boston: Ginn, 1941), pp. 233-249.
37. Sears, P. B., *Deserts on the March* (Norman: Univ. Oklahoma Press, 1935).
38. ——, *This Is Our World* (Norman: Univ. Oklahoma Press, 1937).
39. ——, *et al.*, *This Useful World* (Chicago: Scott, Foresman, 1941).
40. Spiller, G., "The Dynamics of Greatness," *Sociol. Rev. Brit.*, 21 (July, 1929), 218-232.
41. Vogt, William, *Road to Survival* (New York: Sloane, 1948).
42. White, L. A., "Energy and the Development of Civilization," in W. Weaver (ed.), *The Scientists Speak* (New York: Boni & Gaer, 1947), pp. 302-305.
43. Zon, R., *et al.*, *Conservation of Renewable Resources* (Philadelphia: Univ. Pennsylvania Press, 1941).

VIII. The Social Processes Affecting Population

Processes and Factors Affecting Numbers:

MARRIAGE SELECTION AND MARRIAGE DIFFERENTIALS

1. Bossard, J. H. S., "The Age Factor in Marriage," *Amer. J. Sociol.*, 38 (Jan., 1933), 536-547.
2. Duncan, O. D., *et al.*, "The Factor of Age in Marriage," *Amer. J. Sociol.*, 39 (Jan., 1934), 469-482.
3. Notestein, F. W., "Differential Age at Marriage according to Social Class," *Amer. J. Sociol.*, 37 (July, 1931), 22-48.
4. Ogburn, W. F., "Recent Changes in Marriage," *Amer. J. Sociol.*, 41 (Nov., 1935), 285-298.
5. Popenoe, P. B., "Where Are the Marriageable Men?" *Soc. Forces*, 14 (Dec., 1935), 257-262.
6. Schnepp, C. J., and L. A. Roberts, "Residential Propinquity and Mate Selection," *Amer. J. Sociol.*, 58 (July, 1952), 45-50.
7. Stouffer, S. A., and L. M. Spencer, "Marriage and Divorce in Recent Years," *Ann. Amer. Acad. polit. soc. Sci.*, 188 (Nov., 1936), 56-69.
8. Sundal, A. D., and T. C. McCormick, "Age at Marriage and Mate Selection: Madison, Wis., 1937-1943," *Amer. sociol. Rev.*, 16 (Feb., 1951), 37-48.
9. Timmons, B. F., "The Cost of Weddings," *Amer. sociol. Rev.*, 4 (Apr., 1939), 224-233.

BIRTH SELECTION AND FERTILITY DIFFERENTIALS

10. Beebe, G. W., *Contraception and Fertility in*

the Southern Appalachians (Baltimore: Williams & Wilkins, 1942).
11. Davis, K., *Human Society* (New York: Macmillan, 1949), pp. 555-562.
12. ———, and A. Casis, "Traits of Urban and Rural Populations," *Milbank mem. Fund Quart.*, 24 (July, 1946), 23-38.
13. Gamble, C. J., "The College Birth Rate," *J. Hered.*, 38 (Dec., 1947), 355-362.
14. Glick, P. C., "Family Trends in the United States," *Amer. sociol. Rev.*, 7 (Aug., 1942), 505-514.
15. Hagood, M. J., "Rural Population Characteristics" and "Dynamics of Rural Population," in C. C. Taylor (ed.), *Rural Life in the United States* (New York: Knopf, 1948), pp. 217-244.
16. Hill, G. W., and H. T. Christensen, "Some Factors in Family Fertility among Selected Wisconsin Farmers," *Amer. sociol. Rev.*, 7 (Aug., 1942), 498-504.
17. Jaffe, A. J., "Urbanization and Fertility," *Amer. J. Sociol.*, 48 (July, 1942), 48-60.
18. Kiser, C. V., *Group Differentials in Urban Fertility* (Baltimore: Williams & Wilkins, 1942).
19. Krzywicki, L., *Primitive Society and Its Vital Statistics* (London: Macmillan, 1939).
20. Landis, P. H., *Population Problems* (New York: American Book, 1948), pp. 51-182.
21. National Resources Committee, *The Problems of a Changing Population* (Washington: U.S. Government Printing Office, 1938), pp. 119-148.
22. Notestein, F. W., "Class Differences in Fertility," *Ann. Amer. Acad. polit. soc. Sci.*, 237 (Nov., 1936), 26-36.
23. ———, "The Differential Rate of Increase among the Social Classes of the American Population," *Soc. Forces*, 12 (Oct., 1933), 17-33.
24. Osborn, F. O., "Characteristics and Differential Fertility of American Population Groups," *Soc. Forces*, 12 (Oct., 1933), 8-16.
25. Pearl, R., "Biological Factors in Fertility," *Ann. Amer. Acad. soc. Sci.*, 188 (Nov., 1936), 14-25.
26. ———, *The Natural History of Population* (New York: Oxford, 1939).
27. Popenoe, P. B., and E. M. Williams, "Fecundity of Families Dependent on Public Charity," *Amer. J. Sociol.*, 40 (Sept., 1934), 214-220.
28. Smith, T. L., *Population Analysis* (New York: McGraw-Hill, 1948), pp. 193-232.
29. ———, *The Sociology of Rural Life* (New York: Harper, 1947), pp. 134-155.
30. "Social and Psychological Factors Affecting Fertility," *Milbank mem. Fund Quart.* A series of studies appearing since 1943.
31. Stouffer, S. A., "Fertility of Families on Relief," *J. Amer. statist. Assoc.*, 29 (Sept., 1934), 295-300.
32. ———, "Trends in Fertility of Catholics and Non-Catholics," *Amer. J. Sociol.*, 41 (Sept., 1935), 143-166.
33. Thompson, W. S., *Plenty of People* (Lancaster, Pa.: Science Press, 1944), pp. 39-54.
34. ———, *Population Problems* (New York: McGraw-Hill, 1942), pp. 151-215.
35. Tinkel, R. M., "Occupation and Fertility in the United States," *Amer. soc. Rev.*, 17 (Apr., 1952), 178-183.
36. Vance, R. B., *All These People* (Chapel Hill, N.C.: Univ. North Carolina Press, 1945), pp. 62-78, 95-108.
37. Whelpton, P. K., *Needed Population Research* (Lancaster, Pa.: Science Press, 1938), pp. 40-94.
38. ———, and C. V. Kizer, "Trends, Determinants, and Control in Human Fertility," *Ann. Amer. Acad. polit. soc. Sci.*, 237 (Jan., 1945), 112-122.
39. Woofter, T. J., "Factors Sustaining the Birth Rate," *Amer. sociol. Rev.*, 14 (June, 1949), 357-366.
40. Young, K., *Sociology: A Study of Society and Culture* (New York: American Book, 1949), pp. 215-224.

DEATH AND MORBIDITY AND DEATH DIFFERENTIALS

41. Davis, *op. cit.*, pp. 562-586.
42. Dublin, L. I., and A. J. Lotka, *Length of Life: A Study of the Life Table* (New York: Ronald, 1949).
43. ——— and ———, "Trends in Longevity," *Ann. Amer. Acad. polit. soc. Sci.*, 237 (Jan., 1945), 123-133.
44. Landis, *op. cit.*, pp. 183-248.
45. National Resources Committee, *op. cit.*, pp. 166-192.
46. Smith, *Population Analysis, op. cit.*, pp. 233-288.
47. ———, *The Sociology of Rural Life, op. cit.*, pp. 156-171.
48. Thompson, *Plenty of People, op. cit.*, pp. 55-71.
49. ———, *Population Problems, op. cit.*, pp. 216-247.
50. Vance, *op. cit.*, pp. 39-47.

51. Whelpton, *op. cit.*, pp. 95-122.
52. Young, *op. cit.*, pp. 224-232.

Migration: Numerical Aspects; Effects upon the Composition and Integration of the Population

53. Davis, *op. cit.*, pp. 586-592.
54. Day, K. H., and P. H. Landis, "Education and Distance of Migration," *Elem. Sch. J.*, 46 (Dec., 1945), 200-208.
55. Freedman, R., *Recent Migration to Chicago* (Chicago: Univ. Chicago Press, 1951), Chap. 3.
56. ———, and A. H. Hawley, "Education and the Occupation of Migrants in the Depression," *Amer. J. Sociol.*, 56 (Sept., 1950), 161-166.
57. Gee, W., and J. J. Carson, *Rural Depopulation in Certain Tidewater and Piedmont Areas of Virginia.* Institute for Research in the Social Sciences, Monograph III (Richmond: Univ. Virginia, 1929).
58. Gist, N. P., and C. D. Clark, "Intelligence as a Selective Factor in Rural-Urban Migration," *Amer. J. Sociol.*, 44 (July, 1938), 36-58.
59. ———, C. T. Pihlblad, and C. L. Gregory, "Selective Aspects of Rural Migration," *Rur. Sociol.*, 6 (Mar., 1941), 3-15.
60. ———, ———, and ———, *Selective Factors in Migration and Occupation* (Columbia, Mo.: Univ. Missouri Press, 1943).
61. Hawley, A. H., *Human Ecology: A Theory of Community Structure* (New York: Ronald, 1950), pp. 340-345.
62. Hobbs, A. H., *Differentials in Internal Migration* (Philadelphia: Univ. Pennsylvania Press, 1942).
63. ———, "Specificity and Selective Migration," *Amer. sociol. Rev.*, 7 (Dec., 1942), 772-781.
64. Hunt, H. N., *Selective Migration.* University of Iowa Studies, No. 53 (Iowa City, 1921).
65. Landis, *op. cit.*, pp. 387-456.
66. Lively, C. E., and C. Taeuber, *Rural Migration in the United States,* W.P.A. Res. Monograph XIX, (Washington: U.S. Government Printing Office, 1939).
67. Masuoka, Edna C., "Motivations for Migration of Southern-born Notables," *Soc. Forces,* 29 (Mar., 1951), 290-294.
68. Mauldin, W. P., "Selective Migration from Small Towns," *Amer. sociol. Rev.*, 5 (Oct., 1940), 748-758.
69. Moore, E. H., "Mobility Patterns of High School Graduates from a Feeder Community by Decades, 1880-1939," *Soc. Forces,* 19 (Mar., 1941), 381-385.
70. National Resources Committee, *op. cit.*, pp. 83-118.
71. Price, D. O., "Nonwhite Migrants to and from Selected Cities," *Amer. J. Sociol.*, 54 (Nov., 1948), 196-201.
72. Reuss, C. F., "A Qualitative Study of Depopulation in a Remote Rural District: 1900-1930," *Rur. Sociol.*, 2 (Mar., 1937), 66-75.
73. Richards, E. S., "Culture Changes Due to Migration: A Study of Negro Migration to California," *Sociol. soc. Res.*, 26 (Mar.-Apr., 1942), 335-351.
74. Sanford, G. A., "Selective Migration in a Rural Alabama Community," *Amer. sociol. Rev.*, 5 (Oct., 1940), 759-766.
75. Smith, M., "An Urban-Rural Intelligence Gradient," *Sociol. soc. Res.*, 27 (Mar.-Apr., 1943), 307-315.
76. ———, "Mobility of American Congressmen," *Sociol. soc. Res.*, 24 (July-Aug., 1940), 511-525.
77. ———, "Occupational Mobility of Notable Persons," *Sociol. soc. Res.*, 23 (July-Aug., 1939), 503-513.
78. ———, "Some Relationships between Intelligence and Geographical Mobility," *Amer. sociol. Rev.*, 8 (Dec., 1943), 657-665.
79. ———, "The Mobility of Eminent Men," *Sociol. soc. Res.*, 22 (May-June, 1938), 452-461.
80. Smith, T. L., *Population Analysis, op. cit.*, pp. 355-368.
81. ———, *The Sociology of Rural Life, op. cit.*, pp. 172-205.
82. Sorokin, P. A., and C. C. Zimmerman, *Principles of Rural-Urban Sociology* (New York: Holt, 1929), Chaps. XXIV and XXV.
83. ———, ———, and C. J. Galpin, *A Systematic Source Book in Rural Sociology* (Minneapolis: Univ. Minnesota Press, 1932), Vol. III, Chap. XXII.
84. Thomas, D. S., *Research Memorandum on Migration Differentials* (New York: Social Science Research Council, 1938).
85. Zimmerman, C. C., "The Migration to Towns and Cities," *Amer. J. Sociol.*, 32 (Nov., 1926), 450-455.
86. ———, "The Migration to Towns and Cities: II," *Amer. J. Sociol.*, 33 (July, 1927), 105-109.

87. ———, O. D. Duncan, and F. C. Frey., "The Migration to Towns and Cities: III," *Amer. J. Sociol.*, 33 (Sept., 1927), 237-241.

Composition

88. Clark, C. D., and R. L. Roberts, *People of Kansas* (Topeka: Kansas State Planning Board, 1936), pp. 91-116, Chaps. V, VII, X.
89. Hentig, H. von, "The Sex Ratio," *Soc. Forces*, 30 (May, 1952), 443-449.
90. Landis, *op. cit.*, pp. 251-385.
91. Smith, T. L., *Population Analysis, op. cit.*, pp. 27-189.
92. ———, *The Population of Louisiana: Its Composition and Changes*, Louisiana Agricultural Experiment Station Bulletin 293 (Baton Rouge), Chaps. II-VIII.
93. ———, *The Sociology of Rural Life, op. cit.*, pp. 64-100.
94. Thompson, *Population Problems, op. cit.*, pp. 96-127.
95. Vance, *op. cit.*, pp. 39-61.

Eugenic Processes and Qualitative Considerations

96. Jennings, H. S., "Eugenics," *Encyclopedia of the Social Sciences* (New York: Macmillan, 1931), Vol. 5, pp. 617-621.
97. Landis, *op. cit.*, pp. 145-182, 463-473.
98. Lundberg, G. A., *Foundations of Sociology* (New York: Macmillan, 1939), pp. 446-457.
99. National Resources Committee, *op. cit.*, pp. 149-165.
100. Osborn, F., *A Preface to Eugenics* (New York: Harper, 1952).
101. Sims, N. L., *The Problem of Social Change* (New York: Crowell, 1939), pp. 97-118.
102. Thompson, *Plenty of People, op. cit.*, pp. 173-183.
103. ———, *Population Problems, op. cit.*, pp. 341-371.
104. Young, *op. cit.*, pp. 232-234.

IX. Processes of Ecological Organization

Ecological Organization and Basic Processes

1. Alihan, M. A., *Social Ecology: A Critical Analysis* (New York: Columbia Univ. Press, 1938).
2. Bernard, Jessie, *American Community Behavior* (New York: Dryden, 1949), pp. 141-147.
3. Davis, K., *Human Society* (New York: Macmillan, 1949), pp. 310-345.
4. Dawson, C. A., and W. E. Gettys, *An Introduction to Sociology* (New York: Ronald, 1948), pp. 140-212.
5. Firey, W., "Ecological Considerations in Planning for Rurban Fringes," *Amer. sociol. Rev.*, 11 (Aug., 1946), 411-421.
6. ———, "Sentiments and Symbolism as Ecological Variables," *Amer. sociol. Rev.*, 10 (Apr., 1945), 140-148.
7. Gettys, W. E., "Human Ecology and Social Theory," *Soc. Forces*, 18 (May, 1949), 469-476.
8. Hatt, P., "The Concept of Natural Area," *Amer. sociol. Rev.*, 11 (Aug., 1946), 423-427.
9. Hawley, A. H., *Human Ecology: A Theory of Community Structure* (New York: Ronald, 1950), pp. 3-74.
10. Hiller, E. T., *Principles of Sociology* (New York: Harper, 1933), pp. 231-259.
11. Hollingshead, A. B., "A Re-examination of Ecological Theory," *Sociol. soc. Res.*, 31 (Jan.-Feb., 1947), 194-204.
12. ———, "Human Ecology," in R. E. Park (ed.), *An Outline of the Principles of Sociology* (New York: Barnes & Noble, 1939), pp. 63-168.
13. Jonassen, C. T., "Cultural Variables in the Ecology of an Ethnic Group," *Amer. sociol. Rev.*, 14 (Feb., 1949), 32-41.
14. Llewellyn, E. C., and A. Hawthorn, "Human Ecology," in G. Gurvitch and W. E. Moore (eds.), *Twentieth Century Sociology* (New York: Philosophical Library, 1945), pp. 466-499.
15. Lundberg, G. A., *Foundations of Sociology* (New York: Macmillan, 1939), pp. 469-502.
16. McKenzie, R. D., "The Scope of Human Ecology," in E. W. Burgess (ed.), *The Urban Community* (Chicago: Univ. Chicago Press, 1926).
17. Mukerjee, R., *Social Ecology* (London: Longmans, Green, 1945).
18. ———, "Mobility, Ecological and Social," *Soc. Forces*, 21 (Dec., 1942), 154-159.
19. ———, "The Broken Balance of Man and Region," *Sociol. soc. Res.*, 17 (May-June, 1933), 403-408.

20. ———, "The Concepts of Balance and Organization in Social Ecology," *Sociol. soc. Res.*, 16 (July-Aug., 1932), 503-516.
21. Myers, J. K., "Assimilation to the Ecological and Social Systems of a Community," *Amer. sociol. Rev.*, 15 (June, 1950), 367-372.
22. Park, R. E., "Human Ecology," *Amer. J. Sociol.*, 42 (July, 1936), 1-15.
23. ———, "The Concept of Position in Sociology," *Pubs. Amer. sociol. Soc.*, 20 (July, 1926), 1-14.
24. Quinn, J. A., "Ecological versus Social Interaction," *Sociol. soc. Res.*, 18 (July-Aug., 1934), 565-570.
25. ———, *Human Ecology* (New York: Prentice-Hall, 1950), pp. 3-30.
26. ———, "The Nature of Human Ecology—A Re-examination and Redefinition," *Soc Forces*, 18 (Dec., 1939), 161-168.
27. Schaff, A. H., "Culture Factors in Ecological Change on Mindanao in the Philippines," *Soc. Forces*, 27 (Dec., 1948), 119-123.
28. Thompson, J. A., *The System of Animate Nature* (New York: Holt, 1920).
29. Wirth, L., "Human Ecology," *Amer. J. Sociol.* 50 (May, 1945), 483-488.

Settlement Processes and Basic Configuration

30. Anderson, A. H., "Space as Social Cost," *J Farm Econ.*, 32 (Aug., 1950), 411-430.
31. Bartholomew, H., *Urban Land Uses*, Harvard City Planning Series, Vol. IV (Cambridge: Harvard Univ. Press, 1932).
32. Bogue, D. J., *The Structure of the Metropolitan Community* (Ann Arbor: University Michigan Institute for Human Adjustment, Univ. Michigan Press, 1949).
33. Bowers, R. V., "Ecological Patterning of Rochester, New York," *Amer. sociol. Rev.*, 4 (Apr., 1939), 180-189.
34. Burgess, E. W., "The Determination of Gradients in the Growth of the City," *Pubs. Amer. sociol. Soc.*, 21 (1927), 178-184.
35. Davie, M. R., "The Pattern of Urban Growth," in G. P. Murdock (ed.), *Studies in the Science of Society* (New Haven: Yale Univ. Press, 1937), pp. 133-161.
36. Firey, W., *Land Use in Central Boston* (Cambridge: Harvard Univ. Press, 1947).
37. Galpin, C. J., *The Social Anatomy of An Agricultural Village*, Agricultural Experimental Station of the University of Wisconsin, Research Bulletin 34 (Madison, Wis.: 1915).
38. Gist, N. P., "Developing Patterns of Urban Decentralization," *Soc. Forces*, 30 (Mar., 1952), 257-267.
39. Hallenbeck, W. C., *American Urban Communities* (New York: Harper, 1952), pp. 145-169.
40. Harris, C. D., "Suburbs," *Amer. J. Sociol.*, 49 (July, 1943), 1-13.
41. Hawley, *op. cit.*, pp. 234-287.
42. Hoyt, H., *The Structure and Growth of Residential Neighborhoods* (Washington: Federal Housing Administration, 1939).
43. Hurd, R. M., *Principles of City Land Values*, 4th ed. (New York: Real Estate Record and Guide, 1924).
44. James, J., "A Critique of Firey's *Land Use in Central Boston*," *Amer. J. Sociol.*, 54 (Nov., 1948), 228-234.
45. James, P. E., "The Terminology of Regional Description," *Ann. Ass. Amer. Geog.*, 24 (June, 1934), 78-92.
46. Jones, W. D., "Procedures in Investigating Human Occupance of a Region," *Ann. Amer. Ass. Geog.*, 24 (June, 1934), 93-107.
47. McKenzie, R. D., *The Metropolitan Community* (New York: McGraw-Hill, 1933).
48. Quinn, *Human Ecology, op. cit.*, pp. 33-162, 266-290.
49. Thompson, W. S., "The Distribution of Population," *Ann. Amer. Acad. polit. soc. Sci.*, 188 (Nov., 1936), 250-259.
50. Ullman, E., "A Theory of Location of Cities," *Amer. J. Sociol.*, 46 (May, 1941), 853-864.
51. U.S. Census, Preliminary Counts: Series PC-3, No. 8, Rev.; PC-3, No. 10; PC-7, No. 4; Census-BAE, No. 17.
52. Zorbaugh, H. W., "The Natural Areas of the City," *Pubs. Amer. sociol. Soc.*, 20 (July, 1926), 188-197.

Migration: Ecological Significance, Forms, Motivations, Factors

53. Becker, H., "Forms of Population Movement," *Soc. Forces*, 9 (Dec., 1930), 147-160; 9 (Mar., 1931), 351-361.
54. Bogue, D. J., *An Exploratory Study of Migration and Labor Mobility Using Social Security Data*, Studies in Population Distribution, No. 1 (Oxford, Ohio: Scripps Foundation, 1950).
55. ———, and W. S. Thompson, "Migration and

Distance," *Amer. sociol. Rev.*, 14 (Apr., 1949), 236-244.
56. Brunner, E. S., "Internal Migration," *Rur. Sociol.*, 13 (Mar., 1948), 9-21.
57. Dixon, G. I. J., "Land and Human Migrations," *Amer. J. Econ. Sociol.*, 9 (Jan., 1950), 223-234.
58. Foley, D. L., "The Daily Movement of Population into Central Business Districts," *Amer. sociol. Rev.*, 17 (Oct., 1952), 538-543.
59. Freedman, R., and A. H. Hawley, "Migration and Occupational Mobility in the Depression," *Amer. J. Sociol.*, 55 (Sept., 1949), 171-177.
60. Galpin, C. J., and T. B. Manny, *Inter-State Migration among the Native White Population as Indicated by Differences between State of Birth and State of Residence,* (Washington: U.S. Department of Agriculture, 1934).
61. Goodrich, Carter, *et al., Migration and Economic Opportunity* (Philadelphia: Univ. Pennsylvania Press, 1936).
62. Hansen, M. L., *The Atlantic Migration, 1667-1860* (Cambridge: Harvard Univ. Press, 1940).
63. Hauser, P. M., "Population," *Amer. J. Sociol.*, 47 (Mar., 1942), 816-828.
64. Hawley, *op. cit.*, pp. 324-347.
65. Isaacs, J., *The Economics of Migration* (London: Kegan Paul, Trench & Trubner, 1947).
66. Jerome, H., *Migrations and the Business Cycle* (New York: National Bureau of Economic Research, 1926).
67. Kulischer, E. M., *Europe on the Move* (New York: Columbia Univ. Press, 1948).
68. Kuczynski, R. R., *Population Movements* (Oxford: Clarendon Press, 1936).
69. Lively, C. E., "Population Mobility," *Rur. Sociol.*, 1 (Mar., 1936), 40-53.
70. ———, Spatial Mobility of the Rural Population, with Respect to Local Areas," *Amer. J. Sociol.*, 43 (July, 1937), 89-102.
71. Price, D. O., "Distance and Direction as Factors of International Migration, 1935-1940," *Soc. Forces*, 27 (Oct., 1948), 48-53.
72. Quinn, J. A., *Human Ecology, op. cit.*, pp. 372-395.
73. Ravenstein, E. G., "The Laws of Migration," *J. royal Statist. Soc.*, 48 (June, 1885), 167-235; 52 (June, 1888), 241-305.
74. Smith, T. L., *Population Analysis* (New York: McGraw-Hill, 1948), pp. 291-368.
75. Sorokin, P. A., C. C. Zimmerman, and C. J. Galpin, *Systematic Sourcebook for Rural Sociology* (Minneapolis: Univ. Minnesota Press, 1932), Vol. III, 458-627.
76. Stouffer, S. A., "Intervening Opportunities: A Theory Relating Mobility and Distance," *Amer. sociol. Rev.*, 5 (Dec., 1940), 845-867.
77. Taft, D. R., *Human Migration* (New York: Ronald, 1936).
78. Thomas, D. S., *Research Memorandum on Migration Differentials,* Bulletin 43 (New York: Social Science Research Council, 1938).
79. Thompson, W. S., and D. J. Bogue, "Subregional Migration," *Soc. Forces*, 27 (May, 1949), 392-400.
80. Thorndike, E. L., "The Causes of Inter-State Migration," *Sociometry*, 5 (Nov., 1942), 321-335.
81. Thornthwaite, C. W., *Internal Migration in the United States* (Philadelphia: Univ. Pennsylvania Press, 1934).
82. U.S. Census, Series P-20, No. 14.
83. U.S. Census, Series P-20, No. 22.
84. Vance, R. B., *All These People* (Chapel Hill, N.C.: Univ. North Carolina Press, 1945), pp. 109-152.
85. ———, *Research Memorandum on Population Redistribution in the United States* (New York: Social Science Research Council, 1938).
86. Westfeld, A., "The Distance Factor in Migration," *Soc. Forces*, 19 (Dec., 1940), 213-218.
87. Willcox, W. F., *International Migrations* (New York: National Bureau Economic Research, 1931, 1934), 2 vols.

Secondary Dispersal

88. Bogue, D. J., *Metropolitan Decentralization: A Study of Differential Growth;* Studies in Population Distribution, No. 2 (Oxford, Ohio: Scripps Foundation, 1950).
89. Burgess, E. W., "The Growth of the City," in R. E. Park, E. W. Burgess, and R. D. McKenzie (eds.), *The City* (Chicago: Univ. Chicago Press, 1925), pp. 47-58.
90. Cressey, P. F., "Population Succession in Chicago," *Amer. J. Sociol.*, 44 (July, 1938), 59-69.
91. Dawson and Gettys, *op. cit.*, pp. 213-248.
92. Ford, R. G., "Population Succession in Chicago," *Amer. J. Sociol.*, 56 (Sept., 1950), 156-160.

93. Gibbard, H. A., "The Status Factor in Residential Successions," *Amer. J. Sociol.*, 46 (May, 1941), 835-842.
94. Hawley, A. H., "An Ecological Study of Urban Service Institutions," *Amer. sociol. Rev.*, 16 (Oct., 1941), 629-639.
95. ———, *Human Ecology, op. cit.*, pp. 348-431.
96. Hertzler, J. O., *Social Institutions* (Lincoln: Univ. Nebraska Press, 1946), pp. 216-220.
97. Hollingshead, "Human Ecology," *op. cit.*, pp. 103-107, 147-167.
98. Hoyt, Homer, "Forces of Urban Centralization and Decentralization," *Amer. J. sociol.*, 47 (May, 1941), 843-852.
99. McFall, R. J., "Urban Decentralization," in *Economic Essays in Honor of Wesley Clair Mitchell* (New York: Columbia Univ. Press, 1935), pp. 297-307.
100. McKenzie, R. D., "The Ecological Approach to the Study of the Human Community," in R. E. Park *et al.*, *The City* (Chicago: Univ. Chicago Press, 1925), pp. 63-79.
101. ———, "The Scope of Human Ecology," *Pubs. Amer. sociol. Soc.*, 20 (July, 1926), 141-154.
102. Park, R. E., "Succession: An Ecological Concept," *Amer. sociol. Rev.*, 1 (Apr., 1936), 171-179.
103. Quinn, J. A., *Human Ecology, op. cit.*, pp. 295-371.

Regionalization

104. Bertrand, A. L., "Regional Sociology as a Special Discipline," *Soc. Forces*, 31 (Dec., 1952), 132-136.
105. Cahnman, W. J., "The Concept of *Raum* in the Theory of Regionalism," *Amer. sociol. Rev.*, 9 (Oct., 1944), 455-463.
106. Dickinson, R. E., *City, Region, and Regionalism: A Geographical Contribution to Human Ecology* (London: Kegan Paul, Trench & Trubner, 1947).
107. Eldridge, H. T., "The Implications of Regionalism to Folk Sociology with Illustrations from the Southern Regions," *Soc. Forces*, 22 (Oct., 1943), 41-43.
108. Fesler, J. W., "Standardization of Federal Administrative Regions," *Soc. Forces*, 15 (Oct., 1936), 12-21.
109. Gillette, J. M., "Developmental Aspect of Regionalism," *Soc. Forces*, 27 (Oct., 1948), 42-44.
110. Hagood, M. J., "Statistical Methods of Delineation of Regions Applied to Data of Agriculture and Population," *Soc. Forces*, 21 (Mar., 1943), 287-297.
111. Hallenbeck, *op. cit.*, pp. 224-246.
112. Heberle, R., "Regionalism: Some Critical Observations," *Soc. Forces*, 21 (Mar., 1943), 280-287.
113. Hertzler, J. O., "Some Notes on the Social Psychology of Regionalism," *Soc. Forces*, 18 (Mar., 1940), 331-337.
114. ———, "Some Sociological Aspects of American Regionalism," *Soc. Forces*, 18 (Oct., 1939), 17-29.
115. Kollmorgen, W., "Political Regionalism in the United States—Fact or Myth," *Soc. Forces*, 15 (Oct., 1936), 111-122.
116. MacIver, R. M., and C. H. Page, *Society: An Introductory Analysis* (New York: Rinehart, 1949), pp. 341-347.
117. McDougal, M. S., and M. E. H. Rotival, *The Case for Regional Planning* (New Haven: Yale Univ. Press, 1947).
118. Mess, H. A., "Geography in Relation to National and Social Sentiment," *Sociol. Rev. Brit.*, 30 (Apr., 1940), 186-200.
119. Moore, H. E., "Social Scientists Explore the Region," *Soc. Forces*, 16 (May, 1938), 436-474.
120. Morgan, F. W., "Three Aspects of Regional Consciousness," *Sociol. Rev. Brit.*, 31 (June, 1939), 68-88.
121. Mukerjee, R., *Man and His Habitation* (New York: Longmans, Green, 1940).
122. Mumford, L., *The Culture of Cities* (New York: Harcourt, Brace, 1938).
123. National Resources Committee, *Regional Factors in National Planning* (Washington: U.S. Government Printing Office, 1935).
124. Odum, H. W., "A Sociological Approach to the Study and Practice of Regionalism," *Soc. Forces*, 20 (May, 1942), 425-437.
125. ———, "From Community Studies to Regionalism," *Soc. Forces*, 23 (Mar., 1945), 245-258.
126. ———, "Regional Development and Governmental Policy," *Ann. Amer. Acad. polit. soc. Sci.*, 206 (Nov., 1939), 133-141.
127. ———, "The Regional Quality and Balance of America," *Soc. Forces*, 23 (Mar., 1945), 269-284.
128. ———, *Southern Regions of the United States* (Chapel Hill, N.C.: Univ. North Carolina Press, 1937).

129. ——, and H. E. Moore, *American Regionalism* (New York: Holt, 1928).
130. Quinn, J. A., *Human Ecology, op. cit.*, pp. 163-184, 219-265.
131. Riemer, S., "Theoretical Aspects of Regionalism," *Soc. Forces*, 21 (Mar., 1943), 275-280.
132. Simpson, G., "Regionalism," *Soc. Forces*, 26 (Dec., 1941), 185-189.
133. Spengler, J. J., "Regional Differences and the Future of Manufacturing in America," *Sth. Econ. J.*, 7 (Apr., 1941), 475-493.
134. Staley, Eugene, "The Myth of the Continents," *Foreign Affairs*, 19 (Apr., 1941), 481-494.
135. Thompson, W. S., *The Growth of Metropolitan Districts in the United States* (Washington: U.S. Government Printing Office, 1948).
136. Vance, R. B., "Implications of the Concepts 'Region' and 'Regional Planning'," *Pubs. Amer. sociol. Soc.*, 29 (1935), 85-93.
137. Wirth, L., "The Prospects of Regional Research in Relation to Social Planning," *Pubs. Amer. sociol. Soc.*, 29 (1935), 107-114.
138. Woolston, H., *Metropolis: A Study of Urban Communities* (New York: Appleton-Century, 1938).

X. Societal Organization: Processes, Factors, and Components

The Nature and Significance of Societal Organization

1. Barnard, C. I., *Organization and Management* (Cambridge: Harvard Univ. Press, 1948), pp. 143-149.
2. Bennett, J. W., and M. M. Tumin, *Social Life: Structure, Function* (New York: Knopf, 1948), pp. 116-126.
3. Brown, G. G., and J. H. Barnett, "Social Organization and Social Structure," *Amer. Anthrop.*, 44 (Jan.-Mar., 1942), 31-36.
4. Cooley, C. H., *Social Process* (New York: Scribner, 1920), pp. 19-29.
5. Hertzler, J. O., *Social Institutions* (Lincoln: Univ. Nebraska Press, 1946), pp. 12-16.
6. Heberle, R., *Social Movements* (New York: Appleton-Century-Crofts, 1951), pp. 269-274.
7. Homans, G. C., "A Conceptual Scheme for the Study of Social Organization," *Amer. sociol. Rev.*, 12 (Feb., 1947), 13-26.
8. Linton, R., "A Neglected Aspect of Social Organization," *Amer. J. Sociol.*, 45 (May, 1940), 870-886.
9. ——, *The Study of Man* (New York: Appleton-Century, 1936), pp. 253-257.
10. Loomis, C. P., and J. A. Beegle, *Rural Social Systems* (New York: Prentice-Hall, 1950), Pref. and pp. 3-36.
11. Lowie, R. H., *Social Organization* (New York: Rinehart, 1948), pp. 3-14.
12. Malinowski, B., "Man's Culture and Man's Behavior," *Sigma Xi Quart.*, 29 (Oct., 1941), 182-196.
13. Mooney, J. D., *The Principles of Organization* (New York: Harper, 1947), pp. 1-56.
14. Ruesch, J., and G. Bateson, "Structure and Process in Social Relations," *Psychiatry*, 12 (May, 1949), 105-124.
15. Selznick, P., "Foundations of the Theory of Organization," *Amer. sociol. Rev.*, 13 (Feb., 1948), 25-35.
16. Weber, M., *The Theory of Social and Economic Organization* (A. M. Henderson and T. Parsons, trans.) (New York: Oxford, 1947).
17. Williams, R. M., Jr., *American Society: A Sociological Interpretation* (New York: Knopf, 1951), pp. 33-35, 444-448, 455-461, 466-479, 484-485.

Basic Processes:

COOPERATION

18. Bogardus, E. S., "The Long Trail of Cooperation," *Sociol. soc. Res.*, 31 (Sept.-Oct., 1946), 54-62.
19. Deutsch, M., "A Theory of Cooperation and Competition," *Hum. Relat.*, 2 (No. 2, 1949), 129-152.
20. Eaton, J. W., "A Conceptual Theory of Cooperation," *Amer. J. Sociol.*, 54 (Sept., 1948), 126-134.
21. Groves, E. R., and H. E. Moore, *An Introduction to Sociology* (New York: Longmans, Green, 1940), pp. 257-276.
22. Hayes, E. C., "Some Social Relations Restated," *Amer. J. Sociol.*, 31 (Nov., 1925), 333-346.
23. Hiller, E. T., *Principles of Sociology* (New York: Harper, 1933), pp. 162-182, 200-211.
24. ——, *Social Relations and Structures* (New York: Harper, 1947), pp. 115-132, 153-158.
25. Kropotkin, P. A., *Mutual Aid: A Factor in Evolution*, rev. ed., (New York: Knopf, 1917).
26. May, M. A., and L. W. Doob, *Competition and*

Cooperation, Bulletin 25 (New York: Social Science Research Council, 1937).

27. Mead, M., *Cooperation and Competition Among Primitive Peoples* (New York: McGraw-Hill, 1937).
28. Ross, E. A., *Principles of Sociology* (New York: Appleton-Century, 1938), 345-355.
29. Smith, T. L., *The Sociology of Rural Life* (New York: Harper, 1947), pp. 478-498.

SOCIAL PARTICIPATION

30. Allport, G. W., "The Psychology of Participation," *Psychol. Rev.*, 52 (1945), 117-132.
31. Chapin, F. S., *Social Participation Scale* (Minneapolis: Univ. Minnesota Press, 1938).
32. Elliott, M. A., Comment on Paper by S. A. Queen, *Amer. sociol. Rev.*, 6 (June, 1941), 316-319.
33. Hay, D. G., "A Scale for the Measurement of Social Participation of Rural Households," *Rur. Sociol.*, 15 (June, 1950), 141-148.
34. Queen, S. A., "The Concepts Social Disorganization and Social Participation," *Amer. sociol. Rev.*, 6 (June, 1941), 307-316.
35. ———, "Social Participation in Relation to Social Disorganization," *Amer. sociol. Rev.*, 14 (Apr., 1947), 251-257.
36. Young, K., *Sociology: A Study of Society and Culture* (New York: American Book, 1949), 27-28, 260-262, 282-284.

DIVISION OF LABOR AND SPECIALIZATION OF FUNCTION

37. Durkheim, E., *Division of Labor in Society* (G. Simpson, trans.) (New York: Macmillan, 1933).
38. Freedman, R., A. H. Hawley, W. Landecker, and H. Miner, *Principles of Sociology* (New York: Holt, 1952), pp. 151-154.
39. Hiller, *Social Relations and Structures, op. cit.*, pp. 148-153.
40. North, C. C., *Social Differentiations* (Chapel Hill, N.C.: Univ. North Carolina Press, 1926), pp. 8-16, 270-274.
41. Salz, A., "Specialization," *Encyclopedia of the Social Sciences* (New York: Macmillan, 1934), Vol. 14, 279-282.
42. Smith, A., *An Inquiry into the Nature and Causes of the Wealth of Nations* (New York: Modern Library, 1930), Bk. I, Chaps. I-III; Bk. II, Chap. I.
43. Sorokin, P. A., *Society, Culture, and Personality* (New York: Harper, 1947), pp. 276-379.
44. Young, *op. cit.*, pp. 494-498.

OPPOSITION

45. Carr, L. J., "A Situational Approach to Conflict and War," *Soc. Forces*, 24 (Mar., 1946), 300-303.
46. Cooley, *op. cit.*, pp. 35-42, 125-136.
47. Hiller, *Principles of Sociology, op. cit.*, pp. 219-226.
48. MacIver, R. M., and C. H. Page, *Society: An Introductory Analysis* (New York: Rinehart, 1949), pp. 62-70.
49. Ross, *op. cit.*, pp. 204-209.
50. Young, *op. cit.*, pp. 64-69.

INTEGRATION

51. Angell, R. C., "Moral Integration and Interpersonal Integration in American Cities," *Amer. sociol. Rev.*, 14 (Apr., 1949), 245-251.
52. ———, *The Integration of American Society* (New York: McGraw-Hill, 1941).
53. ———, "The Social Integration of Selected American Cities," *Amer. J. Sociol.*, 47 (Jan., 1942), 575-592.
54. Clinard, M. B., "The Group Approach to Social Reintegration," *Amer. sociol. Rev.*, 14 (Apr., 1949), 257-262.
55. Cooley, *op. cit.*, pp. 241-254.
56. Freedman, *et al.*, *op. cit.*, pp. 145-147, 154-155, 489-503.
57. Landecker, W. S., "Smend's Theory of Integration," *Soc. Forces*, 29 (Oct., 1950), 39-48.
58. ———, "Types of Integration and Their Measurement," *Amer. J. sociol.*, 56 (Jan., 1951), 332-340.
59. ———, "Integration and Group Structure: An Area for Research," *Soc. Forces*, 30 (Mar., 1952), 394-400.
60. Loomis, C. P., *Studies in Applied and Theoretical Social Science* (East Lansing: Michigan State College Press, 1950), pp. 10-13.
61. Lundberg, G. A., *Foundations of Sociology* (New York: Macmillan, 1939), pp. 268-277.
62. Parsons, T., and E. A. Shils, *Toward a General Theory of Action* (Cambridge: Harvard Univ. Press, 1951), pp. 202-204, 219-221.
63. Williams, *op. cit.*, pp. 513-532.

Essential Factors and Components:

SOCIAL VALUES

64. Aberle, D. F., "Shared Values in Complex Societies," *Amer. sociol. Rev.*, 15 (Aug., 1950), 495-502.

65. Bain, R., "Natural Science and Value Policy," *Phil. Science,* 14 (July, 1949), 182-192.
66. Becker, H., "Supreme Values and the Sociologist," *Amer. sociol. Rev.,* 6 (Apr., 1941), 155-171.
67. Benoit-Smullyan, E., "Value Judgments and the Social Sciences," *J. Phil.,* 42 (Apr., 1945), 197-210.
68. Bierstedt, R., "The Means-End Schema in Social Theory," *Amer. sociol. Rev.,* 3 (Oct., 1938), 665-671.
69. Bouglé, C., *The Evolution of Values* (Helen S. Sellars, trans.) (New York: Holt, 1926), pp. v-xxxvii, 3-87, 147-181.
70. Cooley, C. H., *Social Process* (New York: Scribner, 1915), pp. 283-348.
71. ———, "The Process of Pecuniary Valuation," *Quart. J. Econ.,* 30 (Nov., 1913), 188-203.
72. ———, "Valuation as a Social Process," *Psychol. Bull.,* 9 (1918-1919), 543-550.
73. Dodd, S. C., "On Classifying Human Values: A Step in the Prediction of Human Valuing," *Amer. Sociol. Rev.,* 16 (Oct., 1951), 645-653.
74. Flewelling, R. T., *The Things That Matter Most* (New York: Ronald, 1946), pp. 17-36.
75. Giddings, F. H., *Civilization and Society* (New York: Holt, 1932), pp. 283-300.
76. Hart, S. L., *Treatise on Values* (New York: Philosophical Library, 1949).
77. Hilliard, A. L., *The Forms of Value: An Extension of Hedonistic Axiology* (New York: Columbia Univ. Press, 1950).
78. Hull, C. L., "Value, Valuation, and Natural Science Method," *Phil. Science,* 11 (July, 1944), 125-141.
79. Jensen, H. E., "Sociology and Fundamental Values," *Soc. Sci.,* 19 (Jan., 1944), 5-12.
80. Kluckhohn, C., *et al.,* "Values and Value-Orientations in the Theory of Action," in Parsons and Shils, *op. cit.,* pp. 388-433.
81. Lundberg, G. A., "Human Values—A Research Program," *Research Studies of the State College of Washington,* 18 (Sept., 1950), 103-111.
82. Malinowski, B., *Freedom and Civilization* (New York: Roy, 1945), pp. 128-137.
83. Mukerjee, R., *The Social Structure of Values* (London: Macmillan, 1949).
84. Perry, R. B., *General Theory of Value* (New York: Longmans, Green, 1926).
85. Parsons, T., "Some Aspects of the Relation between Social Science and Ethics," *Soc. Sci.,* 22 (July, 1947), 213-217.
86. ———, *The Social System* (Glencoe, Ill.: Free Press, 1951), pp. 36-45.
87. ———, and Shils, *op. cit.,* pp. 159-189, 388-433.
88. ———, "The Place of Ultimate Values in Sociological Theory," *Int. J. Ethics,* 45 (Apr., 1935), 282-316.
89. Williams, *op. cit.,* pp. 374-442.

NORMS

For references on norms, see references of Chapter 20.

STATUSES AND ROLES

90. Barnard, C. I., *Industry and Society* (New York: McGraw-Hill, 1946), pp. 46-72.
91. ———, *Organization and Management* (Cambridge: Harvard Univ. Press, 1948), pp. 207-244.
92. Bennett and Tumin, *op. cit.,* pp. 86-115.
93. Benoit-Smullyan, E., "Status, Status Types, and Status Interrelations," *Amer. sociol. Rev.,* 9 (Apr., 1944), 151-161.
94. Brown, J. C., "An Experiment in Role-Taking," *Amer. sociol. Rev.,* 17 (Oct., 1952), 587-597.
95. Cattell, R. B., "The Concept of Social Status," *J. soc. Psychol.,* 15 (May, 1942), 293-308.
96. Cottrell, L. S., Jr., "The Adjustment of the Individual to His Age and Sex Roles," *Amer. sociol. Rev.,* 7 (Oct., 1942), 617-620.
97. Davis, A., "American Status Systems and the Socialization of the Child," *Amer. sociol. Rev.,* 6 (June, 1941), 345-354.
98. Davis, K., "A Conceptual Analysis of Stratification," *Amer. sociol. Rev.,* 7 (June, 1942), 309-321.
99. ———, *Human Society* (New York: Macmillan, 1949), pp. 83-119.
100. Dawson, C. A., and W. E. Gettys, *An Introduction to Sociology* (New York: Ronald, 1948), pp. 415-460.
101. Freedman, *et al., op. cit.,* pp. 111, 147-150.
102. Hiller, *Social Relations and Structures, op. cit.,* pp. 330-543.
103. Hughes, E. C., "Dilemma and Contradictions of Status," *Amer. J. Sociol.,* 50 (Mar., 1945), 353-359.
104. Kaufman, H. F., "Defining Prestige Rank in a Rural Community," *Sociometry,* 8 (May, 1945), 199-207.
105. ———, *Prestige Classes in a New York Rural Community,* Agricultural Experimental Station Memoir, No. 260 (Ithaca: Cornell Univ. Press, 1943).
106. Linton, R., "Problems of Status Personality,"

in *Culture and Personality* (New York: Viking Fund, 1949), pp. 163-171.
107. ———, *The Study of Man, op. cit.*, pp. 113-131.
108. Lundberg, G. A., "The Measurement of Socio-economic Status," *Amer. sociol. Rev.*, 5 (Feb., 1940), 29-39.
109. Mead, G. H., *Philosophy of the Act* (Chicago: Univ. Chicago Press, 1938).
110. Merrill, F. E., and H. W. Eldredge, *Culture and Society* (New York: Prentice-Hall, 1952), pp. 151-158.
111. Newcomb, T. M., *Social Psychology* (New York: Dryden, 1950), pp. 275-287.
112. Parsons, T., *The Social System, op. cit.*, pp. 24-26, 38-40, 58-96.
113. ———, and Shils, *op. cit.*, pp. 23-26, 91-98, 208-218, 349-351.
114. Rose, A. W., "The Adequacy of Women's Expectations for Adult Roles," *Soc. Forces*, 30 (Oct., 1951), 69-77.
115. Schuler, E. A., "Social and Economic Status in a Louisiana Hills Community," *Rur. Sociol.*, 5 (Mar., 1940), 68-84.
116. Toby, Jackson, "Some Variables in Role Conflict Analysis," *Soc. Forces*, 30 (Mar., 1952), 323-327.
117. Warren, R. L., "Cultural, Personal, and Situational Roles," *Sociol. soc. Res.*, 34 (Nov.-Dec., 1949), 104-111.

LEADERSHIP

118. Barnard, *Organization and Management, op. cit.*, pp. 80-110.
119. ———, *The Functions of the Executive* (Cambridge: Harvard Univ. Press, 1940).
120. Bernard, L. L., *Social Psychology* (New York: Holt, 1926), pp. 517-527.
121. Bogardus, E. S., *Leaders and Leadership* (New York: Appleton-Century, 1934).
122. Coyle, Grace L., *Social Process in Organized Groups* (New York: Smith, 1930), pp. 103-126.
123. Crowley, W. H., "Traits of Face-to-Face Leaders," *J. abnorm. soc. Psych.*, 26 (Oct.-Dec., 1931), 404-413.
124. Faris, R. E. L., "The Sociological Causes of Genius," *Amer. sociol. Rev.*, 5 (Oct., 1940), 689-699.
125. Fearing, F., "Psychological Studies of Historical Personalities," *Psychol. Bull.*, 249 (Sept., 1927), 521-539.
126. Frank, L. K., *Society and the Patient* (New Brunswick, N.J.: Rutgers Univ. Press, 1948), pp. 308-338.
127. Gibb, C. A., "Principles and Traits of Leadership," *J. abnorm. soc. Psychol.*, 42 (July, 1947), 267-284.
128. Gouldner, A. W., *Studies in Leadership: Leadership and Democratic Action* (New York: Harper, 1950).
129. Hart, H., *Technique of Social Progress* (New York: Holt, 1931), pp. 532-535, 607-658.
130. Homans, G. C., *The Human Group* (New York: Harcourt, Brace, 1950), pp. 415-440.
131. Jennings, H. H., *Leadership and Isolation: A Study of Personality in Inter-personal Relations* (New York: Longmans, Green, 1950).
132. ———, "Leadership—A Dynamic Interpretation," *J. educ. Sociol.*, 17 (Mar., 1944), 431-433.
133. ———, "Structure of Leadership-Development and Sphere of Influence," *Sociometry*, 1 (July-Oct., 1937), 93-143.
134. Krech, D., and R. C. Crutchfield, *Theory and Problems of Social Psychology* (New York: McGraw-Hill, 1948), pp. 417-439.
135. Krout, M. H., *Introduction to Social Psychology* (New York: Harper, 1942), pp. 636-711.
136. Levine, S., "An Approach to Constructive Leadership," *J. Soc. Issues*, 5 (Winter, 1949), 46-53.
137. McCormick, T. C., *Sociology* (New York: Ronald, 1950), pp. 531-549.
138. Morris, R. T., and M. Seaman, "The Problem of Leadership: An Interdisciplinary Approach," *Amer. J. Sociol.*, 56 (Sept., 1950), 149-155.
139. Murphy, A. J., "A Study of the Leadership Process," *Amer. sociol. Rev.*, 6 (Oct., 1941), 674-687.
140. Pigors, P., *Leadership or Domination* (Boston: Houghton Mifflin, 1935).
141. ———, "Types of Followers," *J. soc. Psychol.*, 5 (Aug., 1934), 378-393.
142. Schmidt, R., "Leadership," *Encyclopedia of the Social Sciences* (New York: Macmillan, 1933), Vol. 9, pp. 282-286.
143. Smith, H. L., and L. M. Krueger, *A Brief Summary of Literature on Leadership*, Bulletin of School of Education, University of Indiana, Vol. IX, No. 4 (Sept., 1933).
144. Smythe, H. H., "Changing Patterns in Negro Leadership," *Soc. Forces*, 29 (Dec., 1950), 191-197.
145. Tead, O., *The Art of Leadership* (New York: Whittlesey House, 1935).
146. Wakeley, R. E., "Selecting Leaders for Agricul-

tural Programs," *Sociometry,* 10 (Nov., 1947), 384-395.
147. Zeleny, L. D., "Social Leadership," *Sociol. soc. Res.,* 33 (July-Aug., 1949), 431-436.
148. Znaniecki, F., *The Social Role of the Man of Knowledge* (New York: Columbia Univ. Press, 1940).

XI. Groups: Nature, Formation, Functions, and Forms

Groups: Place, Nature, Formation, Types, Functions, Distinctions, Problems

1. Angell, R. C., *The Integration of American Society* (New York: McGraw-Hill, 1941), pp. 29-38.
2. Bennett, J. W., and M. M. Tumin, *Social Life* (New York: Knopf, 1948), pp. 138-165.
3. Bernard, J., *American Community Behavior* (New York: Dryden, 1949), pp. 15-38.
4. Bernard, L. L., *Introduction to Sociology* (New York: Crowell, 1942), pp. 851-876.
5. Bierstedt, R., "The Sociology of Majorities," *Amer. sociol. Rev.,* 13 (Dec., 1948), 700-710.
6. Carr, L. J., *Situational Analysis* (New York: Harper, 1948), pp. 3-4, 45-48.
7. Coyle, G. L., *Social Process in Organized Groups* (New York: Smith, 1930).
8. Davis, K., *Human Society* (New York: Macmillan, 1949), pp. 289-309, 346-357.
9. DeGré, G., "Outlines for a Systematic Classification of Social Groups," *Amer. sociol. Rev.,* 14 (Feb., 1949), 145-148.
10. Dolson, F., "Patterns of Voluntary Association among Urban Working Class Families," *Amer. sociol. Rev.,* 16 (Oct., 1951), 687-693.
11. Eubank, E. E., *Concepts of Sociology* (Boston: Heath, 1932), pp. 117-118, 132-135, 138-140, 146-153, 156-168.
12. Francis, E. K., "Minority Groups—A Revision of Concepts," *Brit. J. Sociol.,* 2 (Sept., 1951), 219-230.
13. Freeman, E., *Social Psychology* (New York: Holt, 1936), pp. 367-406.
14. Hawley, A. H., *Human Ecology* (New York: Ronald, 1950), pp. 209-220.
15. Hertzler, J. O., *Social Institutions* (Lincoln: Univ. Nebraska Press, 1946), pp. 17-23.
16. Hiller, E. T., *Social Relations and Structures* (New York: Harper, 1947), pp. 246-290.
17. Homans, G. C., *The Human Group* (New York: Harcourt, Brace, 1950).
18. Krech, D., and R. C. Crutchfield, *Theory and Problems of Social Psychology* (New York: McGraw-Hill, 1948), pp. 366-403.
19. Lewin, K., "Field Theory and Experiment in Social Psychology: Concepts and Methods," *Amer. J. Sociol.,* 44 (May, 1939), 868-896.
20. Lundberg, G. A., *Foundations of Sociology* (New York: Macmillan, 1939), pp. 252-254, 321-322, 339-374.
21. ———, "Some Problems of Group Classification and Measurement," *Amer. sociol. Rev.,* 5 (June, 1940), 351-360.
22. ———, and M. Lawsing, 'The Sociography of Some Community Relations," *Amer. sociol. Rev.,* 2 (June, 1937), 318-335.
23. ———, and M. Steele, "Social Attraction Patterns in a Village," *Sociometry,* 1 (Jan.-Apr., 1938), 375-419.
24. Lundberg, G. A., V. B. Hertzler, and L. Dickinson, "Attraction Patterns in a University," *Sociometry,* 12 (Feb., 1949), 158-169.
25. MacIver, R. M., *Community* (London: Macmillan, 1924), pp. 128-152.
26. ———, and C. H. Page, *Society: An Introductory Analysis* (New York: Rinehart, 1949), pp. 213-237.
27. McGregor, D., "Conditions of Effective Leadership in the Industrial Organization," in T. M. Newcomb and E. L. Hartley (eds.), *Readings in Social Psychology* (New York: Holt, 1947), pp. 427-435.
28. Miller, D. C., and W. A. Form, *Industrial Sociology* (New York: Harper, 1951), pp. 273-307.
29. Moreno, J. L., *Who Shall Survive: A New Approach to the Problem of Human Interpretations* (New York: Nervous and Mental Disease Pub. Co., 1934), Part IV.
30. Smith, T. L., *The Sociology of Rural Life* (New York: Harper, 1947), pp. 324-330.
31. ———, and C. A. McMahan, *The Sociology of Urban Life* (New York: Dryden, 1951), pp. 390-395.
32. Sanderson, D., "A Preliminary Group Classification Based on Structure," *Soc. Forces,* 17 (Dec., 1938), 196-201.
33. ———, "Group Description," *Soc. Forces,* 16 (Mar., 1938), 309-319.
34. Simpson, G., *Emile Durkheim on the Division of Labor* (New York: Macmillan, 1933), Bk. I, Chaps. II, III.
35. Sorokin, P. A., *Society, Culture, and Personality* (New York: Harper, 1947), pp. 367-389, 400-404.

36. ———, C. C. Zimmerman, and C. J. Galpin, *Systematic Sourcebook for Rural Sociology* (Minneapolis: Univ. Minnesota Press, 1930), Vol. I, pp. 307-308.
37. Wilson, L., "The Sociography of Groups," in G. Gurvitch and W. E. Moore (eds.), *Twentieth Century Sociology* (New York: Philosophical Library, 1945), pp. 139-171.
38. Wood, M. M., *The Stranger: A Study in Social Relationships* (New York: Columbia Univ. Press, 1934).
39. Znaniecki, F., "Social Groups as Products of Participating Individuals," *Amer. J. Sociol.*, 44 (Mar., 1939), 799-811.
40. ———, "Social Organization and Institutions," in G. Gurvitch and W. E. Moore (eds.), *Twentieth Century Sociology* (New York: Philosophical Library, 1945), pp. 200-216.

Large-Scale Formal Organizations—Bureaucracy

41. Barnard, C. I., *Organization and Management* (Cambridge: Harvard Univ. Press, 1948).
42. ———, *The Functions of the Executive* (Cambridge: Harvard Univ. Press, 1940).
43. Bendix, R., "Bureaucracy: The Problem and Its Setting," *Amer. sociol. Rev.*, 12 (Oct., 1947), 493-507.
44. Dalton, M., "Conflicts between Staff and Line Managerial Offices," *Amer. sociol. Rev.*, 15 (June, 1950), 342-351.
45. Drucker, P. F., "The New Society: Revolution by Mass Production," *Harper's*, 199 (Sept., 1949), 21-29.
46. Dubin, R., "Division-Making by Management in Industrial Relations," *Amer. J. Sociol.*, 54 (Jan., 1949), 292-297.
47. ———, *Human Relations in Administration: The Sociology of Organization* (New York: Prentice-Hall, 1951).
48. Gaus, J. M., "A Theory of Organization in Public Administration," in *The Frontiers of Public Administration* (Chicago: Univ. Chicago Press, 1936), Chap. V.
49. Gerth, H. H., and C. W. Mills, *From Max Weber: Essays in Sociology* (New York: Oxford, 1946), pp. 196-244.
50. Josephson, E., "Irrational Leadership in Formal Organizations," *Soc. Forces*, 31 (Dec., 1952), 109-117.
51. Hiller, *op. cit.*, pp. 581-587.
52. MacIver and Page, *op. cit.*, pp. 229-237.
53. Merton, R. K., "Bureaucratic Structure and Personality," *Soc. Forces*, 18 (May, 1940), 560-568; or R. K. Merton, *Social Theory and Social Structure* (Glencoe, Ill.: Free Press, 1949), pp. 151-160.
54. ——— (ed.), *Reader in Bureaucracy* (Glencoe, Ill.: Free Press, 1951).
55. ———, "The Machine, the Worker, and the Engineer," *Science*, 105 (Jan. 24, 1947), 79-84.
56. ———, "The Role of the Intellectual in Public Bureaucracy," *Soc. Forces*, 23 (May, 1945), 405-415; or R. K. Merton, *Reader in Bureaucracy* (Glencoe, Ill.: Free Press, 1951), pp. 161-178.
57. Miller and Form, *op. cit.*, pp. 70-71, 144-271, 836-837.
58. Mooney, J. D., *The Principles of Organization* (New York: Harper, 1937).
59. Moore, W. E., *Industrial Relations and the Social Order* (New York: Macmillan, 1951), pp. 71-202, 296-319.
60. Parsons, T., "Professions and Social Structure," *Soc. Forces*, 17 (May, 1939), 457-467; or T. Parsons, *Essays in Sociological Theory, Pure and Applied* (Glencoe, Ill.: Free Press, 1949), pp. 185-199.
61. ———, *The Structure of Social Action* (New York: McGraw-Hill, 1937), pp. 506-509.
62. Reissman, L., "A Study of Role Conceptions in Bureaucracy," *Soc. Forces*, 27 (Mar., 1949), 305-310.
63. Roethlisberger, F. J., and W. J. Dickinson, *Management and the Worker* (Cambridge: Harvard Univ. Press), 1939.
64. Ross, E. A., *Principles of Sociology* (New York: Appleton-Century, 1938), pp. 356-398.
65. Russell, J. D., "Some Reflections Concerning University Administration," *Bull. Amer. Ass. Univ. Prof.*, 35 (Autumn, 1949), 476-489.
66. Selznick, P., An Approach to a Theory of Bureaucracy," *Amer. sociol. Rev.*, 8 (Feb., 1943), 47-54.
67. ———, "Foundation of the Theory of Organization," *Amer. sociol. Rev.*, 13 (Feb., 1948), 25-35.
68. ———, *TVA and the Grass Roots: A Study in the Sociology of Formal Organization* (Berkeley: Univ. California Press, 1949).
69. Simon, H. A., *Administrative Behavior* (New York: Macmillan, 1947).
70. Spindler, G. D., "The Military—A Systematic Analysis," *Soc. Forces*, 27 (Oct., 1948), 83-88.

71. Stogdill, R. M., "The Sociometry of Working Relationships in Formal Organization," *Sociometry,* 12 (Nov., 1949), 276-300.
72. Trecker, H. B., *Group Process in Administration* (New York: Women's Press, 1950).
73. Weber, M., *The Theory of Social and Economic Organization* (A. M. Henderson and T. Parsons, trans.) (New York: Oxford, 1947), pp. 56-64, 136-157, 324-423.
74. Williams, R. M., Jr., *American Society: A Sociological Interpretation* (New York: Knopf, 1951), pp. 174-183, 455-461, 466-479.
75. Young, H., "The Conference Process," *Amer. J. Sociol.,* 46 (Mar., 1941), 708-717.

Communities

76. Bennett and Tumin, *op. cit.,* pp. 387-430.
77. Bernard, J., *American Community Behavior, op. cit.,* pp. 15-37.
78. Bogue, D. J., *The Structure of the Metropolitan Community: A Study of Dominance and Subdominance,* Social Science Research Project, Institute for Human Adjustment (Ann Arbor: Univ. Michigan Press, 1949).
79. Carr, *op. cit.,* pp. 69-88.
80. Davis, *op. cit.,* pp. 310-315.
81. Dawson, C. A., and W. E. Gettys, *An Introduction to Sociology* (New York: Ronald, 1948), pp. 497-525.
82. Ensminger, D., "Rural Neighbors and Communities," in C. C. Taylor (ed.), *Rural Life in the United States* (New York: Knopf, 1949), pp. 55-77.
83. Galpin, C. J., *The Social Anatomy of an Agricultural Community,* Agricultural Experimental Station, University of Wisconsin, Research Bulletin, No. 34 (Madison, Wis., 1915).
84. Hiller, *op. cit.,* pp. 3-11.
85. ———, "The Community as a Social Group," *Amer. sociol. Rev.,* 6 (Apr., 1941), 189-202.
86. Kinneman, J. A., *The Community in American Society* (New York: Crofts, 1947), pp. 3-107.
87. Loomis, C. P., and J. A. Beegle, *Rural Social Systems* (New York: Prentice-Hall, 1950), Part II.
88. Lundberg, G. A., and M. Lawsing, *op. cit.*
89. MacIver, R. M., *Community* (London: Macmillan, 1924).
90. ———, and C. H. Page, *op. cit.,* pp. 281-309.
91. Murdock, G. P., *Social Structure* (New York: Macmillan, 1949), pp. 79-90.
92. Smith, *op. cit.,* pp. 331-342.
93. Zimmerman, C. C., *The Changing Community* (New York: Harper, 1938), pp. 3-115.

XII. Social Institutions and Institutionalization

Institutions: Place, Nature, Functions

1. Ballard, L. V., *Social Institutions* (New York: Appleton-Century, 1936), pp. 3-18.
2. Barnes, H. E., *Social Institutions* (New York: Prentice-Hall, 1942), pp. 3-47.
3. Bennett, J. W., and M. M. Tumin, *Social Life* (New York: Knopf, 1948), pp. 166-196.
4. Bernard, J., *American Family Behavior* (New York: Harper, 1942), pp. 1-24.
5. Chapin, F. S., "A New Definition of Social Institutions," *Soc. Forces,* 6 (Mar., 1928), 375-377.
6. ———, *Contemporary American Institutions* (New York: Harper, 1935).
7. Dawson, C. A., and W. E. Gettys, *An Introduction to Sociology* (New York: Ronald, 1948), pp. 249-261.
8. Gillin, J. P., and J. L. Gillin, *Cultural Sociology* (New York: Macmillan, 1948), pp. 319-331.
9. Hertzler, J. O., *Social Institutions* (Lincoln: Univ. Nebraska Press, 1946), pp. 1-49.
10. Hiller, E. T., *Social Relations and Structures* (New York: Harper, 1947), pp. 219-245.
11. Hughes, E. C., "The Study of Institutions," *Soc. Forces,* 20 (Mar., 1942), 307-311.
12. Lundberg, G. A., *Foundations of Sociology* (New York: Macmillan, 1939), pp. 375-384, 410-420.
13. MacIver, R. M., *Community* (London: Macmillan, 1924), pp. 153-165.
14. ———, and C. H. Page, *Society: An Introductory Analysis* (New York: Rinehart, 1949), pp. 15-22.
15. Malinowski, B., *A Scientific Theory of Culture* (Chapel Hill, N.C.: Univ. North Carolina Press, 1944), pp. 36-66, 62-167.
16. ———, *Freedom and Civilization* (New York: Roy, 1945), pp. 153-171.
17. ———, "The Group and the Individual in Functional Analysis," *Amer. J. Sociol.,* 44 (May, 1939), 938-964.
18. Merrill, F. E., and H. W. Eldredge, *Culture and Society* (New York: Prentice-Hall, 1952), pp. 375-392.

19. Mukerjee, R., *The Social Structure of Values* (London: Macmillan, 1949), pp. 296-308.
20. Panunzio, C., *Major Social Institutions* (New York: Macmillan, 1939), pp. 7-140.
21. Parsons, T., "The Position of Sociological Theory," *Amer. sociol. Rev.*, 13 (Apr., 1948), 156-164; or *Essays on Sociological Theory, Pure and Applied* (Glencoe, Ill.: Free Press, 1949), pp. 3-16.
22. Sawyer, J. E., "Social Structure and Economic Progress," *Papers and Proceedings of Sixty-third Annual Meeting of American Economic Association*, 1951, pp. 321-329.
23. Sumner, W. G., *Folkways* (Boston: Ginn: 1906).
24. ———, and A. G. Keller, *The Science of Society* (New Haven: Yale Univ. Press, 1927), 4 vols.
25. Williams, R. M., Jr., *American Society* (New York: Knopf, 1951), pp. 28-35.
26. Znaniecki, F., "Social Organization and Institutions," in G. Gurvitch and W. E. Moore (eds.), *Twentieth Century Sociology* (New York: Philosophical Library, 1945), pp. 172-217.

Processes of Institutionalization

27. Bernard, J., *op. cit.*, pp. 1-24.
28. Bernard, L. L., *Introduction to Sociology* (New York: Crowell, 1942), pp. 877-900.
29. Chapin, F. S., *Contemporary American Institutions, op. cit.*, pp. 13-23, 319-352.
30. Cooley, C. H., R. C. Angell, and L. J. Carr, *Introductory Sociology* (New York: Scribner, 1933), pp. 406-414.
31. Cuber, C. F., "Some Aspects of Institutional Disorganization," *Amer. sociol. Rev.*, 5 (Aug., 1940), 483-488.
32. Ellsworth, J. S., Jr., *Factory Folkways. A Study of Institutional Structure and Change* (New Haven: Yale Univ. Press, 1952), pp. 89-111.
33. Hertzler, J. O., "Culture Contact and Institutional Change," in E. B. Reuter (ed.), *Race and Culture Contacts* (New York: McGraw-Hill, 1938), pp. 48-56.
34. ———, *Social Institutions, op. cit.*, pp. 50-88, 156-177, 237-308.
35. Hughes, E. C., *The Growth of an Institution: Chicago Real Estate Board* (Chicago: Society for Social Research of the Univ. of Chicago, Series 11, No. 1, 1931).
36. Katz, D., and R. L. Schanck, *Social Psychology* (New York: Wiley, 1938), pp. 169-212.
37. LaPiere, R. T., *Collective Behavior* (New York: McGraw-Hill, 1938), pp. 63-83.
38. Panunzio, *op. cit.*, pp. 392-490.
39. Park, R. E., "Symbiosis and Socialization: A Frame of Reference for the Study of Society," *Amer. J. Sociol.*, 45 (July, 1939), 6-12.
40. Parsons, T., *The Social System* (Glencoe, Ill.: Free Press, 1951), 36-58.

Institutionalized Systems

41. Angell, R. C., *The Integration of American Society* (New York: McGraw-Hill, 1941), pp. 39-189.
42. Ballard, *op. cit.*, pp. 19-479.
43. Barnes, *op. cit.*, pp. 66-877.
44. Chapin, *Contemporary American Institutions, op. cit.*, pp. 27-278.
45. Chapple, E. D., and C. S. Coon, *Principles of Anthropology* (New York: Holt, 1942), pp. 277-694.
46. Davis, K., *Human Society* (New York: Macmillan, 1949), pp. 392-548.
47. Dawson and Gettys, *op. cit.*, pp. 262-288.
48. Hartung, F. E., "Science as an Institution," *Phil. Science*, 18 (Jan., 1951), 35-54.
49. Hawley, A. H., "An Ecological Study of Urban Service Institutions," *Amer. sociol. Rev.*, 6 (Oct., 1941), 629-639.
50. Hertzler, *Social Institutions, op. cit.*, pp. 89-155.
51. Hiller, E. T., "Institutions and Institutional Groups," *Soc. Forces*, 20 (Mar., 1942), 297-307.
52. Lundberg, *op. cit.*, pp. 384-410.
53. MacIver and Page, *op. cit.*, pp. 238-280, 453-506.
54. Murdock, G. P., *Social Structure* (New York: Macmillan, 1949).
55. Panunzio, *op. cit.*, pp. 142-390.
56. Sorokin, P. A., C. C. Zimmerman, and C. J. Galpin, *Systematic Sourcebook in Rural Sociology* (Minneapolis: Univ. Minnesota Press, 1936), Vol. II.
57. Sumner, W. G., and A. G. Keller, *The Science of Society* (New Haven: Yale Univ. Press, 1927), 4 vols.
58. Williams, *op. cit.*, pp. 36-77, 136-346.
59. Wilson, L., and W. L. Kolb, *Sociological Analysis* (New York: Harcourt, Brace, 1949), pp. 513-677.
60. Witmer, Helen L., *Social Work: An Analysis of a Social Institution* (New York: Farrar & Rinehart, 1942).

Professionalization

61. Barnes, H. E., H. Becker, and F. B. Becker, *Contemporary Sociological Theory* (New York: Appleton-Century, 1940), pp. 900-903.
62. Carr-Saunders, A. M., *The Professions: Their Organization and Place in Society* (Oxford: Clarendon Press, 1928).
63. ———, and P. A. Wilson, *The Professions* (Oxford: Clarendon Press, 1933).
64. ———, "The Professions," *Encyclopedia of the Social Sciences* (New York: Macmillan, 1934), Vol. 12, pp. 476-480.
65. Landis, B. Y., *Professional Codes: A Sociological Analysis* (New York: Columbia Univ. Press, 1927).
66. Meadows, P., "Professional Behavior and Industrial Society," *J. Business Univ. Chicago,* 19 (July, 1946), 145-150.
67. Parsons, T., "The Professions and Social Structures," *Soc. Forces,* 17 (May, 1939), 457-467; or *Essays on Sociological Theory, Pure and Applied* (Glencoe, Ill.: Free Press, 1949), pp. 185-199.
68. Ross, E. A., *Principles of Sociology* (New York: Appleton-Century, 1938), pp. 570-582.
69. Taeusch, C. A., *Professional and Business Ethics* (New York: Holt, 1926).
70. ———, "Professional Ethics," *Encyclopedia of the Social Sciences, op. cit.,* Vol. 12, pp. 472-476.

XIII. Differentiation: Nature, Factors, Processes, and Forms

The Place, Nature, Factors, Functions, and Processes of Societal Differentiation

1. Bennett, J. W., and M. M. Tumin, *Social Life* (New York: Knopf, 1948), pp. 127-137.
2. Davis, K., and W. E. Moore, "Some Principles of Stratification," *Amer. sociol. Rev.,* 10 (Apr., 1945), 242-249.
3. Hawley, A. H., *Human Ecology* (New York: Ronald, 1950), pp. 182-205.
4. Landtman, G., *The Origin and Inequality of the Social Classes* (London: Kegan Paul, Trench & Trubner, 1938), pp. 1-14.
5. MacIver, R. M., and C. H. Page, *Society; An Introductory Analysis* (New York: Rinehart, 1949), pp. 384-416, 525-528.
6. Parsons, T., Introduction to Max Weber, *The Theory of Social and Economic Organization* (A. M. Henderson and T. Parsons, trans.) (New York: Oxford, 1947), pp. 18-24).
7. Smith, T. L., and C. A. McMahan, *The Sociology of Urban Life* (New York: Dryden, 1951), pp. 390-391.
8. Sorokin, P. A., *Society, Culture, and Personality* (New York: Harper, 1947), pp. 376-379.
9. ———, C. C. Zimmerman, and C. J. Galpin, *A Systematic Sourcebook in Rural Sociology* (Minneapolis: Univ. Minnesota Press, 1932), Vol. I, pp. 305-335.
10. Wiese, L. von, and H. Becker, *Systematic Sociology* (New York: Wiley, 1932), pp. 281-347.

Major Forms of Societal Differentiation

11. Cooley, C. H., R. C. Angell, and L. J. Carr, *Introductory Sociology* (New York: Scribner, 1933), pp. 219-223.
12. Cox, O. C., *Caste, Class, and Race* (New York: Doubleday, 1948), pp. 317-433.
13. Goldschmidt, W. R., "Class Denominationalism in Rural California Churches," *Amer. J. Sociol.,* 49 (Jan., 1944), 348-355.
14. Hacker, H. M., "Women as a Minority Group," *Soc. Forces,* 30 (Oct., 1951), 60-69.
15. Hiller, E. T., *Social Relations and Structures* (New York: Harper, 1947), pp. 331-580.
16. Komarovsky, M., "Cultural Contradictions and Sex Roles," *Amer. J. Sociol.,* 52 (Nov., 1946), 184-189.
17. Landtman, *op. cit.,* pp. 14-35, 68-226, 233-308.
18. LaPiere, R. T., *Sociology* (New York: McGraw-Hill, 1946), pp. 422-482.
19. Linton, R., "A Neglected Aspect of Social Organization," *Amer. J. Sociol.,* 45 (May, 1940), 870-886.
20. ———, "Age and Sex Categories," *Amer. sociol. Rev.,* 7 (Oct., 1942), 589-603.
21. Mead, M., *Male and Female* (New York: Morrow, 1949).
22. Parsons, T., "Age and Sex in the Social Structure of the United States," *Amer. sociol. Rev.,* 7 (Oct., 1942), 604-616; or in *Essays in Sociological Theory: Pure and Applied* (Glencoe, Ill.: Free Press, 1949), pp. 218-232.
23. ———, *The Social System* (Glencoe, Ill.: Free Press, 1951), pp. 113-200.
24. Sorokin, *op. cit.,* pp. 181-235.
25. ———, Zimmerman, and Galpin, *op. cit.,* Vol. I, pp. 186-249; Vol. III, pp. 226-351, 682-700.
26. Whelpton, P. K., and E. Hollander, "A Standard

Occupational and Industrial Classification of Workers," *Soc. Forces*, 18 (May, 1940), 488-494.

27. Young, K., *Sociology; A Study of Society and Culture* (New York: American Book, 1949), pp. 467-499.

XIV. Stratification: Characteristics, Processes, and Kinds

Stratification: Characteristics, Factors, Processes

1. Barnard, C. I., "Functions and Pathology of Status Systems in Formal Organization," in W. F. Whyte (ed.), *Industry and Society* (New York: McGraw-Hill, 1946), pp. 46-83.
2. Bendix, R., "Social Stratification and Political Power," *Amer. polit. Sci. Rev.*, 46 (June, 1952), 357-375; or Berkeley Institute of Industrial Relations, Reprint No. 44, 1952.
2a. Cattell, R. B., "The Concept of Social Status," *J. soc. Psychol.*, 15 (May, 1942), 293-308.
3. ———, "The Cultural Functions of Social Stratification: Regarding Individual and Group Dynamics," *J. soc. Psychol.*, 21 (1945), 25-55.
4. Chapin, F. S., "A Quantitative Scale for Rating the Home and Social Environment of Middle Class Families in an Urban Environment," *J. educ. Sociol.*, 19 (1928), 99-111.
5. ———, *Measurement of Social Status by Use of the Social Status Scale* (Minneapolis: Univ. Minnesota Press, 1933).
6. Cox, O. C., "Max Weber on Social Stratification: A Critique," *Amer. sociol. Rev.*, 15 (Apr., 1950), 223-227.
7. Davis, A., "American Status Systems and the Socialization of the Child," *Amer. sociol. Rev.*, 6 (Jan., 1945), 345-354.
8. Davis, K., "A Conceptual Analysis of Stratification," *Amer. sociol. Rev.*, 7 (June, 1942), 309-321.
9. ———, *Human Society* (New York: Macmillan, 1949), pp. 91-94.
10. Davis, K., and W. E. Moore, "Some Principles of Stratification," *Amer. sociol. Rev.*, 10 (Apr., 1945), 242-249.
11. Duncan, O. D., and J. W. Arris, "Some Problems of Stratification Research," *Rur. Sociol.*, 16 (Mar., 1951), 17-29.
12. Freedman, R., A. H. Hawley, Q. Landecker, and H. Miner, *Principles of Sociology* (New York: Holt, 1952), pp. 197-215.
13. Goldhamer, H., and E. H. Shils, "Types of Power and Status," *Amer. J. Sociol.*, 45 (Nov., 1939), 171-182.
14. Hall, J., and J. C. Jones, "Social Grading of Occupations," *Brit. J. Sociol.*, 1 (Mar., 1950), 31-55.
15. Hatt, P. K., "Occupation and Social Stratification," *Amer. J. Sociol.*, 55 (May, 1950), 533-543.
16. ———, "Stratification in the Mass Society," *Amer. sociol. Rev.*, 15 (Apr., 1950), 216-222.
17. Hughes, E. C., and H. M. Hughes, *When Peoples Meet: Racial and Ethnic Frontiers* (Glencoe, Ill.: Free Press, 1952), pp. 100-115.
18. Kaufman, H. F., "An Approach to the Study of Urban Stratification," *Amer. sociol. Rev.*, 17 (Aug., 1952), 430-437.
19. ———, "Defining Prestige Rank in a Rural Community," *Sociometry*, 8 (May, 1945), 199-207.
20. Linton, R., "Problems of Status Personality," in S. S. Sargent, and M. W. Smith (eds.), *Culture and Personality* (New York: Viking, 1949), pp. 163-171.
21. Lipset, S. M., and R. Bendix, "Social Status and Social Structure: A Re-examination of Data and Interpretations, I, II," *Brit. J. Sociol.*, 2 (June, 1951), 150-168; 2 (Sept., 1952), 230-254; or Berkeley Institute of Industrial Relations, Reprint No. 35, 1952.
22. Loomis, C. P., and J. A. Beegle, *Rural Social Systems* (New York: Prentice-Hall, 1950), Pt. III.
23. McGuire, C., "Social Stratification and Mobility Patterns," *Amer. sociol. Rev.*, 13 (Apr., 1950), 195-204.
24. Moore, B., Jr., "The Relation between Social Stratification and Social Control," *Sociometry*, 5 (Aug., 1942), 230-250.
25. Moore, W. E., *Industrial Relations and the Social Order* (New York: Macmillan, 1946), pp. 479-498.
26. Mukerjee, R., *The Social Structure of Values* (London: Macmillan, 1949), pp. 247-251.
27. Parsons, T., "An Analytical Approach to the Theory of Social Stratifications," *Am. Jour. Soc.*, 45 (May, 1940), 841-862; or in *Essays in Sociological Theory: Pure and Applied* (Glencoe, Ill.: Free Press, 1949, pp. 166-184).

28. Pfautz, H. W., "The Current Literature on Social Stratification: Critique and Appraisal," *Amer. J. Sociol.*, 58 (Jan., 1953), 391-418.
29. Rosenfeld, E., "Social Stratification in a 'Classless' Society," *Amer. sociol. Rev.*, 16 (Dec., 1951), 766-774.
30. Ross, E. A., *Principles of Sociology* (New York: Appleton-Century, 1938), pp. 401-433.
31. Sewell, W. A., *The Construction and Standardization of a Scale of Measurement of the Socio-Economic Status of Oklahoma Farms,* Technical Bulletin No. 6 (Stillwater, Okla.: Oklahoma Experiment Station, 1941).
32. Simpson, G. E., "Haiti's Social Structure," *Amer. sociol. Rev.*, 6 (Oct., 1941), 640-649.
33. Sorokin, P. A., *Society, Culture, and Personality* (New York: Harper, 1947), pp. 276-295.
34. ———, C. C. Zimmerman, and C. J. Galpin, *A Systematic Sourcebook for Rural Sociology* (Minneapolis: Univ. Minnesota Press, 1932), Vol. I, pp. 362-402.
35. Spier, H., "Social Stratification in the Urban Community," *Amer. sociol. Rev.*, 9 (Apr., 1936), 193-202.
36. Stone, G. P., and W. H. Form, "Instabilities in Status: The Problem of Hierarchy in the Community Study of Status Arrangements," *Amer. sociol. Rev.*, 18 (Apr., 1953), 149-162.
37. Thomas, W. I., *Primitive Behavior* (New York: McGraw-Hill, 1937), pp. 358-416.
38. Williams, R. M., Jr., *American Society: A Sociological Interpretation* (New York: Knopf, 1951), pp. 78-135.

Community or Regional Studies Involving Classes and Class Distinctions

39. Beals, R. L., "Social Stratification in Latin America," *Amer. J. Sociol.*, 58 (Jan., 1953), 327-339.
40. Bell, E. H., "Social Stratification in a Small Community," *Sci. Mon., N.Y.*, 38 (1934), 157-164.
41. ———, *Sublette, Kansas,* Rural Life Studies, No. 2 (Washington: U.S. Government Printing Office, 1942).
42. Blumenthal, A., *Small Town Stuff* (Chicago: Univ. Chicago Press, 1932).
43. Davis, A., B. B. Gardner, and M. R. Gardner, *Deep South: A Social Anthropological Study of Caste and Class* (Chicago: Univ. Chicago Press, 1941).
44. Dollard, J., *Class and Caste in a Southern Town* (New Haven: Yale Univ. Press, 1937).
45. Hicks, G., *Small Town* (New York: Macmillan, 1946).
46. Hollingshead, A. B., *Elmtown's Youth* (New York: Wiley, 1948).
47. ———, "Selected Characteristics of Classes in a Middlewestern Community," *Amer. sociol. Rev.*, 12 (Aug., 1947), 385-395.
48. Kaufman, H. F., *Prestige Classes in a New York Rural Community,* Memoir No. 2 (Ithaca: Cornell Univ. Experiment Station, 1944).
49. Lynd, R. S., and H. M. Lynd, *Middletown in Transition* (New York: Harcourt, Brace, 1937).
50. Mills, C. W., "The Social Life of a Modern Community," *Amer. sociol. Rev.*, 7 (June, 1942), 263-271.
51. Moore, W. E., and R. M. Williams, Jr., "Stratification in the Ante-Bellum South," *Amer. sociol. Rev.*, 7 (June, 1942), 343-351.
52. Rogoff, N., "Social Stratification in France and in the United States," *Amer. J. Sociol.*, 58 (Jan., 1953), 347-357.
53. Useem, J., P. Tangent, and R. Useem, "Stratification in a Prairie Town," *Amer. sociol. Rev.*, 7 (June, 1942), 331-342.
54. Warner, W. L., and P. S. Lunt, *The Social Life of a Modern Community,* Yankee City Series, Vol. I (New Haven: Yale Univ. Press, 1941).
55. ——— and ———, *The Social Status System of a Modern Community,* Yankee City Series, Vol. II (New Haven: Yale Univ. Press, 1942).
56. West, J., *Plainville, U.S.A.* (New York: Columbia Univ. Press, 1945).
57. Wheeler, W., *Social Stratification in a Plains Community* (Minneapolis: Univ. Minnesota Press, 1949).
58. Williams, J. M., *An American Town* (New York: Columbia Univ. Press, 1906).

Kinds of Stratification Systems: Social Class Systems in Contrast to Caste and Estate Systems

59. Adams, R. N., "A Change from Caste to Class in a Peruvian Sierra Town," *Soc. Forces*, 31 (Mar., 1953), 238-244.
60. Aron, R., "Social Structure and the Ruling Class," *Brit. J. Sociol.*, 2 (Mar., 1950), 1-16.
61. Barber, B., and L. S. Lobel, "Fashion in Women's Clothes and the American Social

System," *Soc. Forces,* 31 (Dec., 1952), 124-131.

62. Bennett, J. W., and M. M. Tumin, *Social Life* (New York: Knopf, 1948), pp. 452-492, 570-600.
63. Bernard, J., *American Community Behavior* (New York: Dryden, 1949), pp. 187-201.
64. Blunt, E. A. H., *The Caste System of Northern India* (London: Oxford Univ. Press, 1931).
65. Brooks, M. R., "American Class and Caste: An Appraisal," *Soc. Forces,* 25 (Mar., 1946), 207-211.
66. Centers, R., "Social Class, Occupation, and Imputed Belief," *Amer. J. Sociol.,* 58 (May, 1953), 543-555.
67. ———, *The Psychology of Social Classes* (Princeton: Princeton Univ. Press, 1949).
68. Cooley, C. H., *Social Organization* (New York: Scribner, 1915), pp. 209-238.
69. Cox, O. C., *Caste, Class, and Race* (New York: Doubleday, 1948).
70. Davis, A., *Social Class Influences upon Learning* (Chicago: Univ. Chicago Press, 1951).
71. Davis, K., *Human Society, op. cit.,* pp. 364-391.
72. Espenck, H. J., "Social Attitudes and Social Class," *Brit. J. Sociol.,* 1 (Mar., 1950), 56-66.
73. Freedman *et al., op. cit.,* pp. 228-239, 449-463.
74. Ginsberg, M., "Class Consciousness," *Encyclopedia of the Social Sciences* (New York: Macmillan, 1930), Vol. 3, pp. 536-538.
75. Goldschmidt, W., "Social Classes in America: A Critical Review," *Amer. Anthrop.,* 52 (Oct.-Dec., 1950), 483-498.
76. Gordon, M. M., "Social Class in American Sociology," *Amer. J. Sociol.,* 55 (Nov., 1949), 262-268.
77. Gross, L., "The Use of Class Concepts in Sociological Research," *Amer. J. Sociol.,* 54 (Mar., 1949), 409-421.
78. Harrison, T., "Notes on Class Consciousness and Class Unconsciousness," *Sociol. Rev. Brit.,* 34 (1942), 147-163.
79. Havighurst, R. J., and H. Taba, *Adolescent Character and Personality* (New York: Wiley, 1949), pp. 47-61.
80. Hertzler, J. O., "Some Tendencies toward a Closed Class System in the United States," *Soc. Forces,* 30 (Mar., 1952), 314-323.
81. Hiller, E. T., *Social Relations and Structures* (New York: Harper, 1947), pp. 330-335, 479-580, 599-630, 618-622.
82. Hollingshead, A. B., "Trends in Social Stratification: A Case Study," *Amer. sociol. Rev.,* 17 (Dec., 1952), 679-684.
83. ———, and F. C. Redlich, "Social Stratification and Psychiatric Disorders," *Amer. sociol. Rev.,* 18 (Apr., 1953), 163-169.
84. Homans, G. C., *The Human Group* (New York: Harcourt, Brace, 1950), pp. 362-365.
85. Hutton, J. H., *Caste in India: Its Nature, Function and Origin* (New York: Macmillan, 1947).
86. King, C. F., "The Process of Social Stratification among an Urban Southern Minority Population," *Soc. Forces,* 31 (May, 1953), 352-355.
87. Kluckhohn, C., and F. R. Kluckhohn, "Differentiated Class Conditions and Class Goals," in L. Bryson, L. Finkelstein, and R. M. MacIver (eds.), *Conflicts of Power in Modern Culture* (New York: Harper, 1947), pp. 121-128.
88. Kornhauser, A., "Public Opinion and Social Class," *Amer. J. Sociol.,* 55 (Jan., 1950), 333-345.
89. Landtman, G., *The Origin and Inequality of the Social Classes* (London: Kegan Paul, Trench & Trubner, 1938).
90. Lenski, G. E., "American Social Classes: Statistical Data or Social Groups?" *Amer. J. Sociol.,* 58 (Sept., 1952), 139-144.
91. Liston, P., "Religion and Class Structure," *Ann. Amer. Acad. polit. soc. Sci.,* 256 (Mar., 1948), 84-91.
92. Loomis, C. P., J. A. Beegle, and Longmore, T. W., "Critique of Class as Related to Social Stratification," *Sociometry,* 19 (Nov., 1947), 319-337.
93. Marshall, T. H., "Social Classes: A Preliminary Analysis," *Soc. Rev. Brit.,* 26 (Jan., 1934), 55-76.
94. McConnell, J. C., *The Evolution of Social Classes* (Washington: American Council of Public Affairs, 1942).
95. MacIver, R. M., and C. H. Page, *Society: An Introductory Analysis* (New York: Rinehart, 1949), pp. 348-383.
96. Montague, J. B., Jr., "Research Related to Social Classes in England," *Amer. sociol. Rev.,* 17 (Apr., 1952), 192-196.
97. ———, "Some Aspects of Class, Status, and Power Relations in England," *Soc. Forces,* 30 (Dec., 1951), 134-140.
98. Moore, W. E., *op. cit.,* pp. 568-592.
99. Mukerjee, R., "Caste and Social Change in

India," *Amer. J. Sociol.*, 43 (Nov., 1937), 377-390.
100. Neugarten, B. L., "Social Class and Friendship among School Children," *Amer. J. Sociol.*, 51 (Jan., 1946), 305-313.
101. North, C. C., "Social Classes," in J. S. Roucek (ed.), *Social Control* (New York: Van Nostrand, 1947), pp. 149-166.
102. Olcott, M., "The Caste System of India," *Amer. sociol. Rev.*, 9 (Dec., 1944), 648-657.
103. Page, C. H., *Class and American Sociology* (New York: Dial, 1940).
104. Pfautz, H. W., and O. D. Duncan, "A Critical Evaluation of Warner's Work in Social Stratification," *Amer. sociol. Rev.*, 15 (Apr., 1950), 205-215.
104a. Ross, *op. cit.*, 434-443.
105. Simpson, G. E., "Class Analysis: What Class Is Not," *Amer. sociol. Rev.*, 4 (Dec., 1939), 827-835.
106. Sjoberg, G., "Are Social Classes in America Becoming More Rigid?" *Amer. sociol. Rev.*, 16 (Dec., 1951), 775-783.
107. Smith, T. L., *The Sociology of Rural Life* (New York: Harper, 1947), pp. 344-367.
108. ———, and C. A. McMahan, *The Sociology of Urban Life* (New York: Dryden, 1951), pp. 412-417.
109. Sorokin, P. A., *Social Mobility* (New York: Harper, 1927), pp. 337-345.
110. ———, *Society, Culture, and Personality*, pp. 256-275.
111. Steiner, I. D., "Some Social Values Associated with Objectively and Subjectively Defined Social Class Memberships," *Soc. Forces*, 31 (May, 1953), 327-332.
112. "The People of the United States—A Self-Portrait," *Fortune*, 21 (Feb., 1940), 14ff.
113. Warner, W. L., *American Life* (Chicago: Univ. Chicago Press, 1953).
114. ———, M. Meeker, and K. Eells, *Social Classes in America* (Chicago: Science Research Associates, 1949).

Kinds of Stratification Systems: Ethnic Stratification

115. Boskoff, A., "Negro Class Structure and the Technicways," *Soc. Forces*, 29 (Dec., 1950), 124-131.
116. Cox, *Caste, Class and Race*, *op. cit.*, pp. 317-423.
117. Davis, A., "Caste Economy and Violence," *Amer. J. Sociol.*, 51 (July, 1945), 7-15.
118. ———, *et al.*, *op. cit.*
119. Dollard, *op. cit.*
120. Doyle, B. W., *The Etiquette of Race Relations in the South* (Chicago: Univ. Chicago Press, 1937).
121. Drake, St. Clair, and H. K. Clayton, *Black Metropolis* (New York: Harcourt, Brace, 1945).
122. Golightly, C. L., "Race, Values, and Guilt," *Soc. Forces*, 26 (Dec., 1947), 125-138.
123. Hertzler, J. O., "The Sociology of Anti-Semitism through History," in I. Graeber and S. H. Britt (eds.), *Jews in a Gentile World* (New York: Macmillan, 1942), pp. 62-100.
124. Hill, M. C., and T. D. Ackers, "Social Classes: A Frame of Reference for the Study of Negro Society," *Soc. Forces*, 22 (Oct., 1943), 92-98.
125. ———, and B. C. McCall, "Social Stratification in 'Georgia Town,'" *Amer. sociol. Rev.*, 15 (Dec., 1950), 721-729.
126. Humphrey, N. D., "American Race Relations and Status Structure," *Soc. Sci.*, 22 (Jan., 1947), 19-22.
127. Lash, J. S., "The Race Consciousness of the American Negro: Toward a Re-examination of an Orthodox Critical Concept," *Soc. Forces*, 28 (Oct., 1949, 24-34.
128. Lobb, J., "Caste and Class in Haiti," *Amer. J. Sociol.*, 46 (July, 1940), 23-34.
129. MacIver and Page, *op. cit.*, pp. 394-416.
130. Myrdal, G., *An American Dilemma* (New York: Harper, 1944).
131. Tumin, M. M., "Reciprocity and Stability of Caste in Guatemala," *Amer. sociol. Rev.*, 14 (Feb., 1949), 17-25.
132. Warner, W. L., and A. Davis, "A Comparative Study of American Caste," in E. T. Thompson (ed.), *Race Relations and the Race Problem* (Durham, N.C.: Duke Univ. Press, 1938), Chap. VIII.
133. ———, and P. S. Lunt, *The Social Life of a Modern Community*, *op. cit.*, pp. 211-326.
134. ———, and L. Srole, *The Social Systems of American Ethnic Groups*, Yankee City Series, Vol. III (New Haven: Yale Univ. Press, 1947).
135. Wirth, L., "The Problem of Minority Groups," in R. Linton (ed.), *The Science of Man in the World Crisis* (New York: Columbia Univ. Press, 1945), pp. 347-372.

Kinds of Stratification Systems: Stratification in Large-Scale Organizations

136. Barnard, C. I., *Industry and Society* (New York: McGraw-Hill, 1946), pp. 46-70.
137. ———, *Organization and Management* (Cambridge: Harvard Univ. Press, 1948), pp. 207-244.
138. Hildebrand, G. H., "American Unionism, Social Stratification, and Power," *Amer. J. Sociol.*, 58 (Jan., 1953), 381-390.
139. MacIver, R. M., *The Web of Government* (New York: Macmillan, 1947), pp. 82-113.
140. Warner, W. L., and J. O. Low, *The Social System of a Modern Factory* (New Haven: Yale Univ. Press, 1947).

XV. Social Mobility in the Societal Structure

Social Mobility: Nature, Forms, Conditions, Processes

1. Anderson, H. D., and P. E. Davidson, *Occupational Trends in the United States* (Stanford: Stanford Univ. Press, 1947).
2. Babcock, F. L., *The United States College Graduate* (New York: Macmillan, 1941).
3. Bogardus, E. S., "A Social Distance Scale," *Sociol. soc. Res.*, 17 (Jan.-Feb., 1933), 265-271.
4. Centers, R., "Occupational Mobility of Urban Occupational Strata, "*Amer. sociol. Rev.*, 13 (Apr., 1948), 197-203.
5. Davidson, P. E., and H. D. Anderson, *Occupational Mobility in an American Community* (Stanford: Stanford Univ. Press, 1937).
6. Davis, A., B. B. Gardner, and M. R. Gardner, *Deep South: A Social Anthropological Study of Caste and Class* (Chicago: Univ. Chicago Press, 1941), pp. 171-207.
7. Freedman, R., A. H. Hawley, W. Landecker, and H. Miner, *Principles of Sociology* (New York: Holt, 1952), pp. 455-463.
8. McGuire, C., "Social Stratification and Mobility Patterns," *Amer. sociol. Rev.*, 15 (Apr., 1950), 195-204.
9. Schneider, J., "Social Class, Historical Circumstances and Fame," *Amer. J. Sociol.*, 43 (July, 1937), 37-56.
10. Smith, T. L., *The Sociology of Rural Life* (New York: Harper, 1947), pp. 532-551.
11. ———, and C. A. McMahan, *The Sociology of Urban Life* (New York: Dryden, 1951), pp. 655-658.
12. Sorokin, P. A., "Mobility, Social," *Encyclopedia of the Social Sciences* (New York: Macmillan, 1933), Vol. 10, pp. 554-555.
13. ———, *Social Mobility* (New York: Harper, 1927), pp. 133-214, 346-492.
14. ———, *Society, Culture and Personality* (New York: Harper, 1947), pp. 398-444.
15. ———, *Sociocultural Causality, Space, Time* (Durham, N.C.: Duke Univ. Press, 1943), pp. 113-157.
16. Timasheff, N. S., "Vertical Social Mobility in Communist Society," *Amer. J. Sociol.*, 50 (July, 1944), 9-21.
17. Turner, R. E., "The Experience of Vertical Mobility and Personal Values," *Proc. Pacific sociol. Soc.*, 1951, pp. 88-92.
18. Voitinsky, W. S., *Labor in the United States* (New York: Social Science Research Council, 1938).
19. Warner, W. L., *Democracy in Jonesville* (New York: Harper, 1949), pp. 60-70.
20. Westie, F. R., "Negro-White Status Differentials and Social Distance," *Amer. sociol. Rev.*, 17 (Oct., 1952), 550-558.

Channels of Vertical Social Movement

21. Hatt, P. K., "Occupation and Social Stratification," *Amer. J. Sociol.*, 55 (May, 1950), 533-543.
22. Hertzler, J. O., *Social Institutions* (Lincoln: Univ. Nebraska Press, 1946), pp. 188-190.
23. Ross, E. A., *Principles of Sociology* (New York: Appleton-Century, 1938), pp. 457-468.
24. Roth, J., and R. F. Peck, "Social Class and Social Mobility Factors Related to Marital Adjustment," *Amer. sociol. Rev.*, 16 (Aug., 1951), 478-487.
25. Sorokin, *Social Mobility, op. cit.*, pp. 164-211.
26. Warner, *op. cit.*, pp. 144-148.

Factors Restraining Vertical Mobility

27. "A Revolution in Birth Rates," *Popul. Bull.* (Population Reference Bureau), 5 (July, 1949), 17-21.
28. Adams, S., "Regional Differences in Vertical Mobility in a High-Status Occupation," *Amer. sociol. Rev.*, 15 (Apr., 1950), 228-234.
29. Bell, D., "Labor's Coming of Middle Age," *Fortune*, 49 (Oct., 1951), 114-115, 137-150.

30. Corey, L., *The Crisis of the Middle Class* (New York: Covici, Friede, 1935).
31. Covington, F. C., "Color: A Factor in Social Mobility," *Sociol. soc. Res.*, 15 (Nov., 1930), 145-152.
32. Current Population Reports, *Fertility: April, 1947*, Bureau of the Census, Series P-20, No. 18, June 30, 1948.
33. Drucker, P. F., "Are We Having Too Many Babies?" *Saturday Evening Post*, 222 (May 6, 1950), 40-41, 154-158.
34. ———, "The Employee Society," *Amer. J. Sociol.*, 58 (Jan., 1953), 358-363.
35. Ellis, E., "Social Psychological Correlates of Upward Mobility among Unmarried Career Women," *Amer. sociol. Rev.*, 17 (Oct., 1952), 558-563.
36. Hertzler, J. O., "Some Tendencies toward a Closed Class System in the United States," *Soc. Forces*, 30 (Mar., 1952), 313-323.
37. Lynd, R. S., and H. M. Lynd, *Middletown in Transition* (New York: Harcourt, Brace, 1937), pp. 65-73.
38. McKee, J. B., Status and Power in the Industrial Community: A Comment on Drucker's Thesis," *Amer. J. Sociol.*, 58 (Jan., 1953), 364-370.
39. Meadows, P., "Facts and Figures on the White-Collar Workers," *Technol. Rev.*, 51 (June, 1949), 508-510, 522-528.
40. Mills, C. W., *White Collar: The American Middle Class* (New York: Oxford, 1951).
41. Mulligan, R. A., "Socio-Economic Background and College Enrollment," *Amer. sociol. Rev.*, 16 (Apr., 1951), 188-196.
42. Myrdal, G., *An American Dilemma: The Negro Problem and Modern Democracy* (New York: Harper, 1948), 2 vols.
43. Neugarten, Bernice L., "Social Class and Friendship among School Children," *Amer. J. Sociol.*, 51 (Jan., 1946), 305-313.
44. North, C. C., *Social Differentiation* (Chapel Hill, N.C.: Univ. North Carolina Press, 1926), pp. 254-266.
45. Riesman, D., *The Lonely Crowd: A Study of the Changing American Character* (New Haven: Yale Univ. Press, 1950), pp. 113-174.
46. Sibley, E., "Some Demographic Clues to Stratification," *Amer. sociol. Rev.*, 7 (June, 1942), 322-330.
47. Sjoberg, G., "Are Social Classes in America Becoming More Rigid?" *Amer. sociol. Rev.*, 16 (Dec., 1951), 775-783.
48. Sorokin, P. A., "American Millionaires and Multi-Millionaires," *Soc. Forces*, 3 (Mar., 1922), 627-640.
49. Starck, L., "Union Security and Its Implications," *Ann. Amer. Acad. polit. soc. Sci.*, 248 (Nov., 1946), 62-69.
50. Stephenson, R., "Status Achievement and the Occupational Pyramid," *Soc. Forces*, 31 (Oct., 1952), 75-77.
51. Tannenbaum, F., "Unions in 1950: Not Bread Alone," *The Reporter*, Apr. 11, 1950, pp. 5-10.
52. Warner, W. L., M. Meeker, and K. Eells, *Social Classes in America* (Chicago: Science Research Associates, 1949), pp. 23-29.

XVI. Isolative and Separative Processes

Disorganization: Theoretical Orientation, Characteristics

1. Bernard, J., *American Community Behavior* (New York: Dryden, 1949), pp. 457-553.
2. Blumer, H., "Social Disorganization and Individual Disorganization," *Amer. J. Sociol.*, 42 (May, 1937), 871-877.
3. Elliott, M. A., and F. E. Merrill, *Social Disorganization* (New York: Harper, 1950).
4. Faris, R. E. L., *Social Disorganization* (New York: Ronald, 1948).
5. Frank, L. K., "Society as the Patient," *Amer. J. Sociol.*, 42 (Nov., 1936), 335-344.
6. ———, "What Is Social Order?" *Amer. J. Sociol.*, 49 (Mar., 1944), 470-477.
7. Fuller, R. C., "Sociological Theory and Social Problems," *Soc. Forces*, 15 (May, 1937), 496-502.
8. ———, and R. R. Myers, "Some Aspects of a Theory of Social Problems," *Amer. sociol. Rev.*, 6 (Feb., 1941), 24-32.
9. ——— and ———, "The Natural History of a Social Problem," *Amer. sociol. Rev.*, 6 (June, 1941), 320-329.
10. Hertzler, J. O., *Social Institutions* (Lincoln: Univ. Nebraska Press, 1946), pp. 256-267.
11. Homans, G. C., *The Human Group* (New York: Harcourt, Brace, 1950), pp. 334-368.
12. Kramer, R., 'The Conceptual Status of Social Disorganization," *Amer. J. Sociol.*, 48 (Jan., 1943), 466-474.
13. Llewellyn, K. N., "Group Prejudice and Social Education," in R. M. MacIver (ed.), *Civili-*

zation and Group Relationships (New York: Harper, 1945), pp. 11-28.

14. Lindesmith, A. R., and A. S. Strauss, *Social Psychology* (New York: Dryden, 1949), pp. 329-352.
15. Lundberg, G. A., "Societal Pathology and Sociometry," *Sociometry*, 4 (Feb., 1941), 78-97.
16. Meadows, P., "The Cultural Organization of Action," *Phil. Science*, 13 (Oct., 1946), 332-338.
17. Merrill, F. E., "The Study of Social Problems," *Amer. sociol. Rev.*, 13 (June, 1948), 251-259.
18. Mikesell, W. H., "Maladjustment," in W. H. Mikesell (ed.), *Modern Abnormal Psychology* (New York: Philosophical Library, 1950), pp. 125-160.
19. Mowrer, E. R., *Disorganization, Personal and Social* (Philadelphia: Lippincott, 1942).
20. ———, "Social Crisis and Social Disorganization," *Amer. sociol. Rev.*, 15 (Feb., 1950), 60-66.
21. Queen, S. A., W. B. Bodenhafer, and E. B. Harper, *Social Organization and Disorganization* (New York: Crowell, 1935).
22. Reuter, E. B., *Handbook of Sociology* (New York: Dryden, 1941), pp. 111-113.
23. Rose, A., and C. Rose, *America Divided* (New York: Knopf, 1948), Chap. 10.
24. Sutherland, E. H., "Social Pathology," *Amer. J. Sociol.*, 50 (May, 1945), 429-435.
25. Thomas, W. I., and F. Znaniecki, *The Polish Peasant in Europe and America* (New York: Knopf, 1927), Vol. II, pp. 1127-1133.
26. Walker, W., "Social Problems and the Mores," *Amer. sociol. Rev.*, 1 (Dec., 1936), 922-933.
27. Warren, R. L., "Social Disorganization and the Interrelationship of Cultural Roles," *Amer. sociol. Rev.*, 14 (Feb., 1949), 83-87.
28. Wirth, L., "Ideological Aspects of Social Disorganization," *Amer. sociol. Rev.*, 5 (Aug., 1940), 472-482.
29. Young, D., "Democracy and Minority Groups," in R. M. MacIver (ed.), *Civilization and Group Relationships* (New York: Harper, 1945), pp. 151-159.

Separative Factors and Processes

30. Allport, G. W., "Prejudice: A Problem in Psychological and Social Causation," in T. Parsons and E. A. Shils (eds.), *A General Theory of Action* (Cambridge: Harvard Univ. Press, 1951), pp. 365-387.
31. Bettelheim, B., and M. Janowitz, *The Dynamics of Prejudice: A Psychological and Sociological Study of Veterans* (New York: Harper, 1950).
32. Davis, A. K., "Conflict between Major Social Systems," *Soc. Forces*, 30 (Oct., 1951), 29-36.
33. Davis, K., "Extreme Social Isolation of a Child," *Amer. J. Sociol.*, 45 (Jan., 1940), 554-565.
34. ———, *Human Society* (New York: Macmillan, 1949), pp. 150-151.
35. Gesell, A., *Wolf Child and Human Child* (New York: Harper, 1939).
36. Handlin, O., *The Uprooted* (Boston: Little, Brown, 1951).
37. Hankins, F. H., "Social Discrimination," *Encyclopedia of the Social Sciences* (New York: Macmillan, 1934), Vol. 14, pp. 131-134.
38. Krout, M. H., *Introduction to Social Psychology* (New York: Harper, 1942), pp. 592-604.
39. Lewin, K., *Resolving Social Conflicts* (New York: Harper, 1948), pp. 17-33.
40. Locke, H. J., "Mobility and Family Disorganization," *Amer. sociol. Rev.*, 5 (Aug., 1940), 489-494.
41. MacIver, R. M., and C. H. Page, *Society: An Introductory Analysis* (New York: Rinehart, 1949), pp. 407-416.
42. McWilliams, C., "Does Social Discrimination Really Matter?" *Commentary*, Nov., 1947, pp. 408-415.
43. Merton, R. K., "Discrimination and the American Creed," in R. M. MacIver (ed.), *Discrimination and National Welfare* (New York: Harper, 1949), pp. 99-126.
44. Murdock, G. P., "Ethnocentrism," *Encyclopedia of the Social Sciences* (New York: Macmillan, 1931), Vol. 5, pp. 613-614.
45. Page, C. H., "Bureaucracy's Other Face," *Soc. Forces*, 25 (Oct., 1946), 88-94.
46. Park, R. E., and E. W. Burgess, *Introduction to the Science of Society* (Chicago: Univ. Chicago Press, 1921), pp. 226-277.
47. Reuter, E. B., and C. W. Hart, *Introduction to Sociology* (New York: McGraw-Hill, 1933), pp. 205-231.
48. Rose, and Rose, *op. cit.*, pp. 277-306.
49. Ross, E. A., *Principles of Sociology* (New York: Appleton-Century, 1938), pp. 466-468, 490-500.
50. Roucek, J. S., "Group Discrimination and Culture Clash," in R. M. MacIver (ed.), *Civilization and Group Relationships* (New York: Harper, 1945), pp. 39-69.
51. Singh, J. A. L., and R. M. Zingg, *Wolf Children and Feral Man* (New York: Harper, 1942).

52. Siu, P. C. P., "The Sojourner," *Amer. J. Sociol.*, 58 (July, 1952), 34-44.
53. Small, M. H., "On Some Psychical Relations of Society and Solitude," *Pedagog. Sem.*, 7 (1900), 13-69.
54. Sorokin, P. A., *Social Mobility* (New York: Harper, 1927), pp. 510-545.
55. Stonequist, E. V., *The Marginal Man* (New York: Scribner, 1937).
56. Toynbee, A. J., *A Study of History* (1-vol. ed.) (New York: Oxford, 1947).
57. Wirth, L., "Morale and Minority Groups," *Amer. J. Sociol.*, 47 (Nov., 1941), 415-433.
58. ———, *The Ghetto* (Chicago: Univ. Chicago Press, 1928).
59. ———, "Segregation," *Encyclopedia of the Social Sciences* (New York: Macmillan, 1934), Vol. 13, pp. 643-646.
60. ———, Preface to K. Mannheim, *Ideology and Utopia* (New York: Harcourt, Brace, 1936), p. xxv.
61. Wolf, K. H., *The Sociology of Georg Simmel* (Glencoe, Ill.: Free Press, 1950), pp. 402-408.
62. Young, K., *Sociology: A Study of Society and Culture* (New York: American Book, 1949), pp. 113-118.

XVII. Opposition: Factors and Processes

The Opposition Situation

1. Bernard, L. L., *Introduction to Sociology* (New York: Crowell, 1942), pp. 829-848.
2. Carr, L. J., "A Situational Approach to Conflict and War," *Soc. Forces*, 24 (Mar., 1946), 300-303.
3. Cooley, C. H., *Social Process* (New York: Scribner, 1918), pp. 35-42.
4. Davis, K., *Human Society* (New York: Macmillan, 1949), pp. 157-166.
5. Krout, M. H., *Introduction to Social Psychology* (New York: Harper, 1942), pp. 558-629.
6. MacIver, R. M. (ed.), *Group Relations and Group Antagonisms* (New York: Harper, 1944).
7. Ross, E. A., *Principles of Sociology* (New York: Appleton-Century, 1938), pp. 195-214.
8. Smith, T. L., and C. A. McMahan, *The Sociology of Urban Life* (New York: Dryden, 1951), pp. 588-593.
9. Spykman, N. J., *The Social Theory of Georg Simmel* (Chicago: Univ. Chicago Press, 1925), pp. 112-127.
10. White, H. R., "The Aggressive Forms of Defense Mechanism," in W. H. Mikesell (ed.), *Modern Abnormal Psychology* (New York: Philosophical Library, 1950), pp. 163-207.
11. Wiese L. von, and H. Becker, *Systematic Sociology* (New York: Wiley, 1932), pp. 239-247.
12. Wilson, G., and M. Wilson, *The Analysis of Social Change* (Cambridge: Cambridge Univ. Press, 1945), pp. 125-136.
13. Wilson, L., and W. L. Kolb, *Sociological Analysis* (New York: Harcourt, Brace, 1949), pp. 713-716.
14. Young, K., *Sociology: A Study of Society and Culture* (New York: American Book, 1949), pp. 64-69.
15. Znaniecki, F., *Social Actions* (New York: Farrar & Rinehart, 1936), pp. 313-318.

The Competitive Processes

16. Bernard, J., *American Community Behavior* (New York: Dryden, 1949), pp. 84-102, 133-257.
17. Cooley, C. H., *Human Nature and the Social Order* (New York: Scribner, 1910), pp. 262-282.
18. ———, *Social Process, op. cit.*, pp. 125-136.
19. Gillin, J. L., and J. P. Gillin, *Cultural Sociology* (New York: Macmillan, 1948), pp. 587-610.
20. Hamilton, W. H., "Competition," *Encyclopedia of the Social Sciences* (New York: Macmillan, 1931), Vol. 1, pp. 141-147.
21. May, M. L., and L. W. Doob, *Competition and Cooperation*, Bull. No. 25 (New York: Social Science Research Council, 1937).
22. Reuter, E. B., and C. W. Hart, *Introduction to Sociology* (New York: McGraw-Hill, 1933), pp. 277-296.
23. Ross, *op. cit.*, pp. 204-209, 215-237.
24. Wiese and Becker, *op. cit.*, Chap. 18.

Contravention Processes

25. Gillin and Gillin, *op. cit.*, pp. 611-625.
26. Nimkoff, M. F., "Parent-Child Conflict," *Sociol. soc. Res.*, 14 (Nov.-Dec., 1929), 135-150.
27. ———, "The Relation of Parental Dominance to Parent-Child Conflict," *Soc. Forces*, 9 (June, 1931), 559-563.
28. Pollack, O., "Conservatism in Later Maturity and Old Age," *Amer. sociol. Rev.*, 8 (Apr., 1943), 175-179.

29. Ross, *op. cit.*, pp. 238-254.
30. Simmel, G., *Soziologie* (Leipzig: Drucker and Humblot, 1908).
31. ———, "The Sociology of Conflict," *Amer. J. Sociol.*, 9 (1903-1904), 490-525, 672-689, 798-811.
32. Wiese and Becker, *op. cit.*, pp. 245-246, 260-271.
33. Znaniecki, *op. cit.*, pp. 410-432.

Conflict in General

34. Bernard, J., *op. cit.*, pp. 103-130.
35. ———, "The Conceptualization of Intergroup Relations with Special Reference to Conflict," *Soc. Forces,* 29 (Mar., 1951), 243-251.
36. Cooley, C. H., *Human Nature and the Social Order, op. cit.*, pp. 232-261.
37. ———, *Social Process, op. cit.*, pp. 241-254.
38. Dollard, J., "Hostility and Fear in Social Life," *Soc. Forces,* 17 (Oct., 1938), 15-26.
39. ——— *et al., Frustration and Aggression* (New Haven: Yale Univ. Press, 1939).
40. Lewin, K., *Resolving Social Conflicts* (New York: Harper, 1948).
41. Meadows, P., "Technological Change and Human Conflict," *Personalist,* 29 (Oct., 1948), 396-402.
42. Reuter and Hart, *op. cit.*, pp. 297-318.
43. Ross, *op. cit.*, pp. 195-203, 210-214.
44. Singer, K., *The Idea of Conflict* (Melbourne: Melbourne Univ. Press, 1949).
45. Wiese and Becker, *op. cit.*, pp. 273-280.
46. Williams, R. M., Jr., *The Reduction of Intergroup Tensions* (New York: Social Science Research Council, 1947), pp. 49-77.

Forms of Conflict

ECONOMIC

47. Bernard, J., *op. cit.*, pp. 261-317.
48. Dalton, M., "Conflicts between Staff and Line Managerial Officers," *Amer. sociol. Rev.*, 15 (June, 1950), 342-351.
49. Dawson, C. A., and W. E. Gettys, *An Introduction to Sociology* (New York: Ronald, 1948), pp. 429-434.
50. Faris, R. E. L., *Social Disorganization* (New York: Ronald, 1948), pp. 69-81.
51. Hiller, E. T., *The Strike: A Study in Collective Action* (Chicago: Univ. Chicago Press, 1928).
52. Ross, *op. cit.*, pp. 294-300.
53. Queen, S. A., W. B. Bodenhafer, and E. B. Harper, *Social Organization and Disorganization* (New York: Crowell, 1935), pp. 322-325.
54. Young, *op. cit.*, pp. 416-420.

CLASS

55. Ginsburg, M., "Class Consciousness," *Encyclopedia of the Social Sciences* (New York: Macmillan, 1930), Vol. 3, pp. 536-538.
56. Lorwin, L. L., "Class Struggle," *Encyclopedia of the Social Sciences* (New York: Macmillan, 1930), Vol. 3, pp. 538-542.
57. Moore, B., "A Comparative Analysis of the Class Struggle," *Amer. sociol. Rev.*, 10 (Feb., 1945), 31-37.
58. Ross, *op. cit.*, pp. 275-293.
59. Schweitzer, A., "Ideological Groups," *Amer. sociol. Rev.*, 9 (Aug., 1944), 415-426.
60. Young, *op. cit.*, pp. 534-536.

COMMUNITY, INCLUDING URBAN-RURAL OPPOSITION

61. Anderson, E. L., *We Americans: A Study of Cleavage in an American City* (Cambridge: Harvard Univ. Press, 1937).
62. Bernard, J., *op. cit.*, pp. 103-130.
63. Elliott, M. A., and F. E. Merrill, *Social Disorganization* (New York: Harper, 1941), pp. 808-810, 850-852.
64. Faris, *op. cit.*, pp. 125-163.
65. Kinneman, J. A., *The Community in American Society* (New York: Crofts, 1947), pp. 373-387.
66. Queen *et al., op. cit.*, pp. 221-224.
67. Ross, *op. cit.*, pp. 266-274.
68. Sanderson, D., and R. A. Polson, *Rural Community Organization* (New York: Wiley, 1939), pp. 316-338.
69. Simpson, G., *Conflict and Community: A Study in Social Theory* (New York: T. Simpson, 1937), pp. 41-70.
70. Smith, T. L., *The Sociology of Rural Life* (New York: Harper, 1947), pp. 453-477.
71. Sorokin, P. A., C. C. Zimmerman, and C. J. Galpin, *A Systematic Sourcebook for Rural Sociology* (Minneapolis: Univ. Minnesota Press, 1930), Vol. I, pp. 186-268; Vol. III (1932), pp. 628-700.
72. Thomas, W. I., and F. Znaniecki, *The Polish Peasant in Europe and America* (New York: Knopf, 1927), Vol. II, pp. 1171-1212.
73. Tuck, R. D., *Not with the Fist* (New York: Harcourt, Brace, 1946).

MAJORITY-MINORITY, INCLUDING CONFLICT BETWEEN RACIAL AND NATIONALITY GROUPS

74. Bernard, J., *op. cit.*, pp. 318-355, 388-428.

75. Berry, B., *Race Relations: The Interaction of Ethnic and Racial Groups* (Boston: Houghton Mifflin, 1951), pp. 157-193.
76. Bettelheim, B., and M. Janowitz, "Ethnic Tolerance: A Function of Social and Personal Control," *Amer. J. Sociol.*, 55 (Sept., 1949), 137-145.
77. Dahlke, H. O., "Race and Minority Riots: A Study in the Typology of Violence," *Soc. Forces*, 30 (May, 1952), 419-425.
78. Dawson and Gettys, *op. cit.*, pp. 366-372.
79. Faris, *op. cit.*, pp. 393-407.
80. Hertzler, J. O., "The Sociology of Anti-Semitism through History," in I. Graeber and S. H. Britt (eds.), *Jews in a Gentile World* (New York: Macmillan, 1942), pp. 62-100.
81. LaPiere, R. T., *Sociology* (New York: McGraw-Hill, 1947), pp. 422-449.
82. Lewin, *op. cit.*, pp. 145-200.
83. Locke, A., and B. J. Stern (eds.), *When Peoples Meet* (New York: Hinds, Hayden & Eldredge, 1946).
84. Marden, C. F., *Minorities in American Society* (New York: American Book, 1952), pp. 26-44.
85. Marcson, S., "The Control of Ethnic Conflict," *Soc. Forces*, 24 (Dec., 1945), 161-165.
86. McWilliams, C., "Does Social Discrimination Really Matter?" *Commentary*, Nov., 1947, pp. 408-415.
87. Myrdal, G., *An American Dilemma* (New York: Harper, 1944), 2 vols.
88. Parsons, T., "The Sociology of Modern Anti-Semitism," I. Graeber and S. H. Britt (eds.), *Jews in a Gentile World* (New York: Macmillan, 1942), pp. 101-123.
89. Price, M. T., "The Concept 'Culture Conflict': In What Sense Valid?" *Soc. Forces*, 9 (Dec., 1930), 164-167.
90. Queen *et al.*, *op. cit.*, pp. 411-414.
91. Rose, A., and C. Rose, *America Divided* (New York: Knopf, 1949).
92. Wirth, L., "The Problem of Minority Groups," in R. Linton (ed.), *The Science of Man in the World Crisis* (New York: Columbia Univ. Press, 1943), pp. 347-372.
93. Young, D., *American Minority Peoples* (New York: Harper, 1932).

Religious

94. Bernard, J., *op. cit.*, pp. 356-387.
95. Elliott and Merrill, *op. cit.*, pp. 846-850.
96. Hertzler, J. O., "Religious Institutions," *Ann. Amer. Acad. polit. soc. Sci.*, 256 (Mar., 1948), 1-13.
97. Queen *et al.*, *op. cit.*, pp. 408-411.
98. Ross, *op. cit.*, pp. 301-309.
99. Young, *op. cit.*, pp. 379-381.

War

100. Bernard, L. L., *War and Its Causes* (New York: Holt, 1944).
101. Carr, *op. cit.*
102. Clarkson, J. D., and T. C. Cochran (eds.), *War as a Social Institution* (New York: Columbia Univ. Press, 1944).
103. Dawson and Gettys, *op. cit.*, pp. 315-337.
104. Elliott and Merrill, *op. cit.*, pp. 1019-1020, 1030-1041.
105. Faris, *op. cit.*, pp. 447-454.
106. Kirk, G., "Nationalism, Internationalism and the War," in R. Linton (ed.), *The Science of Man in the World Crisis* (New York: Columbia Univ. Press, 1943), pp. 496-520.
107. Krech, D., and R. C. Crutchfield, *Theory and Problems of Social Psychology* (New York: McGraw-Hill, 1948), pp. 575-622.
108. LaPiere, *op. cit.*, pp. 483-512.
109. McCormick, T. C., *Sociology* (New York: Ronald, 1950), pp. 451-495.
110. Nef, J. U., *War and Human Progress* (Cambridge: Harvard Univ. Press, 1950).
111. Park, R. E., "The Social Function of War," *Amer. J. Sociol.*, 46 (Jan., 1941), 551-570.
112. Queen *et al.*, *op. cit.*, pp. 364-399.
113. Ross, *op. cit.*, pp. 317-325.
114. Salter, Sir A., *et al.*, *The Causes of War: Economic, Industrial, Racial, Religious, Scientific and Political* (New York: Macmillan, 1932).
115. Spier, H., and A. Kabler, *War in Our Time* (New York: Norton, 1939).
116. Waller, W. (ed.), *War in the Twentieth Century* (New York: Dryden, 1940).
117. Wright, Q., *The Causes of War and the Conditions of Peace* (New York: Longmans, Green, 1920).
118. ———, *A Study of War* (Chicago: Univ. Chicago Press, 1942), 2 vols.
119. Young, *op. cit.*, pp. 442-450.

XVIII. Processes of Societal Decadence and Societal Ossification

Social Decadence

1. Becker, H., "Processes of Secularization: An Ideal-Typical Analysis with Special Reference

to Personality Change as Affected by Population Movements," *Sociol. Rev. Brit.*, 24 (Apr.-July, Oct.-Dec., 1932), 138-154, 266-286.

2. Bennett, J. W., and M. M. Tumin, *Social Life* (New York: Knopf, 1948), pp. 601-640.
3. Bernard, L. L., *Social Control* (New York: Macmillan, 1939), pp. 16-49, 152-333.
4. Elliott, M. A., and F. E. Merrill, *Social Disorganization* (New York: Harper, 1941), pp. 787-966.
5. Faris, R. E. L., *Social Disorganization* (New York: Ronald, 1948), pp. 19-49, 371-407.
6. Hertzler, J. O., *Social Institutions* (Lincoln: Univ. Nebraska Press), 1946, pp. 280-292.
7. Ross, E. A., *Principles of Sociology* (New York: Appleton-Century, 1938), pp. 144-191, 559-569, 594-611.
8. Toynbee, A. J., *A Study of History* (1-vol. ed.) (New York: Oxford, 1947), pp. 244-558.
9. Wiese, L. von, and H. Becker, *Systematic Sociology* (New York: Wiley, 1932), pp. 368-384, 391-394.
10. Znaniecki, F., *Social Actions* (New York: Farrar & Rinehart, 1936), pp. 466-505.

Social Ossification

11. Becker, H., "Sargasso Iceberg: A Study in Cultural Lag and Institutional Disintegration," *Amer. J. Sociol.*, 34 (Nov., 1928), 492-506.
12. Cooley, C. H., *Social Organization* (New York: Scribner, 1915), pp. 342-355.
13. Cuber, J. F., "Some Aspects of Institutional Disorganization," *Amer. sociol. Rev.*, 5 (Aug., 1940), 489-494.
14. Elliott and Merrill, *op. cit.*
15. Herman, A. P., *An Approach to Social Problems* (Boston: Ginn, 1949), pp. 406-441.
16. Hertzler, *op. cit.*, pp. 237-255.
17. Merton, R. K., *Social Theory and Social Structure* (Glencoe, Ill.: Free Press, 1949), pp. 153-157, 175-178.
18. Page, C. H., "Bureaucracy's Other Face," *Soc. Forces*, 25 (Oct., 1946), 88-94.
19. Panunzio, C., *Major Social Institutions* (New York: Macmillan, 1939), pp. 468-478.
20. Ross, *op. cit.*, pp. 362-366, 580-582, 585-593, 611-619.
21. Schneider, E. V., "Limitations of Observation in Industrial Sociology," *Soc. Forces*, 28 (Mar., 1950), 279-285.
22. Selznick, P., "An Approach to a Theory of Bureaucracy," *Amer. sociol. Rev.*, 8 (Feb., 1943), 47-54.
23. Spindler, G. D., "The Military: A Systematic Analysis," *Soc. Forces*, 27 (Oct., 1948), 83-88.
24. Waller, W., *The Sociology of Teaching* (New York: Wiley, 1932), pp. 442-447.
25. Wiese and Becker, *op. cit.*, pp. 385-389.

XIX. Social Order and Social Control

Theoretical Orientation, Aspects

1. Bennett, J. W., and M. M. Tumin, *Social Life* (New York: Knopf, 1948), pp. 493-514.
2. Bernard, L. L., *Social Control* (New York: Macmillan, 1939).
3. Brearley, H. C., "The Nature of Social Control," in J. S. Roucek (ed.), *Social Control* (New York: Van Nostrand, 1947), pp. 3-16.
4. Dawson, C. A., and W. E. Gettys, *An Introduction to Sociology* (New York: Ronald, 1948), pp. 631-677.
5. Eliot, T. D., "Human Controls as Situation-Process," *Amer. sociol. Rev.*, 8 (Aug., 1943), 380-388.
6. Eubank, E. E., *The Concepts of Sociology* (Boston: Heath, 1932), pp. 206-257.
7. Everett, H., "Control, Social," *Encyclopedia of the Social Sciences* (New York: Macmillan, 1931), Vol. 4, pp. 344-349.
8. Frank, L. K., "What Is Social Order?" *Amer. J. Sociol.*, 49 (Mar., 1944), 470-477.
9. Giddings, F. H., *Civilization and Society* (New York: Holt, 1932), pp. 64-73.
10. ———, *Studies in the Theory of Human Society* (New York: Macmillan, 1922), pp. 197-208.
11. Gurvitch, G., "Social Control," in G. Gurvitch and W. E. Moore (eds.), *Twentieth Century Sociology* (New York: Philosophical Library, 1945), pp. 267-296.
12. Hollingshead, A. B., "The Concept of Social Control," *Amer. sociol. Rev.*, 6 (Apr., 1941), 217-224.
13. Homans, G. C., *The Human Group* (New York: Harcourt, Brace, 1950), pp. 281-312.
14. Landis, P. H., *Social Control: Social Organization and Disorganization in Process* (Philadelphia: Lippincott, 1939), pp. 7-23.
15. Lemert, E. M., "The Folkways and Social Control," *Amer. sociol. Rev.*, 7 (June, 1942), 394-399.
16. Lumley, F. E., *Means of Social Control* (New York: Century, 1925), pp. 3-30, 395-404.
17. Parsons, T., *The Social System* (Glencoe, Ill.: Free Press, 1951), pp. 249-325.

18. ———, and E. A. Shils, *Toward a General Theory of Action* (Cambridge: Harvard Univ. Press, 1951), pp. 199-204, 219-221, 226-230.
19. Reuter, E. B., and C. W. Hart, *Introduction to Sociology* (New York: McGraw-Hill, 1935), pp. 381-436.
20. Ross, E. A., *Social Control: A Survey of the Foundations of Order* (New York: Macmillan, 1901), pp. 1-6, 49-88, 295-442.
21. Roucek, J. S. (ed.), *Social Control* (New York: Van Nostrand, 1947), Part I.
22. Sanderson, D., *Rural Sociology* (New York: Wiley, 1942), pp. 633-641.
23. Smith, T. L., "Social Cohesion and Social Control," in J. S. Roucek (ed.), *Social Control* (New York: Van Nostrand, 1947), pp. 62-75.
24. Young, K., *Sociology: A Study of Society and Culture* (New York: American Book, 1949), pp. 541-559.

Dominance-Submission: Influence, Power, Authority

25. Barnard, C. I., *The Functions of the Executive* (Cambridge: Harvard Univ. Press, 1940), pp. 161-165.
26. Barnes, H. E., *An Introduction to the History of Sociology* (Chicago: Univ. Chicago Press, 1948), pp. 406-409.
27. Bierstedt, R., "An Analysis of Social Power," *Amer. sociol. Rev.*, 15 (Dec., 1950), 730-738.
28. ———, "The Sociology of Majorities," *Amer. sociol. Rev.*, 13 (Dec., 1948), 700-710.
29. Clapp, O. E., "The Creation of Popular Heroes," *Amer. J. Sociol.*, 54 (Sept., 1948), 135-141.
30. ———, "The Folk Hero," *J. Amer. Folklore*, 62 (Jan.-Mar., 1949), 17-25.
31. Dubin, R., *Human Relations in Administration* (New York: Prentice-Hall, 1951), pp. 172-173, 188-198, 229, 271-280.
32. Goldhamer, H., and E. A. Shils, "Types of Power and Status," *Amer. sociol. Rev.*, 45 (Sept., 1949), 171-182.
33. Jaco, E. G., "Prestige and Esteem as Power Components: An Experimental Analysis," *Sthwest. soc. Sci. Quart.*, 33 (Mar., 1953), 319-327.
34. MacIver, R. M., *The Modern State* (London: Oxford, 1926), pp. 221-231.
35. ———, *The Web of Government* (New York: Macmillan, 1947), pp. 73-113.
36. ———, and C. H. Page, *Society: An Introductory Analysis* (New York: Rinehart, 1949), pp. 146-149, 154-165.
37. Meadows, P., "On the Dynamics of Power: A Case Study," *Sthwest. soc. Sci. Quart.*, 33 (Mar., 1953), 309-318.
38. ———, "Some Notes on the Social Psychology of the Hero," *Sthwest. soc. Sci. Quart.*, 26 (Dec., 1945), 239-247.
39. Sherif, M., and C. W. Sherif, "Some Effects of Power Relations in Molding Opinion," *Sthwest. soc. Sci. Quart.*, 33 (Mar., 1953), 287-296.
40. Sjoberg, G., "Strategy and Social Power: Some Preliminary Formulations," *Sthwest. soc. Sci. Quart.*, 33 (Mar., 1953), 297-308.
41. Ross, E. A., *Social Control* (New York: Macmillan, 1901), pp. 275-290.
42. Russell, B., *Power: A New Social Analysis* (New York: Norton, 1938).
43. Williams, R. M., Jr., *American Society: A Sociological Interpretation* (New York: Knopf, 1951), pp. 200-209.
44. Zeleny, L. D., "The Leadership Process," in J. S. Roucek (ed.), *Social Control* (New York: Van Nostrand, 1947), pp. 278-294.

XX. Processes and Instrumentalities of Societal Regulation

The Mechanisms and Processes That Establish Order

THE NATURE, FUNCTION, FORMATION, TRANSMISSION, AND INCULCATION OF NORMS

1. Bernard, J., *American Family Behavior* (New York: Harper, 1942), pp. 107-112.
2. ———, *American Community Behavior* (New York: Dryden, 1949), pp. 57-83.
3. Davis, K., *Human Society* (New York: Macmillan, 1949), pp. 52-82.
4. Freedman, R., A. H. Hawley, W. Landecker, and H. Miner, *Principles of Sociology* (New York: Holt, 1952), pp. 166-173.
5. Giddings, F. H., *Studies in the Theory of Human Society* (New York: Macmillan, 1922), pp. 190-196.
6. Hiller, E. T., *Social Relations and Structures* (New York: Harper, 1947), pp. 11, 39-61, 89-90, 253-259.
7. Homans, G. C., *The Human Group* (New York: Harcourt, Brace, 1950), pp. 121-127.
8. Linton, R., *The Study of Man* (New York: Appleton-Century, 1936), pp. 271-287.
9. Morgan, J. W., "Notes on Common Values and Social Control," *Soc. Forces*, 27 (May, 1949), 418-421.

10. Odum, H. W., "Notes on the Technicways in Contemporary Society," *Amer. sociol. Rev.*, 2 (June, 1937), 336-346.
11. Sherif, M., *The Psychology of Social Norms* (New York: Harper, 1936).
12. Sorokin, P. A., *Society, Culture and Personality* (New York: Harper, 1947), pp. 70-91, 121-127.
13. Stouffer, S. A., "An Analysis of Conflicting Social Norms," *Amer. sociol. Rev.*, 14 (Dec., 1949), 707-717.

SOCIALIZATION

14. Apple, D., "Learning Theory and Socialization," *Amer. sociol. Rev.*, 16 (Feb., 1951), 23-27.
15. Becker, H., *Through Values to Social Interpretation* (Durham, N.C.: Duke Univ. Press, 1950), pp. 79-91.
16. Bennett, J. W., and M. M. Tumin, *Social Life* (New York: Knopf, 1948), pp. 641-680.
17. Bowman, C. C., "Role-Playing and the Development of Insight," *Soc. Forces*, 28 (Dec., 1949), 195-199.
18. Coulter, C. W., "Social Control and the Conditioning of Personality," in J. S. Roucek (ed.), *Social Control* (New York: Van Nostrand, 1947), pp. 31-44.
19. Davis, A., "Socialization and Adolescent Personality," in T. M. Newcomb and E. L. Hartley (eds.), *Readings in Social Psychology* (New York: Holt, 1947), pp. 139-150.
20. Freeman, G. L., *The Energetics of Human Behavior* (Ithaca: Cornell Univ. Press, 1948), pp. 174-192.
21. Gibson, J. J., "The Implications of Learning Theory for Social Psychology," in J. G. Miller (ed.), *Experiments in Social Process* (New York: McGraw-Hill, 1950), pp. 149-167.
22. Giddings, *op. cit.*, pp. 287-290.
23. Gillin, J. L., and J. P. Gillin, *Cultural Sociology* (New York: Macmillan, 1948), pp. 643-664.
24. Hertzler, J. O., *Social Institutions* (Lincoln: Univ. Nebraska Press, 1946), pp. 162-166.
25. Landis, P. H., *Social Control* (Philadelphia: Lippincott, 1939), pp. 53-148, 331-361.
26. Mead, G. H., *Mind, Self and Society* (Chicago: Univ. Chicago Press, 1939), Part III.
27. Miller, D. C., and W. A. Form, *Industrial Sociology* (New York: Harper, 1951), pp. 519-523.
28. Miller, N. E., and J. Dollard, *Social Learning and Imitation* (New Haven: Yale Univ. Press, 1941), pp. 1-18, 183-202.
29. Murray, H. A., and C. Kluckhohn, "Outline of a Conception of Personality," in C. Kluckhohn and H. A. Murray (eds.), *Personality in Nature, Society and Culture* (New York: Knopf, 1948), pp. 3-32.
30. Park, R. E., "Symbiosis and Socialization: A Frame of Reference for the Study of Society," *Amer. J. Sociol.*, 45 (July, 1939), 1-25.
31. Tolman, E. C., "The Psychology of Social Learning," *J. soc. Issues*, 5 (Suppl., 1949), 5-18.
32. Wilson, L., and W. L. Kolb, *Sociological Analysis* (New York: Harcourt, Brace, 1949), pp. 208-231.
33. Znaniecki, F., "Social Groups as Products of Participating Individuals," *Amer. J. Sociol.*, 44 (May, 1939), 799-811.

UNIFORMATION

34. Bernard, L. L., *Social Control* (New York: Macmillan, 1939), pp. 408-450.
35. Chapple, E. D., and C. S. Coon, *Principles of Anthropology* (New York: Holt, 1942), pp. 484-565.
36. Coyle, G. L., *Social Process in Organized Groups* (New York: Smith, 1930), pp. 144-158.
37. Cressman, L. S., "Ritual the Conserver," *Amer. J. Sociol.*, 35 (Jan., 1930), 564-572.
38. LaPiere, R. T., *Sociology* (New York: McGraw-Hill, 1946), pp. 105-110, 362-363.
39. MacIver, R. M., and C. H. Page, *Sociology: An Introductory Analysis* (New York: Rinehart, 1949), pp. 149-154.
40. Spencer, H., *Principles of Sociology* (New York: Appleton-Century, 1947), Part IV.

THE SANCTIONING PROCESSES

41. Barnard, C. I., *The Functions of the Executive* (Cambridge: Harvard Univ. Press, 1940), pp. 139-142.
42. Bernard, J., *op. cit.*, Chap. VI.
43. Bernard, L. L., *op. cit.*, pp. 96-178.
44. Katz, D., and R. L. Schank, *Social Psychology* (New York: Wiley, 1939), Chap. III.
45. LaPiere, R. T., and P. R. Farnsworth, *Social Psychology* (New York: McGraw-Hill, 1949), pp. 277-284.
46. Lumley, F. E., *Means of Social Control* (New York: Century, 1925), pp. 31-108, 211-314, 339-394.

Agencies of Regulation

47. Bernard, L. L., "The Conflict between Primary Group Attitudes and Derivative Group Ideals in Modern Society," *Amer. J. Sociol.*, 41 (Mar., 1936), 611-623.

48. Hertzler, *op. cit.*, pp. 43-46, 63-65, 156-177, 297-305, 309-324.
49. Hiller, *op. cit.*, pp. 219-262.
50. Katz and Schanck, *op. cit.*, pp. 23, 169-212.
51. Landis, *op. cit.*, pp. 151-327.
52. MacIver, R. M., and C. H. Page, *Society: An Introductory Analysis* (New York: Rinehart, 1949), pp. 453-492.
53. Malinowski, B., *Freedom and Civilization* (New York: Roy, 1945), pp. 264-275.
54. Panunzio, C., *Major Social Institutions* (New York: Macmillan, 1939), pp. 456-465.
55. Ross, E. A., *Social Control: A Survey of the Foundations of Order* (New York: Macmillan, 1901), pp. 106-374.

Public Opinion

56. Albig, W., *Public Opinion* (New York: McGraw-Hill, 1939).
57. Bogardus, E. S., *The Making of Public Opinion* (New York: Association Press, 1951).
58. Childs, H. L., *An Introduction to Public Opinion* (New York: Wiley, 1940), pp. 129-142.
59. Doob, L. W., *Public Opinion and Propaganda* (New York: Holt, 1948).
60. Ginsburg, M., *The Psychology of Society* (London: Methuen, 1921), pp. 137-151.
61. Hertzler, *op. cit.*, pp. 174-177.
62. Landis, P. H., *Social Control* (Philadelphia: Lippincott, 1939), pp. 185-206.
63. Lasswell, H. D., *Democracy through Public Opinion* (Menasha, Wis.: Banta, 1941).
64. Lee, A. M., "Public Opinion," in J. S. Roucek (ed.), *Social Control* (New York: Van Nostrand, 1947), pp. 385-407.
65. Lundberg, G. A., *Foundations of Sociology* (New York: Macmillan, 1939), pp. 185-192.
66. Ogle, M. B., *Public Opinion and Political Dynamics* (Boston: Houghton Mifflin, 1950).
67. Powell, N. J., *The Anatomy of Public Opinion* (New York: Prentice-Hall, 1951).
68. Ross, *op. cit.*, pp. 89-105.

XXI. Processes and Instrumentalities of Societal Maintenance

The Nature and Function of Motivation

1. Burke, K., *A Grammar of Motives* (New York: Prentice-Hall, 1945).
2. ———, *A Rhetoric of Motives* (New York: Prentice-Hall, 1950).
3. ———, *Permanence and Change: An Anatomy of Purpose* (New York: New Republic, Inc., 1935).
4. Cantril, H., *The Psychology of Social Movements* (New York: Wiley, 1941), pp. 30-52.
5. Cartwright, D., "Some Principles of Mass Persuasion," *Human Relations*, 2 (No. 3, 1949), 253-267.
6. Centers, R., "Motivational Aspects of Occupational Stratification," *J. soc. Psychol.*, 28 (Nov., 1948), 187-217.
7. Cooley, C. H., *Social Process* (New York: Scribner, 1918), pp. 125-136.
8. Dewey, R., and W. J. Humber, *The Development of Human Behavior* (New York: Macmillan, 1951), Part I.
9. Foote, N. N., "Identification as the Basis for a Theory of Motivation," *Amer. sociol. Rev.*, 16 (Feb., 1951), 14-21.
10. Hart, H., "The Transmutation of Motivation," *Amer. J. Sociol.*, 35 (Jan., 1930), 588-600.
11. LaPiere, R. T., *Collective Behavior* (New York: McGraw-Hill, 1938), pp. 27-29.
12. MacIver, R. M., *Social Causation* (Boston: Ginn, 1942), pp. 195-223.
13. ———, "The Imputation of Motives," *Amer. J. Sociol.*, 46 (July, 1940), 1-12.
14. Maslow, A. H., "A Theory of Human Motivation," *Psychol. Rev.*, 50 (1943), 370-396.
15. Newcomb, T. M., *Social Psychology* (New York: Dryden, 1950), pp. 74-146, 284-285, 425-427, 649-650.
16. Parsons, T., "The Motivation of Economic Activities," *Canad. J. Econ. polit. Sci.*, 6 (May, 1940), 187-200.
17. ———, "The Position of Sociological Theory," *Amer. sociol. Rev.*, 13 (Apr., 1948), 156-164; or *Essays in Sociological Theory: Pure and Applied* (Glencoe, Ill.: Free Press, 1949), pp. 3-16.
18. ———, *The Social System* (Glencoe, Ill.: Free Press, 1951), pp. 3-23, 29-33, 201-248.
19. Peterson, F., "Cause of Industrial Unrest," *Ann. Amer. Acad. polit. soc. Sci.*, 274 (Mar., 1951), 25-31.
20. Rose, A. W., "Projective Techniques in Sociological Research," *Soc. Forces*, 28 (Dec., 1949), 175-183.
21. Sears, R. B., "Personality Development and Contemporary Culture," *Proc. Amer. philos. Soc.*, 92 (Nov. 12, 1948), 363-370.
22. Sherif, M., *An Outline of Social Psychology* (New York: Harper, 1948), pp. 11-38, 250-273.
23. Williams, R. M., Jr., *American Society: A Soci-*

ological Interpretation (New York: Knopf, 1951), pp. 518-532.
24. Young, P. T., *Motivation in Behavior* (New York: Wiley, 1936).

Social Morale and Morale Building

25. Allport, G. W., "The Nature of Democratic Morale," in G. Watson (ed.), *Civilian Morale* (New York: Reynal and Hitchcock, 1943), pp. 3-18.
26. Angell, J. R., "Radio and National Morale," *Amer. J. Sociol.*, 47 (Nov., 1941), 352-359.
27. Bavelas, A., "Morale and the Training of Leaders," in G. Watson, *Civilian Morale* (New York: Reynal and Hitchcock, 1943), pp. 143-165.
28. Blumer, H., "Morale," in W. F. Ogburn (ed.), *American Society in Wartime* (Chicago: Univ. Chicago Press, 1943), pp. 207-231.
29. Creel, G., "Propaganda and Morale," *Amer. J. Sociol.*, 47 (Nov., 1941), 340-351.
30. Frank, L. K., *Society as the Patient* (New Brunswick, N.J.: Rutgers Univ. Press, 1945), pp. 380-388.
31. Hocking, W. E., *Morale and Its Enemies* (New Haven: Yale Univ. Press, 1918).
32. ———, "The Nature of Morale," *Amer. J. Sociol.*, 47 (Nov., 1941), 302-320.
33. Krech, D., and R. C. Crutchfield, *Theory and Problems of Social Psychology* (New York: McGraw-Hill, 1948), pp. 404-417.
34. Landis, J. M., "Morale and Civilian Defense," *Amer. J. Sociol.*, 47 (Nov., 1941), 331-339.
35. Lewin, K., "Time Perspective and Morale," in G. Watson (ed.), *Civilian Morale* (New York: Reynal and Hitchcock, 1947), pp. 48-70.
36. Lindeman, E. C., "Recreation and Morale," *Amer. J. Sociol.*, 47 (Nov., 1941), 394-405.
37. Lippitt, R., "The Morale of Youth Groups," in G. Watson (ed.), *Civilian Morale* (New York: Reynal and Hitchcock, 1947), pp. 119-142.
38. Miller, D. C., and W. H. Form, *Industrial Sociology* (New York: Harper, 1951), pp. 469-492.
39. Sullivan, H. S., "Psychiatric Aspects of Morale," *Amer. J. Sociol.*, 47 (Nov., 1941), 277-301.
40. Watson, G., "Five Factors in Morale," in G. Watson (ed.), *Civilian Morale* (New York: Reynal and Hitchcock, 1947), pp. 30-47.
41. Wirth, L., "Morale and Minority Groups," *Amer. J. Sociol.*, 47 (Nov., 1941), 415-433.
42. Zentner, H., "Morale: Certain Theoretical Implications of Data in *The American Soldier*," *Amer. Sociol. Rev.*, 16 (June, 1951), 297-310.

Equalization: Freedoms and Rights

43. Anshem, R. N. (ed.), *Freedom, Its Meaning* (New York: Harcourt, Brace, 1940).
44. Brinton, C., "Equality," *Encyclopedia of the Social Sciences* (New York: Macmillan, 1931), Vol. 5, pp. 574-580.
45. Burma, J. H., "Race Relations and Antidiscriminatory Legislation," *Amer. J. Sociol.*, 56 (Mar., 1951), 416-423.
46. Cushman, R. E., "Civil Liberties," *Encyclopedia of the Social Sciences* (New York: Macmillan, 1931), Vol. 3, pp. 509-513.
47. Dickinson, J., "Civil Rights," *Encyclopedia of the Social Sciences* (New York: Macmillan, 1930), Vol. 3, pp. 513-515.
48. Edman, I. (ed.), *Fountainheads of Freedom* (New York: Reynal and Hitchcock, 1941).
49. Eliot, T. D., "Civil Liberties," *Encyclopaedia Britannica* (Chicago: Univ. Chicago Press, 1946), Vol. 5, pp. 742-744.
50. "Freedom of Inquiry and Expression," *Ann. Amer. Acad. polit. soc. Sci.*, 200 (Nov., 1938), entire number.
51. Fosdick, D., *What Is Freedom?* (New York: Harper, 1939).
52. Kallen, H. M. (ed.), *Freedom in the Modern World* (New York: Coward-McCann, 1928).
53. Knight, F. H., "The Meaning of Freedom," in C. H. Perry (ed.), *The Philosophy of American Democracy* (Chicago: Univ. Chicago Press, 1943), pp. 59-86.
54. Laski, H. J., "Liberty," *Encyclopedia of the Social Sciences* (New York: Macmillan, 1933), Vol. 9, pp. 442-447.
55. Lippmann, W., *The Method of Freedom* (New York: Macmillan, 1943).
56. Malinowski, B., *Freedom and Civilization* (New York: Roy, 1945).
57. McIlwain, C. H., "Bills of Rights," *Encyclopedia of the Social Sciences* (New York: Macmillan, 1930), Vol. 2, pp. 544-546.
58. Merton, R. K., "Discrimination and the American Creed," in R. M. MacIver (ed.), *Discrimination and National Welfare* (New York: Harper, 1949), pp. 99-126.
59. Ross, E. A., *Principles of Sociology* (New York: Appleton-Century, 1938), pp. 444-456, 514-526, 542-550.

60. Smith, T. V., *The American Philosophy of Equality* (Chicago: Univ. Chicago Press, 1927).
61. Tawney, R. H., *Equality* (London: Allen & Unwin, 1931).

Adjustment of Unequals and Inequalities of Opportunity

ORDINATION

62. Cattell, R. B., "The Cultural Functions of Social Stratification: I. Regarding the Genetic Basis of Society," *J. soc. Psychol.*, 21 (1945), 3-23.
63. Davis, K., "A Conceptual Analysis of Stratification," *Amer. sociol. Rev.*, 7 (June, 1942), 309-321.
64. ———, *Human Society* (New York: Macmillan, 1949), pp. 366-379.
65. ———, and W. E. Moore, "Some Principles of Stratification," *Amer. sociol. Rev.*, 10 (Apr., 1945), 242-247.
66. Kluckhohn, F. R., "Dominant and Substitute Profiles of Cultural Orientations: Their Significance for the Analysis of Social Stratification," *Soc. Forces*, 28 (May, 1950), 376-391.
67. McConnell, J. W., *The Evolution of Social Classes* (Washington: American Council on Public Affairs, 1942), pp. 71-81.
68. Moore, B., Jr., "The Relation between Social Stratification and Social Control," *Sociometry*, 5 (Aug., 1942), 230-250.
69. Warner, W. L., "Individual Opportunity: A Challenge to the Free Enterprise System," in American Management Association, *Identifying and Developing Potential Political Leaders*, Personnel Series No. 127 (New York, 1949), pp. 3-9.
70. ———, M. Meeker, and K. Eells, *Social Classes in America* (Chicago: Science Research Associates, 1949), pp. 7-11.
71. Wiese, L. von, and H. Becker, *Systematic Sociology* (New York: Wiley, 1932), pp. 257, 348-367.
72. Williams, *op. cit.*, pp. 125-135.

THE MOBILITY PROCESSES: *Adjustment through Physical Mobility*

73. Albig, W., "A Method of Recording Trends in Urban Residential Mobility," *Sociol. soc. Res.*, 21 (Nov.-Dec., 1936), 120-127.
74. Barnes, H. E., *Society in Transition* (New York: Prentice-Hall, 1939), pp. 257-260.
75. Isaacs, J., *Economics of Migration* (London: Kegan Paul, Trench & Trubner, 1947), pp. 70-112.
76. Kulischer, E. M., *Europe on the Move* (New York: Columbia Univ. Press, 1948), pp. 11-12, 16-18.
77. National Resources Committee, *The Problems of a Changing Population* (Washington: U.S. Government Printing Office, 1938), pp. 9-11, 108-112, 116-118.
78. Sorokin, P. A., C. C. Zimmerman, and C. J. Galpin, *Systematic Sourcebook for Rural Sociology* (Minneapolis: Univ. Minnesota Press, 1932), Vol. III, pp. 532-534.
79. Vance, R. B., *Research Memorandum on Population Redistribution within the United States* (New York: Social Science Research Council, 1938), pp. 85-87.

Adjustment through Social Mobility

80. Andrzejewski, S., "Vertical Mobility and Technical Progress," *Soc. Forces*, 29 (Oct., 1950), 48-51.
81. Burma, J. H., "The Measurement of Negro 'Passing,'" *Amer. J. Sociol.*, 52 (July, 1946), 18-22.
82. ———, "How Many Negroes 'Pass'?" *Amer. J. Sociol.*, 52 (May, 1947), 498-500.
83. Centers, R., "Occupational Mobility of Urban Occupational Strata," *Amer. sociol. Rev.*, 13 (Apr., 1948), 197-203.
84. Hertzler, J. O., "Some Tendencies toward a Closed Class System in the United States," *Soc. Forces*, 30 (Mar., 1952), 313-323.
85. Ross, *op. cit.*, pp. 466-468, 533-534.
86. Sorokin, P. A., *Social Mobility* (New York: Harper, 1927), pp. 508-515, 530-546.

Adjustment of Dissension, Conflict, and Differences

ACCOMMODATION

87. Bernard, J., *American Community Behavior* (New York: Dryden, 1949), pp. 47-52, 84-102, 110-113, 305-319, and the discussion of accommodation in connection with each type of conflict examined.
88. Bogardus, E. S., "Reducing Racial Tensions," *Sociol. soc. Res.*, 35 (Sept.-Oct., 1950), 50-57.
89. Chase, S., *Roads to Agreement* (New York: Harper, 1951).
90. Dawson, C. A., and W. E. Gettys, *An Introduction to Sociology* (New York: Ronald, 1948), pp. 299-301, 304-306, 344-345, 377-378, 400-401, 490-493.
91. Du Bois, W. E. B., "Prospect of a World with-

out Race Conflict," *Amer. J. Sociol.*, 49 (Mar., 1944), 450-456.

92. Freeman, F. D., "Theory and Strategy of Action in Race Relations," *Soc. Forces*, 30 (Oct., 1951), 77-87.
93. Gillin, J. L., and J. P. Gillin, *Cultural Sociology* (New York: Macmillan, 1948), pp. 505-522.
94. Gist, N. P., "Accommodation and Assimilation," in S. Eldridge (ed.), *Fundamentals of Sociology: A Situational Analysis* (New York: Crowell, 1950), pp. 402-412.
95. Lewin, K., *Resolving Social Conflicts* (New York: Harper, 1948).
96. Marcson, S., "The Control of Ethnic Conflict," *Soc. Forces*, 24 (Dec., 1945), 161-165.
97. Marden, C. F., *Minorities in America* (New York: American Book, 1952), pp. 460-481.
98. Ogburn, W. F., and M. F. Nimkoff, *Sociology* (Boston: Houghton Mifflin, 1950), pp. 177-185.
99. Park, R. E., and E. W. Burgess, *Introduction to the Science of Sociology* (Chicago: Univ. Chicago Press, 1921), pp. 663-732.
100. Reuter, E. B., and C. W. Hart, *Introduction to Sociology* (New York: McGraw-Hill, 1933), pp. 319-348.
101. Ross, *op. cit.*, pp. 326-338.
102. Singer, K., "The Resolution of Conflict," *Sociol. soc. Res.*, 6 (June, 1948), 230-245.
103. Smith, T. L., *The Sociology of Rural Life* (New York: Harper, 1947), pp. 449-525.
104. Vincent, M. J., *The Accommodation Process in Industry*, Social Science Series, No. 2 (Los Angeles: Univ. Southern California Studies, 1930).
105. Watson, G., *Action for Unity* (New York: Harper, 1947).
106. Williams, R. M., Jr., *The Reduction of Intergroup Tensions* (New York: Social Science Research Council, 1947).
107. Wilson, L., and W. L. Kolb, *Sociological Analysis* (New York: Harcourt, Brace, 1948), pp. 682-712.
108. Young, K., *Sociology: A Study of Society and Culture* (New York: American Book, 1949), pp. 74-77.

SOCIAL ASSIMILATION

109. Duncan, H. G., "A Study of the Process of Assimilation," *Pubs. Amer. sociol. Soc.*, 23 (1929), 184-187.
110. Gillin and Gillin, *op. cit.*, pp. 523-535.
111. Gist, *op. cit.*, pp. 412-420.
112. Glick, C., "The Relation between Position and Status in the Assimilation of Chinese in Hawaii," *Amer. J. Sociol.*, 47 (Mar., 1942), 667-679.
113. Hartly, E. L., and A. Muntz, "A Technique for the Study of the Dynamics of the Racial Saturation Point," *Sociometry*, 3 (Feb., 1940), 14-20.
114. Hiller, E. T., *Principles of Sociology* (New York: Harper, 1933), pp. 376-387.
115. House, F. N., "Social Relations and Social Interaction," *Amer. J. Sociol.*, 31 (Mar., 1926), 617-633.
116. Infeld, H., "The Aged in the Process of Ethnic Assimilation," *Sociometry*, 3 (Oct., 1940), 353-366.
117. Lind, A. W., "Assimilation in Rural Hawaii," *Amer. J. Sociol.*, 45 (Sept., 1939), 200-214.
118. Ogburn and Nimkoff, *op. cit.*, pp. 185-191.
119. Park, R. E., "Assimilation, Social," *Encyclopedia of the Social Sciences* (New York: Macmillan, 1930), Vol. 2, pp. 281-283.
120. ———, "Symbiosis and Socialization: A Frame of Reference for the Study of Society," *Amer. J. Sociol.*, 45 (July, 1939), 1-25.
121. ——— and Burgess, *op. cit.*, pp. 734-774.
122. Reuter and Hart, *op. cit.*, pp. 349-380.
123. Ross, *op. cit.*, pp. 338-340.
124. Smith, T. L., *op. cit.*, pp. 525-527.
125. Woolston, H. B., "The Process of Assimilation," *Soc. Forces*, 23 (May, 1945), 416-424.
126. Young, *op. cit.*, pp. 77-79.

AMALGAMATION

127. Hiller, *op. cit.*, pp. 395-399.
128. Kennedy, R. J. R., "Premarital Residential Propinquity and Ethnic Endogamy," *Amer. J. Sociol.*, 48 (Mar., 1943), 580-584.
129. ———, "Single or Triple Melting Pot?: Intermarriage Trends in New Haven, 1870-1940," *Amer. J. Sociol.*, 49 (Jan., 1944), 331-338.
130. ———, "Single or Triple Melting Pot?: Intermarriage in New Haven, 1870-1950," *Amer. J. Sociol.*, 58 (July, 1952), 56-59.
131. Lowrie, S. H., "Racial and National Intermarriage in a Brazilian City," *Amer. J. Sociol.*, 44 (Mar., 1939), 684-707.
132. Marcson, S., "A Theory of Intermarriage and Assimilation," *Soc. Forces*, 29 (Oct., 1950), 75-78.
133. Nelson, L., "Intermarriage among Nationality Groups in a Rural Area of Minnesota," *Amer. J. Sociol.*, 48 (Mar., 1943), 585-592.
134. Panunzio, C., "Intermarriage in Los Angeles, 1924-33," *Amer. J. Sociol.*, 47 (Mar., 1942), 690-701.

135. Reuter and Hart, *op. cit.*, pp. 353-356.
136. Ross, *op. cit.*, pp. 340-341.
137. Slotkin, J. S., "Social Factors in Amalgamation," *Sociol. soc. Res.*, 26 (Mar.-Apr., 1942), 346-351.

Correction and Prevention of Decadence and Ossification

138. Ross, *op. cit.*, pp. 590-593, 607-608, 612, 618-619, 621-622.

XXII. Processes and Instrumentalities of Societal Reorganization

Historical Reorganizational Concepts

1. "Ages of the World," *Hastings' Encyclopedia of Religion and Ethics* (Edinburgh: Clark, 1908), Vol. III, pp. 183-210.
2. Hertzler, J. O., *History of Utopian Thought* (New York: Macmillan, 1923).
3. ———, "On Golden Ages: Then and Now," *Sth. Atl. Quart.*, 39 (July, 1940), 318-329.
4. ———, *Social Thought of the Ancient Civilizations* (New York: McGraw-Hill, 1936), pp. 32-38, 168, 308-314, 350-351.
5. Kohn, H., 'Messianism," *Encyclopedia of the Social Sciences* (New York: Macmillan, 1933), Vol. 10, pp. 356-364.
6. Morgan, A. E., *Nowhere Was Somewhere* (Chapel Hill, N.C.: Univ. North Carolina Press, 1946), pp. 120-151.
7. Mumford, L., *The Story of Utopias* (New York: Boni & Liveright, 1922).
8. Wallis, W. D., *Culture and Progress* (New York: Whittlesey House, 1930), pp. 230-233, 247, 252-253, 255, 274-292.
9. ———, *Messiahs: Their Role in Civilization* (Washington: American Council on Public Affairs, 1943).

Social Movements in General

10. Blumer, H., "Social Movements," in R. E. Park (ed.), *An Outline of the Principles of Sociology* (New York: Barnes & Noble, 1939), pp. 255-280.
11. Burgess, J. S., "A Study of Modern Social Movements as a Means of Clarifying the Process of Social Action," *Soc. Forces*, 22 (Mar., 1944), 269-275.
12. Cantril, H., *The Psychology of Social Movements* (New York: Wiley, 1941).
13. Davis, J., *Contemporary Social Movements* (New York: Century, 1930).
14. Dawson, C. A., and W. E. Gettys, *An Introduction to Sociology* (New York: Ronald, 1948), pp. 678-714.
15. Faris, R. E. L., *Social Disorganization* (New York: Ronald, 1948), pp. 408-446.
16. Freedman, R., A. H. Hawley, W. Landecker, and H. Miner, *Principles of Sociology* (New York: Holt, 1952), pp. 560-584.
17. Gist, N. P., "Collective Behavior," in S. Eldridge (ed.), *Fundamentals of Sociology: A Situational Analysis* (New York: Crowell, 1950), pp. 423-435.
18. Heberle, R., "Observations on the Sociology of Social Movements," *Amer. sociol. Rev.*, 14 (June, 1949), 346-357.
19. ———, *Social Movements: An Introduction to Political Sociology* (New York: Appleton-Century-Crofts, 1951), pp. 1-366, 454-459.
20. Hertzler, J. O., "American Ancestor Worshipers," *Sth. Atl. Quart.*, 36 (Apr., 1937), 189-200.
21. House, F. N., *The Range of Social Theory* (New York: Holt, 1929), pp. 212-219.
22. Laidler, H. W., *Social-Economic Movements* (New York: Crowell, 1944).
23. LaPiere, R. T., *Collective Behavior* (New York: McGraw-Hill, 1938), pp. 437-554.
24. McCormick, T. C., *Sociology* (New York: Ronald, 1950), pp. 227, 515-528.
25. Meadows, P., "Analysis of Social Movements," *Sociol. soc. Res.*, 27 (Jan.-Feb., 1943), 223-228.
26. ———, "Behavioral Bases of Social Movements," *Sociol. soc. Res.*, 28 (Nov.-Dec., 1943), 112-117.
27. ———, "Movements of Social Withdrawal," *Sociol. soc. Res.*, 29 (Sept.-Oct., 1944), 46-50.
28. ———, "The Dynamics of a Revolutionary Age," to be published in *Revista Mexicana de Sociologia.*
29. Reuter, E. B., and C. W. Hart, *Introduction to Sociology* (New York: McGraw-Hill, 1933), pp. 500-530.
30. Znaniecki, F., *Social Actions* (New York: Farrar and Rinehart, 1936), pp. 409-449.

Social Reform Movements

31. Abel, T., "The Pattern of A Successful Political Movement," *Amer. sociol. Rev.*, 2 (June, 1937), 347-352.
32. Barnes, H. E., "Social Reform Programs and

Movements — Their Historical Development," *Encyclopedia Americana* (New York: Americana Corp., 1949), Vol. 25, pp. 166-186.
33. Boettiger, L. A., "Organic Theory of Social Reform Movements," *Soc. Forces*, 3 (Nov., 1924), 60-64.
34. Cheyney, E. P., *Modern English Reform* (Philadelphia: Univ. Pennsylvania Press, 1931), Chaps. 2-6.
35. Dawson, C., *The Spirit of the Oxford Movement* (New York: Sheed & Ward, 1934).
36. Faris, *op. cit.*, pp. 305-315.
37. Freeman, E., *Social Psychology* (New York: Holt, 1936), pp. 367-406.
38. Fuller, R. C., and R. R. Myers, "The Natural History of a Social Problem," *Amer. sociol. Rev.*, 6 (June, 1941), 320-328.
39. Greer, T. H., *American Social Reform Movements: Their Pattern since 1865* (New York: Prentice-Hall, 1949).
40. Kress, A. J., *Introduction to the Cooperative Movement* (New York: Harper, 1941).
41. Jameson, J. F., *The American Revolution Considered as a Social Movement* (Princeton: Princeton Univ. Press, 1940).
42. Johnson, A., "Agrarian Movements," *Encyclopedia of the Social Sciences* (New York: Macmillan, 1930), Vol. 1, pp. 489-515.
43. Kallen, H. M., "Reformism," *Encyclopedia of the Social Sciences* (New York: Macmillan, 1934), Vol. 13, pp. 194-195.
44. Lee, A. M., "Technique of Social Reform: An Analysis of the New Prohibition Drive," *Amer. sociol. Rev.*, 9 (Feb., 1944), 65-77.
45. Loomis, C. P., and J. A. Beegle, *Rural Social Systems* (New York: Prentice-Hall, 1950), pp. 611-650.
46. McConnell, D. W., "Temperance Movements," *Encyclopedia of the Social Sciences* (New York: Macmillan, 1934), Vol. 14, pp. 567-570.
47. Murray, R. H., *Group Movements throughout the Ages* (New York: Harper, 1936).
48. Schlesinger, A. M., *The American Reformer* (Cambridge: Harvard Univ. Press, 1950).
49. Wagner, D. O., *Social Reformers: Adam Smith to John Dewey* (New York: Macmillan, 1934).
50. Woolston, H. B., "American Intellectuals and Social Reform," *Amer. sociol. Rev.*, 1 (June, 1936), 363-372.

The Resistance to Innovation and Reform

51. Hart, H., *Technique of Social Progress* (New York: Holt, 1931), pp. 619-631.
52. Hertzler, J. O., *Social Progress* (New York: Century, 1928), pp. 110-112.
53. Leighton, A. H., *Human Relations in a Changing World* (New York: Dutton, 1941), pp. 129-146.
54. Ogburn, W. F., and M. F. Nimkoff, *Sociology* (Boston: Houghton Mifflin, 1950), pp. 525-530.
55. Schlesinger, A. M., "The Revolt against Revolt," in A. M. Schlesinger, *The American as Reformer* (Cambridge: Harvard Univ. Press, 1950), pp. 65-96.
56. Stern, B. J., "Resistances to the Adoption of Technological Innovations," in National Resources Committee, *Technological Trends and National Policy* (Washington: U.S. Government Printing Office, 1937), pp. 39-66.
57. ———, "Restraints upon the Utilization of Inventions," *Ann. Amer. Acad. polit. soc. Sci.*, 200 (Nov., 1938), 13-31.

Revolutions

58. Adams, B., *The Theory of Revolutions* (New York: Macmillan, 1913).
59. Bernard, L. L., *Social Control in Its Sociological Aspects* (New York: Macmillan, 1939), pp. 337-374.
60. Brinton, C., *The Anatomy of Revolution* (New York: Norton, 1938).
61. Burns, C. D., *The Principles of Revolution: A Study in Ideals* (London: Allen & Unwin, 1920).
62. Edwards, L. P., *The Natural History of Revolution* (Chicago: Univ. Chicago Press, 1927).
63. Elliott, M. A., and F. M. Merrill, *Social Disorganization* (New York: Harper, 1941), pp. 971-1004.
64. Ellwood, C. A., *Psychology of Human Society* (New York: Appleton, 1925), pp. 250-266.
65. Faris, *op. cit.*, pp. 431-443.
66. Gottschalk, L., "Causes of Revolution," *Amer. J. Sociol.*, 50 (July, 1944), 1-8.
67. Heberle, R., *Social Movements: An Introduction to Political Sociology, op. cit.*, pp. 366-387.
68. Hopper, R., "The Revolutionary Process," *Soc. Forces*, 28 (Mar., 1950), 270-279.
69. Hunter, R., *Revolution: Why, How, When?* (New York: Harper, 1940).

70. Kohn, H., *Revolutions and Dictatorships* (Cambridge: Harvard Univ. Press, 1939).
71. Krout, M. H., *Introduction to Social Psychology* (New York: Harper, 1942), pp. 543-547.
72. Le Bon, C., *The Psychology of Revolutions* (New York: McGraw-Hill, 1947).
73. Lederer, E., "On Revolutions," *Sociol. soc. Res.,* 3 (Feb., 1936), 1-18.
74. MacIver, R. M., *The Web of Government* (New York: Macmillan, 1947), pp. 269-287.
75. Martin, E. D., *Farewell to Revolution* (New York: Norton, 1935).
76. Meadows, P., "Roots of Revolution," *Sociol. soc. Res.,* 30 (Sept.-Oct., 1945), 27-36.
77. ———, Sequence in Revolution," *Amer. sociol. Rev.,* 6 (Oct., 1941), 702-709.
78. ———, "The Situational Dialectic of Revolution," *Soc. Forces,* 20 (Mar., 1942), 391-395.
79. Meusel, A., "Revolution and Counter Revolution," *Encyclopedia of the Social Sciences* (New York: Macmillan, 1934), Vol. 13, pp. 367-376.
80. Parsons, T., *The Social System* (Glencoe, Ill.: Free Press, 1951), pp. 520-533.
81. Reuter and Hart, *op. cit.,* pp. 521-525.
82. Sorokin, P. A., *Man and Society in Calamity* (New York: Dutton, 1942).
83. ———, *Social and Cultural Dynamics* (New York: American Book, 1937).
84. ———, *The Sociology of Revolution* (Philadelphia: Lippincott, 1925).
85. Soule, G., *The Coming American Revolution* (New York: Macmillan, 1934).
86. Turner, R. E., *The Great Cultural Traditions* (New York: McGraw-Hill, 1941), Vol. II. Consult "Revolutionary movements" in Index.
87. Yoder, D., "Current Definitions of Revolution," *Amer. J. Sociol.,* 32 (Nov., 1926), 433-441.
88. ———, "Process in Revolution," *Sociol. soc. Res.,* 12 (Jan.-Feb., 1928), 253-263.
89. Young, K., *Sociology: A Study of Society and Culture* (New York: American Book, 1949), pp. 435-437.

Dictatorships

90. Bainville, J., *Dictators* (London: Jonathan Cape, 1937).
91. Bogardus, E. S., "Fascism as a Social Movement," *Sociol. soc. Res.,* 17 (July-Aug., 1933), 569-574.
92. Brooks, R. C., *Deliver Us from Dictators* (Philadelphia: Univ. Pennsylvania Press, 1935).
93. ———, "Democracies and Dictatorships: The Debit Side of Their Ledgers," *Proc. Amer. philos. Soc.,* 75 (1935), 443-481.
94. Carr, A., *Juggernaut: The Path of Dictatorship* (New York: Viking, 1939).
95. Childs, H. L. (ed.), *Propaganda and Dictatorship* (Princeton: Princeton Univ. Press, 1936).
96. Ford, G. S. (ed.), *Dictatorship in the Modern World* (Minneapolis: Univ. Minnesota Press, 1935).
97. Hertzler, J. O., "The Causal and Contributory Factors of Dictatorship," *Sociol. soc. Res.,* 24 (Sept.-Oct., 1939), 3-21.
98. ———, "Crises and Dictatorship," *Amer. sociol. Rev.,* 5 (Apr., 1940), 157-169.
99. ———, "The Typical Life Cycle of Dictatorships," *Soc. Forces,* 17 (Mar., 1939), 303-309.
100. ———, "Totalitarian Ways of Life," in J. S. Roucek (ed.), *Social Control* (New York: Van Nostrand, 1947), pp. 508-526.
101. ———, "The Effects of Dictatorship," *Sociol. soc. Res.,* 24 (Nov.-Dec., 1939), 111-123.
102. Hoover, C. B., *Dictators and Democracies* (New York: Macmillan, 1937).
103. Kellett, E. E., *The Story of Dictatorship: From the Earliest Times till Today* (New York: Dutton, 1937).
104. Lasswell, H. D., "Garrison State," *Amer. J. Sociol.,* 46 (Jan., 1941), 455-468.
105. Loewenstein, K., "Autocracy versus Democracy in Contemporary Europe," *Amer. polit. Sci. Rev.,* 29 (Aug., 1935), 571-593.
106. MacIver, R. M., *Leviathan and the People* (State University: Louisiana State Univ. Press, 1939).
107. Mannheim, K., "Crises and Culture in the Era of Mass-Democracies and Autarchies," *Sociol. Rev. Brit.,* 26 (Apr., 1934), 105-129.
108. Newmann, S., "The Rule of the Demagogue," *Amer. sociol. Rev.,* 3 (Aug., 1944), 415-426.
109. Perry, R. B., *Shall Not Perish from the Earth* (New York: Vanguard, 1940), pp. 97-129.
110. Rossiter, C. L., *Constitutional Dictatorship: Crisis Government in Modern Democracies* (Princeton: Princeton Univ. Press, 1948).
111. Spearman, D., *Modern Dictatorships* (New York: Columbia Univ. Press, 1939).
112. Spencer, H. R., "Dictatorship," *Encyclopedia of the Social Sciences* (New York: Macmillan, 1931), Vol. 5, pp. 133-136.
113. Stavrianos, L. S., "Schooling under the Dic-

tators," *Curr. Hist.*, 44 (Sept., 1936), 139-146.

114. Tunis, J. R., "The Dictators Discover Sport," *Foreign Affairs*, 14 (July, 1936), 606-617.

Social Planning

115. Adams, E. M., "The Logic of Planning," *Soc. Forces*, 28 (May, 1950), 419-423.
116. *Ann. Amer. Acad. polit. soc. Sci.*, 162 (July, 1932), entire number.
117. Barnard, C. I., "On Planning for World Good," in C. I. Barnard, *Organization and Management* (Cambridge: Harvard Univ. Press, 1948), pp. 134-175.
118. Bessling, J., "Social Reconstruction through National and International Planning," *J. legal polit. Sociol.*, 2 (Apr., 1944), 67-89.
119. Bossard, J. H. S., *Social Change and Social Problems* (New York: Harper, 1938), pp. 794-808.
120. Bunbury, Sir H. N., "Importance of Planning," *Fortnightly Rev.*, 155 (June, 1941), 568-576.
121. Burgess, E. W., "Social Planning and the Mores," *Pubs. Amer. sociol. Soc.*, 29 (Aug., 1935), 1-18.
122. Coil, E. J., "Democracies Must Plan," *Plan. Age*, 5 (May, 1939), 127-155.
123. Cole, G. D. H., *Economic Planning* (New York: Knopf, 1935).
124. Donham, W. B., "Regimentation or Muddling Through," *Ann. Amer. Acad. polit. soc. Sci.*, 176 (Nov., 1934), 162-171.
125. Doob, L. W., *The Plans of Men* (New Haven: Yale Univ. Press, 1940).
126. Flanders, R. E., "Limitations and Possibilities of Economic Planning," *Ann. Amer. Acad. polit. soc. Sci.*, 162 (July, 1932), 27-35.
127. Frank, Jerome, "The Place of the Expert in Democratic Society," *Phil. Science*, 16 (Jan., 1949), 3-24.
128. Freedman *et al.*, *op. cit.*, pp. 622-630.
129. Friedrich, C. J., *The New Belief in the Common Man* (Boston: Little, Brown, 1942), pp. 212-237.
130. Galloway, G. B., *et al.*, *Planning for America* (New York: Holt, 1941).
131. ———, *Postwar Planning in the United States* (New York: Twentieth Cent. Fund, 1942).
132. Giddings, F. H., *Scientific Study of Human Society* (Chapel Hill, N.C.: Univ. North Carolina Press, 1924), pp. 140-171.
133. Hayek, F. A., *Road to Serfdom* (Chicago: Univ. Chicago Press, 1944).
134. Hertzler, J. O., "World Planning: What Is Involved?" *J. legal polit. Sociol.*, 2 (Apr., 1944), 5-16.
135. Ivey, J. E., "Social Planning," *Soc. Forces*, 20 (Dec., 1941), 189-195.
136. Jewkes, J., *Ordeal by Planning* (New York: Macmillan, 1948).
137. Lilienthal, D. E., *TVA: Democracy on the March* (New York: Harper, 1944).
138. Lorwin, L. L., "Planning in a Democracy," *Pubs. Amer. sociol. Soc.*, 29 (Aug., 1935), 41-48.
139. ———, *Time for Planning: A Social-Economic Theory and Program for the Twentieth Century* (New York: American Book, 1949), pp. 577-614.
140. Lynd, R. S., "The Implications of Economic Planning for Sociology," *Amer. sociol. Rev.*, 9 (Feb., 1944), 14-20.
141. Mannheim, K., *Diagnosis of Our Time* (New York: Oxford, 1944).
142. ———, *Freedom, Power, and Democratic Planning* (New York: Oxford, 1950).
143. ———, *Man and Society in an Age of Reconstruction* (London: Kegan Paul, Trench & Trubner, 1941).
144. Martindale, D., and E. D. Monachesi, *Elements of Sociology* (New York: Harper, 1951), pp. 628-669.
145. McDougal, M. S., and E. H. Rotival, *The Case for Regional Planning: With Special Reference to New England* (New Haven: Yale Univ. Press, 1947).
146. McKenzie, F., *et al.*, *Planned Society: Yesterday, Today, Tomorrow* (New York: Prentice-Hall, 1937).
147. Meadows, P., *The Culture of Industrial Man* (Lincoln: Univ. Nebraska Press, 1950), pp. 192-206.
148. ———, "Planning in Mass Society and in Differentiated Society," *J. legal polit. Sociol.*, 2 (Apr., 1944), 17-35.
149. Merriam, C. E., "The Possibilities of Planning," *Amer. J. Sociol.*, 39 (Mar., 1944), 397-407.
150. Merton, R. K., "The Unanticipated Consequences of Purposive Social Action," *Amer. sociol. Rev.*, 1 (Dec., 1936), 894-904.
151. Moore, W. E., "Control and Accountability in a Planned Economy," *J. legal polit. Sociol.*, 2 (Apr., 1944), 67-89.
152. Odum, H. W., "The Case for Regional-National

Social Planning," *Soc. Forces,* 13 (Oct., 1934), 6-23.
153. Pritchett, C. H., "Organization for Regional Planning," *Soc. Forces,* 23 (Mar., 1945), 387-394.
154. Riemer, Svend, "Social Planning and Social Organization," *Amer. J. Sociol.,* 52 (May, 1947), 508-516.
155. Rodgers, C., *American Planning: Past, Present, Future* (New York: Harper, 1947).
156. Selznick, P., *TVA and the Grass Roots* (Berkeley: Univ. California Press, 1949).
157. Sorokin, P. A., "Is Accurate Social Planning Possible?" *Amer. sociol. Rev.,* 1 (Feb., 1936), 12-29.
158. Soule, G., *A Planned Society* (New York: Macmillan, 1932).
159. Spier, H., "Freedom and Social Planning," *Amer. J. Sociol.,* 42 (Jan., 1937), 453-483.
160. Staley, E., "What Types of Planning Are Compatible with Free Institutions?" *Plan. Age,* 6 (Feb., 1940), 37-51.
161. Vance, R. B., "The Place of Planning in Social Dynamics," *Soc. Forces,* 23 (Mar., 1945), 331-334.
162. Ward, B., "Limits of Economic Planning," *Foreign Affairs,* 27 (1949), 246-262.
163. Ward, L. F., *Dynamic Sociology* (New York: Appleton, 1883), 2 vols.
164. ———, *Psychic Factors in Civilization* (Boston: Ginn, 1906).
165. ———, *Pure Sociology* (New York: Macmillan, 1907).
166. Wirth, L., "The Prospects of Regional Research in Relation to Social Planning," *Pubs. Amer. sociol. Soc.,* 29 (Aug., 1935), 107-114.
167. Woods, A. L., "The Structure of Social Planning," *Soc. Forces,* 22 (May, 1944), 388-398.
168. Wootton, B., *Freedom under Planning* (Chapel Hill, N.C.: Univ. North Carolina Press, 1945).
169. Young, *op. cit.,* pp. 577-614.
170. Znaniecki, F., "Sociological Ignorance in Social Planning," *Sociol. soc. Res.,* 30 (Nov.-Dec., 1945), 87-100.

Utilization of Social Theory and the Products of Social Research

171. Bain, R., "Natural Science and Value-Policy," *Phil. Science,* 16 (July, 1949), 182-192.
172. ———, "Sociology as a Natural Science," *Amer. J. Sociol.,* 52 (July, 1947), 9-16.
173. ———, "The Concept of Complexity in Sociology," *Soc. Forces,* 8 (Dec., 1929), 222-231; 8 (Mar., 1930), 369-378.
174. Bierstedt, R., "Social Science and Social Policy," *Bull. Amer. Ass. Univ. Prof.,* 29 (Summer, 1948), 310-319.
175. Chapin, F. S .,"Social Theory and Social Action," *Amer. sociol. Rev.,* 1 (Feb., 1936), 1-11.
176. ———, "Social Obstacles to the Acceptance of Existing Social Science Knowledge," *Soc. Forces,* 26 (Oct., 1947), 7-12.
177. Glass, D. V., "The Application of Social Research," *Brit. J. Sociol.,* 1 (Mar., 1950), 17-30.
178. Goldenweiser, E. H., "Research and Policy," *J. Amer. statist. Ass.,* 39 (Mar., 1944), 1-9.
179. Hankins, F. H., "Social Science and Social Action," *Amer. sociol. Rev.,* 4 (Feb., 1939), 1-15.
180. Hauser, P. M., "Are the Social Sciences Ready?" *Amer. sociol. Rev.,* 11 (Aug., 1946), 379-384.
181. Hauser, P. M., "Social Science and Social Engineering," *Phil. Science,* 16 (July, 1949), 209-218.
182. Lundberg, G. A., "Alleged Obstacles to Social Science," *Sci. Mon., N.Y.,* 70 (May, 1950), 299-305.
183. ———, *Can Science Save Us?* (New York: Longmans, Green, 1947).
184. ———, "The Future of the Social Sciences," *Sci. Mon., N.Y.,* 53 (Oct., 1941), 346-359.
185. ———, "The Proximate Future of American Sociology: The Growth of Scientific Method," *Amer. J. Sociol.,* 50 (May, 1945), 502-513.
186. Lynd, R. S., *Knowledge for What?* (Princeton: Princeton Univ. Press, 1939).
187. Merton, R. K., "The Bearing of Empirical Research upon the Development of Social Theory," *Amer. sociol. Rev.,* 13 (Oct., 1948), 505-515; or in R. K. Merton, *Social Theory and Social Structure* (Glencoe, Ill.: Free Press, 1949), pp. 97-111.
188. ———, "The Bearing of Sociological Theory on Empirical Research," in R. K. Merton, *Social Theory and Social Structure* (Glencoe, Ill.: Free Press, 1949), pp. 83-96.
189. ———, "The Role of Applied Social Science in the Formation of Policy: A Research Mem-

orandum," *Phil. Science,* 16 (July, 1949), 161-181.

190. Odum, H. W., *Understanding Society* (New York: Macmillan, 1947), pp. 661-665, 690-693.

191. Parsons, T., "The Present Position and Prospects of Systematic Theory in Sociology," in G. Gurvitch and W. E. Moore (eds.), *Twentieth Century Sociology* (New York: Philosophical Library, 1945), pp. 42-69.

192. ———, "The Role of Social Theory in Social Research," *Amer. sociol. Rev.,* 3 (Sept., 1938), 13-20.

193. "Questions for Sociology: An Informal Round Table Symposium," *Soc. Forces,* 13 (Dec., 1934), 165-223.

194. Selltiz, C., and S. W. Cook, "Can Research in Social Science Be Both Socially Useful and Scientifically Meaningful?" *Amer. sociol. Rev.,* 13 (Aug., 1948), 454-459.

195. Shils, E. A., "Social Science and Social Policy," *Phil. Science,* 16 (July, 1949), 219-242.

196. Sombart, W., "Sociology: What It Is and What It Ought to Be," *Amer. J. Sociol.,* 55 (Sept., 1949), 178-193.

197. Wirth, L., "Responsibility of the Social Sciences," *Ann. Amer. Acad. polit. soc. Sci.,* 255 (Jan., 1948), 143-151.

198. Young, D., "Limiting Factors in the Development of the Social Sciences," *Proc. Amer. phil. Soc.,* 92 (No. 5, Nov. 12, 1948), 325-335.

INDEX

Lightning Source UK Ltd.
Milton Keynes UK
UKHW021253070119
335137UK00014B/655/P

9 781330 288061